IOWANS OF THE MIGHTY EIGHTH

by Charles Day Taylor

Turner
PUBLISHING COMPANY
Nashville, Tennessee

TURNER PUBLISHING COMPANY

www.turnerpublishing.com

Copyright © 2005, Charles Day Taylor
No part of this book may be reproduced or transmitted in any form or by any means,
electronic or mechanical, including photocopying, recording, or by any information
storage and retrieval system, without permission in writing from the publisher.

Turner Publishing Company Staff:
Randy Baumgardner, Editor
Peter Zuniga, Designer

Library of Congress Control No. 2005923896

ISBN 978-1-68162-377-1

Limited Edition

0 9 8 7 6 5 4 3 2 1

Contents

Acknowledgments 4
Preface 5
Brief History of the Mighty Eighth 6
Purpose 8
The Pre-War Years 10
Call to Arms 14
Home Front 16
Training 20
Deployment 28
Life On the English Home Front 33
Bases 38
Logistics 47
Base Life 57
Special Units 71
Targets 80
Missions 91
Special Missions 121
Victory 125
POW - Prisoner of War 134
Prisoners of War 158
Evades 162
Internees 165
Rememberance 167
Roster of Iowa Veterans of the Eighth Air Force 175
Killed In Action 193
Deceased 251
Medals 297
Biographies 305
Picture Credits 471
Bibliography 473
Suggested Reading 474
Index 475

ACKNOWLEDGMENTS

Special thanks in the four years of interviewing, preparation and writing of this project to:

- Sharon Avery, State Historical Society of Iowa, Des Moines for her unwavering assistance and dedication in retrieving World War II casualty files for this project.

- Duff Coleman, Monticello, Iowa and Steve Elliott, Cherokee, Iowa, for photographic and interview assistance in their area.

- Kay Cunningham, Waterloo, for permission to use numerous photographs from the files of her late husband Gerald, a 7th Photo Reconnaissance Group intelligence officer.

- Raj and Hema Patel, Ramada Inn, Newton, for lodging to write and compose away from telephone, computer, television and chores at home.

- Dave Popelka, of Sigler Publishing, Ames, for guidance in organizing my material and patience with my lack of publishing technicalities.

- Encouragement from friends and relatives to preserve the experiences and memories of Iowa Eighth Air Force veterans.

- Each Eighth Air Force veteran interviewed and their families for their gracious hospitality and cooperation often on a moment's notice, to tell their stories. No finer people exist.

- My son Charles for skill, attention to detail and authenticity in his artwork depicting principle American and German aircraft in the European Theater of Operations of World War II.

- My wife Jane for putting up with four years of "my one great adventure."

PREFACE

Nineteen forty-five marked the end of the most devastating war known to mankind. In the decades since, it has faded in the memory of the participants and become a cloudy myth of many of the younger generation. It deserves better understanding, for World War II has touched the lives of all those living today and will continue to do so for the next few generations at least. It is not unique in this respect, for other major wars in our past have affected our laws, our society and even our very existence as a nation. As well as opening the nuclear age, World War II made a major contribution to American military tradition at its best. It was a war fought for a cause that was well understood and our participation was precipitated as the immediate result of a sudden, damaging blow to our forces. How our Armed Services rallied from their wounds, how the home front leaped to man the factories, and how our fighting men in the air, on the sea and on the land carried the flight to the enemy is indeed an inspiring story.

Truly global in scope, massive in manpower and destruction, rich in heroic deed and scarred with countless examples of man's inhumanity to man, the Second World War has been written about by historians, playwrights and novelists. Yet most of these authors suffered from the myopia of being participants in the events described or have looked at the war from the sole viewpoint of one or another of the combatants. To understand history is to better understand how to avoid future cataclysm.

Pearl Harbor, Bataan, Corregidor, Kasserine and Cassino, the Solomons, Leyte Gulf, Midway, Okinawa and Normandy, the Ardennes and Iwo Jima are stamped on American memories as deeply as are other names on the minds of other participants.

– James L. Collins, Jr., Brigadier General, US Army Chief of Military History, Dept. of the Army

* Illustrated World War II Encyclopedia, Volume I, Copyright 1972. 1978 Orbis Publishing LTD, Jaspard Polus, Monaco, 1966.

BRIEF HISTORY OF THE MIGHTY EIGHTH

In World War II, the Eighth Air Force became the greatest air armada of any country in any war, reaching a total strength of 200,000 persons by June, 1944. It has been estimated that more than 350,000 Americans served in the Eighth Air Force during the three years of the war in Europe. At one time the Eighth Air Force could fly more than 2,000 bombers and more than 1,000 fighter on a mission. Hence, the title "Mighty Eighth."

The Eighth Air Force was constituted in the U.S. Army Air Forces on January 19, 1942, and activated at Savannah, Georgia nine days later. Eighth Air Force Bomber Command Headquarters was moved to England in February, 1942. The building of airstrips and base facilities began as well as the build-up of bomber and fighter groups, support personnel and aircraft to deploy there. In the early stages of America's war on Germany, what began with meager availability of aircraft and trained personnel would eventually become a steady flow of both as American war industry reached peak production and military bases overflowed with trainees.

The mission of the Eight Air Force: destroy the Luftwaffe and the industrial might of Nazi Germany. This would be accomplished by daylight strategic bombing of military targets, transportation, fuel and war production centers of all types, while England's Royal Air Force bombed Axis targets at night. American involvement began in June, 1942 with borrowed aircraft when the 15th Bomb Squadron of the Eighth Air Force flew Royal Air Force A-20 Bostons during a British bombing mission at Hazebrauck, France. In July, 1942, the 15th led the first combat mission of the Eighth Air Force when they bombed airfields in Holland using British A-20 aircraft. Two American crews were lost on this first mission. The 31st Fighter Group became involved when they flew six British Spit-

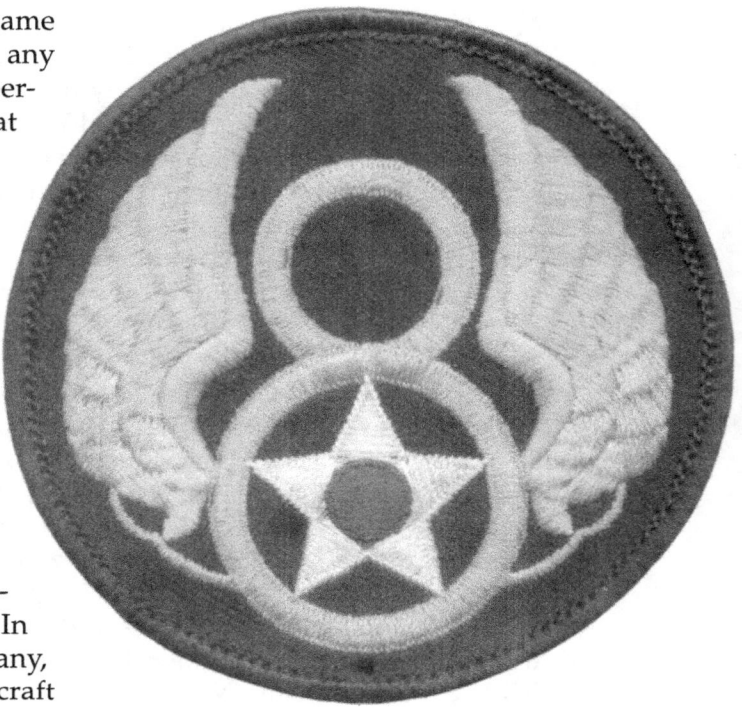

fire fighters over the French coastal area on July 26, 1942. Twelve B-17 bombers of the 97th Bomb Group flew the first Eighth Air Force heavy bomber raid on a mission to Rouen, France. The lead plane of that mission was flown by Paul Tibbets who would later fly the "Enola Gay" when it dropped the atomic bomb on Hiroshima, Japan in August, 1945.

The Eighth Air Force would eventually be comprised of nearly eighty bomber and fighter groups, and additional weather, reconnaissance, troop carrier, rescue, radio counter measures, and leaflet squadrons, air depots, and headquarters personnel at an equal number of bases hastily constructed in Eastern England. Bomber and fighter groups, in addition to air crews would include ordnance and chemical personnel, armorers, mechanics, radio and instrument specialists, structural and aircraft repair, medical, finance, postal, military police, fire fighters, quartermaster, clerical, intelligence, mess hall and service personnel.

In 1944 alone, the Eighth Air Force flew 1.7 million operational hours and consumed 522 million gallons of gasoline to drop 430,000 tons of bombs against enemy targets. Bomber crews and fighter pilots would destroy over 6,000 enemy aircraft in the air. An additional 2,000 enemy aircraft were accounted for by fighter strafing attacks, and another 2630 were destroyed when enemy production plants were bombed. Fighters would destroy 3,652 locomotives, 5,702 fright cars, and 3,436 trucks. Ground crews in 1944 loaded 3 million bombs and 53 million rounds of 50 caliber ammunition. In addition to maintenance of aircraft for maximum bombing efforts, 25 thousand vehicles had to be serviced, maintained and repaired. Airstrips had to be maintained, supplies of food, clothing and organizational equipment had to be guaranteed.

The inevitable cost in lives by members of the Eighth Air Force from 1942 to Victory in Europe, V-E Day, May 7, 1945, was over 47,000 casualties. This included 26,000 killed in action of which nearly 500 were Iowans. Many more lost their lives in non-combat related accidents. Another twenty-eight thousand fighter pilots and air crewmen would be taken prisoner of war.

Eighth Air Force personnel would be awarded seventeen Congressional Medals of Honor, 2210 Distinguished Service Crosses, eleven Distinguished Service Medals, 864 Silver Stars, 207 Legion of Merit medals, 46,000 Distinguished Flying Crosses, 478 Soldiers Medals, nearly 3,000 Bronze Star Medals, 7,000 Purple Heart Medals and 442,000 Air Medals. There were 261 fighter pilots that became "Aces." Thirty-one of these had more than fifteen aircraft "kills."

The Eighth Air Force has continued to serve in every armed conflict the United States has faced since World War II. It is presently headquartered at Barksdale Air Force Base, Shreveport, Louisiana. In the 1991 Gulf War, B-52s of the 8th Air Force flew some of the initial strikes. They took off from their home base at Barksdale, and flew to the Middle East where they loosened their guided missiles against Iraq and then returned home. It is estimated that more than one million persons have been assigned or attached to the Eighth Air Force since its inception in World War II and remains one of the most powerful air striking forces in the world.

-Col. Therman E Moore, Chaplain
U.S. Air Force Academy
Eighth Air Force Memorial Service
8 October 1989

Purpose

History books, over time, have devoted less space to some historical events. What used to fill chapters may now be reduced to a few pages or even paragraphs despite its significance in history. To do this to World War II, to set humanities' greatest struggle for survival on a back burner does not seem fitting. If the outcome had been reversed, (and it very well could have been), the lives of all persons throughout the world would now be entirely different.

It was not my intent in this book to create another re-write of events leading to World War II, battles, statistics, methods employed or strategy. Rather I concentrate on the personal experiences of Iowans who were a part of the Eighth Air Force, the largest air armada and single military unit ever assembled. As an associate member of the Eighth Air Force Historical Society I listened in awe to stories and experiences of missions flown and recollection of friends and crewmembers lost in combat. I came to the conclusion these memories should be preserved so future generations may appreciate the struggle and sacrifice made by Americans in World War II. How little our youth appear to know of history, its bearing on their lives and the terrible cost it took for the freedoms they take for granted

Nearly five hundred Iowans in the Eighth Air Force were killed in action in the embattled skies over Europe during World War II. Many others lost their lives in accidents in route to, during and return from the European Theater of Operations. It is unknown how many Iowans were based in England with the Eighth Air Force in World War II, survived, and in the fifty plus years hence, succumbed to illness or age or moved to other States for employment or retirement.

My intent in this book was to interview as many surviving Iowa veterans of the Eighth Air Force as possible who were also members of the Eighth Air Force Historical Society, an Association comprised primarily of Eighth Air Force veterans. Through them I describe what life was like when suddenly thrust into military service to America's call to duty at a time when our country was almost totally unprepared to fight a war. Other chapters include their training, deployment to the United Kingdom, base life and experiences during missions flown to gain air superiority and destroy Germany's industrial and economic systems. Nearly 28,000 aircrew men of the Eighth Air Force were shot down and taken prisoner of war. A chapter is devoted to the conditions and existence suffered at the hands of their captors and a death march for seemingly endless days and nights in one of Europe's worst winters on record. A section is devoted to those that evaded capture and were aided by Underground members in Nazi-occupied countries to return them to Allied military control as well as those forced down and

interned in neutral countries. After Victory in Europe Eighth Air Force members returned home to resume their lives and careers. Many maintained a close relationship with aviation by flying home-built aircraft, continuing to fly privately, or joined Air National Guard and Reserve units. Some made the Air Force a career.

A biographical section contains the interviews conducted with each veteran highlighting their training, deployment and missions flown to include their most memorable experience. The interviews are supplied with a current photograph of them and a photograph taken during the war years. Also included are photographs of their air or ground crew and candid snapshots while based in England, lasting memories that were hung on the walls of their homes or in photograph albums. Sometimes humorous, sometimes tragic and choked with emotion the Eighth Air Force veterans told of friends lost and near death experiences against fighter attacks, flak barrages and struggles to maintain flight in shattered aircraft during return to their base. The home front is not ignored, without whose sacrifices and gallant efforts in production centers the military could not have accomplished victory.

From files of the Iowa Historical Society photographs of each Iowan are included that was killed in action and able to be identified as with the Eighth Air Force.

To America's "Greatest Generation," this book is dedicated. The way World War II was thrust upon them, and without any great sense of patriotism, they knew they had a job to do and just went out and did it. As their numbers dwindle with time everyone should be reminded of all the fine young men and women who gave their lives that we might live in a free, more decent and humane world.

Chapter One

THE PRE-WAR YEARS

In the twenty years following the end of World War I political and economic chaos spread worldwide. Dynasties had been toppled, new regimes formed, new countries established and borders re-aligned that bred bitterness and hatred. In Europe cities and towns had been destroyed, people were dislocated and struggling to survive when there were shortages of food and jobs. People groped for solutions and were ready to follow anyone who promised them hope and a way out of their misery. Individuals stepped forth on the public platform and gained control of governments bent on ruthless revenge and expansionism. The world became one crisis after another that could only lead to one result – World War II.

Germany- Near the end of World War I, a blockade of German ports left millions in that country dying from starvation and disease. Setbacks on the battlefield forced Germany to seek an armistice to the war and did so after consulting with President Wilson of the United States. Wilson had proposed a plan for world peace where each nation would reduce their armaments to a minimum. Trade barriers would be removed by all countries; all people would have the right of self-determination with rulers of their own choosing; countries' frontiers would correspond as closely as possible to their national groupings; and in colonies the interests of all persons would have equal weight.

Wilson proposed a League of Nations charged with keeping the peace and guaranteeing the independence and security of all countries. Based on these principles Germany asked for an Armistice to end World War I. A peace conference was called with representatives of the victorious nations to determine terms of the armistice which would be dictated to Germany rather than negotiated. This included reduction of military forces, ban on manufacture of war materials, loss of German colonies and occupied territories and payment of huge sums of money for war reparations. The delegates hammered out the terms of the Armistice which were to be signed by the Germans on a formal document known as the Treaty of Versailles. It would take six months from the time the peace conference convened to the actual signing. Bickering began immediately as to shares from the spoils of war. Countries promised certain territorial gains by other nations as a reward for entering the war on the side of the Allies had some or all of their promises reneged. The fate of millions of people within the affected areas was decided by a handful of politicians from the principle participants in the war. Dissention reigned within the conference. Alignment of some borders by ethnic and language led only to more bitterness and hatred. When terms of the Armistice was presented to Germany their representatives were stunned in disbelief at the conditions that had been stipulated. Germany was inclined to refuse the terms based on huge sums of war reparations they were to pay and admission of guilt for starting the war. They even considered resumption of the war. They acquiesced, however, and signed the Treaty.

Under terms of the Treaty Germany could not have an army of more than one hundred thousand men and no air force. Manufacture of airplanes, submarines and war materials was forbidden. They had to cede large territories of land to Poland, the Alsace-Lorraine Region was returned to France and German colonies in Africa were to be surrendered. German islands in the Pacific were ceded to Japan including a portion of China. Germans were dissatisfied with the existing government and small political parties began to flourish. The German Communist Party attempted to overthrow the government. Another political party, the German Worker's Party was created and joined by a down and out Austrian named Adolf Hitler who had been a decorated corporal in the German Army.

Chapter One

Hitler, bitter by the terms of the Armistice ending World War I rose quickly in the Party and began a climb in national popularity. He promised to restore Germany's prosperity and position in the world. He attempted to seize control of the government in 1923 and was arrested for treason. Sentenced to five years in prison he served only nine months during which time he wrote "Mein Kamp," a book wherein he set forth what he believed should be the future of Germany. He blamed Jews and communists for Germany's plight in the world. Hitler finished second in elections against President Hindenburg held in 1932 but his party, now the National Socialist German Workers Party, gained in popularity. The Party finished second in the election causing Hindenburg to name Hitler his Chancellor. When Hindenburg died the following year Hitler was named President, a title he changed to Fuhrer (leader). He quickly abolished all other political parties and began a reign of terror.

Italy-Inflation, strikes, unemployment and lack of leadership within the country played into the hands of Benito Mussolini who came to power as Italy's dictator. Like Hitler, Mussolini also played upon people's fear and frustrations. Using national pride and supporters with violent tactics he was handed the leadership of his country. Mussolini as a newspaper editor called for a meeting attended mostly by unemployed veterans of the war where he outlined his proposals for Fascism. In an ensuing election for Parliament, Mussolini was soundly defeated. But no political party had a majority. The government was immobilized. Strikes, riots, mutiny within the Army existed. Some turned to communism as a way out of their predicament. Fascism began strong-arm tactics to keep Mussolini's movement alive. Fascists began street battles with socialists, communists and union organizers. Mussolini gained police, military and public support when his followers marched on city governments and threatened overthrow unless public work projects were established to provide jobs for the unemployed. Mussolini was offered a cabinet post by the country's premier to avoid his army of followers from marching on the Capital. During an audience with the King, Mussolini was invited to establish a new government with himself as Premier.

Japan-was also in political chaos with ever changing leadership, lack of direction and assassinations of Cabinet officials by members of the military trying to gain control of the government. Japan was highly over-populated. There was a limited amount of arable ground to grow food. The country had limited natural resources causing them to rely on trade for oil and raw materials. In addition to food and goods, they needed living space. Under terms of the Treaty of Versailles, Japan was given the previous controlled German Mariana, Caroline, and Marshall islands and a province in China. They already controlled Korea, Formosa and islands north of Japan won during a 1905 war with Russia. The military took control over Manchuria. After a skirmish with Chinese troops, Japan invaded China in 1937 and all out war with China began that was only slowed down by the country's vast area and natural barriers. Large sections of China were overrun and cities pillaged. The city of Nanking alone suffered over forty thousand men, women and children slaughtered.

France-under terms of the Armistice had the Alsace-Lorraine region returned to them. The Rhineland area was to be demilitarized to provide a buffer zone between them and Germany. France occupied the highly industrialized Ruhr area of Germany for default on war reparation payments. When workers walked off the job the German government provided financial support for the workers. When money ran low the government printed millions of marks to continue support payments, but inflation ran wild. It took a wheelbarrow full of money to buy a loaf of bread and people burned money for heat. The government encouraged the workers to return to work and reparation payments were resumed.

China- China was under constant internal strife. Two political parties emerged as dominant forces, the Nationalists under General Chiang Kai-shek and the Communists under Chou En-lai. When the Japanese invaded China, General Chiang and communist guerila leader MaoTse-tung joined forces to fight the Japanese. The Chinese military had few modern weapons. The Japanese overran virtually all of China's port cities leaving only the Burma Road, a twisting, winding mountainous road from Burma to China in which to sustain the country. China would receive support from Great Britain in the form of ground forces. Before World War II started for the United States, aerial support was received from the American Volunteer Group (Flying Tigers) to fight the Japanese.

Spain-a military plot to overthrow the left-wing government began in 1936. General Francisco Franco and his revolutionists represented the Nationalists on one side while the Republicans or Loyalists supported by Communists fought on the other side. It was a time for Germany to test its expanding military denied by terms of the Armistice ending World War I. Hitler wanted revenge for the terms dictated to Germany and purposely ignored military limitations placed on the country. He began building an army, a navy and an air force. Lightning fast tactics were tested in Spain with amazing results enabling Franco and his forces to gain control of the government after a three-year war. The League of Nations stood idly by and watched. No means of enforcement was taken through the combined power of many nations against Germany and its violations of the Treaty of Versailles.

League of Nations-Germany through negotiations with President Wilson of the United States declared an armistice ending the fighting in World War I. Representatives of Allied nations met at Paris to determine a settlement with Germany regarding its penalties for starting the war. Formal surrender terms were negotiated between the victors that led to breach of promises, and bitterness regarding distribution of the "spoils." President Wilson had proposed a League of Nations that set forth ideals for the world to live by in peace, a worldwide democracy, with equality for all. In part he proposed country's borders be aligned by race, language, and ethnic-type. In doing so the representatives making the critical decisions created more bitterness and conflict than was corrected. When violations of world order occurred the League was ineffective in maintaining order, resorting to arbitration as a main means to resolve differences with only a slap of the hand as a deterrent.

Russia- A revolution was taking place to overthrow the Czarist regime and replace it with a Bolshevik state. Red armies of the Bolsheviks and white armies of the Czar clashed in a drawn out civil war that lasted five years and killed millions. Disease and hunger had also swept the country when the Bolsheviks under Lenin and Stalin gained control. They called for worldwide revolution that would make everyone equal, devoid of social class. Their movement spread communist sympathizers to almost every country to gain support and create internal chaos.

Finland- In 1939, the USSR invaded Finnish territory for "defensive purposes." Finland, greatly outnumbered and with inferior weapons, was able to use cold weather, terrain and irregular warfare tactics to its advantage to beat back the Soviet advance. But they invaded Finland again in February, 1940, until a cease-fire was ordered in March, 1940, that allowed the Soviets to take control of the country. Although the Soviet Union was condemned by the League of Nations for its actions, no sanctions were imposed on them.

United States- During the years following World War I, the United States, except for participation in the Paris peace conference, maintained a position of isolationism. Although Woodrow Wilson had stipulated a 14 point peace plan for ending WWI including the League of Nations, the country maintained a hands off posture while other countries struggled with their problems and outside forces. It was not until hostilities began to have worldwide implications that America reluctantly began to prepare for its own defense over the outspoken cries of many that maintained isolationist ideals. The Selective Service Act began to draft for the armed services and American industry geared to turn out war materials that were provided to friendly warring countries first under "cash and carry" and then under Lend Lease. When America was attacked it found itself almost totally unprepared for war. It would require time to train and build up its armed forces, and supply them with the necessary military goods and armament to do their job.

Such were the conditions existing in countries that would greatly impact the world from World War I until the late 1930s. Then all hell broke loose. Italy invaded Ethiopia in1935. Hitler's military marched into the Rhineland and occupied it without opposition from France or Britain. It was Hitler's intent to unite the German speaking country of Austria with Germany. Hitler threatened Austria with war if the Austrian Nazi Party was not legalized in that country and given a role in administration of the government. In 1938 Austria invited the German Army to occupy their country to avoid bloodshed.

Next was Czechoslovakia to be invaded without bloodshed when Britain and France backed down from pledges to come to the Czechs aid. Hitler's pretense for invasion was that the Germans residing in the Sudetenland were a persecuted minority and he was re-uniting them with Germany. Portions of Czechoslovakia were also ceded to Poland and Hungary.

In 1939 Nazi Germany and Russia sign a non-aggression pact. Italy invaded Albania and on September 1,1939, Germany invaded and over ran Poland. The Soviet Union occupied Eastern Poland as its share of the spoils. Meanwhile the United States declared neutrality and the Soviet Union was ousted by the League of Nations. In

Chapter One

the next two years Denmark, Norway, Belgium, the Netherlands, Luxembourg and France fell to the German war machine. Rumania was forced to cede portions of its country to Hungary and Bulgaria and Germany was given exclusive right to all of Rumania's oil production. Germany also invaded Libya and with Italy and Bulgaria, invaded Yugoslavia. Italy attacked Greece and had to be rescued by Germany after being beaten. The German invasion of Russia in June, 1941, lightly assisted by Rumania, Hungary, Italy, Slovakia and Albania, left plans to invade Great Britain "on temporary hold." Hermann Goring, head of the German Luftwaffe, convinced Hitler that aerial bombardment alone would bring the English to their knees and sue for peace. He was wrong, it only stiffened their resistance and will to fight. The Royal Air Force, though greatly outnumbered, defeated the Germans in the air during what became known as The Battle of Britain. With subsequent entry of the United States into the war and Germany fighting in all directions, Germany placed a permanent "hold" on the invasion of Great Britain.

Italy invaded and conquered Ethiopia. Greece invaded Turkey but was beaten back. Twice Russia invaded Finland. Japan had taken Manchuria, invaded China and was now looking to the Dutch East Indies, Malaya, and the Philippines. The United States placed an embargo on oil shipments to Japan, abolished trade with the Japanese and encouraged the Dutch and English holding colonial territories in those countries rich in oil and rubber and other raw materials, to follow in America's footsteps. Japan occupied French Indo-China, an obvious stepping off zone for possible attacks in Asia. The Japanese refused to leave China in return for a lift of the embargoes placed on them. They launched attacks on American military bases in Hawaii and the Philippines, invaded Thailand, Malaya, Guam, and Borneo and American owned Wake Island after an initial attack failed. The world was at war.

Chapter Two

CALL TO ARMS

The attack on America's naval and air bases on the Hawaiian Island of Oahu on Sunday, December 7, 1941, by military forces of Japan caught the United States woefully unprepared for war. The United States military was under-manned and under-trained. Compulsory military training, required by the Selective Service Act, had not been enacted by Congress until 1940. Weaponry was either outdated, non-existent, or not in sufficient numbers to wage war. Toy rifles, cars or trucks as make believe tanks and broomsticks as machine guns were used in training because there wasn't enough of the real item to go around. Many weapons were leftovers from World War I. Before America's entry into World War II military goods and armaments produced in the United States were shipped to Britain and Russia to help them in their fight against Nazi Germany. War directly involving America was threatening and American industry was in its infancy of gearing for modern war production.

Americans were stunned, outraged, furious and anxious to exact revenge for the sneak attack at Pearl Harbor. Recruiting stations were deluged with volunteers. Every one wanted to help in the war effort to, as a World War II song put, "Sap the Jap." Then Germany declared war on the United States on December ll, 1941.

As in other states, all across Iowa young men left colleges and farms, postmen, mechanics, accountants, defense plant and construction workers, left the security of their lives to enlist in all the military services. Those still in high school would follow upon graduation. Others would continue to enlist or be drafted. Volunteers nationally included future Presidents Bush, Nixon, Johnson, Ford; Hollywood celebrities Jimmy Stewart, Clark Gable, Alan Ladd, Glenn Miller, and Gene Autry; sports personalities Joe Dimaggio, Joe Lewis and numerous other baseball, football and basketball standouts.

Suddenly servicemen were everywhere. Train stations and bus terminals were jammed with soldiers, sailors and marines in route to and from furloughs, duty or training stations or overseas. As available men at the home front decreased a popular song written by Loesser and Schwartz and sung by Kitty Kallen summed up what men were left. "They're either too young or too old, they're either too bald or too bold."

When the Selective Service Act was enacted, all men between the ages of 21 and 35 were required to register with their local draft boards. Deferment from the draft was based on being a conscientious objector to war, sole financial supporter of a family or in an essential occupation such as farming. Most men felt it their moral obligation to be drafted or enlist in the military and wore the uniform with pride. Iowans were predominantly sworn into military service at Camp Dodge or Ft. Des Moines. Some had enlisted into the military up to two years before the attack on Pearl Harbor. After war was declared many enlisted immediately, volunteered when they reached enlistment age or knew their Draft Board would soon call their number. Wives, mothers, fathers and girlfriends saw them off as they were sent to basic training. Married men were able to have their wives live near bases where they took specialized military training before going overseas.

Many recruits away from home for the first time were thrown into their new homes, "barracks," with others from all over the United States at locations they had never heard of, many of which were hastily established with the advent of war. "The recruit suddenly found himself in an alien world of doctors with inch-long needles and half-inch crewcuts, of fat supply sergeants who doled out drab uniforms that did not always fit. The recruit gave up his civilian identity for a rank and serial number. He learned a new vocabulary, "chow" for food, "on the double" for hurrying,

Chapter Two

Beverly Jean Moses, Des Moines, left, and Gleanna Roberts, Iowa City, right, both lost their lives in airplane crashes as Women's Air Service Pilots.

"SNAFU" for situation normal, all fouled up, and "SOS" for the chipped beef and gravy abomination that was served to him on toast at six in the morning."[1] Men who had never made a bed before now had to make them neat, tight and quick. Their meager civilian possessions and military items were stored in either foot or wall lockers or a combination of both. Restrooms, "Latrines," had no partitions between toilets and showers were in open rooms containing multiple shower heads. Food was not like mom used to make.

To not be in uniform allayed suspicion on a person's courage or conviction, mental or physical health. Nearly 16 million Americans would wear the uniform in World War II. This included women who would perform duties previously done by men, freeing the men for the battlefront whether in the air, on land or sea. The Women's Auxiliary Ferrying Squadron, (WAFS), also known as WASPS(Women's Air Service Pilots) flew planes from factories to overseas points of debarkation or to Army Air bases in the United States. They underwent pilot training. Some lost their lives in crashes. Most were better pilots than men but received no credit for service to their country until the 1970s. Fort Des Moines, Iowa, was an officer candidate school for the Women's Army Auxiliary Corps. They would eventually perform over 200 different Army jobs freeing men for the battlefield. Men and women alike would suffer loneliness, separation from loved ones and the shock of being taken from civilian life.

---

1 *Time-Life Books, The Home Front*, U.S.A. Copyright 1977, page 7

Iowans of the Mighty Eighth

Chapter Three

Home Front

Little attention was paid to the notion of civil defense until World War II. When cities in Europe and Asia were bombed, citizens were trained on fire fighting, rescue of bombing victims, mass evacuations, airplane spotting and air raid alert training. All knew when the air raid sirens wailed it was time to take shelter at designated sites. When war came to America, Americans realized they could also be targeted by long-range bombers. The Office of Civil Defense was established in 1941. Thousands of volunteers were enlisted as ambulance drivers, airplane spotters and air raid wardens. In actuality, it was limited to the enforcement of blackout regulations in coastal cities. Air raid wardens were in charge of keeping all lights turned off during the periodic blackouts. The wardens wore white helmets, arm bands that bore a red arch on a white triangle inside a blue circle, and were authorized to carry whistles.

Nearly everyone on the home front volunteered in campaigns to collect scrap metals of all kinds, rubber, paper, silk and nylon for powder bags, milkweed for life vests, and bacon grease in the manufacture of explosives. Children peeled off tin foil from cigarette and gum wrappers and scoured neighborhoods for scrap metals, old tires, rubber boots and garden hoses. In addition to aiding the war effort by supplying resources for recycling, the collection drives served as a morale booster for Americans. They felt they were doing their part.

Everyone able to planted Victory Gardens ranging from massive gardens to planting vegetables

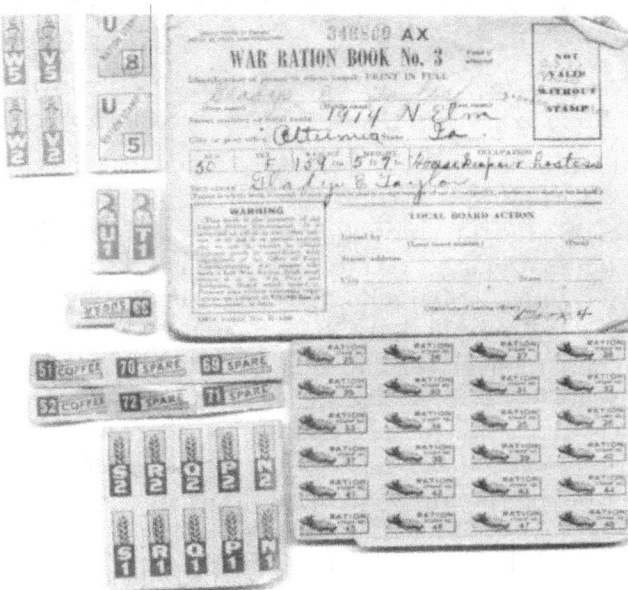

Assorted Ration Stamps of Gladys Taylor, Ottumwa, IA

Air Raid Warden Armband

Ten Cent Stamp Album

Chapter Three

in flower boxes. Every available space was used. Vegetable gardens accounted for the majority of vegetables in the population's diet, eased the necessity for tin used in canned goods, and created a healthier American. Many persons deferred from the Draft or rejected from the military were products of the Depression when poor diet over time affected the health of the men now appearing at recruiting/enlistment stations.

The major sacrifice in the war years was rationing of essential items. Items people had previously taken for granted. Gasoline, sugar and rubber were imported. National sources or synthetic products were not adequate to supply both the war effort and home front. Canned foods were rationed because tin was needed for armaments and military food packaging. Shoes were in short supply because the materials were needed for servicemen. Rationing was a daily reminder America was at war and everyone had to sacrifice. Every sacrifice was a contribution to the war effort.

Americans made do with what they had. They patched or repaired what wore out. Women painted stocking seams on their legs or wore cotton stockings. Nylon had gone to war. Workers had to carpool. The public used railroads for transportation. Coffee drinkers reused coffee grounds; smokers rolled their own cigarettes from tobacco because cigarettes went mostly to the military; coffee drinkers sparingly added sugar to their cup; meat was stretched in casseroles; appliances were treated with care because they were not replaceable and less butter was used on toast. With every bus depot, train station and airport filled with servicemen on the move to and from training camps or points of debarkation for overseas, fuel for the home was rationed. In winter there was barely enough fuel to heat homes and temperatures were recommended they be set at 65 degrees.

To help finance the war, millions of dollars were raised from nickels and dimes spent by children purchasing war stamps. War Bond drives with the aid of radio and film celebrities also raised millions of dollars. Bonds also helped to fight inflation by absorbing excess wages earned by workers in war production plants and factories.

One of the biggest frustrations on the home front was not being able to buy what you want

Pauline Mairs, Marshalltown, as an Iowa State College student was paid to perform tests on the new Norden bombsight. During World War II she entered the Army Medical Corps and became a dietician in a military hospital in North Carolina.

Those least affected by the effects of food rationing were farmers. Marvis Henrickson Varland, Radcliffe, Iowa was a young farm wife with one child when World War II began. "As far as food rationing, it didn't affect us at all. We gew or raised what we needed and had plenty to eat. It was the other items, gas, tires, and machinery parts that were hard to get. You had to take care of what you had. Dresses and children's clothing were made from the cloth of feed and flour sacks."

Helen (Dvorak) Rogness, Cedar Rapids, was a "Rosie the Riveter" in Detroit during World War II. She operated a rivet gun attaching metal covering on wings of B-24 bombers.

Vivian Dennis, Conrad, worked on the production line at Fisher Controls, Marshalltown, which fulfilled wartime government contracts for the military.

when you wanted it. There was never enough to go around and long lines formed for what was available. Family cars were no longer produced nor were toasters, refrigerators, irons or washing machines. Food items were limited to an average of twelve pounds of butter a year, 28 ounces of meat a week, one pound of coffee every five weeks, twelve ounces of sugar a week. Cigarettes were hard to find. Everyday items normally taken for granted were also limited: laundry soap, facial tissue, and liquor. Spirits remained high despite empty showrooms and grocery shelves. Sacrifice was a sense of duty. Everyone believed victory would come and with it, the promise of plenty.

Unemployment disappeared. With men away in service, industry recruited women. Over six million women took jobs during the war. They came out of the home to work in war plants, doing their part in the all-out effort on the home front. Rosie the Riveter was their symbol. Their presence also helped to improve working conditions, the establishment of cafeterias and cleaner rest rooms. There was no limit to the jobs they were prepared to do and could perform. It ranged from driving steamrollers, welding, riveting, and operating cranes to driving garbage trucks and taxis.

In production plants workers were making products that could directly affect the life of a loved one at war. There were instances of servicemen's lives being saved by an item that was made by his wife or mother. Many women used their own talents as nurse's aides or helped the Red Cross in canteens providing food, entertainment and company to servicemen. Many soldiers, sailors, marines or airmen away from home were invited into private homes for a home-cooked meal.

Women in the workforce were faced with the problem of discrimination, until they proved what they could do. But they also faced problems of transportation, shopping, cooking and caring for their children, in addition to working their shift. They were also earning their own paychecks and becoming more independent.

A fortunate few newly married women were able to travel to cities or towns near their husband's military training where they obtained employment and living quarters to be with their spouse as much as possible before his deployment overseas.

It took the catastrophe at Pearl Harbor to put America's plants and factories into full production converting from peacetime goods to wartime armaments. During the war over 200,000 companies, big and small converted to war production. The world's largest airplane factory, half a mile long and a quarter of a mile wide was built at Willow Run, Michigan, producing the B-24 Liberator bomber comprised of 100,000 parts. Also complicating the problem of production were hundreds of design changes. At its peak of produc-

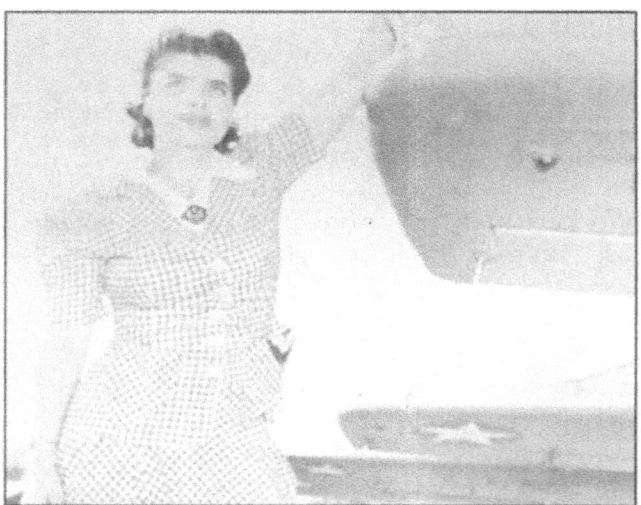

Mary Cunningham, Waterloo, poses at plane's wing, Randolph Field, Texas. Her Husband Gerald was an intelligence officer with the 7th Photo Reconnaissance Group, Mount Farm, England.

B-24 Production

tion, Willow Run was able to produce a B-24 bomber every 63 minutes.

Detroit car factories were the obvious places to manufacture wheeled and tracked vehicles, the most famous being the jeep. Mass production techniques used there were also used to produce weapons of every sort including airplane engines. Orders for airplanes and other equipment required production potential be enlarged and plants increased in capacity. Boeing, Douglas, Bell, Lockheed and Curtis-Wright Aircraft companies all expanded. Airplanes became faster, stronger, more agile and capable of longer flying range. Henry Kaiser mass-produced the Liberty ship to transport troops, tanks, airplanes, food, ammunition and other essential goods where ever needed worldwide. His shipbuilders, at one time, were able to build a ship in 80 and a half hours.

Americans were reminded every day there was a war on, taking part in air raid drills, coping with shortages and rationing, planting vegetable gardens, collecting scrap metal and hearing pleas to buy War Bonds on the radio, in movie theaters and on posters. Always lurking was the unspoken fear that haunted everyone on the home front, the possibility of receiving a telegram reporting the death, wounding or missing in action of a loved one in battle. Keeping busy left less time to reflect on this possibility.

Mim Peters, Grinnell, Iowa, was married just six weeks before America's entry into World War II. Her husband Bob subsequently entered the military. With the advent of rationing and a newborn child, Mim's sister registered the newborn for ration stamps to ensure the baby would have milk (canned). "You lived with the fear that you might get the telegram reporting your husband's death. We realized we couldn't get mail everyday. When the mail arrived it was six or seven letters at a time. It was particularly frustrating before D-Day when servicemen weren't allowed to write and I got no mail. Not realizing what was going on I got real worried something had happen."

Mim Peters, Grinnell, Iowa

World War II was a period of tremendous growth for the United States spurred on by technological advances in war production, mechanization in farming, advances in science and research, education in specialized subjects and population growth. While much of wartime production was geared toward the destruction of human life, it also went toward its preservation – DDT, penicillin, dried blood plasma, sulfa drugs, synthetic fuels, radar and of course atomic energy.

Willow Run

Iowans of the Mighty Eighth

Chapter Four

TRAINING

They were college students and farm boys or worked in a variety of jobs prior to the outbreak of war. They answered the call of their country and most enlisted into military service at Camp Dodge or Fort Des Moines, Iowa. Many had done little travelling beyond their county area of the State of Iowa. The next few years would take them places many had never heard of or dreamed about. The exigencies of war caused boys to become men overnight with awesome responsibilities and only partially experience the carefree existence of youth. They would be changed forever.

After induction into military service they were sent to Basic Training. Basic was not intensive in nature. A couple weeks was spent on marching, military code of conduct, testing and classification to determine their future role in the military. The most common sites used for Basic Training included Jefferson Barracks, St. Louis, Missouri; Sheppard Field, Wichita Falls, Texas; St Petersburg and Miami Beach, Florida; Buckley Field, Colorado and Amarillo, Texas.

Before being shipped overseas, air and ground crews and support personnel had to be trained quickly, a war was on. This meant men with no military experience and no experience in the area for which they were being trained had to be taught and become highly proficient. Lives depended on it. They were tested to determine their individual aptitudes and then began to learn a myriad of specialties such as engines, hydraulics, weather, aerial navigation, communications, munitions, weapons and flight. A few were actually sent to training schools for a specialization they had worked in during civilian life. Many were hurried directly to the war zone and would learn "on the job." Other's training would take two years to complete before they were deployed overseas.

Training Classes at Chanute Field, Illinois

Chapter Four

Military training sites and schools sprang up overnight. Schools some attended were often at opposite ends of the United States and required long train rides to reach their destination while others were fortunate to attend training in a general geographic area or even within the same state. A program entitled College Training Detachment (CTD) utilized colleges and universities to teach mathematics, weather, physics and other courses including basics of flight until openings for further stages of pilot training could be scheduled. Although other Iowa colleges and universities participated in this program, Coe College, Cedar Rapids; Iowa Wesleyan at Mount Pleasant, Grinnell College, Grinnell and Morningside College at Sioux City were schools interviewed Iowans attended for CTD Training. Aircraft manufacturers such as Bell, Lockheed, North American, and Boeing provided specialized instruction in mechanics and engineering. Skills would be developed many would use in post-war employment, but at the time they were trained for roles on an air or ground crew team whose sole purpose was the strategic bombing and destruction of an enemy and its ability to wage war.

As mechanics they would learn routine maintenance and repair on fighter and bomber aircraft engines, engine overhaul, and replacement if necessary, as well as hydraulics in operating landing gear, bomb bay doors and gun turrets. Mechanics Schools were located primarily at Amarillo, and Wichita Falls, TX; Biloxi, MS; TX; Rantoul, IL; Aurora and Denver, CO.

Armorers would learn mounting and repair of machine guns. They would be able to take the guns apart and re-assemble them virtually blindfolded as well as learn to load ammunition, bombs and install rocket launchers under fighter aircraft. Training sites were at Lowry and Buckley Fields, Colorado, both in the Denver area and at the Aberdeen, Maryland Proving Grounds.

Personnel working in Sub-depots would be overhauling and replacing thousands of aircraft engines and parts, and making major structural repairs under constant time restraints to maintain a maximum effort during all missions.

Radio Schools were conducted at Sioux Falls, SD; Chicago and Scott Field, IL; Madison and Milwaukee, WI; and Langley, Virginia. Other schools included those for instrument specialists, flight engineers, electronics, radar, meteorology, clerical, sheet metal, aerial photography and interpretation, teletype, drafting, supply, ordnance, chemicals, and fire fighting. Cooks had to be trained to feed thousands, as well as truck drivers for supply, military police for security, chaplains, and medical assistants. Each airplane, fighter or bomber, required an army of support personnel in order for it to fly into combat. Without them there would be no mission.

Aircrews would undergo training to form themselves into a combat team. A heavy bomber crew usually consists of ten men, the Pilot, Co-pilot, Bombardier, Navigator, Engineer who doubled at Top Turret Gunner, Radio Operator, Two Waist Gunners, Tail Gunner and Ball Turret Gunner. A fighter has a crew of one, the Pilot.

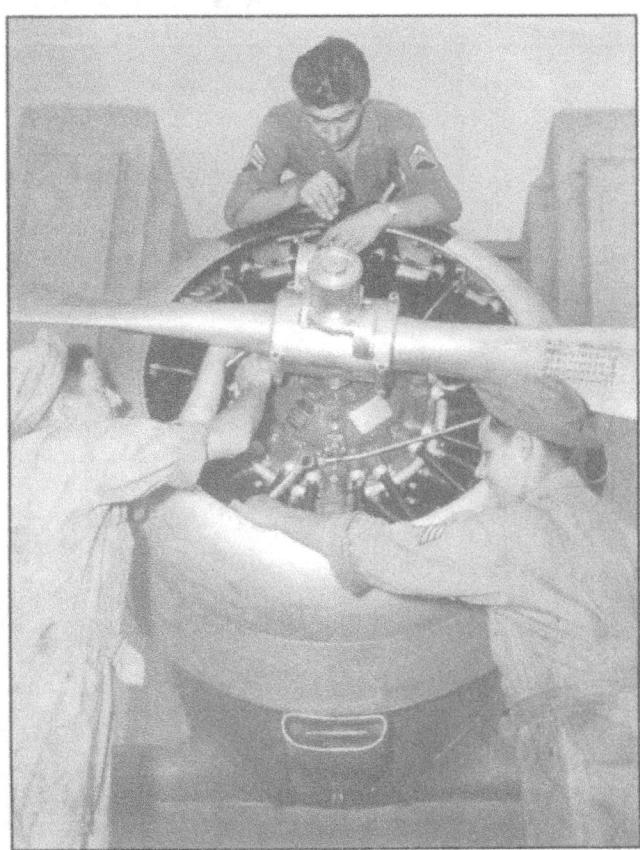

Pilot training required at least four phases of training to include Pre-flight, Basic Flight, Primary Flight and Advanced Flight Training., It could take up to two years of successful training before a pilot and crew would be deployed to overseas combat. At any point in their pilot training cadets could be "washed out," because they were unable to master the skills involved, sometimes eliminated on the whim of instructors, or as nation-wide training expanded, eliminated because of too many pilot applicants in the program and a need existed in other specialties. Some aviation cadets dropped out voluntarily and opted for training in other skills.

Pre-flight included up to two months training primarily at San Antonio, Texas and Santa Ana, California, in the theory of flight, navigation, aircraft recognition, Morse Code and always marching, calisthenics and military discipline. Then it was off to Primary Flight School at one of twenty-seven different locations predominantly in Texas, California and Arizona where flying was performed usually in a single engine airplane with a low wing. At Primary, for approximately five months they learned to takeoff, land, recover from spins and stalls, aerobatics and soloed. This was supplemented by hours of ground school in the classroom.

Nineteen different locations were mentioned where Basic Flight Training was taken. Basic involved flying another monoplane with an enclosed canopy, fixed landing gear and a more powerful engine. After five weeks flying and successful completion of training, cadets destined as bomber pilots were sent to twin-engine flight training. Afterward they were commissioned as Second Lieutenants. First Pilot training involved flying the four-engine bombers and ground school to include engineering of the plane, engines, mechanical and emergency features. Upon graduation each was assigned an aircrew and sent to a designated airbase for training to become combat ready and eventual overseas assignment.

Pilot training for transition to the B-17 bomber was held at such sites as Roswell and Hobbs, NM; Columbus, OH; Sebring,FL; Boca Raton, FL and Pyote, TX. Training on the B-24 included locations at San Diego, CA; Liberal, KS and Ft Worth, TX. Additional transition training was taken at various locations in the United States for the C-47 cargo plane, P-47 Thunderbolt fighter and B-26 medium bomber.

The Pilot is the airplane commander responsible for the safety and efficiency of the crew twenty-four hours a day. He must know each member of his crew individually, his idiosyncrasies, capabilities and shortcomings. He must maintain morale, discipline and monitor training of his crew. The

Training at Randolph Field, Texas

Learning to load ammunition at Randolph Field, San Antonio, Texas

Chapter Four

lives of all crewmembers may depend on how well each person performs his duties.

The Co-pilot is the Pilot's right-hand man. He must also be able to fly the airplane under all conditions, be proficient in engine operation, a qualified instrument pilot, able to navigate by day or night, able to operate all radio equipment, fly in formation and maintain a log of performance data.

Navigators are responsible for getting the aircraft in formation to and from the target on an assigned route requiring directional changes. The route is designed to minimize exposure to anti-aircraft fire, and weather conditions. He must know the position of the airplane at all times. He must determine the geographic position by: (1) Pilotage-visual reference to landmarks on the ground, particularly on the bomb run (2) Dead Reckoning – determine the position of the airplane by keeping an account of the track and distance flown from the point of departure or last known position (3) Radio – make use of various radio aids to determine position, and (4) Celestial – determine position by reference to two or more celestial bodies. He must maintain a log, constant contact with the pilot regarding course, air speed and changes in flight. Iowans who served as navigators with the Eighth Air Force in World War II received training at Hondo, Big Springs, Houston and San Marcus, Texas; Langley Field, Virginia and Monroe, Louisiana.

Sheppard Field, Wichita Falls, Texas

Bombardier in Training

The Bombardier is in the nose of the airplane. Trained in operation of the highly secret Norden bombsight he is in complete control of the airplane during the final minutes of the bomb run over the target. Instrumentation attached to the bombsight allows the bombardier to transmit to the pilot directional changes to put the bombs on target. This is the most critical time of the whole mission when the aircraft must fly at a constant speed and altitude to put the bombs on target. Any change without opportunity to correct his bombsight can cause the bombs to miss their target. At this time the bomber is exposed to accurate anti-aircraft barrage and enemy fighters. The bombardier must know his bombing instruments, racks, switches, controls, releases, doors and linkages are in first-class operating condition. He must be able to make adjustments and minor repairs in flight, operate all gun positions, load and fuse his own bombs, understand bombing problems, probabilities, and bombing errors, be versed in aircraft identification and assist the navigator if needed or incapacitated. Bombardier training was held at Big Springs, Midland, Houston and Childress, TX; Roswell, Deming and Albuquerque, NM.

Gunners protect the flanks, rear, underside, top and nose of the bombers. Bombers were not pressurized and would fly at altitudes up to 30,000 feet causing temperatures within the aircraft to reach 50-60 degrees below zero. Wearing heated suits, fleece-lined caps, gloves, jackets, boots and pants, goggles, throat microphones, and oxygen masks they would still have to be able to fire their machine guns at enemy aircraft while spent cartridges piled up at their feet. The two waist gunners firing single .50 caliber machine guns mounted in side windows would also have to "dance" to avoid colliding with each other in maneuvering to fire their weapons. Nose, top turret and tail gunners would fire twin .50-caliber machine guns in their positions. Ball turret gunners were generally the smallest of the gunners. For most of the flight to and from the target they would be confined in the turret in a cramped position in the "belly" of the aircraft, constantly on alert for enemy fighters. Gunners must have a fine sense of timing, be familiar with the coverage area of all gun positions and be ready to bring his guns to bear as conditions may warrant. They should be experts in aircraft identification and how to maintain their weapons and clear jams. Gunnery schools were held at sixteen different locations but primarily Las Vegas, NV; Laredo and Harlingen, TX; Kingman and Yuma, AZ.

Ball Turret Instruction

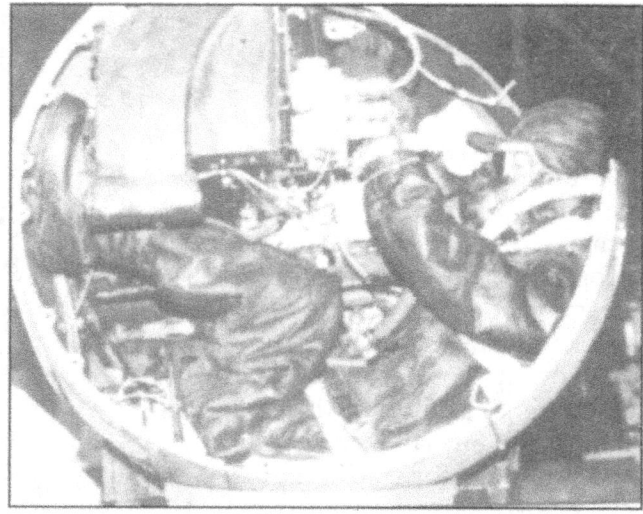
Ball Turret Gunner

The Engineer is supposed to know more about the airplane than any other crewmember, particularly the engines and armament. Working closely with the Co-pilot he will check engine operation, fuel consumption and operation of all equipment. He must be able to cock, lock and load the bomb racks, and know how to strip, clean and re-assemble guns. The engineer should have a general knowledge of radio equipment and assist in tuning transmitters and receivers. He will also double as a

AT-6 fighter training aircraft

top turret gunner during the bomb run. Flight Engineers were trained at Wichita Falls and Amarillo, TX; Ardmore, OK; Seattle, WA; Denver, CO; Rantoul, IL; New Orleans, LA and Biloxi, MS.

The Radio Operator is responsible for ensuring his equipment is operating to maintain communications within the aircraft, the formation and contact with command. He must report the airplane's position every thirty minutes, maintain a log, assist the navigator in taking fixes and understand navigational aids in the airplane. He may also be a gunner during periods of combat and render first aid if needed.

Before deployment overseas bomber crews completed a final phase of training. After they had completed their specialized training, gunners, radiomen, navigators, bombardiers, pilots and co-pilots reported to air bases where they met for the first time, the other men who would comprise their crew. Overseas training was taken at 41 different locations. These bases were widely scattered throughout the United States and included Sioux City, IA. For the next two months they would perform their individual specialties in practice missions to mold themselves into an effective combat team. Practice allowed for deficiencies to be strengthened and knowledge gained of each other's tendencies, strengths and weaknesses. As they were to find out in combat, each crewmember was dependent on the other to not only do his job, but to survive. From then on until they were deployed to the United Kingdom and completed the required number of missions for rotation back to the United States, they would eat, sleep and play together and know practically everything there was to know about each others' personal lives.

Donald Thompson, Central City, Iowa, served in the 384th Bomb Group. In an article written by him for the Cedar Rapids Gazette in August, 1984, he recalled receiving his pilot's wings two months before his twentieth birthday. Now came the responsibility of molding himself and his crew into an effective combat team. It was a memorable day for him, as a nineteen-year old, when he and his crew walked out on the flight line to his newly assigned B-17 that would take them to England and combat.

The average age of pilots in one Bomb Group in World War II was twenty. Faced with the reality of lost youth, responsible for the lives of others in a kill or be killed situation, scores of young airmen completed 25-35 missions before turning twenty years of age.

Training is training. No one is shooting at you. Still over 18,000 airmen died in training accidents in the United States.

Future bomber pilots in formation at Ellington Field, Texas.

Plane banking over Randolph Field

HEAVY BOMBER CREW POSITIONS

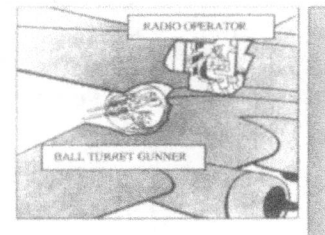

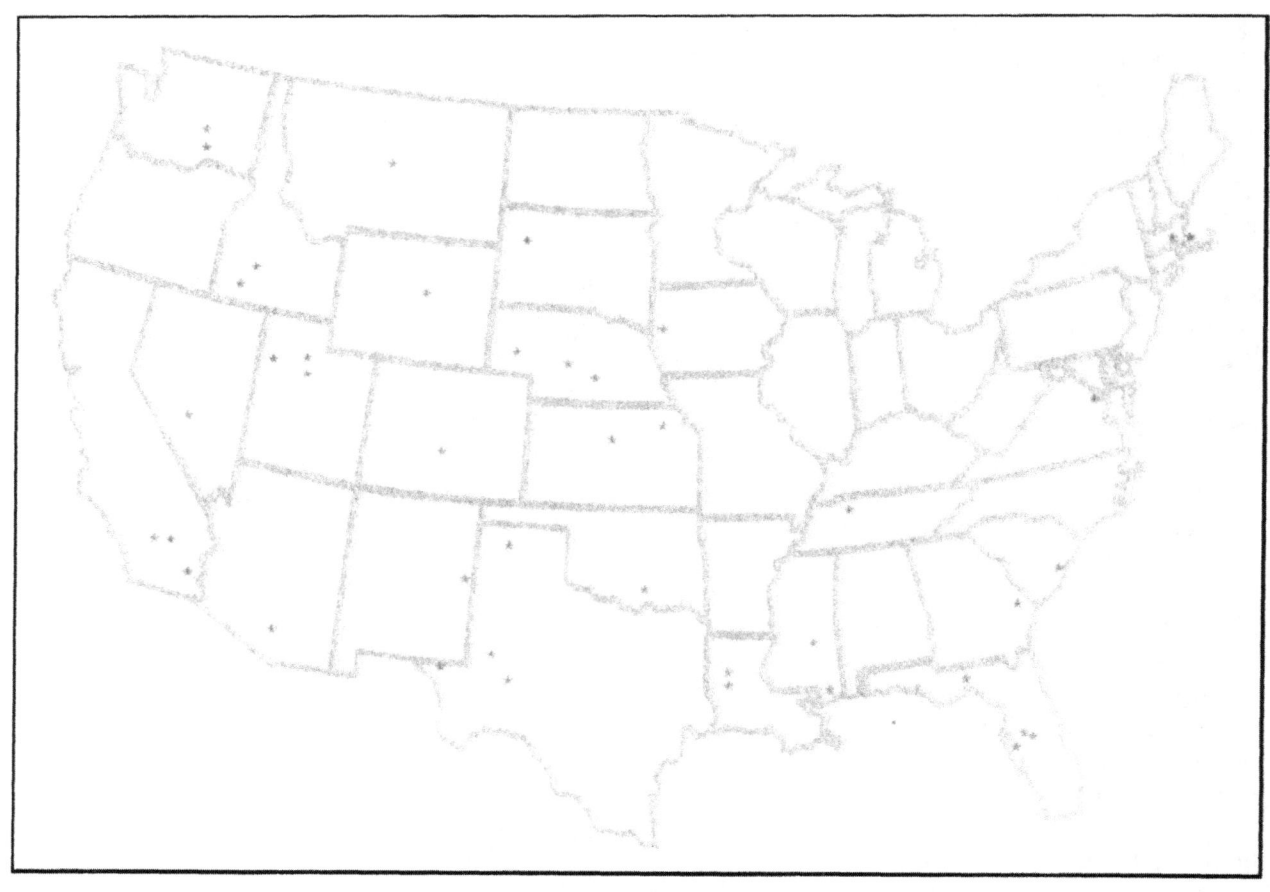

Locations where Iowans of the Eighth Air Force In World War II completed overseas training in preparation for deployment to the European Theater of Operations

Alexandria, LA	Kearney, NE	Tallahassee, FL
Ardmore, OK	Kearns, UT	Tampa, FL
Avon Park, FL	Lake Charles, LA	Tonapah, NV
Blythe, CA	Langley, VA	Topeka, KS
Boise, ID	Lewistown, MT	Walla Walla, WA
Boston, MA	McCook, NE	Wendover, UT
Casper, WY	Meridian, MS	Westover, MA
Charleston, SC	Mountain Home, ID	
Clovis, NM	Muroc, CA	
Colorado Springs, CO	Pyote, TX	
Dalhart, TX	Rapid City, SD	
DeRitter, LA	Riverside, CA	
Dyersburg, TN	Salina, KS	
El Paso, TX	Salt Lake City, UT	
Ephrata, WA	Savannah, GA	
Grand Island, NE	Sioux City, IA	
Gulfport, MS	St. Petersburg, FL	

Chapter Four

LOCATIONS WHERE IOWANS TOOK PRE-FLIGHT, PRIMARY, BASIC AND ADVANCED PHASES OF PILOT TRAINING

Albany, GA	Blytheville, AR	Fayetteville, AR	Independence, KS	Malden, MO	Pyote, TX	Scottsdale, AZ	Tulare, CA
Alexandria, LA	Camden, SC	Ft Stockton, TX	Jackson, MS	Marfa, TX	Pine Bluff, AR	Shaw Field, GA	Victorville, CA
Altus, OK	Rantoul, IL	Ft Sumner, NM	King City, CA	Merced, CA	Phoenix, AZ	Sherman, TX	Visalia, CA
Amarillo, TX	Chico, CA	Frederick, OK	Las Vegas, NV	Moffitt Field, CA	Riverside, CA	Stamford, TX	Waco, TX
Arcadia, FL	Coffeyville, KS	Garden City, KS	Lemoore, CA	Montgomery, AL	Roswell, NM	Stockton, CA	
Bakersfield	Coleman, TX	Glendale, AZ	Lubbock, TX	Omaha, NE	Sacramento, CA	Sumter, SC	
Bonham, TX	Corsicana, TX	Greenville, TX	Luke AAB, AZ	Ontario, CA	Santa Ana, CA	Taft, CA	
Brady, TX	Cuero, TX	Hemet, CA	McAllen, TX	Paris, TX	San Angelo, TX	Tampa, FL	
Blythe, CA	Douglas, AZ	Houston, TX	McBride, MO	Pecos, TX	San Antonio, TX	Tucson, AZ	

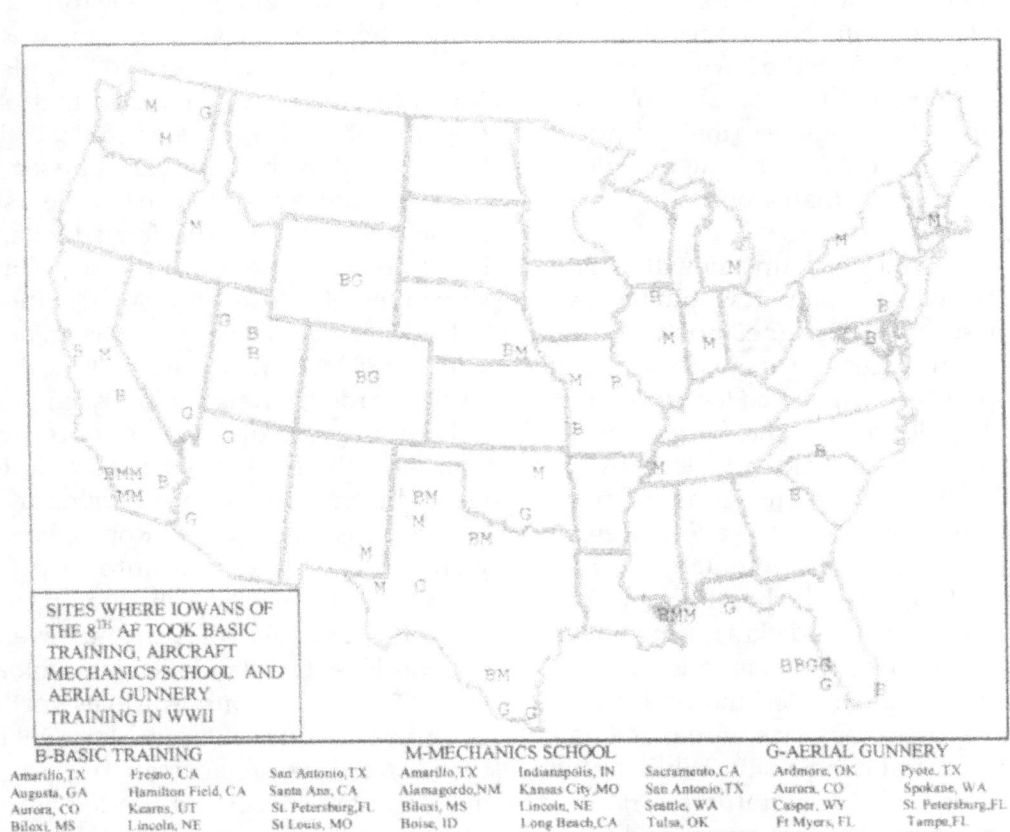

SITES WHERE IOWANS OF THE 8TH AF TOOK BASIC TRAINING, AIRCRAFT MECHANICS SCHOOL AND AERIAL GUNNERY TRAINING IN WWII

B-BASIC TRAINING			M-MECHANICS SCHOOL		G-AERIAL GUNNERY	
Amarillo, TX	Fresno, CA	San Antonio, TX	Amarillo, TX	Indianapolis, IN	Sacramento, CA	Ardmore, OK	Pyote, TX
Augusta, GA	Hamilton Field, CA	Santa Ana, CA	Alamagordo, NM	Kansas City, MO	San Antonio, TX	Aurora, CO	Spokane, WA
Aurora, CO	Kearns, UT	St. Petersburg, FL	Biloxi, MS	Lincoln, NE	Seattle, WA	Casper, WY	St. Petersburg, FL
Biloxi, MS	Lincoln, NE	St Louis, MO	Boise, ID	Long Beach, CA	Tulsa, OK	Ft Myers, FL	Tampa, FL
Charlotte, NC	Miami Beach, FL	Valley Forge, PA	Boston, MA	Los Angeles, CA	Willow Run, MI	Harlingen, TX	Wendover, UT
Cheyenne, WY	Neosho, MO	Wichita Falls, TX	Dyersburg, TN	Lubbock, TX	Wichita Falls, TX	Kingman, AZ	Yuma, AZ
Clearwater, FL	Provo, UT		El Paso, TX	New Jersey	Yakima, WA	Laredo, TX	
Denver, CO	Riverside, CA		Glendale, CA	Niagara Falls, NY		Las Vegas, NV	
Ft. Meade, MD	Rockford, IL		Gulfport, MS	Rantoul, IL		Panama City, FL	

Chapter Five

DEPLOYMENT

After training as a crew to mold themselves into a combat ready team, next came deployment to England and the European Theater of Operations. If they had the opportunity this was the last chance for them all to say goodbye to loved ones. For twenty-six thousand men of the Eighth Air Force it would be the last goodbye. Ahead lay an uncertain future. They didn't know what to expect or their individual fate. They embarked to a country where they were "adopted" by its people and treated with as much concern as one of the family. Yet ground crews and support personnel would be faced with working long hours often under extreme weather conditions and pressure from command. Aircrews would experience total fear, the horrors of mortal combat, suffer emotional turmoil and for many, make associations that would last their entire life. All would receive limited reward and experience loneliness, frustration, exhaustion and personal loss on a daily basis.

Bomber crews would pick up a new B-17 or B-24 bomber in the United States. It would be flown to either the base of their assigned bomber group or, if they were replacement crews, the aircraft would be dropped off at specified locations in Ireland, Scotland, Wales or England for retro-fitting to make the airplane combat ready. Usually this meant addition of armor plating, guns and bomb racks. The crews would report to a Replacement Center and, after a period of orientation, would then be assigned to a specific bomb group. B-17 aircraft were flown to England via a northern route from Bangor, ME, to Goose Bay, Labrador; Gandor, Newfoundland; Greenland, Iceland and then to Britain. Some of these stops may or may not have been omitted as a refueling point. While not always the case, some B-24 aircraft were flown a southern route through South America and Africa to England. Additionally, bomber crews, ground crew personnel and fighter pilots reported to ports of debarkation on the East Coast where they boarded the "Queen Mary," "Queen Elizabeth" or other ocean liners and troop ships for the cross-Atlantic trip.

However they were deployed, danger lurked. Sailing on the huge luxury liners turned troop ships, as many as 20,000 soldiers, sailors and airmen were aboard. The five day trip meant twenty to thirty men sleeping in rooms normally reserved for two to three people. They had to be fed and accommodated as to personal hygiene. Many had never sailed on the ocean and depending on the seas, size of the ship and weather, seasickness was a problem. The danger of being torpedoed by German U-boats was constant. Lowell Rothbart, an aircraft mechanic with the 20th Fighter Group at Kings Cliffe, England, recalled that on arrival in England aboard the "Queen Elizabeth" the ship had to drop anchor five miles at sea because no dock space was available to handle a ship the size of the "QE." Troops were ferried to land on small boats taking five days to unload. This made the ship vulnerable to attack from both the air and sea.

Cecil Cooper, Ottumwa, was an aerial gunner with the 392nd Bomb Group at Wendling, England. Cecil boarded a Kaiser Liberty ship to cross the Atlantic in a convoy. "The sea never seemed to be calm and the boat listed from side to side and heaved from bow to stern causing most of us on board to become seasick. Ropes were tied along walkways for grabbing onto to prevent being swept overboard. The only good part of the voyage was a contingent of Army nurses also aboard."

Leon Hoegh, Atlantic, was a cook assigned to the 303rd Bomb Group at Molesworth, England. Leon boarded the "Queen Mary" with eighteen thousand other American troops. "The ship moved out at sunset and headed North on a zig-zag course to prevent submarine attack. The captain turned the ship wide open at night when smoke from the diesel engines couldn't be detected on the horizon. There were sixteen of us staying in a room designed to accommodate two people. We got to sleep in the room every other night. The odd night we had to find our own place to sleep, on deck or on stairways. There was vomit everywhere from those that got seasick."

Elmer Johansmeier, Burlington, was a mechanic with the 2003 Ordnance and Maintenance Company in support of the Eighth Air Force at Risley, England. Elmer boarded the "QE" with 23,000 other troops. "Bunks were stacked clear to the ceiling. Troops spent 24 hours below decks and 24 hours above deck." To feed this number of soldiers required a constant "chow" line. Elmer was designated a ship's runner requiring he be on duty 24 hours a day. He had the benefit of sleeping in a headquarters compartment and have access to the dining room at any time.

Edward Kelly, Corydon, sailed on the "Ile de France" ocean liner for Scotland and the 44th Bomb Group at Shipdham, England. "It was a terrible trip. The seas were rough, stormy and "everyone got sick."

John Beckman, Ankeny, in November, 1944, boarded the "USS Wakefield" at Camp Miles Standish, Boston, Massachusetts. "I think I was seasick before I got out of Boston harbor. The seas were rough and everyone down below was sick."

Ray Marner, Iowa City, was a Personnel and Supply Sergeant assigned to the 44th Bomb Group at Shipdham. He boarded the "S.S. Chantilly" at New York. "The ship was in bad repair. The crew was composed mainly of Hindu natives from Calcutta, India. We joined 74 other ships to form a convoy. The "Chantilly" was the only ship carrying troops and was placed near the rear of the convoy with only three other ships behind us. It took seventeen days to sail to Glasgow, Scotland. We had poor sleeping arrangements, seasickness and the worst food any of us had ever eaten."

Russell Orwig, Bettendorf, was an aerial gunner with the 386th Bomb Group at Boxted, England. Russell boarded the "Queen Elizabeth" for a five day sail across the Atlantic to Scotland. "Near the end of the voyage the ship turned 180 degrees and sailed for half a day before turning back on course. This action was taken to avoid a German U-boat "Wolf Pack" converging on the "QE" course.

A similar experience occurred to Marvin Otto, with the 100th Service Group at Rattlesden, England. He boarded the "Aquatania" at New York with 22,000 other soldiers. "We took one day longer to get to England because German subma-

Marino Pusateri, Cedar Rapids, on right, aboard ship in route to the ETO and 942nd Topographics Engineers attached to the Eighth Air Force.

rines were spotted ahead of us and we detoured around them."

Bob Messerly, Janesville, was with the 80th Medical Unit assigned to the 486th Bomb Group at Sudbury, England. Bob boarded a ship as part of a convoy that would take fourteen days to cross the Atlantic. They sailed into a storm in route. "When the storm cleared no other ships in the convoy were in sight. A young soldier on board ship was crying "I don't want to die. The Germans are going to get us." The convoy reformed after the storm and proceeded to England with a destroyer escort.

Fred Marold, Waterloo, performed clerical duties in the communications section of the 44th Bomb Group at Shipdham, England. He boarded a troop ship at Camp Kilmer, New Jersey and sailed for Glasgow, Scotland, in a convoy of ships. "The first ten days of the voyage were uneventful. The night of March 10 at 630PM a tanker in the convoy was hit and sunk by torpedoes fired from German submarines. Troops were ordered to stay on deck. Later that night another tanker was torpedoed and sunk. The balance of the voyage was without incident."

Les Portwood, Boone, was a dental technician at the 21st Air Depot Group near Ipswich, England. He sailed aboard the "Anthon Castle" ocean liner as part of a 454-ship convoy for Glasgow, Scotland. In route a soldier on his ship opened a porthole at night exposing light from the interior of the ship. The soldier was court-martialed and the ship was pulled from the convoy to make it to Scotland on its own.

Donald Richards, Waterloo, was with the 2006th Ordnance Company based near Melchbourne, England, in support of the Eighth Air Force. He boarded the ocean liner "Aquatania" in July, 1943. "One night out of the United States the ship ran into a German sub and outran it. A 'wolf pack' of submarines was waiting for the liner. The ship's Captain turned everything off on the ship, drifted out of the ring of submarines and then headed for Scotland."

Everett Sandersfeld, South Amana, was an aircraft mechanic assigned to the 385th Bomb Group at Knettishall, England. Everett boarded the "Aquatania" for Scotland. "The rough seas tossed the ship around like a cork. Water swept over the deck and ran under our bunks. Oatmeal served on board was thick with little white worms so I subsisted on candy bars for most of the trip."

Thousands of American soldiers sailed from the East Coast to ports in England and Scotland. German submarines that operated alone and in 'wolf packs' attacked supply convoys to England and Russia and inflicted heavy losses to the merchant marine in men, ships and material. They were also lying in wait within visual distance of American cities to attack shipping. While they were a constant threat to all shipping, why troop ships were able to avoid being struck is unknown. Ocean liners such as the "Queen Mary," "Queen Elizabeth" and the "Aquatania" were able to sail from New York to England in five days. Following a zig-zag course their speed allowed them to outrun submarines. Even with German U-boat knowledge of such great ships carrying troops it seems a miracle they succeeded in delivering their cargo to the war zone without harm.

Fantail of troop ship in route to England

George Clark, Ames,. "We spent sixteen days in a convoy. Our ship was eighteen thousand tons. We hit a sleet storm in the North Atlantic. There were two Victory ships ahead of us that would go over a wave and go down a trough where other waves would wash over the bow of the ships. At times the rear "screws" would be out of the water. I was in G Deck. The only thing below me was the hold of the ship. Bunks were stacked five high and I was in the top bunk. We took turns in the bunks. For twenty-four hours we were down below and the next twenty-four hours we were on deck where we slept. Each time we moved we had to take our gear with us. During the storm water in the latrines would wash all over the deck where we were. Guys got seasick and it was a mess."

Flying to England meant taking either the northern or southern route. Flying up and over the North Atlantic was the shortest of routes via Labrador or Newfoundland, Greenland, and Iceland all for refueling purposes and then on to England. Many airmen in route to the air battle over Europe would lose their lives to navigation or flight inexperience, mechanical or equipment failures, lack of fuel attributed to weather, navigation or equipment, crashes and unknown causes.

Leon Mehring, Cedar Rapids, Iowa, left Georgia on January 7, 1945. After refueling at Bangor, Maine Leon and his crew landed at Goose Bay, Labrador where snow was thirty feet high on both sides of the runway. When taking off in a blinding snowstorm the propeller on number four-engine hit a snow bank and the engine started to vibrate. They were denied permission to return to base because the next plane after theirs had crashed on takeoff. They proceeded to Greenland on three engines. Unable to land there because of weather, the crew proceeded to Iceland, had a propeller change and then flew on to England, taking ten days to make the trip.

George Berry, Winterset, aerial gunner with the 447th Bomb Group at Rattlesden, England, flew with his crew from Bangor, Maine to Goose Bay, Labrador. From there, in route to Iceland, the wings of their aircraft "iced up." "We got lost and our gas tanks were about down to zero. We had thrown out everything we could to lose weight including our radio equipment except for one, when our radio operator finally got a hold of Iceland to direct us in. We had to stay there thirty-one days until the aircraft was repaired before we flew out. Each day there we had only four hours of daylight and the wind seemed like it blew a hundred miles an hour."

Ward Britson, Radcliffe, aerial gunner with the 93rd Bomb Group at Hardwick, England, was supposed to fly from New Hampshire to Goose Bay, Labrador, then to Iceland and on to Prestwick, Scotland. They carried extra fuel in wing tanks but nearing Iceland found their transfer pumps allowing extra fuel to enter the engines didn't work. They were forced to turn back only to find the nearest base, Greenland, was "socked in" due to weather. With only fifteen minutes of fuel remaining and being one hour from Labrador their transfer pumps began working. They landed at Labrador and stayed five days because of a snowstorm then resumed their trip.

Marvin Ford, Tipton, was a flight engineer and aerial gunner with the 381st Bomb Group at Ridgewell, England. Flying through Goose Bay, Labrador in route to Belfast, Ireland, "we had to spend ten days at Goose Bay because of bad weather. Flying into Goose Bay in heavy fog we broke out from the fog at just four hundred feet above ground. We found the runway lighted by smudge pots. "I've never been so scared."

Hjalmar Hellberg, Jr, Marshalltown, was a ball turret gunner with the 379th Bomb Group at Kimbolton, England. "I had never seen snow like they had at Labrador. Except for the runways, they rolled the snow to flatten it. It built up covering the buildings so you had to go downhill into the mess hall. While there a fueling truck hit a wing of our airplane causing a delay to repair it."

Francis Kapler, Waterloo, was a pilot with the 385th Bomb Group at Great Ashfield, England. In route to England his aircraft was struck by lightning while over New York State. "It appeared as if there was a ball of fire off the nose of the aircraft. Our instruments were going haywire and the lightning had melted some of our wiring. We landed at Iceland and spent three days there while the whole airplane was re-wired.

Carl Kitchen, Waterloo, was a Co-pilot with the 490th Bomb Group at Eye, England. "We flew to Gander, Newfoundland for re-fueling where the temperature was 45 degrees below zero. We took off in a blizzard for Iceland where we spent Christmas, 1944.

Gilbert Lindberg, West Branch was to fly from New Hampshire to Gander, Newfoundland and then to Iceland in route to England. Near Labrador "our compass wasn't faithful. I was watching the negative compass which indicated we were flying in a southerly direction. I called the navigator and asked how we were doing. He replied that we were right on. I asked him if he had checked other compasses and our position. After a moment of silence he said "Oh my God." We were going the wrong direction."

Robert Megchelsen, Washington, was an aerial gunner with the 91st Bomb Group at Bassingbourn, England. From Presque Isle, Maine, Robert and his crew flew to Newfoundland where they stayed for two weeks because of snow and bad weather. Other aircraft being ferried to England were also forced to land at Newfoundland because of the weather and the airplanes began to backup on the base.

Flying the southern route under normal circumstances would take longer to reach England. It was not without its problems too. Wide stretches of open water had to be crossed and Allied bases for rest, refueling, and equipment repair were not readily available.

Howard Hobbs, Morning Sun, Iowa, left Walla Walla, Washington, for Florida with his crew for the final phase of training before deployment overseas. Encountering engine trouble in route they were forced to land at Lubbock, Texas on two engines, nearly out of fuel and barely missing a freight train near the end of the runway. They caught a train to Florida. On September 1, 1943, they were off to Snetterton Heath, England, home of the 96th Bomb Group. The trip would take thirteen days via Trinidad; Brazil; Dakar, Africa; and the French Morocco.

Willard Higdon, 458th Bomb Group traveled the same route. In Africa they flew into a dust storm. Their compasses went crazy and they became lost, landing out of fuel at Rio Del Oro, Africa. They were reported missing since they didn't arrive at Dakar. The crew was taken by boat to the Canary Islands, then to Spain and after a bus trip to Gibraltar, flown to their base at Horsham-St Faith, England.

Part of the wreckage of Darwin Joliffe's aircraft at McCook AAC Base

Darwin Joliffe, Dayton, was an aerial gunner with the 446th Bomb Group at Bungay, England. Darwin was initially ordered to the Pacific Theater of Operations. After a series of aircraft equipment failures and a crash landing at McCook, Nebraska, Army Air Base, he and his crew were reassigned to the European Theater and routed through Florida, Puerto Rico, South America and Africa. On arrival in South America, his pilot was relieved of his duties due to mental stress. Given another pilot they continued the balance of their flight.

Howard Linn, Hubbard, was a flight engineer and aerial gunner with the 492nd Bomb Group at North Pickenham, England. Howard and his crew were routed through Trinidad, British Guinea, Brazil and Africa, a ten day trip touching four continents.

Loyd Morse, Fort Dodge, was a pilot with the 448th Bomb Group at Seething, England. Getting to England took longer than was expected. While at Puerto Rico, ground crews, while preflighting the engines to Loyd's aircraft, accidentally released the brakes. When the plane started rolling the brakes were applied with such force the nose wheel collapsed dumping the plane on its nose. It was thirty days before the aircraft was repaired and Loyd and his crew continued their trip.

Deployment also meant leaving the United States and loved ones far behind. A new adventure began from which no one knew whether or not they would return. Each pondered his own fate without knowing what lay ahead. They knew they had a job to do and went about it with a sense of purpose. They would lose their youth, see and experience things that would stay with them forever. Some would come back and lead normal lives putting the past behind them. Others would bear physical and mental scars forever. A few would carry a self-imposed guilt that would haunt them for years. "Why did I survive when some of my friends or fellow crewmembers didn't?"

Those that survived were a part of the mightiest air armada ever assembled. To their dying day they carry a special pride in their individual bomber or fighter group, in the Eighth Air Force, and the fact that they were right in the middle of one of the most historical events in the history of mankind.

Chapter Six

Chapter Six
LIFE ON THE ENGLISH HOME FRONT

The Munich Pact of 1938 between Germany and England allowed the Germans to invade the Sudetenland of Czechoslovakia, a pre-dominantly German speaking portion of that country. Czech diplomats were not represented at the conference and were told of the decision between Hitler and Prime Minister Chamberlain after it was reached. Germany agreed they would not pursue any further territorial gains, however it was Hitler's intent to invade Poland and overrun the country before England and France could mobilize and come to Poland's aid from a treaty of alliance signed between the countries. A treaty had also been secretly signed between the Soviet Union and Germany to allow Germany to invade Poland without Soviet interference. Hitler's armies invaded Poland on September 1, 1939 and conquered the country in a mere 36 days. By May, 1940, Germany had overrun Holland, Belgium, Norway and most of France pinning the remnants of Allied armies on the beaches at Dunkirk. Only by German troops pausing to rest and re-supply were the Allied forces allowed to escape capture and annihilation by a massive evacuation using every type of boat available, both civilian and military. The evacuation saved over 340,000 allied soldiers to fight again and was deemed the "Miracle of Dunkirk."

The evacuation of Dunkirk saved thousand of lives to fight again. What was lost were massive amounts of arms and munitions to wage a war. American help began to arrive with Lend Lease. Supply ships by the thousands braved the North Atlantic in convoys to feed, clothe and arm Britain. Women were mobilized into factories for production of military goods. A Home Guard of older men were utilized as observers, guards and other duties to relieve able bodied men for the armed forces.

With German troops now just a scant 18 miles from the British port of Dover, all England expected an imminent invasion and massive bombing of their homeland. An invasion date of September 21, 1940 was set and termed Operation Sea Lion. Field Marshall Herman Goering, in command of German Luftwaffe forces convinced Hitler an invasion would not be necessary to conquer England. His air forces now based just across the English Channel would bring England to its knees by attacking its channel ports and shipping, bombing cities, aircraft manufacturing facilities and bases. This would bring the Royal Air Force into the air and he boasted, they would be eliminated. What wasn't considered was the resolve of the people of England and the daring of the Royal Air Force (RAF).

What became known as the Battle of Britain began on July 10, 1940. Radar gave advanced warning of incoming flights of German fighters and bombers. Anti-aircraft weapons and the skill of the RAF shot down hundreds of German planes. The RAF, greatly outnumbered in the air, managed in the next five months, to shoot down twice as many German planes as they had losses. With appalling losses during daylight bombings of London, Germany resorted to bombing English cities by night. By November when it was apparent the British could not be defeated through the air, Hitler put off the planned invasion and turned his attention toward an invasion of Russia.

Charlie Huggins, Mendlesham, an English Army veteran of World War I was utilized as a drill sergeant training new English recruits. A member of the Home Guard he also patrolled beaches armed only with a night stick. It was his belief that if Germany had invaded England instead of trying to defeat them by air "We wouldn't have had a chance."

Germany waged an indiscriminate bombing of English civilian centers. Attacks against military targets were minimal. A nighttime blackout for the duration of the war was imposed and enforced in

Joan (Lock) Allen, Plotter, ATS

all cities and towns. Blackout curtains were drawn on house windows, factories, or any other occupied building. Windows on shops and buildings were taped to prevent shattering and causing serious harm from explosions. Gas masks were issued for fear that bombs being dropped might contain lethal gas, a carry-over from World War I when poisonous gas was widely used on the battlefield. The gas masks were described as giving a Mickey Mouse appearance. Barrage balloons floated over the London by cable anchored on the ground to prevent low level bombing attacks. Homemade air raid shelters were built in gardens and backyards. In London people sought shelter in the Underground, London's mass transit system far below street level. Even then people were killed when bombs pierced through to the tunnels or exploded at entrances. For their protection children in major cities were sent to the countryside to live with relatives or friends.

Joan (Lock) Allen, Carshalton, Surrey, England, now of Panora, Iowa, was a Plotter in the Auxilliary Territorial Service (ATS), basically the British Army. Her job was to plot everything that moved on the ground, air and sea, giving course and speed. Her family home was in a suburb about twenty miles from London. She recalls spending all night in their air raid shelter until the "All Clear" at dawn. Her family home was severely damaged three times from bombs although not sustaining a direct hit. Windows and doors were blown out and household goods, irreplaceable because of shortages and rationing, were destroyed.

Joan will never forget the day war was declared "My girlfriend and I decided we would pass the time. We walked on down to the next block and I told my friend "There are getting to be a lot more up there(airplanes)." " What are they going to do?' she asked. I said "probably practicing." We were jabbering away walking down the street. After about a mile we saw airplanes forming up, the sky was full of them. My girlfriend said "you're right there are a lot of them." They started flying over us. Zoom, Zoom, Zoom, we looked up "they're Germans" They started machine gunning us. They were coming treetop high. We jumped behind a tree and bullets whizzed by us. She looked at me and I looked at her. I said "I don't know about you but I'm going home." We ran home. When I got there out of breath mom was standing in the air raid shelter doorway. Sirens were going off. She was the only one home. She said "Oh, I'm so glad you're here, I don't know what to do." I said "I don't know either mom but get out of the doorway."

Chapter Six

Germany lost the Battle of Britain in its efforts to bring England to its knees and sue for peace. The arrival of the Eighth Air Force and its gradual build-up of bomber and fighter groups took awhile but eventually air superiority was gained by Allied forces. Bombings and fighter attacks on England by the Germans could not be sustained on a continual basis and became sporadic. Instead, V-1 and V-2 rockets launched from sites in Germany began to be directed toward England. The V-1 also known as the "buzz bomb" or "doodle-bug" was packed with explosives and enough fuel to at least reach the English coast. When it ran out of fuel it would dive to earth and explode. Noisy with a distinctive "putt putt" sound, its speed and visibility made it susceptible to anti-aircraft guns. Allied fighters were also able to fly faster than the rocket and shoot down the majority of those launched before they could touch ground. Many of those that did make it unscathed exploded harmlessly in the countryside. Yet many landed in population centers and lives were lost. With development of the V-2, the rocket was launched vertically, reached super-sonic speeds and was virtually invisible. Without warning devastating explosions would occur where ever they fell. Some have said that although they were invisible they had a sort of whistle to them and you learned to take cover when you heard the sound. Others would notice a red fireball descending to earth and knew it to be the V-2.

An island nation and limited in natural resources, Britain was dependent on the sea lanes for survival. German U-boats attacked convoys sinking ships from the United States bringing thousands of essential items. The loss of ships, the bombings, and the necessity of using everything they had for the war effort, severe rationing was imposed on sugar, butter, meat, gasoline, clothes and hundreds of other precious commodities. The government imposed a near starvation diet on its people. They were issued ration stamps based on their family size and allowed so much per week. Then there was no guarantee they would be able to get the items. Store shelves were bare. When someone would hear talk of a truck coming with grocery items, lines would form. In the distribution, supplies might run out and some would get nothing. To step out of a line for anything meant a person would lose their place.

Pat Eberle, from Kempston, Bedford, England, now Scranton, Iowa, recalls that as a child she was "kind of sickly." "I saw my first orange when I was five, my first banana when I was seven. My mother gave me a banana, I cried. I didn't know what to do with it. I didn't know how to eat it. I'd stand in line, and stand and stand. Once I fainted. My mother got out of line and came to me "oh my poor darling what has happened to you? See what you've done now, your father won't get his sausages. You should never have done that."

Flying Buzz Bomb

Diving Buzz Bomb

Jean Cadwallader formerly of Bishops Stortford, Hertz, England, now of Coon Rapids, Iowa, remembers when her mother was able to get a fresh, brown egg. "All four of us in the family stood around and watched mother cook the egg. When it was done she put it on a plate and cut it into four pieces so we each could have some."

Parachutes recovered from downed airmen or crashed airplanes was made into underwear and clothes. Old army blankets were made into suits, jackets or pants. Victory gardens supplemented their starvation diet. Local wildlife, primarily rabbits were chased down and caught for meat. Joan Allen summed it up best, "You learned that today might be your last. You didn't worry about tomorrow because you were worrying about today. That's how we lived." Glenda Braland, Cambridge, England, now residing in Story City, Iowa added, "if you had a husband or father in service, God knows where and not knowing if they were dead or alive, and at the same time we had to contend with bombs, finding food every day, and if you were bombed you had to find a place to live. Would your relatives ever find you?"

An invasion did occur however. A "Friendly Invasion," beginning in 1942 of American GIs, a quarter of a million of them airmen of the Eighth Air Force. Eventually English cities and towns would be filled with air and ground crew and support personnel, as well as other Allied servicemen and women, sight seeing, attending concerts, dances, clubs and pubs. The beleaguered British, already suffering from the austerity of two years of war, met the well paid, outgoing American with skepticism at first. They were "cocky" and "knew it all." It didn't take long for the servicemen to endear themselves to the English. In addition to aiding in their economy and coming to their aid, they knew also, the Americans were far from home as were their own sons in service. Americans were soon invited to English homes for meals on weekends. Their gratitude was best expressed in sharing their meager rations when in doing so they were doing without themselves.

Village pubs near air bases were very popular. GIs also attended movies and dances in towns and hosted monthly dances on their air base. English mothers and fathers warned their daughters "Don't bring a Yank home, don't go out with them." Despite these warnings truckloads of English girls were brought to the dances. By some strange coincidence the trucks, sometimes were not nearly as full on the return trip. It caused one Commanding Officer of a base to issue a "generous" order demanding that all civilians must be off the base by Wednesday following the Saturday night dance.

With the secrecy surrounding D-Day, the Allied invasion of France, a similar incident occurred at Martlesham Heath, home of the 356th Fighter Group involving English girls from the surrounding area employed on the base. On the eve of D-Day at 1400 hours (2:00 P.M.), the base was sealed off and no one was allowed to leave the base. Personnel returning from leaves or passes were allowed back on base, but once there, they had to stay. This also meant the English girls were being forced to stay on base with several thousand American servicemen.

This was not accepted well by the girl's families. When they failed to return home from work that evening a number of English mothers were quite upset that their daughters were penned in at the base and some appeared at the base to take the girls home. They were allowed into Martlesham, but they too, were not allowed out. This was definitely not furthering British-American relationships.

When the English wives and mothers failed to return, the fathers got into the act. Six of them demanded entrance to the field, ready to return with their families. After all, it was suppertime and the cooks were gone. They gained entrance, and like all the others, were forced to remain there. Finally the vicar of the church of Ipswich got into the act. Besieged by parents wanting their daughters home, the Anglican minister appeared at the main gate to the base, demanding the townspeople be released. He was allowed onto the base and, like the rest, was not allowed to return until after the invasion was over. There were a lot of very upset English country folk over this affair, but no complaints were ever heard from any of the English girls.

Thousands of marriages or promises of marriage of English women and American GIs would result from airbase dances, parties and acquaintances made in the communities. While some would not endure and others were empty promises, many lasting marriages arose from the "Friendly Invasion." British War Bride Clubs and Trans-Atlantic Brides-Parents Associations (TBPA) sprang up in America after the war. They combined to receive discount charter flights to and from England and remain active chapters. The four English ladies pictured below married American GIs.

Leon Mehring, 305th Bomb Group stationed at Chelveston, England, now of Cedar Rapids, Iowa, met Vera Handshaw at a dance. They celebrated their 59th wedding anniversary in the year 2004. They had five children.

While far from inclusive other English warbrides of Iowans include Mrs Joyce (Evans) Van Duyn, Iowa City, formerly of Wolverhampton, England; Mrs Nancy Grubb, Holstein; Mrs. Robert White, Burlington; Mrs Elmer Steven, Spencer and Mrs Laverne Varenhorst, Storm Lake.

Not everyone was pleased with the 'American Invasion." The complaint of most English men was that "the trouble with Americans are they are over-paid, over-sexed and over here." What endeared the English people to the Americans most was their kind and generous treatment of the English children. Parties, particularly at Christmas, were hosted at many air bases for local English children. Truckloads of children from the surrounding area were transported to bases where purchased and handmade gifts were given to each child. Plenty of food was served. Many children tasted ice cream for the first time. Chocolate, chewing gum and cookies were generously distributed.

Glenda Braland was in Infant School for five to six year olds. "American convoys always went by our school. The teachers would let children out of school to stand by the fence along the road. The Americans would throw us candy as they went by, then we would share what we got." Pat Eberle knew where the American convoys passed near her home. With a girlfriend they changed out of their school clothes into old clothes, put dirt on their faces and stood by the road. "Yanks came by and threw us candy and cookies. Then we changed back to our school clothes, washed the dirt off our faces and took our "sweets" home. We knew that if we looked poor we would get more.

The people of England suffered and sacrificed, but persevered. With American help they kept their chin up and were finally able to celebrate the end of a six year blackout on V-E Day with, as a song of the time said, "When the lights come on again, all over the world."

Leon & Vera Mehring

Brit Ladies -From the left, Marion Joan Allen, Carshalton, Surrey, England(Panora, Iowa); Glenda Braland, Cambridge, England(Story City, Iowa); Jean Cadwallader, Bishops Stortford, Hertz, England(Coon Rapids, Iowa) and Pat Eberle, Kempston, Bedford, England(Scranton, Iowa).

Allen's Wedding – S/Sgt Glenn Allen and bride Joan (Lock) of Carshalton, Surrey, England

Iowans of the Mighty Eighth

Chapter Seven

BASES

One of the marvels of WWII was the land acquisition, design and construction of air bases on an emergent basis for the Eighth Air Force predominantly in the area of England known as East Anglia. Shortly after the Eighth Air Force was created on January 25, 1942, movement of its Headquarters and meager allotment of aircraft and personnel began. The Eighth flew its first combat mission in June of that year from airfields and in aircraft borrowed from the Royal Air Force. The "Mighty Eighth" would need heavy, medium and light bombardment groups, fighter, fighter training, and troop carrier groups.

These would be supported by Special Operations Squadrons and Groups, Air/Sea Rescue, Photographic and Weather Reconnaissance, Radio Countermeasures and Night Leaflet Squadrons.

Sites for airfields had to be selected and built with three intersecting runways inside a perimeter track with taxiways and hard stands for parking aircraft. Each base required a control tower, hangars for aircraft maintenance, service and repair, buildings for briefing, administrative, command, medical personnel, supply, weather, photographic and intelligence personnel, chapels, military police, officer and enlisted men's clubs, mess halls, barracks, and facilities for bomb and fuel storage, communications and base defense. Supply lines were required to ensure a constant flow of fuel, bombs, ammunition, vehicles of all types, spare and replacement parts, and food and service items.

It would take time. In addition to training air and ground crews and deploying them to England, aircraft had to roll off America's assembly plants and ferried to England. British support was the key to success in massing strategic bombardment and fighter forces within striking distance of Germany. The British, despite manpower shortages constructed most of the airfields required for America's flying operations. U.S. Army Engineer Battalions constructed the balance. Limited in natural resources much of the material for con-

Control tower 96th BG, Snetterton Heath, England

B-17s parked at 91st BG, Bassingbourn, England

struction of the bases had to be imported, but as airfields were hurriedly constructed and aircraft and trained personnel arrived in England, the Eighth began to grow.

Planning on what bomber and fighter groups were required to carry out the mission of the Eighth, location of bases and complement varied as the war progressed. Yet attacks on the enemy during its growing period had to be made. Construction of the magnitude envisioned in such a short time span required careful planning that was constantly altered by changes in what units would be assigned, number and type of aircraft and personnel required. It was hard for military planners to predict when aircraft from American production centers would be completed, and of those what would be allocated to the Eighth Air Force. Needs of other American air forces in a global war had to be considered. Twelve units initially assigned to the Eighth Air Force were re-assigned to the Twelfth Air Force in North Africa and six units transferred to the Ninth Air Force also based in England to fly support for the cross-Channel invasion of Europe.

One hundred fifty-eight airfields were allocated to the Eighth Air Force although not all would be used or constructed. Eighty-two operational units were assigned to the Eighth at one time or another and as many as ninety airfields were used. Units in a short time span were stationed at as many as five different bases before re-assignment or stabilization at a station. Repair facilities, storage depots training and special operations were also established at other locations. The balance of bases allocated to the Eighth were returned to the Royal Air Force or not constructed as planned. So many bases existed in such a confined space flight patterns, communications, assembly after takeoff and landings in overlapping air space required careful planning. English weather was not especially cooperative causing collisions in fog and low cloud cover.

Nine airfields were used in Ireland as training, storage, replacement centers and retro-fit of newly arrived aircraft.

Control Tower 392nd BG Wendling, England

Control Tower, 390th BG, Framlingham, England

UNITS AND PRIMARY BASES OF THE EIGHTH AIR FORCE IN BRITAIN

EIGHTH AIR FORCE HQTRS AND BOMBER COMMAND HQTRS-
High Wycombe

EIGHTH AIR FORCE FIGHTER COMMAND HQTRS- Bushey Hall

1ST AIR DIVISION HQTRS-
Brampton Grange

2ND AIR DIVISION HQTRS-
Ketteringham Hall

3RD AIR DIVISION HQTRS-
Elveden Hall

BOMBER AND FIGHTER GROUP LOCATIONS:
1ST FG-Colerne (transf to 12th AF)
3RD PHOTO-Steeple Morden (transf to 12th AF)
4TH FG-Debden
7TH PHOTO-Mount Farm
14TH FG-Atcham (transf to 12th AF)
20TH FG-Kings Cliffe
25TH BG-Watton
31ST FG-Merston (transf to 12th AF)
34TH BG-Mendelsham
44TH BG-Shipdham
52ND FG-Goxhill (transf to 12th AF)
55TH FG-Wormingford
56TH FG-Boxted
60TH TCG-Aldermaston (transf to 12th AF)
62ND TCG-Keevil (transf to 12th AF)
64th TCG-Ramsbury (transf to 12th AF)
67TH RECON-Membury (transf to 9th AF)
78TH FG-Duxford
82ND FG-Maydown, Northern Ireland (transf to 12th AF)
91ST BG-Bassingbourn
92ND BG-Podington

Chapter Seven

93RD BG-Hardwick
94TH BG-Bury St. Edmunds
95TH BG-Horham
96TH BG-Snetterton Heath
97TH BG-Grafton Underwood (transf to 12th AF)
100TH BG-Thorpe Abbotts
301ST BG-Podington
303RD BG-Molesworth
305TH BG-Chelveston
306TH BG-Thurleigh
315 TCG-Aldermaston (transf to 9th AF)
322 BG-Andrews Field (transf to 9th AF)
323RD BG-Earls Colne (transf to 9th AF)
339TH FG-Fowlmere
350TH FG-Snailwell (transf to 12th AF)
351ST BG-Polebrook
352ND FG-Bodney
353RD FG-Raydon
355TH FG-Steeple Morden
356TH FG-Martleson Heath
357TH FG-Leiston
358TH FG-Leiston (transf to 9th AF)
359TH FG-East Wretham
361ST FG-Bottisham
364TH FG-Honington
379TH BG-Kimbolton
381ST BG-Ridgewell
384TH BG-Grafton Underwood
385TH BG-Great Ashfield
386TH BG-Great Dunmow
387TH BG-Chipping Ongar (transf 9th AF)
388TH BG-Knettishall
389TH BG-Hethel
390TH BG-Framlingham
392ND BG-Wendling
398TH BG-Nuthampstead
401ST BG-Deenethorpe
445TH BG-Tibenham
446TH BG-Bungay
447TH BG-Rattlesden
448TH BG-Seething
452ND BG Deopham Green
453RD BG-Old Buckenham
457TH BG-Glatton
458TH BG-Horsham St Faith
466TH BG-Attlebridge
467TH BG-Rackheath
479TH BG-Wattisham
482ND BG-Alconbury
486TH BG Sudbury
487TH BG-Lavenham
489TH BG-Halesworth
490TH BG-Eye
491ST BG-North Pickenham

492ND BG/801ST BG-Harrington
493RD BG-Debach
495TH FTG-Atcham
496TH FTG-Goxhill

5TH EMERGENCY RESCUE SQUADRON-Boxted

15TH BS-Molesworth (transf to 12th AF)

RADIO COUNTERMEASURES SQUADRON-Cheddington

NIGHT LEAFLET SDN- Cheddington
BASE AIR DEPOTS-
Warton
Burtonwood
STRATEGIC AIR DEPOTS-
Alconbury
Watton
Honington
Wattisham
Stansted
BASES TEMPORARILY USED BY EIGHTH AIR FORCE BOMBER AND FIGHTER GROUPS-
Asche
Bovingdon
Chalgrove
Chievres, Belgium
Eglington, N. Ireland
High Ercall
Hitcham
Ibsley
Kirston in Lindsey
Little Walden
Oulton
St. Dizier, Belgium
Sculthorpe
Westhampnettt

BASES IN IRELAND USED BY 8TH AF-
BASE AIR DEPOT-Langford Lodge
COMBAT CREW REPLACEMENT CENTERS-
Mullaghmore
Toome
Cluntoe
Greencastle
Nuts Corner

FERRYING AND TRANSPORT BASE-
Maghaberry

Chapter Seven

379th Bomb Group, Kimbollton, England

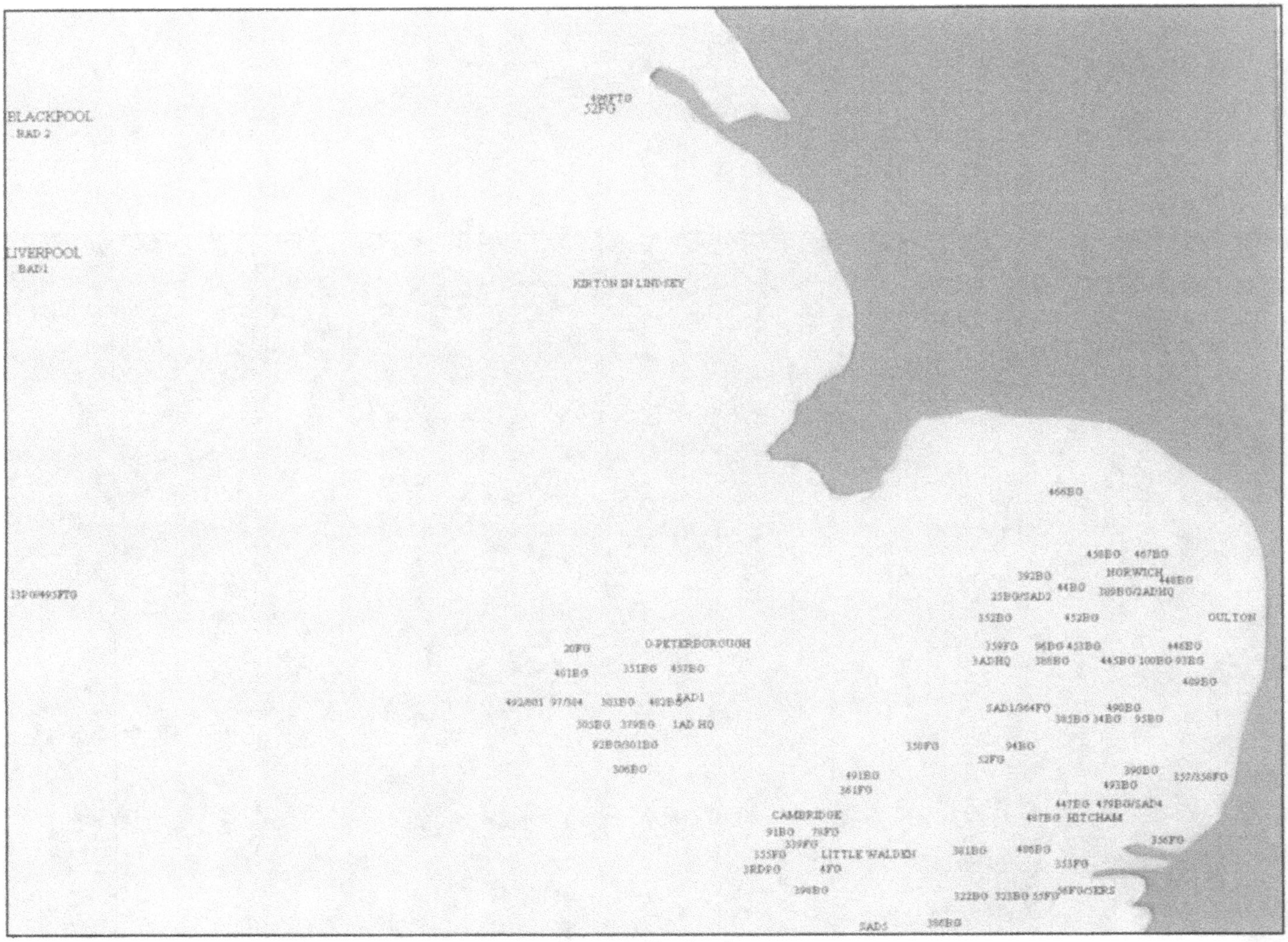

Iowans of the Mighty Eighth

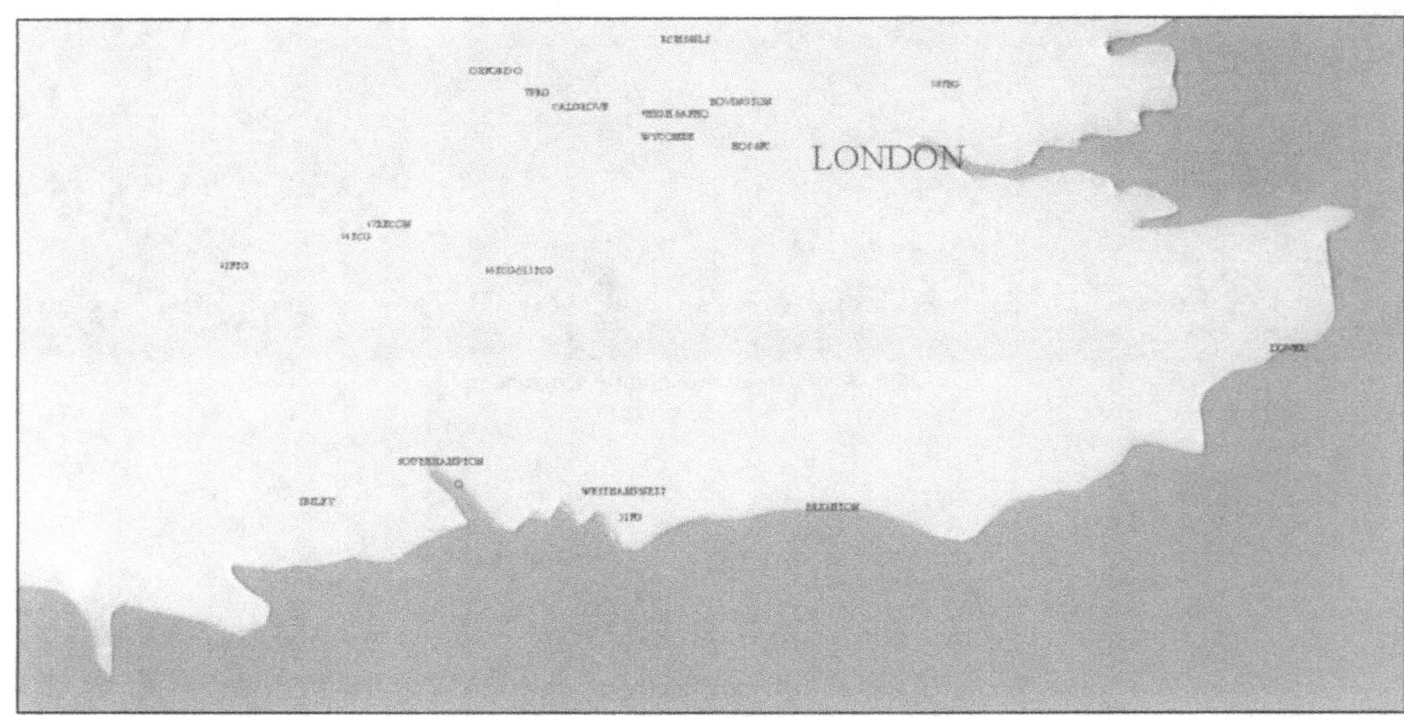

Bases in England

Bases in England

Chapter Seven

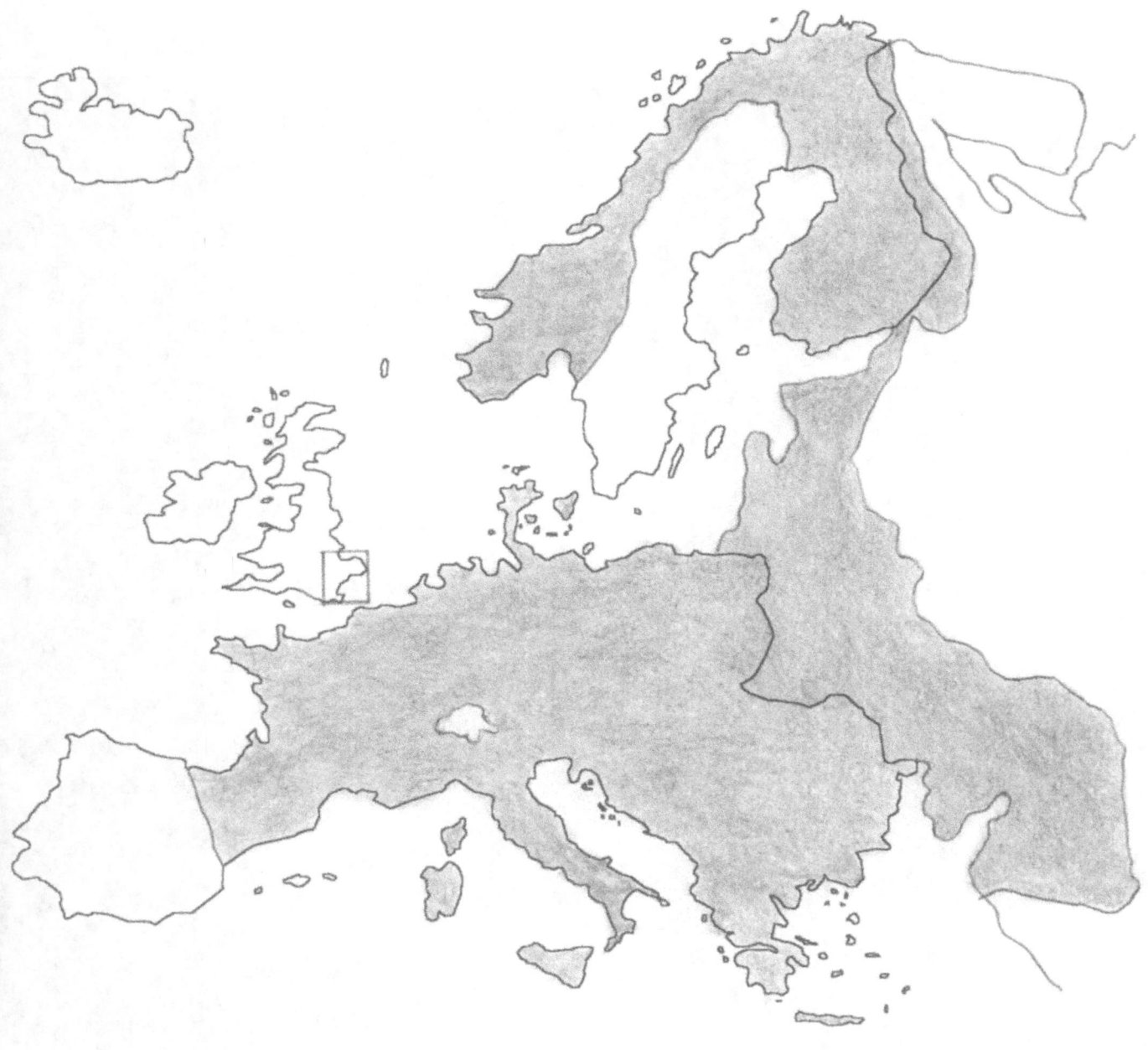

Shaded area indicates Nazi occupied territory and Axis satellites of Northern Europe, excluding portions of North Africa, at time of deployment of Eighth Air Force to England. Boxed area is location of most Eighth Air Force bases.

Bases in Ireland

Chapter Eight

LOGISTICS

World War II dramatized as never before the importance of the essentially non-dramatic functions of transportation, supply and maintenance. An enormous effort was required to receive, support and sustain Eighth Air Force bomber and fighter units and ground personnel in World War II. Measures for logistic mobilization were not in place when the Eighth Air Force was born and moved to England to commence operations against Germany. Numerous problems arose over the next two-year span that had to be resolved and eliminated before an effective system of transportation, supply and maintenance was achieved. The late start that was made in providing a logistical system meant that problems had to be resolved stateside and in-theater which took time. Time was limited to stop the German war machine running rampant over Europe. As a result, bases became a training school in support of an air force. A bad situation to be in. Industrial mobilization, unit buildup, stateside logistics support, facility expansion and modernization, training and equipping of personnel, and organization of air logistics activities should have been in place from the time war was threatening until the time it actually struck.

There was lack of emphasis on logistics training prior to the war with too few personnel knowledgeable of logistics and its functions. This was corrected through a training program for military personnel and technical training programs for civilian employees recruited to work in stateside depots. Unskilled and untrained workers were also sent to the United Kingdom to help man rapidly expanding depots using production line methods for simplicity. British support was a key to success by providing materials for and construction of ninety-one airfields required for American flying operations. Britain also contained a core of civilians with maintenance and supply skills. On the maintenance side personnel that graduated from technical schools were cycled through air depot groups for formal training before re-assignment to air service groups.

The aviation industry prior to World War II was pre-occupied with research and development and aircraft production in small lots. After declaration of war aircraft companies were faced with the challenge of trying to convert to a mass production ethos.

Raw materials had to be supplied from which war material and essential civilian products were made, plants and factories equipped to manufacture the tools of war and the plants staffed with people who had the right skills.

Plans in advance of war should have provided for more effective civilian war agencies. While the military put much effort into planning, plans were often incomplete. Military leadership did not seek advice from industry leaders or consult with elected officials. The proliferation of civilian, civil-military and military organizations, often with overlapping functions and lacking authority, resulted in duplication of effort, confusion and frustration that was counter-productive and retarded efforts to build and sustain the logistics support necessary to conduct large air operations. For example, there were four organizations involved in munitions planning, the consequence of which hampered production and effectiveness of Allied bombing. Demand constantly exceeded production because of overestimation of capacity by those producing the munitions. Like other problems of supply and maintenance, it took time for them to be ironed out, but again, time was of the essence. The military potential of a nation is directly proportional to the nations logistic potential. Resources of all countries are limited and delays or inefficiency in harnessing logistic resources surely cost lives and could have cost victory.

The desperate need for aircraft in all theaters of the war required the repair of crippled or damaged planes causing an additional strain on air depot and operational groups with shortages of special skills, equipment and materials to meet operational demands.

By strict adherence to standards of inspection and maintenance the interval between overhaul or engine change was lengthened and increased the force available for flying operations. Meanwhile, Lockheed and other aircraft companies sent employees to the United Kingdom for in-theater support.

Initial planning was made for airfields to house bomber and fighter groups as well as projections by type of aircraft and numbers to cover attrition, transit, services, training and modifications. Logistical requirements beyond personnel strength and munitions required resulted in war plans that were incomplete. Funds available to the Air Corps to build complete aircraft created a critical shortage of spare parts. Operational planning had taken precedence over logistical planning.

Before World War II the Army Air Corps had fewer than 2,000 airplanes. Overhaul of planes and engines in small depots posed no problem but with a rapidly expanding Air Force it was impossible to meet steadily growing maintenance demands. Bomber and fighter groups were set up to carry the war to Germany but not a Depot Group to perform major maintenance and supply distribution. It was not until 1943 that base air depots and advance depots were established to ease the demands for overhaul, engine changes and take care of abnormal battle damage and repair. Depot field teams or mobile aircraft repair teams were established to repair aircraft too badly damaged to fly to the depot. Depot modernization and expansion stateside, along with the addition of eight depots and many sub-depots in England meant that capacity outstripped the availability of qualified technicians.

U.S. forces in the United Kingdom relied on merchant shipping that was subject to German U-boat attacks. U-boats caused the loss of millions of tons of cargo in 1942. Because of shipping losses, shortages in spare parts for superchargers, bombsights and vehicles were frequent. The losses steadily declined through use of war ship escorted convoys, attacks on German naval installations and losses to the German submarine fleet. While monthly losses decreased, problems with manifest and cargo markings often delayed deliveries to units. Ships commonly arrived in the United Kingdom without a copy of the manifest or loading information. Improvements were realized by dividing the British Isles into two geographic zones and Northern Ireland a third zone. Ships in the United States were then loaded with supplies based on zones that reduced the amount of intra-theater transportation required within the United Kingdom. Until the Air Forces took over segregation and distribution of their own supplies from ship to consuming unit, they starved.

Al Razor, Collins, Iowa, was a truck driver with the 2457th Quartermaster Truck Company attached to the Eighth Air Force at Wattisham, England. At dock-side in Liverpool, Al's truck was loaded with P-47 fighter drop tanks. His orders read only "To Whom it May Concern". At that stage of the war drop tanks for fighter aircraft had not been used and no one knew what the drop tanks were. He spent three days and nights trying to deliver the tanks to Eighth Air Force bases and had driven all the way to Wales before it was determined where the shipment was to have been delivered.

The Eighth's trucks were pooled into a single organization and were effective and efficient in moving supplies from port to base and laterally between bases. Operation requirements would not permit delays associated with waiting for parts from the United States. Local procurement and manufacture was initiated and partially alleviated some of the shortages. Supply support received from the British was significant as the U.S. suffered losses of shipping. Common supplies were pooled which reduced pipeline time and transport burdens. The British dispensed all the petroleum, oil and lubricants even though most of it came from the U.S. By the beginning of 1944 supply items were cataloged and spare parts were at satisfactory levels.

Eighth Air Force logistics prior to 1944 was the story of brute force logistics. Problems had to be solved by innovation and adaptation. It was not until leadership was able to synchronize logistics and operations that they were able to provide responsive, effective, and efficient logistical support to the theaters of operation. Valuable assistance was provided by the Army Service Forces with items common to the Army and the Air Force but never before in the history of warfare was there more rapid and far-reaching scientific and technological developments in weapons. The Air Force Service Command provided stateside depot, technical, research and development and acquisition support to the Eighth Air Force.

Chapter Eight

Principle American Fighter and Bomber Aircraft Used by the Eighth Air Force

Lockheed P-38 Lightning "Shorty" flown by Richard "Steamboat" Garrett of the 20th Fighter Group, Kings Cliffe, England, and maintained by crew chief Lowell Rothbart, Dewitt, Iowa. Engine-Two Allison V 1710, 12 cylinder liquid cooled, 1,385 HP, wing span -52ft 1 in; length-37ft 11 in; height-12 ft 10 in, weight,-20,000 lbs loaded; speed-395 at 20,000 ft; ceiling-39,000 ft; range-425 miles; armament-one 20 mm cannon, four machine guns, 2,000 lbs in bombs

Republic P-47D-25. named "Angel" of the 356th FG based at Martlesham, England and maintained by Byrl Elliott, Cherokee, Iowa, as instrument specialist. Engine-Pratt & Whitney 18 cylinder radial, air cooled, 2,000 hp. Wingspan-40 ft 11 in; length-36 ft 2 in; height-14 ft 7in; weight-19,426 lbs; maximum speed-427 mph; ceiling-42,000ft; range-474 miles; armament-6-8 machine guns, 2,500 lbs bombs.

Iowans of the Mighty Eighth

North American P-51D, "Nooky Booky IV" flown by Leonard "Kit" Carson of Clear Lake, Iowa, with the 357th FG based at Leiston, England. Carson was an "Ace" credited with 18 1/2 aerial victories and other enemy planes destroyed on the ground. Engine-Packard V-1650-7 12 cylinder V, liquid cooled, 1612 hp; Wingspan-37 ft; Length-32 ft 3 in; height-13 ft 8 in; Weight-11,815 lbs; speed-436 mph at 25,000 ft; ceiling-42,000 ft; range-949 miles, armament-6 machine guns and 2,000 lbs of bombs.

De Haviland Mosquito manufactured in Great Britain and shown in markings of 25thBG based at Watton, England. Two Squadrons conducted weather and scouting flights over the European Continent as well as photographic missions. Engine-two Rolls Royce Merlin, 12 cylinder, liquid cooled, 1250 hp; Wingspan-54 ft 3 in; length-40 ft 10 in; height-15 ft 3 in; weight- 21,823 lbs; Speed-380 mph at 21,000 ft; Ceiling-31,000 ft; Range-1200 miles; Armament-2,000 lbs bombs-crew of two.

Chapter Eight

Boeing B-17G Bomber. Wing Span 103 ft 9 in, Length 74 ft 4 in; four Wright R-1820-97 Cyclone engines with 1000 hp @ 2300 rpm @ 25,000ft. Gross Weight 40,260 lbs. Top Speed 302 mph, Ceiling 36,400 ft, Range 3,750 miles. Crew of ten. Bomb load 5,600 lbs. Armament 11-.50 caliber machine guns. Plane has markings of 381st Bomb Group, Debach, England. Named "Pella Tulip" after the Iowa town. Plane was able to fly back to its base on two engines and 300 holes in aircraft after 14 October 1944 raid on Cologne, Germany.

Consolidated B-24J, Wingspan 110 ft, Length 67ft 4 in, 4 Pratt & Whitney R-1830-65 Twin Wasp, 14 cylinder radial, air cooled engines, 1,217 hp each. Maximum speed 290 mph at 25,000 ft, Ceiling 28,098 ft., range 2,098 miles. Crew of 8-10, Armament 10 machine guns, 12,803 lbs. of bombs. Plane shown was named "Sierra Blanca", and was with the 492nd BG, North Pickenham, England. Paul Gidel, Lake City, flew as tail gunner on this aircraft until battle damage caused them to land in neutral Sweden where they were interned for the duration of the war. However, Paul and as many other internees as could be loaded in a B-24 were flown out of Sweden in the middle of a night and returned to Allied hands.

Iowans of the Mighty Eighth

Martin B-26 Marauder "Miss Muriel" of the 386th BG at Boxted, England, in which Russell Orwig, Bettendorf, Iowa, flew as tailgunner. Designated a medium bomber, the B-26 was powered by two Pratt & Whitney 18 cylinder, air cooled engines of 2,000 hp each. WIngspan-71 ft 2 in; length-58ft 4 in; height-21 ft 6 in; weight-37,000 lbs; maximum speed-281 mph at 15,000 ft; ceiling-21,000 ft; range-1,149 miles, armament-12 machine guns, 5,000 lbs bombs, crew of seven.

Chapter Eight

PRINCIPLE GERMAN AIRCRAFT FLOWN BY THE LUFTWAFFE

Focke Wulf FW 190A-8 of Jg/300 based at Lobnitz, during October-November, 1944. This aircraft was flown by Unteroffizier Ernst Schoder as part of the Defense of the Reich operations. Specifications: Wing Span-34 ft 5.5 in; Length-29 ft 5 in; Height-12 ft 11.5 in; Engine 2,100 hp BMW 801 D-2 14 cylinder radial piston; Performance-408 mph (max); Weight 10,800 lbs (gross); Armament-two 7.9 mm machine guns, four .20 mm MG 151 cannons.

Messerschmitt Bf 109K-4 from 1/JG 27. The aircraft is in the Defense of the Reich identification markings. Eighth Air Force bombing forced the transfer of fighter units back to Germany. JG 27 is identified by its green band around the rear fuselage. Specifications: Wing Span 32 ft 9 in; Length-29 ft; Height-8 ft 2 in; Engine-Daimer Benz DB 605 ASCM, 12 cylinder, liquid cooled, 2,000 hp; performance-451 mph (max); Weight 7,448 lbs (gross); Ceiling-41,118 ft, Range-355 miles; Armament-one 30 mm cannon, 2-15 mm cannons.

Messerschmitt Bf. 110G-2; Engine-2 1475 hp Daiier Benz 12 cylinder, liquid cooled, Wing Span-53ft 4 in; length-39 ft 8 1/2 in; height-11 ft 6 in; weight-9,920 lb empty; Speed-349 mph at 23,000 ft; Armament-two 20 mm cannons, four 7.92 mm machine guns, one 7.92 mm manually aimed machine gun in rear cockpit.

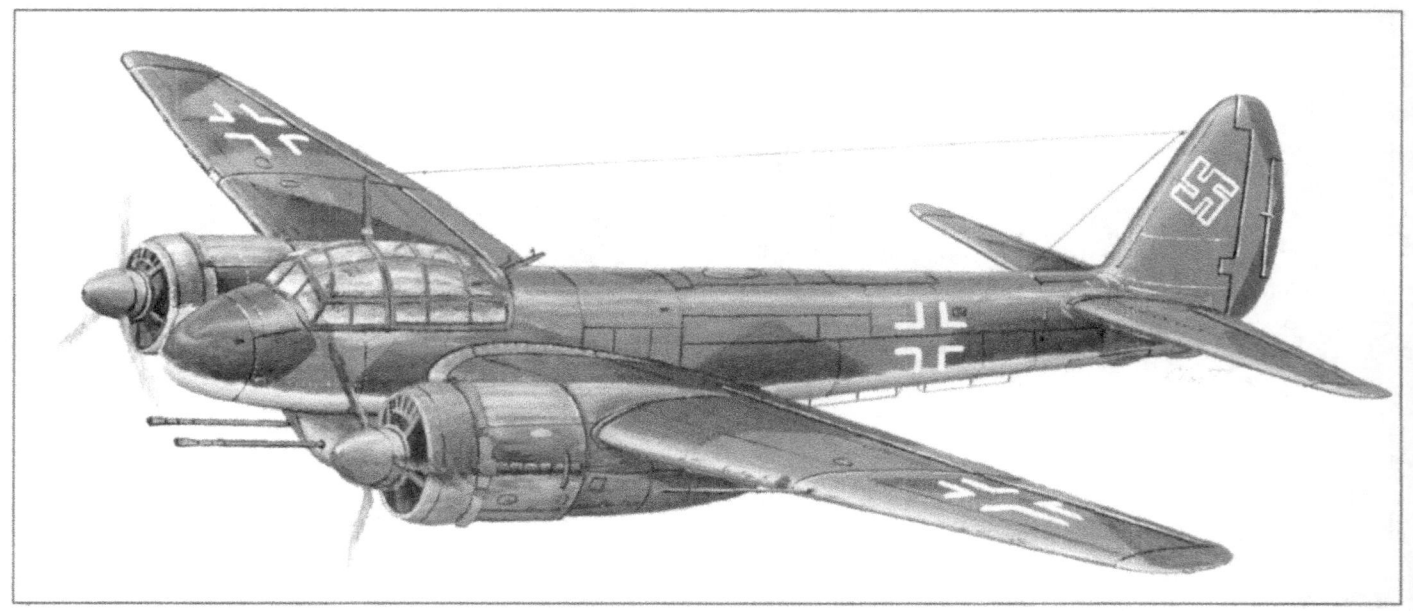

Junkers, JU-88 A14, two 1,340 hp Junkers 12 cylinder inverted-vee liquid cooled engines; Wing Span-65 ft, 10 1/2 in, length-47 2 1/2 in, height-15ft 11 in; weight-17,637 lbs; Speed-269 mph, ceiling 26,500 ft; Armament-various versions on all models. Two 7.92 mm MG 81 firing forward from gondola, two MG FF cannon under nose for anti-shipping role.

Chapter Eight

Messerschmitt Me 163 B-1a, Engine-Waltger HWK 509 A-2 rocket, Wing Span-30 ft 7 in; length 19 ft 3 in; height-9 ft 1 in; weight-9,072 lbs; maximum speed-596 mph at 10,000 ft; ceiling-39,802 ft; range-80 miles; armament-two 30 mm cannon.

Messerschmitt Me262 A-1, Engine-two Junkers Jumo 004 B-1 turbojets with a thrust of 1,986 lbs, Wing Span-41 ft 1 in; length-34 ft 9 in; height-10 ft 10 in; weight- 14,099 lbs; maximum speed 539 mph at 13,000 ft; ceiling 37,964 ft; range 662 miles; armament-four 30 mm cannon.

Iowans of the Mighty Eighth

Messerschmitt ME-410A1, Engine-two 1,850 hp Daimler Benz 603 A, 12 cylinders, liquid cooled; Wing span- 53 ft 9 in; length- 41 ft; height- 14 ft; Weight- 21,276 lbs; Maximum speed- 387 mph at 22,000 ft; ceiling- 23,000 ft; ramge- 1,050 miles loaded. Armament-t-two 20 mm cannon, four machine guns, 2,200 lbs of bombs.

HIGH ALTITUDE FLIGHT CLOTHING AND BODY ARMOR

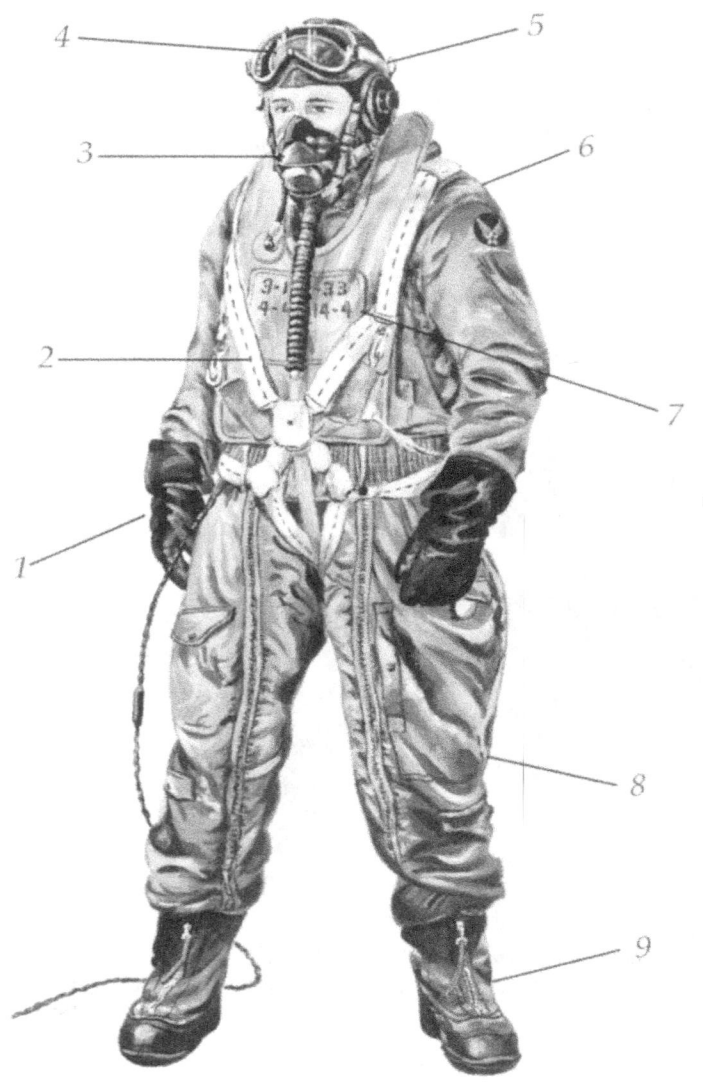

1. A-11 Gloves
2. A-4 QAC Parachute Harness (attachable chest pack not shown)
3. A-14 Oxygen Mask
4. B-8 Goggles
5. A-11 Flying Helmet
6. B-15 Jacket
7. B-4 "Mae West" Life Vest
8. A-11 Trousers
9. A-6 Boots

Chapter Nine

Base Life

As soon a base was nearing completion movement of aircraft and personnel continued the constant flood to England to take up residency. In addition to operational needs in sustaining an air force at each base, personal needs had to be provided for up to ten thousand men and women at larger bases.

Living quarters were predominately pre-fabricated buildings (Nissen Huts) although some bases that were occupied were former Royal Air Force bases with permanent living quarters. Enlisted men slept in quarters separate from officers. A single coal stove in the center of the hut provided the only heat. Coal or coke was rationed and required occasional "midnight requisitioning" from supplies to try and keep warm. Some have said the stoves were not there to keep you warm but to keep you from freezing to death. English weather of fog, cold, rain and snow occasionally punctuated with sunshine didn't help living conditions in non-insulated buildings. Bill Werner, Muscatine, First Strategic Air Depot, "we had to move to plywood barracks that weren't insulated and heated only by a pot-bellied stove that burned coke."

Marvin Otto, Atla, 100th Service Group erected Nissen huts, mechanical facilities, bomb and ammunition dumps at new bases under construction.

Donald Richards, Waterloo, was assigned to the 2006th Ordnance Company at Melchbourne, England. In addition to making metal parts and tools from metal casings, operating engine lathes, milling machines, drill presses and power hack saws, Donald constructed Nissen huts, tools and parts, for all branches of military service including the British.

Lebron Fox, Jamaica, was an aircraft mechanic with the 351st Bomb Group at Polebrook, England. He organized a cleanup crew of newly constructed bases, replaced aircraft tires, and serviced oxygen and hydraulic systems. He helped devise a way pilot and co-pilots could easily remove windows in the cockpit in case their aircraft had to be ditched in water.

Aircrews were considered temporary residents. They rotated in, and if successful in completing their required number of missions, rotated back to the United States for re-assignment to other duties. Their tenure on base depended on how soon they could complete their missions or were killed in action, taken prisoner of war or wounded beyond reinstatement to flight duty. Aircrew members spent as little as two

Billy Hancock, Perry, inside Nissen Hut, 379th BG, Kimbolton, England

Dick Lynch, Conrad, outside Nissen Hut, 44th BG, Shipdham, England

months on base while some were there over a year. Depending on the need for air crews and airplanes, they practiced bombing, assembly in the air after take-off, formation flying, gunnery practice and learned British communication procedures before going on their first mission. If they weren't in the air there was always classroom training leaving little time for sleep or relaxation. Other than occasional trips to London or nearby cities, free time was spent at officer's or enlisted men's clubs participating in perpetual card games, playing ping-pong, shooting pool or unwinding at the bar until it was shut down because of an impending mission.

Orville Whitcanack, flight engineer with the 493rd Bomb Group at Debach had just such an occasion to unwind, but he stayed behind in his barracks while the rest of his crew went for a few drinks. They returned minus one of the crew. "Where's Moore?" he asked. "He got drunk, passed out and we got tired of dragging him so we left him on the perimeter road." Flabbergasted, Orville said "What's the matter with you guys someone will run over him." Their reply: "Naw, we put flares at each end of him." An army truck later delivered Moore to the barracks.

For aircrews, periods of relaxation were prized, to write letters, reflect on their experiences, deal with inner thoughts, or just unwind and have a good time to get away from the war. Mission day meant they would be roused from sleep in the early morning hours, fed, briefed and sent on missions that could last over nine or ten hours. As they approached enemy territory they began a battle against enemy fighters. On the run to the target they had to fly through box barrages of "flak" that riddled airplanes and human bodies. They had to deal with survival not only of the massive bombing raids, but human error, weather, equipment and mechanical failure. They experienced airplanes exploding and disintegrating all around them, expecting at any time it would happen to them. They saw airplanes on fire leaving formation or spinning out of control heading earthward and counted the parachutes of those leaving their stricken aircraft on its way to the ground.

No words can express the feeling of seeing men falling from broken airplanes wearing no parachutes, or no one exiting an aircraft on its way to the ground. Those that made it home faced empty bunks in their huts from lost friends and crews and lived with the fear that they would have to do it all again tomorrow.

Bases provided spiritual guidance to deal with combat stress and other personal matters. Charles Fix, Spirit Lake, was a chaplain assigned to a supply unit at Standsted, England, before transfer to the 9th Air Force. Charles provided regular religious services on the base, private consultation with personnel on emotional and family matters and was on the flight line for prayer prior to mission takeoff. He regularly visited hospitals to give aid and comfort to the sick and wounded.

It took more than aircrews to fly the planes into combat. Ground support personnel covering a multitude of specialties were the permanent residents. Trained and deployed to England they were there for the duration of the war. For every airman that took to the air another score or more had to support him on the ground. Ordnance personnel were required to supply and load a variety of bombs depending on the mission. Armorers ensured weapons were cleaned and repaired if necessary and ammunition was on hand and loaded in the aircraft. Instrument specialists repaired everything from bombsights to radios. Meteorologists and photo-reconnaissance personnel flew pre-mission flights to gather intelligence data. Fire fighters and medical personnel were at the ready when damaged aircraft returned to base or crashed on takeoff and landing. Military police provided base security. Clerical personnel performed administrative tasks and sorted and delivered much sought after letters and packages. Truck drivers at transportation units and storage depots were responsible for an endless amount and variety of supplies they delivered to each base from bombs to toilet paper. Medical personnel took care of the sick, wounded and dental hygiene. Cooks were responsible for feeding all base personnel at all hours and chaplains tended to the religious needs of the servicemen. Service groups managed clubs providing relaxation in separate facilities for the officer and the enlisted man. The American Red Cross established service field clubs at designated bases for additional entertainment, refreshments and parties. Repair depots provided engine overhaul and repair to aircraft that couldn't be locally repaired. World War II dramatized as never before the importance of the essentially non-dramatic functions of those behind the scenes. All were critically important to the overall success of the Eighth Air Force mission.

Armament crews maintained aircraft machine guns to ensure they were cleaned after each mission, repaired if necessary and functioning properly. On bombers the machine guns were installed and loaded prior to take off. Bomb racks were loaded with the correct type of bombs designated for the mission. On fighter aircraft, bombs or external fuel tanks, depending on the range of mission required, were hung on bomb racks under the wings or fuselage. Guns in the wings had to be bore-sighted so bullets from both wings would converge at a prescribed distance.

Roger Robinson, Davenport, was an armorer with the First Fighter Group, the first group to arrive in England in August, 1942. The unit was transferred to the 12th Air Force in North Africa where sand made cleaning and proper functioning of weapons difficult to maintain. Roger was later assigned to a fighter group with the 15th Air Force in Italy.

John Betten, Kanawha, was assigned as a truck driver at the 482nd Bomb Group at Alconbury. His main duty was loading bombs aboard bombers and assisted in recovery of wounded from aircraft that returned from missions.

George Chipman, Estherville, was an ordnance officer with the 453rd Bomb Group at Old Buckenham. George had forty men under his charge to clean and oil guns after missions, repair guns and insure gun turrets, auto pilots and instruments were in proper working order.

Morris Steffen, Cumberland, was with the 1735th Ordnance Company assigned to the 385th Bomb Group at Great Ashfield. He was responsible for the storage and issue of ammunition, bombs and bomb fuses at the base. He handled bomb hoists to lift and transport bombs and supervised unloading of bombs after their arrival at the base from British ports. Machine gun bullets had to be hand-loaded into links.

Marvin Otto, Alta, was with the 100th Service Group at Rattlesden. Marvin supervised bomb and ammunition delivery and maintained a perpetual inventory of stock levels. Machine gun bullets were received loose in packing and had to be hand-loaded into links.

Arthur Petersen, Mason City, was an ordnance and weapons specialist with the 305th Bomb Group both at Grafton Underwood and at Chelveston. He received extensive training in ammunition, bombs, fuses, gases and weapons. His duties with the 305th included loading loose armor-piercing ammunition, tracers and incendiary. 50 caliber ammunition in belt links. Bombs of the type required for each mission were assembled and loaded in aircraft bomb bay racks. Art also maintained custody of bomb fuses.

Rationing of food in America ensured military personnel stateside and in overseas assignments would be fed. Some perishables were purchased locally from the struggling British who had limited food supplies, including mutton, lamb chops, brussel sprouts and other vegetables. Enterprising farmers would sell fresh eggs to airbase personnel. To ease this burden powdered eggs and milk were used, but fresh eggs were sometimes available at breakfast on mission days. An occasional steak after a mission was a rare treat. Canned meat, everyone's favorite – Spam, was left to the ingenuity of the cooks to disguise its preparation.

Leon Hoegh, Atlantic, was a cook with the 303rd Bomb Group at Molesworth. He worked in a mess hall providing meals for 425 base personnel. Open 24 hours food had to be available all the time for ground crews and medics. As supplies coming from the United States became more plentiful there was less dependence on food purchased locally. Meat came frozen including chickens that had not been gutted and the feet still on. Fresh milk was given to English children so powdered milk was used at the base. Bread was purchased from the English. "We cooked food in sixty gallon pots heated by coke. Mutton was shipped in to us as carcasses. The smell of mutton was over-powering and a lot of guys couldn't handle it. The vegetables we got, potatoes, carrots, brussel sprouts, were wormy, but we cooked them anyway. About

Art Petersen, Mason City, armorer, 305th BG, Chelveston, England

Bomb Storage at 390th Bomb Group, Framlingham, England

sixty per cent of the fresh stuff that was shipped to us was spoiled by the time we got it. We made coffee in large pots, sixty gallons at a time. A guy who was on KP during the day came back to the mess hall at night and some how used one of the pots to do his laundry. He got by with it. Coffee was made in the pot the next day. When the pot was drained one of the guy's socks was found in the bottom."

Medical personnel had to tend to dental needs, illnesses, injuries from accidents and those wounded who made it back to base from combat over the skies of Europe.

Les Portwood, Boone, was assigned to the 21st Air Depot Group of the Fourth Strategic Air Depot at a small village near Ipswich, England. Les worked in the dental clinic of the base hospital and responded to all emergencies in and around the base with other medical personnel. This included the recovery of bodies from crash sites and wounded aboard returning aircraft. Emergency first aid was provided for wounded before they could be transported to a major medical facility.

Stanley Patterson, Mason City, was with the 305th Bomb Group at Chelveston, England. Stan operated the base dispensary, completed medical reports and dealt with "sick call". He was a member of the emergency crew that waited by the runway and removed casualties from aircraft that returned from missions or were in nearby crashes. He recalled recovering twenty bodies from a collision of two B-17 bombers over Chelveston.

Robert Messerly, Janesville, was with the 80th Medical Unit assigned to the 486th Bomb Group at Sudbury, England. Part of his duties included meeting inbound aircraft with casualties aboard and rendering temporary first aid in route to the base hospital.

Clerical personnel worked behind the scenes to perform a myriad of administrative tasks for the base commander. Whether it was ordering supplies, administering pay, mail, typing reports or orders, or maintaining personnel files each organization would have operated in chaos and could not have functioned without them.

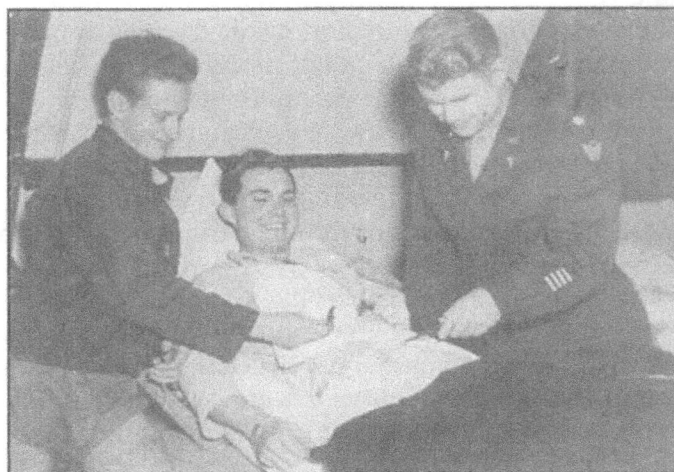
Roberly Howe, Central City, on left, Gunner, 100th BG, Thorpe Abbotts, England compares shrapnel from wounded man with his own wound.

Les Portwood, Boone, medic, second row, sixth from left, 21st Air Depot Group, Ipswich.

"Lamb Stew Again"

Robert Kloser, Carroll, distributes "mail call" at First Air Depot, Burtonwood, England.

Chapter Nine

Elmer Steven, Spencer, was a teletype maintenance mechanic at the 339th Fighter Group, Fowlmere, England.

Clele Baker, Waverly, typed orders and letters dictated to him at Eighth Air Force Headquarters.

Fred Marold, Waterloo, performed clerical duties in the communications section of the 44th Bomb Group at Shipdham.

Elmer Ferrel, Iowa City, was a message center clerk copying military orders and performing other clerical duties with the 108th ACS Squadron

Robert Kloser, Carroll, worked in the orderly room of the 15th Bomb Squadron at Molesworth, England, before arrival of the 303rd Bomb Group. His unit was transferred to the 12th Air Force in North Africa, but Bob was successful in transferring back to the Base Air Depot at Burtonwood, England, where he performed mailroom duties.

It took all the money, resources and innovation the United States could muster to supply America's men and women fighting a prolonged global war, across two vast oceans thousands of miles apart. To ensure the right equipment, ammunition, fuel, bombs, parts, food and supplies were at the right location, at the right time in the right amount required a monumental coordinated team effort. Things didn't always work out the way they were planned but the job got done. It took Americans in plants and factories, railroads, merchant marine, truck drivers, and administrators to organize what was needed and get it to England. At British ports, rail stations and centers, truck drivers hauled supplies to Base Air Depots. Advance or strategic air depots would receive their inventory of stocks from Base Air Depots and further distribute supplies to individual bases.

Glenn Allen, Panora, an automotive equipment mechanic attached to Eighth Air Force, Headquarters and Headquarters Squadron hauled supplies from British ports.

Al Razor, Collins, a truck driver with the 2487th Quartermaster Trucking Company delivered bombs and other supplies to Eighth Air Force bases over East Anglia.

Maynard Johnson, Sibley, was in charge of 25 drivers and a fleet of trucks with the 2465th Trucking Company at the First Strategic Air Depot, Honington. They picked up bombs at rail depots and delivered them to the depot for dispersal to bases.

Elmer Johansmeier, Burlington, was with the 2003 Ordnance Maintenance Company. He traveled all over England providing maintenance to jeeps, trucks, bulldozers and cranes.

Robert White, Burlington, was a supply sergeant with the 99th Station Complement at Bury St Edmunds with the 94th Bomb Group and the 420th Sub-Depot at Debach, England with the 493rd Bomb Group.

The quality of maintenance was often the margin of difference between the life and death of an aircrew or the success or failure of a mission. The greatly increased rate of air operations, the high incidence of battle damage and the growing complexity of mili-

Views in repair shop at Strategic Air Depot 3, Watton, England, where Bill Clark, Ames, Iowa, repaired damaged aircraft instruments and special equipment or component parts were manufactured. "I just repaired them and put them back on the shelf for future use". Bill also made local flights to test instrument reliability. "Some instruments required adjustment every fifteen minutes during a mission."

Trucks getting ready to move out after loading supplies from Storage Depot

tary planes during World War II made maintenance one of the most vital functions in waging an air war.

Maintenance system operations were flexible and the amount of maintenance was determined by the availability of equipment, supplies and manpower. Prior to Mid-1944 heavy bomber maintenance organizations were constantly challenged by having to expend labor and parts to keep war-weary aircraft flying since replacement aircraft were not available in sufficient quantities to stabilize aircraft availability with respect to losses.

Command sweated the results of each mission as much as the ground crew. They knew they would be on the receiving end of pressure from Headquarters, Division and Wing superiors for a maximum effort on the next mission already being planned. Mechanics worked all day and long into the night often in extreme weather conditions servicing and maintaining aircraft assigned to them for the next mission. With no pre-war experience working on airplanes, the determination and skill devoted to "their" airplanes saved countless aircrews. Many sent to England during the beginning of Eighth Air Force build-up had little or no formal training and had to learn "on the job".

Bill Zachar, Davenport, was an aircraft mechanic with the 303rd Bomb Group at Molesworth, England. "We were green, pioneers and we didn't know what we were doing." Bill credits his crew chief with expert training and supervision in turning his mechanics into "seasoned veterans". After flight crews had left on their mission Bill would catch sleep until the aircraft returned. He would also hold wallets and some personal effects of the flight crew until they returned. If they returned. Aircraft engines rebuilt at a facility at Birmingham, England, saved time and work of overhauling engines at Sub-Depots. "We installed the engines ourselves." Bill went through seven aircraft either lost in combat or retired as battle weary. One of the B-17s flew 135 missions.

Everett Sandersfeld, South Amana, was an aircraft mechanic at the 385th Bomb Group, Knettishall, England. He had no formal aircraft engine training other than two weeks in a classroom. He credits his crew chief with providing most of his training "on the job".

They worked on the aircraft while the aircrew slept, met them in the morning getting ready for takeoff and were waiting for them if and when they returned from missions. Roy Picht, Ames, Iowa, was a Crew Chief with the 458th Bomb Group at Horsham St. Faith, England. Roy had a five-man crew assigned to one B-24 working twelve to fourteen hour shifts. "We were close to the air crew, we never got any medals, but our reward was the safe return of the crew."

Woody Heitland, Ackley, was an aircraft mechanic with the 398th Bomb Group at Nuthampstead. "We never got too close to the aircrew, it made it that much harder if the crew was lost. If they did return we could spend the rest of the day and night getting their planes ready for the next mission."

Delph Hruska, Fort Dodge, was an aircraft mechanic crew chief supervising four other mechanics with the 389th Bomb Group at Hethel. In addition to routine maintenance and repair, engine sump pumps were checked for metal filings, which, if found, required engine replacement often overnight. "Generators were a problem, it seemed some burned out every mission and had to be changed. After the planes left for a mission we slept in a shack near the hard stand until they returned. We never got close to knowing the aircrews because we went through five different planes that didn't return from missions."

Maurice Brandenburger, Des Moines, Supply Sergeant, 445th BG, Tibenham, England, "On a mission in September, 1944, thirty of our bomb group's aircraft were lost. Hardly any came back. Those that made it, most were so shot up they were no longer flyable. It was a tough night at the base with a lot of

Everett Sandersfeld, 385th BG

Robert Manahl, 384th BG

long faces. We didn't know any of the air crews and didn't want to know them because you didn't want a friend lost in action."

Arlon Nessa, Hubbard, was an aircraft mechanic crew chief over three mechanics with the 91st Bomb Group at Bassingbourn. Their responsibility included change of engines, tires, wings, installation of fuel tanks and pre-flight the aircraft before the aircrew left on its mission. When and if the aircrew returned, work started all over again. Initially billeted in barracks with aircrews, it was found to have a demoralizing effect on the ground crews when aircraft and crews were lost and they were eventually assigned separate quarters.

Leslie Pedersen, West Branch was a P-51 fighter mechanic responsible for service and maintenance of one airplane and work performed on it by other specialists. He installed drop tanks for long-range missions, pre-flighted the aircraft and had it warmed and ready for takeoff when the pilot arrived. A strong bond existed between Les and his pilot who flew every mission without a mechanical hitch until war's end.

George Roepke, Traer, was a crew chief with the 357th Fighter Group at Leiston. During his tour of duty George went through two P-51 Mustang fighters and three pilots. One of the P-51s failed to return from a mission and it was believed the pilot killed. At a Group reunion after the war he was surprised to see the pilot in attendance. He had bailed out of his airplane and taken Prisoner of War.

Verne Josifek, Cedar Rapids was a P-51 aircraft mechanic with the 361st Fighter Group at Bottisham and Little Walden. Verne was assigned to maintain and service an airplane piloted by another Iowan, Robert Ward of Toledo. A strong bond existed between the two. Before each mission Verne would give Bob a lucky silver dollar. In return Bob would give Verne his little black book containing a listing of everyone who owed him money from gambling. Then Bob would relieve himself on the plane's tail wheel and go on the mission. On return, the lucky dollar and black book would change hands again.

Crews replaced engines, installed superchargers, horizontal stabilizers, oil coolers, landing gear, tires, tail wheels, brakes, generators, regulators, radio equipment and spark plugs. To have one airplane return to base because of a mechanical malfunction reduced the effectiveness of the mission and increased the hazards exposed to others. Airplanes had to be fueled, engines finely tuned, instruments, radios, and turrets checked to ensure they were functioning properly.

Gaylord Henryson, Story City, was an aircraft mechanic crew chief with the 91st Bomb Group at Bassingbourn. "We would be on the flight line on missions to preflight the aircraft and top off fuel tanks while other crews loaded ammo, bombs and checked instruments."

Roger Cox, Des Moines, 453rd BG, Old Buckenham, England, was attached to the Royal Air Force where he installed radar in their aircraft. The radar was supposed to divert V-2 rockets fired from Germany. "The rocket had four fins on the back. They were fired toward London. The RAF would take to the air and manipulate the radar to flip the fins and send them off course and hopefully into the English Channel."

Ray Marner, Iowa City, was with the 357th Fighter Group at Leiston and delivered and installed drop tanks of P-51 fighters enabling them to increase their escort duty range. Engines were checked for fuel, oil and coolant leaks.

Kenneth Ranson, Cedar Rapids, was an aircraft mechanic crew chief with the 20th Fighter Group at Kings

Ground crews at work on B-24

Ray Schmelzer, Postville, on right, Crew Chief, 479th FG, Wattisham

Byrl Elliott, Cherokee, on left, Instrument Specialist, 356th FG, Martlesham Heath

Cliffe and maintained aircraft flown by four different pilots all of whom finished their tour of duty. Ken was able to sneak aboard a B-17 bomber and fly three missions as a tail gunner and see the fighter plane he maintained flying escort with the bomber formation.

Rex McDowell, Waterloo, was an aircraft mechanic with the 44th Bomb Group at Shipdham. He helped fuel the aircraft and maintain engines and systems of his assigned B-24 bomber including replacement of rubber fuel tanks.

The work performed by aircraft mechanics didn't go unnoticed from aircrews whose lives depended on their bomber or fighter flying without mechanical problems. Command at each base was under pressure to assure their superiors the maximum number of aircraft would be available for any scheduled mission.

Donald Eastwood, Red Oak, 452 Bomb Group, Deopham Green, was awarded a meritorious citation for having aircraft under his maintenance control fly fifty-eight straight missions without a mechanical abort.

Wes Franklin, Des Moines, Crew Chief, 34th BG, Mendelsham, England, was awarded the Bronze Star Medal for the aircraft under his control and supervision completing fifty-one bombardment missions against the enemy without being forced to return because of mechanical difficulty or failure. "Also without the loss of a man."

Leighton Ford, Marion, 96th Bomb Group, Snetterton Heath, received a commendation for keeping a B-17 bomber over the target for sixty-eight straight missions without a turn back for mechanical trouble.

Verne Josifek, Cedar Rapids, Crew Chief, 361st Fighter Group, Little Walden, England, received the Bronze Star Medal for keeping his assigned P-51 Mustang fighter in operating condition for 200 hours without any mechanical problems resulting in aborted missions. At one point Verne had gotten 900 hours out of an engine without an engine change.

Lowell Rothbart, Dewitt, 20th Fighter Group, Kings Cliffe, was in charge of seventeen men performing maintenance and repair of a squadron of aircraft. His fighter group had the best P-51 maintenance record in the Eighth Air Force.

Base Air Depot (BAD) personnel assembled aircraft shipped to England and made modifications to aircraft flown across the Atlantic to make them combat ready. Aircraft flown from America were reported to have been left at Prestwick, Scotland; Nuts Corner, Ireland and Valley, Wales. Air Transport Group pilots would then fly the planes to a BAD base. Major battle damage was repaired that couldn't be performed by Sub-Sepots or base units because of limited equipment and facilities. BADs received stores of parts, equipment, vehicles, medical and chemical supplies, ammunition, bombs and general supplies for stockpiling and dispersal to advance depots nearer individual bases. Major engine overhauls were performed on a mass basis. The great number of aircraft, fighter, bomber, reconnaissance, and other flight units consumed an enormous amount of fuel and oil. Tanker trucks delivered fuel on a constant basis to satisfy operational demands.

Leighton Ford, Marion, in center, Crew Chief, 96th BG, Snetterton Heath, England

Advanced or Sub-Depots repaired aircraft, performed major engine overhauls, retrieved aircraft that had been forced down but were flyable, and scavenged parts from severely damaged aircraft that were to be scrapped and at crash sites. Replacement aircraft was not always available nor were parts able to be stockpiled until America's plants and factories achieved maximum production. Until supplies caught up to and surpassed demand, aircraft parts in some instances, were hand-made in base shops. Command elements maintained constant pressure to ensure the maximum number of aircraft were available for dispatch on each mission. Flak and bullet holes had to be repaired as well as operational cabling, wiring, wings, ailerons, stabilizers, flaps and tails. Sub-depots also served as an advance storage facility from where a limited number of bases could receive supplies.

Aircrews had to give repaired aircraft "shakedown" flights before they could be placed back on operational lists. One such test flight was made by Bob Houser, Des Moines, 306th Bomb Group, Thurleigh, England, and his crew. The official report stated "fuel fumes were strong in the aircraft at take off and increased as they were flying" They decided to land. Flames came from #3 supercharger and engulfed the bomb bay area and spread rapidly. On landing the ship nosed over and swerved off the runway. The Flight Engineer suffered burns and a broken leg. The aircrew escaped from the burning aircraft and ran in case of explosion. Bob escaped out the front hatch and almost ran in the direction of the

Chapter Nine

still rotating propellers. After taking one step in the wrong direction he ran forward from under the aircraft. The plane was a total loss.

Gilbert Douglas, Storm Lake worked at Base Air Depot #2, Burtonwood, England. "We furnished 90 percent of all engines to the Eighth Air Force. We had a 9 cylinder and an 18 cylinder line doing constant engine overhauls."

Dale Frank, Winterset, was with the 475th Sub-Depot at Mendelsham, England. As crew chief Dale repaired bullet and flak holes in aircraft and provided major re-construction of tail sections, wing stabilizers and fuselages.

Robert Myers, Tiffin, was assigned to Base Air Depot #2, Wharton, England, where ten thousand personnel were assigned to fulfill engine overhaul, structural support repair from battle damage and modifications to aircraft for Eighth Air Force bases under its territorial assignment. P-51 Mustang fighter planes arriving at British ports in crates would be taken to the base and assembled. Modifications included installation of armor plating on the outside of B-24 bombers next to the pilot and co-pilot positions; oxygen bottles and life raft positions in the B-24 were moved from where they were installed at the factory; gas tanks installed behind the pilot in the P-51; and radio and instrument modifications were made. War-weary bombers had their bomb bay doors riveted shut and were used to drop supplies through escape hatches to the Underground on low-level flights.

Dick Vanduyn, Iowa City, was also assigned to Base Air Depot #2. Before entering military service he worked on a line crew with American Telegraph and Telephone. When he arrived at Wharton it was a relatively new base and Dick installed telephones all over the base including hangars. "Eighteen American soldiers operated the switchboard at night. During the day British girls ran the switchboard."

Germany lost the Battle of Britain in 1940 during their attacks on English cities, air production centers, ports and shipping in preparation for an invasion of England. This diminished their reserve of experienced pilots. The invasion of Russia engaged them in a two-front war, further spreading their resources. Arrival of the Eighth Air Force and success of the RAF in the Battle of Britain, reduced bomb and fighter attacks against England. In their place V-1 and V-2 rockets from sites in Germany were launched against England.

A radar system gave advanced warning of enemy formations or V-1 rockets destined for England and fighters would be dispatched to intercept them. Although air superiority had been won by allied forces, attacks still occurred at American bases which had limited anti-aircraft defenses. Luftwaffe bombers made night bombing attacks on bases or fighters followed American bombers back to their bases and attacked them while they were trying to land. In a diary maintained by Staff Sergeant Byrl Elliott. Cherokee, Iowa, of the 356th Fighter Group, Martlesham Heath, England, the following entries were made:

"Buzz bombs from June 6,"44 up till now Oct 19, 44. The last month they have come down to tree top height. I don't like it!"

"Pretty big raid last nite mostly incendiaries started a lot of fires but didn't do much damage, a lot of them were duds. Feb 13, 1944, 2100 hrs"

"Four buzz bombs directly over our bks. Tonite, flak boys shot one down directly overhead. Boy that was close!! Sept 23, 1944. They are sure sending them a long ways"

"Big raid the nite of Feb 3rd around 0400 till 0600 all the new ack ack got in a good nite. I sure didn't get much sleep that nite. Buzz bomb hit around three hundred yds from our hut, busted up some of our huts. No casualties. Oct 25, 745 PM. It knocked me off my bike."

"January 27, 1944. Hell of a big bunch of Jerry upstairs tonite, most since we've been here. Ack-ack boys are tossing up everything but the kitchen sink."

"Nine buzz-bombs over last nite at 3:30 to 4AM. Five went directly over our area, sure glad they didn't decide to land or run out of gas. Aug 31, 44. Eight more tonite Sept 1, 44 about the last I imagine. Like Hell!! Sept 20, 1944"

"I wish to hell these buzz bombs would leave me alone, I'm trying to write letters, Oct 6, 1944"

"One of our pilots got a picture of a V-2 rocket in his gun camera at 3,000 feet and going up. About all you could see was its trail. 25 or 30 buzz bombs over last nite, Nov 19, 1944, 2000 hrs."

Found cause of recent explosions around camp. Rocket bombs, no noise except when they hit. They make a pretty big hole in the ground. Oct 10, 1944"

"They finally got one of those rocket bombs on our area tonite. I was going down to the Red Cross. Wont know till morning if it got any one. Oct 25, 1944 745PM:

"Fifteen shot down so far tonite, buzz bombs, 8pm, Nov 10, 44 and they are still coming! Alert lasted one half-hour. 29 bombs were shot down, three got thru."

"Buzz bomb at 1945 hrs hit on skeet range back of M.P. area, nine boys went to hospital. Don't think any one was killed out right. Blew in a few buildings including the east wall of our hangar. Nov 14, 44"

Another incident recalled by Staff Sergeant Elliott was upon his recent arrival at Martlesham Heath, assigned as an instrument specialist. Three Luftwaffe

JU 88s attacked the base on a night bombing mission. One plane was shot down, crashing on the base. Pumped full of adrenaline the newly arrived GI's rushed to the scene despite the base still being under attack. "We really wanted to get a look at their aircraft and see what the dreaded Nazis were like", he recalled. What they found was their first initiation to the horrors and cruelty of war. Sprawled in the grass along the runway was a young German crewman, who had been pitched from the crashing Junkers. Short in stature, his blond hair was smeared with blood. Blood pulsed from a gaping wound in his chest, large enough to view destroyed internal organs. He died quickly, screaming "Mutter" "Mutter" for his mother and reaching out for the awe-struck American soldiers.

After the raid was over, they went through the German's papers. He was 19 years old, three years younger than the Americans who watched him die. Fifty years later, Byrl could not speak of the incident without tears welling in his eyes.

Bicycles were everywhere. Purchased from the British, they were the chief form of transportation on base and short trips off base, usually to area pubs. When piled outside mess halls or other facilities, or the need demanded it, bicycle ownership often changed hands daily. Many a G.I. riding bicycles at night during blackout and unable to see where they were going or feeling the effects of pub potions, had accidents. A road leading from the 34th Bomb Group to Mendlesham had a creek running across the road. To prevent erosion and making the road passable, concrete was poured where the creek crossed the road. Moss formed making the road slick. G.I.s returning from pubs rode down the dip in the road, hit the slick surface and sent sprawling to the ground. They could be heard loudly cussing and swearing at the bicycles. After all it was the bicycle's fault. More than one airman was rescued from deep ditches alongside roadways.

At war's end, knowing the G.I.s couldn't take the bicycles home with them, British civilians from whom they had purchased the bicycles refused to buy them back. This caused many base bicycles to be stacked and run over with heavy equipment destroying them. Claude Conklin rescued four for the Higgins family who owned a nearby pub and with whom he had become close friends.

Nancy Foster, Cedar Falls, was a Red Cross volunteer assigned to Base Air Depot #2 at Wharton, England, where airmen could be served refreshments, play cards, ping pong and billiards or attend parties at the club.

Both air and ground crew personnel adopted pets whether obtained locally or obtained in route to England during their deployment to the European Theater of Operations. The most unusual however was "Lady Moe" an African burrow flown to England from North Africa by an aircrew of the 96th Bomb Group at Snetterton Heath. The flight required "Lady Moe" be outfitted with an oxygen mask and heated suit to survive the rigors of high altitude flight. The official mascot

Her Ladyship "Lady Moe"

Bob Manahl and ground crew personnel, 384th BG, Grafton Underwood

Red Cross Clubmobile, somewhere in England at 8th AF Base

Chapter Nine

of the Bomb Group, she was adopted by and cared for by all base personnel

In addition to movies on the base, movies played in the English towns. A trip to town, usually by bicycle or hitching a ride wouldn't be complete, and was more likely the reason for, a visit to a local pub for the warm beer known as 'bitters'.

The English, wary at first of the American, soon welcomed the GIs at the pubs and treated them with respect. It didn't take long for the Americans to be-

Blue Lion Pub outside 492nd BG-Pickenham, England

The Flying Fortress Pub outside Great Ashfield, England.

Leroy Edward, Mt Pleasant, second from left, and crew on pass in London

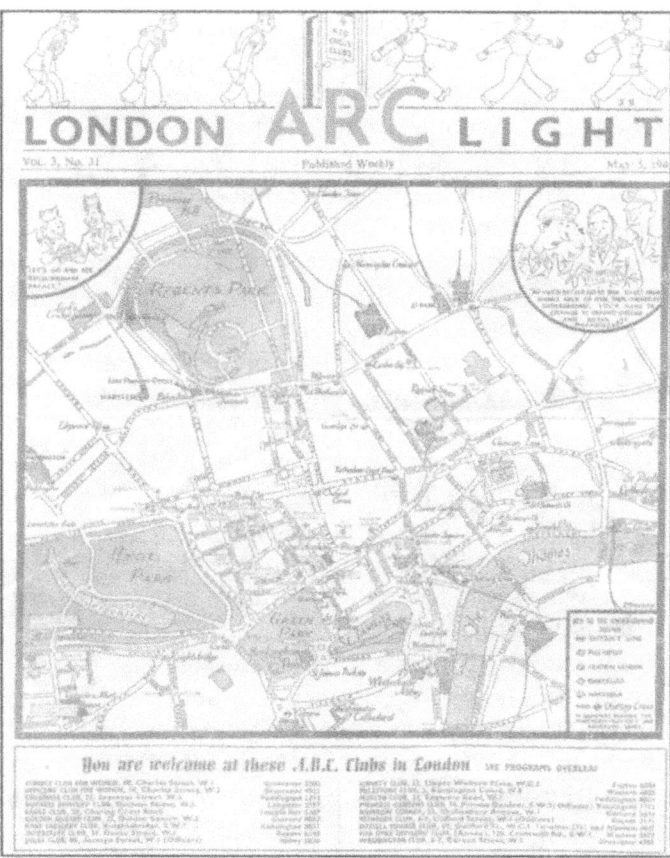
Red Cross Map and Daily Schedule of Events

Theater Schedule

come part of the community. Pubs near the bases were recalled with fond memories such as "The Chequers","Woodman Inn", "The Flying Fortress".

Claude Conklin of Belle Plaine and many members of the 34th Bomb Group at Mendlesham frequented a pub named "The Fleece". It was a favorite of the base mess sergeant, a friend and important ally, but Claude preferred "The Oak", a two-story home with the ground floor converted into a pub. To Claude and his crew it was "Charlie's", after the owner Charlie Huggins and his family with whom a lifelong friendship was established. Charlie would serve warm light or dark beer tapped from wooden kegs.

Three day passes found many Americans going to London or other major cities to site see, attend concerts, plays and rest. They could always go to British and American clubs frequented by local girls for their company and dancing. For those so inclined, the "Picadilly Commando", (lady of the evening) came out after blackout for profitable private interludes.

Dances held at Eighth Air Force bases would be attended by British girls trucked in from nearby cities and towns. Glenn Miller's orchestra was in constant demand and also had regularly scheduled radio shows beamed to American troops on the continent.

Verne Josifek, Cedar Rapids, played in a band at the 361st Fighter Group, Little Walden, England. The band was successful in playing at jobs three nights a week. High-ranking officers liked the band and would often send a staff car to the flight line to pick up Verne to get him to band jobs. The band played at the Stage Door Canteen in the Rainbow Corner Red Cross Club in London on both V-E and V-J Days.

Ollie Joiner, Monroe, was director of the band at the 364th Fighter Group, Honington, England. The band played at English clubs for free scotch or beer

Photo taken by friend of Everett Sandersfeld, S. Amana, on eve of Glenn Miller's disappearance.

Verne Josifek, aircraft mechanic, Cedar Rapids, on trumpet with "The Mustangs" band at 361st FG, Little Walden

The "Skyliners" at 92nd BG, Podington, England. Bob Dougherty is trombone player second from left.

Chapter Nine

and a minor monetary payment. Red Cross dances were played for free. "I believe it helped morale of the soldiers." Their band, the Goldbricks was selected to play at a ball hosted by the Duke of Grafton.

Robert Dougherty, Ft Madison, 92nd BG, Podington, England, carried his trombone with him while in service. Aboard ship in route to the European Theater of Operations he played in a band aboard ship with USO personnel that entertained the troops. While at the 92nd BG, he played in a base band called "The Skyliners" when not flying missions.

Facing Christmas away from home and families while at war was an especially lonely, dispirited time. Missions were flown and more airmen lost their lives. Perhaps more than a good-will gesture, but remembering their own loved ones back home and seeing the ration-starved, poor and orphaned children in England, many air bases responded to the most holy of days. Parties were organized for children living near the bases.

At Wendling, the 392nd Bomb Group trucked 130 orphan and refugee children to their base. The children were shown cartoons and given an inside tour of a B-24. Then they were fed all the food they could eat including candy, cakes, fruit, and jello. Santa Claus distributed gifts, purchased from GI donations, to all the children.

The 359th Fighter Group at East Wretham through the efforts of a base chaplain organized a party for 200 orphans and school children from nearby villages. Jeep rides, games, cartoons and plenty of food, candy and ice cream preceded the arrival of Santa Claus and presents for all.

The 401st Bomb Group at Deenethorpe hosted a party for 650 children plying them with fruit, ice cream, turkey and cranberry sauce.

Singer Francis Langford and Comedian Bob Hope at 306th BG, Thurleigh, England.

Manor House, Risely, England, where Glenn Miller entertained servicemen. Band played from roof of mess hall on left of main structure to G.I.s sitting on lawn.

Santa and Kids - Scenes at base Christmas Parties for English children and orphans

GIs with kids

Each squadron of the 384th at Grafton Underwood adopted a war orphan paying for his food and clothing up to the age of fifteen.

Six B-17 bombers were loaded with toys either purchased, made or had sent from the United States. The planes flew to Nantes, France where the toys were distributed to war orphans.

A party was hosted by the 305th Bomb Group at Chelveston where they fed British children from nearby villages and made sure Santa Claus arrived to give them all presents.

At Ridgewell, home of the 381st Bomb Group, a chaplain visited churches and schools in nearby villages. He saw the deprivation in the children who had not tasted an orange, banana or Hershey bar. Toys were not available in war-torn England. He organized a group of volunteers to gather toys and candy from PX rations, prepare ice cream, cookies, sandwiches and fresh fruit. Trucks were sent to the village and gathered 350 children. A giant Christmas tree, Santa Claus and base musicians were on hand to greet them. Tables had been filled with food. Gifts were labeled for each child. In an article for the "8th AF News, David McCarthy stated, " the tired, dispirited fliers began to slouch into the building and stood moodily viewing, with unseen eyes, the excited children. Then one pushed away from the wall to help a child unwrap a gift; another and another followed until the hall was filled with happy, laughing youngsters, of all ages, playing together." Later, "as the evening drew to a close, the soft strains of "Silent Night" filled the room and our leather-jacketed fliers, grasping those small hands, stood taller, with renewed faith, and unashamedly wept for joy as their voices sounded throughout the hall." The chaplain "had once again, saved the day. He proved, not only to the tiny British children, but to his beloved young fliers as well, that there was indeed a "Father Christmas" and that "Peace on Earth" would once again prevail.

Christmas for English orphans, 305th BG, Chelveston, 1944

388th BG, Knettishall, England. Everett Sandersfeld, S. Amana, bottom row, middle of three men.

Christmas Party at Strategic Air Depot #3, Watton, England, with British guests.

Chapter Ten

Chapter Ten
SPECIAL UNITS

PROPAGANDA LEAFLETS

Special squadrons of the Eighth Air Force dropped psychological bombs over Germany and Axis-occupied countries. They were propaganda leaflets designed to create doubt and fear in the German military, reduce their willingness to continue fighting and inform them on the true progress of the war. Containers were packed with leaflets, a special bomb designed to explode on a time-delay after it left a bomber and allow a wide dispersal of the material. This was completed on an ever increasing scale with millions of leaflets sent fluttering to the enemy on the ground encouraging them to cease resistance and promised good treatment if they surrendered. German military leaders imposed threats of punishment on any soldier caught with a leaflet in his possession. The threats evidently went unheeded. Many captured soldiers had leaflets in their possession when they surrendered or used the leaflets to surrender.

The leaflets were prepared by the Army's Psychological Warfare Division and unlike German and Japanese posters and propaganda material, was effective by telling the truth. This was especially important nearer the end of the war when leaflets were dropped over retreating German armies.

Jim Brown, Mason City, was assigned to a Composite Squadron of the 305th Bomb Group. He flew a black B-17 bomber at night dropping propaganda leaflets over Nazi-occupied Europe as well as weapons and supplies to underground resistance groups. Because of blackout conditions in all of England, Jim was required to take off and land in total darkness. Pinpoint lights along the runway allowed him to take off from his base. Other pinpoint lights, visible from only one direction at low altitude allowed him to find his base runway at night and land. On his thirteenth mission a German night fighter attacked his bomber. Despite shooting down the night fighter it had inflicted damage to his airplane to the extent he and his crew were forced to "bail out" over German-occupied Holland. Jim and his crew were taken prisoner of war.

Richard Taylor, Cedar Rapids, was a pilot with the 388th Bomb Group at Knettishall, England. As the war closed in on the Germans, his crew dropped propaganda leaflets which announced "Sie Kommen" (We're Coming) to convince enemy troops to surrender.

Everett Dexter, Marshalltown, was an aerial gunner with the 406th Night Leaflet Squadron at Cheddington, England. Everett flew forty-one missions. "We would fly at night over Axis territory dropping leaflets to as many as five different locations. One night over Germany we found ourselves in the middle of a British formation flying to a target. To avoid mid-air collision, the pilot turned on all of our aircraft's lights and made his way out of the formation."

Bob Suckow, Newton, was a B-24 pilot with the 445th Bomb Group at Tibenham, England. Bob spoke fluent German and was used by the British Broad-

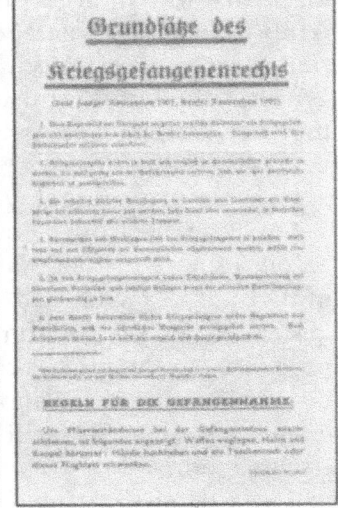

One of the millions of propaganda leaflets dropped over Germany and occupied countries by Special Leaflet Squadrons of the Eighth Air Force. It promises to the German solider food, medical attention, good treatment and removal from the war zone if he surrenders.

casting Company to beam propaganda over Germany advising civilians it was not our intent to kill or injure civilians in the bombing raids but to end the war as soon as possible.

By 1945 Germany's Army and Luftwaffe was essentially out of food, gas, ammunition, transport and will to continue fighting. Their cities were leveled and German soldiers began to surrender in droves. Some would continue to fight to the end.

Photographic Reconnaissance

To support the strategy of daylight precision bombing it was necessary to gain intelligence on intended targets whether it was in oil, transportation, aircraft, or in armaments and munitions industries. Photographic Reconnaissance Squadrons (Photo Recon) were formed using the P-38 Lighting fighter equipped with cameras in the nose of the aircraft. Extremely fast and devoid of guns, the P-38 flew over enemy-held territory to photograph enemy activity in widespread geographic areas to determine enemy strength, defenses, location and movement. Intended targets were photographed to assist mission planners in verifying intelligence data gathered from other sources. Photographs provided intelligence personnel and mission planners, shortly after return of the aircraft, a view of an intended target that could be studied and analyzed for long periods of time. They could then determine what was in the immediate surrounding area of the target and identify areas of the target where concentrated bombing should be directed. Bombardiers were also afforded visible identification of targets through their bombsights. After a mission targets were photographed to assess damage inflicted. Periodic return photographic missions allowed mission planners to monitor progress of restoration efforts at the target and determine when and if future missions against the same target were needed.

For example, from reconnaissance photographs of an oil refinery or fuel plant, oil experts could determine the most vital and vulnerable sections of the target and its production capacity. After a mission, post-strike photographs could assess how much production was reduced and the time required for the enemy to repair the facility to bring it to normal capacity again.

The British Spitfire fighter was also used by American pilots for long-rang photographic flights. The P-51 Mustang fighter was used near the end of the war for high altitude photography. Gerald Glaza, Cedar Rapids, was a pilot with the

Gerald Glaza, Cedar Rapids sitting on top of his Spitfire, 7th Photo Recon

British Spitfire with American markings flown by 7th Photo Recon Group. Art print by Charles R. Taylor, Montezuma, Iowa, depicts Spitfire on photo mission over German synthetic fuel refinery.

7th Photo Recon Group and flew both the British Spitfire and the P-51. While on a low-level mission over enemy territory his aircraft received anti-aircraft hits that forced him to crash land. Gerald escaped capture by German troops and was able to make it back to the safety of Allied-held territory.

Low-level photo recon missions were flown over Northern France prior to the D-Day invasion to gain intelligence on German coastal defenses and troop concentrations. The British Mosquito twin-engine aircraft and the American B-26 Martin Marauder medium bomber were employed for night photographic missions.

Gerald Cunningham, Waterloo, was an Intelligence Officer with the 13th Squadron of the 7th Photo Recon Group at Mount Farm, England, responsible for analyzing and interpreting reconnaissance photographs taken by the pilots before they were sent to Eighth Air Force Headquarters.

James Hoy, Eldora, was based at High Wycombe, Eighth Air Force Headquarters where reconnaissance photographs received final interpretation, bomb damage reports typed and distributed, models made of proposed targets and maps made of enemy territory.

Vernon Grubb, Kingsley, was a crew chief with the 7th Photo Recon Group and serviced aircraft assigned to him. "Missions were flown unarmed. In place of machine guns the aircraft were armed with cameras to take pre-mission and post-mission photographs of targets. My first pilot was shot down and eventually made his way back to England." Vernon's second pilot was fellow Iowan Gerald Glaza of Cedar Rapids. "We had no losses because of a mechanic malfunction."

WEATHER RECCONAISANCE

In England the Eighth Air Force had two enemies, the Germans and the weather. The value of accurate weather forecasting was immense for bombers and fighters to take off from their bases, assemble safely on time, fly to and visually bomb their targets and make it back to their bases. Weather forecasting played a vital role in the successful dismantling of the German war machine and production centers, supply and support of ground forces and date of one of the most historic invasions in history. It was also responsible for the loss of hundreds of American lives from crash landings, mid-air collisions and extra time over enemy targets..

Incoming frontal systems from the Atlantic Ocean naturally reached the United Kingdom first as the fronts moved across Northern Europe. Gathering weather data in Britain during the early stage of American involvement in World War II gave both British and American weather forecasters the means to predict weather conditions at individual bases and track the systems over enemy targets. However, unpredictable English weather still caused havoc in control of missions, whether it would remain a "go", be cancelled or aborted in route.

Planners required more reliable data if they were to do a better job of forecasting weather. In particular information on weather conditions over the Atlantic Ocean was needed. Royal Air Force units and American bomb groups flew reconnaissance missions over

Pre-invasion photo reconnaissance of Omaha Beach showing TNT explosives on top of beach obstacles

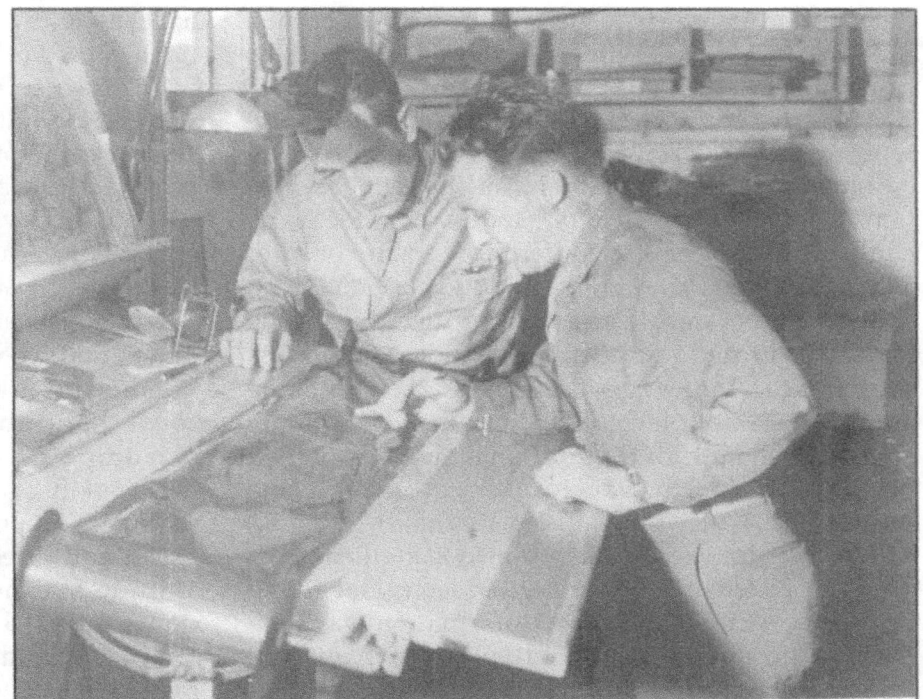

Gerald Cunningham, Waterloo, closest to camera, 7th Photo Recon Group

the Atlantic following specified oceanic tracks. Ten tracks were flown, eight by the RAF and two by the Eighth Air Force to obtain weather data.

Beginning in the Fall of 1943 regular Atlantic Ocean weather reconnaissance flights were made in specially equipped B-17 and B-24 bombers with meteorology trained specialists aboard. After organizational changes in April, 1944, units were consolidated and renamed. The 652nd Squadron of the 25th Bomb Group became the primary weather squadron from personnel of the former 8th Weather Reconnaissance Squadron of the 802 Recon Group. Other squadrons of the 25th, the 653rd Squadron flew the twin engine Mosquito on weather reconnaissance missions over Europe and as scout planes in advance of bomber formations. The 654th Squadron also flew the Mosquito on photo reconnaissance and chaff-dispensing missions.

Eventually using the B-17 bomber, the 652nd Squadron flew an Atlantic route code named EPICURE. Four missions a day were flown, two departed in daylight and two at night in any kind of weather. Their route took them from Watton, home of the 652nd BG, to Land's End, England, and out over the Atlantic. After confirming instrument settings their flight leveled out between 950 and 1800 feet for a distance of 500 miles. Observations of weather conditions were taken every 50 miles recording visibility, precipitation, turbulence, airframe icing, cloud types and tenths of sky covered by each layer, dry and wet bulb temperatures and barometer readings. Every 100 miles a wind was determined using drift meters and smoke bombs or flares as markers. Wind speed and direction was calculated.

After each wind check the aircraft descended to 50 to 100 feet above the water to provide a near sea level barometer reading. At the 500-mile mark, observations were taken at every 1000-foot level as the plane climbed in a box or step pattern to a ceiling of 25 to 30 thousand feet. The heights of cloud bases and tops and any temperature inversions were noted. Then the plane was turned south and made a descending approach to the Azores islands with observations made at every 1,000-foot level. The crews rested 24 hours and made the return flight to England code-named SHARON, using the reverse pattern flown to the Azores.

Weather data was put into a five digit number group, encoded and transmitted in secret cipher to a British receiving station. The information was then teletyped to a British headquarters and relayed to all British and American bases for use by base weather forecasters.

Paul Scherb, Waterloo, was assigned to the 18th and 21st Weather Squadrons at Hethel and Bungay, England. Trained in weather forecasting and weather phenomenon he had to determine weather conditions to and from mission targets and over American bases. His staff of weather forecasters worked in shifts twenty-four hours a day, seven days a week accumulating weather data, plotting it on charts and making predictions

The other route flown by the Eighth Air Force was code named ALLAH that flew westerly south of Ireland for 700 miles, turned south for about 700 miles and then eastward back to England. The same weather observations and readings were made as on the EPICURE and SHARON routes.

Sydney Thomas, Waterloo, was a weather officer with the 25th Bomb Group and flew the SHARON and ALLAH missions. Highly trained in meteorology Sydney continued to fly weather missions after V-E Day until September of 1945. The extended duty was to assist all military services in return of servicemen and equipment to the United States. He then served as weather officer at Bad Kissengen, Germany, as part of American occupation forces.

The aircrews flew the heavy weather flights in all kinds of weather and over a large expanse of water on missions that lasted twelve to fifteen hours in length. Their aircraft carried an extra two thousand gallons of fuel that was always a hazard at takeoff. Instrumentation by today's standards was barely adequate. Navigators had to be extremely skillful in guiding the aircraft out and back over a vast expanse of ocean with few, if any, of today's modern navigational aids. Accidents occurred. Ninety-one men lost their lives.

Dave Hamilton, Des Moines, flew the long missions to the Azores as a waist gunner. An aircrew Dave trained with was lost without a trace on one mission. Although he was not with the crew on that mission an Air Force Museum publication erroneously listed Dave as with the crew and killed in action.

Floyd Nielsen, Pocahontas, 25th Bomb Group: "At Lands End we would fly toward Iceland. Every one hundred miles we would go down to twenty-five feet above the ocean to take a pressure reading. We would also drop a smoke bomb onto the water, take a sighting, then fly at a ninety-degree angle to take another reading. From those readings we could predict wind speed and direction. We would then climb back to altitude for another one hundred miles and drop down and do the same thing. When we got near Iceland we would be at thirty thousand feet and fly a fifty-mile box to determine what is now known as the jet stream. Our flights would be ten to twelve

Chapter Ten

hours long. When you were down to twenty-five feet above the ocean it was like being in a bowl with water above you on all sides."

Weather forecasters were also aided by the capture of the ENIGMA, a German code machine which produced coded messages that had been unbreakable by the best Allied cryptographers. An Enigma machine along with German weather codebooks was taken from a captured U-boat. The British were able to break the German code. In addition to knowledge of German military operational plans in advance, coded messages from German ships and weather stations in Greenland, Ireland and occupied Europe were decoded and provided weather conditions all over Europe on a daily basis including Berlin.

Wayne Stellish, Aurelia, in front of checkered trailer at end of runway, 306th

Accurate weather forecasting played an important role in the invasion of the European continent on June 6, 1944, D-Day. Although heavy rain and high winds lashed the British Isles and English Channel beforehand, weather forecasters were able to predict a high pressure system developing which would provide "a window of opportunity" for invasion on June 6.

Joseph Barnes, Mason City, was a navigator with the 392nd Bomb Group at Wendling, England. "There were numerous "stand down" times of up to eleven days when our Group did not fly a mission because of weather."

Bases would employ a B-17 with a weather spotter aboard to determine ice formation levels, cloud formations and visibility at various altitudes over Eighth Air Force bases prior to launching missions The plane would then land and participate in pre-mission briefings to air crews.

Other problems arose during "forming up", the time bomber and fighter aircraft would get into formation after takeoff. Bases were often next door or within a few miles of each other. In foggy or heavy overcast weather mid-air collisions occurred between aircraft taking off and gaining altitude despite speed, rate of climb and direction procedures to prevent this from happening.

Harold Jackson, Waterloo, was a radio operator with the 44th Bomb Group at Shipdham, England. Scheduled for a mission to bomb targets in Berlin his squadron had to take off in dense fog. "We were lined up nose to tail and took off at thirty second intervals, turned at a prescribed time and climbed in order to form up for the mission. There were a lot of collisions at times because of the weather."

Duane Kritchman, Des Moines, was a ball turret gunner with the 92nd Bomb Group at Podington, England. His squadron was taking off in dense fog for a mission when a bomber failed to get airborne and ran off the runway into woods beyond their airfield. The next plane was already on its takeoff run and stopped halfway down the runway after hearing a radio command to cease taking off or saw warning flares. He turned his aircraft around and began taxiing back on the runway. The next aircraft either didn't hear the radio command or see the flares and with throttles wide open began its takeoff. The two planes collided and exploded killing all aboard both aircraft."

Wayne Stellish, Aurelia, while with the 306th Bomb Group at Thurleigh, England, had primary duties inside a checked caravan trailer at the end of the base runway. He had to make visual contact with all aircraft taking off and landing. In foggy weather he help aircraft line up on the runway using flares, radio contact with the pilot or lamp signals

Weather over targets and over England changed. On arrival at the target, aircrews often found weather that was promised to be clear had turned sour, was obscured by fog or overcast or enemy smoke screens covered entire industrial areas. It was often difficult to visibly locate targets until radar-bombing technology arrived. Until then, scout planes for some bomb groups, flew to targets in the British Mosquito or P-51 Mustang in advance of bomber formations and report weather conditions.

Raymond Carlson, Walcott, was a navigator with the 466th Bomb Group at Attlebridge, England. Thick overcast prevented bombers from his Group from gathering into formation . They proceeded singly to Northern France where the Group was able to form up for the run to the target. "We found our formation flying through clouds so dense we could barely see our wing man. At that time a group of B-17s flew through our formation from the right. The next five to ten minutes was spent doing evasive action to prevent mid-air collisions."

Iowans of the Mighty Eighth

Joseph Pfiffner, Waterloo, was an aerial gunner with the 458th Bomb Group at Horsham St. Faith, England. "Because of weather conditions our Group flew to Belgium to form up. A weather front had moved and we were required to fly in fog. Our wings began to ice up and our plane went into a dive. The pilot ordered us to bail out. I hadn't tightened the parachute harness around myself and when the chute opened it nearly tore me apart."

Richard Steelman, Fort Dodge, was a B-24 pilot with the 93rd Bomb Group at Hardwick, England. On his fourth mission "we took off in heavy overcast to "form up". When we finally broke into the clear we couldn't find our Group. We flew an oval pattern to try and find them all the while using precious fuel. We flew the mission by hooking onto another bomb group. When we returned we had to land at an Allied base in France because we didn't have enough fuel to make it back to England."

Returning aircraft, some often hard-pressed by battle damage or fuel depletion, found it nearly impossible to find their bases when enveloped in fog, heavy overcast or snow storms. Identifiable features on the ground were also obscured. Many aircrews were forced to land at other bases, emergency airstrips, or made it to their own base only by the fortune of good luck. For others luck sometimes ran out. Mid-air collisions or crashes resulted taking lives of the crew and often civilians on the ground. Because fog was such a problem a system called "Fido" was employed at emergency landing strips near the English Channel. The landing strips were re-designed to be exceedingly long and wide. Petrol was burned around the runways to burn away fog.

Burl Beam, Martensdale, was a B-17 pilot with the 398th Bomb Group at Nuthampstead, England. Returning to England from one mission "we were down to one thousand feet. Actually there was no visibility at all. We were down so low I saw a tree coming at us through the fog. I gave the engines full throttle and pulled up and away just in time to miss it. Our radio operator was able to get us to an auxiliary field."

Allen Gartman, Maquoketa, was a tail gunner with the 34th Bomb Group at Mendolesham, England. Scheduled to fly a relay mission it was snowing when Allen and his crew took off. When they returned to base "it was a complete 'whiteout'". On approaching their base the pilot suddenly gunned the airplane and gained altitude. "We weren't anywhere near the direction of the runway. On our second attempt to land I looked out one side of the plane and saw a hangar. On the other side there were trees that were higher than us. On the third try the pilot made it."

Glen Hill, Fairfield, was an aerial gunner and toggelier also with the 466th Bomb Group. Glen was part of a skeleton crew that flew to Scotland to dispose of their war-weary B-24 "Dirty Gertie". "The weather was miserable, overcast, slush on the runway. It took us three tries to get airborne. On the way to Scotland a British Spitfire flew along side us and tried to make hand signals to us. Since we didn't have radio contact with him we didn't know until later that he was trying to tell us the airfield in Scotland was "socked in" and to return to our base. When we got to Scotland we made numerous attempts to land. We couldn't see much and couldn't line up with the runway. All at once I saw us heading for a church steeple and yelled at the pilot. He pulled up in time for one wing to go over the steeple. We were able to finally land."

Russell Logue, Norwalk, was a radio operator with the 392nd Bomb Group at Wendling, England. When he returned from a mission "our base was fogged in and we were about out of fuel. The pilot asked the crew if they should bail out to which one crewman replied "we should climb up a little bit first because we just flew under a cow's belly. We climbed to 5000 feet, headed the plane out to sea and bailed out. As we floated down our bombar-

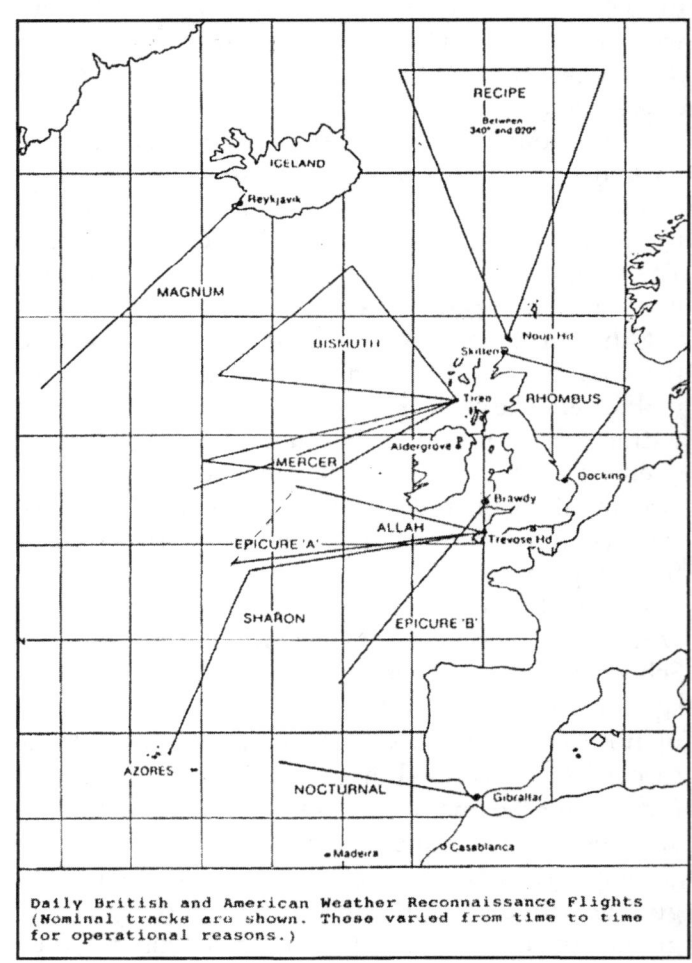

Daily British and American Weather Reconnaissance Flights (Nominal tracks are shown. These varied from time to time for operational reasons.)

Chapter Ten

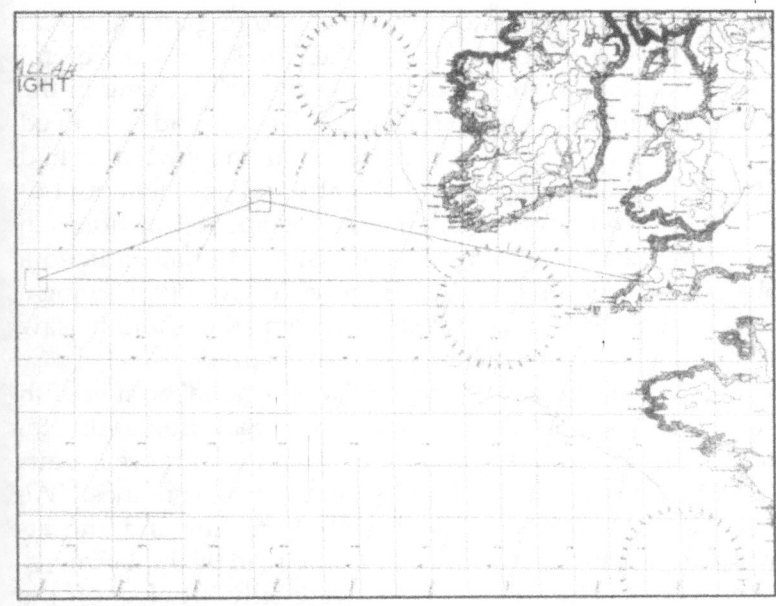
ALLAH Flight Route

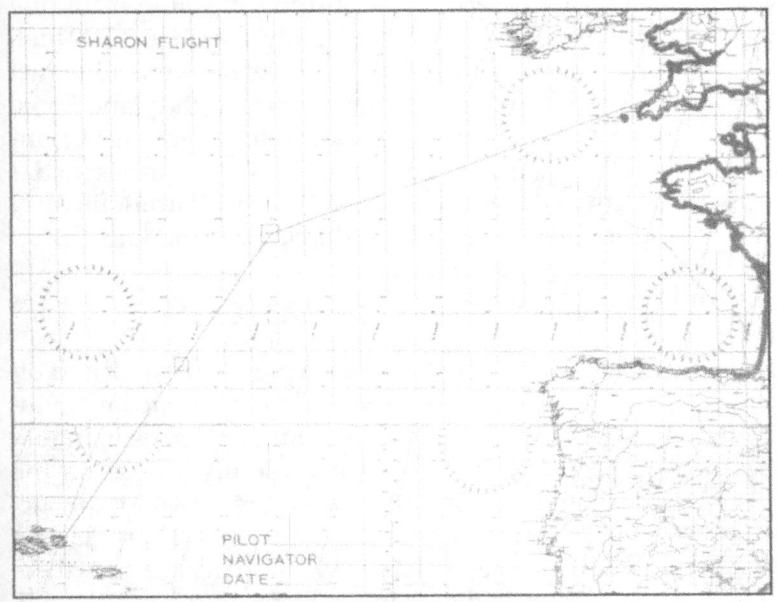
SHARON Flight Route

dier was singing "There will be a hot time in the town of Berlin".

Orville Myers, Panora, was an aerial gunner with the 93rd Bomb Group at Hardwick, England. Returning from one mission "we ran into a snowstorm. You couldn't even see our wingtips. There were a lot of mid-air collisions between our planes, but our pilot got us out of there and we flew on to Scotland."

Blair Rossow, Panora, was an aerial gunner with the 34th Bomb Group at Mendelsham, England. On one mission fog caused his aircraft to "ice up". "We couldn't climb, dropped our bombs on a target of opportunity and returned to base which was also fogged in. We came in on a radar beam looking out for church steeples and landed at a base that wasn't our own." While landing in fog after another mission "Two bombers collided in mid-air. Some of the guys were able to parachute to safety but base anti-aircraft guns opened up on them thinking it was Germans trying to shoot down our planes when they landed."

Ellsworth Shields, Waverly, was a radio operator/gunner with the 458th Bomb Group at Horsham St. Faith. "Once, in heavy fog we were trying to land when we spotted another B-24 right below us also trying to land. If that other plane would have moved a little higher it would have been twenty men and two planes gone."

Radio Countermeasures

German anti-aircraft batteries were able to direct their fire at bomber formations using radar known as Wurzburg with knowledge of aircraft speed, altitude and location. Estimates range up to 60%, the number of Eighth Air Force bomber losses in World War II to anti-aircraft guns throwing shells into the air that would explode at specified altitudes and send splintering shrapnel in all directions (flak). Transmitters were devised and placed in bombers to "jam" the radar and reduce losses in men, aircraft and battle damage. Another widespread tactic was the use of "window" or "chaff", aluminum foil strips dropped from bombers to reflect German radar beams. As the war progressed technological advances became more sophisticated to confuse German radar operators.

Jack Jones, Panora, was trained as a radio operator and assigned to the 453rd Bomb Group at Old Buckenham, England. He flew thirty-five missions sitting behind the pilot with three transmitters and one receiver., "Every time I would pickup a German radar signal I would jam it and record the time. It worked. We would see flak being shot in perfect patterns but it would explode either way below, behind or above us."

Bob Boice, Waterloo, flew thirty-five missions with the 91st Bomb Group at Bassingbourn, England as waist gunner/radio operator. He was also responsible for dropping "chaf" from their bomber to confuse German radar and anti-aircraft batteries.

John Frampton, Reinbeck, was a toggelier with the 94th Bomb Group at Bury St. Edmunds, England. On a mission to bomb submarine pens at Kiel, Germany with bombs designed to penetrate thick concrete "German ships in the harbor were throwing up heavy flak. We dropped "chaff" out of our airplanes in hopes of confusing German radar systems."

AIR/SEA RESCUE

The B-17 and B-24 bombers were not designed to stay afloat if they had to be "ditched" at sea. They often broke apart on landing and sank within moments or stayed afloat for only a short while. Problems arose with emergency equipment being antiquated or ability to be safely stowed aboard the aircraft. The Eighth Air Force relied on British Air/Sea Rescue organizations to locate downed flyers, provide aircraft for search missions, their communications network and patrol boats to pick up survivors. Americans were trained by the British until Catalina flying boats were supplied for an Eighth Air Force air/sea rescue squadron in January, 1945.

War-weary P-47 Thunderbolt fighters with long-range capability were previously used to locate and stay with downed aircrews in the North Sea and English Channel until British patrol boats could arrive to pluck them out of the water. Iowa Eighth Air Force veterans interviewed who were rescued from the icy waters included:

Bill Baltisburger, Marshalltown, was a navigator with the 452nd Bomb Group at Deopham Green, England. In May, 1944, German fighter aircraft attacked Bill's bomber setting it afire and causing it to be out of control and spiraling down to earth. The crew parachuted from the airplane and landed in the English Channel. "It was thirty minutes before we were rescued. It wouldn't have taken much longer for us to have died from over-exposure."

Thomas Estes, Aurelia, was a pilot with the 384th Bomb Group at Grafton Underwood, England. After a bombing raid on Hamburg, Germany, Tom's bomber formation was attacked by German fighters. With gunners out of ammunition and three engines of his aircraft disabled Tom was forced to land in the North Sea. The entire crew was able to exit the aircraft and get aboard two life rafts that were inflated. "We drifted for two days before we spotted a Danish fishing trawler. We were able to convince the skipper of the boat to take us to England." A British aircraft also spotted Tom and his crew and radioed Air/Sea Rescue who dispatched a boat for them.

Francis Kapler, Waterloo, was a B-17 Co-pilot with the 385th Bomb Group at Great Ashfield, England. During one mission weather prevented Francis's bomb group from holding formation. "We passed right over the island of Helgoland, bristling with German anti-aircraft guns. They knocked out two engines that began wind milling. We lost speed and couldn't maintain altitude even after throwing out everything we could. We had turned back to England and had flown for about an hour when we knew we weren't going to make it. I made a dead stick landing in the North Sea in fifteen-foot swells. We had practiced ditching procedures so each man knew what he had to do. We inflated two life rafts and got them out but a third one wouldn't inflate. We spent four hours in the water bobbing up and down. We had radioed a "Mayday" signal. Eventually we saw a P-38 flying a search pattern so we shot off some flares and he saw us. Later a British boat picked us up."

Bill Tomasek, Waucoma, was an aerial gunner with the 388th Bomb Group at Knettishall, England. Returning from a bombing mission over France his aircraft was hit by flak knocking out two engines. "We knew we couldn't make it back to England and attempted to land on Jersey Island held by the Germans. They wouldn't let us. We were only fifty feet off the ground. It was so foggy the German fighters couldn't see us so we kept on by shifting gasoline from one engine to another and eventually got up to 2,500 feet. The navigator didn't know where we were. Our fuel was running out so we parachuted from the plane. Some bailed out over land and some into the English Channel. Everyone who landed in the water was rescued. I landed on a lilac bush near an English farmhouse and within fifteen minutes was having tea and tarts."

CLANDESTINE OPERATIONS

Clandestine operations are a part of any war and often make the difference not only in the outcome of individual battles or offensives, but the war itself. Intelligence data gathered by Japanese operatives on the Hawaiian island of Oahu was one reason for their success in the December 7, 1941, attack on Pearl Harbor, Hawaii and other American military installations there which catapulted the United States into World War II. The United States had broken the Japanese military message code and was able to gain intelligence throughout the war from message intercepts. Unfortunately significant information was not acted upon to prevent the attack on Pearl Harbor. Advance information gleaned from message intercepts did allow the United States to learn of Japanese plans to invade Midway island in June, 1942. Battle plans were successfully carried out that delivered a sounding defeat to the Japanese Navy. The battle turned the tide in the Allies favor in the Pacific Theater of Operations and eventually led their defeat three years later.

From a captured German code machine named Enigma, Allied cryptographers were able to break the previously unbreakable German military message code. This proved invaluable to military planners in obtain-

Chapter Ten

ing intelligence data on German military unit strengths, deployment and battle intent as well as weather data from German weather stations throughout Europe.

During war-time combatant countries anticipate their enemies will utilize spies in an attempt to obtain intelligence data or military secrets. German operatives were sent to the United States, Canada and England as well as other countries. Allied countries sent their operatives into Germany and Nazi-occupied countries. Many operatives were caught immediately upon entering the United States while other escaped detection and relayed military information back to Germany. This became obvious when American airmen were shot down and captured. They faced questioning by interrogators knowledgeable of the United States who were armed with personal data on them. Under warfare rules of the Geneva Convention prisoners of war are required to only give their name, rank and serial number. German interrogators often cited knowledge of the prisoners unit, date when he arrived in the United Kingdom and names of his wife or mother and hometown. Most of this information was obviously obtained from local newspapers in the United States.

It was rightly assumed by the German military that Underground and resistance workers in occupied countries would conduct sabotage, relay military information to friendly countries and aid downed Allied flyers by establishing safe houses and lines of escape. Those suspected of being in the Underground were subjected to torture to obtain information on the Underground network. Torture usually led to execution. Those caught in the act were also subjected to torture before they were exterminated. Despite knowledge of their fate if caught, resistance and underground workers in Nazi-occupied countries continually risked death to aid the Allied cause. Their goal, some feel, was to maintain the honor of their country and its people.

Intelligence data obtained from underground operatives, particularly in advance of an invasion, was of enemy strengths, deployment and defenses. Sabotage behind enemy lines incident to the D-Day invasion was carried out to disrupt movement of the Germany military machine regarding reinforcements and supplies.

Many an Allied airman that was shot down behind enemy lines owed their lives to Resistance forces in France, Belgium and Holland. George Clark, Ames, 398th BG and William Baltisburger, Marshalltown, 452nd BG, both escaped from German captors and hidden by French Resistance workers until they could be returned to American military control. Loyd Morse, Ft Dodge, 448th BG, had been interned in neutral Switzerland after being shot down. He escaped and was aided by the French Resistance until he could reach American ground forces.

Henry Glover, Sanborn, 379th BG, spent three months hiding in French barns and attics of homes until he could be returned to England by boat. James Wilson, Waterloo, 379th BG, avoided capture by German military forces in Holland for nearly a year. The Dutch Underground hid him until he was able to cross the Rhine River by boat and reach Canadian ground troops.

Gerald Miller, Des Moines, 458th BG, was aided by Belgium resistance workers the moment he landed on the ground after parachuting from his stricken aircraft. For three months he and four other Allied airmen were hid in the home and barn of two elderly Belgian women under the nose of German troops stationed in the area until advancing American troops arrived.

James Brown, Mason City, was not so fortunate. He was aided by the Dutch Underground and moved to Belgium where German "plants" in the Belgian underground turned him over to German military authorities and he was sent to a Prisoner of War camp. He later learned after the war one of the "plants" was executed, one committed suicide and one was sentenced to prison for twenty years.

Before arrival of the Eighth Air Force in England, the Royal Air Force aided Underground and Resistance partisans by supplying them with supplies and personnel to coordinate resistance efforts or spy activity. The 801st Bomb Group of the Eighth Air Force, later re-designated the 492nd Bomb Group was formed to assist in clandestine operations with the primary duty of dropping parachute canisters filled with radio equipment, food, clothing, weapons and ammunition as well as operatives, behind German lines. This required low-level, night-time flights over enemy territory flying B-24 Liberator bombers painted black. Pre-arranged drop zones were designated that would allow those on the ground to safely retrieve the dropped supplies without capture by German forces or a person parachuted from the aircraft. Resistance forces waiting on the ground were equipped with radio beacons or lamps to direct the aircraft to the drop zones. Short-range radios were also used with which to talk directly to an aircrew and give directions. Small aircraft were sometimes used to land in a field to pick up a downed airman or unload a person for clandestine operations.

Other units of the Eighth also dropped supplies to Underground fighters. Bill Baltisburger, Marshalltown, 452nd BG, "we dropped weapons and ammunition and had two underground people in our bomb bay. After they pushed out the ammo they jumped out too." Howard Croner, Estherville, 452nd BG, "in July, 1944, we dropped food and supplies to Freedom French Marquis who were assisting U.S. forces after our invasion of Southern France."

Chapter Eleven
TARGETS

The Eighth Air Force was established to destroy the Luftwaffe and the industrial might of Nazi Germany. This was to be accomplished by daylight strategic bombing, precision bombing of selected targets. The British Royal Air Force preferred to bomb German cities by night on the theory they would demoralize the German people and by carpet bombing potentially destroy industrial and military targets as well. Hitler had ordered indiscriminate fire bombing of British cities and population centers of no military value. Retaliation in kind by the British was well justified. Prior to arrival of the Eighth Air Force, the RAF had been battling Germany's Luftwaffe for two years in the skies over England. They were experienced in night mass bombings and it was the policy they would stick with in attacking Germany's industry and civilian centers.

An agreement reached between England's Prime Minister Churchill and American President Roosevelt called for a combined offensive of British and American air forces against Germany. 'Round the clock" bombing with the British bombing at night and the Americans conducting daylight strategic bombing during the day were to bring about the progressive destruction of the German military, industrial and economic system. In turn the morale of the German people would be undermined and an invasion of Europe could be launched with an expectation of success. The initial priorities for attack included submarine and naval facilities, oil refineries and fuel plants, transportation facilities, and industrial and manufacturing facilities producing aircraft, tanks and guns.

The Ninth Air Force with medium bombers and fighters in England; the Twelfth Air Force from bases in North Africa and the Fifteenth Air Force based in Italy were later brought into the combined offensive and attacked targets in France, Belgium, Italy and other countries under Nazi occupation.

The 8th AF and Royal Air Force Bomber Command hammered at Germany day and night in one of the bitterest and most protracted struggles in the history of warfare. But it would take years. Air bases in England had to be built, a massive supply line established for food, fuel, ammunition, parts and a million and one supply items that had to be shipped to England. To support the war effort, plants and factories in the United States had to be built, expanded or modernized to produce war materials and air and ground crews trained. Aircraft rolling off America's assembly lines had to be allocated to hundreds of fighter and bomber groups across two oceans.

The price of being unprepared for war would be paid until 1944 when production and training reached its peak to offset previous losses and maximum blows could be delivered to the enemy with three thousand plane raids. Eventually the Eighth Air Force would reach a complement of nearly 300,000 officers and enlisted men. Long-range fighters would be able to escort bombers all the way to their targets and back. Fighters would take the offensive against aircraft and transportation targets. The Luftwaffe was pushed back from coastal areas by fuel shortages to defend high risk industries. A reduction in the presence of the Luftwaffe near the invasion area on D-Day proved that repeated attacks on selected targets over the course of two years could pave the way for June 6, 1944, when Allied armies stormed the beaches of Normandy to begin the invasion of Europe.

When America entered the war the Army Air Corps had a total complement of a few thousand personnel and 800 obsolete airplanes. The B-17 had been developed but production halted until war clouds appeared they would engulf America. When the first Eighth Air Force aircraft arrived in England in July, 1942, with their meager allotment of aircraft, few pilots had experience in multi-engine aircraft, navigators, bombardiers and gunners also had limited training. British bases were used. Due to lack of available aircraft some missions were flown with borrowed RAF aircraft.

Chapter Eleven

Frank Hinds, Marion, was a flight engineer with the 303rd Bomb Group at Molesworth, England. When the build-up of Eighth Air Force aircraft began "there were times we could only muster ten or twelve planes in our Group for a mission."

It would take time to build up a force of fighters and bombers to carry out the combined offensive. As the build-up of the Eighth Air Force progressed, German anti-aircraft batteries and fighter aircraft took a heavy toll on American bomber forces. American fighters had limited fuel range and could not escort the bombers to the target. As soon as the escort turned back to England, German fighters would attack the bombers in swarms. The losses in crews and aircraft could not be easily replaced.

Wallace Albert, Marengo, was a B-24 tail gunner with the 392nd Bomb Group at Wendling, England. Wallace participated in the August, 1943, raid on Rumanian oil refineries at Ploesti. Of 177 aircraft sent on the mission, 122 made it to the target and forty-two airplanes crashed or were shot down.

James Goff, Sioux City, was a navigator with the 95th Bomb Group at Horham, England. during a mission to bomb ball bearing plants at Schweinfurt, Germany, on October 14, 1943. The bomber formation was attacked twice by German fighters in a running battle that lasted four hours. In route to the target sixty-two bombers were shot down or forced to turn back due to battle damage. German fighters landed, rearmed, refueled and attacked the bombers on their way back to England shooting down another thirty-two aircraft.

On October 10, 1943 during a bombing raid on Munster, Germany, without fighter escort, James's formation was attacked by a force of 300 Germany fighters. Twenty-seven of forty-one bombers of the 13th Combat Wing were shot down.

Loren Darling, Waterloo, was an aerial gunner with the 100th Bomb Group at Thorpe Abbotts, England, and also participated in the Munster raid. Twelve of the thirteen bombers in Loren's squadron were shot down, Loren's airplane being the sole survivor. He was wounded with over eighty metal fragments in his head. A thumb was severed from his hand but was successfully re-attached at his base hospital.

In that one week, October 8-14, 1943, one hundred eighty-three bombers were lost to enemy action.

Kenneth Oseth, Cedar Rapids, aerial gunner with the 94th Bomb Group at Bury St. Edmunds flew to their target with twenty aircraft. All others had turned back to England and the group of twenty had not received a recall notice. Ten of the twenty bombers were shot down by German fighters.

Bill Vance, Des Moines, was a ball turret gunner with the 381st Bomb Group at Ridgewell, England. During an August 17, 1943 raid on ball bearing plants at Schweinfurt, his group lost eleven bombers to German fighters. Two other bomb groups lost ten aircraft each.

The principle of daylight strategic bombing was the right tactic, but because of heavy losses in the early stages of the campaign and the fact that crews and aircraft could not be immediately replaced, the doctrine began to be in doubt whether or not it would succeed. But aircrews would learn by experience, build-up of the Eighth Air Force would continue, new tactics would be devised and technological advances made to minimize losses. The Luftwaffe, except over targets, would be virtually eliminated and Germany's industry and transportation would grind to a halt.

NAVAL FACILITIES

Every replacement part, every drop of gas, every bomb, including thousands of supply items had to be shipped 3,000 miles across the ocean to England. Germany's submarines had to be attacked to prevent their wholesale slaughter of merchant marine ships. Submarine pens and naval facilities were bombed at Lorient, Fr; St.Nazaire, Fr; Brest, Fr; Wilhelmshaven, Kiel, Duisberg, Hamburg and Bremen,GE. The type of bombs used by the Allies against the thick concrete protecting the submarines virtually bounced off the submarine pens and caused little damage. Other means were employed to eliminate the U-boat threat until concrete piercing bombs could be developed. Ships crossed the Atlantic from America in convoys protected on the flanks by war ships with depth bombs. Intercepts of German radio transmissions gleaned information regarding "wolf pack" numbers, locations and routes. Aerial observation of waters around convoys and travel routes also detected submarines. Aggressive action on the high seas caused the Germans to suffer a high rate of submarine losses and naval targets dropped down on the priority list of targets.

Harvey Miller, Clarksville, aerial gunner with the 486th Bomb Group at Sudbury, England recalled submarine pens were well protected by German fighters and anti-aircraft batteries. "The concrete pens were so thick bombs didn't do any damage."

Bill Baltisburger, Marshalltown, navigator with the 452nd Bomb Group at Deopham Green, England, said "twenty feet of concrete protected the submarne pens at Bremen. Bombs just bounced off. Flak was the toughest I'd seen. We got the hell shot out of us, my pilot was killed and the Co-Pilot and myself wounded."

Iowans of the Mighty Eighth

Dwight Hohl, Argyle, was a pilot with the 445th Bomb Group at Tibenham, England. "Conventional bombs had not been able to penetrate the thick concrete of the submarine pens at Bordeaux, France during previous missions. We dropped napalm to burn oxygen and suffocate German troops occupying the pens."

Robert Nelson, Sioux City, Ball Turret Gunner, 94th BG, Bury St. Edmunds, England, on a mission to bomb submarine pens at Kiel, Germany, "we had to make two passes over the target before we could see what we were supposed to bomb. We had armor piercing bombs that were supposed to penetrate fortifications protecting the German subs. "Flak" was intense especially on the second pass. We got a lot of holes in our plane but no one got hurt except our flight engineer. A piece of "flak" hit him in the chest. He was wearing a flak suit but the shrapnel still penetrated the suit and he received a minor wound."

Reconnaissance photograph of submarine pens at Lorient in advanced stages of construction. (1) sub pen partially roofed in (2) dredger clearing channel (3) new foundations being laid (4) railway tracks being laid and diverted (5) new quays being prepared (6) camouflage on roof of sub pen to represent a road.

AIRCRAFT

The campaign to destroy German aircraft and its production centers was one of the bloodiest struggles in aerial warfare. American bombers groups suffered losses of up to sixty planes on a single mission. Ten men were in each bomber crew. Losses in the early stages of the campaign couldn't be tolerated for long without long-range fighter aircraft able to escort the bombers all the way to their target and back to England. High numbers of German fighters would also be shot down in the battle for control of the skies over Europe. Coinciding with destruction of aircraft production facilities what started off with American inferiority in aircraft numbers in 1942 became on a par with the Luftwaffe in numbers during 1943. In 1944 until the end of the war, superiority in the air was gained by the Allies.

Bomber formations began to penetrate further into the heartland of Germany. This caused the Luftwaffe to be stretched to the limit in defense of the Fatherland. Germany began to expand its fighter industry in response to buildup of the Eighth Air Force. Bomber production was halted and those facilities were converted to produce fighter aircraft. Germany also constructed airfields throughout France, Belgium and Holland. Fighters from these fields attacked bomber formations from the moment they crossed the English Channel. The Luftwaffe had to be eliminated at all costs if strategic bombing of enemy industry on a conclusive scale was to become a reality.

Attacks on airfields required Germans to fill craters in runways, repair hangars, living quarters and aircraft wrecked by bombs or strafing. Factories at Regensburg, Kassel, Augsburg, Querem, Furth, Leipzig, Warnemunde, Strasbourg, Marienburg, Neustadt, Egeln, Rostock, Baden Baden, Oschersleben, Merignac, Poznan, Stuttgart, Bunkau and other locations were bombed time and again. In early 1944 long-range American fighters carrying extra fuel in drop tanks began to escort bombers all the way to targets deep in Germany. They shot down German fighters attacking bomber formations and strafed airfields destroying German aircraft sitting on the ground. Despite bombings to aircraft factories Albert Speer, Hitler's Minister of Armaments was able to increase fighter production by dispersal of production facilities. Instead of a huge plant producing aircraft engines and fighter aircraft which could be easily bombed, production was spread out into countless small plants and even in caves. Although production of fighter aircraft increased, Germany was limited in what planes they could get in the air because of a lack of trained pilots and shortages of fuel. Experienced German pilots were forced to fly until they were killed or wounded and unable to fly again. Losses to the Eighth dwindled as German fighters were destroyed. They were still a factor in bombing raids from D-Day to the end of the war when the Luftwaffe consolidated their bases deeper in the Fatherland due to fuel restrictions and mass attacks were made on American bomber formations as they approached their target.

Robert McElree, Oelwein, was an aerial gunner with the 351st Bomb Group at Polebrook, England. During a March, 1944 raid on Berlin "we lost sixty-nine heavy bombers. What a mess. I saw pieces of planes flying past us. We went back two days later and had little or no opposition."

As late as October, 1944 enemy fighters still took a toll of American bombers. John Swift, Manchester, a Co-pilot with the 94th Bomb Group at Bury St. Edmunds, England, had his bomb group attacked just prior to the bomb run after American fighter escort had been lured away from the formation. "Forty to fifty German fighters came in from our tail in three or four waves stacked in stair step formation . Of the twelve bombers in his squadron, nine were shot down and one crashed landed in Belgium."

In November, 1944, Jim Haas, Perry, was a bombardier with the 398th Bomb Group at Nuthampstead, England. During a mission to bomb targets in Nuernberg, Germany, "we were attacked by German ME-109 fighters. They slaughtered us. We lost nine of our twelve planes. We were really shot up but we flew into clouds to escape them or they would have probably gotten us too." Air superiority was gained to the extent the German air force was hardly present during the D-Day landings at Normandy in June, 1944 or the balance of the war except for last ditch efforts and appearance of newly developed jet fighter aircraft.

OIL

War could not be waged without oil. Militaries demand a lot of it, and it must be readily available for use in airplanes, tanks, trucks, armored cars, and ships. Attacks on oil refineries were intended to immobilize the Luftwaffe and ground forces. Beginning in 1944, Germany's oil resources were relentlessly attacked. It would take time to have an adverse effect on the military because of their large stores of oil. Germany also had large amounts of a low grade coal with which to make synthetic fuels. Brux, Czechoslovakia, was the largest producer of synthetic oil in the world and was bombed nine times by the

Hartwell -Recon photo of damage assessment on Hartwell, Caen Carpiquet airfield

Rostock - Pre-attack photo reconnaissance of Rostock/Marienehe Heinkel Aircraft Factory

Newburg airfield destroyed 21 March, 1945.

Iowans of the Mighty Eighth

Eighth and Fifteenth Air Forces and the Royal Air Force. Rothensee synthetic fuel plant near the city of Magdeburg was bombed fourteen times by the Eighth Air Force. Merseburg, near Leipzig, Germany, was bombed twenty-one times.

In September, 1944, the Ploesti oil fields in Rumania were captured by the Russians thereby cutting off those resources for the German military machine. Coupled with the effects of attacks on synthetic oil and refineries, production was greatly reduced and placed a great strain on Germany's military. In September, 1944, weather caused a lull in bombing oil targets and allowed Germany to repair some facilities and bring in concentrated anti-aircraft batteries for defense. The refineries were also heavily protected by fighters from nearby German airbases. Despite heavy American losses from continual bombings, oil production was reduced to the extent coke ovens were employed to extract much needed oil from coal.

Bob Brown, Fort Dodge, was an aerial gunner with the 95th Bomb Group at Horham, England. He described the anti-aircraft battery concentration around Merseburg as "intense and damned accurate". A piece of shrapnel penetrated Bob's aircraft and struck his navigator between the eyes killing him instantly. Two engines to his airplane were disabled but the crew was able to fly it back to England.

Stanley Davidson, Ames, was a Co-pilot with the 303rd Bomb Group at Molesworth, England. He described the industrial area around Merseburg as "ringed with anti-aircraft guns equipped to determine bomber's flight pattern and altitude with accuracy. Flak knocked out three of his four engines requiring they bail out over Germany. Stan was taken prisoner of war.

Robert Chrisjohn, Alden, was a pilot with the 306th Bomb Group at Thurleigh, England. Nine of his bomb group's aircraft were lost on a mission to bomb the oil facility at Ruhland, Germany. "One German fighter pilot brought his fighter up from behind and just missed hitting our wing. He saluted us as he flew by."

Staver Hyndman, Cherokee, was a pilot with the 398th Bomb Group at Nuthampstead, England. He described the synthetic oil refinery at Merseburg as a

Aerial view of heavily defended synthetic oil refinery at Merseburg, Germany.

Misburg refinery burns after Allied attack.

Destruction of Bremen refinery

Chapter Eleven

"heavily defended area. Anti-aircraft batteries ringed the city and some of the Luftwaffe's best fighter pilots were nearby. Only three of thirteen aircraft in my squadron returned from a November, 1944 raid. Ten were shot down by German fighters."

Relentless attacks were made on German facilities at Sterkrade, Misburg, Bottrop, Hamburg, Mereseberg, Lutzkendorf, Zeitz, Bolhlen, Magdeberg, Ludwigshaven, Ruhland, Hanover, Bremen, Ostermoor, Emmerich, Leuna, Politz, Brux, Salzburg and other locations. Attacks had been made by the 12th Air Force on the large refinery at Ploesti in Rumania. Elements of the Eighth Air Force participated in raids on this oil field.

By mid 1944 oil targets became a top priority. Ploesti was captured by the Russians, production at existing facilities was decreased or halted, and German reserves were being exhausted. Soon there was an immediate need for every drop of oil produced. Aircraft and tanks of the German war machine ground to a halt. Tanks were abandoned on the battlefield for want of fuel. Fighter aircraft sat on airfields with empty tanks.

Dwight Hohl, Argyle, was a pilot with the 445th Bomb Group at Tibenham, England. Lack of fuel for the German war machine became so acute that "during the latter stages of the war, horses and oxen pulled German planes to the end of their runway to conserve fuel."

When resistance ceased, mass bombing attacks by Allied bombers and fighters were made to a multitude of targets designed to finish off the Third Reich.

Hjalmar Hellberg, JR, Marshalltown, was an aerial gunner with the 379th Bomb Group at Kimbollton, England,. On a February 3, 1945, mission to Berlin, "Over a thousand bombers took part in this raid while other bombers attacked other targets. When the lead plane dropped its bombs over Berlin the last planes in the raid hadn't left England yet."

Bill Vint, Beaman, was a toggelier with the 96th Bomb Group at Snetterton Heath and was also on the 1,000 bomber raid. After their bomb run and turn for home "we tuned the aircraft's radio to the British Broadcasting Company to listen to an account of our raid. The bombing was so intense that while returning to base we could see bombers coming and going to and from the target as far as the eye could see."

TRANSPORTATION

Germany had one of the most complete railroad networks in the world. It possessed large numbers of locomotives, rail cars and track confiscated from countries it had conquered. British and American attacks were made on rail systems to prevent troops, reinforcements and supplies from reaching the battle

Reconnaissance photo taken on V-E Day of damage inflicted on Magdeburg oil facility

front. War material produced from factories, and raw goods shipped to the factories were delayed or failed to arrive at their destination. It took awhile for the bombings to have an effect on German factories. The huge amounts of rail equipment and ability to quickly repair damaged rail yards by emergency crews placed at all important centers with stores of extra switches and rail were able to put the German rail system back in operation with minimum delay. The bombings were repeated to create further delays in factories from want of items required for production and distribution of items it had produced. Rail centers all over Germany particularly in the highly industrial centers were targeted. Prior to the Normandy invasion and immediately thereafter rail bridges and lines were attacked to prevent movement of German troops, reinforcements and supplies to the front lines.

Fighter planes took the offensive in 1944 and attacked rolling train stock destroying locomotives, freight and oil cars. Trucks, tanks, and armored cars in troop and supply convoys were attacked. Freed from escort duty fighters were highly successful in destroying hundreds of locomotives, rail cars and trucks bearing troops and supplies denied further use by the German military.

Bill Knowling, Iowa City, was a P-47 and P-51 fighter pilot with the 353rd Fighter Group at Raydon,

Iowans of the Mighty Eighth

England. He flew sixty-nine missions as escort to bomber formations and strafed troop convoys, airfields and railroad traffic.

Bob Ward, Toledo, was a P-51 fighter pilot with the 361st Fighter Group. He began a strafing run at a German train when he saw a farmer riding in a horse drawn cart between him and the train. The farmer panicked probably thinking he was to be attacked and drove his cart into the side of the train.

Bob Abernathy, Mason City, flew seventy-two missions in P-47s and P-51s with the 353rd Fighter Group. While escorting bombers was his primary duty "if we had time and fuel after escort we could attack any target of opportunity, bridges, tanks, convoys, and trains." He became an "Ace" while escorting bombers on a mission to Dresden by shooting down his fifth enemy plane, one of Germany's ME-262 jet fighters.

Railroad marshalling yards and junctions attacked included those at Zweibrucken, Munster, Beyubm, Limburg, Dillenburg, Kaiserslautern, Aschaffenburg, Berlin, Northeim, Ludwigslust, Salzwedel, Treuchtlinger, Alsfeld, Ausbach, Marburg, Wittenberg, Simmern, Lichtenfels, Reutlingen, Bruchsal, Kassel, Crailshelm, Villingen, Kitzengen, Hamm, Offenburg, Fulda, Siegen, Rhein, Bebra, Orianburg, Chemnitz, and Frankfurt.

Other Targets

<u>Ordnance, Armaments and Munition</u> factories at: Kaiserslautern, Hamburg, Essen, Dusseldorf, Weimar, Berlin, Frankfurt, Orianburg, Weimar, Bremen, Brunswick, Chemnitz, Cologne, Stuttgart, Brandenberg, Friedrichstadt, and Pilsen, CZ.

<u>Ball bearing plants</u> at:
Schweinfurt, Kassel, Stuttgart, Berlin and Munich

<u>Rocket testing facilities</u> at:

Photographic Reconnaissance of Berlin Railroad Marshalling Yard, 13Mar45

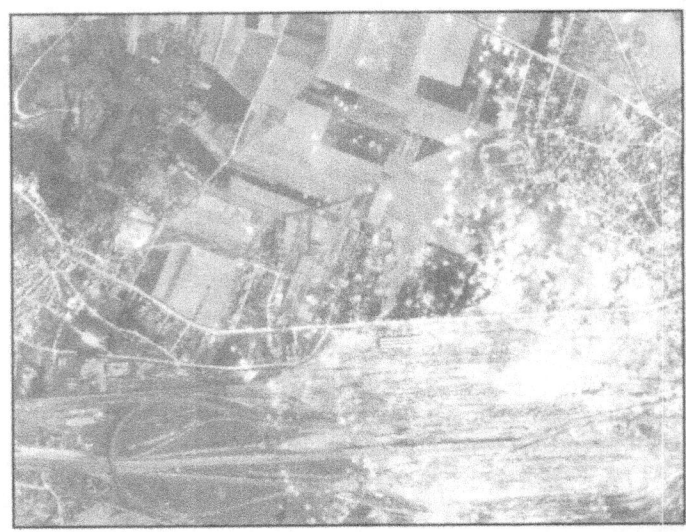
Photo reconnaissance of damage inflicted on Vaires railroad marshalling yards, Paris

Photographic reconnaissance of German industrial complex, 13Mar45

V-E Day partial photograph of railroad facilities, Bremen

Chapter Eleven

Peenemunde, Fallersleben and related hydrogen peroxide plants at Friedrichshaven, Rheinfelden, Hollriegelskreuth and Dusseldorf.

Also targeted and attacked were communication sites at Neukirchen, synthetic rubber at Halle, electric generators at Mannheim, chemical plants at Saarbrucken, Ludwingshaven and Leuna and industry in Fredrichshauven, Rheinfelden, Duffelldorf, Brunswick, Bremen

Strategic targets were not restricted to Germany. Industrial and manufacturing sites in occupied France, Czechoslovakia, Poland, and Austria were bombed. The output of military equipment was significantly reduced and in many cases completely halted creating shortages in Germany's ability to wage and prolong a war.

The dismantling of German industry and economy took two years before its military was significantly weakened to gamble on an invasion of the continent. Despite the bombings, Germany still had strong and well-equipped ground forces. Pre-invasion bombardment of enemy occupied territory was designed to further weaken its transportation system. It was intended to eliminate German fighters from the invasion area by pushing their operational airstrips deeper within Germany and create long distances for them to fly and therefore expend more fuel. Coastal defenses, military and transportation targets were bombed over a large area in Normandy to disguise where the planned invasion would was to take place. Photographic reconnaissance of invasion areas were made to gain intelligence on where and what type of coastal defenses existed.

Eighth Air Force aircrews flew two and as many as three missions on D-Day in support of the allied invasion on June 6, 1944, bombing enemy troop concentrations, road junctions, bridges and communication centers. Fighters attacked convoys bringing supplies and reinforcements to the battlefront.

John Meyer, Waverly, was a bombardier with the 466th Bomb Group at Attlebridge, England. "The night of June 5, 1944, our base was closed down. No one was allowed to leave and we were told to go to bed early. We knew then that this was it. We were awakened at eleven o'clock that night, ate, and went to mission briefing. We would be bombing at low altitude just ahead of our landing forces. We had to be at a precise location at a precise time. This was one of the greatest times in history, and here I was taking part in it."

Robert Peters, Grinnell, was a navigator with the 455th Bomb Group at Tibenham, England. His first mission was in support of the D-Day invasion when his crew bombed railroad yards at St. Lo, France. "It was unbelievable, even at 20,000 feet, to see the En-

1942 Aerial reconnaissance photograph of Skoda Armaments Plant, Pilsen, Czechoslovakia. Facilities received extensive bombardment by Eighth Air Force.

glish Channel filled with ships and boats from the invasion. The sky was filled with airplanes going to and from France on bombing and strafing missions."

Post-invasion photograph of Normandy invasion area showing results of pre-invasion bombardment.

In the days following the invasion, the Eighth Air Force would continue to fly support missions to ensure ground troops had secured a foothold on the continent; major defensive positions of the enemy were attacked and this eventually the Allied "break out" into France.

Joe Pfiffner, Waterloo, an aerial gunner with the 458th Bomb Group at Horsham St. Faith, England, began his overseas tour of duty as a B-24 crew member hauling gasoline in wing tanks to forward bases in support of General Patton's armored force.

Germany made a last gasp offensive effort on December 16, 1944, which became known as the Battle of the Bulge. Weather prevented retaliation by air forces, and allowed a spearhead of German tanks and ground troops to penetrate deep into Allied-held territory. When weather permitted flying, Eighth Air Force aircraft dropped much needed supplies and ammunition to American ground forces. German troop concentrations and armored forces, convoys, bridges and roads were bombed to alleviate possible dire consequences for some American forces that were surrounded in Belgium. Their stubborn resistance, resupply by air and arrival of armored forces caught

German forces with over-extended supply lines and their offensive ground to a halt for want of fuel.

Ed Kelly, Corydon, was an aerial gunner with the 44th Bomb Group at Shipdam, England. During the Battle of the Bulge, Ed's crew flew low-level missions in support of ground forces. "Armament was stripped from our B-24s. Crates of supplies were roped together in the bomb bay area and hooked to bomb releases. When alerted, the bomb bay was emptied and we in the back of the plane pushed other supplies out. Then all hell broke loose. We saw a German officer firing his pistol at our plane. A machine gun on the ground managed to shoot off part of the wing on the plane next to us. The plane went into the ground, hitting a tree. A guy on one plane got to his feet entangled in the ropes attached to the supplies, and was dragged out of his plane."

Wayne Zeigler, Iowa Falls, was a B-17 pilot with the 385th Bomb Group at Great Ashfield, England. On January 2, 1945, on a mission to bomb German Tiger tanks behind the front lines during the Battle of the Bulge, three engines of his airplane were lost. The crew was forced to bail out and fortunately landed twenty miles behind American front lines.

The Eighth would fly more supply missions in support of ground forces. Next came the crossing of the Rhine River, the last natural barrier in Germany blocking the way to Berlin. British and American airborne forces parachuted into enemy rear areas after initial crossings of the Rhine River had been made by British forces. The Eighth Air Force flew low-level supply missions to support the paratroopers.

Lavern Peters, Bedford, was an aerial gunner with the 389th Bomb Group at Norwich, England. On March 24, 1945, the bomb bay of his and nearly 250 other bombers were filled medical supplies, ammunition and weapons. The supply drop was to be made flying at a 400 foot level. Lavern could see dead American paratroopers hanging in trees, shot before they could get free of their parachutes. The aircraft were easy prey for small arms fire from the ground and fourteen bombers were lost on the mission.

Darrell Reed, Cherokee, was a radio operator/gunner with the 445th Bomb Group at Tibenham, England. Waiting to take-off on the mission, Darrell noticed the sky filled with C-47 cargo planes carrying paratroopers and pulling gliders filled with airborne troops. Flying into their cargo drop zone at 150 feet, Darrell could see the destruction of war, dead animals and men, towns on fire and wrecked gliders. The pilot slowed the bomber almost to a stall and sounded an alarm bell, alerting the crew to release the cargo. Darrell lost his balance and was ready to fall out of his aircraft, when an Associated Press re-

"Bombs Away" toward a German target

porter flying as observer grabbed Darrell's parachute harness and pulled him to safety. A crewman was seen falling out of another aircraft.

Dick Lynch, Conrad, was an aerial gunner with the 44th Bomb Group at Shipdam, England, and also flew on the supply mission. "The airplanes flying on both sides of me were hit by ground fire and crashed. We crossed the drop zone into the area where the gliders landed and then bullets began flying. A crew on our wing went down and blew sky high, then another; it was terrible. I wasn't scared until after we got back across the Rhine; then I was really nervous. We had 22 holes in our plane."

SUMMARY

Daylight strategic bombing of German targets destroyed aircraft plants, caused Germany loss of pilots through attrition, precluded intensive training of additional pilots, and loss of aviation fuel with which to continue defense of their country.

Ball bearings which every vehicle and aircraft required in order to operate was attacked at production centers often with heavy losses. Albert Speer, Hitler's Minister of Armaments believed the Allies did not use enough heavy bombs to completely destroy the facilities nor make continued attacks on the facilities to bring armaments plants to a standstill. Bombings must have had a greater effect than believed. American ball bearings were flown to Sweden to give to Germany in exchange for release of some Allied internees.

Attacks on the oil industry affected both the air and ground forces of Germany. Repeated attacks created shortages of fuel for the Luftwaffe. Later in the war their aircraft could not get off the ground to attack Allied bombers and fighters. Tanks ground to a halt with no fuel to continue fighting. Tanks and trucks were abandoned on the battlefield.

By attacking the German transportation system the Allies made it impossible for railroads to meet transportation requirements including supply to manufacturers and transportation of finished products. As resilient as German workers were in getting factories back into operation after bombings, partly due to failure of bombs to destroy machinery, production lagged and portions of factories and plants had to be dispersed, some to caves, in order to prevent wholesale destruction. Transportation of troops, armaments and supplies to ground forces eventually came to a standstill.

While initially listed as a target objective, electric power was not heavily and repeatedly attacked. Destruction of power plants would have stopped production of all industry that was attacked individually as well as having a demoralizing effect on civilian life.

The Eighth Air Force, RAF, and other assisting air forces were given the tools to do their job. Despite setbacks and heavy losses of both men and aircraft under the most difficult of situations, they did their job well and proved the case of daylight strategic bombing by helping to bring Nazi Germany to its knees.

Hitler once boasted "we will build a Reich to last a thousand years." – He was wrong.

He also said "Give me four years and I promise you, you won't recognize your towns."

He was right.

Iowans of the Mighty Eighth

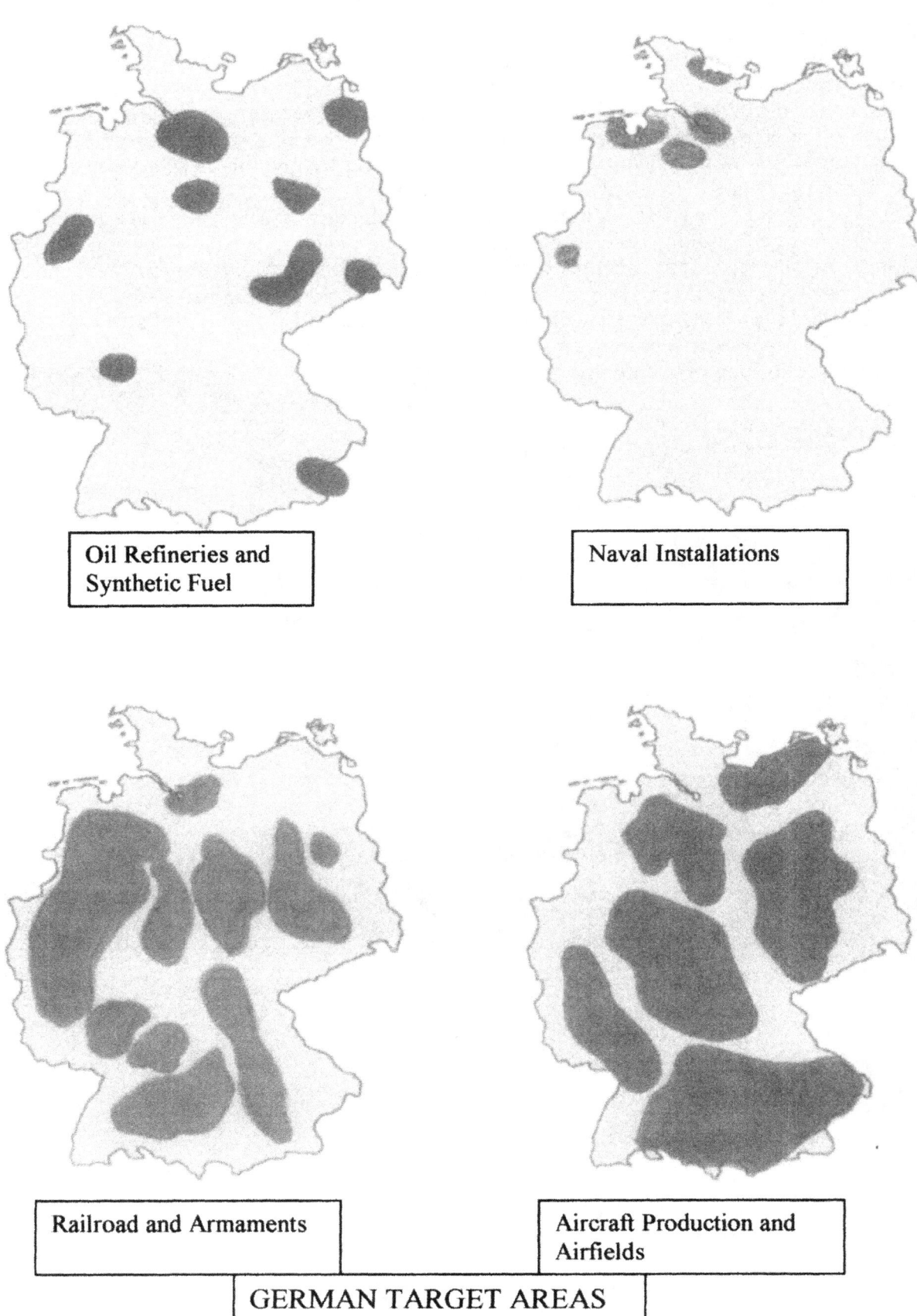

GERMAN TARGET AREAS

Chapter Twelve

MISSIONS

MISSION PREPARATION

The months and years of training, the buildup of aircraft and personnel in England, movement of ordnance, munitions, supply, mechanics, repair, food, medicine and other essential items to newly constructed bases to sustain an air offensive comes down to one thing- missions.

The Eighth Air Force set out to destroy Germany's industrial and economical system by high altitude daylight bombing of strategic targets with large formations of heavy bombers. To do that a military organization doesn't just fly in a fleet of aircraft, load them with fuel and bombs and take off and bomb Berlin, Brunswick, Regensburg, or Merseburg, Germany. Behind the scene preparation involved thousands of personnel and man-hours in a beehive of activity and planning to put an effective air force in the air. Once in the air that fleet had to organize itself to provide for its own defense to and over enemy territory and effectively put its bombs on target. Once bombs were released then the armada had to reorganize itself again and fight its way back home.

Based on a priority of targets described in the previous chapter, once a mission was ordered by Eighth Air Force Bomber Command, notification went down the chain of command. Headquarters notified Divisions, Divisions notified Wings and Wings notified Groups. Each layer of command had their specific duties to perform and orders to issue with details of the mission. Many questions had to be asked through the command structure and answers given on a priority basis. What type of ordnance was required to destroy the target? How many tons of ordnance was required? How many aircraft are required? What bomb groups to use? Can the Bomb Groups provide the required number of aircraft and crews? Combat losses and aircraft with battle damage that could not be readily repaired affected a bomb group's capability as well as aircraft that could fly if repairs could be made on time. What route would they take to the

Snow covered B-17 at 100th Bg, Thorpe Abbotts, England

target to avoid the greatest amount of enemy anti-aircraft batteries and enemy fighters? Where will enemy fighters most likely attack the bombers? Where is anti-aircraft fire expected? What altitude should they fly? Can fighter escort be provided for the bombers? What fighter groups are to be employed as escort? How far can the fighters escort the bombers? If not all the way to the target and back, where and when will the fighters provide escort on the return flight? What is the weather forecast over the bases and over the target?

In the Eighth Air Force, the First Division complement comprised B-17 bombers in four Combat Wings, three Bomb Groups to a wing and three or four squadrons of ten to fourteen aircraft in each squadron made up a Group. The Second Division was comprised of B-24 bombers with the same complement as the First Division except the Second Division and a Third Division had five combat wings.

Weather was the overall controlling factor whether or not a mission would be a "go" or "no go". Weather forecasters constantly monitored weather conditions over the bomber and fighter bases and intended target. The Eighth Air Force operated from over sixty bases within a confined space. Visibility in taking off, assembly into formation and landing back at base was extremely critical. Unless a mission was a "must", a mission would be cancelled if bad weather were predicted over Eighth Air Force bases. Even if weather over the target area was favorable, takeoff under hazardous conditions could lead to formation disorganization, late assembly and collisions or crashes. English weather turned out to be highly fickle and often turned on weather forecasters.

Keith Shirk, Des Moines, Pilot, 389th BG: Fog required an instrument takeoff on December 19, 1944, for a mission behind German lines during the Battle of the Bulge. "We could only see two runway lights ahead of the plane so I asked the Co-pilot to watch the lights on the right side and the engineer to watch the lights on the left and to let me know if we were getting close to them. At 90 m.p.h. the engineer shouted "look out we are running off the runway, we're going to hit the lights". I called full flaps-emergency power and hauled back on the yoke and we jumped into the air. I kicked the right rudder. As the flaps came down the nose wanted to come up so I had to hold a lot of pressure on the yoke to keep the plane level. We didn't have enough speed to fly so we had to get back down to the runway. It seemed to take a long time to hold the plane down and get back to the runway. We finally bounced at about 110 m.p.h. I felt we could hold it so called 'gear up'. As the speed continued to increase we started to climb. We raised the flaps slowly. By the time we got the flaps up we were at 700 feet and broke out into the clear."

Leon Mehring, Cedar Rapids, Waist Gunner, 305th BG: On February 23, 1945, a mission to bomb Wurzbug, Germany, "Fog was so bad we couldn't see across the street. Solid clouds ranged up to 12,000 feet. We were told it is a "must" mission and the weatherman predicted the front would lift by the time we got back to England in the afternoon. At takeoff we couldn't see the runway lights on either side. The pilot lined up in what he hoped was the middle of the runway and told the crew to watch for runway lights and let him know what side they were on so he could use the brakes to keep them on the runway. We made it off the ground and didn't break into the clear until about 15,000 feet. There were three other bomb groups within five miles of us also taking off within the solid weather front."

When Groups were alerted of an impending mission sufficient lead time had to be allowed for preparation. Generally this was a daily occurrence. One mission to prepare for after another. A mission alert would be posted to all affected personnel. A red flag would be raised over bases. In Officer and Enlisted

"Socked in" Base. Control tower at 466th BG, Attlebridge, England

Men's Clubs, a red light went on over the bar and it was closed down. Bases became a beehive of activity. Weather and operations officers, ordnance and armaments sections, aircraft mechanics, photographic personnel, mess halls, transportation and all barracks were alerted.

Crews and planes are chosen for the mission based on what was available or could be made available on time. Aircraft are loaded with bombs and fueled. The intelligence officer duplicates photographs of the target from photo reconnaissance files (targets previously photographed by reconnaissance planes) and gathers other intelligence data on the target such as defenses and ground features near the target. Maps and flak charts are gathered for the bombardier, navigator and pilot. Courses and distances are plotted, and times for assembly established. Weather forecasters provide expected wind direction, velocity at air and ground speeds, drift and temperatures on the chosen route. Weather conditions on the ground at the target are forecast including drift, wind speeds and headings at the bombing altitude. This data is computed for settings on the bombsight

Elmer Prusha, Tama, Bombardier, 303rd BG: On August 5, 1944, during a mission to Liege, Belgium, cloud cover prevented release of their bombs on the target. The entire formation circled to make a second bomb run. On the second run another formation also closing on the target "screwed up" calibrations on Elmer's bomb sight and required the formation to circle again and make a third run on the target. This time through a break in the clouds and at the right moment Elmer was able to sight the target and release his bombs. The objective was destroyed. Elmer received the Distinguished Flying Cross for his actions on this mission.

Once the time for launching a mission has been set, ordnance personnel transported bombs to each

Chapter Twelve

aircraft scheduled to fly on a mission where they were loaded in the aircraft bomb bay. Fuses were screwed on the bombs and made safe from unexpected detonation with a pin and wire. Belted ammunition and .50 caliber machine guns were distributed to the aircraft for the aerial gunners to setup on their arrival. Mechanics also rose early to pre-flight airplanes before takeoff. Engines were started and run up to check oil pressure, turbocharger and magneto performance as well as test electrical and hydraulic functions aboard the aircraft. After the engines were checked they were shut down and the airplane's fuel tanks refilled. The ground crews may have worked all night to get aircraft back into combat readiness.

James Pierce, Grinnell, Ball Turret Gunner, 303rd BG: His eleventh mission was a bomb raid on Leipzig, Germany. Their airplane unknowingly to them, had been shorted 500 gallons of fuel in preparation for the mission. Over the English Channel the pilot realized they were not going to make it back to their base but managed to bring the aircraft over land as fuel ran out. He gave the order for the crew to bail out. James was the third crewmember out the escape hatch. At that time the airplane was down to about 3,000 feet. He remembered thinking of everything in his lifetime on the way down until he landed in a wheat field. Others were not so fortunate. One crewmember opened his parachute too soon. It caught on the airplane and he was dragged down with it. The pilot stayed too long with the airplane, failed to jump, and died in the crash.

Groups set up a time schedule to allow for crews to be wakened, dress, and eat breakfast. No one likes to be wakened at two or three o'clock in the morning. Crews were allowed limited time to wash, shave, use the latrine and dress before going to breakfast. Shaving was essential to ensure a secure, lifesaving fit of oxygen masks. Food consisted of powdered milk and eggs. Fresh eggs were reserved for aircrews on mission day. In the last half of the war when supply routes were firmly established, fresh eggs were more frequently available. Coffee, juice, cereal, toast and pancakes were also included in the meal as filling and easily digestible. Pre-packaged food was available for crews as supplemental food during long missions.

James Hamilton, Council Bluffs, Pilot, 95th BG: "Getting up in the middle of the night, eating breakfast and going to briefings, we just wanted to get the mission over with."

Gerald Thompson, Pilot, Des Moines, 91st BG, Bassingbourn, England, "on the evening before a mission there was a posting of the crews that were to participate the following day. We got up at three or four in the morning for preparation and briefing. When we returned from a mission it was sometimes as late as eight in the evening. We were de-briefed on events of the mission and information we had on enemy opposition. Our crew flew missions on three successive days before we got a day off. During the Battle of the Bulge we flew nine missions in ten days. In order to succeed on a mission one had to free one's mind for the task by accepting the idea that you would not live through it."

Francis Hinds, Marion, Flight Engineer/Top Turret Gunner, 303rd BG: During his second mission, while sporting a goatee, his oxygen mask froze. The goatee caused the mask to pull away from his mouth and he collapsed unconscious. Another crewman grabbed a portable oxygen tank and applied it to Frank reviving him and saving his life. Frank was a top turret gunner. A 20mm shell from a German fighter plane ripped through Frank's turret. Had he not collapsed he would have been killed by the shell.

Kermit Neubauer, Iowa Falls, Tail Gunner, 94th BG: On three occasions Kermit was awakened in the wee small hours of the morning and told he was flying as a replacement gunner although he hadn't been scheduled.

After breakfast aircrews attended briefings. Lead crews, crews that would lead and command formations were wakened earlier than other flight crews to attend a pre-briefing where details of the mission were outlined. While they were being briefed other crews involved in the mission would be wakened.

Leon Huggard, Plainfield, Radio Operator, 458th BG: During a bomb raid on Metz, Germany, Leon's aircraft flew as lead plane for his bomb group. His aircraft got caught in the prop wash of the Group flying ahead of him. This made his airplane and the Deputy lead plane flying alongside, pitch up and down. Their two wings collided tearing off ten feet of wing from Leon's aircraft. Their plane went into a dive that pinned the crewmembers to the floor of the plane. The pilot was able to gain control of the airplane and they returned to England only five miles per hour over stalling speed.

Joseph Barnes, Mason City, Navigator, 392nd BG: "We had the opportunity to reduce our required number of missions from thirty-five to thirty by being a lead crew, but all of us in the crew voted to turn it down. In our crew we had an eighteen-year old tail gunner that completed thirty-five missions and an Engineer who was in his 30's."

William Baltisburger, Marshalltown, Navigator, 452nd BG: "Lead crews went to a Pre-briefing meeting the night before missions. We would walk into the Officer's Club about 5:30 or 6:00 P.M. That's' when the ball went up over the bar. There was red, white and a green ball. The white ball meant a raid was a "maybe", As soon as a mission was ordered the clubs would be called and they would change the balls. Green meant no mission the next day. Red meant a mission was on and the clubs closed all activities at the bar."

In briefing rooms a large map covered with a curtain was at the end of the room. When the briefing started the curtain would be pulled back to reveal the destination of the mission and route they were to fly designated with colored string or yarn. Crews were generally given a pep talk on importance of the target before an enlarged photograph of the target was shown on a screen. Enemy defenses and details of the target and surrounding area would be presented. The weather officer went over forecast conditions. Times for takeoff, assembly and other checkpoints would also be given. After the briefing bombardiers and navigators would attend a separate briefing where they were given maps and flight plans. Each navigator had to continually know the location of his aircraft despite flying with others, in case of damage or mechanical failure that might cause them to leave the bomber formation. Bombardiers studied target photographs to ensure absolute identification. Gunners were briefed on where enemy fighters were most likely to be encountered, tactics and where fighter escort would rendezvous with them. Radio operators received the day's wireless codes, radio call signs and frequencies.

Ken Newsom, Des Moines, Aerial Gunner, 486th BG, Sudbury, England, "most of our missions we took off at night. They used to get us up at eleven o'clock or midnight. We would go eat and then attend the general briefing. When they pulled the cover off the flag and you saw the red yarn from our base to the target, you could hear a pin drop. About one-third of

Tom Page, Osceola, 94th BG, Bury St. Edmunds, at plane side getting dressed for mission

the time when we would get up that early and go through all the routine they would cancel the mission."

Following the briefing, items had to be issued to the crew that included heavy flight clothing and electrical flight suits, escape kits, flak suits, flak helmets, parachutes, oxygen masks, and Mae West life jackets. Time also had to be allowed for crews to be transported to their aircraft, load their equipment and prepare for takeoff. Crews had to be ready at a given signal to start their engines. Gunners inspected and installed their weapons. Radios were checked for operation. An inspection of the aircraft had to be made of tires, engines, wings, tail assembly, fuselage and operating systems.

Chapter Twelve

Takeoff and Assembly

A green flare shot from the control tower signaled all aircraft to start their engines. Pilots ran up the engines just as the mechanics had done previously, and monitored their performance on gauges and instruments with the Flight Engineer. On another signal from the control tower aircraft moved to the edge of the taxiway and began taxiing to the end of the runway in an order prescribed during the briefing. Position in the formation after assembly determined order of takeoff. To personnel on the base and nearby residents, the noise was deafening. Imagine thirty-six aircraft scheduled for a mission at a base. That meant 144 engines running at the same time and brakes squealing as planes proceeded to the end of the runway in stop and go fashion.

Another signal was given for takeoff. Planes headed down the runway at thirty to forty-five second intervals. The failure of an engine at the moment of lift off or shortly thereafter could cause a crash. Reduced visibility was a danger on takeoff in order to stay lined up on the runway but also any event that might occur on the runway itself.

Clayton Scott, Osceola, Bombardier, 492nd BG: "An RAF Spitfire taking off from our base attempted a barrel-roll just off the end of the runway. He was turning back to land in the opposite direction but didn't make it. His engine "konked out"." Clayton and a friend were walking from the briefing room for their mission and saw the fighter coming right at them. They dove into a roadside ditch full of mud and water. "The Spitfire hit the tops of trees then knocked over a large tree directly across the road from us. The airplane skidded through the rear of the base Finance Office coming to rest near our briefing room. The wings and engine were torn off and the pilot's body thrown out. The wheels, guns and ammunition were scattered between us and where the fuselage came to rest." Russell Orwig, Bettendorf, Aerial Gunner, 386th BG: A fatal mishap nearly occurred during takeoff on a mission. A 4,000 pound bomb load had been loaded in their B-26, "Miss Muriel". While rolling down the runway to takeoff the Co-Pilot in reaching to adjust flaps accidentally retracted their landing gear causing them to belly-land on the runway. When they came to a stop Russell scrambled out an escape hatch in the side of the fuselage under the tail.

After takeoff each bomber climbed at a predetermined rate of climb by a prescribed route to an assembly area. This was a pre-determined area by location and altitude. In bad weather there was always the risk of collision. Each bomb group had a designated assembly area at an altitude that varied according to cloud conditions and weather. Precise headings and speeds had to be flown. Bomb Groups often were in close proximity to each other on the ground and flight procedures had to be followed to the letter to avoid collision in fog or clouds.

Thomas Page, Osceola, Tail Gunner, 94th Bomb Group, witnessed two mid-air collisions in his bomb group while they flew in formation. On one occasion he noticed debris flying past his tail gunner windows. A lower flying bomber bounced upwards in turbulence. It's propellers severed another B-17 in half causing it to immediately go nose down to earth. The other plane managed to climb and circle with its nose broken off and flight deck crushed. He saw the bombardier fall out of the aircraft with no parachute. No parachutes were seen escaping from the two aircraft.

Ed Kelly, Corydon, Aerial Gunner, 44th Bomb Group: "immediately on takeoff we lost engine number three. In a very short time number four engine went out. We were informed that our field was fogged in and that we would have to proceed to an air base in Scotland." The crew dumped everything they could within the plane to lighten their load. This included their bombs which were jettisoned somewhere over The Wash of England. They made it safely to the base in Scotland. "If it had not been for the skill of the pilot we would not have made it."

Assembling a vast armada of bombers into battle formation was never easy. Even with unlimited visibility the task demanded precise control in order to form and place each bomber box at the required position and altitude at a given time. Frequent overcast made assembly difficult and on occasion caused

"Miss Muriel" on the ground after Co-Pilot accidentally retracted landing gear on takeoff

missions to be aborted. With time, practice and experience assembly procedures became more successful. Chaos could result if weather deteriorated after take-off.

Raymond Carlson, Walcott, Navigator, 466th Bomb Group: A March 4, 1945, mission was scheduled to bomb a German jet airfield at Kitzingen, Germany. Thick overcast prevented bombers of the 466th from gathering into formation. They proceeded singly to Northern France where they formed for the remaining flight to the target. "We found our formation flying through clouds so dense, we could barely see our wing man. At that time a group of B-17s flew through our formation from the right. The next five to ten minutes was spent in evasive action to prevent mid-air collisions. As a result, our formation was completely scattered and we abandoned the mission. Approximately eight or nine of us that were still in reasonable formation formed on a lead plane and started home together."

Clarence Schuchman, Hawkeye, Pilot, 457th Bomb Group: March 20, 1944, was a scheduled mission to Frankfurt, Germany, to bomb the Alfred Treves plant, manufacturer of 50% of Germany's aircraft and submarine piston rings and 75% of their hydraulic brakes. The mission was aborted when only 80 miles from Frankfurt due to bad weather and lack of visibility. In leading the top squadron, Clarence rolled out of a left turn. The right wing man did not and came directly at them for what was about to be a mid-air collision. Clarence's co-pilot pulled the stick back in his lap. Clarence opened the throttle wide open and they went over on their back going into a spin., They recovered after a 10,000 foot fall. Out of formation in bad weather they were on their own. They broke into the clear at one point to discover three ME-109 German fighters beneath them. The enemy did not attempt to engage them and Clarence headed for the nearest cloudbank for cover. Everyone in their bomb group saw them go down in a spin and took it for granted they crashed. No one knew a B-17 could recover from a tailspin with a full bomb load.

Individual aircraft were forced to leave their bomb group and return to their base because of mechanical problems or accidents within the aircraft that prevented them from continuing the mission. In one instance a mission was aborted because of religious observance.

David Alfrey, Waterloo, Flight Engineer/Aerial Gunner, 487th Bomb Group: David's aircraft hit an air pocket at 25,000 feet causing doors of his aircraft to pop open including the bomb bay doors. The airplane

B-17 of 305th BG assembles off wing of Ivan Lindaman, Aplington

went into a diving spin. David recalled seeing the Pilot and Co-pilot with their feet on the instrument panel as leverage attempting to pull the airplane out of the dive. All other crew members were pinned against the sides of the plane by centrifugal force. The pilot was able to pull the airplane out of the dive at about 10,000 feet.

Charles Boyer, Ft Madison, Flight Engineer/Aerial Gunner, 93rd Bomb Group: In June, 1943, Charles and his crew were attached to the Ninth Air Force and trained in preparation for the low level raid on the Ploesti Oil Refineries in Romania. On August l, 1943, in route to Ploesti for the raid, fittings came loose on their gas tanks when they were halfway to the target. Loss of fuel required they return to base. In view of the heavy losses sustained during this raid, this quirk of fate probably saved his life.

Howard Cropp, Cedar Rapids, Pilot, 401st Bomb Group: On Easter Sunday, 1945, the weather was cold and temperatures inside the aircraft required he talk to each crew member every fifteen minutes to make sure their oxygen masks had not frozen and they were still breathing normally. As they neared their target, the mission was cancelled at the last minute because of the religious holiday. The entire formation of bombers returned to their bases after their bomb loads were jettisoned in the area of Great Britain known as "The Wash".

Bernie Palmquist, Red Oak, Aerial Gunner, 100th Bomb Group: "While forming up after takeoff, the top turret gunner was firing flares from a Very pistol as a signal when a live flare flew back into a box of flares, starting a very quick and smoky fire. The pilot called for "ready to bail out" and the men in the rear grabbed for their parachutes. The plane went into a tight spin and everyone was pinned back to the fuselage. As the airplane flattened somewhat, but still in steep descent, they tried to open the main hatch just in front of the tail. The door was made to open with an emergency handle that pulled the hinge pins and the door out when exiting the airplane for escape. As they pulled the handle, the top pin pulled out. The cable broke leaving the bottom pin stuck tight. The top of the door gapped open enough to start through, but a body with a chute and harness was too bulky to get through. The first man got stuck. The next man kicked him on through and got stuck himself. The next man then pushed him out, etc. The fifth man out was the spare ball gunner taking my place. He was a big boy and got stuck tight. While the last man was pushing him he accidentally pulled his ripcord. His chest pack was outside. It opened pulling him outside and back, striking the tail and breaking his back. The last man got stuck and had no one left to help him. He got his chute outside and pulled the rip cord. Out he went, the chute gave him a hard jerk and the next second he hit the ground. Three or four hundred yards away, the plane went into the ground. It had a full bomb and gas load. The explosion created a large crater in the ground. The four officers in front were still aboard. Why they didn't get out no one knows, they had plenty of time and an escape hatch in the nose section."

After assembly by Bomb Group, the formation flew to another assembly point where other Bomb Groups met them to form a Combat Wing. The Wing then flew to another point to assemble into a Division and begin their cross-Channel flight to the mainland of Europe. Each Squadron, Group and Wing was assigned specific locations within a large formation whether it was lead crew, in a high or low position or "tail end Charlie". Various formation patterns were flown to provide the maximum firepower against attacking enemy fighter aircraft and also to provide a concentration of bombs on the target during the bomb run.

In heavy overcast and with strict adherence to speed and rates of climb and timing, aircraft sometimes found themselves breaking into the clear scattered over a wide range that caused increased assembly time. Bombers often emerged and could not locate their group. They were forced to join a formation from another group.

Richard Steelman, Fort Dodge, Pilot, 93rd Bomb Group: Richard took off in heavy overcast to "form up" with his Squadron and Group. After he broke into clear weather his Group could not be found. He was forced to fly an oval pattern to try and find them, meanwhile using precious fuel. Unsuccessful in finding them he continued the mission with another bomb group. On the homeward trip he realized there was not suf-ficient fuel to make it back to base. "May Day" calls went unanswered. He was able to land at a base about twenty miles from Dunkirk, France. After receiving fuel they returned to England. Two RAF Spitfire fighters flew alongside and checked them out to make sure there was an American crew aboard. Germans sometimes used captured American fighters and bombers to infiltrate bomb groups and shoot down aircraft

Joe Pfiffner, Waterloo, Aerial Gunner, 458th Bomb Group: Joe's first mission was on October 26, 1944, a bomb raid on a target at Perleburg, Germany. Due to weather conditions their Group flew to Belgium before "forming up". A weather front had moved in and they were required to fly in fog. The wings on Joe's aircraft "iced up" and the airplane went into a dive. The pilot ordered the crew to bail out. Joe bailed out but hadn't tightened the harness around himself. When the chute opened he learned his mistake as it "nearly tore me apart". Floating toward earth he noticed a big town below. He attempted to drift away from the town but his parachute canopy nearly collapsed. He landed in a pasture with other crewmembers and saw civilians rushing toward them with pitchforks. Fortunately American GIs arrived to prevent any mistaken identity that they were Germans.

Groups often had to form up between layers of clouds. As the size of the 8th grew, so did congestion over East Anglia. Bomb Groups used flares, flashing lights and brightly painted, war-weary aircraft to identify themselves in "forming up" during assembly. Often a pilot or co-pilot in the lead aircraft sat in the tail-gunner's position to watch the formation and report to the command pilot on formation progress or problems.

After aircraft had reached ten thousand feet the aircrew went on oxygen. Every fifteen minutes an

B-17s of 305th BG, Chelveston, assemble over heavy overcast

oxygen mask check was made of every crewmember on each plane to ensure their oxygen was working. Faulty equipment or a disconnected line could lead to unconsciousness or death. Victims were generally unaware of what was happening to them as drowsiness took over.

Jim Mairs, Marshalltown, Navigator, 398th Bomb Group: "When flying at high altitudes the temperature inside our aircraft was 35-50 degrees below zero. The thin air required the crew wear oxygen masks anytime above ten thousand feet. An oxygen check with each crewmember every ten minutes was required. Each crewmember was required to respond whether or not they were all right. On one mission the tail gunner did not respond to an oxygen check. A waist gunner took an oxygen bottle and went to check on him. When the waist gunner did not come back or respond to his own oxygen check the other waist gunner went to see what was wrong. He found both men passed out. Condensation had caused the tail gunner's mask to freeze and cut off his oxygen supply. The waist gunner's bottle had run out of oxygen. Both men were revived."

Prior to going on oxygen, the bombardier or a crewmember went to the bomb bay and removed the safety pins from the bombs. Heated flying suits were plugged in and switched on, and the ball turret gunner went to his position. After Division assembly was made the main bomber stream headed for the target. Altitudes over enemy territory ranged from twenty to thirty thousand feet with a temperature inside aircraft from forty to sixty degrees below zero.

Ralph Trout, Logan, Aerial Gunner, 398th Bomb Group: After takeoff and assembly Ralph entered the ball turret, plugged in his intercom and heated suit extension cord onto his suit. After donning his oxygen mask he had to keep watch for enemy fighters. Suddenly it felt cold. He checked all the connections from his clothing and everything seemed all right. He had one last place to check. The heated suit extension cord in the outlet under the seat. Literally standing on his head to reach the plug in the small turret, he managed with considerable difficulty to lock the plug in the outlet. Warmth began to come into his suit. Had he not been able to do so he would have frozen to death.

Milo Noble, Cherokee, Aerial Gunner/Togglier, 466th Bomb Group: During a mission to bomb Berlin, Milo's electrically heated flying suit shorted out and lost temperature. At their altitude in a non-pressurized airplane, temperature within the aircraft was thirty to forty degrees below zero. Milo had to continually bang his hand against the side of the nose turret to maintain circulation in his fingers and be able to release his bombs on cue. He was successful, target strikes were good and Milo knew he had done his part.

Loren Darling, Waterloo, Aerial Gunner, 100th Bomb Group: In December, 1943, in route to bomb targets at Bordeaux, France, Loren's heated flight suit shorted out. It was sixty degrees below zero within the aircraft. He had only two choices, either bail out over enemy territory and be captured or stick with the aircraft and try to keep from freezing to death. He decided to remain with the aircraft. On return to base his legs were frozen. While in the base hospital gangrene began to set in and it was feared his legs would have to be amputated. A doctor assigned five nurses to rub Loren's legs with a medical salve on a 24-hour basis. Eventually color returned to his legs and he fully recovered.

Gunners test fired their guns. Radio communications were monitored for any mission recall or other coded messages. Other than that, radio silence was generally maintained.

Ward Britson, Radcliffe, Aerial Gunner, 93rd Bomb Group: After takeoff and assembly into formation Ward tested his guns while over the English Channel. They didn't work. He took the guns apart and put them back together in time to re-test them while over Belgium. This time they worked.

Chapter Twelve

FIGHTER ESCORT AND OPERATIONS

In the early stages of the Eighth Air Force buildup in England, the primary role of American fighter squadrons was protective support of bomber aircraft operations against intervention by the German Luftwaffe. American fighter planes were hampered by their limited operating range and could only provide bomber escort to that distance which their remaining fuel supply would allow them to return to their base. This was generally the German border. The Luftwaffe, well aware of this would wait until American fighters had to disengage from escort duty and attack the bomber formation all the way to their target or their own limit of endurance. They could then return to their bases, refuel, rearm and takeoff to attack the bombers as they returned to England.

The range of American fighter aircraft, basically the P-51 Mustang, P-47 Thunderbolt, and the P-38 Lightning varied because of different fuel capacity and consumption rates. As a result, bombers were escorted by one type of fighter until they had to break off the escort because of fuel limitations. Another type of aircraft from a different fighter group would then take up the escort from a checkpoint until it also reached its range limit. If, during escort, fighters had to engage the enemy near the end of their escort, they would not have enough fuel to make it back to base. Beyond that, the bombers were on their own until they reached their target, dropped their bombs and were within range of protective fighters on the return flight to England.

Jim Halverson, Spencer, P-47 fighter pilot, 356th Fighter Group: "We were told not to fly at full throttle all the time because we had just enough fuel to make it back to base if we conserved some of it."

Bill Knowling, Iowa City, P-47 and P-51 fighter pilot, 353rd Fighter Group: Bill flew thirty-five missions in the P-47 before the Group replaced the Thunderbolt because of its lack of fuel range, with the P-51.

As American bombers made their approach to their target, German fighters "ganged up" on them with head on attacks in an attempt to shoot down the lead bombers. Well aware that all bombers in the formation dropped their bombs when the lead aircraft released their bombs, the Luftwaffe, in attacking head on tried to cause disruption of the formation with resulting failure of bombs to hit their target.

Drop tanks containing additional fuel were adapted to be suspended under the fuselage and wings of the fighters and provide additional distance for escort duty. American fighters, instead of turning back near the German border were able to make a shallow penetration into Germany during escort. If, on the way to the target, the Luftwaffe attacked the bombers, American fighters dropped their external fuel tanks for more maneuverability in dog fighting and engage the enemy. This consumed precious fuel and reduced the distance they could continue with their escort. But it proved effective. Bomber losses dropped dramatically the further fighter escort was afforded.

By late 1943 and early 1944 external and internal fuel tanks on P-51s were increased. The P-51D with a Rolls Royce engine could fly over 400 miles per hour at 25,000 feet. Its nearly 1,000 mile range was nearly doubled and it then became possible for American fighter aircraft to escort bombers all the way to their target and back to England. Meanwhile Eighth Air Force fighter groups received additional long-range fighter aircraft that increased the size of squadrons flying bomber support.

Combined with efforts by the 9th and 15th Air Forces, all fighter groups were ordered to go on the offensive, to hit the enemy in the air, on the ground and in the factories to eliminate the Luftwaffe. Dive bombing and strafing of targets was encouraged. Fighters flying protective cover for the bombers freed other squadrons to roam the skies in advance of the bomber stream to try and locate the Luftwaffe forming up for an attack. If freed from escort duty, American planes strafed German airfields to destroy aircraft and facilities on the ground as well as other targets such as train locomotives, rail centers, convoys and troop concentrations. The effort, in advance of D-Day, was carried out with such success the Luftwaffe was not a factor when Allied armies invaded the European continent at Normandy on June 6, 1944. However American fighter plane losses mounted during this offensive because of their vulnerability at low altitude to ground fire and light anti-aircraft weapons. More than one pilot also "bounced" the ground on their strafing attacks. Losses to dive-bombing and strafing accounted for more losses than in aerial combat.

Even with the appearance of new German jet fighters, some success was scored in downing them both on the ground and in the air. American P-51s were able to score victories over the faster jet. Robert Abernathy, Mason City, 353rd Fighter Group, Raydon, England. "Ab's" fighter group changed from the P-47 to the longer range P-51 in late 1944. On April 10, 1945, "Ab" became a fighter "Ace" when he closed head on with a German ME-262 jet. "Ab" got off the first shots and the jet "flamed right away". "The plane began a slow spiral to the ground and I followed it all the way down until it exploded in some woods."

Aerial gunners also scored victories despite technical inability to track the jets with their guns and the speed of the jets. George Hoffman, Leon, tail gunner, 303rd Bomb Group, "I saw this ME-262 coming out of the sun to attack my plane from the rear. I fired a steady stream of bullets at the jet and saw it break up and plunge to earth after it passed under our plane."

The overall offensive contributed greatly to German losses of aircraft and experienced pilots. The goal of virtually eliminating the Luftwaffe from the air and gaining air superiority was attained well before war's end. German fighter aircraft was still plentiful despite bombings to their factories, but fuel was limited from repeated attacks on German oil refineries and synthetic fuel plants. Combat attrition left Luftwaffe pilots with very little training who were pressed into action, and despite lack of experience and high losses incurred, proved themselves a determined foe in defensive of their homeland. "Last ditch" mass attacks on bomber formations were made from what resources the Luftwaffe had left and Allied fighters scored lop-sided aerial victories. "Flak", however, from German anti-aircraft weapons still took its toll on bombers. This was reduced over German as Allied ground troops fought their way through Germany and closed on Berlin.

Fighter operations, except for purpose, were basically the same as for bomber operations. An alert for a major escort operation was issued that provided the target, route of the bombers, check points, flak and enemy fighter concentrations, the bomber's altitude and time of arrival at rendezvous points where escort was to commence.

Weather at takeoff over bases and check points where fighters were to rendezvous with the bombers was an ever present concern. As at bomber bases, all personnel on the base were alerted including mess halls, armaments sections, mechanics, weather and intelligence personnel.

Ground crews on mission day were awakened to do an engine pre-flight check., External drop tanks were filled and internal fuel tanks "topped off". Radios were checked for operating condition, armament checked guns and charged them. Oxygen, supplied automatically at ten thousand feet, was checked to ensure it was fully charged.

Meanwhile pilots were awakened for breakfast followed by mission briefing. The briefing, detailed times, altitude and points where bombers were to be met. Weather provided clouds, wind and tempera-

P-51s assemble off wing of bomber formation

tures expected at various altitudes. Intelligence provided information where flak was likely to be encountered as well as where they might expect contact with enemy fighters.

Robert Shuler, Des Moines, was a draftsman for squadron intelligence with the 20th Fighter Group at Kingscliffe, England. His job was to make maps and charts for pilots and in his spare time painted names, slogans and pictures on pilot's assigned aircraft.

After briefing pilots were issued flight clothes and gear that included oxygen mask, Mae West inflatable life jacket, parachute, maps and escape kit. Pilots were driven to their aircraft where, as with bomber crews, a visual check was made of their aircraft with the crew chief. The pilot, particularly in the last year and a half of the war with long-range fighters available, would be in his aircraft for several hours. Before takeoff, it was prudent to urinate.

Robert Ward, Toledo, 361st Fighter Group, was a proficient gambler. Many officers on base owed him money from gambling that he kept posted in a little black book. Before each mission Bob's crew chief would give Bob a "lucky" silver dollar to carry in his flight suit. Bob, on the other hand, would give his little black book to the crew chief and then ceremoniously urinate on the tail wheel of his plane. On return from a mission the silver dollar and black book would change hands to their original owner.

While fighter aircraft are equipped with a relief tube resembling a funnel with a line going to the outside of the plane, it was cumbersome. At high altitude it was cold and several layers of clothing had to be dealt with. Relief could also come at an inopportune time and was to be kept to a minimum. On one occasion while over enemy territory Bob was using the relief tube. While attempting to fly with one hand and use the relief tube with the other, the funnel failed to drain properly. With a full funnel he accidentally hit his own gun button. The sound of his own guns going off was very similar to the sound of .30mm fire from German aircraft. He immediately took evasive action wondering where the guy on his tail came from. He realized quickly what had happened, but now what had previously been sitting in the funnel was everywhere inside the cockpit. The unwanted liquid instantly froze to the inside of the canopy and on his instrument panel. He had to scrape it off to see. As he landed back at his base, the frozen material began to thaw as he parked his aircraft. The ground crew who had to clean up the mess found the relief tube twisted somewhere before it exited the aircraft.

Given the signal for takeoff, fighters could run down the runway two at a time. At some airfields where they were grass runways, four planes could take off at once. Lighter and faster than bombers, fighter squadrons could take off and assemble into formation in a matter of minutes. Once airborne, they began a direct course to the bombers for rendezvous.

Initially, in 1942 and 1943 fighter escort remained with the bombers and attacked enemy fighters when they began to attack the bombers. As mentioned earlier, in latter 1943 and early 1944 fighter forces had been built up with long-range capability and ordered to take the offensive. Some squadrons were able to range from the escort to pursue enemy aircraft while others remained as escort. After strafing or aerial combat, fighters were often widely scattered and frequently returned home on their own. It was on these occasions many fighters suddenly appeared and flew protective escort for battle damaged bombers who were defenseless against enemy fighter attack. Fighters also radioed positions for air/sea rescue, and on occasion directed bombers back to their base or an emergency field in inclement weather.

Robert Dougherty, Ft Madison, Aerial Gunner, 92nd BG, Podington, England, on a mission to bomb targets at Bremen, Germany, "Flak knocked out our number three engine. We lost speed and altitude and dropped out of formation. Then flak got our number four engine. We lost more altitude and speed and were all alone. Four German Focke-Wolfe fighters flew alongside us just out of machine gun range evidently looking over their "sitting duck". To make things worse none of our machine guns worked. They were froze probably because we lost altitude so fast condensation on the guns froze. We tracked them with our guns anyway. When all hope for survival seemed to be lost, suddenly, ten American P-51 fighters appeared and drove the enemy fighters away."

Jerome Yearous, Cedar Falls, Flight Engineer, 306th BG, Thurleigh, England, "over Brandenburg, Germany, we got hit by about thirty-five German fighters. Eight American P-51 fighters plowed right into them. I saw five German planes go down. I think one P-51 got three of them. We were hit by "flak" that cut wires and caused our wheels to go down and flaps lock in the full flap postion. We had to run at full power to stay aloft and made no forward progress. We were six to eight hundred miles from England and an easy mark for both flak and German fighters. I knew where the short was and went into the bomb bay and repaired the wires. We were then able to make it back to England and land safely."

Eugene Stientjes, Pella, 93rd Bomb Group: "We lost two engines on a mission to Holland. Unable to hold altitude we attempted to return to England. To lighten our load we threw everything we could out of the aircraft. Meanwhile weather had closed in over England and visibility was down to 700 feet. An American P-47 Thunderbolt fighter flew as escort for us and signaled us where our airfield was."

Harlyn Turner, Dubuque, 446th Bomb Group: "On a raid on Munich we got hit by flak. One engine was shot out. We were unable to keep up with the rest of our formation and became stragglers. The Luftwaffe began to attack us to finish us off when American P-51s and P-38s suddenly roared by our plane and drove off the German fighters. Then they escorted us safely back to our base."

James Van Ginkel, Atlantic, 466th Bomb Group: "I owe my life to the P-51 Mustang and its ability to escort bombers all the way to and from targets."

Charles Claude, Corwith, 398th Bomb Group: "Over Dresden we got hit pretty bad by flak. Coming off the bomb run we were leaving a vapor trail behind number three engine from fuel leaks. Number four

Escort duty

engine was smoking bad so we transferred fuel from it. We had to break formation. Two P-51 Mustang fighters flew alongside as escort until we found an emergency field in France behind American lines and landed there."

Lyle Latimer, Farragut, 44th Bomb Group: "On a mission to Hamburg, we took heavy flak on the bomb run. Our left waist gunner was wounded. Our radioman although drenched by gasoline spray from three crippled engines rendered first aid to the gunner. Alone over the North Sea and subject to attack by Luftwaffe fighters, an American P-51 fighter flew alongside and escorted u all the way back to our base."

Kermit Neubauer, Iowa Falls, 94th Bomb Group: "On a raid to Mersberg our navigator was wounded, our oxygen system destroyed, our hydraulics ruined, number four engine was shot out and there was a large hole in the right wing. We were forced to drop in altitude and lost our way. We found out we were over Guernsey Island held by the Germans and they began shooting at us. An American P-51 fighters arrived and guided us back to England."

James O'Connor, Peosta, 388th Bomb Group: "After a raid on Madgeburg we lost number two engine. We were forced to drop out of formation deep in the heart of Germany and try to make it back to base alone. Another engine had taken a flak hit and began to lose oil and pressure. We lost altitude and our chances of survival against enemy fighters were slim. Fortunately American P-51s and P-47s flew alongside and escorted us back to the English Channel. We crossed the Channel at about 1,000 feet and were down to our last few hundred feet when we arrived at our base."

Albert Nichols, Des Moines, Pilot, 452nd BG, Deopham Green, England, during the bomb run over Politz, Germany, "two engines were lost to flak. We had to drop out of formation and try and make it back to England alone. A P-51 Mustang flew escort with us over Germany. From 26,000 feet we could fly to Sweden and be interned or try to make England. We chose to try for England knowing that if we couldn't make it and had to land in the North Sea it meant certain death. We were able to make it to our base through gradual descent and landed out of gas."

After return to their base pilots were de-briefed. This consisted of several questions regarding enemy fighter opposition, allied aircraft in distress or shot down, and information on enemy troop movements. Any information was gleaned from the pilots of an intelligence nature that would benefit rescue, determine losses, or benefit ground forces or future aerial missions. Pilots also claimed victories with a written claim detailing circumstances. Their gun camera film was removed from the aircraft for processing and verification.

As at bomber bases, when aircraft returned from a mission, work for the ground crews began again. Aircraft had to be serviced that included installation of new drop tanks, guns removed for cleaning, examination and repair if necessary. Armorers reinstalled the guns and filled the magazines with new ammunition. New gun cameras were installed, fuel tanks filled and oxygen pumped into the aircraft's system. The aircraft had to be maintained in combat readiness at all times and ready for takeoff on a moment's notice.

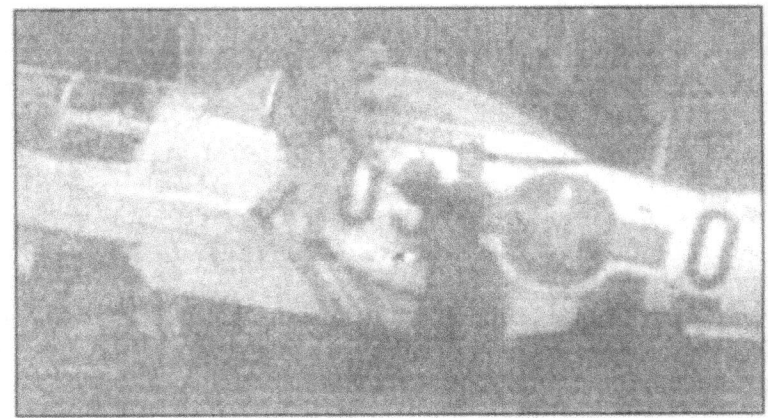
Ground Crew of 356th FG repairing P-51 of 355th Fighter Group that made emergency landing at their base.

"Little Friend", a P-51 Mustang flying escort off a bomber wing.

Chapter Twelve

Flight to the Target

The route taken to the target by bomber formations was rarely a direct flight from where they assembled, to the Initial Point (IP), a landmark or location where the bombers turned to make a bomb run over the target. Enemy fighter aircraft was always a major threat. Routes were not only taken to deceive the enemy as to the intended target but to avoid heavy concentrations of anti-aircraft fire in route and known locations of enemy fighters. This couldn't always be avoided. Anti-aircraft batteries were placed on river barges, railroad cars, and surrounded vital war industries throughout the country.

James Haas, Perry, Bombardier, 398th Bomb Group: "After we crossed the French coast we were hit by "flak" which put our aircraft in a spin. The pilot was able to level the airplane. Our number three engine was smoking. The fire stopped after we feathered the engine and pulled the fire extinguisher handle. Number four engine was unharmed but number two engine began wind milling. The cowling had been ripped away and revealed exploded cylinders that were dripping oil and fuel. Number one engine also began wind milling out of control. With these problems, the pilot turned back toward England. The crew reported they were unharmed except no word came from the ball turret gunner. He was found unharmed, but in shock staring at a large hole in his turret only inches from his face that had been blown out by debris from the number two engine. He was pulled from the turret, wrapped in a blanket, his wrists and face massaged and given inhalants to which he responded."

George Berry, Winterset, Aerial Gunner, 447th Bomb Group: On one mission to bomb Berlin a plane flying off to the side of us in the formation took an anti-aircraft hit in engine number three and began leaking fuel. The propeller was "feathered" and engine number four was shut down. The plane was off to the side and above us. He veered over the top of us spraying gasoline all over us and the rest of the formation behind us. It was lucky we and the whole formation didn't catch fire."

George Popelka, Cedar Rapids, Bombardier, 390th Bomb Group: "During a mission to Aachen, Germany, "flak" knocked out two of our engines. Unable to maintain altitude we bailed out over American-held territory except for the Pilot and Co-pilot who went down with the airplane and were killed. One other crewmember, too frozen with fear to pull the rip cord, fell to earth without opening his parachute.

Wayne Zeigler, Iowa Falls, Pilot, 385th Bomb Group: In route to bomb German tanks during the

German Railroad flak guns

Surveillance Photo of destroyed German Flak Gun Position

Battle of the Bulge, Wayne lost both engines on the right wing of his aircraft. Unable to maintain speed and altitude he turned back hoping to reach Allied territory. By the time they were down to twelve thousand feet the number three engine was out of oil and coming apart causing severe vibration and shaking the aircraft to the point it was uncontrollable. The plane was put on auto-pilot and the crew bailed out. "When I saw the ground coming up through a break in the clouds I pulled the ripcord. I was falling headfirst. Suddenly the main chute opened. It jerked me draining the blood from my head and I blacked out. When I came to the canopy was bobbing over my head. Everything was quiet and peaceful. I heard an airplane engine diving and getting louder. My first thought was that a German fighter had spotted me. I looked around frantically but couldn't see anything. The sound faded away and right away started to come back. I thought he's coming back to finish me off and I expected machine gun bullets to come through from somewhere but the roar faded away again. Right away it started getting real loud. My B-17 had broken away from the auto-pilot and came diving out of the clouds right at me. I thought it was going to snag my chute, but about 100 yards out it flopped over on its right wing and dove into the ground under me. It blew up in a ball of fire and completely disappeared. The concussion and sound of the explosion hit me in two or three seconds and blew me backwards. I landed on my left hip. It was like an explosion in my head when it snapped down on my chest and I bit through my tongue." Fortunately, Wayne landed near a small town in France and despite some anxious moments with civilians holding a pitchfork at his head while he lay on the ground, he convinced them he was an American and was given medical treatment. The German Army had just retreated from the area.

Because of shorter distances to fly to make contact with Allied bomber formations. German fighters could attack bombers in route to the target, return to their base, re-fuel and re-arm and attack the bombers on their withdrawal from Germany. Enemy fighters varied their attack methods. Head on attacks was made to shoot down lead aircraft. The Luftwaffe was well aware that all other American bombers in the formation bombed when the lead aircraft released its bombs. To shoot down the lead aircraft would hopefully cause chaos within the formation and ineffective bombing results. Other methods were a hit and run tactic by diving down on formations, particularly those on the outskirts of the formation with the least amount of defensive firepower or to approach the formation from behind. In the earlier stages of the war when American fighters were limited in their range of escort duty, the Luftwaffe would be poised to attack when the American fighters had reached the limit of their range and had to return to England for fuel. With the advent of drop tanks and long-range fighters that could escort the bombers all the way to the target and back, the Luftwaffe was aggressively hunted and gradually reduced to the extent they became less and less a factor in bombing missions.

Bob Boice, Waterloo, Radio Operator/Aerial Gunner, 91st Bomb Group: "At the beginning of our bomb run thirty German ME-109 fighters attacked us. We had seven or eight of our planes go down. They shot the hell out of the rest of us. We had one hundred-thirty holes in our plane. We lost one engine and had to salvo our bomb load to keep up with the rest of our formation. We had a runaway propeller on one engine all the way back to base. We radioed an emergency to our base. The pilot was wounded and the Co-pilot landed the plane OK."

Marvin Ford, Tipton, Flight Engineer/Aerial Gunner, 381st Bomb Group: "On a mission to Leipzig German ME-109 fighters attacked us in route to the target and on the way back to base. The Germans

Bomber Formation

Contrail formation

Bomber formations in route to target

knew how far to stay out from the formation and fire their .20 mm cannons. Our .50 caliber machine guns couldn't reach them."

Francis Prendergast, Callendar, Navigator, 447th Bomb Group: On a mission to bomb aircraft repair facilities north of Berlin, German fighters attacked the bomber formation. Francis was able to shoot down a Focke-Wulf 190. "He dove close to our plane, within 150 feet I pulled the trigger on my machine gun and hit him across the fuselage. I could see the pilot and saw him flinch like he got hit. He went down and I didn't see him parachute out."

Robert McElree, Oelwein, Flight Engineer/Aerial Gunner, 351st Bomb Group: On December 31, 1943, Robert flew an eleven hour mission to bomb an aircraft plant at Bordeaux, France. Because of the distance there was no fighter escort. "The target was clouded over so we went to another target even further away. There was a lot of flak and fighters. One plane behind us got hit and was all on fire. We lost eight or nine planes that day. No one made it back to base. Aircraft were running out of fuel and the crews bailing out. We had to land at an English base. The airplane ahead of us ran out of gas when it hit the runway. We were coming in behind it and had to swerve to miss hitting it. We counted over 200 holes in our airplane and then stopped counting."

Jack Weaver, Estherville, Radio Operator/Aerial Gunner, 384th Bomb Group: During a mission to bomb targets at Oberpfoffenhofen, Germany, "fighters came through the formation head on. We lost two engines and had one engine on fire, so we had to leave the formation and limp back to England."

James Goff, Sioux City, Navigator, 95th Bomb Group: On October 10, 1943, on a bomb raid to Munster, Germany, two hundred twenty-nine B-17s were to fly a diversion over the North Sea to split the German fighter force. "The lead bomber developed electrical problems that knocked out their radio All efforts of the lead crew to communicate the problem to the deputy leader failed. When the lead ship turned back to England everyone followed. German radar operators were then able to send all their squadrons to engage the main bomber force as it approached Munster. When they neared their bomb run, American escort fighters had reached the extent of their range and turned back to England. A second force of P-47 Thunderbolt fighters scheduled for escort duty with the bombers were still back in England unable to takeoff because of fog. It was then 300 Luftwaffe fighters began to attack in wave after wave. In the furious battle that followed burning planes and parachutes filled the air. Gunners stood ankle deep in shell casings while German fighters kept coming. They concentrated on the 100th Bomb Group flying low position and within minutes only one Fortress remained. They then turned to the 390th Bomb Group flying high position. In the next few minutes, nine bombers went down and five from the 95th were shot down. The American bombers were in danger of complete annihilation. Despite the vicious action, the lead bombardier put the bombs exactly on target."

Laverne Peters, Bedford, Aerial Gunner, 389th Bomb Group: "On April 7, 1945, the German Luftwaffe instituted "ramstaffel, suicide missions against American bombers.

Germany's Luftwaffe commander Hermann Goering recruited 300 pilots to ram 300 American bombers. The trade-off was supposed to be the loss of 300 pilots against 3000 American air crewmen. The pilots were instructed to begin firing at a bomber from long range and continue all the way to the point of ramming the aircraft. The pilot was supposed to bail out at the last moment, if possible. Several instances of ramming did occur, one of which killed my commanding officer. A German ME-109 crashed across the cockpit area of the lead bomber cutting off the nose of the aircraft causing it to crash into the wing of another bomber. Both bombers went down."

The appearance of the German jet fighter late in the war created havoc. Gunners could not track the jet to shoot it down and no Allied fighters could match its speed in aerial combat. However some successes were scored. Fortunately for the Allies the jet came too little too late as did other German scientific advances that could be employed for war purposes.

Earnest Degan, Des Moines, Aerial Gunner, 487th BG, Lavenham, England: "A German jet, the ME-262 once flew alongside our plane. We didn't know what it was. It didn't have a propeller. We never heard of jets. The pilot waved to us and flew off."

George Hoffman, Leon, Aerial Gunner, 303rd Bomb Group: "During one mission I spotted a new German

German ME-410 diving away after hit and run attack on bomber formation

jet, the ME-262 coming out of the sun to attack our aircraft from the rear. I fired a steady stream of bullets at the jet and saw it break up and plunge to earth after it passed under us. I was superstitious that if I claimed credit for the kill I would be killed next. I didn't report it. The 262 put twenty-five bullet holes in the tail section around me."

Walter Lienemann, Minburn, Aerial Gunner, 392nd Bomb Group: During a bombing mission to Munich, Germany, we took numerous flak hits and our navigator was wounded. At the time I was throwing out "chaf" in an attempt to confuse German radar controlled anti-aircraft batteries. When I returned to my gun position a German jet, an ME-262 dove on us. I didn't have my gun charged. The jet attacked and shot down a plane next to us. I grabbed my gun, charged it, and got off some bursts. I saw the German pilot when he went through the formation. I was too late to get him."

Carl Kitchen, Waterloo, Pilot, 490th Bomb Group: "On my last mission, to Czechoslovakia, our Group was attacked by the new German jet, the ME-262. Our formation was all spread out due to a navigation error and we were in the middle. In trying to "form up" the jet hit us and shot down two B-17s. Gunners couldn't track the jets and get shots off at them."

Downed B17

Jack Perrin, Cherokee, Aerial Gunner, 390th Bomb Group: "I saw the new jet fighter, the ME-262 and called out the fighter's approach on our formation. He blasted the right wing and fuel tank of a B-17 on my right. The bomber went down but the crew was able to parachute out of the airplane. I continued to call out the 262's position, but couldn't talk fast enough because the jet's speed was too fast. He knew there was no way a hand-held .50 caliber machine gun nor any of the power-operated gun turrets could track a jet to get shots at it."

Willard Branch, Davenport, Aerial Gunner, 401st Bomb Group: "We were attacked twice by the new German jet. No damage was sustained to our aircraft but the jets were successful in downing others."

Chapter Twelve

The Bomb Run

The Initial Point was a prominent landmark where bombers turned toward the target. Bundles of aluminum foil strips called 'Chaff' were sometimes dropped from the aircraft to create spurious images on enemy radar to reduce the accuracy of anti-aircraft fire. During the bomb run the bombardier was in control of the aircraft and flew the plane by Automatic Flight Control Equipment. The bombs were released at a point predetermined by data obtained during the briefing and entered into the bombsight. When the target was centered in the bombsight the bombs were triggered automatically. All other aircraft released their bombs when the lead aircraft released its bombs. Instead of a bombardier other aircraft in the group may have used another crewmember, called a togglier to watch when the lead planes released their bombs. He would then release his aircraft's bombs.

William Vint, Beaman, Togglier/Aerial Gunner, 96th Bomb Group:"A togglier sits in the bombardier's position in the nose of the aircraft but without a bombsight. The Norden bombsight was carried in only about six of the thirty-six airplanes in a Bomb Group. When bombs were dropped by the bombardier in the lead aircraft, the togglier in following aircraft release their bombs."

Herbert Reis, Early, Navigator, 453rd Bomb Group: "On a mission our bombardier passed out while on the bomb run. He had lost his oxygen. While he was being tended to I operated the toggle switch to drop our bombs when the lead plane dropped theirs."

Bruce Rust, Sheffield, Aerial Gunner, 94th Bomb Group: "On a mission to Berlin, the lead aircraft for the raid used a toggelier to signal when the Group was to drop their bombs. Forty miles from the target, while leaning forward, the bill of the toggelier's cap hit the bomb switch and released his bombs. All other aircraft then dropped their bombs. The formation had to abort the mission before they could reach the target area."

John Frampton, Reinbeck, Aerial Gunner, 94th Bomb Group: "When aircrews were reduced from ten men to nine, I was grounded and helped ground crews in maintenance. I wanted to fly and got back on flight status as a toggelier and flew twelve more missions."

Bomb runs were supposed to be chosen to avoid heavy anti-aircraft concentrations to the maximum extent possible. This was virtually impossible to achieve. Targets of maximum importance to the enemy such as oil refineries and synthetic fuel plants were ringed with hundreds of anti-aircraft batteries.

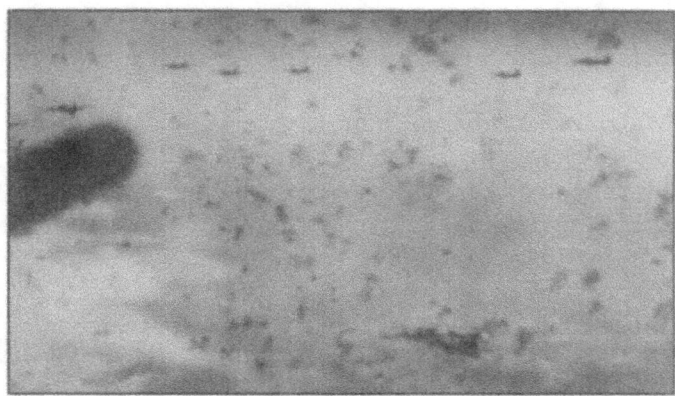
Heavy flak

German anti-aircraft fire, "flak" being fired at formation of bombers during bomb run.

If the lead bomber fell to enemy anti-aircraft fire on the bomb run, a deputy lead plane flying as wing on the lead aircraft took over as the lead. The bomb run was the most frightening of experiences. The enemy fighters had gone. Gone back to their base to re-fuel and re-arm and wait for the bombers when they finished the bomb run. "Flak" was the killer of bombers and accounted for more bomber aircraft downed in World War II than by enemy fighters. The bombers were required to fly at a designated altitude, straight and level with their bomb bay doors open that slowed their speed. German anti-aircraft gunners knew this and fired shells at a point in front of the bombers which exploded at set altitudes. Called a box barrage, their guns were capable of firing shells that could reach altitudes flown by the bombers. When they exploded, pieces of the shell burst in all directions and ripped through bombers like they were made of paper. "Chaff" dropped by the bombers to confuse German radar was therefore most effective when overcast skies prevented visual observation of American bombers.

Marlyn Gillespie, West Des Moines, Pilot, 305th BG, Chelveston, England: "We had to make three passes over the target bnefore we could release our bombs. One pass you want to get out of there. Two passes is fatal. Three passes they obliterated our squadron. I lost my number one and two engines on the left wing to "flak".

John Woolway, Des Moines, Aerial Gunner, 453rd BG, Old Buckenham: "On an October 12, 1944, mission, while on the bomb run, we were flying straight and level. A flight of B-17 bombers passed through our formation. It was like everyone for themselves. One B-17 clipped our left wing and tore off three and a half fee of it. The collision knocked me to the floor of the aircraft. When I stood up I had my parachute on. I don't know how or remember putting it on. The pilot never lost control of the plane and we made it back to England and landed at an airfield at Mansten, England."

Ken Newsom, Des Moines, Aerial Gunner, 486th BG, Sudbury, England: "On a mission to Bremen, Germany, I flew as a replacement. During the bomb run I heard a big thump. A German .88 shell came up right through the plane's radio compartment and exploded above us. No one was injured. It must have been set to detonate at a specific altitude and we were just lucky. During missions when anti-aircraft shells are being shot at us and the "flak" starts flying you crunch up like trying to squeeze into the shell of a turtle."

Thomas Wright, Des Moines, 453rd BG, Old Buckeham, England: "During a mission to Mainz, Germany, the German gunners were right on target. To comprehend the awesome sounds, visualize hundreds of rocks continually striking both sides of your automobile out of a clear blue sky. The shrapnel from the "flak" would go right through the airplane. The very core of the airplane's structure began to shudder and the engines were sputtering. The intense roaring of these sounds when combined with the shouting on the intercom made all of us feel that "this is it". My drift meter was struck and shattered to pieces. Better it than me since I was right in the path."

Lyle Dirks, Ocheydedan, Pilot, 379th BG, Kimbolton, England: "During one mission I flew a bomber usually reserved for my commanding officer. Plexi-glass windows in the front of the aircraft were of abnormal thickness for protection. During the mission a piece of shrapnel from "flak" struck the windshield in front of me and failed to enter the aircraft. Normal plexi-glass would have been broken and I wouldn't be here now."

Ray Pritchard, Des Moines, Aerial Gunner, 384th BG, Grafton Underwood: "During a bombing raid on the Skoda Armament Works at Pilsen, Czechoslovakia, we had to make three bomb runs on the target before it could be seen visually. The flak was murderous. When we got back our tail gunner had a large hole in the tail section right behind his position. We found him lying on his back laughing and looking up where the flak had come through the plane and missed him."

So much of a bomber is made up of vital parts, the engines, fuel tanks, electrical, hydraulic, oxygen and control systems, surfaces, bombs and nine to ten men per plane. Enemy gunners simply had to fire their weapons at one location knowing the aircraft had to fly through it. The odds were in their favor. At least with enemy fighters the aircrew could defend itself. Not so

Bombs Away from B-17 of Chuck Sessions, Cedar Rapids, 490th BG

Bombs Away for B-17s of 379th BG

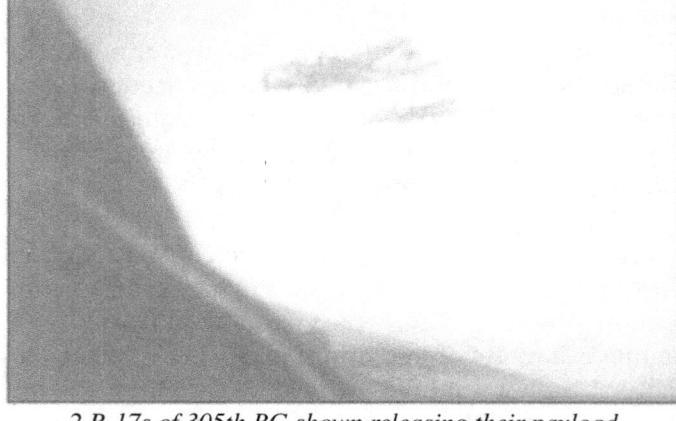
2 B-17s of 305th BG shown releasing their payload

Chapter Twelve

with "flak". Aircraft were perforated with flak and in many cases returned to their base in England with two to three hundred holes in the aircraft with no one injured nor vital parts of the aircraft damaged. In other instances a single hole in an aircraft made by "flak" was known to kill a crewmember.

To describe what the bomb run was like can only come from those who had the experience. Bomber crews were over enemy territory. To be shot down meant dying in the crash of the aircraft; bailing out and being taken prisoner of war or in many instances being able to maintain control of the aircraft long enough to return to Allied-held territory. To be seriously wounded on any portion of the mission meant help was up to eight hours away. Even their stories cannot fully relate what it was like to fly in bouncing aircraft through constant explosions around them that sent hot metal fragments flying in all directions, or slashing attacks by enemy fighters sending bullets and cannon shells ripping through aircraft. Many aircrews were able to make it back to their base or the safety of Allied lines through the skill of their pilot, teamwork of the crew or durability of their aircraft when the airplane shouldn't have been able to fly at all. When airplanes disintegrated or broke apart when hit by flak or enemy fighters whole crews were lost yet some managed to survive. Contained in the individual biography section are stories of close calls and strange twists of fate that saved lives. A sudden movement to the side or turning of their head at the right moment meant a difference of life or death.

Bill Carter, Ames, Aerial Gunner, 303rd Bomb Group: While over Koblenz, Germany, on a bombing mission, "flak" knocked out two of their aircraft's engines. Then their armed bombs "hung up" in the bomb bay and required a crew member climb into the open bomb bay area and manually release them. Bill's pilot took a wrong direction heading after being hit by flak that caused a fire within the aircraft. Loss of fuel caused Bill and his crew to make a crash landing near Tournier, France.

Richard Werner, Van Horne, Aerial Gunner, 384th BG, Grafton Underwood: "A big "flak" burst hit below our plane. It was like a big puff ball. From where I was in the tail of the plane I could really feel the concussion. It lifted me off the floor of the plane. We just wanted to finish our missions and get out of the war."

Wilmer Link, Dubuque, Flight Engineer, 379th Bomb Group: "We got hit over the target. "Flak" knocked out rudder control cables preventing the pilot from turning off the bomb run. While the rest of the formation turned toward England, we flew deeper into enemy territory. We had a "green" Co-pilot who didn't realize for a long time his controls worked. We hitched onto another Bomb Group and flew towards home. Flak had also cut hydraulic lines and we lost the fluid. To pre-

One of the first uses of napalm bombs, 490th Bomb Group, Eye, England

B-24 hit by flak goes down. Crew parachuted from aircraft and taken Prisoner of War

vent landing with no brakes we urinated in the hydraulic tank behind the Co-pilot's seat and wrapped the leak in the line with rags. It worked and we didn't lose hydraulic pressure until we landed and stopped."

Lyle Latimer, Farragut, Aerial Gunner, 44th Bomb Group: "Heavy flak was thrown at our formation on the bomb run. My left waist gunner was wounded in his upper leg. The radioman although drenched by gasoline spray from three crippled engines rendered first aid to the gunner and then took over his gun position. Alone over the North Sea and subject to Luftwaffe fighter attack, an American P-51 Mustang fighter flew alongside and escorted us all the way back to base."

Loren Schipull, Eagle Grove, Pilot, 398th Bomb Group: "Turning on the bomb run and seeing the flak ahead of us, I never thought we would make it through it. I was hit in the hand by a piece of flak but was not seriously wounded. I never received serious damage to my aircraft and never lost a crewmember to wounds

Mack Farmer, Clarinda, Radio Operator/Aerial Gunner, 306th Bomb Group: "While flying as lead aircraft a

German anti-aircraft shell exploded outside my plane. A piece of flak hit me in the chest. Luckily I was wearing a flak vest, however the force twisted me off my chair, knocked me through a door of my compartment and I fell into the bomb bay area. Flak also cut the hose of my oxygen mask and I passed out. A radar operator gave me artificial respiration and a portable oxygen bottle which saved my life."

George Berry, Winterset, Aerial Gunner, 447th Bomb Group: "While on a mission to bomb German submarine pens at Kiel, a P-51 Mustang fighter plane flew alongside our plane during the bomb run. I looked at the pilot and we waved to each other. I then heard a "boom" and the next thing I knew he was gone. What used to be his airplane was a ball of fire and he was gone. He took a direct hit."

Darwin Joliffe, Dayton, Aerial Gunner, 446th Bomb Group: "During a February, 1944, mission to Berlin, "flak" was intense. To me it seemed like four bursts around us. One in front and two on the sides. You didn't want to be there when the fourth one exploded." While on a mission to Frankfurt, "flak" shorted out wiring causing his aircraft to fill with smoke. "We dropped out of formation and most of us went into the bomb bay area with oxygen bottles to get ready to bail out when someone found the problem. "Flak" had cut a wire. It was repaired and we flew back to base. All missions were scary. With "flak" bursting outside I don't see how we got through it."

Clem Marsden, Ames, Navigator, 457th Bomb Group: Clem was wounded in the back from a piece of "flak" and another piece was found imbedded in his parachute. Only one crewmember was lost to enemy action when a piece of "flak" tore through the ball turret and struck the gunner in the head.

Glenn Hill, Fairfield, Togglier/Aerial Gunner, 466th Bomb Group: "Flak guns opened up on us. It was like shooting ducks. A lot of planes was hit and went down. No parachutes were seen coming from them. We got hit in the bottom of the plane but we were still able to continue. The tail gunner's parachute had an .88 shell go through it. If he needed it, it was worthless."

Harold Brookhiser, Wever, Togglier/Aerial Gunner, 92nd Bomb Group: On a mission to Dresden, Germany, it was decided not to drop our bombs on the first bomb run. Instead "chaff" was thrown out in an attempt to confuse anti-aircraft batteries and German radar operators. The formation made another bomb run and we released our bombs on target. "We got hit by "flak" in the wing. The hole was so large you could have jumped through it. An .88mm shell went through the bottom of the plane and out the top without exploding. It came through right behind the pilot's seat. I got hit by a piece of flak in the chest. I was wearing my flak vest which protected me. It felt like someone hit me with a hammer."

Norm Strom, Des Moines, Pilot, 92nd BG, Podington, England: "On one mission we took a direct hit from "flak" in the bomb bay area when the doors were open but we were able to fly home with a huge hole in the side of he plane."

Donald Broadbent, Des Moines, Bombardier, 487th BG, Lavenham, England: "While on the bomb run with the bomb bay doors open, a German .88 shell went through the bomb bay without striking any of the bombs and exited through the top of the aircraft. Hydraulics to the bomb bay doors were severed and the doors had to be hand-cranked shut after "bombs away"".

Victor Schweer, West Liberty, Tail Gunner, 100th Bomb Group: "Flak blew out the entire tail gunner's dome and a large part of the aircraft's tail. My guns had jammed and I had just crawled out of the tail gunner's position when I felt a hell of a jolt, a tremendous gust of air, and our plane started vibrating.

Bennett Fischer, Vinton, Bombardier, 91st Bomb Group: On a February 3, 1945, mission to bomb Berlin and Dresden, Germany, a B-17 flying alongside of Bennett's aircraft contained Robert Carpenter, a close friend from Cedar Rapids. The aircraft took a direct hit from "flak" in the middle of the fuselage. The airplane separated into two sections then blew apart and tumbled in pieces to the ground. His friend tried to escape the stricken airplane and had inadvertently pulled the ripcord on his parachute within the airplane. Despite the inflated parachute he put it on but was knocked unconscious. Amazingly he woke up dangling from his parachute in a tree, but was taken prisoner of war. When the airplane blew apart, his parachute, already open, inflated and he floated to earth. On another mission Bennett escaped certain death when "flak" pierced the nose of his airplane where the bombardier sat. For some reason the bombardier's seat was missing that day from his aircraft and required he sit lower in the nose than normal. The flak passed over his head.

Claude Conklin, Belle Plaine, Aerial Gunner, 34th Bomb Group: Suspended under the belly of the B-17 in the ball turret Claude soon found that if he lined the bottom of the turret with flak suits it afforded him some measure of protection from the flak fragments exploding around him. He was still small enough and had plenty of room to maneuver and his visibility was not affected.

Clarence Henderson, Cedar Rapids, Aerial Gunner, 303rd Bomb Group: "During the start of the bomb run on Dresden, Germany, our pilot had to urinate. He relieved himself in a fuse can, opened his window at the cockpit and emptied the can. The contents sprayed over the windows of the plane and froze. At that time we were hit by flak that knocked out the number two engine and set it afire. The propeller began wind milling out of control. From my ball turret position I radioed the pilot oil was leaking from the engine and running down the side of the plane. Then gas began leaking threatening to ignite the plane with its full bomb load. Suddenly I couldn't breathe. My oxygen line had been hit by flak and was broken. I was able to get out of the turret and was handed a walk around oxygen bottle by the radio operator. The aircraft was put into a dive to try and put out the engine fire. Pins were replaced in the bombs and fuel transferred from the number two engine. Down to 800 feet and still behind enemy lines, American P-51s were radioed for escort assistance. We released our bombs in the countryside and returned to base without further incident."

Milo Noble, Cherokee, Togglier/Aerial Gunner, 466th Bomb Group: "During one mission we got hit in the right wing with "flak". The .88mm shell pierced the underside of the wing and exploded above the wing. We made it back to base and when we examined the wing we found the shell had grazed the side of the fuel tank and the main wing spar. The main wire cable controlling the function of the aileron on that wing was frayed and only three tiny strands of wire were all that kept the pilot in control of the aircraft."

Loren Darling, Waterloo, Aerial Gunner, 100th Bomb Group: On October 10, 1943, a mission was scheduled to bomb railroad marshalling yards at Munster, Germany. Loren's aircraft had survived an attack by over two hundred German fighter planes prior to the bomb run. Once over the target, flak filled the sky and shredded American bombers. A flak burst on the left side of Loren's aircraft wounded the left waist gunner. Loren, in the right waist was thrown against the side of his aircraft by the explosion and broke his jaw. He was wounded in the head by over eighty metal fragments from the shell. Unknown to him his left hand also sustained a severe wound. Loren continued to man his post firing at enemy fighters after the bomb run. Two of their engines had been shot out, they were losing altitude and leaking fuel from flak hits in the wing. After receiving an emergency shot of morphine for his wounds he assisted other crewmembers in throwing out all the equipment they could to reduce the weight of their aircraft. As his aircraft skimmed across the English Channel at water level they needed to gain altitude to avoid crashing into the White Cliffs of Dover. They were barely able to clear the cliffs but brushed the tops of trees at cliff's edge. Heavy mists had settled in over the English countryside. Loren, now in the Co-pilot's seat assisted the Pilot in locating their base where they made a successful landing. When the left mitten was taken off his hand, his thumb came with it. Doctors were able to successfully re-attach his thumb. Loren had to wear a magnetic cap to try and draw metal splinters from his head that had not been removed during medical treatment. Four teeth had to be removed to allow Loren to be fed after his broken jaw was wired shut. For his wounds Loren received the Purple Heart Medal. For his actions he was awarded the Silver Star pinned on him personally by Eighth Air Force Commanding General Curtis LeMay.

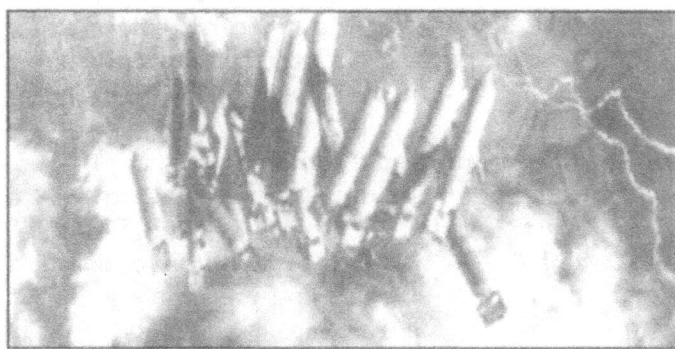

"Bombs Away" Salvo of bomb load over Germany

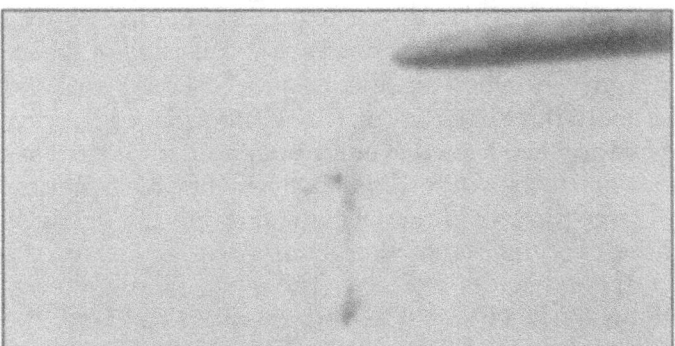

B-17 goes straight down after hit by flak and severed in two on bomb run, no parachutes exited plane

B-17's left stabilizer sheared off by bombs dropped by aircraft in formation above them

Iowans of the Mighty Eighth

RETURN TO ENGLAND

After "bombs away", aircraft flew to a rally point, a location for the bombers to re-form for a defensive flight back to England. Their aircraft were now lighter. Fuel had been consumed and their bomb load dropped. Their return speed could be increased but they still had to contend with flak from anti-aircraft batteries on their return and hordes of enemy fighters. On occasion no enemy fighters were encountered the entire mission or until after the bomb run. Allied fighters flew to a mutual rendezvous point to meet the bombers and deal with the Luftwaffe should they appear. Early in the war fighter escort on withdrawal would have been just over the European coast because of limited fuel range, but after development of drop tanks and long-range fighters, escort was provided the entire mission.

Clarence Hightshoe, Iowa City, Navigator, 384th Bomb Group: "Thank the Lord I was only 5'10 1/2" and not 5'11" tall. "Suddenly right in front of us was a burst of "flak". We were feeling pretty safe with our escort and had just removed our steel helmets. We were descending, as the French coast was almost directly below us. Flak suits were coming off along with our oxygen masks that we had worn for about five hours. I had just picked up my head set. It consisted of the intercom ears joined together by an adjustable steel band of about three-quarters inch in width. I placed it on my head and had leaned over the bombardier to orient my position to the White Cliffs of Dover when the flak burst. A large piece of shrapnel came through the plexiglas nose over the bombardier's shoulders. It sheared the steel band across my head. There was no tug, no any thing, the headphones fell, one on each side of me. The flak then passed through the pilots instrument panel popping out most of the glass covers, proceeded upward and imbedded itself in a sheet of one half inch armor plating along side the co-pilot's head." The shrapnel had sheared the steel band on his headset without harming a hair on his head.

Ronald Higdon, Iowa City, Aerial Gunner, 392nd Bomb Group: On a bombing mission in support of the invasion of southern France their bomb load could not be dropped because of an electrical malfunction. On the return trip to England with a full bomb load, the plane was hit by flak from anti-aircraft fire. A shell came through the catwalk in the bomb bay area and hit the shackle holding the top bomb in the racks. The shell failed to explode. The shackle kept the shell from going through oxygen tanks which would have destroyed the plane and crew. The pilot gave the crew the opportunity to bail out of the damaged plane but also told them he was going to try and take them home. No one bailed out and they returned to base safely.

Orville Whitcanack, Cantril, Flight Engineer, 493rd Bomb Group: As his bomb group returned from a mission they were flying along the Rhine River in Germany. Suddenly a plane next to Orville's took a direct hit from flak, burst into flames, broke up and went down. "I was looking at the plane. It was so close I could see one guy's face and his eyes. He was there on minute and the next was gone. It gives you a weird feeling to see your buddies go that way." The Germans had anti-aircraft guns mounted on barges floating up and down the Rhine River.

Cleon Wood, Cedar Falls, Flight Engineer/Aerial Gunner, 452nd Bomb Group: "On the return flight to England our formation came under heavy fighter attack by German FW-190 fighters. The fighters attacked from the rear of the formation. The plane next to mine had its tail broken off and then exploded. My plane's horizontal stabilizer was hit by .20 mm cannon fire and flew apart. It didn't affect the ability of the plane to fly and we returned to base safely."

James Goff, Sioux City, Navigator, 95th Bomb Group: During an October 9, 1943, mission to bomb a Focke-Wulf Plant at Marienburg, Poland, we saw no German fighters, only a German observation plane that shadowed our formation. We bombed the plant unmolested and headed for home. As we flew out over the North Sea we relaxed and brought out peanut butter sandwiches and hot soup which had been sent along for the long flight. We never got to eat. Our tail gunner called out that German fighters were approaching fast from our rear. The fighters stayed out of range of our machine guns and fired rockets and .37mm cannon. Our wingman took a rocket in the number three engine and the burning Fortress plunged earthward. Seven parachutes were seen to exit the plane. The last two parachutes were on fire. Thirty bombers were lost that day."

Kermit Neubauer, Iowa Falls, Aerial Gunner, 94th Bomb Group: After "bombs away" during a raid on Mersberg, Germany, and heading home we were suddenly attacked by German fighter planes which annihilated our high squadron and then came after my squadron which was flying in the lead. Our navigator was wounded, our oxygen system was destroyed, our hydraulics ruined, number four engine was shot out and there was a large hole in the right wing. With no oxygen system and we were forced to drop in altitude. We lost our way and found out we were over German held Guernsey Island in the English Channel. We received small arms fire from German troops stationed there. An American P-51 fighter arrived to guide us back to England. On arrival over our base with no hydraulics, the landing gear of our plane had to be hand-cranked down. Since we didn't have any brakes it was decided that as the airplane touched down on the run-

Chapter Twelve

way the crew would let out a parachute at each waist gunner's position to inflate and slow the airplane. One parachute opened ahead of the other and caused the plane to "ground loop". We stopped and no one was seriously injured."

Thomas Estes, Aurelia, Pilot, 384th Bomb Group: "Seventy-eight of the 109 airplanes that flew a mission to Hamburg on July 25, 1944, suffered some sort of flak damage. Many had engines or vital control surfaces damaged and fell back out of formation. At the rally point twenty-five miles east of Hamburg our six bomb groups began the return to England. This is where the German fighters hit us with orders to pursue as far as their fuel would allow. While we were over the North Sea a second attack was mounted by German twin-engine fighters from Holland.

If no enemy aircraft appeared or were not in the area after the bomb run, fighters were free in some instances to take the offensive and bomb or strafe targets of opportunity. Other fighters found bomber stragglers with combat damage and escorted them as far as the bomber could fly, whether it be back to England or a crash landing in Europe to ward off any attacking Luftwaffe fighters.

Ralph Pender, Cedar Falls, Flight Engineer, 388th Bomb Group: "Our aircraft took flak hits in the wing that punctured the fuel tanks. Luckily the aircraft didn't explode but the holes in the wing were too large for the self-sealing tanks to prevent leakage of all our gas. We were able to make it back to France and land at an airstrip American ground forces had captured the previous day. We spent three days there repairing the aircraft and getting fuel to fly back to England. German fighters strafed us but we were in bunkers and no one got hurt. When we got back to our base our footlockers in our barracks had been looted. No one expected us to return from the mission after they saw us go down."

John Ruppert, Iowa City, Aerial Gunner, 447th Bomb Group: "On my thirteenth mission we lost one engine from flak and realized we would not make it back to our base. Our pilot gave us the chance to bail out over territory recently taken from the Nazis. The pilot indicated he was going to try and land at a former Luftwaffe air base in France. The crew decided to say with the plane. Despite the poor condition of the bombed out runway we landed safely."

Robert Fitzgerald, Milford, Bombardier, 100th Bomb Group: While on a mission to bomb targets at Chemnitz, Germany, an engine of his aircraft was shot out while flying over battlefield front lines. The engine's propeller would not feather. As a result they lagged behind the rest of the bomber formation. They continued on to their target alone lacking air speed and vulnerable to

B-17 of Alva McCalley, Hazelton, 306th BG, "bellied in" in Belgium, Winter '44,

enemy fighter attack. Unable to make the return flight to England the pilot was forced to land their bomber at a French fighter airstrip. It took three days for the crew to "hitchhike" back to their base.

Harley Reisgaard, Exira, Aerial Gunner, 452nd Bomb Group: While over Frankfurt, Germany, flak knocked out one engine of his aircraft. Shortly thereafter, two other engines were lost. Unable to maintain altitude, everything available in the aircraft was thrown out to reduce their weight. The pilot was able to fly the aircraft until they were behind Allied lines to avoid capture by the Germans. He belly-landed in a wheat field in France. "We sat in the radio room in crash position. We had been trained on what to do. It wasn't too bad, the pilot did a great job. American soldiers showed up right away and took us to an airstrip where there was another B-17 that had been forced to land and was repaired, so we flew it back to our base."

Chuck Sessions, Cedar Rapids, Pilot, 490th Bomb Group: "Heavy flak taken by our plane caused engine failure and made it impossible for us to return to our base. I made a forced landing at Eindhoven, Holland, behind Allied lines. We were picked up by British forces and returned to England. "

Jack Modlin, Dawson, Flight Engineer/Aerial Gunner was in the same aircrew as

Rudy Nelson, Cedar Rapids, Pilot, 95th Bomb Group: During a mission to Frankfurt, Germany, "They threw everything they had at us (flak). We lost three engines and with only one engine we were losing altitude and running out of gas. We spotted a temporary landing strip made of steel mats in Belgium just behind the front lines. A crashed C-47 sat at the end of the runway. Rudy sat the plane down and was able to stop it in front of the C-47."

Jerrold Jacobsen, Cedar Falls, Bombardier, 467th Bomb Group: "On a bombing mission to Czechoslovakia one engine malfunctioned and quit running at the start of our bomb run. Another engine was lost when hit by flak. We were able to make it back to France where we made a forced landing near a town close to the Belgium border that had recently been taken by Allied ground forces."

Charles Claude, Corwith, Pilot, 398th Bomb Group: "While over Dresden, Germany, we got shot up pretty bad by flak. Coming off the bomb run we were leaving a vapor trail behind number three engine from fuel leaks. Number four engine was smoking bad so we transferred fuel from it. We were south of Berlin and had to break formation. Two P-51 Mustang fighters flew along side as escort. We were losing gas fast and knew we couldn't make it back to England. We found an emergency field in France behind American lines and landed there."

Merlin Bruning, Carroll, Aerial Gunner, 34th Bomb Group: "On my fifth mission flak knocked out one engine starting a fire. Extinguishers and feathering the propeller failed to put out the fire. Then two other engines failed. My pilot put us down in a field behind American lines in France. On landing, one propeller that was wind milling broke off the engine and tore a six foot section off the wing. The French told us there was another B-17 nearby and the only thing wrong with it was the wheels wouldn't retract. We flew it back to England and landed at an RAF base."

Robert Harken, Ackley, Pilot, 466th Bomb Group: "My tail gunner was lost on one mission when his oxygen system failed and he fell unconscious. We were flying alone and susceptible to enemy fighter attack. I secured escort from an American P-51 Mustang fighter and flew to the nearest air base in Allied hands to get aid for the gunner. We were shot at by both Germans and Americans before I was able to land at a British base in Belgium. It was too late for the tail gunner. He could not be revived and died."

Charles Buckley, Iowa City, Aerial Gunner, 392nd Bomb Group: Coming back from a raid on Lauta, Germany and after taking numerous "flak" hits, Charles' Flight Engineer advised the pilot they only had fifteen minutes of fuel remaining. The pilot believed they could still make England or at least get back over Allied lines. After fifteen minutes the engines quit while they were northeast of Paris. They bailed out and the airplane went down taking the nose gunner and navigator with it. Why they hadn't bailed out remains a mystery. Charles and the rest of his crew were safe in American hands and were taken to Paris for transport back to England.

Thomas Gallagher, Cedar Rapids, Flight Engineer/Aerial Gunner, 100th Bomb Group: In addition to receiving intense "flak" while over Berlin, Tom's aircraft was attacked by German jets, the ME-262, which used the bomber's contrails as cover to approach them from the rear. The number two and four engines of Tom's aircraft were hit. Control cables were knocked out on the rear stabilizer and a Tokyo gas tank exploded taking off eight feet of a wing. While they lost altitude rapidly the pilot maintained an East heading toward Poland. As they descended from 32,000 to 9,000 feet they made it over Allied lines but a burst of fire exploded between the number two engine and the fuselage. A piece of shrapnel passed behind the pilot and hit Tom, wounding him. At 3,000 feet the plane stopped losing altitude and a pasture was found on which to land. The crew evacuated the aircraft for fear of further explosions when oxygen lines were hissing

B-17 of Jim Haas, Perry, 398th BG, makes safe belly landing at emergency landing field in England.

After the bomb run aircrews often discovered some or all of their bombs had not fully released from the shackles that held them until they reached the target. The bombs were armed and had to be jettisoned from the aircraft before they could land. The only alternative was to replace safety pins and wires in the bombs and attempt a landing, but this was risky.

Gilbert Lindberg, West Branch, Pilot, 384th Bomb Group: During a mission to Anklam, Germany, "Everyone else dropped their bombs except us. With the bomb load still aboard and the mission requiring eleven hours flight time, we were running low on fuel. The bombardier discovered he had forgotten to turn on the intervolumeter switch. The bombs were dropped in the countryside and we were able to make it back to base on the remaining fuel."

John DeLorbe, Waterloo, Radio Operator, 96th Bomb Group: While on the bomb run, John looked out the window above him to see another B-17 out of formation and directly above them with the bomb bay doors open. Its whole salvo of bombs dropped between the front and rear wings of John's aircraft without striking them.

Charles Buckley, Iowa City, Aerial Gunner, 392nd Bomb Group: After a bomb raid on a Salzburg, Austria, fuel plant, Charles' top turret gunner noticed another B-24 above them with its bomb bay doors open. The aircraft had not dropped its bomb load. The bombs were

Chapter Twelve

released while over Charles's airplane. One bomb struck his plane a foot and a half away from Charles knocking out the left tail and stabilizer. They were headed in a westerly direction toward England. Weather in England had deteriorated to the extent landing back at their base was impossible. All aircraft in the formation were ordered to turn around and land at the nearest friendly air base in France. Because of damage Charles's pilot could not turn their aircraft back to France nor land in England because of weather. It was decided to abandon their airplane while at ten thousand feet. After the crew bailed out the airplane went into a steep dive and then exploded when it was at about two thousand feet. The crew believed the pilot had stayed with the airplane and was killed. When the pilot let loose of the controls, the airplane went into its dive pinning him in the top turret area by centrifugal force. When it exploded the force of the blast propelled him out the bomb bay area. He was still able to pull the ripcord on his parachute and land safely. He suffered only a black eye.

Earl Brindley, Atlantic, Radio Operator, 398th Bomb Group: Earl flew what he described as the RDX raid. "Bombs containing plastic explosives were stored in the Group's bomb dumps. They knew the war was about over and these explosives were very unstable. To get rid of them, it was decided to drop them over Germany but the crews were ordered to drop them in a string, not all at once. Some guy salvoed all his bombs. As they fell they hit each other and exploded near where the 601st Squadron was flying and several bombers were blown apart. Shrapnel from the explosions punctured our transfer lines and leaked gas into our bomb bay. We crawled into the bomb bay and used rags to try and halt the flow of gas. The bomb bay doors were open and we couldn't close them for fear of sparks setting off the gas. We landed in Austria with the bomb bay doors open."

Jim Haas, Perry, Bombardier, 398th Bomb Group: "After "bombs away" over Berlin one bomb "hung up" and did not release from its shackles." Without a parachute Jim climbed into the bomb bay area and was successful in getting it to drop. "I was scared to death. Any sudden jolt or movement of the plane that would cause me to lose balance, I would have been a goner."

Lee Gingery, Shenandoah, Radio Operator, 351st Bomb Group: During one mission a bomb "hung up" on the bomb racks. Lee had to climb into the open area of the bomb bay where the temperature was between 30 to 60 degrees below zero and while under intense anti-aircraft fire, released the bomb manually.

Earl Fouts, Marshalltown, Aerial Gunner, 457th Bomb Group: In route to a mission over Germany with

Buckley's B-24 with left stabilizer damaged by bombs dropped by above aircraft

armed bombs, Earl's entire formation was ordered to return to England. The mission had been "scrubbed". Earl climbed into the bomb bay area to re-install the pins in the bombs disarming them before they could land back at his base.

Kenneth Hansen, Cedar Rapids, Flight Engineer/Aerial Gunner, 96th Bomb Group: During one mission his aircraft had been loaded with five hundred pound bombs. After "bombs away" over the target, one bomb failed to release from one shackle and was left dangling in a downward position. The propeller on the bomb had fully spun out and was in danger of exploding at any moment. Ken entered the bomb bay area and was not able to dislodge the bomb. Tying one end of a rope around a part of the bomb bay and the other end around his parachute harness Ken climbed as high as he could in the bomb bay and jumped up and down on the bomb until it fell to earth. Ken fell through the bomb bay and was himself dangling by the rope under the aircraft. He was able to climb back into the airplane.

What are the odds? Raymond Carlson, Walcott, Navigator, 466th Bomb Group: On a mission to bomb an ordnance plant at Berlin, "we were the last group into the target and had to stay under the contrails of the flights before us in order to bomb visual at 18,000 feet." The bombs in Raymond's aircraft "hung up" in the bomb bay and were not released on target. On the return flight to his base it was decided to kick the bombs loose on a Northern Germany farm field. The explosions created a huge crater in the field. Much later, after the war, Raymond was employed with the "Quad City Times" newspaper. A young German typesetter was hired in his department. Raymond and the young German became good friends and regular golfing partners. Raymond eventually learned the German farm on which his aircraft dropped their bombs on March 18, 1945, belonged to his typesetter's father. The crater created by the bombs filled with rain and was used to water cattle.

Home At Last

As the bombers neared England and dropped below ten thousand feet, crewmembers no longer needed oxygen masks. Damaged aircraft unable to make it back to their base headed for any nearest airfield. An IFF (identification friend or foe) transmitter was turned on so the crew could identify themselves as friendly to intercepting Allied fighters or by colored flares pre-determined to be "the colors of the day" or by flashing a special code letter by Aldis lamp. This was essential in case a bomber was flying alone because of battle damage or some mechanical failure. They were required to identify themselves using one of the signals to prove they were not the enemy flying a captured aircraft.

At each base ambulance and fire fighting crews stood by for aircraft with casualties aboard, or severe battle damage that would cause anything but a normal landing. Ground crews waited and watched the skies for their aircraft to return and counted them as they made their pass in preparation for landing. Aircraft signified they had casualties aboard by firing two red flares and were given priority in landing. After landing they turned off the runway at the first possible taxiway or nearest hard stand where an ambulance was waiting. Bombers normally landed in a set pattern 10-20 seconds apart. Aircraft with severe battle damage posed a problem for other landing aircraft in case they crashed and blocked the runway.

Galen Wiley, Boone, Pilot, 305th Bomb Group: On approach to his base the left landing gear would not lock into place. All efforts failed to secure the gear and Galen was told to attempt a one wheel landing on the grass next to the runway. "because they thought the soft ground would be better." With his crew in crash position Galen was able to keep the left wing horizontal until reduced speed lowered it gently to the ground. No one was seriously injured. Said Galen's navigator, "Galen did a masterful job. What a great pilot!"

Bob Reeves, Waterloo, Aerial Gunner, 91st Bomb Group: "We landed at Bassingbourn with the full load of bombs and "greased it on", but as we turned off the runway one of our main tires blew out. We thought the bombs would blow next. You should have seen us get out of that plane and run for our lives. We returned from another mission with 158 flak holes in our aircraft."

Leroy Edwards, Mt Pleasant, Aerial Gunner, 100th Bomb Group: "Over Chemnitz, Germany, we got hit and lost one engine. Coming back we had to put down near Rochester, England. There were 300 to 500 foot hills in the area and we were skimming the tops of them. Trying to make a final approach we lost another engine. The pilot picked out a wheat field on slanted ground. We landed and slid on wet ground. The remaining gas didn't explode but the navigator was trapped in the airplane. We had to kick out the plexiglass nose of the plane to get him free. The prop from number three engine in landing had cut through the side of the plane and put a big gash in his head."

Russell Knight, Iowa City, Aerial Gunner, 466th BG, Attlebridge, England: "On one mission we were carrying 150 pound cluster bombs. On our way back to England we were near the English Channel when we heard a big noise and saw one of our bomb bay doors fly back past us. One cluster of three bombs hadn"t released when we dropped our bombs. Two of the bombs fell free but one bomb was still hung on cables and was swinging under our plane. We couldn't land or would be blown apart. We didn't have any tools to cut the bomb loose. One guy on our crew had a mess kit and a fingernail file. We were told to fly up and down the English Channel and try to free the bomb. If we were going to run out of gas before we could get it free, then we were supposed to bail out and let the plane fall into the Channel. Taking turns we were successful in filing through three-quarter inch steel cable with the finger-

B-24 Home at Last

Galen Wiley's B-17 after one-wheeled landing at Chelveston, England

Chapter Twelve

nail file and release the bomb into the water. We then flew back to our base"

Donald Connell, Waterloo, Flight Engineer/Aerial Gunner, 91st Bomb Group: On one mission two engines had been shot out and a third engine was not running properly. Hit at a high altitude they were able to drift back to England although they lost altitude steadily. Their brake system had also been shot out. Don's pilot made a landing at an emergency landing strip and stopped only after the airplane rolled off the end of the runway. No one was injured.

Staver Hyndman, Cherokee, Pilot, 398th Bomb Group: A cannon shell from a Luftwaffe fighter wounded his navigator in the groin area. Other cannon hits shot out two engines and caused minor damage to a third engine. His plane's entire hydraulic system was shredded and the electrical system damaged. They realized they were not going to make it back to England. He attempted a wheels-down landing with no brakes at a Royal Air Force base in Belgium. As he tried to land on a muddy field, the landing gear folded. Staver was able to spin the airplane around to a stop before they would crash into a construction area at the end of the runway. No one was injured in the landing.

John Megchelsen, Washington, Aerial Gunner, 91st Bomb Group: "Our horizontal stabilizers were shot up, one front tire was rendered flat, the tail wheel was shot off and the windshield was cracked. Numerous hits in the wings and fuselage was also taken. When they landed back at Bassingbourn on only one tire, they came to a stop only after they ran off the runway. No one was hurt.

Donald Fagen, Keota, Aerial Gunner, 100th Bomb Group: Over Berlin the number four engine of Don's aircraft was hit by flak. The back of the right wing was on fire. The Co-pilot put the plane into a steep dive and was able to put out the fire. After he recovered from the dive another engine stopped running and another engine was not running good. As they crossed the English channel on one engine and nearing the closest air base, Don's pilot was advised by the control tower to "go around" and get in the landing pattern. He replied, "like Hell, we're coming in."

Robert Peters, Grinnell, Navigator, 445th Bomb Group: As their aircraft returned to base one engine had been damaged and was not working. Their left landing gear had been destroyed by flak. Bob's pilot tried a one-legged landing with no brakes. It was decided the crew would open parachutes out the waist gunner's windows in a braking attempt. "The pilot brought the plane down beautifully on the right wheel, holding it there. When the parachutes were opened the one on

Staver Hyndman's B-17 after landing with no brakes

the left side inflated prematurely and caused us to make an immediate left turn off the runway. But we stopped and everyone was safe with no injuries."

Warren Ryan, Grinnell, Radio Operator, 96th Bomb Group: Over Hohenbudburg, Germany, Warren's aircraft took several flak hits that cut hydraulic lines. With no brakes Warren's pilot landed the airplane at the beginning of the runway. "We rolled and rolled and were finally stopped by a parked truck." No one was injured.

Father James O'Connor, Peosta, Co-Pilot, 388th Bomb Group: Over Schweinfurt, Germany, to bomb ball bearing plants, "the sky was black with flak, the worst I had ever seen. Flak was exploding all around our aircraft, tossing us around and shredding our plane with shrapnel. Flak had taken out the rudder and trim cables and at the moment of landing back at our base, we suddenly realized flak had also punctured one of our wheels. We had no way of knowing before landing that a tire was punctured. To be surprised by a blowout while landing at about 65 m.p.h. was a roller coaster experience. This happened to us when we returned from two other missions. Each time we managed to pull off the runway into the infield in order to clear the landing strip for other incoming ships, some of which, had wounded aboard, were damaged or dangerously low on fuel."

Vern Nyhus, Mason City, Radio Operator/Gunner, 390th Bomb Group: Flak on our missions was always accurate and we would come back to base with a lot of holes in our plane. When an anti-aircraft shell exploded it would throw the airplane upward. You could hear the shrapnel hitting the plane. We had an engine knocked out on one mission that caused the whole plane to shake and vibrate when the engine's propeller windmilled out of control. We made it back to base and when we landed the wind milling prop broke loose and flew away from the plane."

Another problem on landing back at their home base was weather. The ever changeable, unpredictable English weather. When it was known weather would be unfavorable over the base at takeoff, over the target, or over the base on return, a mission may not be scheduled. Weather that was supposed to clear, sometimes didn't. Weather that was supposed to be clear, often changed for the worse. Returning to their base in fog, snow and heavy overcast was equally as difficult as taking off and assembling into formation to start a mission.

Leon Mehring, Cedar Rapids, Aerial Gunner, 305th Bomb Group: When we returned to England the weather front had not moved. The base commander decided to let the Group's planes down by circling and descending so many feet per minute, but everyone was on their own. There was bound to be some collisions. Every crewmember was at his position in the airplane blinking lamps on and off to warn other planes of their presence. Round and round we went over the English Channel for what seemed an eternity before we broke out in the clear, over water. When we did another B-17 was flying in formation with us." The two planes never saw each other and were both heading directly at a large ship in front of them. Leon's plane broke left and the other plane went right. Our navigator was lost and we were running low on fuel. If we couldn't find a landing field we would have to crash land. The co-pilot suddenly saw a long flame off to the right. It was an emergency field on the coast that burned fuel along the runway to lift the fog. "We landed when one engine was sputtering from lack of fuel. Before we came to a stop at the end of the runway two more engines had cut out. We taxied only a short way on one engine when it ran out of fuel."

Russell Logue, Norwalk, Radio Operator, 392nd Bomb Group: "We returned to Wendling in a snowstorm with only two working engines. The other two had been shot out by flak during the mission." Unable to see their runway, Russell took a radio direction finding and relayed the information to the pilot. He continued to give the pilot headings so directional corrections could be made. "The first pass we flew right down the runway but we were too far down it before the pilot saw it, so we flew past and went around again. On our second try we landed on the snow covered runway. Unable to stop we slid off the end of the runway and stopped in a ditch. No one was hurt."

James Hamilton, Council Bluffs, Pilot, 95th Bomb Group: "We got shot up pretty bad during the bomb run. We lost two engines and a third one was running at only half power. We broke from the formation and began a gradual descent of about one hundred feet per minute. We had to hide in clouds from German fighters. We made it back to England and landed on an airstrip in East Anglia. Coming over the tops of trees I saw two runways. One had concrete obstructions on it to prevent anyone from landing on it. I gave what power the plane had left to make it to the second airstrip. I couldn't get the plane stopped and we ran off the end of the runway."

"On another mission we had no hydraulics so the wheels had to be hand-cranked down. When we landed we couldn't stop until we ran off the runway, through a fence and into a kale patch."

George Armington, Sioux Center, 379th BG, inspects battle damage.

Inspecting battle damage after return from a mission

Eugene Stientjes, Pella, Pilot, 93rd Bomb Group: Two engines were lost on a mission to Holland. Unable to hold altitude we attempted to return to England. We threw everything we could out of the aircraft to lighten our load. Weather had closed in over England and visibility was down to 700 feet. An American P-47 Thunderbolt fighter flew as escort and signaled us where our airfield was. "Our wheels reached the fully down position just as we hit the runway."

Burl Beam, Martensdale, Pilot, 398th Bomb Group: Returning to England from one mission their base was "socked in" due to weather with visibility down to one thousand feet. "Actually there was no visibility at all. We were down so low I saw a tree coming at us through the fog. I gave the engines full throttle and pulled up and away just in time to miss it. Our radio operator was able to get us to an auxiliary field."

Bud Jenson, Cedar Rapids, Radio Operator, 379th BG, Kimbolton, England: "On a raid to Merseburg we had two engines knocked out from "flak". We kept losing altitude and threw out everything we could to maintain altitude. When we dropped the ball turret out, our plane jumped up from loss of weight. We were trying to call MFDF stations to find out where we were. They would call back our coordinates. We navigated back to England on radio calls and were able to make one last pass at an emergency field before we landed there out of gas."

Allen Gartman, Maquoketa, Aerial Gunner, 34th Bomb Group: On return to our base the weather was a complete "white out". As we approached our base I looked out the window and thought "it won't be long now and we'll be on the ground". That thought was interrupted when the pilot gunned the airplane and gained altitude. We weren't anywhere near the direction of the runway. The second time trying to land I looked out one side and going by was a hangar and on the other side there were trees and they were higher than we were. I thought "Oh, boy, this is it". On the third approach he made it, he couldn't see where we were going. That was strictly flying by the seat of your pants."

After landing and parking, crews emptied their aircraft. It was inspected for battle damage and mechanical problems reported to crew chiefs. Previously issued equipment was turned in and crews reported to a briefing room complex for interrogation by intelligence personnel. Common questions posed were whether or not the target was hit, where they encountered "flak" and enemy fighter opposition, enemy fighter tactics, bombers seen to be hit and go down, parachutes seen exiting stricken aircraft, and claims for enemy fighters shot down.

Don Fennell, tailgunner, 305th BG, Chelveston, had a replacement gunner for him on mission when German fighters severely damaged rear of his aircraft killing the replacement.

Houser Plane on fire

Houser's B-17 broke apart after landing.

Iowans of the Mighty Eighth

Howard Breson, Dubuque, Crew Chief, 96th BG, Snetterton Heath, England: Howard was on the flight line directing two aircraft to their parking hard stands. The planes had just returned from a bombing mission to Kassel, Germany. In one of the bombers a ball turret gunner had a .50 caliber bullet jammed in his weapon and while trying to clear his guns, the bullet fired. It struck Howard in the right calf of his leg and "blew if off".

Film from bomb strike cameras was developed, reviewed and reports filed to higher command which included aircraft damage, enemy aircraft claims and the location and strength of flak. Missing in action forms had to be completed for crews and individuals. Return of a mission meant ground crew's work began again. Routine maintenance was performed on each bomber and minor damage repaired to ready them for a possible mission the next day. Fuel tanks and oxygen systems were replenished and the bomber brought to a serviceable standard as quickly as possible. Major battle damage and engineering problems was a different story. Ground crews might have to work all night to get an aircraft ready for the next day. In cases when this was impossible and required major structure and engineering repair, the aircraft was flown to a Base Air Depot (BAD) or repair made at the base by a mobile team from a BAD.

Following de-briefing the aircrews were released. The resilient ones went to the Officer's or NCO clubs for a drink and to relive the mission all over again. For most, however, it meant bed and rest. In just a few hours they might have to do it all over again.

Ground crew "sweating out return of aircraft from mission. Gaylord Henryson, Story City, Crew Chief, 91st BG, in center with raised bill of cap

Ambulances at 305th BG, Chelveston, wait return of aircraft from mission to give aid to the wounded and rush them to the base hospital.

Chapter Thirteen

SPECIAL MISSIONS

Ground Support - The dismantling of German industry and economy took two years before its military was significantly weakened to gamble on an invasion of the continent. Despite the bombings Germany still had strong and well-equipped ground forces. Pre-invasion bombardment of enemy occupied territory was designed to further weaken its transportation system. It was intended to eliminate German fighters from the invasion area by pushing their operational airstrips deeper within Germany and create long distances for them to fly and therefore expend more fuel. Coastal defenses, military and transportation targets were bombed over a large area in Normandy to disguise where the planned invasion was to take place. Photographic reconnaissance of invasion areas was made to gain intelligence on where and what type of coastal defenses existed.

Eighth Air Force aircrews flew two and as many as three missions on D-Day in support of the allied invasion on June 6, 1944, bombing enemy troop concentrations, road junctions, bridges and communication centers. Fighters attacked convoys bringing supplies and reinforcements to the battlefront.

John Meyer, Waverly, was a bombardier with the 466th Bomb Group at Attlebridge, England. "The night of June 5, 1944, our base was closed down. No one was allowed to leave and we were told to go to bed early. We knew then that this was it. We were awakened at eleven o'clock that night, ate, and went to mission briefing. We would be bombing at low altitude just ahead of our landing forces. We had to be at a precise location at a precise time. This was one of the greatest times in history and here I was taking part in it."

Robert Peters, Grinnell, was a navigator with the 445th Bomb Group at Tibenham, England. His first mission was in support of the D-Day invasion when his crew bombed railroad yards at St. Lo, France. "It was unbelievable, even at 20,000 feet, to see the English Channel filled with ships and boats from the invasion. The sky was filled with airplanes going to and from France on bombing and strafing missions."

Post-invasion photograph of Normandy invasion area showing results of pre-invasion bombardment.

121

Wallace Albert, Marengo, aerial gunner, 392nd Bomb Group: Three missions were flown on D-Day in support of the invasion. "The first mission I could see ships leaving the English ports. The second mission they were midway and the third mission there were so many ships in the English Channel you could walk across the Channel on their decks."

Dr. J.J. Cecil, Spirit Lake, pilot, 466th Bomb Group: "We flew raids against villages that gave access to roads leading to the invasion beach, bridges, rail and road junctions and German airfields."

Warren Dedrickson, Clarinda, aerial gunner, 466th Bomb Group: "My twenty-third mission was flown in support of D-Day. I was awestruck to see the largest invasion fleet ever assembled below me. It was quite a sight to see."

In the days following the invasion the Eighth Air Force would continue to fly support missions support to ensure ground troops had secured a foothold on the continent, major defensive positions of the enemy were attacked and eventually the Allies "broke out" into France.

Stanley Potter, Marion, bombardier, 385th Bomb Group: Assigned to a low-level mission to bomb a bridge that would prevent German reinforcements from reaching the front lines after D-Day, "we popped over a large hill into a valley. We came upon the bridge too fast to release our bombs. German tanks were massing near the bridge, so we acted as if we were flying away and then came back. We dropped our bombs right in the middle of the tanks and our gunners were strafing the ground as we flew. We bombed the living hell out of them. Tanks were flying through the air."

Joe Pfiffner, Waterloo, an aerial gunner with the 458th Bomb Group at Horsham St. Faith, England began his overseas tour of duty as a B-24 crew member hauling gasoline in wing tanks to forward bases in support of General Patton's armored force.

Raymond Carlson, Walcott, navigator, 466th Bomb Group: We flew our B-24s loaded with gasoline on low-level flights to France in support of Patton's armor. Flying at only 200 feet we landed at captured airfields. Troops swarmed all over our plane to unload the fuel the instant we stopped."

Germany made a "last gasp" effort to take the offensive on December 16, 1944, which became known as the Battle of the Bulge. Weather prevented retaliation by allied air forces and allowed a spearhead of Germans tanks and ground troops to penetrate deep into Allied-held territory. When weather permitted flying, Eighth Air Force aircraft dropped much needed supplies and ammunition to American ground forces. German troop concentrations and armored forces, convoys, bridges and roads were bombed to alleviate possible dire consequences for some American forces that were surrounded in Belgium. Their stubborn resistance, re-supply by air and arrival of armored forces caught German forces with over-extended supply lines and their offensive ground to a halt for want of fuel.

Ed Kelly, Corydon, was an aerial gunner with the 44th Bomb Group at Shipdham, England. During the Battle of the Bulge Ed's crew flew low-level missions in support of ground forces. "Armament was stripped from our B-24s. Crates of supplies were roped together in the bomb bay area and hooked to bomb releases. When alerted the bomb bay was emptied and we in the back of the plane pushed other supplies out. Then all hell broke loose. We saw a German officer firing his pistol at our plane. A machine gun on the ground managed to shoot off part of the wing on the plane next to us. The plane went into the ground hitting a tree. A guy on one plane got his feet entangled in the ropes attached to the supplies and was dragged out of his plane."

Wayne Zeigler, Iowa Falls, was a B-17 pilot with the 385th Bomb Group at Great Ashfield, England. On January 2, 1945, on a mission to bomb German Tiger tanks behind the front lines during the Battle of the Bulge, three engines of his airplane were lost. The crew was forced to bail out and fortunately landed twenty miles behind American front lines.

Robert Harken, Ackley, pilot, 466th Bomb Group: Bob flew Christmas Day, 1944; January 1, 1945 and three days in between hauling gasoline in support of General Patton's Third Army trying to reach surrounded American forces in the Battle of the Bulge.

Ellsworth Shields, Waverly, radio operator/aerial gunner, 458th Bomb Group: Ellsworth flew nine missions hauling gasoline in five gallon cans to support General Patton's advance through France. "The gas fumes n the bombers were very heavy. All that was needed was a spark and you would blow up. Our flight engineer used to say "I'm going to keep the bomb bay doors partially open to let fresh air come in all the time."

The Eighth would fly more supply missions in support of ground forces. Next came the crossing of the Rhine River, the last natural barrier in Germany blocking the way to Berlin. British and American airborne forces parachuted into enemy rear areas after initial crossings of the Rhine River had been made by British forces. The Eighth Air Force flew low-level supply missions to support the paratroopers.

Lavern Peters, Bedford, was an aerial gunner with the 389th Bomb Group at Norwich, England. On March 24, 1945, the bomb bay area of his and nearly

Chapter Thirteen

250 other bombers were filled with medical supplies, ammunition and weapons. The supply drop was to be made flying at a 400 foot level. Lavern could see dead American paratroopers hanging in trees, shot before they could get free of their parachutes. The aircraft were easy prey for small arms fire from the ground and fourteen bombers were lost on the mission.

Darrell Reed, Cherokee, was a radio operator/gunner with the 445th Bomb group at Tibenham, England. Waiting to take-off on the mission Darrell noticed the sky filled with C-47 cargo planes carrying paratroopers and pulling gliders filled with airborne troops. Flying into their cargo drop zone at 150 feet Darrell could see the destruction of war, dead animals and men, towns on fire and wrecked gliders. The pilot slowed the bomber almost to a stall and sounded an alarm bell alerting the crew to release the cargo. Darrell lost his balance and was ready to fall out of his aircraft when an Associated Press reporter flying as observer grabbed Darrell's parachute harness and pulled him to safety. A crewman was seen falling out of another aircraft.

Dick Lynch, Conrad, was an aerial gunner with the 44th Bomb Group a Shipdam, England, and also flew on the supply mission. "The airplanes flying on both sides of me were hit by ground fire and crashed. We crossed the drop zone into the area where the gliders landed and then bullets began flying. A crew on our wing went down and blew sky high, then another, it was terrible. I wasn't scared until after we got back across the Rhine then I really was nervous. We had twenty-two holes in our plane."

Glenn Hill, Fairfield, aerial gunner, 466th Bomb Group flew a low-level bombing mission down the Ruhr Valley. "Flak guns opened up on us. It was like shooting ducks. A lot of planes were hit and went down. No parachutes were seen coming from them. We got hit but were still able to continue. The tail gunner's parachute had an .88mm shell go through it. If he needed it, it was worthless."

Shuttle Misssions

Six current Eighth Air Force Historical Society members participated in a shuttle mission to Poltava, Russia, on June 26, 1944:
Howard Croner, Estherville, Flight Engineer/Aerial Gunner, 452nd Bomb Group
Marion Ferguson, Washington, Radio Operator/Aerial Gunner, 452nd Bomb Group

Portion of aircraft destroyed at Poltava

Frederick Miller, Des Moines, Aerial Gunner, 458th Bomb Group
Raymond Schleihs, Johnston, Pilot, 390th Bomb Group
Richard Taylor, Cedar Rapids, Pilot, 388th Bomb Group
Vernon Torreson, Wallingford, Radio Operator/Aerial Gunner, 452nd Bomb Group

Plans called for a target at Ruhland, Germany, south of Berlin to be bombed. The distance back to England was too great for the fuel capacity of the B-17 to make a return flight. Arrangements had been made with the Russian government for the aircraft to fly on to Poltava where they would be re-fueled, re-armed and another target bombed in Germany on their return flight to England. Unknown to the bomber formation a German fighter plane shadowed the formation to its destination. That night with the aircraft parked on the Poltava airstrip, the Luftwaffe attacked the base for one hour bombing and strafing the aircraft. Little or ineffective anti-aircraft fire was directed against the attackers. Russian night fighters had a half-hour advance notice of the Luftwaffe's approach but failed to make contact with the enemy. Of the seventy-one aircraft that landed at Poltava, estimates ranged between forty-seven to sixty B-17s destroyed and many others damaged as well as loss of fuel and ordnance supplies. The bomber crews sought safety of slit trenches when aircraft sirens wailed the approach of enemy aircraft and could only watch helplessly as the attack took place. It took three weeks for the crews to be picked up and returned to England through North Africa. Said Howard Croner, " No one who was there will ever forget that night on the airfield at Poltava."

George Popelka, Cedar Rapids, 390th Bomb Group participated on a later Russian shuttle mission. They were to bomb a target in Poland and fly on to Poltava.

Iowans of the Mighty Eighth

While over Poland their aircraft was hit by "flak" and disabled to the extent they fell behind the rest of their bomber formation. Unable to make it to Poltava they landed at the nearest Russian airstrip they could find. Their aircraft was deemed not repairable. George and his crew were fortunate to be flown to Egypt by the Russians. From there American transport flew them through Libya and Casablanca, Morocco back to England.

Frederick Miller, Des Moines, Bombsight and Auto-Pilot Mechanic, 390th BG, Framlingham, England: "Each aircraft on the mission took a ground crew person with a specialty to make needed repairs once we landed in Russia. I also served as waist gunner. That evening German aircraft bombed and strafed the Russian airfield and destroyed the majority of the American bombers. We were at an airfield near there and believed they would come and bomb us the next night so we took off and flew to a Fifteenth Air Force airfield in Italy."

George Popelka, Cedar Rapids, on center camel during rest stop on way back to England from Poltava mission.

Chapter Fourteen
VICTORY

On June 6, 1944, D-Day, Allied armies invaded the European continent and began to sweep across France toward Germany. The underbelly of Europe had also been invaded at Sicily and Italy and American and allied forces advanced northward. After stubborn resistance Rome was captured in June, 1944. In the East, Russian armies, after halting German forces at the door step of their capital, began a Spring and Summer offensive that made major advances toward Germany when heavy German armored forces were defeated and oil refineries at Ploesti were captured. The British Royal Air Force and American 8th, 9th and 15th Air Forces continued their assault on Germany aircraft and armament production centers, transportation and oil facilities. They supported ground forces and gradually eliminated the Luftwaffe as a defending force.

In July, 1944, a bomb plot to kill Hitler by some members of his General Staff and others within the hierarchy of the Third Reich failed. Revenge was taken against those both responsible and believed involved.

In August, 1944, American and allied armies from Southern France linked with invading forces from Normandy. Paris was liberated late in the month. The Polish Home Army began an uprising against German forces in Warsaw.

Greece, Yugoslavia, and Norway were liberated. Allied armies captured the port city of Antwerp, Belgium, which began their liberation of that country and crossed the German frontier. Russian armies captured the capital of Hungary. Hitler's Third Reich was crumbling but resistance grew as armies advanced closer to the German capital. Heavy fighting both in the air and on the ground remained.

In December, 1944, Germany massed its armored and ground forces for a last gasp effort for victory by launching a surprise offensive through the Ardennes. It was nearly successful. Over-stretched from fuel, ammunition and supply lines, American forces were surrounded in one of Europe's worst winters on record in what was termed The Battle of the Bulge Outnumbered and nearly out of food and ammunition the troops held on until they were relieved by on-rushing American armored forces.

By the Spring of 1945 advancing American and British ground forces had captured major industrial cities in Germany. The Rhine River was breached and as Allied armies captured the countryside, Russian forces lay siege to the German capital.

The German war machine virtually ceased to exist. The German Army had its back to the wall and also nearly out of fuel, food, and ammunition, began to surrender in droves. Only the diehards remained in Berlin where they were systematically eliminated by Russian forces. Adolph Hitler in his underground bunker in the heart of Berlin still believed wonder weapons, which existed only in his mind, would save the Third Reich from destruction and bring ultimate victory.

On April 28, Italian partisans killed Mussolini, the dictator of Italy. Hitler, on April 30th, finally realized all was lost and fearing capture by the Russians, committed suicide along with his mistress Eva Braun, Joseph Goebbels, his Minister of Propaganda and his family.

On May 7, 1945, German military forces, now under Admiral Doenitz, signed an unconditional surrender at Rheims, France, and the next day Victory in Europe was proclaimed. World War II in the European Theater of Operations, was over.

For Europeans the celebration was indescribable. Bob Houser, 306th BG, Thurleigh, was in Paris the evening of V-E Day where "they were dancing in the streets" celebrating the end of the war. Lowell Blizzard, 96th BG, Snetterton Heath, was on leave in Edinburgh, Scotland, where he took part in the celebration with people singing and dancing in the streets.

Floyd Nielsen, Pocahontas, 25th BG, Watton: "I celebrated by getting on top of our barracks roof, which was a flat roof, and shooting off a whole case of different colored flares with a Very pistol."

James Bottenfield, 452nd BG, Deopham Green: "On V-E Day we were told not to leave the base but we sneaked off anyway. They closed all the bars because of how we might celebrate. Some guys were shooting off flares in a Very pistol and caught some English farmer's haystacks on fire. When some guys started shooting their .45 caliber pistols in the air things were called to a halt."

Richard Lynch, Conrad, 44th BG, Shipdham: "No one at our base was excited. Just another day. I wondered how the people at home were taking it."

George Hoffman, Leon, 303rd BG, Molesworth, had completed his required number of missions and believed he was on one of the first boats to arrive in New York harbor following V-E Day. "The reception and partying taking place in New York harbor for the returnees was wild, to say the least."

Jim Hoy, Eldora, second from right, and friends celebrate VE-Day

Warren Ryan, Grinnell, 96th BG, Snetterton Heath, had learned his wife was pregnant while he was overseas. He returned to the United States by boat after completing his tour and boarded a train for St. Louis. When the train arrived there he learned the war in Europe was over. He made it home in time to be at his wife Clara's side when the baby was born two days later.

Keith Shirk's last mission was on March 9, 1945, a raid on Munster, Germany. He returned home to Grundy Center and arrived on May 8, 1945, V-E Day.

On May 12, 1945, fifteen hundred United States heavy bombers and fighters, in battle formation, flew a victory salute over England.

For American forces in Europe victory was short-lived. More work remained. Liberated prisoners of war had to be returned to American military custody. Civilians in countries under Nazi rule had subsisted on starvation rations and had to be fed. American forces were required to occupy Germany. Those that were returned to the United States began training for possible re-deployment to the Pacific Theater of Operations. The Japanese, by this stage of the war would soon lose the Philippines, Okinawa, Borneo, Thailand, New Guinea, China and had been pushed back to their home islands vowing to die to the last man. They still had to be defeated.

While most prisoners of war were liberated by Allied armies just prior to V-E Day, the vast numbers of them that had been interned throughout Germany, Poland and Austria, required time to transport them back to Allied hands for medical attention, de-lousing, clothing, food, and processing. After the POWs had been moved to the nearest airstrip that could accommodate bombers and transport aircraft a massive airlift of POWs was orchestrated. Numerous aircrews volunteered to fly the "Revival" flights and return the POWs.

Thomas McElherne, Ames, 388th BG, Knettishall, was a prisoner of war. The Germans evacuated his camp and the POWs ordered to walk to escape onrushing Allied ground forces. At night they stayed in any nearby woods or in farm buildings. One morning near Denmark, the POWs woke to find their German guards gone. They were soon liberated by English soldiers and flew by transport plane to France and then trucked to Camp Lucky Strike, a processing center for POWs. In route they saw soldiers celebrating. They learned Germany had surrendered.

Earl Brindley, Atlantic, Radio Operator/Aerial Gunner, 398th Bomb Group: Earl flew two missions to pick up American prisoners of war from Stalag Luft I at Barth, Germany. "We had orders not to shut down our engines when we landed on a former German airstrip. POWs were waiting in plane load groups. As soon as each bomber landed and taxied to a POW group, they were herded aboard the aircraft and it took off for Camp Lucky Strike, a POW processing camp near Le Havre, France."

Ralph Pender, Cedar Falls, Flight Engineer, 388th Bomb Group: "After V-E Day we flew to Germany to pick up American prisoners of war and flew them back to England."

Howard Cropp, Cedar Rapids, pilot, 401st Bomb Group: "We flew to Linz, Austria, where we picked up English prisoners of war and returned them to England."

Lee Gingery, Shenandoah, Radio Operator, 351st Bomb Group: "The most worthwhile and totally in-

Chapter Fourteen

teresting experience of my military career was flying with a skeleton crew to Linz, Austria, for the purpose of transporting Frenchmen back to France who had recently been released from Mauthausen Concentration Camp. Two to three hundred prisoners had been dying each day at the camp from exhaustion and malnutrition under Nazi rule. I made two trips there."

Norman Mutchler, Waverly, Pilot, 486th Bomb Group: "We flew a low-level flight at about 500 feet to Linz, Austria, where thirty-two French slave laborers were picked up and flown to Paris. I had to be sprayed with delousing powder before and after the mission to avoid being infested by the refugees who were poor, starved and looked like animals."

William Rich, Clear Lake, Pilot, 487th Bomb Group: "In June, 1945, we delivered boxed food to an airport near Linz, Austria, for starving civilians. French prisoners of war, men, women and children were taken aboard our plane and flown to a steel mat landing strip near Paris. The POWs were off-loaded and we returned to England. To return the people to their homeland, feed the starving people and attend to their needs was extremely heart warming."

Jack Perrin, Cherokee, 390th BG, Framlingham, England, was part of an aircrew that flew to Linz, Austria, to pick up Allied prisoners of war. Jack had earlier learned that a constant companion of his at Cherokee was a POW somewhere in Europe. After he returned from the mission, aircrews lined up along the sidewalk leading to the mess hall to allow the POWs to eat first. "This guy walked past me and I couldn't tell but I thought it was Jim. The guy had lost so much weight. When I saw the back of his head I knew it was Jim and yelled out his name. What a reunion! We spent seven days in London partying and I almost missed my plane to fly back home to America."

Ground crew personnel including mechanics, armorers, ordnance and other base personnel who had dutifully kept the bombers and fighters flying throughout the war, were treated with tour flights of Germany, and targeted areas of Holland and France. The purpose was for them to see firsthand, the destruction inflicted by the Eighth Air Force as a result of their tireless efforts to keep their aircraft in the air. They were a crucial part of the over-all team that brought victory to the free world and deserved to witness results of their "behind the scenes" efforts to crush Hitler's Third Reich.

Even before the war in Europe was over, missions were flown to Holland to drop food to the Dutch population who had lived on starvation diets under Nazi rule. The countryside had been flooded by the Germans to prevent advances by Allied armies into the country. Arrangements were made with the Germans to allow American bombers to fly a corridor through the country in order to drop food to the starving Dutch. To stray outside the limitations of the corridor meant the bombers would be fired upon with the risk of being shot down. On May 1, 1945, American bombers began their "Chow Hound" missions. The Dutch were expecting them and marked targets where the low flying bombers were to drop the food. Ground crew personnel got into the act by flying the mission to help kick the food containers out of bomb bay areas. Most food missions, however, were flown immediately after Victory in Europe had been won.

Jack Fernhout, West Des Moines, Aerial Gunner, 95th BG, Horham, England: "We came in at low-level and pushed the bales of food out the bomb bay doors. They had a cross formed by muslin on a field as a target for us. We went on our own, there was no formation flown. From my tail position I threw out a large tin of English "bully beef". I watched the tin crash through the roof of a house. I can still see the red tiles on the roof explode when it hit. I hope no one was hurt. Some people were killed by falling food parcels."

Lowell Blizzard, Oskaloosa, Mechanic/Crew Chief, 96th Bomb Group: "To see the Dutch people

Sign painted on roof of building greets bombers dropping food to the Dutch "The moment we all expected. Thank you!!"

waving and rushing to the food parcels as they were dropped was extremely heartwarming."

Donald Lynam, Greenfield, aerial gunner, 493rd Bomb Group: "Still held by the Germans, the Netherlands had been flooded to prevent the Allies from taking the territory. The Dutch people were reduced to near starvation under Nazi rule. Despite war, the Germans allowed American airplanes to drop food to the Dutch with the provision they would not be fired on if they flew a certain route. It was a heartwarming mission to see the starving people waving and smiling at the American formations when food was dropped to them."

Ralph Pender, Cedar Falls, Engineer, 388th Bomb Group: "Ralph flew two missions to Holland to drop food to the Dutch. "They outlined a large circle we were to drop the supplies in. The food was in "gunny sacks' loaded in the bomb bay area of our plane. Some sacks got "hung up" and I had to go down in the bomb bay and kick them free. We had to make three passes over the drop zone to empty the plane."

Jack Perrin, Cherokee, aerial gunner, 390th Bomb Group: "A large "X" had been drawn on a soccer field as a target for American bombardiers. The canned goods and other supplies missed, crashing through the roof of a nearby barn, smashing out the side walls allowing livestock in the barn to escape."

Robert Schreiner, Waterloo, aerial gunner, 493rd Bomb Group: "I flew two food missions to Holland. It was very heart warming to be greeted with the people on rooftops, spelling out "Thanks, Yanks" in tulips and waving in appreciation."

Laverne Sedore, Fairfield, Pilot, 493rd Bomb Group: "Our bombers were loaded with food. We flew across the Channel at low altitude and dropped the food on a racetrack on the outskirts of Amsterdam. These people knew we were coming. They were there by the thousands. We came over so low, we could see their mouths were open and they were waving like crazy. We did that for two consecutive days. It was a real upper."

Russell Clingan, Des Moines, 100th BG, Thorpe Abbots, England, had already completed his tour of missions but remained in England to fly food missions to the Dutch.

John Beckman, Ankeny, 490th BG, Eye, England, flew twenty-eight combat missions and finished off his tour with two "Chowhound" missions over Holland.

As men finished their tour of duty in Europe they were rotated back to the United States for re-assignment to other duties. Some were able to fly back aboard war-weary aircraft while others returned on ships ranging from ocean liners converted to carrying troops to Kaiser built Victory ships and cargo vessels. Many had finished their required number of missions before V-E Day, quietly arrived in New York and boarded trains for their next reporting station and furlough home. After V-E Day, the volume of returning servicemen at first appeared astronomical.

Harbor at Liverpool, England. Heading Home

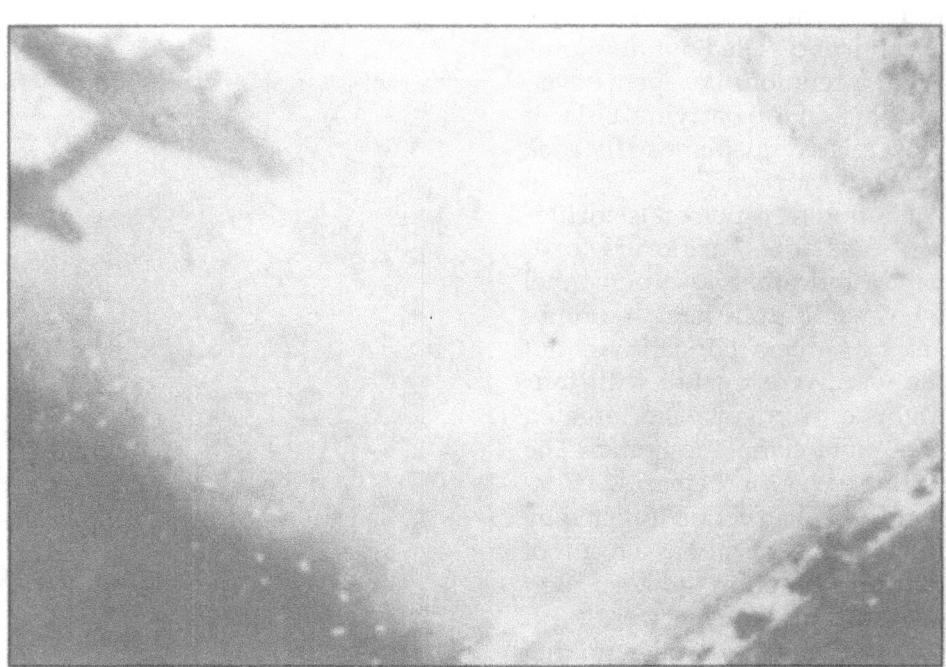

Shadow on ground of B-17 dropping food suplies to the Dutch. White specks on lower left corner are food parcels falling to the ground.

Chapter Fourteen

By July, 1945, planes carrying Eighth Air Force personnel left England at the rate of one plane every twenty minutes. Over two thousand bombers carrying nearly forty-two thousand men had been re-deployed to the United States. They would trickle in from Europe for months after the war had ended.

The voyage home met with the same problems they experienced going to Europe-storms and seasickness. John DeLorbe, Waterloo, returned to the United States in May, 1945, aboard a Victory ship. The voyage was highlighted by "a storm with deep wave troughs that would lift the rear of the ship out of the water." "The ship's propellers would cause the ship to shudder each time they spun in open air."

Jim Haas, Perry, spent ten days aboard ship returning to America. "Most of the trip was spent in a storm. I got seasick and just wanted to die. I just got over flying my thirty-five missions. I couldn't eat or get my head off the pillow."

Wilmer Link, Dubuque, boarded the "George Washington" in December, 1945. While at sea his ship ran into a severe storm. "We were hit sideways nearly capsizing. An SOS was sent but ship's personnel finally gained control of the ship for the balance of the trip."

Dick Van Duyn, Iowa City, returned to the United States in February, 1946, aboard a Liberty Ship in rough seas and storms. "The ship's captain had to sail south through the Azores to get into calmer waters."

Donald Richards, Waterloo, returned to the United States in January, 1946, aboard the "U.S.S. Wasp". "One day out of England, instead of returning to port to avoid a storm, the ship's Captain sailed South running directly into the storm. An SOS was sent after part of the deck was torn from the ship. Hangar decks and lower decks were awash from seawater. The ship was able to continue and make it to America. All personnel were without food for three days during the trip until repairs could be made."

Erwin Stamp, Holstein, was part of occupation forces in Germany and didn't return to the United States until the end of March, 1946. The ship he sailed on encountered two storms, which virtually lifted the ship out of the water and caused widespread seasickness.

For others no storms were encountered during the voyage home yet the ships were over-

Children carrying food supplies dropped by Allied aircraft.

One of the starving Dutch children who was a recipient of much needed food.

crowded and sailing time seemed an eternity, especially long when filled with the anticipation of finally getting home.

Wallace Albert, Marengo, sailed home aboard an old German luxury liner by a southern route that took twenty-one days to make it to New York

Maynard Johnson, Sibley, sailed home on a cargo ship that took seventeen days to make the voyage.

Lowell Rothbart, Dewitt, was aboard a Kaiser Liberty ship that took seventeen days to sail from England to New York. The ship had boiler trouble necessitating a stop at Newfoundland for repair. While there it snowed three feet in a three hour period. When they arrived in New York, the ship was quarantined because two men had died in route and were kept in the ship's cooler.

Bob Peters, Grinnell, returned to the United States in October, 1944 aboard the "Queen Mary". "Singer/dancer/actor Fred Astaire was also aboard and spent almost every waking moment entertaining the troops."

Les Portwood, Boone, sailed home aboard a Victory ship and docked in New York harbor the day the war ended with Japan. A band playing "Sentimental Journey" was on hand to greet them.

Combat wounded returned to the United States aboard ships during all stages of the war. This includes hospital ships, ships converted to a hospital ship and aboard ocean liners carrying other troops. Kermit Neubauer, Iowa Falls, had completed his required number of missions for rotation back to the United States. In November, 1944, he boarded the "Queen Mary" along with 2,500 wounded soldiers and 3,000 other military personnel heading home. Kermit volunteered to help take care of the wounded during the night. He was so happy to see the Statute of Liberty he tossed his helmet overboard at the Statute's feet.

Everett Dexter, Marshalltown, sailed back to America aboard a hospital ship and assisted the medical staff tending to wounded GIs aboard.

Glen Hill, Fairfield, returned to the United States in May, 1945, aboard a Liberty Ship that had been converted to a hospital ship. Aboard were American prisoners of war freed from German prison camps. Glenn and others volunteered to do work on the ship which otherwise would have to be done by the POWs. "They were thin, poor, just like animals. Many got seasick-felt sorry for the poor devils."

Jimmy Wilson, Waterloo, was shot down over Germany. He avoided capture for more than a year before making it back to American control. "When we arrived in New York harbor I saw a sight I shall never forget: the Statute of Liberty. What a thrill! I shall never forget that moment. When I saw her I said a little prayer. I thanked God for being with me and for bringing me home safe. I vowed that when I got back home and if I got married and had a home of my own I would fly the Stars and Stripes out in front of my house every single day of my life. And I have kept that promise."

Others were able to fly home. Gene Person, Ft. Dodge, left England with scheduled stops at Iceland and Labrador. His plane landed at Labrador with only fifteen minutes fuel remaining.

Ward Britson, Radcliffe, was to fly from Scotland through the Azores and Newfoundland to Massachusetts. When they landed in the Azores a leak in a fuel tank was discovered that required a delay in getting it repaired. In the meantime, his pilot with thirty-nine missions to his credit began celebrating their return to America too early. He got into trouble with local military authorities and it was another five days before the matter was cleared, or forgotten, and they resumed their flight.

Others were not so fortunate. After surviving combat missions, they were lost on flights home from weather-related crashes, lack of fuel or mechanical problems. Herbert Autenreith, Jefferson, 351st BG, was one such returnee only minutes away from New York City when his aircraft crashed into the Atlantic Ocean from lack of fuel.

Those members of the Eighth Air Force that didn't return to the United States immediately after V-E Day were utilized to close American bases in England, ferry aircraft and serve as part of the occupation forces in Germany.

Ross King, Sioux City; Ivan Lindaman, Aplington; Leon Mehring, Cedar Rapids; and Arthur Petersen, Mason City, were all members of the 305th Bomb Group at Chelveston, England, that after the war in Europe ended, were sent to St. Trond, Belgium, to participate in a program named "Casey Jones". The Group photographed Europe, Iceland and the North Pole from 20,000 feet. Late in 1945, they moved to a German Air Base at Leichfield, Germany, near Munich, to continue photographic missions which included North Africa.

Other members of the Eighth served a variety of occupational force duties that included John Frampton, Reinbeck, who guarded captured German SS troops. Sydney Thomas, Waterloo, served as Weather Officer and flew missions until September, 1945, when he was re-assigned as weather officer in Germany aiding aircraft returning to the United States and other non-combat related missions. Ray Marner, Iowa City, spent eight months at a former Luftwaffe airfield at Neubiberg in aircraft mechanics. Robert

Chapter Fourteen

Myers, Tiffin, was Chief of Maintenance at Schweinfurt, Germany for American P-47 fighters based there. Ken Ranson, Cedar Rapids, was sent to Paris where he assisted in staging loaded bombers destined for Berlin in the early stages of the Berlin Airlift. George Roepke, Traer, was also sent to Neubiberg air base near Munich and saw the deplorable state of concentration camp prisoners at Dachau. Jack Frost, Des Moines, was part of occupation forces at a former Luftwaffe air base. Bruce Rust, Sheffield, in addition to his normal duties, in Germany, worked as a bouncer at a nightclub frequented by American troops. George Zachar, Davenport, was flown to Casablanca to service transport planes that were to ferry troops to the Far East in preparation for the invasion of Japan, if needed. While there, word came the Atomic Bomb had been dropped on Japan.

George Berry, Winterset, remained behind at his base at Rattlesden, England, to help clean up and close the base for return to the Royal Air Force. "I was on the last truck to leave the base."

Wayne Stellish, Aurelia, was assigned to the 306th BG at Thurleigh, England. He was one of the last members of the 306th to leave the base long after V-E Day. There was one B-17 left and ten servicemen remaining at the base. Before we took off to go to Gielbestadt, Germany, for occupation duty I walked through the previously busy headquarters building. "Nothing much was there anymore. The cold wind was banging the window shutters against the side of the building. It was like a ghost town now."

Those that returned to the United States after finishing their required number of missions for rotation and those returning after victory was won in Europe were either discharged on an earned point system or given new assignments. New assignments were either as instructors, training on the B-29 bomber for possible deployment to the Pacific Theater of Operations to help defeat Japan, or given temporary assignments until it could be decided what to do with them. The influx of returnees from Europe left the military unprepared as what to do with thousands of men. Many were granted furloughs and extended furloughs after that. Like many ground crew personnel who were sent to the European Theater of Operations in the early stages of the Eighth Air Force build-up, Arlan Nessa, Hubbard, and Bert Jenson, Cedar Rapids, in three years never received a furlough. Art Petersen, Mason City, served thirty-seven months in the Army Air Corps. His parents never saw him in uniform until after he had received his discharge.

Other returned personnel were assigned to a base and given nothing to do but report in each day. Others were in serious preparation for the Pacific.

The front page of the "Des Moines Tribune" newspaper dated May 12, 1945, proclaimed "Veterans of Europe and North Africa Won't Go to Pacific." "No more fighting for these men" guaranteed General Eisenhower, regarding combat soldiers who had fought in both North Africa and Europe. Whether or not this pertained to air forces is not known. In April, 1945 over 200,000 men were shipped to the European Theater of Operations. To re-deploy them from Europe to the Far East would take two months by ship.

It was planned well in advance of the German surrender that the Eighth Air Force would be re-deployed to the Pacific to assist the 20th Air Force in bombing Japan. American forces had island hopped in the Pacific and captured islands in a string advancing toward Japan. With the capture of Guam, Tinian and Saipan in the Marianas, bases were now established that were within fuel range of B-29 bombers to bomb Japan.

Okinawa, the largest of the Japanese Ryukyu Islands was to be invaded in April, 1945, and once secured, would be a base for the Eighth Air Force to help in bombing Japan. Capture of Okinawa would disrupt sea communications and supply of Japanese forces in China and like the Marianas, well within bombing range.

Capture of Okinawa was slow. Japanese forces were well fortified in limestone caves and fighting to the last man. Build-up of the Eighth Air Force on the island was delayed. Three newly trained crews of the 346th Bomb Group were each assigned to a bomb group of the 20th Air Force in the Marianas to gain combat experience ahead of the rest of their Group. They would then be qualified to brief their group on what to expect once the balance of the 346th arrived on Okinawa, which was expected to be in August, 1945.

Doug Keen, Cherokee, was a B-29 aerial gunner with the 346th Bomb Group(VH) Very Heavy, of the Eighth Air Force. He and his crew were assigned to gain combat experience with the 330th Bomb Group of the 20th Air Force at Guam. "Our crew flew eleven combat missions against Japan. We flew both day and night missions that lasted 12-13 hours each. When Marines captured Iwo Jima, B-29 crews were really grateful for this emergency landing field. We landed on Iwo twice." When the two Atomic Bombs were dropped on Hiroshima and Nagasaki, Japan, in August, 1945, Japan sued for peace. Doug's last two missions were to pick up Allied prisoners of war at Osaka and the show of force fly-over Tokyo Bay during surrender proceedings aboard the "U.S.S. Missouri".

The 346th Bomb Group of the Eighth Air Force arrived on Okinawa as the war was ending and flew no missions. The three combat crews of the Eighth assigned to Bomb Groups of the 20th Air Force remain the only Eighth Air Force crews to bomb the Empire of Japan.

Some air force personnel stationed on Okinawa were transferred to the Eighth in advance of arrival of the 346th Bomb Group. W. L. Sypal, Des Moines, was a communications specialist with the 507th Fighter Group of the 20th Air Force at Ie Shima, a small island off the coast of Okinawa. "When Doolittle showed up to command Eighth Air Force units sent to the Pacific he told us "you are now in the 8th, change those patches"." (Air Force patches on uniforms.)

Robert Boice, Waterloo, was sent to the Pacific after serving in Europe where he flew thirty-five combat missions as radio operator/waist gunner. He returned from England in November, 1944, and was sent to the China/Burma Theater of Operations where he was part of a crew that hauled gasoline in B-24 bombers over "The Hump" from India to China. He made ninety trips over the Himalayas before being re-assigned to a DC-4 crew that evacuated troops from India. On one mission he bailed out of his aircraft into a jungle during a monsoon when his plane ran out of fuel on approach to their runway.

Dropping of the Atomic Bombs on Japan ended the most devastating war in history and without doubt saved millions of lives if the Japanese home island would have had to be invaded. Thousands of Eighth Air Force veterans in training for re-deployment to the Pacific Theater of Operations were now discharged from military service to resume their civilian lives and careers. Many would retain their association with the Air Force either as a career or in the Air Force Reserve or Air National Guard.

World War II claimed not only millions of lives of combatants, but millions of innocent civilians as a result of combat, bombing of the civilian population, organized extermination in concentration camps, massacre from racial hatred and bigotry, siege of cities and starvation from loss of food supply. By the time Japan was defeated, the loss of human life in World War II was the highest of any war in history and estimated to have been between 45 to 50 million people. It has been estimated that Russia lost seven million civilians, Chine ten million, Poland six million and Germany over two million. Military losses included nearly fifteen million from Russia, China over one million, Japan one and a half million, Yugoslavia nearly two million and Germany nearly three million.

Hitler's regime had displaced hundreds of thousands of people through slave labor and internment in concentration camps. At their moment of freedom thousands were still dying daily from starvation. An emergency airlift was required to prevent further deaths and return of the prisoners to their homeland. For many, freedom came too late. Their condition had deteriorated too far for recovery. Many would survive and search for years for their displaced loved ones or relatives. Some would be successful while most would not.

It would take years for the re-construction of Europe. It was politically disorganized, economically flattened and its labor force stripped by large-scale movement of its people. Bombing and fighting had left industry crippled in the war zones as well as agriculture through flooding and a scorched earth policy for advancing and retreating armies. Transportation systems, especially railroads as a priority target, were in need of massive repair. Most major cities of Europe had been reduced to rubble. Houses, stores, factories, schools had been obliterated.

To say the future looked bleak would be a gross under-statement. There were shortages of everything, food, medicine, housing, clothing, fuel, a distribution system for products and imports, machinery and seed to grow crops, and livestock and feed. Everywhere there was destruction and desolation. Dead still remained buried in the rubble of cities and the stench of decay was everywhere.

Life after the war ended became a struggle to survive as much as the war itself. People lived in caves, in hollowed out portions of the rubble in cities, basements of bombed out buildings or no where at all. By necessity they were consumed with finding shelter and the next meal. Thousands would starve to death. Germany was divided into four zones under the military control of Russia, France, England and the United States. Berlin, within the Russian zone was also divided into four occupational zones. When Russia denied access through their zone of Germany to supply Berliners within the French, English and America zones of Berlin, a massive airlift through an air corridor was required. Supply aircraft flew non-stop to bring food, fuel, medicine and other critical material and goods to the free people of Berlin. Massive American aid in the years immediately following World War II through the Marshall Plan helped lay the foundation on which European countries could and did recover.

On February 26, 1946, the last bomber of the Eighth Air Force took off from England at Honington Air Base to return to the United States. The last base used by the Eighth Air Force was officially returned to control of the Royal Air Force. The love affair between

Chapter Fourteen

the American G.I. and the people of England however, was not over. It has endured to this day.

"All the fine young men" who went off to war in World War II, without fanfare but with a sense of duty to their country, served and served well. They gave the best years of their lives to defeat Nazi Germany, lost their youth and grew up in a hurry. Many had completed thirty-five combat missions when they were nineteen and twenty years old. The youngest Eighth Air Force aircrew man completed twenty-six missions when he was seventeen years, one month and seven days old.

They flew in non-pressurized, unheated aircraft, where the temperature was as much as sixty degrees below zero. During their first combat experience they suddenly realized they were in a war and someone else was shooting back at them. They endured frostbite, collisions, "flak", enemy fighters, friendly fire and unfriendly weather and never turned back from a mission because of enemy action. They knew they were going to live or die together. Despite losses, fear, exhaustion, unbearable apprehension and loneliness their morale never broke. They kept going on until they finished their allotted missions or had been killed, wounded, or captured, whichever came first. What made them get into their fighters and bombers for each mission and keep going was their own pride and fear of not letting their buddies down. They were extraordinary men responding to extraordinary circumstances, knew the importance of what they were doing, and could see they were affecting the outcome of the war. They did their job and proved the case of daylight strategic bombing by weakening the Nazi war machine and its ability to wage war. Their role in destroying Germany's economic and industrial capability was immeasurable to ground forces that were required to take and occupy the country right to the heart of Berlin.

During the greatest airborne confrontation in history, the Eighth Air Force destroyed over 5,200 enemy aircraft in the air, 4,200 on the ground and 4,600 locomotives. In addition, countless bridges, armament and aircraft factories, oil and synthetic fuel refineries, railroad yards, tanks, shipping, and rocket sites were destroyed as well as providing support to Allied forces fighting on the ground.

The cost of war to the Eighth Air Force was not in the 6500 heavy bombers and 3300 fighters lost to combat, salvage, and non-operational losses. The cost was not in the millions of gallons of fuel and oil, food, equipment and materiel of all types. The cost of the war in Europe was in the 26,000 Eighth Air Force personnel killed in action, nearly one-tenth of all Americans killed in World War II, and the lasting effect their loss had on their comrades and concerned American families. For those who survived, "it was a great experience but I wouldn't want to do it over again."

Famed General, Jimmy Doolittle, a Commanding Officer of the Eighth Air Force, defined a hero as a person who does his duty with a sense of purpose. That qualifies each and every serviceman and woman and all on the home front in World War II who did their job to bring about Victory.

Interview of Iowa Eighth Air Force veterans some fifty-five plus years after the war, to a man, did not consider themselves a hero. To them, it was a part of the times in which they lived. To them "the real heroes were the ones that didn't make it back." "We had years of life they never did. We greatly honor their memory."

Chapter Fifteen

POW – PRISONER OF WAR

The three-year air war over Europe was a deadly affair. The Eighth Air Force sent thousands of bombers, fighters, weather and reconnaissance aircraft over German occupied territory following a policy of daylight strategic bombing. As air battles were waged in the skies, airmen were shot down at an alarming rate. Attacks by German fighter aircraft, anti-aircraft gun barrages and even equipment failure would cause air crewmen to die, shot in their airplanes when attacked, when their aircraft was blown apart or go down uncontrollably to crash. A fortunate few managed to survive by parachuting from their stricken airplane only to land in enemy held territory. Some evade capture but most were taken prisoner of war (POW).

It has been estimated that over 28,000 members of the Eighth Air Force were POWs during World War II. Some were able to escape capture when aided by members of various countries' underground forces. Local partisans fed, clothed, and hid airmen until they could arrange transportation to Allied control. Others found safe haven in neutral countries where they sat out the war.

For others, capture meant subsistence on a near starvation diet afford them by their captors, inadequate clothing and protection against the elements, unsanitary toilet facilities, uncertain water, barracks, mattresses and blankets infested with bugs, lice and vermin, exposure to a wide variety of sicknesses and possible epidemics. In addition to receiving no or little mail from their relatives the hardest adjustment for them to make was loss of freedom, dignity and ever-persistent boredom. It is a miracle any survived. Their own leadership and organizational structure established within the camps, combined with individual ingenuity and will to live enabled them to subsist and endure. The Red Cross provided food parcels to prison camps. One parcel a week was to be given to each prisoner.

The American Red Cross utilized 13,500 volunteers who packed six hundred thousand parcels a week. The United States sent nearly 28 million food parcels to International Red Cross Headquarters at Geneva, Switzerland, who in turn forwarded the parcels by train to nations holding POWs. As many as fifty boxcars a day were loaded with Red Cross goods for Germany. In addition the Red Cross and YMCA sent books, glasses, sports equipment, musical instruments and most importantly, mail, for the POWs. As the fortunes of war soured for the Germans, it was obvious they could hardly feed themselves let alone the POWs and quality of food went from bad to worse. Red Cross parcels were used by the Germans for their own benefit and those doled out to POWs became less frequent and had to be shared with as many as ten other POWs rather than one parcel per POW per week. If it had not been for the parcels that were received, there was no question many POWs would not have survived

Each prison camp had either a senior officer who was in charge of a compound at the camp or a Man of Confidence in the case of enlisted men. They were the prisoner's spokesperson with the prison commandant. The International Red Cross based in Switzerland, made periodic inspections of the prison camps not only in Germany but also in the United States to monitor treatment of prisoners. Findings in need of correction and recommendations for improvement of conditions within the camps were discussed with the commandant. At most camps in Germany, Red Cross recommendations were ignored and in some prison camps treatment became worse.

Unless a person has experienced it themselves, no one can imagine the loss of dignity, degradation, mental anguish and primitive environment to which POWs were subjected. The loss of freedom, particularly to an American, was hard to bear, but bear they did. With compassion for their fellow internee and Yankee ingenuity they made the most of their situation and most all survived. They adapted themselves to a situation completely foreign to their nature. The camps were run like a military organization with committees for food rationing, clothing, recreation,

Chapter Fifteen

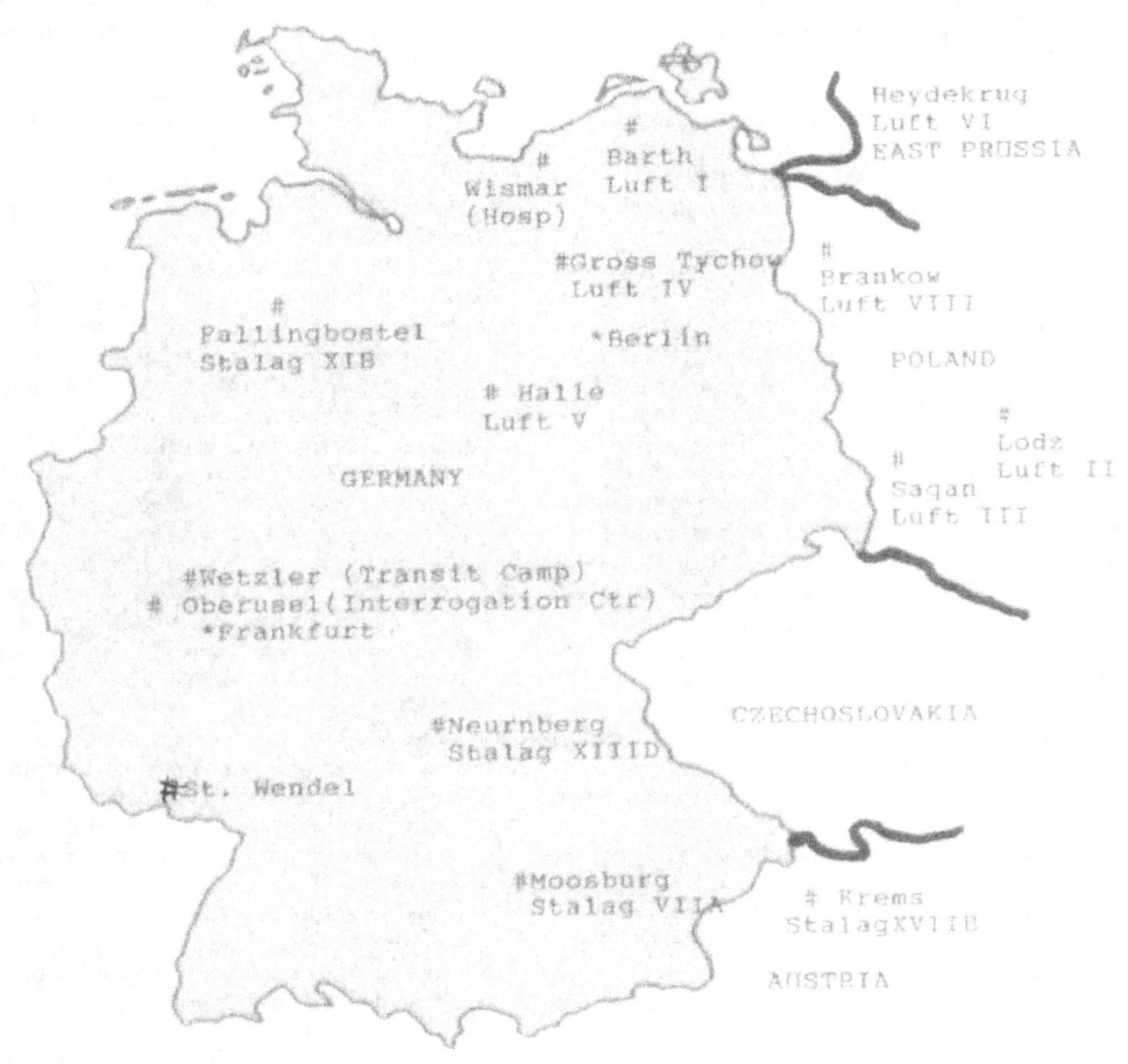

= Stalag Luft – Prisoner of War Camps for Airmen
   Stalag was a Prisoner of War Camp for captured ground forces but also included some enlisted airmen

Germany maintained over 119 Stalag Prison Camps and sub-camps; 8 Stalag Luft Camps; 48 Dulags or Transit Camps; 17 Jlags or Ilags-Civilian Internment Camps; 4 Marinelags-Prisoner of War Camps for sailors; 41 Oflags-Camps for Officers.

Iowans of the Mighty Eighth

sports, Red Cross parcels, mail, supply, medical attention, religious services and escape.

As the war progressed and Allied armies began to close the ring around Germany the POWs were forced to evacuate their prison camps in one of Europe's coldest winters on record. They had to march through snow in sub-zero weather, in some cases for over eighty days, covering 600 miles with little or no food or shelter. Some were shipped in railroad boxcars for some distances with no room to lie or sit down, no toilet facilities, no protection against the weather and again no food or water.

The Germans had numerous POW camps, called a Stalag, scattered over France, Germany, Poland, Austria and East Prussia. Some prison camps held only airmen. Some only aircrew officers. Stalag had the word Luft added to it meaning air. Following is a listing of German Stalag Luft prisoner of war camps and their location during the war. Some locations listed as Germany are actually in Poland having gained its freedom from Nazi control after World War II. Iowa POWs interviewed were interned at most of these Stalag Lufts and also at regular Stalags. It is not known where all Iowans of the Mighty Eighth, listed at the end of this Chapter, were held as POW.

Dulag Luft Transit camp, initially at Oberursel, then Frankfurt, then Wetzler

Luftwaffen Laz	Wismar (hospital for airmen)
Stalag Luft I	Barth
Stalag Luft II	Litzmannstadt, GE now Lodz, Poland
Stalag Luft III	Sagan, Poland
Stalag Luft IV	Gross Tychow, Poland
Stalag Luft V	Halle, GE
Stalag Luft VI	Heydekrug, East Prussia, 1944
Stalag Luft VI	St. Wendel, Aug-Sep 1944
Stalag Luft VIII	Bankau, GE, now Poland

Interviewed POWs were interned at the following additional Stalags

Stalag VIIA	Moosburg
Stalag XIB	Fallingbostel
Stalag XIIID	Nuernberg
Stalag XVIIB	Krems an der Donau, Austria

A listing of prison camps in Germany disclosed 119 Stalag camps; 8 Stalag Luft camps; 48 Dulags or transit camps; 17 Jlag or Ilags civilian internment camps; 4 marinelags, camps for sailors and 41 Oflags, camps for officers.

Stan Davidson, Ames, Iowa, was interned at Barth. He was the pilot of a B-17 bomber hit by flak over Germany. Three engines of his airplane were knocked out causing him to order his crew to bail out. Stan himself landed in a forested area and escaped capture until he attempted to walk through a small village and was caught.

Bill Mehegan, Cedar Rapids, Iowa, was interned at Barth. He had to bail out of his aircraft over Germany after it received two direct hits from German flak guns. Only Bill and the flight engineer of his crew survived the hits. He was immediately captured by German troops.

John Butler, Washington, Iowa, was interned at Barth. His bomber was attacked by enemy fighter aircraft whose shells started a fire aboard his airplane. As John attempted to put out the fire with an extinguisher additional fire from the German fighter caused an explosion mashing John against an escape hatch of his bomber. He opened the hatch and "was dangling half in and half out of the airplane" while it was in a diving spin. The next thing he knew he was falling in space and pulled the ripcord to his parachute. He landed on the roof of a house in a small German town. The town's Chief of Police clubbed John in the back of the head, took him into custody and then marched him through the town kicking him as he walked. He was put in a jail cell and later turned over to German troops.

James Brown, Mason City, was interned at Sagan, Poland. Jim flew night missions dropping propaganda leaflets. His aircraft was attacked by a German night fighter while they were over Holland. Gunners were able to shoot down the German fighter but not before it set fire to Jim's bomber causing the crew to bail out. Jim evaded capture for nearly a month as he was shuttled through the Dutch Underground in order to try and get him back to Allied hands. He was turned in to German authorities by a man and woman working for the Germans

George Sterler, Sheldon, Iowa, was interned at Sagan. His bomber was attacked by German fighter planes. Their shells caused a portion of the wing on George's bomber to be ripped from the aircraft and send it into a spiraling dive. The bomber exploded sending George out of the plane. Fortunately he was wearing his parachute and pulled the ripcord to inflate it. He broke his leg when he landed on the ground. German soldiers arrived to capture George before civilians armed with pitchforks could get to him.

W. A. Singer, Ames, Iowa, was interned at Sagan. While his aircraft was turning on the bomb run toward the target, Bill's aircraft was hit by German anti-aircraft fire knocking out two engines, damaging a third and wounding Bill. A German fighter also attacked his bomber causing further damage. Bill's pilot made a forced landing in a potato field. Civilians armed with pitchforks were seen running to them but German soldiers captured them before the civilians could get there.

Willard Spangler, Everly, Iowa, was interned at Sagan. On August 2, 1944, while over France his aircraft took three direct hits from German anti-aircraft flak. Willard, as Co-pilot was wounded in the neck, shoulder and back when one of the hits knocked out the number three engine next to his crew position. He was rendered unconscious but awoke to find the nose of his aircraft had been blown away and the plane was on fire. All of his crew had bailed out except his bombardier who was trapped in the wreckage. Willard stayed with his airplane and made a forced landing but was taken prisoner of war.

Hap Westbrook, Ames, Iowa, was interned at Sagan. German fighters attacked Hap's B-24 bomber before they could reach their target and drop their bombs. Two engines to the bomber were knocked out and a third engine was on fire. Hap had been wounded in the shoulder and leg. The crew bailed out of the bomber and Hap landed in the North Sea. It was estimated a person could survive only 15-20 minutes in the icy waters. Hap lost consciousness and was in the water four hours before being pulled aboard a Swedish fishing boat. After it was discovered he had a pulse, Hap was revived and eventually turned over to German military authority.

Fred Abigt, Cedar Rapids, was interned at Gross Tychow. Fred was a B-17 waist gunner on a mission to bomb a chemical plant at Saarbrucken, Germany. His bomber was hit by flak on the bomb run with the bomb bay doors open. Wounded in the eyes and with lines to his oxygen and heated suit severed Fred bailed out of his aircraft. He landed on the top of a large pine tree but managed to get out of his parachute harness and drop to a snow bank on the ground. Wearing only wool stockings on his feet he began walking and after several hours wound up right bad at the tall pine tree. A member of the German Home Guard took Fred into custody, fed him, dressed his wounds and frozen feet before turning him over to German troops.

Ivan Hunter, Gowrie, Iowa, was interned at Gross Tychow. Ivan was on his thirty-third mission, a raid on a German airfield at Weisbaden when flak knocked out one engine to his aircraft. Struggling to maintain altitude the engine caught on fire and the aircrew bailed out of the airplane. Ivan was captured immediately by German ground forces.

Howard Linn, Hubbard, Iowa, was interned at Gross Tychow. He was flying his second mission, a raid on Brunswick, Germany, when his B-24 bomber was attacked by enemy fighters. The number three engine burst into flames causing the leading edge of the wing to also catch fire. Howard and three other crew members bailed out of the aircraft before it exploded killing the balance of his aircrew. Howard landed in a forest clearing and evaded capture until the next day when a German boy spotted him and turned him in to a policeman.

Merlin Dyvig, Humboldt, Iowa, was interned at Gross Tychow. Merlin was on a bombing raid over Wilhelmshaven, Germany when his aircraft took two direct hits in the left wing and one in the right wing from German flak guns. Leaking fuel caught one engine on fire. The aircrew bailed out of the aircraft except for the pilot and navigator. Merlin free fell "for half a day" until he pulled the ripcord on his parachute. Merlin landed in the middle of a German anti-aircraft battery and immediately taken prisoner.

Melvin Wile, Pomeroy, Iowa, was an engineer/gunner on his tenth mission in December of 1943 when, over Germany, his aircraft was hit by flak knocking out its engines. Melvin was wounded in an arm and leg by machine gun bullets from enemy fighters. Melvin and his crew crash-landed. The impact threw Melvin and his tailgunner from the airplane. All other crew members were able to walk away from the wreckage. The tailgunner subsequently died from his wounds. Melvin received medical treatment at various German hospitals before being sent to Stalag Luft VI at Heydekrug, East Prussia.

Hubert Campney, Emmetsburg, Iowa, was interned at Stalag Luft VI at St Wendel, Germany. He was on his seventeenth mission as a ball turret gunner to bomb electric generators at Mannheim, Germany. His aircraft was hit by German flak knocking out two engines and causing the plane to lock in an upward climbing pattern. Hydraulic controls were knocked out of the aircraft requiring other crewmembers to hand crank the ball turret to a position Hubert could climb out of it. The bail out order had been given by the pilot and other crew members were in the process of exiting the aircraft. Howard could not find his parachute. He finally spotted it bouncing on the floor of the aircraft near the open door and managed to reach it before it could bounce out of the plane. He was immediately captured when he landed on the ground. After the POW camp at St Wendel was evacuated, Hubert was sent to the POW camp at Gross Tychow.

Carroll Bogard, Mason City, Iowa, was initially interned at St. Wendel, Germany. Carroll was a ball turret gunner on a raid on Hamburg, Germany when his aircraft took direct hits from German flak guns. After his aircraft began uncontrollable Carroll bailed out of his bomber and landed in a forest clearing where German troops were camped.

Victor Johnson, Nashua, Iowa, was interned at Nuernberg, Germany. Victor was a B-24 gunner on his fourteenth mission when his aircraft took a direct hit from flak guns. The number four engine was destroyed and his aircraft caught fire. The bail out order was given and Victor pulled the ripcord to his parachute as he left the airplane. He passed out from lack of oxygen and regained consciousness as he was floating to earth. He was captured immediately by German soldiers.

Thomas McElherne, Ames, Iowa, was interned at Fallingbostel, Germany. Tom was a flight engineer and top turret gunner on a B-17 bomber on a raid to Dortmund, Germany when anti-aircraft fire made direct hits on the wings of his aircraft. Leaking fuel started a fire in the bomb bay area of the airplane and the crew immediately bailed out. Tom landed in a wooded area and was captured by German troops when children pointed out where he was. Tom's pilot was killed by civilians and another crew member severely beaten before German troops rescued him.

Howard Hobbs, Morning Sun, Iowa, was interned at Krem an der Donau, Austria. Howard was a B-17 flight engineer and top turret gunner on a mission to Augsburg, Germany. An engine malfunctioned causing the aircraft to lose speed and fall out of formation. They continued to the target but anti-aircraft fire knocked out another engine and Howard was wounded. When a third engine began to malfunction the pilot ordered his crew to bail out. When he landed on the ground Howard was immediately surrounded by German civilians who took him to an inn until German soldiers could arrive.

Howard Greiner, Albia, Iowa, was interned in a Stalag Luft Hospital at Oberursel, Germany. Howard was a B-17 pilot on his second mission when German flak caused loss of three engines, oxygen, hydraulics and radio systems. The aircraft caught fire and the crew parachuted from the airplane. Howard landed on the ground with such force it broke his leg. He was taken prisoner of war, forced to walk on his broken leg and did not receive medical attention for several days.

Glenn Underwood, Shenandoah, Iowa, was a tailgunner on a mission over Merignac, France when enemy fighters attacked his aircraft. Two engines were shot out. Unable to make it back to England, Glenn's pilot made a forced landing behind German lines and the crew was taken prisoner of war.

Ellsworth Gustafson, Des Moines, was a tailgunner with the 493rd BG, at Little Walden, England. In route to bomb a target in Germany his aircraft received direct hits from anti-aircraft fire that caused his plane to explode. "I was blown out of the plane and fell through space. I saw a big thunderhead cloud below me and when I fell through it, it caused me to tumble

POW crew at bottom of hill

POW crew walking – Unidentified American air crews taken prisoner of war after being shot down over Germany

Carrying parachute

over and over. I pulled on the ripcord on my parachute and collapsed it when I got out of the clouds. When I tried to open it again, the lines were all tangled in my legs and the chute was wrapped around me. I saw the ground coming up at me and I managed to get it open. I landed in a bomb crater. A German machine gunner was shooting at me. I managed to raise an arm in surrender. He came up to me and yelled "Heil Hitler". I asked him if he spoke English. He drew a knife and put it under my chin and asked "You English?" He knocked me down. I said "Nix, English. Americano." He didn't seem to understand and for some reason I yelled "Chicago". He asked "you, Chicago?" I said yes. He came up to me and gave me a big hug and patted me on the back like we were long lost brothers. I learned he had a brother in Chicago and from then on I could do no wrong."

Jean Ray, Colfax, Iowa, Radio Operator, 100th Bomb Group, Thorpe Abbotts, England. Jean and his crew made a forced landing behind enemy lines after another plane in their bomb group struck the tail and rear stabilizers of their aircraft during a mission in September, 1943.

German civilians were killed during Allied bombings and their homes destroyed. Next came the daily search for food and water for survival. The civilians were enraged and encouraged by German leadership to take revenge on Allied airmen. An argument could be said they started the war and did it to others, but as in all wars, it is the innocent which suffer the most. Many American airmen when parachuting into enemy-held territory were killed by civilian captors. Melvin Wile, Pomeroy, recalled "before going to the prisoner of war camp we were nearly lynched by a mob of German people for bombing their city but was protected by the German guards."

Captured allied airmen were usually transported to Frankfurt, the Luftwaffe Aircrew Interrogation Center. Each new POW was locked in solitary confinement and interrogated while still trying to recover from the effects of being shot down, captured and in many instances, wounded. They would then be sent to a transit camp for as long as a week or more before continuing their journey to a prisoner of war camp with other POWs. The usual greeting at Frankfurt was "For you the war is over." German intelligence officers would attempt to glean information from the prisoner regarding targets, bomb loads, organizational data, strength of numbers or on equipment such as the American Norden bombsight. According to the Geneva Convention Articles of War the POW was only required to give him name, rank and serial number. This was drilled into each soldier before combat. Answers really didn't matter, German intelligence had complete files on captured Air Corps personnel including personal information that was probably taken from American newspapers.

After attempts to gain information and even threats to shoot the prisoner as a spy he was sent by truck or train to a Stalag Luft. Howard Hobbs had to ride in a railroad cattle car for days with only a bucket between him and other POWs for a toilet. In that period of time they received one tub of an unknown soup. He received little or no attention to his wounds until he reached his POW camp.

During interview of POWs the following conditions in their prison camps were disclosed. Their comments are augmented by International Red Cross inspection reports reported by Military Intelligence after the end of World War II and obtained from www.B-24.net/pow web site.

Stalag Luft I – Barth, Germany

The camp consisted of two compounds with seven barracks to a compound. With increasing numbers of prisoners arriving at the camp three additional compounds were built. Three of the compounds were considered unsatisfactory due to a complete lack of adequate cooking, washing and toilet facilities. Over 7700 American officers were interned at the camp. Each barracks contained triple-tiered wooden beds equipped with mattresses filled with wood chips.

Unidentified American captured by German authorities and soldiers

Some compounds contained a kitchen barracks, theater room, church room, library and study room used by all compounds. Maintenance of the buildings was completely lacking due to German resistance to provide equipment and material for repairs. Many of the buildings were not weather proof to protect the POWs from the northern German climate. Stan Davidson of Ames was issued two blankets on arrival at the camp and had to sleep in his clothes in order to stay warm.

Treatment was considered fairly good however that position deteriorated and guards were given liberal use of weapons to shoot at prisoners. One American was killed and one British officer wounded during an air raid when POWs were supposed to be inside their barracks. The commandant tended to inflict mass punishment for individual infractions of rules.

Germans provided rations to each compound. POWs were then responsible for preparation of the food in that compound. Red Cross parcels were issued one per person per week. In the latter stages of the war no Red Cross parcels were distributed and German rations dropped to less than 800 calories a man. Men became so weak they could not stand. Prisoners had to guard garbage cans to prevent other starving POWs from eating what garbage there was and becoming sick. Previously the POWs received about six potatoes, a small amount of bread, margarine, jam, and occasionally a small piece of horsemeat, two vegetables, and tea or coffee. A thin barley soup was sometimes prepared.

Stan Davidson believed the bread was made of sawdust. He received a small portion of horsemeat about every two weeks and shared a Red Cross parcel with another POW whenever one was received, which was about every two weeks. John Butler of Washington found bits of glass and metal in the bread he ate and had only a small portion of potatoes, imitation coffee and occasionally some oleomargarine to eat.

Poor sanitation was a detriment to the health of the POWs. One bath house with only ten shower heads dispensing cold water served over 4,000 prisoners. Once a month Stan Davidson was able to take a warm water shower. The same shower facilities were used as a delousing area for outbreaks of lice and bed bugs. No facilities existed for disposal of garbage that could not be burned. Lack of a drainage system caused latrines and wash drains to flood the area around barracks.

Fuel rations to heat barracks' stoves were insufficient and a cause for many illnesses particularly upper respiratory diseases. Two doctors taken prisoner of war cared for the whole prison camp. Their efforts were hampered by lack of medical supplies and facilities to care for the prisoners. The Germans issued no clothing. The Red Cross was able to supply blankets and clothing in late 1944.

It took seven months to receive a piece of mail from home. POWs were allowed to mail a specified number of letters and postcards per month. German supplies of letter writing materials were low and normal rations were not issued. For the POWs religious needs, the Germans provided clergymen for the camp.

Sports equipment provided by American organizations allowed the men to play football, baseball and volleyball. Musical instruments were provided and two bands were formed at Barth which played concerts and provided background music for theatrical productions. Bill Mehegan of Cedar Rapids was instrumental in organizing stage plays at the camp. Plays were written from books in the prison library. Guards on leave in Berlin and other cities would often return with much needed props for the plays.

7th Photographic Reconnaissance Group aerial photograph of Stalag 1, Bath, Germany, taken in April, 1944.

Chapter Fifteen

Educational programs were organized and classes on a variety of topics were held until overcrowding eliminated available classroom space. Other men relieved their boredom through creative work such as woodcarving, painting, drawing and constructing models. One POW who had flown with Jimmy Doolittle on the famous raid on Tokyo early in the war made paints from boiled down soup can labels and brushes fashioned from human hair to create paintings. Cans in Red Cross parcels were saved and made into pots and pans. Every available item was used in some way to make life more adaptable.

An article printed in the December, 1998 issue of the "8th AF News", Volume 98 Number 4, written by Earl Wassom, 466th Bomb Group, is about an event that occurred at Stalag 1, Barth, Germany. With permission of the 8th AF News, it is re-printed here.

"In war-time, a place called Barth was Hell. It was a prisoner of war camp located only a few miles south of the Baltic Sea in Northern Germany. Downed aircrews were interned there after having been shot down and captured by the enemy. Ten thousand were held there as prisoners. The camp was divided into four administrative compounds with 2,500 airmen in each unit. These "guests of the Germans" were elite and quality men-leaders and brave American youths. They had been effective in their aerial combat activity against Nazi Germany. But now, their role had dramatically changed. Internment brought suffering beyond belief; the unending frigid weather, the unpredictable behavior of the guards. Inadequate food, lice, sickness, boredom, death by starvation or by exposure, was their unchanging agenda. Yet there were times when the spirits of the Prisoners of War were lifted. It was always through their own methods of creativity and ingenious that this happened. One ongoing "high" occurred when each new contingent of "guests" arrived in the camp. Up-to-date uncensored information became immediately available. The reports brought in by these new POW's gave fresh, unbiased running accounts of how the war was progressing on both the Eastern Front with the Russians and on the Western Front. The increasing numbers of bombers and fighters appearing in the air overhead brought silent but exuberant joy and hope to Barth's imprisoned. As optimism flourished small group conversations centered on the war's end and their freedom. Liberation was on everyone's lips. The war was indeed winding down!

Talk of being home for Christmas became a Utopian Dream. Although all embraced the Dream, not all were optimistic. This difference in opinion brought about the "Bet at Barth". A wager was on. New life came to the camp. But what was there to wager? There was no money, no freedom or 3-day passes to London, no material possessions for the loser to forfeit, no points or promotions to be gained or lost. In a heated conversation, two men got carried away in their claims. An optimistic airman bet a pessimistic one on the following terms. "If we aren't home by Christmas, I will kiss your ass before the whole group formation right after head-count on Christmas morning." They shook hands. The bet was on! Well, the optimist hadn't counted on the Battle of the Bulge in early December. Consequently, the war was prolonged and they were still in Barth on Christmas Day, 1944.

Christmas morning was cold, there was snow on the ground and frigid air was blowing in off the Baltic Sea. The body count for the compound began, each man was counted "ein..zwe..drei..vier..funf..sechs..sieben..acht..." Under ordinary circumstances, when the counting was completed and the German guards were satisfied that everyone was accounted for, the group split up and everyone went to their barracks. But this time, everybody stayed in formation. The two betting "Kriegies" walked out of the formation and went into the barracks. No one else moved! The guards were puzzled. They didn't know what was going on. Soon, the two men came back out of the barracks. One was carrying a bucket of water with a towel over the other arm. The second one marched to the front of the formation, turned his back toward the assembled troops and guards, pulled down his pants and stooped over. The other took the towel, dipped it in the soapy water and washed his posterior. The whole formation was standing there looking and laughing. The German guards and dignitaries of Barth stood gazing in amazement, they didn't know what was going on. Then the optimist bent over and kissed his opponent on the rear! A mighty cheer went up from over 2,000 men. Then the puzzled guards joined in the fun.

Nothing changed on Christmas day-the same black bread and thin soup, sparse and flavorless. As evening fell, the weather worsened, the barracks were cold, the last of the daily allotted coal briquettes were reduced to nothing but white ash. Boredom was settling in and the prisoners anticipated another long miserable night. Suddenly, the door opened, a voice shouted, "The curfew has been lifted for tonight! We're going to have a Christmas service over in the next compound." The weather was bitterly cold, the new fallen snow crunched under the feet of the men as they quickly shuffled towards their congregating comrades in the distance.

The nightly curfew always kept men inside – this Christmas night's reprieve allowed them to be outside after dark for the first time. Above, the stars were shining brightly and were high in the northern skies; the dim flicker of Aurora Borealis added a magical touch as the troops assembled. Gratitude was felt in their hearts…a lone singer led out with one of the world's most familiar and loved carols. Other joined in and soon there was joyful worship ringing throughout the camp.

"Silent night! Holy night!
All is calm, all is bright.."

The German guards marching their assigned beats stopped in their tracks…they turned their heads toward the music. The words were unfamiliar but they recognized the tune…after all, Stille Nacht, Heilige Nacht was composed by a German. They loosened up, smiled, and joined in the celebration; the praise became bilingual.

" Round yon virgin, mother and Child."
" Cinsam wacht nurdas traute hoch heilige Paar"
"Holy Infant, so tender and mild."
" Holder Knabe im lockigen Hoiar"
"Sleep in heavenly peace. Sleep in heavenly peace."
"Schlaf in himmlischer ruh!"
"Schlaf in himmlischer ruh."

The Bet at Barth had paid off. Everyone had won! As the words of the carol rang in their hearts, there was a literal fulfillment. Tonight they would sleep in peace. War and internment did not have the power to destroy the meaning and beauty of the special day.

It was Christmas. They were not at home. But they declared, "Next year we will be!" And they were!

At the end of April, 1945, the Russian Army was closing in on Barth. The Germans abandoned the camp and fled. American POWs were evacuated by air, a process that took two weeks to complete.

Stalag Luft III – Sagan, Poland

Germany had problems feeding its own people and its military. Providing food for POWs was therefore at the bottom of the military's priorities. Rations at all camps failed to meet requirements of the Geneva Convention and were insufficient to sustain health. Red Cross parcels which contained high nutrition foods and intended to be rationed to each prisoner depended on German transportation services which were being bombed. Individual camp commandants may have withheld parcels as a form of group punishment.

The POW camp at Sagan consisted of compounds for Americans, British and Canadians, and for Rus-

Barracks at Stalag Luft II, Sagan

sian and Polish prisoners. Two twelve foot high barbed wire fences surrounded the prison. The inner wire was electrically charged. Another fence twelve feet inside the other two was a no trespass zone. Anyone going beyond that fence could be shot. Barracks were of pre-fabricated plywood built off the ground in the American zone to prevent escape. Guard dogs and guards roamed the compounds at night while guard towers, placed every 150 feet around the camp were manned by guards with machine guns. One brick of coal was issued to each POW per week to heat their barracks. No shower facilities existed, toilets were a concrete tank with holes in it, and mattresses and pillows were filled with bug infested straw.

Jim Brown of Mason City described the food at Sagan as "soup that had worms in it but we ate them anyway. Bread was like sawdust with rodent holes in it. Packages and letters sent from home never reached me." Hap Westbrook of Ames described the food at Sagan as "a watery soup containing unidentified objects that were alive and a dark bread made of sawdust. Each POW was supposed to receive one Red Cross parcel a week but that rarely happened."

George Sterler, Sheldon; W.A. Singer, Ames; Willard Spangler, Everly and Hap Westbrook, Ames, were either wounded or received injuries when they were shot down. It was several days before Sterler received medical treatment for his broken leg. He was confined to a German Luft hospital until his leg healed and then sent to Stalag Luft III. W.A. Singer received treatment for his wounds at a rural hospital before being sent to Frankfurt and interrogation. After shipment to Stalag Luft III he required further hospitalization for his wounds which wouldn't heal. He suffered an allergic reaction to sulpha drugs administered to him and his head was put in a plaster cast. He remained in the prison hospital most of his internment. Westbrook received medical treatment for his wounds while at the interrogation center. Spangler received no medical treatment from his German captors for his wounds. He had to rely on what care could be afforded him by Allied doctors also interned at the prison camp

Sagan was the scene of "The Great Escape" by long-time Canadian and British airmen prisoners of war. On a night in March, 1944, after ingenious and exhaustive efforts in digging a tunnel over a long period of time, seventy-six POWs escaped through the tunnel before the exit opening outside the POW camp was discovered by a German sentry. Four POWs were captured at the exit end of the tunnel. The manhunt to recapture the prisoners that had gotten away drained German military resources and caused turmoil throughout the country. All that had escaped were re-captured except three who were able to completely make it back to England. In retribution, fifty of the escapees were shot. The escape was the subject of a movie titled "The Great Escape" and detailed in a book "Stalag Luft III" written by Arthur D Durand, A Touchstone Book published by Simon & Schuster, Inc, Copyright 1988.

At the end of January, 1945, as the Russian Army began to close on Sagan, the prison camp was evacuated. All POWs were marched to Spremburg, Germany where they were loaded aboard box cars and trained to Stalag XIIID at Nuernberg, Germany. They were later evacuated again, and forced to march to Stalag VIIA at Moosburg, Germany.

STALAG LUFT IV – GROSS TYCHOW, POMERANIA

In October, 1944, the camp was under construction with construction of five compounds to hold an anticipated 6,400 American POWs. New barracks had been built with no ventilation or bathing facilities. Toilet facilities were considered adequate. POWs from Stalag Luft VI at Heydekrug and later POWs from St. Wendel were sent to Stalag Luft IV and caused overcrowding. Forty wooden huts were built to house prisoners, 200 to a hut. There were not enough beds constructed and POWs were sleeping on the floor many without mattresses or only mattresses partially filled with wood shavings. Howard Linn, Hubbard, Iowa, stated his mattress filled with wood shavings was infested with fleas and lice. Merlin Dyvig, Humboldt, Iowa, had been issued two blankets but slept on the floor of his barracks in a German burial bag filled with shredded paper. None of the huts could be heated and only five stoves were seen in the entire camp. Each POW was issued two blankets.

There were two open air latrines in each compound. Each hut had one latrine with two seats for the 200 men. Russian slave laborers were forced to empty the latrines but did so only on an irregular basis. There were no facilities for washing or showers. Two outside pump wells provided water for the camp. Water had to be carried into the barracks from the outside for washing and bathing. Fleas, lice and bed bugs were common but the Germans provided no insecticide for delousing.

Food was no worse than at other POW camps. Each of the five compounds had a kitchen for preparing what rations the Germans provided but only five or six utensils in which to prepare the food. Rations consisted of a small daily portion of bread, margarine, and boiled potatoes or a soup made from potatoes. One half ounce of meat was allowed daily. The POWs occasionally received cheese, jam or sugar once a week. Ivan Hunter, Gowrie, Iowa, described the food at Stalag Luft IV as an unknown stew once a day with a third of a loaf of sawdust bread. Red Cross parcels containing high nutrition food, instead of being issued once a week to each prisoner, were, according to Howard Linn, Hubbard, Iowa, issued once a week, but had to be shared with seven other POWs. Merlin Dyvig, Humboldt, Iowa, was required to have a "bowl buddy" for food. Their German ration was poured into a bowl to be shared with another POW. The food was a soup of either turnips or potatoes filled with worms which were eaten. Any meat in the soup was believed to be dog meat. Merlin contracted trench mouth during his captivity and lost his teeth. "Red Cross parcels are all that kept us alive."

Carroll Bogard, Mason City, Iowa was transferred to Stalag Luft IV after the POW camp at St. Wendel was evacuated. He described one soup as "ball bearing soup" made of hard peas and dehydrated cabbage that gave everyone diarrhea. Other than the soup he received one cup of potatoes a day. A Red Cross parcel had to be shared with four other POWs.

Clothing supplies were insufficient. Clothing sent to the camp by the Red Cross never arrived or was not accounted for in order to distribute them. The German policy was to withhold the issuance of Red Cross clothing to American POWs. Men went a month without changing clothes. Warm clothing for winter was not distributed. During their captivity, American POWs were never issued clothing, stockings or underwear.

Two captured American doctors tended to prisoner's health needs in a 130-bed infirmary for 10,000 POWs. Except for skin disease cases, beds had no sheets. Patients often had to sleep on the floor. There was one bathtub in the infirmary and no facilities or equipment for major surgery. One dentist served the needs of the entire camp. The Germans brought dental equipment to the camp two or three times a week.

As the camp filled with POWs recreation committees filled the need for escape from boredom by organizing and finding POWs qualified to teach classes in a wide variety of topics. No sports equipment was available nor musical instruments other than what was brought to the camp by POWs from other Stalags.

After the war American and British POWs reported that POWs that arrived at the camp were required to run a distance of about three kilometers from the train station to the prison camp. During the run German soldiers would prod the POWs with bayonets on their end of their rifles that caused puncture wounds to the buttocks, neck, back and legs. Wounds varied from a break in the skin to wounds three inches deep. Reports estimated over one hundred POWs were bayoneted during the course of the run. Carroll Bogard of Mason City recalled being run from the train station to the camp but was not bayoneted.

The prison commandant was considered harsh and inconsiderate to the needs of POWs. except on Christmas Eve, 1944. All lights to the prison camp were turned on and POWs were given extra German rations and a Red Cross parcel. POWs were allowed out of their barracks until midnight. Howard Linn described it "as lighting a candle in an otherwise dark world." Carroll Bogard described the one night out as "like going to Las Vegas. The little bit of freedom. It's the little things we missed."

In February, 1945, the Russian Army was closing toward Stalag IV. The Germans began a forced evacuation of the camp. Rather than a mass exodus, groups of POWs under guard left the camp by different routes, all on forced marches in the worst European winter on record.

Stalag Luft VI – Heydekrug, East Prussia

American POWs arrived at this Stalag in February, 1944. The camp consisted of three compounds with ten barracks to a compound. Barracks were constructed of brick but an additional twelve wooden huts had to be built to accommodate increasing numbers of POWs. Men slept in two-tiered bunks, had new tables and stools. Heating was considered satisfactory. Additional facilities included a wash house, a chapel/theater building and seven barracks which served as an infirmary.

Rations of German food were considered poor. Each prisoner was allowed a small portion of potatoes per day. Fresh vegetables were not available. After initial stocks of Red Cross were exhausted no more were distributed.

The Red Cross provided the prisoners with clothing and the YMCA sent sports and recreation equipment. Educational classes were established with POW instructors. The internees were also able to establish a band, a choir and a dramatic group to put on plays.

The advance of the Russian Army forced the Germans to evacuate the camp the latter part of June and early July, 1944. The POWs were transported to Stalag Luft IV at Gross Tychow, Germany. Melvin Wile made the transfer to Stalag Luft IV by coal barge.

Stalag Luft VI – St Wendel, Germany

Internment at this camp was short-lived for two Iowans, Hubert Campney of Emmetsburg and Carroll Bogard of Mason City. The camp was evacuated when American ground troops began to close on the area. Both were transported in railroad boxcars to Stalag Luft IV near Gross Tychow, Germany, a trip that took five and a half days. The boxcars were loaded with so many POWs it was impossible to sit or lay down. They received no food or water during the trip. Only a bucket placed in each boxcar served as a latrine. The floors of the boxcars were covered with vomit, urine and excrement that soiled clothing when attempts were made to sit or lay down. "The stench was terrible." Twice during the trip railroad yards were bombed by American planes. German troops took cover leaving the POWs locked in the boxcars.

Stalag Luft 7B – Moosburg, Germany

Late in World War II Moosburg was used as a prison camp for nearly 15,000 officers and enlisted men evacuated from other prison camps. POWs of different nationalities were segregated by compound. Each barracks was divided into two sections by a central room that contained a water faucet and tables for washing and eating. Prisoners slept in three tiered bunks. Sacks filled with excelsior served as a mattress. As the influx of prisoners from other camps increased, prisoners slept on floors, tables, and on the ground.

Chapter Fifteen

The overcrowding caused the treatment of prisoners to be harsh. Mass punishment was inflicted on the whole POW population for individual infractions or, believed by some, to be inability of the guards to control the prisoners.

As at all prison camps, Red Cross parcels were the main source of nutrition for the POWs. Initially issued one parcel per week per POW, the rations were later cut in half. Because of the arrival of additional prisoners the reserve supply of the parcels held by the Germans soon became exhausted. German rations consisted of an ersatz coffee and a few biscuits for breakfast. Dinner was boiled potatoes or sometimes a barley soup. A loaf of bread was divided between five men. Supper was more potatoes.

Captured American doctors treated patients in a 120-bed infirmary and were faced with a constant shortage of medical supplies. Those POWs with serious ailments were taken to a prison hospital outside the camp for treatment.

A POW was lucky to take a shower once every two weeks. Latrines were emptied only when they were about to overflow. No chemicals were provided by the Germans to neutralize the odor permeating the area.

Clothing was in short supply. Clothing that arrived from the Red Cross was not sufficient to replenish supplies issued new arrivals and that worn out by existing prisoners. When Red Cross inspectors discovered clothing stored in warehouses by the Germans instead of distributing them to the prisoners, complaints were made to the camp commandant, but to no avail.

The addition of thousands of POWs marched to Moosburg from other camps included over 4,000 that arrived from Sagan, Poland. This created a lack of space for recreational sports and educational classes were eliminated for need for housing space. Barracks that previously housed 200 now had 300 POWs. German rations became worse, sanitary systems were inadequate and there was no hot water. Boilers were installed for hot water and each POW was allowed a pint of hot water twice daily.

By April, 1945, more POWs evacuated from other camps to prevent their liberation by Allied forces, arrived to add to the confusion and disorganization

Drawing of camp scene, Moosburg, by POW Bob Neary, from book "Stalag Luft III – Sagan-Nuernberg-Moosburg, Copyright 1946, North Wales, PA

at Moosburg. This didn't last long. Elements of the American Army liberated the POWs at Moosburg at month's end.

STALAG XIB – FALLINGBOSTEL, GERMANY

Thomas McElherne, Ames, Iowa, was sent to Fallingbostel after his B-17 bomber was shot down by anti-aircraft fire. Tom was assigned to a barracks that was fenced in and also contained Russian prisoners of war. His barracks contained one table and a stove. The only fuel for the stove was a tree stump placed inside the fence with an axe. The only time prisoners were allowed outside the barracks was to chop up the tree stump for firewood. His bed contained only slats on which to sleep on. The number of slats in each bed dwindled as they were burned in the barracks stove to heat their building. Food was a soup that an unknown vegetable had been cooked in and removed. Food provided by the Germans also consisted of three boiled potatoes and perhaps some bread. He received only two Red Cross parcels during his internment which were shared with three or four other prisoners. The only toilet was "just a hole in the ground". As Allied armies began to close on the area in early 1945, the POWs at Fallingbostel were evacuated and marched in the direction of Denmark.

STALAG XIIID – NUERNBERG, GERMANY

Conditions at Stalag XIIID were deplorable. American POWs that arrived at the camp

Iowans of the Mighty Eighth

Were given no supplies, utensils to eat with, and very little food. No Red Cross parcels were on hand to supplement German rations. The prison was infested with lice, fleas and bed bugs. No repellent was issued by the Germans to combat them and the parasites bit every exposed part of a person's body. Prisoners had to sleep on floors that were soiled from overflowing latrines and prisoners suffering from diarrhea. Showers were available only once every two weeks. German daily food rations consisted of a small portion of bread, potatoes and worm-filled dehydrated vegetables. Coal rationed to the prisoners was used for cooking while their barracks went unheated.

Victor Johnson, Nashua, Iowa, was interned at Nuernberg after his capture. The only food he received at the camp was a green soup that tasted like grass and became known as "green death soup". Weevils in the soup were eaten. "Gray death" was a flour soup the consistency of water. He was given a dark bread which he toasted in order to eat it. As a result of the food many POWs had diarrhea and dysentery.

The approximate 10,000 prisoners housed at Nuernberg for three months were issued one Red Cross food parcel in April, 1945. They were forced to march to Stalag VIIA at

Moosburg, a distance that took sixteen days to complete travelling no more than 20 kilometers a day. Food parcels were delivered to the prisoners at various points on the march. After arrival at Moosburg they had only another nine days to wait to be liberated by the American Army.

Stalag XVIIB – Krems, Austria

By the end of World War II, Stalag XVIIB held nearly 30,000 POWs from many countries. Americans occupied five compounds. Each compound contained four double barracks. The center of each barracks contained a washroom in the center of the building that had six sinks. One stove in each barracks had to supply heat and cooking facilities on a small ration of coal for about 200 men housed there. Beds were triple decked. Because of a shortage of blankets men slept two to a bed for added warmth.

Other prison facilities included one barrack for an infirmary. Other barracks were divided into sections for a library, chapel, theater, food and clothing distribution, and repair shop. for shoes and clothing, a gymnasium and a chapel.

Latrines were open pits in the ground situated away from the barracks. A central bathing station had only cold water taps for the rare occasions there was water pressure. POWs received a hot shower about once every two months.

Two electrically charged wire fences surrounded the camp. Streetlights lit the perimeter of compounds. Watchtower guards armed with machine guns also used searchlights to scan the prison camp.

POWs relied on card games, checkers, chess, other indoor games and books to pass their time. A public address system was utilized to play programs of music and information. Classes covering a variety of topics were taught to the POWs by in-

Camp Scenes at Stalag XIII-D, Nuernberg, Germany. Drawings by Bob Neary, from book titled "Stalag Luft III, Sagan-Nuernberg, Moosburg" Copyright 1946, North Wales PA.

Barracks interior

Cook stove in barracks

Chapter Fifteen

structor POWs. Evening discussion groups were formed and directed by POWs that were experienced in certain areas.

Treatment at the camp was considered brutal at times. Certain guards threatened and even struck POWs with gun butts. The camp commandant had received no complaints but promised to remove guards unsuited for their work.

On April 8, 1945, 4000 POWs of Stalag XVIIB were evacuated and marched 281 miles to Branau, Austria. On May 3, 1945, the prison camp at Krems was liberated by members of the American 13th Armored Division.

Howard Hobbs, Morning Sun, Iowa, was interned at Stalag XVIIB during April, 1944. Food rationed to the POWs consisted of a half loaf of bread and a tub of imitation coffee for breakfast. At noon he was served a small portion of boiled potatoes and a thin soup containing either rutabagas, turnips, onions and a portion of a poor quality meat. As the war progressed badly for the Germans, food went from bad to worse and less frequent. Red Cross parcels which had been doled out one parcel per week to each POW became one parcel for five to six men. "POWs established a library, chapel, and classrooms for continuing education. Classes were taught by fellow POWs on a variety of subjects. Two bands were formed after musical instruments were sent to the camp by the Red Cross."

Jean Ray, Colfax, was a POW for twenty months. He and friends in his barracks drew pictures to relieve boredom and divert constant thoughts of home. They were allowed to write home only on postcards at specified intervals. Colored pencils, crayons, and paper supplied by the Red Cross could not be used for correspondence. Following liberation in May, 1945, Jean saved the following examples of POW art made by him and other POWs at Krems.

Jean Ray's notation: "I drew this picture in 1944 of Brks 17, as it kind of had something in common with our camp #17B and reverse, B-17. My Brks was across the street on the main road through the camp. This looks better than it really was. Although better than the Brks we lived in at Sioux Falls, South Dakota Radio School. We kind of took our prep training for POWs there." Other prisoner of war art include:

Chapel drawing by Jean Ray

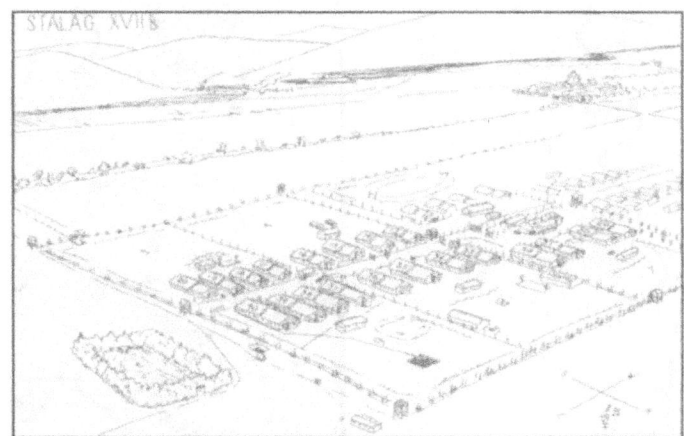

Stalag XVIIB Kremms, Austria

Drawing of barracks at Stalag XVIIB.

Iowans of the Mighty Eighth

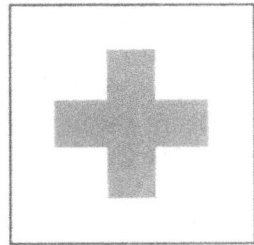

Contents of American Red Cross Parcels:

1 Can Powdered Milk-16oz
1 Can Corned Beef
1 Can Salmon
1 Can Margarine-16oz
1 Can Nescafe Coffee-4oz
1 Can Prunes or Raisins
2 Chocolate Bars-4oz
5 pkgs Cigarettes
1 Can Spam
1 Can Liver Paste
1 Can Cheese
Biscuits-K-Ration
1 Can Jam
1 Box Sugar-8oz
2 bars Soap

German Stuka Dive bomber, by Jean Ray

German Fighter, ME-109. White paper was cut to form clouds and taped to background, by Jean Ray

Barracks, Stalag XVIIB, Kremms, Austria

Guard Tower at Stalag XVIIB, Kremms, Austria

Flight Suit drawing by Jean Ray

Chapter Fifteen

FORCED MARCHES

As Russian, British and American armies advanced in Germany and its occupied territories, prisoner of war camps were evacuated en masse or by groups to other prison camps. German troops feared capture by the Russians and retribution from their invasion of Russia. They hoped if the end of the war was near for them they would be able to surrender to British or American forces. The POWs were moved by forced march guarded by young and radical German soldiers or by elderly soldiers who suffered as much from the march as the POWs. Some POWs were evacuated by railroad boxcars and others endured a combination of forced march and railroad transportation.

The intent of the evacuation may have been, as some believed, a last ditch effort by Hitler to deny the POWs liberation by advancing ground forces and use them as hostages. A more feasible explanation was to deny the highly trained, experienced POWs a chance to fight again against Germany. As the Third Reich was obviously crumbling, freeing the prisoners and utilizing the number of German troops required in all the POWs camps to maintain security and control would amount to a sizeable battle force that could have been used in defense of the Fatherland.

When the POW camps were evacuated artillery fire and battle sounds could be heard by the prison population. They knew the Allies were advancing and expected liberation within days. As the din of battle became closer and louder their dreams of going home were dashed by the evacuation orders. Taking what they could carry the POWs were sent out in one of Europe's coldest winters on record and forced to walk up to 600 miles over a span of eighty-two days. During that time they were given little or no food and water except what they could steal, barter or find. They slept in open country, barns, forests, or whatever shelter they could find or devise. Many suffered from frostbite, dysentery, pneumonia, typhus, blisters or a number of other ailments due to their weakened condition from months of prison camp existence on starvation diets. Walking for hours in snow and below-zero weather with biting winds and inadequate, lice-infested clothing prisoners would fall during the march or pass out. They would be helped by their fellow POW, but still, many died, needlessly, in one of man's greatest inhumanities to man.

STALAG LUFT III – SAGAN, POLAND

On January 27, 1945, with the Russian Army but thirty miles away and dreams of liberation on the minds of every POW, the prisoners were given thirty minutes to gather what belongings they wanted to take with them and be ready to evacuate the camp. Most took what food there was, blankets, and all of the winter clothing they could wear. It was snowing outside, the winds created blizzard-like conditions and the temperature was below zero degrees Fahrenheit. The camp was evacuated by compounds and marched down a road leading West away from the advancing Russians. No POW would have believed the Germans would move them. No one knew where they were going or how far. German guards were ordered to shoot anyone trying to escape.

Hap Westbrook of Ames, Iowa, recalled "we marched for six days covering sixty miles. I developed frostbite in my right foot and was barely able to walk. To stop meant being shot by guards. At a rest stop I fashioned a sled for my foot to relieve pressure on it and with an arm around a friend supporting me, was able to continue the march. At another rest stop, in a vacant pottery factory, I was able to discharge fluid that had swollen my feet and lance the openings."

Bob Brown, Mason City, Iowa, stated "we made sleds to pull our belongings in the snow. At one time I passed out during the march but other POWs helped me until I could make it on my own again. If they had left me as I lay I would have died or been shot."

At the pottery plant they were fed bread and margarine. A loaf of bread had to last eight men two days. The march continued until they reached Spremberg, Germany. The men were forced to stand in knee-deep snow while a roll call was taken to make sure there were no escapes. They were given a cup of barley soup before they were loaded onto railroad boxcars which would take them to Nuernburg, Germany, site of another prisoner of war camp. W.A. Singer of Ames, Iowa, and George Sterler, Sheldon, Iowa, described the boxcars as 40 and 8s, which meant room for forty men or eight horses. "We weren't given any food or water during the trip. It was impossible to lay or sit down there was so many of us in each railroad car. Men got sick with diarrhea. We had no sanitary facilities so the floor of each car was filled with urine, vomit and excrement. Our clothing was covered with it. The stench was terrible."

After twenty-four hours the POWs received some bread and margarine and got water the following day. At one stop the prisoners were allowed to de-train to relieve themselves, the first time in forty-eight hours. Then it was back on the train to Stalag XIIID, Nuernberg, a rodent and vermin infested prison camp with no provisions to feed the newly arrived POWs.

On April 4, 1945, the Nuernberg prison camp was

evacuated before the American Army arrived. The POWs were marched ninety miles to Moosburg, Germany, site of Stalag VIIA, described by Westbrook as "a vermin-ridden hellhole".

During the ninety-mile march American fighter planes strafed the column of POWs. Victor Johnson, Nashua, Iowa, said " Three American p-51s came over and one strafed us, then must have realized what was going on and kept the other two planes from attacking. From then on we had a plane over us everyday keeping track of our progress and where we were going." Fortunately the strafing did not kill any POWs who immediately used white clothing to spell out "POWS" on the ground.

Victor described the march as "sleeping in ditches, woods and barnyards." Without food or water except for what could be bartered from farmers or found in the countryside, men drank water from ditches in which others previous to them had relieved themselves.

W.A. Singer thought of escape. He and two other POWs ran across a plowed field into some woods. They wound up walking in circles for hours. The only food they had was a jar of jam and a jar of margarine. One of the escapees got sick. They spent the night in a rabbit hutch in the woods while a tank battle took place near them. With their condition deteriorating the trio decided to get re-captured. They approached a house in a nearby village and were met by a Hungarian SS Officer who promptly took them to a jail. They were treated well and given food. After a few days, American soldiers arrived in the town and Bill was liberated. He was later taken by truck to the POW camp at Moosburg, Germany, the original destination of the march.

The POWs at Moosburg and those that arrived there in early April, 1945, were liberated by Patton's Third Army on April 29. Jim Brown recalled "we could see American tanks on the hilltops surrounding the camp. It wasn't long before Patton's tank crashed through the prison gates liberating the prisoners.

Army field kitchens were set up to feed the POWs until cargo planes could arrive to fly them out to Camp Lucky Strike at Le Havre, France. Willard Spanger weighed just 96 pounds at the time of his liberation

Stalag Luft IV – Gross Tychow, Germany

Seven Iowans interviewed were interned at Stalag Luft IV. The POWs knew that Allied armies advancing through Germany were near. Artillery fire could be heard and they felt their liberation was only a matter of days. The Germans had other ideas and on February 5, 1945, evacuated the prison camp holding between six to ten thousand POWs. The prisoners were given a Red Cross parcel, divided into groups and marched out of Stalag IV under guard. Each Iowan interviewed would be part of the forced march but all would wind up going different routes and be liberated at different locations.

Without exception the POWs slept where they could find shelter whether it be in a barn or forest and in many instances open fields. They were provided little or no food and water. Some were able to forage from the land, steal or barter from farmers and reportedly even eat raw rats for subsistence. As at Stalag Luft III, the prisoners walked in knee deep snow during sub-zero weather, drank contaminated water, and also had dysentery, soiled clothing, blisters, frostbite, lice, and typhus. Their starvation diet led to disease, suffering and death. Some POWs unable to continue became stragglers and were shot.

The group Fred Abigt of Cedar Rapids, Iowa, was in had no guards. The Germans left leaving his group

POW with blanket over shoulder

POWs in snow

the choice of staying at the camp until liberated or walk toward Allied lines. 'We started walking toward the Baltic Sea and Schweinemunde. Farmers fed us along the way. We split up into small groups and slept in barns. After eighty-six days on the road we met elements of the British Second Army." Fred was sent to Brussells, Belgium and eventually flown to Camp Lucky Strike near Le Havre, France.

Carroll Bogard, Mason City, Iowa, had earlier been transferred from Stalag Luft VI. "I made a backpack out of a shirt to carry my belongings. From February 6 to May 4, 1945, we walked across Northern Poland and Germany and stayed on the road until we were liberated by the British Seventh Army at Lauenburg near Hamburg. We had no food except a piece of bread every three weeks. I would find raw potatoes deep in manure piles where they were stored. I would brush them off as best I could before eating them. I remember we walked twenty-five miles on Valentines Day. When we stopped we slept outside and I had one cup of millet soup. We normally slept in barns when we could, but four days we stopped and slept in a gymnasium. The floor was covered with guys. Everyone had dysentery. I went through three sets of clothes. I sneaked away one day and went to a British POW Camp where I saw Russian laborers diving into mud piles to retrieve horse bones thrown into the mud by British soldiers cutting meat off of the bones. They ate like animals looking at each other like dogs protecting their food and watching out for anyone else who might try and take it from them."

Hubert Campney, Emmetsburg, Iowa, had transferred from Stalag Luft VI to Stalag Luft IV. "With Russian troops closing in on our camp we were evacuated and forced to march for eighty-two days without food and water except what could be foraged on the way from the land or traded with farmers. We arrived at Moosburg in early April and remained there until American troops liberated the camp on April 29, 1945." Merlin Dyvig, Humboldt, Iowa, and others were evacuated in advance of February 6. They were forced to march for a week to reach a train that was to take them to Nuernburg, Germany. "We were herded into box cars and rode for fifteen days without food and only a half cup of water a day. The trip lasted longer than normal because Allied aircraft bombed railroad tracks ahead and behind us. At one stop, in the rain, a trainload of Russian women prisoners brought us water." In April, 1945, Merlin was forced to march again, to Moosburg where he was one of the POWs liberated by General Patton's armored force on April 29. "Patton's tank broke down the front gate to the camp and entered the compound. We were free! A skinny guy climbed the flagpole at the camp and tore down the German swastika flag and put up an American flag. There wasn't a dry eye in the place. When I was captured I weighed 185 pounds. When liberated I was down to 127.

Ivan Hunter, Gowrie, Iowa, in January, 1945 rode eight days in a locked railroad boxcar to Nuernberg, Germany, and Stalag XIIID. In April, 1945, he was forced to march ninety miles to Moosburg, Germany where Stalag VIIA was located. The POWs were forced to live off the land as they walked for two weeks. Red Cross parcels given to them before they left were used to trade soap, cigarettes and candy for food with German civilians on the way. Ivan was also liberated on April 29.

Howard Linn, Hubbard, Iowa, was told when evacuating the camp in February, 1945, they would be walking for two or three days and to take with them what they needed and could carry. "We marched for fifty-two days in snow, ice and cold. We slept on open ground and in barns on straw covered with manure. We scrounged food from the countryside. Dysentery and illness reduced our group from two thousand to fifteen hundred. We developed a buddy system for sleeping in the cold by sharing blankets, overcoats and body heat to survive. We arrived at Hanover, Germany, at the end of March. Then they moved us again. We marched another thirty-five days and stopped in woods. The guards suddenly disappeared and later four English soldiers in a jeep drove up to our encampment. They told us to walk toward American lines which we reached the next day."

Melvin Wile, Pomery, Iowa, "we began walking all over Germany. For the next eighty-six days we marched 686 miles often with nothing to eat. We once had one loaf of bread for fourteen guys. At the end of the march we were put in an opera house. An American plane flew over and dropped leaflets saying the First Army was coming. We were liberated on April 26, 1945."

STALAG XIB – FALLINGBOSTEL, GERMANY

POWs at Fallingbostel were evacuated in groups of several hundred at a time. Guarded by elderly German soldiers Thomas McElherne walked during the day and at night slept in nearby woods or farm buildings. "One morning near Denmark we woke up to find the German guards gone. Right after that we were liberated by English soldiers. We saw American trucks pulling howitzers and walked in the direction the jeeps came from until we were told to congregate near a captured airstrip. Transport planes were arranged to fly us to France and then we were trucked to Camp Lucky Strike."

STALAG XIIID – NUERNBERG, GERMANY

Nuernberg was a collection point for those POWs evacuated from Sagan, Poland, and some of the groups that were evacuated from Gross Tychow, Germany. Victor Johnson, Nashua, Iowa, was initially sent to Nuernberg after his capture and marched ninety miles to Moosberg after other POWs arrived and the American Army began to close in on the city. "They marched us out of the camp in early April, 1945, after taking our flight clothes away from us. They gave us an overcoat, blanket, shoes, and a Red Cross parcel. Guarded by elderly German guards we lived off the land until we reached Moosburg and were liberated by Patton on April 29. When the tanks crashed through the main gate we all went crazy with happiness."

STALAG XVIIB – KREMS, AUSTRIA

On April 8, 1945, as Allied armies closed in on Germany, the prisoners of Stalag XVIIB were evacuated from their camp by the Germans. Howard Hobbs, Morning Sun, Iowa, stated "every prisoner packed what he felt were essentials. Under-aged German guards marched us for seventeen days until they reached Branau, Hitler's birthplace. We slept in the open and lived off the land. Food provided by the Germans was on a sporadic basis and a limited amount of Red Cross parcels were doled out to the prisoners. At Branau, we built shelter out of logs and pine boughs and waited. One week later American tanks rumbled into our camp and we were free at last." A month later Howard stepped off the train at Burlington, Iowa, met by his brother.

Following is a diary written by Jean Ray, 100th Bomb Group, Thorpe Abbotts, England, that described experiences during a forced march after evacuation of Stalag Luft XVIIB on April 8, 1945. The diary was transcribed to typewritten form for purposes of clarity and condensation.

"April 8, 1945. Sunday noon was 4,000 American Prisoners of War left Krems, Austria, in advance of the Russian onslaught. The sound of artillery could be plainly heard. We left a few men there because they were physically unable to march. We were taken in groups of 500 at 15 minutes intervals. I remember our last look of camp, what a place. Toilet paper streamers were all about the place. The porches were torn off the barracks used for fires. Patches of tarpaper missing here and there giving the place its fitting name "Desolation". We carried _ American Red Cross parcel for food per man, also one blanket, one overcoat, ten packs of cigs, ten bars soap, three packs of French cigs, one towel, four socks, shaving kit, one short, one undershirt, one sewing kit as well as eating utensils. Our worldly destination. Our group leaders are Charlie Balmer, Don Edder and Frank Arlenger as interpreter. We have no destination, no camp to go to, just keeping on the move until the end of the war, keeping out of battle zones which is pretty hard to do in this country. Most of us have been prisoners going on two years with not much physical exertion due to lack of proper food, etc. So it will indeed be a hard march especially the task of procuring food. Today we walked eighteen kilometers over moutainous terrain, beautiful scenery under different circumstances. We arrived in a little village eight o'clock this evening and we are to sleep on the other side in a field. Going through the town to gain the field picket fences, pieces of timber and other things were rapidly confiscated for cooking fires. The next few days can best be brought to date by a brief summary of what has happened up to now. There has been days because the Germans do not give us much food, it consists of a thin soup each day and sometimes bread and potatoes of miserable rations. Strange to say few men have fell by the wayside. We're marching on guts alone, not food. We have had air raids everyday. Soap and cigarettes are very valuable in this country and are a good measure for procuring food from the civilians. The first stage we made it was quite easy on the small farms up in the mountains but since we have been following the Danube Valley it has been very difficult. Due to the large amounts of ....and other military authorities however I can assure you the people themselves are a long way from starving. Our main trouble or worry is the S.S. troops in larger cities and Gestapo. The civilians are afraid of both. Already some of our boys sneaking off into the hills have been shot by some. As a whole most of the Austrian people are very friendly except in the bombed out areas such as we're in now. Passing through……..we ran into a group of Hungarian Jews who were prisoners. Also took a five-minute break where one lay dead in the ditch with the top of his head blown off. Also on the outskirts of this city we passed through a political prisoners camp or (concentration camp) they were under heavy S.S. guard. Each wore the concentration prisoner's garb. A very pitiful looking group of people as some were in the early teen ages. I might add that it was a huge stone quarry they were laboring in. That just about brings us up to the present with the insertion that it is very easy to escape from our guards but personally I can't see the percentage the way things stand as a whole. We walk fifty minutes and rest ten. Last night we camped on a dummy smudge pot field some thirteen kilometers from Linz. We all sweated coming through this city using a G.I. expression for such. We heard it had been heavily bombed and it was. The Russians dropped several flares and bombs next to the field we camped on. At any rate today we came through Linz and it was really bombed on the outskirts. We saw one bomb crater after another. Also many 500 pound duds lying about with their fins pulled. In the city itself people greeted us with a non too friendly look. Large buildings were nothing but masses of rubble. Windows in countless shops were boarded up. Pieces of shrapnel had torn into trees, automobiles and such things. That impeded their flight. In closing and in doing so bringing this up to date. Today has been a hard strenuous one going through air raids and the wrath of the civilians in the large city of Linz. Also the length and rapidness of today's march. Its most eight o'clock now and I'm writing by a cooking fire. I'm very tired as is every one else, also quite hungry, they likewise, also its going to rain and we're sleeping in an apple orchard. So ends this date, April 18, 1945.

"April 19, 1945. Started out at seven o'clock in the morning. Three boiled potatoes and a hot brew for breakfast. Thirteen kilometers out of Linz we marched by a huge German airdrome. At this same time the air raid sirens blew an alert. Most of the ships dispersed. There were ME-109s and JU-88s. Also most of the pilots were Hungarian. I might add too that there's almost every nationality one can think of fighting with the Germans. I saw English soldiers with Volkstrum bands on, like wise Russian, Italian, Hungarian, Czech, etc. At any rate we took an hour break near the southwestern edge of the air field. Flak guns mostly light stuff were located on the adjoining fields. P-38s came down for a look see and the flak gunners let go with poor luck. Along today's route old shot-up fuselages and portions of packed fuselages were along the highway. The wind is blowing up from the North. Its quite cold lying out along the highway here. Well there goes the call to start marching again. We're all weary as almost all of us had for dinner but two slices of bread. Well in ending we came nineteen kilometers today. Fortunately men from Geneva are here and we are sleeping in barns tonight. Also fairly decent rations. So ends the day. Rations today, one-fifth loaf bread, spoonful sugar, butter, coffee, one-tenth pound of meat."

"April 20, 1945. Today was by far the most exciting one of them all. Nothing on the road but first of all after marching almost thirty kilometers we are to receive a twenty-four hour layover on a farm operated by Hungarians. We arrived here about six o'clock. All of us quite weary. We were assigned to different places in the barns but we preferred to camp outside being a good night for such things. I'll try to briefly describe the type farms most of these are. Their very old and built in a form of a square, more on a stockade order with a courtyard in the center. Cow barns, horse barns, fowl runs, storage spaces all adjoin one another in the square, usually with huge gates on each side of the square. The houses generally are tile-roofed with the barns having thatched ones. Painting is nothing more than whitewash. Some of them one could call picturesque. This farm seemed to be sort of a resting place for jaded horses used by the German military. So much of the hauling is done by these animals due to a shortage of motor transportation. At any rate tonight for supper we received barley soup about the same time we were officially notified that five truck loads of Red Cross parcels were in route to here. God knows this was most welcome news. Ten minutes later it was verified by some of our boys who were getting chow and saw two of the trucks themselves, led by a jeep. What a grand sight. So with this exciting news most of us turned in for the night with our spirits bubbling."

"April 21, 1945. Today is a day of rest also the day we receive our Red Cross parcels. We prepared our breakfast about eight o'clock which consisted of coffee and bread. The rest of the morning I spent in working on my pack and trading. Managed to pick up quite a number of kartoffels(spuds) for soap. Some of the "trader horns" are really in operations, sneaking into town, trading clothes, soap, cigarettes for such eatables as bread, beans, flour, eggs, milk, bacon, etc. Its most interesting to watch the traders. Its almost always customary for the traders, as soon as we hit our nightly stops, to drop packs and beeline for the nearest farm house which is usually swarming with G.I.s at the drop of a hat. At eleven o'clock today five formations of our heavy bombers were seen flying overhead. Almost simultaneously the other Red Cross trucks came roaring, all white with huge red crosses painted on them. These were met with a rousing cheer. Up to five o'clock I spent most of the time cleaning up, peeling spuds and shooting the breeze with some of the boys. They have just called for the men to get our Red Cross parcels. All in all we received one Canadian and one French one between the two of us however the American ones are the best. We fried potatoes for supper and packed our new food in our bulging bags. So ends the day and tomorrow we march at seven o'clock."

"April 22, 1945. Started out at seven. Storm clouds scudding across the skies. Not much of anything happened today with the exception it was a cold, steely day, a miserable one. Reached our shelter at seven o'clock, ate supper and turned in."

Iowans of the Mighty Eighth

"April 23, 1945. Same as yesterday, a blue rainy, blustery day. The roads we traveled on are a muddy mess and could hardly be called anything but the back trails of Austria. We arrived at shelter about five o'clock, ate and turned in for our twenty-four hour stay."

"April 24, 1945. We stayed in a leaky barn last night but it seemed to me like a millionaire's mansion after the raid and cold. Speaking of cold it surprises me the so few men have acquired colds on this march from being out in all types of weather. Some of the men have already been out of camp from early morning trading, lugging in much booty in the way of eggs, meat and bread. Myself not being up to par I didn't go out until about four in the afternoon. To go out you've got to sneak past the guards. Sometimes they shoot a little. Another fellow and I walked to a little village about three kilometers from camp. Even at that late hour generosity was still keen. A very kindly old house Frau gave me about a pound of good meat as well as three pounds of pure wheat flour while a French Kommando Kreigie sneaked me ten pounds of graham flour, two generous portions of bread and a piece of roasted duck. Also an apple. Having done well enough we trudged on back to camp through open fields. There is a little danger in this as one never knows when someone will take a shot at you. I always have that queer feeling of being watched all the time. All in all I'd rather be out on the road than in a prison camp. We have lots of freedom and none of that hateful barbed wire. Although marching twenty-five kilometers a day is quite a ....back. We ate a good supper tonight. Fried potatoes, meat, flap jacks and a chocolate drink. Most men are in what we call a combine. Two men or more go together on food and so forth, also in trading camp duties, etc. My buddy and I have been in such a deal for most two years. It works out much better this way, two heads are better than one and I must say we've cooked up some good meals in our times. I might add that the greater percentage of the Austrian people were very generous and kind people. After all they've been through however this doesn't include the man-child ones. Out of ink from here on out pencil will have to do. At seven o'clock tonight bombing of a heavy sort could be heard in the southwest. At nine o'clock we turned in for a good night's sleep for tomorrow its the road again."

"April 25, 1945. Last night we had another air raid alarm . One ship flew right over our barn barely clearing. I though it was going to cave in. It's a clear but cold morning and my feet are quite cold. We had barley soup and coffee for breakfast left over from yesterday. If we depended on Jerry rations for this march many of us would never reach our destination. We fell out on the march at eight o'clock heading in a southwesterly direction. Today proved to be a most interesting one. Rumor has it that we're going to arrive to our final destination today. At any rate we marched out of hill country. The beautiful snow capped Austrian Alps were visible down into the level river valley country. A little ways from the outskirts of .... an air raid alarm sounded and ten formations of heavy bombers with fighter escort were clearly seen flying over .... headed in towards the Munich area. No ordinary flak was sent up but long streamers of smoke came all the way up from the ground towards the formations. We all took it to be some sort of a rocket. Also a little farther along two P-51's came down on the first of our groups of marching men. I should say one came down the other one circled lazily around higher above the other one to give it protection. He later came back to our group. We exposed the American flag. I'm glad he recognized who we were because if he hadn't his little flying arsenal might have cut us to ribbons. At any rate he flew low and waggled his wings at us, climbed high into the heavens. We sent our cheers and hand waving with him. We passed a huge power plant going into....... Halfway through........two P-51s came down and gave the flak batteries hell as well as blowing a German observation ship to hell. Flak bursts were right over our heads about1000 feet. Heavy and light flak batteries have been all along the trail today. We heard the news today as we usually do from our newsman. It seems as though the United States told Germany that all German officers and enlisted in charge of moving prisoners would be held directly responsible for any cruelty or unjust actions on the road. In answer through neutral sources Germany made the agreement that she would put the moving groups of war prisoners into camps until they were either re-captured or the termination of the war. All told today we walked thirty-two kilometers from hill country to plain country back up into hilly, wooded country and our destination was reached tomorrow. I'll describe it as I'm too tired for further writing."

"April 26, 1945. Last night we arrived at this beautiful prison camp if one could possibly conceive such a thing unless he were German. Its nothing more than a pine forest with a swath of trees cut out all around the forest to signify the boundary lines within which we are to stay which in itself is a farce. The water facilities which on other cases proved fairly easy due to rivers, mountain streams and pumps, but here its nothing more than springs located along the very steepest and most thick undergrowth on the other side of the river. Most of us haven't nothing more

Chapter Fifteen

than cans to get water in. By the time one scrambles up and down a steep descent for water he has little left. Not only are there 4,000 of us but other nationalities as well, French, English and Russians lousy with typhus and cholera. We've done practically the same things as yesterday in the way of preparing our camp life. Also today we received three French Red Cross parcels per four men. Shots can be heard around here every hour of the day as some of the boys often stray too far. No one pays any attention to it for we know of old that the Krauts can hit their mark when they want to. So once again I must end another day in this God forsaken hole with smart and sting of hazy camp fires in nostrils and the damp, dark, smell of a large forest."

"April 28, 1945. Today is by far the most miserable one I've ever spent in my life and I have seen some hard ones in the past twenty months. This morning started off with a gray heavy overcast sky. As a result we were blessed with a cold, drizzly rain. Naturally our pine bough and moss roof soon became saturated and began to leak here and there. Soon it was like standing outdoors. It was difficult to keep a fire going due to wet wood. In going for wood our heavy, issue overcoats soon soaked through causing cold damp clothes to be worn all day. For dinner we cooked up a batch of hot millet which tasted exceptionally well as it was something hot in the belly. Our bed was wet. Also most everything else we possessed. I'm sure that 4,000 more miserable men couldn't be found the world over than right here in Austria. So passes a bad day and tonight may even be worse if it starts a steady rain again. Nevertheless we're going to hit a wet bed tonight. Others are going to stay up all night crouched over a fire rather than sleep in wet blankets. Lets hope for the sun tomorrow."

"April 29, 1945. Good old sunshine has at last finding its way through the trees and everyone is busy trying to dry their meager possessions out. On awakening this morning I found my eyes acting strangely. Blurred vision and a slight ache as well as being slightly puffed up. This is due to wood smoke. Most everyone of late suffers from such an affliction. Some are quite bad. A great number of fellows are still suffering from loose bowel conditions. A most pitiful one in a case like this as there is not enough food and it leaves a fellow quite weak. Quite exciting things happened last night over the airways. It seems as though Himmler sent an unconditional surrender to Truman and Churchill but failed to contact Stalin. This was rejected. For an instant we had the war over. Air raids are here every day and some say they can hear artillery fire but I believe its bombing. With our blankets somewhat dryer than last night we are going to bed early. We received one American no. 10 and an English Red Cross parcel for four men. It revived any dampened spirits and my partner and I really worked it over."

"April 30, 1945. Rained during the night and today as usual was heavily overcast with the sun peeping through once in a great while. At noon today our group went on chow detail. We received one Red Cross box full of beans, 250 pounds of potatoes, twenty-five pounds of meat and a little salt as well as twenty-five loaves of bread. All of this is for 500 men for meals we received in the form of soups. But due to the German's slovenly sanitary conditions we cook our own, what there is of it. We went on our usual wood detail as well as water which took up the rest of the day. For supper we had hot cakes made out of flour acquired on the road, can of sardines, four English biscuits, cocoa drink, Jerry meat stew with a few spuds and carrots thrown in. Also four thin slices of bread with jam. The reason for this splurge is that Major Beaumonte passed an order the men should not leave the camp for water as "Blood and Guts" is mighty close and we are almost encircled. Also he stated that those having quantities of Red Cross food should eat it up as we should be liberated within the next twenty-four hours. Then too we are located near the river from which we get our water. We were cautioned not to go down there if we heard any action. For the last four nights early and late in the evening we can hear old Patton's artillery fire and tonight it sounds very close. The morale of the men is very high but I have never seen it different. Every time we hear explosions we cheer. I might add the Germans blew the bridge up crossing the …. River. Patton is reported at…….fourteen kilometers from here. So with all the good news we retired to the sack(bed). Oh yes its started snowing, boy, there goes the artillery again."

"May 1, 1945. Woke up this morning in pools of icy water as our trustworthy roof leaked again. Fortunately it was snow instead of rain so most of the morning was spent in drying out our lean-to. Wet wood is a wonderful for eyes as it is burning right now. I am sitting before a very cherry fire. Its about six in the evening and very exciting things have happened of which I will try to relate. About four o'clock I was down on the river getting water when artillery shells started bursting on the other side. I got the hell out of there. Also our Major is supposedly surrendering this camp along with the German Colonel. At any rate they are down the road about five kilometers with the American flag. We were ordered that when transportation comes we are not to make an emotional display but get into the trucks as ordered. Already we are organized for such a move. Also in case tanks come breaking through the timber don't climb trees but run at right tangles of them. My partner returned from the river and saw eight tanks going into the village from which a white flag is hung from the church steeple. Wow, they're getting close. I forecast a most exciting evening. Also minutes of seven we were liberated from German bondage. We are once more soldiers of the United States Army. As Major Beaumonte and Don Edder came in camp escorted by a captain in Patton's tank corps he looked like God himself. I can write no more as I can't think right. God I'm happy."

"May 2, 1945. Rained all night again but the excitement keeps a man's spirits up. About eleven o'clock this morning the G.I.s came to camp and disarmed the guards. Boy what a sight. Our good old G.I.s with steel helmets and battle gear on, figuratively speaking (loaded for bear). All the Germans were lined up with their hands on top of their head and I mean they stayed there as our boys didn't take no pains with 'em. Bags, packs canteens, rifles were immediately grabbed by the "Kriegies" for .... everyone is excited but not nearly so much as could be expected. It seems so unreal. Now we have the last laugh on the Jerrys who have kicked us around for the last two years and shot some of our boys in camp. May the dirty bastards rot in hell. No more starving, no more Rouse Appell."

"May 3, 1945. Today as usual we were blessed with a rainy day. As yet no new development on moving out of the woods. Also only a promise of G.I. chow but this can't be helped due to the rapid advance of the army ahead of supplies. Also as the Germans blew up all bridges crossing the …..River and our Engineers have all but completed a pontoon bridge across it. There are three resistance pockets around our area.

Mainly S.S. troops and Hitler Youth snipers. We confiscated everything within a twenty kilometer radius, buses, fire trucks, ambulances, civilian cars, horses, wagons, bicycles, motor cycles, every sort of vehicle imaginable. Run them till the gas gives out then turn them over along the road. The woods are simply a mad house, guns going off at all times, deer hunting with machine guns. Also rounding up German prisoners we take everything they got. Make 'em put their hands on top of their heads and confiscate anything we want. And I or no one else feels a bit sorry for them. We sent our foraging parties in trucks armed to the teeth with German weapons. Bread milk, eggs, flour, meat, rice, beans, noodles and millet were brought in and issued out. Also many of us just walked into the nearest farm house and told them we were staying all night to which they heartily agreed with us. Also taking a few chickens and other eating materials as we left in the morning. It seems a hard thing to do but, us or them and it damned sure won't be us. Actually if an outsider could

Freed POWs celebrate around liberating American tank at Stalag VII, Moosburg, Germany

have a bird's eye view of the situation and the comings and going of the "Kriegies" back and forth to camp would think a three ring circus were in town. To say it's the most laughable thing that's ever happened, seeing is believing. More jeeps just came in I'm going up and see if they have any extra food on their persons. Other than that not much happened today so I'll say adieu until the morrow."

"May 4, 1945. Had lots of fun today. My buddy and I awoke early this morning for a heavy day of liberating. We ate a hurried breakfast of Jerry black bread and coffee. ……is about six miles from our camp and we left about seven o'clock that morning. Many of our comrades were up for the same reason we were. In fact everyone was in very good spirits even though it is a lousy goddamned day. My buddy Phillips is sure a scroungy looking bastard. He tells me I'm no bed of roses mitt red kimmel eyes, no hair and a scraggly beard. We are armed with "Jerry" guns. I possess a very vicious looking "burp" gun plus ample rounds. Phillips has a "Tommy gun" of German vintage plus ammo. We've had quite a big time pre-flighting these jobs. Also lots of our former guards have been found scattered all over the place quite dead."

Freedom at last for at least 40,000 airmen of various American air forces, and thousands more from other branches of the military. After months and years of cold, sickness, starvation, deprivation and then needlessly forced to march in bitter cold and snow for miles, came the emotional experience of being free which words cannot describe. Each POW had his own unique story of misery during captivity and feelings on liberation.

CAMP LUCKY STRIKE

A temporary collection camp for liberated prisoners of war was located at Le Havre, France, named Camp Lucky Strike. It was here as well as other replacement depots freed POWs received de-lousing,

Chapter Fifteen

shaves, showers, haircuts, new issue of clothing, medical treatment, decent food, and back pay. Ships arrived to transport them back to the United States for furlough and re-assignment or discharge. Some POWs were flown back to England to their original bomber or fighter group for the same processing.

Aftermath

It took months and even years for many POWs to adjust to eating good food without getting sick after living a near starvation existence. Many suffered illnesses, injuries and nightmares that plagued them their entire lives. Others would remain bitter over their treatment and refuse to talk of their experiences to friends or family while others talked freely. Some measure of revenge was gained through the Nuremberg War Crimes trials. Some prison guards and officers were executed while others, who treated their POWs humanely, were even invited as guests to post-war prisoner of war reunions.

Merlin Dyvig, Humbotdt, Iowa, felt, "the best thing that ever happened to me was being captured and placed in a prisoner of war camp. No matter how bad things get in life it will never be as bad as that."

Most all POWs were forced to adapt themselves to a mode of living completely foreign to their nature. They became resourceful in improving their living conditions, developed an ability to live in harmony with others under the most trying of circumstances and conditions, and in addition to a clearer sense of values, strengthened a love of their country and loyalty to each other. They became a "band of brothers".

"Many unfortunate people will never understand the love one man may have for another be it one hour, one minute or eternity. But of those who saw action I'm sure they above all understand. They know the companionship of one man to another of every breed, stripe and personality, for in the years of the service by necessity they are mingled with thousands of personalities and every type of man in existence. In that respect, we have come out of this war with a much broader view, and understanding that many men would never attain in two lifetimes while we reached it in a few years. Thus my story starts and in its three years of beginning to end, I have seen with the eyes of thousands."

Jean Ray
Colfax, Iowa
Radio Operator
100th Bomb Group
Ex-POW, Stalag XVII-B

Forced March Summary of Iowans Interviewed

Jim Brown, Bill Singer, George Sterler and Hap Westbrook forced march from Sagan, Luft III to Spremberg, GE. Then rode in railroad boxcars to Nuernberg, then 90 mile march to Moosberg

Carroll Bogard and Hubert Campney rode in railroad boxcars to from Stalag Luft VI to Stalag Luft IV. Bogard then marched three months across N. Germany and N. Poland to Lauenburg
Campney marched 86 days from Luft IV to Moosburg.

Tom McElherne marched from Stalag XIB to near the Denmark border.

Howard Linn marched 52 days from Luft IV to Hanover, GE. 35 more days to unknown area.

Fred Abigt marched for 86 days from Luft IV to Baltic Sea area

Merlin Dyvig and Ivan Hunter rode 8 days in locked box car from Luft IV to Nuernberg, then marched 90 miles to Moosburg

Howard Hobbs marched 17 days from Krems, to Braunau, Austria

After years of captivity and going home it was impossible for the POWs to describe what it meant to sail past the Statute of Liberty. Most just stared in reverent silence with tears streaming down their faces.

"I had never fully realized before going overseas just how wonderful this country of ours is. I had always taken for granted my complete liberty, freedom of speech and countless luxuries that I considered my heritage as an American. My experience of oppression and want in prison camp has changed my perspective completely. I think I have learned my lesson well and feel that I shall never forget it. I am an American. And I am grateful."

Bob Neary, North Wales, PA

Iowans of the Mighty Eighth

Chapter Sixteen

PRISONERS OF WAR

The following Iowans of the Eighth Air Force were shot down by enemy fighters or anti-aircraft fire or forced to make emergency landings behind enemy lines and taken prisoner of war. Listing is by hometown at time of entry into military service. Experiences of those in bold type are contained in Chapter Fifteen, POW Prisoner of War and Chapter Twenty-Two, Biographies.

Fred Abigt, 388th BG, Cedar Rapids
Howard J. Adams, 384th BG, Wilton Jct.
Carl A. Anderson, 392nd BG, Perry
Donald E. Anderson, 423rd BS, Ottumwa
Edwin P. Anderson, 489th BG, Audubon
Joseph W. Anderson, 94th BG, Denison
Frank L. Arnold, 306th BG, Des Moines
Harold L. Basbcock, 401st BG, Des Moines
Robert R. Bagley, 445th BG, Audubon
Boyd E. Baker, 351st BG, Perry
Joseph C. Beasley, 379th BG, Hamburg
Charles W. Beigel, 466th BG, Onawa
John N. Beilstein, 379th BG, Davenport
Robert E. Bembenek, 93rd BG, Clinton
Ben A. Bereskin, 467th BG, Sioux City
Gordon C. Bergquist, 305th BG, Alta
Keith L. Berve, 96th BG, Radcliffe
Charles M. Betzel, 91st BG, Davenport
Samuel M. Bishop, 379th BG, Churdan

Ernest P. Boat, 303rd BG, Sully
James R. Boatright, 448th BG, Council Bluffs
Willis D. Boatright, 96th BG, Monroe
William D. Brooks, 100th BG, Waterloo
James R. Brown, 487th BG, Mason City
Richard K. Brown, 390th BG, Cedar Falls
Robert O. Brown, 390th BG, West Bend
Verlyn G. Brown, 351st BG, Estherville
Rollo L. Budde, 92nd BG, Iowa
Edward C. Burlingham, 95th BG, Walnut
Ralph P. Butler, 306th BG, Muscatine
Hubert P. Campney, 452nd BG, Emmetsburg
John B. Carder, 357th FG, Red Oak
Paul V. Carlson, 100th BG, Sioux City
Robert D. Carpenter, 100th BG, Cedar Rapids
Stanley P. Carson, 100th BG, Woodburn
Stanley W. Cebuhar, 379th BG, Albia
Rodger G. Christensen, 381st BG, Marne

Lloyd N. Christman, 351st BG, Cedar Rapids
Paul R. Clark, 457th BG, Cedar Rapids
Lemoine H. Clausen, 44th BG, Blairstown
John W. Claussen, 487th BG, Sioux City
Neal V. Clyman, 381st BG, Bloomfield
Elmer C. Colt, 446th BG, Sioux City
Russell C. Conrow, 398th BG, Waterloo
Douglas M. Conway, 401st BG, Ankeny
Ray Cook, 305th BG, Ames,
Clifford T. Combs, 489th BG, Aurelia
William F. Cornelius, 100th BG, Glidden
Richard E. Cotton, 446th BG, Sioux City
Jesse Cox, 401st BG, Boone
Ronald D. Cox, 401st BG, Washington
Stanley V. Davidson, 358BG, Ames
John C. Davis, 447th BG, Ottumwa
Robert G. Dawson, 493rd BG, Clinton
Donald W. Decker, 492nd BG, Creston
Sydney H. Dengle, 95th BG, Des Moines

Chapter Sixteen

Ross W. Detillion, 100th BG, St Marys
Charles M. Dewild, 466th BG, Pella
Delbert R. Dimig, 385th BG, Mapleton
Christian A. Dinkel, 306th BG, Council Bluffs
Laurence E. Doyle, 91st BG, Waterloo
Robert J. Duffy, 389th BG, Iowa City
Homer P. Dumont, 91st BG, Sigourney
Edward Every, 388th BG, Hampton
Robert, W. Fillman, 3385th BG, Des Moines
Pete J. Fischer, 100th BG, Council Bluffs
Thomas L. Flaherty, 492nd BG, Waterloo
Keith E. Foster, 379th BG, Cromwell
Collin W. Fritz, 447th BG, Des Moines
Harry L. Fullerton, 305th BG, Washington
Donald L. Gallagher, 388th BG, Cedar Rapids
Thomas L. Gallager, 100th BG, Cedar Rapids
Marion A. Gard, 492ndd BG, Marshalltown
Richard Gaskel, 447th BG, Sioux City
Charles J. Gast, 305th BG, Steamboat Rock
Herbert Gerbers, 482nd BG, Holstein
James D. Gibson, 100th BG, Des Moines
James B. Gilleon, 389th BG, Dubuque
Robert P. Gilroy, 384th BG, Davenport
Glen C. Gladfelder, 452nd BG, Des Moines
Howard W. Greiner, 466th BG, Wellman
Robert L. Gudgel, 388th BG, Boone
Nelson O. Gunnar, 100th BG, Des Moines
Ellsworth E. Gustafson, 493rd BG, Des Moines
William R. Haines, 93rd BG, Sioux City

Lorin W. Hamann, 303rd BG, St. Olaf
Melvin T. Hames, 390th BG, Williams
Robert H. Hannaman, 458th BG, Dubuque
Robert W. Hare, 95th BG, Battle Creek
Ernest K. Harker, 305th BG, Okoboji
Vernon H. Harms, 303rd BG, New Hartford
Donald G. Harrer, 381st BG, Mason City
James Haugen, 446th BG, Soldier
John W. Hayes, 381st BG, Des Moines
Guy R. Hemenway, 91st BG, Dubuque
Howard W. Hobbs, 96th BG, Morning Sun
William E. Hoff, 452nd BG, Algona
Carl C. Hoover, 92nd BG, Sioux City
Donald K. Hopp, 381st BG, Glenwood
Earl Howard, 92nd BG, Des Moines
Donald R. Huddle, 306th BG, Red Oak
Frank H. Hudson, 390th BG, Waterloo
Robert D. Huff, 389th BG, Fontanelle
Samuel D. Humphrey, 381st BG, Clinton
Ivan F. Hunter, 100th BG, Gowrie
Marion A. Iverson, 487th BG, Dolliver
Andrew G. Jackson, 492nd BG, Eldora
Myron G. Jackson, 44th BG, Cedar Falls
Robert E. Jackson, 97th BG, Estherville
Daniel A. Janish, 390th BG, Des Moines
Leo E. Jeane, 303rd BG, Mt. Pleasant
Dale J. Johnson, 96th BG, Washta
Robert H. Johnson, 392nd BG, Wall Lake
Victor L. Johnson, 92nd BG, Charles City
Eldon R. Jones, 381st BG, Red Oak
Maynard L. Jones, 445th BG, Des Moines

Harold M. Jordan, 96th BG, Oskaloosa
Gordon D. Joslin, 392nd BG, Holstein
Lavern D. Kassa, 388th BG, Hanlontown
Earl R. Kearney, 398th BG, Oakland
Donald K. Kehm, 100th BG, Ft. Dodge
William G. Kelly, 388th BG, Hastings
Rolla C. Kilgore, 95th BG, Des Moines
Noel L. Kincart, 466th BG, Bloomfield
Jack H. King, 384th BG, Ottumwa
Charles A. Kipka, 95th BG, Grundy Center
Donald H. Kitzman, 91st BG, What Cheer
Rex C. Knap, 489th BG, Hinton
Albert P. Knight, 92nd BG, Ft. Madison
Joseph H. Koenig, 447th BG, Halbur
Robert M. Koenig, 384th BG, Lemars
Bernard F. Kozik, 100th BG, Elberon
Jack J. Krejci, 392nd BG, Council Bluffs
Max F. Kruse, 96th BG, Clinton
James J. Krutosku, 389th BG, Carroll
Maurice Lampe, 392nd BG, Ft Madison
Gordon M. Lane, 100th BG, Mapleton
Lloyd Lauger, 392nd BG, Mt. Pleasant
Robert L. Leclere, 388th BG, Manchester
Robert D. Lerow, 448th BG, Harvey
Clarence A. Liddick, 96th BGH, Casey
Vern R. Lines, 100th BG, Rockford
Howard A. Linn, 492nd BG Radcliffe
Robert P. Livingston, 303rd BG, Des Moines
Stewart B. Livingston, 452nd BG, Scranton
Harry R. Long, 381st BG, Des Moines
Richard T. Longman, 96th BG, Clinton
Wayne L. Lough, 385th BG, Ollie
Winston F. Lowe, 94th BG, Cedar Rapids

Iowans of the Mighty Eighth

Aaron J. Lowry, 94th BG, Fontanelle
Richard H. Lowry, 398th BG, Iowa
Derwood E. Macklin, 379th BG, Adel
Earl E. Macksey, 305th BG, Oskaloosa
Norman J. Macloud, 388th BG, Sioux City
Dallas V. Madland, 446th BG, Linwood
Wallace J. Maxon, 446th BG Marble Rock
Charles A. McBride, 487th BG, Muscatine
Harold S. McCarty, 388th BG, Donnellson
Thomas E McElherne, 388th BG, Ames
Roland P. McGee, 94th BG, Council Bluffs
Robert H. McGreevy, 381st BG, Ackley
George W. McMullin, 100th BG, Casey
Harold E. McMurray, 91st BG, Des Moines
William D. Mehegan, 453rd BG, Cedar Rapids
Charles E. Messeri, 448th BG, Council Bluffs
Donald G. Meston, 100th BG, Council Bluffs
Eugene S. Mettler, 467th BG, Des Moines
William C. Metz, 388th BG, Sioux City
James R. Meyer, 445th BG, Sioux City
Albert E. Miller, 458th BG, Missouri Valley
Dewitt A. Miller, 392nd BG, Council Bluffs
Homer L. Miller, 447th BG, Yale
Willard H. Miller, 100th BG, Iowa
Marlin C. Monson, 452nd BG, Forest City
James M. Moorhead, 381st BG, Winterset
James L. Morrison, 401st BG, Grinnell
Max R. Morrow, 457th BG, Seymour
Kenneth R. Morse, 44th BG, Eagle Grove
Duane D. Mowry, 452nd BG, Audubon

James W. Mulder, 388th BG, Orange City
George T. Nacos, 453rd BG, Dubuque
Lawrence W. Neuhauser, 306th BG, Clarksville
Charles A. Newell, 305th BG, Audubon
Robert R. Nichols, 489th BG, Ft. Madison
Fred W. Nicklas, 351st BG, Washta
Ernest F. Nonneman, 96th BG, Hartley
Lloyd R. Nodstrom, 388th BG, Davenport
Henry A. Norgaard, 493rd BG, Council Bluffs
Donald G. Norvet, 95th BG, Forest City
Irvin J. Olson, 100th BG, Postville
Phillip W. Ong, 100th BG, Mason City
Charles R. Parkhill, 452nd BG, Iowa
Charles J. Passica, 453rd BG, Ft. Dodge
Edward H. Patterson, 389th BG, Iowa City
Dean M. Peppmeir, 446th BG, Truro
Gilbert F. Perry, 384th BG, Dakota City
Kelvin H. Pierce, 487th BG, Storm Lake
Robert W. Pike, 493rd BG, Ft. Madison
Donald F. Pilcher, 91st BG, Anamosa
Theodore E. Pollard, 306th BG, Boone
Vemise G. Polly, 490th BG, Sioux City
John T. Powers, 448th BG, Delmar
John Rabenold, Unit Unk-Ottumwa
Mile A. Raim, 385th BG, Cedar Rapids
Gerald J. Ralston, 392nd BG, Des Moines
John Rasko, 351st BG, Blockton
Robert J. Rasmussen, 398th BG, Sioux City
Vernon Rathbun, 94th BG, Waterloo
Jean E. Ray, 100th BG, Newton
Burl L. Renolds, 100th BG, Tingley
Earl L. Richardson, 100th BG, Washington

Paul D. Richardson, 457th BG, Albia
Lloyd J. Roberts, 445th BG, Oskaloosa
Walter R. Rolfe, 458th BG, Council Bluffs
Donald G. Ruggles, 100th BG, Scranton
Rudolph R. Rust, 379th BG, Burlington
Marion W. Saffell, 93rd BG, Des Moines
Frank W. Sage, 452nd BG, Colfax
Frank A. Saunders, 303rd BG, Dubuque
Arthur W. Schinker, 303rd BG, Norway
John A. Schmidt, Jr., 93rd BG, Council Bluffs
Russell L. Schultz, 384th BG, Ft. Dodge
Dale E. Scott, 401st BG, Sidney
Frank G. Scott, 487th BG, Storm Lake
Myron Seiberling, 385th BG, Mitchellville
John F. Sherrets, 92nd BG, Quasqueton
Kenneth W. Simmons, 389th BG, Newell
William A. Singer, 384th BG, Newton
Loren G. Smith, 392nd BG, Ottumwa
Myron L. Sorden, 306th BG, Indianola
Donald G. Soseman, 305th BG, Nevada
Willard Spangler, 388th BG, Everly
Melvin J. Spencer, 95th BG, Mason City
Arthur Staton, Jr., 452nd BG, Audubon
Eugene R. Stephens, 453rd BG, Waterloo
George T. Sterler, 96th BG, Ashton
Gerald H. Steussy, 100th BG, Algona
Lowell F. Stevenson, 303rd BG, Des Moines
George E. Stewart, 303rd BG, Chester
Norman D. Stuckey, 91st BG, Udell
Gerald L. Swanger, 92nd BG, Cromwell

Chapter Sixteen

Wendall K. Thieman, 95th BG, Waterloo
Blaine E. Thomas, 303rd BG, Council Bluffs
Richard S. Thomas, 447th BG, Des Moines
Robert E. Thompson, 392nd BG, Clare
Carroll O. Tiegland, 92nd BG, Ames
Jack L. Timmins, 3303rd BG, Des Moines
John W. Tomke, 306th BG, Clarion
Charles W. Turner, 390th BG, Waterloo
Glenn Underwood, 447th BG, Shenandoah
Warren L. Vaneschen, 94th BG, Ackley
Raymond D. Vogel, 467th BG, Clinton
Wilbur J. Vogel, 448th BG, Dubuque
Frank Vratny, 487th BG, Lehigh
Billy R. Walker, 385th BG, Des Moines
Ramond T. Walton, 392nd BG, Clinton
Robert W. Ward, 91st BG, Boone
Walter E. Ward, 94th BG, Vinton
Joseph F. Waters, 392nd BG, Carroll
Dale R. Watson, 445th BG, Belknap
John M. Watson, 351st BG, Glidden
Donald E. Watts, 445th BG, Ionia
John E. Wells, 92nd BG, Sioux City
Hartley A. Westbrook, 44th BG, Coon Rapids
Dale T. Westell, 390th BG, Pocahontas
Charles E. Whitacre, 467th BG, Dallas Center
Frank R. Whitehead, Jr., 390th BG, Marshalltown
Frank L. Whittington, 486th BG, Dubuque
Melvin V. Wile, 389th BG, Marathon
James J. Wolfe, 447th BG, Danville
Stephen H. Wurtz, 305th BG, Underwood

EVADEES

Bomber crews and fighter pilots received battle damage to the extent they were unable to make it back to their base in England. Forced or crash landings were made behind enemy lines or the air crews had to parachute from their aircraft into Axis held territory. More often than not this meant capture and internment as a prisoner of war. Some were able to avoid capture by being far enough away from German troops they were able to successfully hide and eventually make their way to Allied control. A lot depended on the stage of the war at the time. Toward the latter stages Allied armies were advancing into Germany and were not far from where airmen landed or parachuted. Earlier in the war escape from capture required the helping hand of resistance or underground groups and common citizens of occupied countries. All countries occupied by Germany had individuals who at the risk of their own lives and quite often their entire family, assisted Allied airmen who were downed behind enemy lines. They fed, hid, clothed them, provided false identity papers and made contacts with groups who were able to return the airmen to Allied control to fight again. The following Iowans of the Eighth Air Force were shot down, made forced landings or parachuted behind enemy lines, evaded capture and returned to Allied hands:

William Baltisburger, 452nd BG, Marshalltown
Joseph C. Beasley, 379th BG, Hamburg
John N. Beilstein, 379th BG, Davenport
Robert L. Bobcat, 448th BG, St Charles
Charles S. Bowman, 445th BG, Marshalltown
Nelson A. Branch, 448th BG, Webster City
Everett L. Childs, 384th BG, Manchester
George F. Clark, 389th BG, Ames
Robert H. Copley, 305th BG Davenport
Thomas C. Gallagher, 100th BG, Cedar Rapids
Gerald Glaza, 7th Photo Recon, Cedar Rapids

Henry Glover, 379th BG, Sanborn
Lewis J. Gracik, 379th BG, Washington
Keith R. Haight, 384th BG, Winfield
Max I. Harder, 379th BG, Harlan
Clarence Hightshoe, 398th BG, Iowa City
John E. Hurley, 448th BG, Des Moines
Dwight F. Kelley, 100th BG, Hastings
Harold J. Killian, 93rd BG, Council Bluffs
Clarence I. Larrew, 493rd BG, Boone
Verne H. Lewis 457th BG, Des Moines
Glen A. McCabe 351st BG, Mt Pleasant
Robert M. McCowen, 95th BG, Waterloo

Gerald K. Miller, 458th BG, Des Moines
Donald S. Mohr, 379th BG, North English
Raymond J. Murphy, 91st BG, Des Moines
George T. Nasos, 453rd BG, Dubuque
Hal J. Nelson, 452nd BG, Iowa City
Grover C. Nordman, Jr., 91st BG, Des Moines
Wendell W. Oge, 390th BG, Burlington
Ronald W. Reed, 493rd BG, Ringstead
Charles J. Vejda, 466th BG, Cedar Rapids
Wilbur E. Volz, 447th BG, Edwardsville
John Whitney, 91st BG, Des Moines
James R Wilson, 379th BG, Waterloo

Clarence Hightshoe, 384th Bomb Group, Iowa City, was on a mission to Ludwigshaven, Germany to bomb a chemical plant on September 4, 1944. Immediately after "bombs away" his aircraft was hit by flak knocking out the plane's electrical and hydraulic systems. They lost altitude and received additional hits from flak knocking out the ball turret and most of his left wing. Unable to parachute from the aircraft Clarence and his crew crash-landed in a field near a woods. The crew exited the airplane and while being shot at by ground fire, rushed to the woods. The crew decided to split up in pairs and try and make it to safety. After finding a place to hide, Clarence and his ball turret gunner slept during the day and walked at night. They hid under brush from German soldiers they spotted in the area and who walked dangerously near them. They left the safety of the woods and entered open farm country. After following a hedgerow to a high point on the ground they rested. While there they spotted an American jeep on a road below them. The pondered how to surrender to your own troops without getting mistakenly shot. They waited until another jeep came down the road and left the hedgerow only to be confronted by machine guns pointed at them. Clarence yelled "We're Americans". The soldiers on the business end of the machine guns were an advance American patrol also following the hedgerow on the front lines. The day before the patrol had picked up additional members of Clarence's crew.

William Baltisburger, 452nd BG, Marshalltown, was part of a two man crew flying a B-17 bomber loaded with explosives with the intent of crashing the plane into an important bridge behind enemy lines. Before the plane hit the target Bill and the pilot were to parachute to safety and be picked up by French resistance members who would guide them back to Allied control. The target was hit, but German troops captured Bill and the pilot. After two weeks in captivity Bill and the pilot were to be moved to another location. During a lax moment they saw their chance to escape and ran for it. Hiding and moving in a westerly direction for two weeks they were aided by a farmer who contacted members of the resistance and returned them to the American side of the front lines.

George Clark, 389th BG, Ames, was forced to parachute from his stricken bomber and landed behind enemy lines where he was captured by German S.S. troops. For the next several days he was shuttled and transferred from one location to another before finally being loaded on a trained destined for a prisoner of war camp. On the fourth day during the trip George and six other Americans were able to jump from the moving train. They walked cross-country until they met a French farmer who fed and hid them from the Germans until American ground forces captured the area.

Henry Glover, Sanborn, was a radio operator with the 379th Bomb Group. While on a mission his aircraft was hit by "flak". Unable to fly back to England the pilot crash landed the plane in France. Henry and his crew got out of their aircraft and ran. While German troops searched for them, they hid in haystacks, barn lofts and attics of French homes until underground forces were able to return them to England in a boat.

James Wilson, Waterloo, was a flight engineer and top turret gunner with the 379th Bomb Group. On May 7, 1944, during a mission to bomb Berlin, Germany, enemy fighters and anti-aircraft fire disabled his aircraft and set it afire. Jim and three other crew members parachuted from the aircraft over what was German-occupied Holland. When Jim landed on the ground German soldiers were coming after them. A sixteen year old Dutch boy appeared and told them to follow him. The men were hidden in a small cave for three days and nights. The fourth day they were transported by car to a home near a church in a small town where they hid for almost three months. Area German troops were looking for a person who had killed a Nazi sympathizer and it was risky to stay in one place too long. Germans had a habit of looking for people and arresting them after curfew. Each night Jim and his crew would sneak into the church to spend the night in a space behind the organ. In the morning they would return to the house.

The Dutch Underground decided to move the airmen. The crew was given false identification and rode by train with a member of the Underground. They were to exit the train when the Underground man did. On the train Jim was almost caught. He wore his Waterloo High School class ring and usually turned it upside down to show only a gold band. He inadvertently had his ring turned upward and a man sitting next to him was trying to read the inscription on it, but said nothing. After exiting the train Jim was taken to a camp hidden in some woods where he spent the next six weeks. He was then sent to a farm near a small town where he slept in a barn and helped with the farm work. They were then shipped by truck at night with others under the identity of farm laborers given a holiday. Two truckloads were to cross the Rhine River. Jim's truck, the second one, was delayed. The first truck load of laborers were machine-gunned. Jim fled hiding in some woods. The next day he saw a farmer who agreed to help him. Jim spent the winter in a barn near a small village.

In March, 1945, Jim and his tail gunner crossed the Rhine River in a small boat, and despite German patrols made it to the other side and reach Canadian ground forces. Jim was subsequently turned over to the American Army and sent home. "When we arrived in New York harbor I saw a sight I shall never forget: The Statue of Liberty. What a thrill! I shall never forget that moment. When I saw her I said a little prayer. I thanked God for being with me, for bringing me home safe, and I vowed that when I got back home and if I got married and had a home of my own I would fly the Stars and Stripes out in front of my house every single day of my life. And I have kept that promise."

John Hurley, Des Moines, was a Co-Pilot was the 448th Bomb Group. On his twelfth mission his aircraft was hit by German anti-aircraft guns. John and his crew bailed out of their stricken plane. John was aided by the French Underground to avoid capture by German forces and was eventually returned to Allied control.

Gerald Miller, Des Moines, was a Radio Operator and Top Turret Gunner with the 458th BG, Horsham St. Faith, England. On July 12, 1944, while on the bomb run over railroad marshalling yards at Munich, Germany, the number three-engine of his aircraft was hit by "flak". "We couldn't keep up with our bomb group so we peeled off losing speed and altitude. Our pilot gave us the choice of landing in Switzerland or try to make it back to England. We elected to try for England. While over Belgium we ran out of gas. The pilot ordered everyone to bail out. I remember our tail gunner wouldn't jump. The pilot told the crew he has to jump cause we were going down and were going to crash. One guy yelled back to the pilot, "he's gone, I pushed him".

"At the time we were only about sixteen miles into Belgium from the German border. After I bailed out of the plane I landed headfirst in some trees. After I cut myself loose and fell to the ground I took off running and saw two guys following me. They caught up with me and motioned for me to follow them. They were part of the "Army Blanche", the Belgian Resistance to Germany."

"I was taken to an old castle where I was told to put on some women's clothing and get rid of my American flight clothes. After dark I was led through a forest to a spot where I was to cover myself with leaves and branches and wait. I was then taken to a farmhouse where I was fed wine. I hid in their barn and then for two or three nights traveled at night with the guides and hid in the daytime. After hiding in a potato field I was taken to a big farmhouse where two elderly ladies were hiding five other American flyers. One of them had been at the farmhouse for over a year. We were now only one mile from the French border near the town of Blarnegeis. The roads were well patrolled by German forces."

We spent our days learning to speak French and playing cards. If the house was to be searched there were panels in the walls that could be opened and closed to allow us to hide in the walls. We could climb to the third floor of the house where there was a cupola on top of the roof where we could see the country-side and German troops on the roads near there."

One morning we woke up and heard shooting. A tank battle was going on near the town. The Germans pulled out of the area and American G.I.s showed up and got out of their tanks. As a group the six of us walked to them. They pointed their guns at us. We told them we were Americans. They didn't believe us. We showed them our dog tags.

They still didn't believe us and started asking us all kinds of questions about America and where we were from. After I said I was from Iowa, a sergeant left and came back with a Lieutenant Colonel also from Des Moines. It didn't take long to prove we were Americans."

Chapter Sixteen

INTERNEES

Aircrews attempting to return from missions with damaged planes or with seriously wounded crewmen aboard that could not survive the long flight back to England were faced with limited alternatives. They could land behind German lines or Axis-held territory and be taken prisoner of war; try to make Allied-held territory or friendly country and land wherever possible; try to make England and risk having to ditch in the English Channel or North Sea; or for some, because of the route taken to or from their mission, land in a neutral country where they would be interned for the duration of the war.

Internment in a neutral country meant living in a resort or hotel set aside for those interned with good food and freedom of movement, except escape. To escape and be captured meant prison for the duration of the war. Many crews faced with the dilemma of whether to try and make it back to England in their damaged plane or land in a neutral country, chose returning to base. Others had no choice and had to land at the earliest opportunity or face a crash landing or death of a wounded crewmember. Some it must be presumed, landed in Switzerland or Sweden to finish out the war far from harm's way. Navigational errors caused other aircraft to violate a neutral country's air space and The Hague Convention of 1907 stated that a country that formally declared neutrality during wartime would not to be invaded. It had the right to trade with countries at war in order to provide food and goods for its people. The neutral had to prevent troops or planes from crossing its territory or air space, respect blockades and embargoes imposed on it and refuse to send troops, war material or money to any country at war. Both the Axis and Allied countries in World War II tried to influence neutral nations to ally themselves with one side or the other, put pressure on the neutral to allow troops to pass through its territory, or not trade strategic war materials with another country. Neutrals because of their ports, island, or raw materials were under constant pressure from Germany.

Denmark, Norway, The Netherlands, Belgium and Luxembourg were unfortunate. Small, defenseless countries they were in the path of the German war machine and were simply overrun. Finland was attacked by Russia and had to defend itself and at times had help from the Germans. Switzerland, Sweden, Spain, Portugal, Turkey and Ireland were able to remain neutral, however neutral countries at one time or another were partial to one side or another during the war either in thought or actions and sometimes as the fortunes of war changed. Sweden was rich in iron ore that was shipped to Germany and at one time allowed German troops to cross its territory. Ireland allowed the United States to establish a Base Air Depot that modified bombers in route to England that had come fresh from American factories. Portugal and Spain, recovering from a civil war and strategically located at the entrance to the Mediterranean Sea, was a haven for spies and intrigue for both sides during the war.

Iowans of the Mighty Eighth

Over 150 American B-17 and B-24 bombers and their crews were interned in Switzerland and an untold number in Sweden during World War II.

The following Iowans of the Eighth Air Force were shot down or made forced landings in neutral countries during World War II and interned until cessation of hostilities:

William G. Blackbum, 491st BG, Malvern
Harold R. Chambers, 44th BG, LaPorte City
Aldrich A. Drahos, 448th BG, Cedar Rapids
Lawrence L. Feyerabend, 384th BG, Council Bluffs
Leask H. Herman, 93rd BG, Waterloo
Carol C. Highsmith, 381st BG, Hawarden
David J. Hotle, 392nd BG, West Chester
John R. Jaquis, 44th BG, Jefferson
Alvin W. Jaspers, 390th BG, Steamboat Rock
Francis Johnson, 92nd BG, Cedar Rapids
Robert M. Krumm, 457th BG, Van Horne
John J. Milliken, 448th BG, Corning
Loyd Morse, 448th BG, Fort Dodge
Donald T. Nagle, 490th BG, Davenport
Robert Preis, 493BG, West Burlington
Edaard B. Vaderweid, 44th BG, Sioux Center

Listing of POWs, Evadees, and those Interned taken from "The Mighty Eighth Roll of Honor", Eighth Air Force Memorial Museum Foundation Publication, 1977 by Paul M. Andrews and William H. Adams. Additional names were added to the listing based on information obtained from individual interviews.

Francis Johnson, Cedar Rapids, was a tail gunner with the 92nd Bomb Group. In February, 1945 while on a mission to bomb Berlin, his aircraft received hits from German anti-aircraft batteries causing the loss of one engine and malfunctioning of another engine. Crippled, they fell behind their formation and lost altitude. They were faced with the possibility of having to ditch in the North Sea but were able to reach Malmo, Sweden, where Francis and his crew were interned for the remainder of the war.

Loyd Morse, Fort Dodge, was a B-24 pilot with the 448th Bomb Group. On a bombing mission to Munich, Germany, his aircraft was hit by "flak" causing loss of fuel. Unable to make it back to England, Loyd landed in Switzerland. Loyd and his crew were billeted in a resort hotel. With no special duties to perform and nothing to do, boredom became the biggest problem for the internees. Loyd and two other officers decided to escape aware that capture meant prison. They boarded a freight train and hid in cars the train was transporting to northeast Switzerland. Loyd spoke sufficient German at that point to obtain railroad tickets that took them to the city of Geneva. While on the train they sat across from three German officers. At Geneva they were assisted by the French Underground who hiked them through the mountains for ten days to reach American ground forces.

Robert Preis, West Burlington, was a pilot with the 493rd Bomb Group on a mission to bomb Berlin when an engine of their aircraft malfunctioned and had to be "feathered". This caused them to drop out of formation because of lack of power and fuel and decided to return to their base while still over Germany. They were hit by "flak" causing the loss of another engine and wound up over Sweden. A Swedish fighter plane intercepted them and motioned them to the ground. On landing they lost another engine but landed safe. "We had 168 flak holes in our aircraft. We were later told that if you fly across any part of Sweden you must land or be shot down. A Major in the Swedish Army entered the plane and recited the Rules of the Geneva Convention on Neutral Countries and told us we would be interned for the duration of the war." They were billeted in a retirement home and had freedom of movement to go anywhere but escape. When the war ended Robert assisted in repairing interned American aircraft and flying them back to England.

Chapter Seventeen

REMEMBERANCE

The war was over. Returning servicemen now looked to the future. Their youth had been taken from them. They had matured and encountered experiences beyond their years. They were filled with a sense of purpose as they returned home, sought employment or took advantage of the G.I. Bill of Rights to attend college. The married re-united with their spouses and began to build a life together. Those who had put marriage "on hold" until after the war were now free to resume their plans.

To a few the military suited their needs and chose to remain on active duty and make the Air Force their career. Chaplain Charles Fix, Spirit Lake, retired as a Lieutenant Colonel. Clayton Scott, Osceola, retired as a Lieutenant Colonel and George Kesselring, Guthrie Center, retired as Major. Charles Buckley, Iowa City, re-enlisted in the Air Force thirteen years after the end of World War II and retired nineteen years later. Glenn Underwood, Shenandoah, re-entered military service during the Korean War and Harlyn Turner, Dubuque, re-entered the Air Force two years after the end of World War II and served as a B-29 aerial gunner. Merlin Bruning, Carroll, received his discharge at the end of World War II but re-enlisted in the U.S. Army, took airborne training and served in Korea, then became a Green Beret and served a tour in Viet Nam.

After the end of World War II, Air Force Reserve and Iowa Air National Guard units soon filled with Eighth Air Force veterans who served various terms of enlistment tours including many who retired as higher ranking officers. Flying was "in their blood" and Reserve and National Guard units allowed them to pursue their individual careers yet maintain an association with military aviation. Galen Wiley flew for thirty years with the Iowa Air National Guard at Boone. Both he and Claude Conklin of Belle Plaine serve on the airport commission of their respective communities. Robert Chrisjohn, Alden, served as Deputy Commanding Officer of his Air Guard unit and Assistant Adjutant General in Iowa's State Headquarters. He retired as a one-star general. Hap Westbrook, Ames, helped organize the Iowa Air Guard and became its first Chief Pilot.

Some Eighth Air Force officer aircrew received only a separation from service instead of a discharge at the end of the war, subject to recall at the needs of the service. The outbreak of the Korean War was such a need. Many Iowa veterans were recalled during the Korean War. Although most were given stateside duties because of their experience, Claude Conklin flew fourteen combat missions as a B-29 aerial gunner. Bill Singer, Ames, an attorney, served as Assistant Staff Judge Advocate at Strategic Air Command Headquarters near Omaha, Nebraska, and retired as a Colonel after twenty-six years service.

Former non-pilot air and ground crew veterans took flying lessons. Former pilots upgraded their flying skills for both pleasure and commercial purposes. Robert Kelley, Lisbon, built his own experimental aircraft in the basement of his home and flew it during his business career and retirement. Robert Reeves, Waterloo, a former aerial gunner, owned five airplanes that he either flew or leased to technical schools for use in aviation classes. Leon Hanna, Havelock, a former navigator, owned and flew twenty-two different airplanes during his lifetime. Hap Westbrook, managed three different airports, marketed airplanes for various aircraft companies and operated a flying service for practically his entire life. He was inducted into the Iowa Aviation Hall of Fame.

Following the end of World War II and for nearly sixty years hence, movies continue to be made of major events or battles during the war. Books written by historians, correspondents and veterans told of combat experiences including some published by Iowans. The advent of television also brought World War II to the public through movie re-runs, movies made special for television, documentaries, and serial programs.

Iowans of the Mighty Eighth

  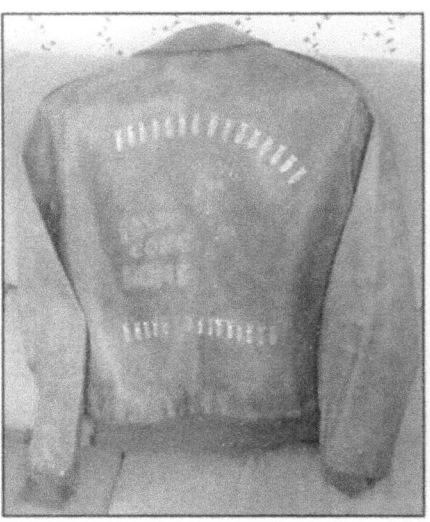

From the left: Queenie – Blair Rossow, Panora, 34th BG ; Tomahawk Warrior – Marvin Ford, Tipton, 381st BG ; Lassie Come Home – Robert Megchelsen, Washington, 91st BG; (Below): Jacket with B24 bomber – "Little Rollo", Harlyn Turner, Dubuque, 446th BG; Jacket with bombs and plane – Kenneth Oseth, Cedar Rapids, 446th BG; Jacket with 2 flags – Kenneth Newson, Des Moines, 486th BG

 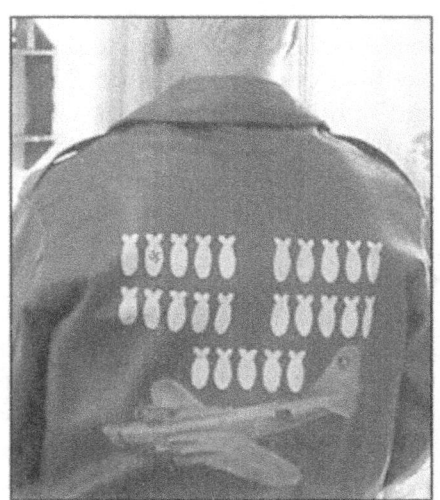 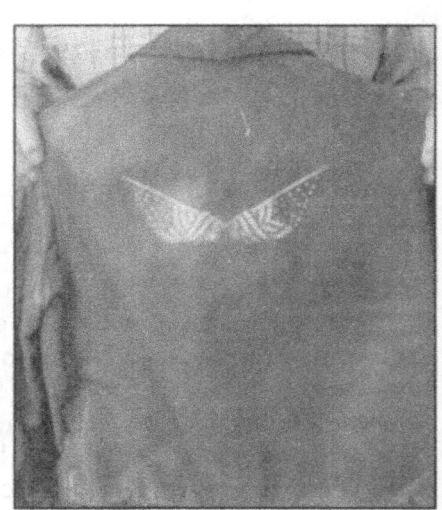

All have played an important role in keeping history alive, education of current and future generations on the horrors of war and the fact that freedom isn't free.

The World War II era was as never before in American history, perhaps in part that it was a total team effort by every patriotic American. Children in scrap drives, men and women in defense plants, technological advances that gave the upper hand, public support of war bond drives, every soldier, sailor, marine, coast guardsman, merchant marine and airman, everyone sacrificed and pulled together for one goal – to win, regardless of cost.

Some servicemen that returned from World War II chose to put the past behind them and remain anonymous. Others corresponded with and met individually with those closest to them that had served together. A strong bond and camaraderie had developed with the men they had fought alongside. Army and Marine combat units, Navy ship crews and Air Corps Groups formed Unit Associations with newsletters and periodic reunions to continue their comradeship. Military unit associations were formed between those who shared the most unique of experiences, the life and death struggle involved in a global war. To witness slaughter and death on a daily basis and experience extreme fear, terror, and horror would be impossible for anyone to fathom unless it happened to them. To lose comrades and friends, to survive together in war from near death experiences, welded these men into a bond of perpetual brotherhood.

Their wartime memories continued to surface in their daily life. Nearly every Eighth Air Force veteran interviewed had his own "niche" in his home where he displayed with pride his individual and/or crew photograph, candid snapshots, and medals display. Other memorabilia included pieces of "flak" which had riddled their aircraft, bomb safety pins, and one item highly sought after by collectors of militaria, the A-2 flight jacket painted with the name of the his air-

Chapter Seventeen

From top left: Bob Peters, Grinnell, 445th BG; Three plates of Lavern Peters, Bedford, 389th BG; Bronze Star Plate of Wesley Franklin, Des Moines, 34th BG; and Hjalmer Hellberg, Marshalltown, 379th BG

plane, nose art and bombing missions. They have long outgrown their jackets, many of which have deteriorated with raveled cuffs, torn lining or cracked leather. Regardless, they remain a prized possession of their owner testifying to their contribution and service within the Eighth Air Force and World War II.

Pride in their service, unit and airplane is also shown by personalized car license plates, bumper stickers, decals, shirts and hats imprinted with the Eighth Air Force logo or their unit designation purchased from their parent unit PX or Eighth Air Force Historical Society.

It was not until 1975 that Veterans of the Eighth Air Force formed a national organization adopting the name, Eighth Air Force Historical Society to preserve for all time the accomplishments and history of the "Mighty Eighth". National reunions were organized that provided the opportunity for veterans of the Eighth to get together. The Society maintains a clearing house that reunites veterans with associates of their parent bomber or fighter group and a national magazine was established.

From the national organization, individual States formed Chapters so veterans within the same geographic area could meet for fellowship, sharing wartime experiences and perpetuating the goals of the National organization.

In Iowa, a Chapter was formed in the summer of 1983 and the first of annual reunions held the following year. The state was divided into geographic "Wings" to allow smaller semi-annual meetings. Despite losing members to Father Time, veterans of the Eighth continue to surface and join the Historical Society. Associate members, relatives of Eighth Air Force veterans or persons interested in military or aviation history are able to join and take part in all activities as well as serve on the State Board of Directors. All meetings are intended to be fellowship in nature with a stipulated goal of preserving for all time, the accomplishments and history of the "Mighty Eighth".

In remembrance whole museums emerged and existing museums required renovation to house World War II artifacts, memorabilia, aircraft and equipment to educate future generations and pay homage to those who participated in the war. The Eighth Air Force Memorial Museum Foundation was formed as an educational-informational body in 1977 to perpetuate the history of the 8th AF by establishing museum exhibits in various air museums in the US and elsewhere. The Foundation's goal is to inform the public about the 350,000 members of the WWII 8th AF in Europe, the "big picture" of WWII 8th AF, and internationally memorializing the 350,000 who served, 47,000 casualties and 26,000 KIA in WWII.

Gerald Miller, Des Moines, third from left, and balance of his crew reunite fifty-nine years after being shot down and evading capture.

Unable to leave the monastery at New Mellery Abbey, Peosta, Father James O'Connor's crew of "La-Dee-Doo" come to the Abbey to reunite with him.

Their activities have included donation of a photo collection to the Library of Congress, an 8th AF document collection at Maxwell AFB, Alabama, and an archival depository at Pennsylvania State University. Money from annual membership dues were donated to help build the 8th AF exhibit at the American Air Museum within the British War Museum at Duxford, England and their restoration of a B-17 bomber and P-47 fighter plane. Contributions were also made toward an Eighth Air Force Exhibit at the Experimental Aircraft Association Museum, Oshkosh, Wisconsin; preservation of the "Memphis Belle" B-17 at Memphis, Tennessee; World War II control tower at the Air Force Museum, Dayton, Ohio; "Hall of the B-24 Legions" exhibit at Pueblo, Colorado; and 8th Air Force Museum at Barksdale, Louisiana. Base locator maps were placed in exhibits at the Commemorative Air Force Museum, Midland, Texas; Duxford, Oshkosh, and Weeks Air Museum, Orlando, Florida. Sixty-one aviation art prints by British artist Keith Hill were also placed in the museum at Oshkosh.

Eighth Air Force Museum at Pooler, Georgia near Savannah.

In 1996 construction of an Eighth Air Force Museum located at Pooler, Georgia, near Savannah, was completed to be the home of "The Mighty Eighth" and house the core of Eighth Air Force exhibits, a central PX and membership record center. In addition to the ever-growing museum, its Memorial Gardens, Chapel of the Fallen Angels and archives make it a unique learning experience for visitors.

Other air museums throughout the United States and in Britain maintain Eighth Air Force displays and memorabilia including the Air Force Museum at Dayton, Ohio, Air Force Academy at Colorado Springs, Colorado, Strategic Air Command Museum near Omaha, Nebraska, and the Pima Air Museum near Phoenix, Arizona. Within Iowa, Eighth Air Force displays have been included in air museums being built at Sioux City and Ankeny, Iowa. Bomb and fighter group associations have memorial monuments not only at the Savannah museum but also the Air Force Museum and the Air Force Academy.

The strong bond that existed between the British people and American servicemen during World War II can best be described through the words of England's wartime Prime Minister, Winston Churchill, who said: "Our two countries, parted long ago by war, were brought together again by war in a unity and understanding such as we had never known. Through long years of endeavor and endurance we shared all things, and though we lost so much we found a lasting friendship. We shall never forget those gallant American soldiers, sailors and airmen who fought with us, some in our own ranks, countless others from our shores. Those who did not return the best memorial is the fellowship of our two countries, which by their valor they created and by their sacrifice they have preserved."

And the English didn't forget when it was over, over there. At former airbases, Friends of the Eighth, are English contact persons well versed in the history of the Eighth who will gladly give of their time to assist visitors and tours. Memorials have been erected at the site of former air bases in memory of fighter or bomb groups that were stationed there.

 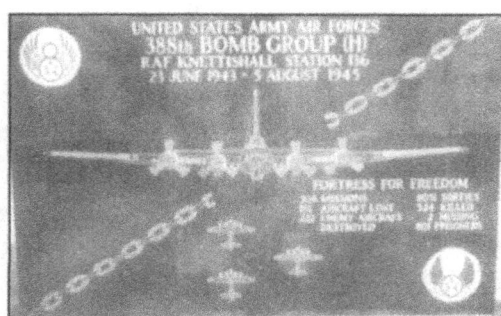 

Memorials at former bases 92nd BG, Podington; 88th Knettishall; 379th BG, Kimbolton

Chapter Seventeen

Derelict control towers at Bassingbourn (91st BG), Thorpe Abbotts (100th BG), Framlingham (390th BG) and Seething (448th BG) have been restored and turned into museums.

In 1977 Her Majesty the Queen officially opened the American Air Museum building at The Imperial War Museum, Duxford, England. Funding for the building came from America and Britain but 6.5 million dollars was allocated from the National Lottery in England for the project. The museum contains the finest collection of historic American combat aircraft outside the United States and serves as testimony to Anglo-American cooperation in peace and war during the twentieth century.

Churches in close proximity to former bases are adorned with stained glass windows as a tribute to the American fliers of the unit based near there.

The American Cemetery at Madingley, near Cambridge, the only World War II cemetery in the British Isles, was the site of a temporary cemetery in 1944. On land donated by the University of Cambridge, an impressive memorial chapel was built with a huge sculpted map of the European Theater showing the progress of the war with brass ships and airplanes. On one wall and on the ceiling is a beautiful mosaic showing airplanes flying toward a blue-tiled glory of final rest. Around the ceiling of the chapel are inscribed these words: "In proud and grateful memory

Derelict tower

Control tower at Framlingham, 390th BG, 1974 and 1984 after restoration

American Air Museum building, Imperial War Museum, Duxford, England.

91st BG, Bassingbourn

American Cemetery at Madingley, England.

Iowans of the Mighty Eighth

of those men of the United States Army Air Force who, from these friendly isles, flew their final flight and met their God. They knew not the hour, the day, nor the manner of their passing when, far from home, they were called to join that heroic band of airmen who had gone before. May they rest in peace." Outside is a reflecting pool, statues, and a 427 foot wall on which are recorded the names of 5,126 Americans (mostly airmen) missing in action, lost or buried at sea, or those "Unknowns" whose remains were either never found or positively identified prior to interment. The cemetery is immaculately maintained and landscaped around 3,812 white marble headstones of those killed in action and interned there.

A chapel within St Paul's Cathedral in London commemorates the common sacrifice of British and American servicemen in World War II and especially those twenty-eight thousand American servicemen that were killed or missing in action. The names of the Americans are recorded in its Roll of Honor. The Roll of Honor is a large book in a glass case with the names of the Americans inscribed on the pages. A page is turned each day.

The friendship that developed between the British people and American servicemen has not died in the sixty years since the end of World War II. Younger English generations became well versed in the history of the Eighth, collected artifacts and memorabilia and became active in restoration projects. Roger Freeman, was a curious young boy who lived near an American airbase in World War II and befriended by the airmen. He watched the daily operations of the base, counted the planes going out on missions, counted them returning and witnessed the horrors of war through crashes, dead and wounded. An Englishman, he has become the foremost authority on the history of the Eighth Air Force and authored three books on the Eighth and aviation in World War II. Mr. Freeman is on the Board of Directors of the Eighth Air Force Memorial Museum Foundation at Savannah, Georgia, and frequent guest speaker at aviation functions.

Reflecting pool at Madingly

Chapel at Madingly

Church windows from left: 355th FG, Steeple Morden; 385th BG, Great Ashfield; "The Crusaders" and "Window of Friendship and Peace"; 386th BG, Little Easton (Great Dunmow).

Chapter Seventeen

Long after the end of World War II many veterans of the Eighth have returned to the European continent to visit locations where they were interned as Prisoners of War, crashed or made forced landings and cities they had bombed on missions. Howard Linn, Hubbard, returned to a small village in Germany and befriended the man, who as a fifteen year old boy, caused his capture after he had bailed out of his stricken bomber.

Wayne Zeigler, Iowa Falls, had to parachute from his bomber while over France. While drifting to earth near a French town, Wayne was chased by his own airplane that had broken free from its automatic pilot control. At the last possible moment, the plane rolled over and crashed. The nearby explosion caused Wayne to land hard on the ground and he was knocked unconscious. When he awoke, a man and a boy were standing over him with a pitchfork pointed menacingly at him in case he was a German soldier. Other French citizens rushed to the scene telling the man not to kill him, he was an American. The French City of St. Quentin had just been liberated from the Germans. Wayne was treated as a hero and spent three weeks in a makeshift hospital at the city recuperating from injuries of his fall.

In 1997 Wayne wrote officials of the city for information on visiting the site of his plane crash. He received an immediate response. The St. Quentin Tourist Bureau provided maps of the area, reservations for him at a hotel on the town square, arranged local transportation, and included a copy of a page from a local book that detailed his plane crash. Headlines of city newspapers announced Wayne's arrival as a son of "Uncle Sam". "We will never forget the soldiers that came (liberated us)." The mayors of four towns met Wayne. He attended non-stop receptions and a banquet in his honor. He was presented with numerous gifts, medallions, and salvaged parts of his airplane that included an engraved 4x6 inch section of the plane's aluminum skin. "My plane was the only one that had ever gone down in their area and I am the only crew member to return to St. Quentin. The French people were so grateful to the Americans for liberating them." Wayne also met the boy, now a man, who held the pitchfork over him until it was determined he, was not a German soldier.

Many veterans of the Eighth have returned to England on their own to visit their former base, surrounding area, and perhaps a favorite pub.

After individual fighter and bomber group associations were formed, group tours were organized to

Russell Logue, Norwalk, 392nd BG, Wendling, returns to "The Ploughshare" pub.

return to their former bases in England. Rather than sit at home remembering, veterans took the sentimental journey back to where they were teenagers and experiencing the greatest adventure of their life. Their experiences were of a kind not to be forgotten. Although any remaining buildings were abandoned and dilapidated, the airfield overgrown with weeds or gone forever, turned to farmland, housing or commercial enterprise, and the planes long ago gone to scrap save for a few that have been restored, they return for one last look. In their minds they can still see the bustle of activity on mission day, hear the roar of engines, bursts of "flak" and feel the relief of landing safely back from a mission. British hosts arranged special events, tours and banquets to commemorate their return and are quick to tell them "Thanks Yanks. Thanks for coming when we needed you."

One tour in 1996 by the 44th Bomb Group Association, which was based at Shipdham, England, included a visit to a French town where a memorial to the 44th was dedicated. On the tour was a woman, who as a two-year old, lost her father in 1944 when his bomber was shot down near the town and he was killed. No remains were found at the crash site. His plane had exploded on contact with the ground and burned. Dick Lynch, Conrad, was on the tour. "After the dedication a man came forward and told of another memorial in a woods outside the town. We walked about a half-mile into the woods and found a fenced in memorial dedicated the lady's father and crew. A man came forward and gave the lady her father's dog tags he had saved for 52 years."

Eudora Seyfer wrote an account entitled "Reflections" after she accompanied her husband George on a return trip to his former airbase with the 353rd

Iowans of the Mighty Eighth

Fighter Group at Raydon, England. With her express permission, a portion of that account is reproduced here. The account was additionally published in "Little Friends" by Philip Kaplan, Copyright 1991, Random House, pages 240-241, and in "Mature Outlook Magazine" by Meredith Publishing, date unknown.

"Our husbands, some with thinning gray hair, some with slightly arthritic limbs, several with vials of heart medicine tucked handily in their pockets, lean forward in their seats peering out the bus windows through the tops of their bifocals,-excited and anxious as little boys. Each wears a specially ordered cap with 353rd Fighter Group, Eighth Air Force, printed on the front. They are looking for what's left of Raydon Airfield where they lived for two long, lonesome years during World War II."

"I say, it must be near here,' says our travel agent in dignified British English. (His maps of England do not show old World War II airfields.)

"Look!" Suddenly one of the men points across a flat field toward a bulky black shadow looming against a blue horizon. "That's a hangar!"

"That has to be Raydon.' Says another voice with a funny catch.

"Our visit has been carefully planned, even written up in the village newspaper,. First we are to stop at the Peabody farm. Mr. Peabody now owns most of the land that was once Raydon Airfield."

" 'Welcome back to Raydon.' Peabody says as he boards the bus. 'As you can see, there is no longer an airfield here, but more of Raydon survives than most World War II airfields. I'd like to show you about."

"The big bus pulls onto blacktop road and stops amid a cluster of metal Quonset-type buildings. These are the remaining buildings, now used by the government. And here too, is the big black hangar."

"The men fan out among the buildings. The three who were pilots head toward the hangar, those who were mechanics, armorers and radiomen head toward other buildings. I follow my husband, who walks on the remains of the runway. Weeds are growing through the cracks in the old cement."

"Slowly the men drift back toward the bus. I sense a sort of sadness, a letdown. Is the really Raydon? Are these few old buildings in the middle of a farm field all that's left to show for the years spent here? So long ago, the memories faint. Was it real-that war? Reluctantly they board the bus.

"Then from a farm beyond the lane, a woman calls to us. "Wait! Wait!" She runs toward the bus holding something in her hand.

"She reaches the group breathless and laughing. "Forty years ago when you were here I was a little girl living on my father's farm. One of you hit a baseball over the fence into our farmyard. I found it, but I didn't throw it back. I kept it all these years.' She smiles sheepishly. "When I read you were coming, I thought you'd want to see it.'

"The men gather around, laughing, each holding the old baseball for a moment. Then passing it on. Somehow it proves that Raydon was real, that the 353rd Fighter Group was here-and that the men young and vital and strong enough to hit a baseball way over into that farmyard. We thank her and climb back onto the bus. There is a spirit of joy now.

"On to town. Two hundred people live in Raydon. Most of them are here to celebrate the day with us. There are races and games in the schoolyard. Inside, a pot-luck supper is waiting: chicken pies, Cornish pasties, potted shrimp. "You are the first group to come." They tell us.

"The next morning, we dress in our best clothes. The bus takes us to the tiny Anglican Church built in the year 1200 and packed to capacity this Sunday morning. The Americans sit together in the front. When the service ends, Charley Graham stands and asks to say a word.

" 'We have a gift for you.' He holds the check, our collective gift. 'We have one thousand American dollars to be spent in any way you choose. We ask only one thing: that a little of it be spent for a plaque in this church remembering the men of the 353rd Fighter Group who served at Raydon so that our children and our grand children, when they come to visit, will know that we were here.'

"There is silence in the ancient church; the organ begins to play "The Star-Spangled Banner.' I look down the rows and see tears on every cheek. How strange life is, I think. An old baseball brought those long-ago days back to life, and a little plaque will keep them living.

"We walk from the cool stone church into the bright morning. We say good-bye and board the bus."

Chapter Eighteen

Alphabetical Roster of Iowa Veterans of the Eighth Air Force

Following is a listing of nearly 2,000 Iowans who are veterans of the Eighth Air Force in World War II. The listing originated from membership records of the Eighth Air Force Historical Society and was known to be incomplete. Not all veterans of the "Mighty Eighth" belong to the Historical Society. Some have chosen to belong instead to unit associations of their individual bomber or fighter group while others have opted to not belong to any organization. Some veterans of the Eighth are possibly not aware of any Eighth Air Force association with which to ally and others, I am sure, became deceased before any organizations were formed. Attempts to obtain the names of all Iowans that served in the "Mighty Eighth" in World War II and their hometowns disclosed no official records were maintained or existed with that information. County and State veterans records reflect those who served in the Army Air Corps but not the unit in which they were assigned.

Bomber and fighter group Associations of the Eighth Air Force formed after the war were contacted by letter for names of Iowans in their units. This met with a degree of success. Names were obtained through the diligent efforts of Association contact persons and were, in most instances, those Iowa veterans who chose to become members of unit associations after the war. A few units published history books on their bomber or fighter groups that contained a listing of personnel by hometown. Names retrieved from the books however were of those Iowans in the unit at the time of publication and not necessarily all that served during its existence.

Aircrew members served in their Groups from the time of arrival in England until they completed their required number of missions and were rotated back to the United States. This ranged from as little as three months to over a year. Rotation of these aircrew personnel was like a revolving door while ground crew members were stationed with a unit for the duration of the war. During interviews conducted for this publication additional names of Iowans who possibly served with the Eighth Air Force were disclosed and once confirmed, were added to the listing. Iowans killed in action from State Historical Society records are also included in the listing.

The listing is far from complete and numerically may only scratch the surface of Iowans that actually served in the Eighth Air Force in World War II. Well over two thousand men from the far reaches of one State, served in one single military unit in World War II that was not state originated. How many served in other Air Force units, the Navy, Coast Guard, Marines, and Army had to have been in the thousands. Total commitment.

Iowans of the Mighty Eighth

-A-

Robert Abernathy-Mason City, 353rd FG
Fred Abigt-Cedar Rapids, 388th BG, POW
Adolph Abraham-Cedar Rapids, 448th BG, KIA
Billy Adams, Sigourney, Unit Unk, KIA
Carl R Adams-Washington, 490th BG,KIA
Elwin Adams-Numa, 490th BG
Howard Adams-Wilton Junction,384th BG, POW
John Adams-Council Bluffs, 34th BG
Leroy Adams-Cedar Rapids, 322nd BG
Norman Adams-Marshalltown, 94th BG
Ora Adams-Eldora, 453rd BG
William Adams-Waterloo, KIA
Max Adkins-Marshalltown,398th BG
Donald Ahlwardt-Danbury, 94th BG, KIA
Lloyd Ahnen-Creston, 389th BG
Clarence Ahrens-Estherville, 379th BG
Dale Albaugh-Ottumwa, 20th FG
Edwin Albers-Walnut, 78th FG
Wallace Alberts-Marengo, 392nd BG
Stanley Alden-Shellsburg, 487th BG
Paul H Alexander-Winterset, 92nd BG
Ray Allbright-Des Moines, 357th FG
Charles Allen-Montezuma, 301st BG
Dudley Allen-Des Moines, 306th BG
James Allen-Panora, HQs 8th AF
Norbert Allen-Des Moines, 44th BG,KIA
Donald Alvestad-Roland, 390th BG, KIA
William Amundson-Sioux City, 8th AFHQ
John D Ancell-Ottumwa, 390th BG
William Anciaux-Exira, 466th BG
Richard K Anderson-West Bend, 100th BG, KIA
Burke Anderson-Adel, 489th BG
Carl Anderson-Perry, 382nd BG, POW
Clarence Anderson-Atlantic, 25th BG
Dale Anderson-Des Moines, 52nd FG, KIA
Donald Anderson-Ottumwa, 306th BG, POW
Edwin Anderson-Audubon, 489th BG, POW
Ernest Anderson-Lake Mills, 52nd FG,KIA
Erwin J Anderson-Mason City, 493rd BG
Herschel Anderson-Ames, 96th BG
Robert H Anderson-Mason City, KIA
Russell Anderson-Muscatine, 78th FG
James Archer-Cherokee, 447th BG
Gerald Archibald-Manson, 490th BG
John Arihood-Grandview, 91st BG, KIA
Leon Armalavage-Davenport, 78th FG
Paul Armentrout-Anita, 446th BG
George Armington, SIoux Center, 379th BG
Donald Armstrong-Tipton
Robert Arn-Iowa City, 385th BG
Eldon J Arnold-Creston, 493rd BG
Frank Arnold-Des Moines, 306th BG , POW
Melvin Aronson-Sioux City, 447th BG
Robert Artes-Britt, 4th FG
Leo Arts-Iowa, 92nd BG
Howard Askelson-Gilbert,78th FG
Harold L Aucker-Mason City, 448th BG, KIA
Gerhard Ausborn-Sac City, 31st FG
Herbert D Autenreith-Jefferson, 351st BG
Hubert D Autenreith-Creston, 493rd BG, KIA
James Avitt-Berwick, 306th BG
Herman Azinger-Keokuk,78th FG

-B-

Jay Baas-Oskaloosa, 305th BG, KIA
Harold Babcock-Des Moines, 401st BG, POW
Edwin Bachman-Montezuma, 95th BG, KIA
Lee Baddgor-Davenport, 94th BG
Leonard Badding-Urbana, 447th BG
Lester Baer-Dubuque, 453rd BG
Charles Bagley-Audubon-398th BG, KIA
Robert Bagley-Audubon, 445th BG, POW
Edwin C Bailey-Red Oak, 34th BG,KIA
Alvin R Baird-Alton, 493rd BG
Robert Baird-Des Moines, 95th BG
Boyd Baker-Perry, 351st BG, POW
Clele Baker-Waverly, 8AFHQ
Frank M Baker-Bancroft, 493rd BG
John L Baker-Villisca, 82nd FG, KIA
Lowell D Baker- Sharpsburg, 457th BG, KIA
Ray Baker-Des Moines, 20th FG
Arthur Baldwin, Iowa Cityh, 457th BG
Warren G Ball-Cummings, 303rd BG, KIA
Bruce Ballard-Odebolt, 95th BG
William Baltisburger-Marshalltown, 452nd BG, E
Anthony O Bamburg-Lemars, 487th BG, KIA
Delmar C Banes-Iowa City, 487th BG
Frank Bangs-Dows, 447th BG
Robert Banker-Albia, 95th BG
Thomas D Baranett-Farley, 305th BG, KIA
Charles Barker-Floris, 490th BG
Joseph Barnes-Mason City, 392nd BG
Joseph M Barnes-Wapello-392nd BG
Lawrence L Barnett-Lamoni, 490th BG, KIA
Richard Barnhart-Waterloo
Benjamin C Barron-Corydon, 55th FG, KIA
Harold Barton-Sioux City, 392nd BG, KIA
John R Bassler-Dubuque
Clyde A Bates-Marshalltown, 487th BG
David Baumhover-Carroll, 467th BG
John M Baumhover-Dubuque
Charles Bausch-Bettendorf, 490th BG
Bruce Bavender-Marshalltown, 487th BG
John E Baxter-Chariton, 100th BG
Walton Beach-Northwood, 390th BG
William E Beach-Shenandoah, 353rd BG
Darrell Beachan-Dubuque, 20th FG
Burl Beam-Martensdale, 398th BG
Gerald Beaman-Cedar Rapids, 7th Recon
Joseph C Beasley-Hamburg, 379th BG, POW, E
Edward Beaty-Ames, 447th BG
Charles T Becker-Dubuque
James Becker-Independence, 78th FG
John Becker-Waterloo, 392nd BG, KIA
Jack M Beckman-Burlington, 355th FG, KIA
John Beckman, Ankeny, 490th BG
Homer H Beede-Kellerton, 389th BG
Francis G Beedle-Sioux City, 100th BG, KIA
Charles Beigel-Onawa, 466th BG, POW
Willis Beightol-Webster City, 93rd BG
John Beilstein-Davenport, 379th BG, POW, E
Paul H Bellamy-Greeley, 390th BG, KIA
Wesley Belleson-Jewell, 458th BG
Joe Belluchi-Des Moines, 01SD
Tony Beltrane-Des Moines, 492nd BG
Robeert E Bembenek-Clintn, 93rd BG, POW
George Benedict-Davis City, 452nd BG, KIA
Norbert Bengford-Odebolt, 389th BG, KIA
Kenneth A Bennett-Iowa City, 303rd BG, KIA

Chapter Eighteen

Willard K Benson-Kellogg, KIA
Max Benthuysen-Des Moines, 389th BG
Raymond Benton-Guthrie Center, 305th BG, KIA
Robert F Benz-Des Moines, 392nd BG, KIA
C W Berdo-Washington, 93rd BG
Ben Bereskin-Sioux City, 467th BG, POW
Julius Berger-Durango,IA, 379th BG
Marvin Berggren, Cedar Rapids, Unit Unk.
Gordon Bergquist-Alta, 305th BG, POW
Harold Berk-Rockford-447th BG
Robert Bernbenek-Clinton, 93rdd BG, POW
Bernard A Bernstein-Des Moines,306th BG, KIA
Harry Bernstein-Brooklyn, 457th BG, KIA
Charles Berry-Cedar Rapids, 94th BG
George Berry-Winterset, 447th BG
Donald R Bertch-Polk City, 390th BG
Keith Berve-Radcliffe, 96th BG, POW
Beverly Besh-Denver, 447th BG
Robert E Betson, Des Moines, 487th BG
John Betten-Kanawha, 482ndd BG
James Bettis-Burlington, 91st BG, KIA
Roy Bettis-Iowa, 392nd BG
Charles Betzel-Davenport, 91st BG, POW
Robert Biegler-Sioux City, 447th BG
Clarence H Biermann-West Union, 390th BG
Robert Billings-Des Moines, 389th BG
John Bimson-Des Niubesm 93rd BG
George Bird-Hampton, 447th BG
Carl S Bishop-Des Moines,91st BG, KIA
Edwin Bishop-Red Oak, 34th BG, KIA
Samuel Bishop-Churdan, 379th BG
Guilford N Black-Ottumwa, 385th BG, KIA
Robert J Black-Cedar Rapids, 390th BG
William Blackburn-Malvern, 491st BG, I
James Blankenship-Council Bluffs, 447th BG
Otho W. Blankenship, Jr-Sioux City, 390th BG
John R Blaylock-Council Bluffs, 351st BG, KIA
Lowell Blizzard, Oskaloosa, 96th BG
Kenneth Blount-Des Moines, 490th BG
David Blue-Chariton, 388th BG, KIA
Ernest Boat-Sully, 303rd BG
Jonas Boatright-Council Bluffs, 448th BG
Willis Boatright-Monroe, 96th BG, POW
Robert Bobcat-St Charles, 448th BG, E

Robert Bocheck,-Cedar Rapids, 93rd BG
Laurence L Bockeloo-Clinton, 490th BG, KIA
Bernard Bockes-Dubuque, 467th BG
Leonard E Boden-Commanche, 487th BG
Carroll Bogard-Mason City, 466th BG
Roy Boggs-Iowa City, 44th BG
Robert Bohlken-Denison, 490th BG
Frank Bohnenkamp-West Point, 20th FG
Robert Boice-Waterloo, 91st BG
Kenneth Boles-Newton, 02SD
Oscar Bond-Logan, 4th FG
William Boone, Delaware, 389th BG, KIA
Richard A Booth-Tama, 487th BG
Harry Bootsma-Sibley, 94th BG
C L Boretsky-Cedar Rapids, 4th FG
Vincent Borneman-Dumont, 447th BG
Robert Bosworth-Oskaloosa, 78th FG
James Bottenfield-W. Des Moines, 452nd BG
Robert Bottorff-Ottumwa, 92nd BG, KIA
Perr Bowen-Red Oak, 389th BG
William Bowing-Malvern, 92nd BG
Charles S Bowman-Marshalltown, 445th BG, E
Arthur S Boyd-West Des Moines, 388th BG,KIA
Charles Boyer-Ft Madison, 93rd BG
Carroll Brackey-Lake Mills, 303rd BG
Raymond E Bradley-Creston,388th BG, KIA
Nelson Branch-Webster City, 448th BG, E
Willard Branch-Davenport, 401st BG
Lawrence J Brandenburg-Lamoni, Unit Unk, KIA
Leslie O Brandenburg-Strawberry Point, 457th BG, KIA
Maurice Brandenburger-Des Moines, 445th BG
Kenneth Braymen-Shenandoah, 359th FG
Raymond P Brecht-Watkins, 36th BS, KIA
Duane Bredensteiner-Shenandoah, 487th BG
Glenn Breitback-Dubuque, 447th BG
Judean Brekken-Story City, 490th BG
Carl Breson-Dubuque, 96th BG
Howard Breson-Dubuque, 96th BG
Albert Bricker-Greenfield, 303rd BG, KIA
Max P Brim-Osceola, 100th BG, KIA
Earl Brindley-Atlantic, 398th BG

Larry E Brink-Waterloo, 92nd BG
William Brinkman-Pocahontas, 379th BG, KIA
Reuben Britson-Radcliffe, 93rd BG
Willard Britton-Ft Madison, 447th BG
Arthur D Brody-Des Moines, KIA
Warren Brones-sioux City, 447th BG
Harold Brookhiser-Wever, 92nd BG
Delbert Brookhurst-Muscatine, 4 57th BG
Howard E Brooks, Otho, 390th BG, KIA
Robert Brooks-Des Moines, 351st BG
William Brooks-Waterloo, 100th BG, POW
Lambert P Brostrom-Sioux City, 91st BG, KIA
Kenneth E Brouhard-Nevada, 487th BG
Milan Brouser-Nora Springs, 94th BG
Dale Brown-Bonaparte, 100th BG, KIA
George Brown-Waterloo, 369th FG
Ivan Brown- Grant City,489th BG
James Brown-Mason City, 305th BG, POW
Lynn R Brown, JR-Waterloo, 447th BG, KIA
Richard K Brown-Cedar Falls, 390th BG, POW
Robert Brown-Fairfield, 491st BG
Robert Brown-Ft Dodge, 95th BG
Robert Brown-Cedar Falls, 93rdd BG, KIA
Robert J Brown-Des Moines, 390th BG
Robert J Brown-Forest City, 390th BG
Robert O Brown-West Bend, 390th BG
Verlyn Brown-Estherville, 351st BG, POW
William Brown-Des Moines, 384th BG
Ken Brucker-Sioux City, 457th BG,
Merlin Bruning, Carroll, 34th BG
Donald Brunmayer-Burlington, 93rd BG
Duane Brunner-Bettendorf, 306th BG
Beryl Bryant-Clarinda, 490th BG
Gene Bryson-Spencer, 379th BG
Robert Buchanan-Tipton, 492nd BG, KIA
Lowell Buchmillere-Jefferson, 56th FG, KIA
Charles Buckley-Iowa City, 392nd BG
Robert D Buckley-Ogden, KIA
Rollo Budde-Iowa, 92nd BG, POW
Ralph B Budke-Ft Madison, 487th BG
Gerald J Budrevich-Des Moines, 13th PR, KIA
Ralph Buechler-Iowa, 389th BG
Stanley R Buffington-Mason City,493rd BG
George Bullaard-Storm Lake, 95th BG
Elmer Burgart-Ionia, 95th BG

Iowans of the Mighty Eighth

Otis Burger-Cedar Rapids, 78th FG
Donald T Burke-Charlotte, 491st BG, KIA
James Burke-Cedar Rapids, 78th FG
Vernon Burke-Audubon, 385th BG, KIA
William R Burkett-Jefferson, 353rd FG, KIA
Marvin Burkgren-Dayton, 8AFHQ
Edward Burlingham-Walnut, 95th BG, POW
Howard Burmeister-Davenport, 385th
Willard Burns-Council Bluffs
Thomas Burris-What Cheer, 305th BG
Bennie Burrows-Muscatine, 490th BG
Franklin Buseman-Garner, 495th FG
Edward W Bush-Galva, 389th BG, KIA
James A Bussey-Bussey, 364th FG, KIA
John Butler-Washington, 490th BG, POW
Ralph Butler-Muscatine, 306th BG,,POW
Elmer L Byers-Hartley, 487th BG
Vic I Byers-Denison, 353rd FG

-C-

Kenneth Cagwin-Marshalltown, 381st BG
James G Cahalan-Mason City, 487th BG
Warren Callahan-Dysart, 447th BG
Ellsworth Campbell-Oelwein, 95th BG, KIA
James A Campbell-Keokuk, 447th BG, KIA
H A Campbell-Des Moines, 389th BG
Thomas Campbell-Cummings, 303rd BG, KIA
William Campbell-Indianola, 452nd BG
Hubert Campney-Emmetsburg, 452nd BG, POW
Benjamin Caplan-Des Moines, 93rd BG, KIA
Frank Cardamon-Des Moines, 96th BG
John Carder-Red Oak, 357th FG, POW
Paul Carlson-Sioux City, 100th BG, POW
Raymond Carlson-Walcott, 466th BG
Robert T Carlson-Belle Plaine, 390th BG
Russell Carlson-Des Moines, 384th BG
Nicholas J Carmello-Oelwein, 493rd BG
Robert Carmen-Montrose, Unit Unk, KIA
C L Carmichael-Corning, 55th FG
Robert Carpenter-Cedar Rapids, 100th BG, POW
Ellison W Carradus-Manchester, 493rd BG
Gerald R Carris-Keota, 452nd BG, KIA

Howard I Carroll-Sumner, 390th BG
James Carron-Bettendorf, 01SD
Kenneth Carson-West Point, 94th BG
Leonard K Carson-Ayreshire, 357th FG
Stanley Carson-Woodburn, 100th BG, KIA
Francis Ray Carter-Hedrick, 390th BG
Lawrence E Carter-Burlington, 390th BG
William Carter-Ames, 303rd BG
Charles G Cassaday-Dension, 27th Recon, KIA
R M Caughlan-Council Bluffs, 379th BG
Stanley Cebuhar-Albia, 379th BG, POW
J J Cecil-Spirit Lake, 466th BG
August Cerrveti-Madrin, 490th BG
Harold Chambers-LaPorte City, 4 4th BG, I
Oliver W Chapman-Waterloo, 492nd BG
Everett Childs-Manchester, 384th BG, E
George Chipman-Estherville, 453rd BG
Charles Chopard-Edgewood, 78th FG
Robert Chrisjohn-Alden, 306th BG
Daundel Chrissinger-Mt Pleasant, 20th FG
Fred W Christiansen-Davenport, 487th BG
Harold R Christensen, Eagle Grove, 91st BG, KIA
Rodger Christensen-Marne, 381st BG, POW
Warren Christensen-Ogden, 93rd BG
Lloyd Christman-Cedar Rapids, 351st BG, POW
Edward F Christofferson-Muscatine, 390th BG
Richard S Christopher-Sidney, 353rd FG
George Clark-Ames, 389th BG, E
James O Clark-Chariton, 388th BG, KIA
Loren Clark-Lake City, 357th FG
Paul Clark-Cedar Rapids, 457th BG, POW
Robert Clark-Cedar Rapids, 91st BG
Robert J Clark- Ames, 493rd BG
Warren Clark-Havelock, OBDIV
William Clark-Ames, 03SD
Charles Claude-Corwith, 398th BG
Charles C Clausen-Exira, 487th BG
John Claussen-Sioux City, 487th BG, POW
Lemoin Claussen-Blairstown, 44th BG, POW
Howard Clemens-Atlantic, 96th BG
Franklin Clemons-Bettendorf, 306th BG, KIA
James Cline-Perry, 96th BG, KIA
Russell Clingan-Des Moines, 100th BG
Neal Clyman-Bloomfield, 381st BG, POW

William Cochran-Elmira, 487th BG, KIA
Donald Codling-Davenpot, 93rd BG
William H Cogdill-Ruthven, 390th BG
Irwin Cohen-Council Bluffs, 452nd BG, KIA
Royce Colby-Terril, 491st BG
Howard F. Coleman-Toledo, 361st FG
Marvin Collett-West Union, 357th FG
Frank Collings-Cedar Rapids, 100th BG
Robert Collins-Osceola, 466th BG
Elmer Colt-Sioux City, 446th BG, POW
Clifford Combs-Aurelia, 389th BG, POW
Home Comeggs-Des Moines, 385th BG, KIA
Bruce Compton-Ida Grove, 359th FG
Robert Conger-Ottumwa, 78th FG
Claude Conklin-Belle Plaine, 34th BG
William Conklin-Lisbon, 447th BG
Craig Conley-McCallsburg, 305th BG, KIA
Paul Conley-Council Bluffs, 447th BG
Donald Connell-Waterloo, 91st BG
Dick D Connelley-Ottumwa, 359th FG, KIA
Don Connelly-Clinton, 34th BG
Edward Connolly-Dubuque, 379th BG, KIA
Russell Conrow-Waterloo, 398th BG, POW
Clayton Conte-Marshalltown- 445th BG
Douglas Conway-Ankeny, 401st BG, POW
Mervin W Cook-Des Moines, 94th BG, KIA
Ray Cook-Ames, 305th BG, POW
Francis E Cooke-Fonda, 401st BG, KIA
Alfred Cooper-Seymour, 446th BG
Cecil Cooper-Ottumwa, 392nd BG
Robert P Cooper-Stuart, 351st BG, KIA
William H Cooper-Council Bluffs, 4 87th BG
Robert Copley-Davenport, 305th BG, E
Blaine Corbin-Nevada, 91st BG, KIA
Delmar Corderman-Sac City, 306th BG
William Cordray-Charles City, 448th BG
Willis Core-Indianola, 389th BG, KIA
William Cornelius-Glidden, 100th BG, POW
Frederick C Corey-Des Moines, 390th BG
Ray I Cornick-Davenport, 352nd FG, KIA
Donald Corrigan-Waukee, 353rd FG
Edwin D Costello-Cedar Rapids, 487th BG
Richard Cotton-Sioux City, 446th BG, POW

Chapter Eighteen

John Couching-Davenport, 479th FG
Dallas Couchman-Sewal, 490th BG, KIA
Darrell Courtney-Logan, 34th BG
Louis Cowley-Sioux City, 303rd BG, KIA
Eugene Cox-Sioux City, 95th BG
Jesse Cox-Boone, 401st BG, POW
Roger Cox-Des Moines, 453rd BG
Ronald Cox-Washington, 401st BG, POW
Leroy Coy, Randolph, 388th BG, KIA
Robert Cramer-Audubon-447th BG
Winston Crandell-W,Des Moines, 466th BG
Melvin Craper-Ames, 392nd BG
Eugene Crawford-Winfield, 305th BG
Ralph Crawford-Clarinda, 379th BG
William Cregar-Newell, Unit unk
Clayton Croft-Shenandoah, 390th BG, KIA
Dale D Croft-Ft Dodge, 100th BG
Robert Croker-Bode, 339th FG
Robert Crone-Conesville, 351st BG
Howard Croner-Estherville, 452nd BG
Howard Cropp, Cedar Rapids, 401st BG
Harry Crosby-Oskaloosa, 100th BG
William Cross-Corning, 34th BG
Charles Crouse-Cedar Rapids, 507th FG
E L Crowder-Davenport, 490th BG
Howard Crummer-Webster City, 486th BG
Leroy Cruse-Terril, 351st BG, KIA
J R Culber-Sioux City, 487th BG
Darrell Cunningham-Monona, 389th BG
Gerald Cunningham-Waterloo, 7th Recon
Charles F Curtis-Clinton, 390th BG
William Cutting-Des Moines, 381st BG, KIA

-D-

Kermit O Dahlen-Thompson, 4th FG, KIA
Abel Dahlgran-Riverton, 447th BG
Max Dailey-Des Moines, 93rd BG, KIA
Wendell L. Daily-Waterloo, 389th BG, KIA
Sydney Dangle-Des Moines,95th BG
Charles D Danielson-Ottumwa, 487th BG
Brad Daniels-Council Bluffs, 490th BG
Joseph Danner-Dubuque, 305th BG
Loren F Darling-Waterloo, 100th BG
Henry R. Darlington-Des Moines, 92nd BG
Charles Daskam-Cressco, 458th BG, KIA
Gale Daudel-Maquoketa, 445th BG
Kenneth E Davidson-Murray, 487th BG
Stan Davidson-Ames, 303rd BG, POW
John Davis-Cedar Rapids, 447th BG
John C Davis-Ottumwa, 447th BG, POW
Richard Davis-Ft Doge, 4th FG
Robert Dawson-Clinton, 493rd BG, POW
Gerret DeBruin-Rock Valley, 3rd CCRC
Donald Decker-Creston, 492nd BG, POW
Merewyn Decker-Waukon, 447th BG
Warren Dedrickson-Clarinda, 466th BG
Heinz Deetlefon-Ft Dodge, Unit Unk, KIA
Earnest Degan-Des Moines, 487th BG
Harold Degraw-Spirit Lake, 95th BG
Elmer DeJager-Akron, 95th BG
Prosdocimo J DellaBetta-Chariton, Unit Unk, KIA
John DeLorbe-Waterloo, 96th BG
Robert Demery-Ft Dodge, 392nd BG, KIA
Sydney H Dengle,-Des Moines, 95th BG, POW
Lee Denin-Cedar Rapids, 487th BG
Daryl Dennis-Conrad, 486th BG
John N Dennison-Bellevue, 306th BG, KIA
James Denny-Cedar Falls, 390th BG, KIA
Roscoe Depenning-Newton, 466th BG
Ross Detillion-St Marys, 100th BG, POW
Heinz Detlefsen-Manning, 479th FG
Camille F Devaney-Cascade, 351st BG, KIA
Clarence Deverware-Clarence, 457th BG
Donald C Dewey-Spring Hill, 445th BG, KIA
Charles Dewild-Pella, 446th BG, POW
Everett Dexter-Marshalltown406S
Paul Diamond-Cedar Rapids, 490th BG
Felix Diaz-Osage, 446th BG, KIA
David R Dickerson-Union, Unit Unk, KIA
Melvin E Dicks, Columbus Junction, 390th BG
Robert W Dideriksen-Shenandoah, 14th PR, KIA
Don S Differding-Walker, 385th BG, KIA
Marvin E Dille-Belle Plaine, Unit Unk, KIA
Donald Dillon-Red Oak, 78th FG
John Dillon-Boone, 479th FG

Delbert R. Dimig-Mapleton, 385th BG, POW
George Dimond-Keokuk, 78th FG
Christian Dinkel-Council Bluffs, 306th BG, POW
Llyle Dirks-Ocheydedn, 379th BG
Robert L Dittmer-Elkader, 490th BG, KIA
Robert Doerr-Dubuque, Unit Unk
Eugene Domanico-Des Moines, 447th BG
Ray Dombrowski-Mason City, 18th WX
Edward Donovan-Spirit Lake, 490th BG
Warren T. Doolittle-Webster City, 92nd BG
Victor E Doorley-Cedar Falls, Unit Unk, KIA
Robert V Dougherty-Ft Madison, 92nd BG
Fred R. Douglas-Dubuque, 452nd BG, KIA
Gilbert Douglas-Storm Lake, BAD2
George Douroumes-Boone, 458th BG, KIA
Carl Doyle-Waterloo, 20th FG
Lawrence Doyle-Waterloo, 91st BG, POW
Aldrich Drahos-Cedar Rapids, 448th BG, I
Bernard Driscoll-Iowa City, 467th BG
John Droessler-Bancroft, 447th BG
Joseph Droz-Fairfield, 95th BG
Allen Duff-Des Moines, 392nd BG
John Duff-Des Moines, 398th BG
Gerald Duffy-Davenport, 379th BG, KIA
Robert J Duffy-Iowa City, 389th BG, POW
Peter Duin-Humboldt, 467th BG
Charles Dulin-Cedaar Rapids, 94th BG, KIA
Homer Dumont, Sigourney, 91st BG,POW
Maynard Dunker-Muscatine, 92nd BG, KIA
Stanley Durrett-Burlington, 34th BG, KIA
Wayne Dutler,-Des Niubesm 94th BG, KIA
J L Dvorak-Cedar Rapids, 479th FG
Merlin Dyvig-Humboldt, 95th BG

-E-

Emmett Earnest-Mediapolis, 353rd FG
John Earnest-Washington, 339th FG
Donald Eastwood-Red Oak, 452nd BG
Leo C Eaves-Ottumwa, 487th BG
Earl Echwert-Clinton, 479th FG

Iowans of the Mighty Eighth

Floyd Eckrosh-Des Moines, 448th BG, KIA
Ray Edens-Clinton, 305th BG
Laverne Edgeton-Grinnell, 303rd BG
Stephen Edginton-Muscatine, 398th BG, KIA
Lyle Edmondson-Washington, 379th BG, KIA
Leroy Edwards-Mt Pleasant, 100th BG
Herbert Egenes-Story City, Unit Unk, KIA
Nellins Egge-Inwood, 303rd BG, KIA
Robert Eitbreim-Des Moines, 479th FG
Stanley Elder-West Liberty, 490th BG
Frank Elkins-Nevada, 353rd FG
Beryl Elliott, Cherokee, 306th BG
Max Ellis-Centerville, 34th BG
Marvin Elvert-Boone, 34th BG
Charles Emerson-Council Bluffs, 100th BG, KIA
James Emerson-Volga, 453rd BG, KIA
Virgil Emerson-Cambridge, 96th BG, KIA
John Emmons-Nashua, 93rd BG
Ernest Engeman-Ft Madison, 398th BG, KIA
Leon C England-Ames, 384th BG
Carlie English-Centerville, 20th FG
Martin Engstrand-Clarinda, 490th BG
Jack Eppler-Des Moines, 306th BG, KIA
Norman Erbe-Urbandale, 457th BG
John Erbes-Radcliffe, 385th BG
Roland Erdman-Renwick, 466th BG, KIA
John Esau-Burlington, 20th FG
Robert Esbeck-Crescent, 357th FG
Thomas Estes-Aurelia, 384th BG
Dale Estle-Ledyard, 466th BG, KIA
Lawrence Everett-Lacey, 458th BG
Leland Evers-Council Bluffs, 452nd BG, KIA
Edward Every-Hampton, 388th BG, POW

-F-

Donald Fagen-Keota, 100th BG
Ralph Fahl-Cedar Rapids, 490th BG
Carl Fahmow-Schleswig, 94th BG
Donald Fahrenkrog-Persia, 447th BG
Mack Farmer-Clarinda, 306th BG
Dale Farnham-Algona, Unit Unk
Gayl A Farnum-Fayette, 92nd BG
Phillip Fassler-Cherokee, 351st BG
Fred Faust-Monticello, 93rd BG
Robert Feese-Albia, 388th BG, KIA
Richard Felton-Dickens, 389th BG
Don Fennell-Muscatine, 385th BG

Marion Ferguson-Washington, 452nd BG
John Fernhout-Des Moines, 95th BG
Elmer Ferrel-Iowa City, 02SD
Robert L Ferris-Dubuque, Unit Unk
Charles Fetters-Forest City, 34th BG
Elton M Fewson-Clarinda, 487th BG
Lawrence Feyerabend-Council Bluffs, 384th BG
Robert Fillman-Des Moines, 385th BG, POW
C W Fink-Deloit, 453rd BG
Robert Finkle-Marshalltown, 491st BG
Gerald A Finnegan-Lawler, 493rd BG
Bennett Fischer-Vinton, 91st BG
Pete Fischer-Council Bluffs, 100th BG, POW
Duward Fish-Jefferson, 479th FG
Frank Fish-Cambridge, 78th FG
Byron Fisher-Danbury, 56th FG, KIA
Donald Fisher-Keswick, 490th BG
Howard Fisher-Ames, 466th BG
Virgil Fisher-Williams, 458th BG
John Fitch-Des Moines, 384th BG, KIA
William Fitch-Cedar Rapids, 160th TRS, KIA
Robert Fitzgerald-Milford, 100th BG
Paul J Fitzgibbons-Duquesne, 390th BG
Charles Fix-Spirit Lake, 02SD
Thomas Flaherty-Waterloo, 492nd BG, POW
William Flaherty-Waterloo, 390th BG
Paul Flanery-Wintgerset, 491st BG
Harold Flaugh-Winterset, 44th BG, KIA
John Fleege-Beresford, 392nd BG, KIA
John Flior-Cedar Rapids, 490th BG
Donald Floden-Des Moines, 351st BG
Robert Florine-Sutherland, 7th PR
Theodore Fluegel-Cedar Rapids, 94th BG, KIA
Homer Flynn-Marshalltown, 389th BG
William Focht-Des Moines, 487th BG, KIA
Bert Foote-Cedar Rapids, 479th FG
Leighton Ford-Marion, 96th BG
Marvin Ford-Tipton, 381st BG
Russell Ford-Marion, 96th BG, KIA
Anthony Forte-Des Moines, 390th BG, KIA
Gene Foss-Waterloo, 457th BG
Keith Foster-Cromwell, 379th BG, POW
Victor Foster-Cedar Falls, BD2
Howard Found-Keokuk, 458th BG, KIA
Earl Fouts-Marshalltown, 457th BG
Francis Fowler-Cedar Rapids, 482S
Lebren Fox-Jamaica, 351st BG
Roger Fox-Wheatland, 467th BG
Robert Frakes-Sioux City, 20th FG

John Frampton-Reinbeck, 94th BG
Dale Frank-Winterset, 34th BG
Wesley Franklin-Clive, 34th BG
Clyde Frese-Nora Springs, 20th FG
Harley Frese-Grundy Center, 20th FG
George A Freund-Dubuque, 305th BG
Thorpe Friar-Grimes, 489th BG
Raymond Friedmann-Alton, 96th BG, KIA
James Friend-Council Bluffs, 385th BG, KIA
Collin W Fritz,-Des Moines, 447th BG, POW
Lyle Fritz-Des Moines, 447th BG
Francis Froah-Newton, 447th BG
Jack Frost-Des Moines, 306th BG
Edward Fry-Kalona, 357th FG
Lyle Frye-Clayton, 447th BG
Harry Fullerton-Washington, 305th BG, POW

-G-

William Gabrilson-Davenport, 4th FG
Robert Galbraith, Kellerton, 93rd BG, KIA
Verlin Gale-Maxwell, 384th BG
Donald Gallagher-Cedar Rapids, 388th BG, POW
Thomas Gallagher-Cedar Rapids, 100th BG, POW, E
Eugene Gallup-Logan, 392ndBG, KIA
Robert Gamble-Mason City, 452nd BG, KIA
Helmer W Gangstad-Webster City, 447th BG, KIA
Darwin Gant-Dana, Unit Unk, KIA
Marion Gard-Marshalltown, 492nd BG, POW
Donald Gardner-Cedar Rapids, 94th BG
Jesse Gardner- Bagley, 34th BG
Richard Garrett-Ferguson, 20th FG
Allen Gartman-Maquoketa, 94th BG
Richard Gaskel-Sioux City, 447th BG, POW
Charles Gast-Steamboat Rock, 305th BG, POW
Delmar Gavin-Dubuque, 479th FG
Herbert Gerbers-Holstein, 482nd BG, POW
Leon Gebert-Iowa City, 467th BG
Richard A Gee-Knoxville, 55th FG, KIA
Fred Geitz-Des Moines, 306th BG
Earl Genthe-Dubuque, Unit Unk
Ralph A Gentz-Dubuque, 390th BG
Herman L Gerstandt-Paullina, 487th BG
James Gibson-Onawa, 447th BG
James Gibson-Des Moines, 100th BG,

Chapter Eighteen

POW
Paul Gidel-Carroll, 492nd BG
Roger Gilbert-Des Moines, 447th BG
Roger W Gilbert- Des Moines, 25th BG
Chester A Gillen-Bramesburg, 390th BG
James Gilleon-Dubuque, 389th BG, POW
William R Gillette-Fostoria, 487th BG
John Gilligan-Sioux City, 453rd BG, KIA
Edward Gillmeier-Des Moines, 388th BG, KIA
John Gilroy-Davenport, 490th BG
Robert Gilroy-Davenport, 384th BG, POW
Arthur Ginder-Des Moines, 91st BG, KIA
Marvin Gingerich-Kalona, 389th BG
Lee Gingery-Shenandoah, 351st BG
Carroll Gjerde-Radcliffe, 4522nd BG, KIA
Glen Gladfelder-Des Moines, 452nd BG
Kenneth Glasscock-Stuart, 44th BG, KIA
Gerald Glaza-Cedar Rapids, 7th PR, E
Louis Glaza-Cedar Falls, 95th BG
John Gloriso-Wesley, 353rd FG
Henry Glover-Sanborn-379th BG, E
Henry Glover-Salix, 447th BG
H Goebbel-Bussey, 93rd BG
Clair Goel-Mason City, Unit Unk, KIA
Harold Goettsch-Davenport, 448th BG
James Goff-Sioux City, 95th BG
James Golbski-Bettendorf, 453rd BG, KIA
Glenn Gommela-Manson, 489th BG
Robert Gorman-Waverly, 384th BG, KIA
Woodrow Gottsch-Sutherland, 95th BG\
Lewis Gracik-Washington, 379th BG, E
William Grady-Cedar Rapids, 453rd BG, KIA
Milton Graham-Fairfield, 353rd FG
Helmer Grangstad-Webster City, 447th BG, KIA
Donald Granneman-Waterloo, 467th BG
Robert Granp-Clariooon, 20th FG
Douglas Granzow-Iowa Falls, Unit Unk
Melvin Graper-Ames, 392nd BG, KIA
Orland Graper-Rockford-445th BG, KIA
Carlton Graszkruger-Belle Plaine, 95th BG
Milton Grawe-Dyersbille, 95th BG
Gerald R Gray-Chelsea, 390th BG

Willard Gray-Washington, 456th FG
James W Green, Jr.-Sigourney, 453rd BG
Robert Green-Cedar Rapids, 351st BG
Robert Green-Osage, 306th BG, KIA
William Green-Newhall, Unit Unk
Gene Greenwood-Winterset, 100thBG
George Greenwood-Winterset, Unit Unk
Howard Greiner-Albia, 466th BG
William Griffin-Carlisle, 446th BG
Keith Griffith-Swea City, 95th BG
Franklin M Grigg-Bronson, 401st BG, KIA
George Grimes-Albia, 44th BG, KIA
Richard Grow-Mason City, 352nd FG, KIA
Vernon Grubb-Kingsley, 7th PR
Orvan Grudle-Glenwood, 389th BG
Joseph Grundon-Sac City, 303rd BG
Robert Gudgel-Boone, 388th BG, POW
Ronald Guerttman-Des Moines, 379th BG
Clifton Guinn-Armstrong, 94th BG
Vernon Gunion-Jefferson, 389th BG
Nelson Gunnar-Des Moines, 100th BG, POW
Max Gunsolley-Brooklyn, Unit Unk, KIA
Ellsworth Gustafson-Des Moines, 493rd BG, POW

-H-

James Haas-Perry, 398th BG
William Haas-Dubuque, Unit Unk
Arnold Hackbarth-Waterloo, 389th BG
Hank Hagedorn-Spirit Lake, 398th BG
Keith Haight-Winfield, 384th BG, E
William Haines-Sioux City, 93rd BG, POW
Albert Haiserman-Manchester, 390th BG
Clifford R Hall-Sioux City, 390th BG
Delbert Hall-Arnolds Park, 93rd BG
George Hall, JR-Des Moines, Unit Unk, KIA
John Hall-Benton, 447th BG
Loyd Hally-Huxley, 353rd FG, KIA
James Halverson-Spencer, 356th FG
Lorin Hamann-St Olak, 303rd BG, POW
Melvin Hames-Williams, 390th BG, POW
David R Hamilton-Des Moines, 25th BG
David Hamilton-Des Moines, 100th BG
James Hamilton-Council Bluffs, 95th BG
Clem Hammond-Dubuque, 34th BG
Paul Hammond-Mason City, 379th BG, KIA
Wesley Hammond-Council Bluffs, 20th FG

Billy Hancock-Perry, 379th BG
Warren Handley-Des Moines, 384th BG, KIA
Rex Hanft-Muscatine, 8HQ
Allen Haning-Farragut, 78th FG
Leo Hanna-Havelock, 392nd BG
Robert Hannaman-Dubuque, 458th BG, POW
Dan Hannan-Johnston, 452nd BG
Charles G Hansen-Clinton, 487th BG
Dallas Hansen-Audubon, 479th FG
Ervin Hansen-Griswold, 446th BG
Harold G Hansen-Council Bluffs, 390th BG
Kenneth Hansen-Cedar Rpaids, 96th BG
Henry Hanson-Clinton, 94th BG
Winfield Hanssen-Carroll, 389th BG
Wallace Harbeck-Sioux City, 3rd CCRC
Max I. Harder-Harlan, 379th BG, E
Robert Hare-Battle Creek, 95th BG, POW
George Hargis-Manly, 01SD
Melvin Haried-Sioux City, 78th FG
Robert Harken-Ackley, 466th BG
Ernest Harker-Okoboji-305th BG, POW
Paul Harkin-Cumming, 361st FG
James Harl-Bloomfield, Unit Unk, KIA
Vernon Harms-New Hartford, 303rd BG, POW
Robert Harnies-Clinton, 20th FG
Jonas Harper-Mt Pleasant, 390th BG
Ray Harr-Des Moines, 379th BG
Albertus Harrenstein-Grundy Center, 388th BG, KIA
Donald Harrer-Mason City 381st BG, POW
Joe Harris-Haverhill, 91st BG
J R Harris-Perry, 479th FG
Paul Hartkoph-Atlantic, 490th BG, KIA
Gene C Hartley-New Hampton, 389th BG
Gary Hartman-Akron, 385th BG
Harley Hartman-Parkersburg, 466th BG
Raymond I Hartman-Hinton, 390th BG
George Hartz-Newhall, 351st BG
Wesley Harwood-Council Bluffs, 20th FG
Arthur B Hauge-Forest City, 493rd BG
James Haugen-Soldier, 446th BG, POW
Raymond E Haury-Letts, 390th BG
Keith Hausman-Cedar Rapids, 95th BG
John Hayes-Des Moines, 381st BG, POW
Roger Hayes-Mason City, 93rd BG, KIA
Russell Hayes-Waterloo, 389th BG
Paul D Hayward-Independence,

Iowans of the Mighty Eighth

493rd BG
Erwin Hebbeln-Davenport, 96th BG
Robert Hegg-Waverly, 100th BG, KIA
Melvin Heinke-Cedar Rapids, 93rd BG
Arnold Heise-Clarion, 92nd BG
Woodrow Heitland-Ackley, 398th BG
Carl Heline-Marcus, Unit Unk, KIA
Hjalmar Hellberg-Marshalltown, 379th BG
Guy Hemenway-Dubuque, 91st BG, POW
Clarence Henderson-Cedar Rapids, 303rd BG
Gaylord Henryson-Cedar Rapids, 91st BG
Russell Henson-Des Moines, 4th FG
Robert Hentges-Sioux City, 457th BG
Kenneth Herman-Traer, Unit Unk, KIA
Leask Hermann-Waterloo, 93rd BG, I
Robert Herald-Eldora, 94th BG
Harry Herbert-Marshalltown, 3rd CCRC
Paul H Herrold-Grinnell, 17th BG
Martin R Hertz-Laurens, 92nd BG
Donald Hess-Sioux City, 392nd BG, KIA
Don Hesse-Wellsburg, 447th BG
Delbert Hesseltine-Oxford, 490th BG
Merle Hest-Waterloo, 467th BG
Dwayne Heubner-Postville, 389th BG, KIA
Cleve Hewitt-Webster, 479th FG
Harold Q Hicks-Highland Center, 487th BG
Ronald Higden-Iowa City, 392nd BG
Carol Highsmith-Hawarden, 381st BG, I
Clarence Hightshoe-Iowa City, 384th BG, E
Robert Hilderbrand-Marshalltown, 401st BG
C L Hill-Sibley, 390th BG
Glenn Hill-Fairfield, 466th BG
O K Hill-Vinton, 44th BG
Raymond Hill-Spirit Lake, 20th FG
Tom Hill-Des Moines, BAD2
Virgil Hill-Gilman, 447th BG
Willard Hill-Waterloo, 487th BG
Hugh Hilton-Ottumwa, Unit Unk, KIA
Francis Hinds-Marion, 303rd BG
James S Hiner-Osage, 458th BG
Donald Hink-Clinton, 78th Fg
Stanley E Histed-Keokuk, 388th BG, KIA
Howard Hobbs-Morning Sun, 96th BG, POW
Clairmont Hobensee-Havelock, 447th BG
Robert Hodson-Eldon, 96th BG, KIA
Leon Hoegh-Atlantic, 303rd BG

Kenneth Hoff-Ft Dodge, 94th BG
William Hoff-Algona, 452nd BG, POW
George Hoffman-Leon, 303rd BG
Laverne H Hoffman-Monticello, 390th BG
Lnan Hoffman-Clinton, 20th FG
Lyle R Hoffman-Rockford, 493rd BG
Clayton Hohl-Sutherland, 390th BG
Dwight Hohl-Argyle, 445th BG
Robert Hoke-Pella, 303rd BG
Clair J Holcomb-Waterloo, 390th BG
Carlton Holden-Iowa City, 490th BG
Albert H Holiday-Glenwood, Unit Unk, KIA
Dewey H Hollis-Waterloo, 479th FG, KIA
Forrest Hollister-Newton, 20th FG
Elbet Holloway-Des Moines, 78th FG
Robert Holscher-Dubuque, 306th BG
David Holte-West Chester, 392nd BG
Paul Hood-Clare, 93rd BG
William Hook-Dubuque, 490th BG
Carl Hoover-Sioux City, 92nd BG, POW
Lloyd Hoover-Mitchellville, 78th FG
Donald Hopp-Glenwood, 381st BG, POW
Philip S Horton-Osage, 390th BG
William Hosper-Waterloo, 446th BG
Don Hoth-Waverly, 92nd BG
David J Hotle-West Chester, 392nd BG, I
Billy R Hough-Hubbard, 487th BG
Robert Houser-Des Moines, 306th BG
Lester Hovden-Ridgeway, 359th FG, KIA
Glenn C Hovey-Fairfield, 4th BG, KIA
Charles J Howard-Council Bluffs, 17th BG, KIA
Dale Howard-Neola, 389th BG
Delbert Howard-Bloomfield, 389th BG
Earl Howard-Des Moines, 92nd BG, POW
Roberly Howe-Central City, 100th BG
James Hoy-Eldora, 325th Recon
George Hratz-Muscatine, 78th FG
Delph Hruska-Ft Dodge, 389th BG
Gaylord F Hubbard-Blockton, 44th BG, KIA
Richard Hubbard, Council Bluffs, 379th BG
Lornen Hubbell-Rolfe-94th BG
Donald Huddle-Red Oak, 306th BG, POW
Frank Hudson-Waterloo, 390th BG
Dwayne H Huebner-Postville, 389th BG, KIA
Ervin G Huebner-Sabula, 487th BG
Milten H Huebner-Sumner, 356th FG, KIA

Robert Huff-Fontanelle, 389th BG, POW
Richard Huffman-Boone, 490th BG
Galen Hufford-W. Des Moines, 93rd BG
Leon Huggard-Plainfield, 458th BG
Hayden Hughes-Washington, 448th BG, KIA
Richard Hughes-Sioux City, 447th BG
Wilbur F Hughes-Grinnell, 364th FG
Harter B Hull-Des Moines, 487th BG
David A Humke-Des Moines, Unit Unk, KIA
Edward Humphal-Sumner, 78th FG
Howard Humphrey-Postville, 94th BG, KIA
Samuel Humphrey-Clinton, 381st BG, POW
Gail R Hunter, -Atlantic, 387th BG, KIA
Ivan Hunter-Gowrie, 100th BG, POW
John Hurley-Des Moines, 448th BG, E
Dean Huston-Ames, 352nd FG
James Huston-Olds, 93rd BG, KIA
John M Huston-Olds, 487th BG
Harold Hutchcroft-Middletown, 392nd BG
Charles Hutchison-Des Moines, 0001V
Ernest W Hutton-Ollie, 445th BG, KIA
Staver Hyndman-Cherokee, 398th BG

-I-

Donald Ibeling-Mt Vernon, 398th BG
Eugene Ilten-Cedar Rapids, 381st BG
William C Ingalls-Madison, 390th BG
Aaron Inger-Marion, 25th BG
Richard S Ingham-Boonesville, 390th BG
Dean Ingram-Council Bluffs, 479th FG
Paul Ingvoldstad-Ames, 323rd MBG
John Inman-Grinnell, 95th BG, KIA
Donald Irey-Clarence, BAD2
Donald Ivanovich-Des Moines, 497th BG
Marin Iverson-Dolliver, 487th BG, POW
Robert Ivoebren-Harlan, 34th BG

-J-

Andrew Jackson-Eldora, 492nd BG, POW
Harold Jackson-Waterloo, 44th BG
Myron Jackson-Cedar Falls,, 44th BG, POW
Robert Jackson-Estherville, 97th BG, POW
Thomas Jackson-Cherokee, 490th BG
Eugene Jacobs, Marengo, Unit Unk.

Chapter Eighteen

Myron G Jacobs-Muscatine, 44th BG, KIA
Jerold Jacobsen-Cedar Falls, 467th BG
Alan R Jacobson-Britt, 78th FG, KIA
Gail Jacobson-Des Moines, 479th FG
Leslie Jacobson-Spencer, 93rd BG
Otto Jagels-Livermore, BAD2
Robert James-Sioux City, 78th FG
Daniel Janish-Des Moines, 390th BG, POW
Elwood Jansen-Davenport, 801st BG
Alfred Janss-Atlantic, 467th BG, KIA
Donald Janss-Belle Plaine, 93rd BG
Reinard B Janssen-Lake View, 390th BG
John Jaquis-Jefferson, 44th BG, I
Alvin Jaspers-Steamboat Rock, 390th BG, I
Leo Jeane-Mt Pleasant, 303rd BG, POW
Donald W Jeffrey-Des Moines, 384th BG, KIA
Aldon H Jensen-Massena, 392nd BG
Elmer Jensen-Newell, BAD2
Harold Jensen-Ringsted, 95th BG
Alfred Joensen-Ames, 446th BG
Elmer Johanasmeier-Burlington, Unit Unk
Arthur Johnson-Ft Dodge, 389th BG
Claire Johnson-Iowa, Unit Unk
Dale Johnson-Washta, 96th BG, POW
Francis Johnson-Cedar Rapids, 92nd BG, I
George E Johnson-Creston, 487th BG
George L Johnson-New Sharon, 91st BG, KIA
Gerry Johnson-Spencer, 01SD
Guy W Johnson,-Parkersburg, 44th BG, KIA
Harry Johnson-Davenport, 381st BG, KIA
Joel Johnson-Newton, 490th BG
Lawrence Johnson-Centerville, 94th BG
Maynard Johnson-Sibley, 1SAD
Olin Johnson-Rockwell City, 445th BG, KIA
Oscar Johnson-Sioux City, 467th BG
Raleigh Johnson-Belle Plaine, 447th BG
Robert Johnson-Wall Lake, 392nd BG, POW
Russell Johnson-Griswold-490th BG
Victor Johnson-Nashua, 92nd BG, POW
Wayne J Johnson-Des Moines, 390th BG
Guy W Johnson-Parkersburg, 44th BG, KIA
Donald Johnston-Des Moines, 95th BG
Ollie Joiner-Monroe, 364th FG
Darwin Joliffe-Dayton, 446th BG
Dale Jones-Chariton, 20th FG
Donald D Jones-Cherokee, 487th BG
Eldon Jones-Red Oak, 381st BG, POW

Jack Jones-Des Moines, 389th BG
Jack Jones-Panora, 453rd BG
Maynard Jones-Des Moines, 445th BG, POW
Robert Jones-Cedar Rapids, 20th FG
Harold Jordan-Oskaloosa, 96th BG, POW
Ray Jordison-Ft Dodge, 305th BG
Carl H Jorgensen-Des Moines, 303rd BG, KIA
Verne Josifek-Cedar Rapids, 361st FG
Gordon Joslin-Holstein-392nd BG, POW
Jesse Joyce, Jr-Zearing, 303rd BG, KIA
Henry Judge-Marshalltown, 96th BG
William Juno-Dubuque, 389th BG

-K-

Maurice Kahl-Lehigh, 458th BG
Bernard Kajewski-Waterloo, 91st BG
Joseph P Kane-Dubuque, Unit Unk
Malvern L Kaplan-Waterloo, 390th BG
Francis Kapler-Waterloo, 385th BG
John Kappmeyer, Harpers Ferry, 306th BG
Maynard Karris-Des Moines, 490th BG
William Karsten-What Cheer, 490th BG
Lavern Kassa-Hanlontown 388th BG, POW
Charles Kaufman-Mason City, 445th BG
John W Kaufman-Dubuque, 390th BG
Earl Kearney-Oakland, 398th BG, POW
Thomas J Keefe, Jr-Charles City, 96th BG, KIA
Lowell Keeler-Marshalltown, 381st BG
Donald Kehm-Ft Dodge, 100th BG, POW
Rollie Keith-Linden, 490th BG
Dwight F Kelley-Hastings, 100th BG, E
Harry A Kelley,JR-Blencoe, 351st BG, KIA
Joseph Kelley-Delta, 491st BG, KIA
Oren H Kelley-Atlantic, 315TCG, KIA
Robert Kelley-Lisbon, 384th BG
Dale Kellogg-Ionia, 03SD
Clyde Kelly-Spencer,389th BG
Dwight Kelly-Hastdings, 100th BG
Edward Kelly-Corydon, 44th BG
William Kelly-Hastings, 388th BG, POW
I Kelson-Cedar Rapids, 457th BG
Gilbert O Kemmann-Lowden, 385th BG, KIA
Edward J Kempker-Lemars, 392nd BG, KIA
Harold Kendall-Chariton 93rdd BG
Howard Kendall-West Liberty, 490th BG
Donald Kendrick-Edgewood, BAD2

Michael Kennedy-Storm Lake, 93rd BG, KIA
Charles Kepke-Grundy Center, 95th BG
Raphael Kernan-Meservey, 92nd BG
Russell Kerr-Bettendorf, 447th BG
George Kesselring-Guthrie Center, 91st BG
Arthur Ketelsen-Ames, 351st BG
Darrell Kiddie-Des Moines, 303rd BG
Glenn Kilbourn-Waterloo, OCO4
Rolla Kilgore-Des Moines, 95th BG, POW
Norbert Kill-Mapleton, 91st BG, KIA
Dale C Killion-Denison, 379th BG, KIA
Harold Killian-Council Bluffs, 93rd BG, E
Vance Kimm-Blairstown, 78th FG
Noel Kincart-Bloomfield, 466th BG, POW
Jerry Kinel-Auburn, 389th BG
Donald King-Grinnell, Unit Unk
Jack King-Ottumwa, 384th BG, POW
Ross King-Sioux City, 305th BG
David Kingery, Ottumwa, 359th FG
Everett Kinney-Mt Pleasant, 01SD
Thomas Kinney-Des Moines, 447th BG
Ken Kinyon-Iowa City, 457th BG
Charles A Kipka-Grundy Center, 95th BG, POW
Clifford Kirkpatrick-Grand River, 91st BG, KIA
Carl Kitchen-Cedar Rapids, 490th BG
Donald H Kitzman-What Cheer, 91st BG, POW
Vern Kitzrow-Des Moines, 398th BG
Kenneth Klippel-Iowa Falls, 390th BG
Melverne Klindt-Creston, 3rd CCRC
George Kline-Grafton, 95th BG
Marvin Kline-Sioux City, 93rd BG
Robert Kloser-Carroll, 0002V
Donald Klosterman-Sibley, 385th BG
Lester Kluever-Atlantic, 92nd BG
Rex C Knap-Hinton, 489th BG, POW
Albert Knight-Ft Madison, 92nd BG, KIA
Russell Knight-Iowa City, 466th BG
Kenneth Knoke-Elkader, 78th FG
Donald Knoll-Marshalltown, 467th BG
Edmund B Knoll-Garner, 466th BG, KIA
William Knowling-Iowa City, 353rd FG
Robert W Knutson-Davenport, 401st BG, KIA
Martin N Koch-Duuque, 487th BG
Kenneth E Koehler-Davenport, 390th BG
Lloyd Koehler-Rockford, 7th PR
Joseph Koenig-Halbur, 447th BG, POW
Robert Koenig-Lemars, 384th BG, POW
Thomas K Kohlhaas-Algona, 384th BG,

Iowans of the Mighty Eighth

KIA
Norbert D Koll-Mapleton, 91st BG, KIA
Karle Kolmerer-Muscatine, 390th BG, KIA
Richard E Kono-Waterloo, 390th BG
Herb Konrad-Lacona, 486th BG
Lawrence W Kooima-Rock Valley, 306th BG, KIA
Donald G Kopf-Muscatine, 351st BG, KIA
William E Kopf-Des Moines, 384th BG, KIA
Charles Koppernolle-Atlantic, 466th BG
Bernard Kozik-Elberon, 100th BG, POW
Robert E Kraft-Mapleton, Unit Unk, KIA
Roger Krakow-Davenport, 447th BG
Kenneth Kramer-Steamboat Rock
Jack Krejci-Council Bluffs, 392nd BG, POW
Duane Kritchman-Des Moines, 92nd BG
Svend Krogh-Hampton, 392nd BG, KIA
Richard Kroon-Sioux Center, 78th FG
Norman Kropf-Cedar Rapids, 392nd BG, KIA
Dana Krouse-Bondurant, BAD2
Orville Krumm-Paullina, 447th BG
Robert Krumm-Van Horne, 457th BG, I
Max Kruse-Clinton, 96th BG, POW
Myron Kruse-Charles City, 457th BG
William G Kruse-Dubuque, Unit Unk
James Krutosku-Carroll, 389th BG, POW
Robert Kudej-Des Moines, 392nd BG, KIA
Theodore F Kuhlmeier-Ft Dodge, 492nd BG, KIA
Donald Kuhn-Dubuque, 445th BG
Kenneth Kurtenbach-Waterloo, 303rd BG
Oliver Kurtz-Walcott, 487th BG
Edward Kussman-Council Bluffs, 385th BG, KIA
Kenneth Kuyper-Sanborn, 801st BG

-L-

Joseph Lamansky-Pleasant Plain, 447th BG, KIA
Paul Lambert-Des Moines, 493rd BG
Maurice Lampe-Ft Madison, 392nd BG, POW
Kenneth Lancaster-Maquoketa, 94th BG
Robert H Landen-Ida Grove, 94th BG, KIA
Gordon Lane-Mapleton, 100th BG, POW
Harry Lang-Des Moines, 381st BG
Byrd Lange-Des Moines, 93rd BG
Merlin Lange-Dubuque, 20th FG
Lloyd Langer-Mt Pleasant, 392nd BG, POW
Clarence Larrew-Boone, 493rd BG, E
Carl Larsen-Fertile, 7th PR
Glenn N Larsen-Badger, 490th BG, KIA
George N Larsen-Grinnell, 44th BG, KIA
Robert W Larson-Thompson, 353rd FG, KIA
Tom Larson-Ft Dodge, OBDiv
Richard Lasher-Polk City, 447th BG
Lyle Latimer-Farragut, 44th BG
William Latta-Madrid, 389th BG
Robert Laucamp-Tipton, 44th BG, KIA
Donald Laughery-Adair, 447th BG
Tillman O Lawr-Des Moines, Unit Unk, KIA
Dale B Leaf-Marshalltown, 4th FG, KIA
Richard Lechner-Sioux City, 91st BG
Robert LeClere-Manchester, 388th BG, POW
Walter Lee-Boone, 479th FG
Leonard D Leeds-Cherokee, 379th BG, KIA
Daniel Lefever-Davenport, 447th BG
Cal Leidenfrost-Davenport, 490th BG
Earl Lemons-Iowa City, 490th BG
Jon Lenthold-Dubuque, 389th BG
Daniel Lenton-Blairstown, 78th FG
Thomas Lenz-Belmond, 493rd BG
Lester E Leonard-Davenport, 390th BG
Robert Lerow-Harvey, 448th BG, POW
David M Lesher-Waterloo, 401st BG, KIA
Robert Lester-Des Moines, 490th BG
Dale Lewellan-Conway, 447th BG
Burton E Lewis, Cherokee, 390th BG
Jack Lewis-Des Moines, 479th FG
Joseph W Lewis-West Branch, 390th BG, KIA
Richard C Lewis-Cedar Rapids, 92nd BG
Robert Lewis-Mason City, 96th BG, KIA
Thomas W Lewis-Indianola, 93rdd BG, KIA
Verne Lewis-Des Moines, 457th BG, E
Howard Libbey-Ft Dodge, 447th BG
Albert C Lichter-algona, 357th FG
Phil Lichty-Mason City, 305th BG, KIA
Clarence Liddick-Casey, 96th BG, POW
Robert Liebold-Des Moines, 353rd FG
Walter Lienemann-Minburn, 392nd BG
Joseph Lillis-Williamsburg, 487th BG
Ivan Lindaman-Aplington, 305th BG
Gilbert Lindberg-West Branch, 384th BG
Lowell Lindbloom-Iowa, 379th BG, KIA
Charles E Lindquist-Burlington, 457th BG, KIA
Vern Lines-Rockford, 100th BG, POW
Everett Lingle-Corning, 447th BG
Wilmer Link-Dubuque, 379th BG
Howard Linn-Radcliffe, 492nd BG, POW
Ed Lipovak-Iowa, 457th BG
Raymond Lischer-Creston, 100th BG
Robert Livingston-Des Moines, 303rd BG, POW
Stewart Livingston-Scranton, 452nd BG, POW
George Loder-Des Moines, 387th FG
Bernard Logsdon-Leon, 467th BG
Russell Logue-Norwalk, 392nd BG
Tony L Longarich-Des Moines, 390th BG
Harry Long-Burlington, 447th BG, POW
Robert J Long-Marshalltown, 487th BG
Richard Longman-Clinton, 96th BG, POW
John Longnecker-Newton, 20th FG
? Lonn, Red Oak, 96th BG
Bruce Lord-Iowa Falls, 486th BG
Walter Lough-Ollie, 385th BG, POW
Robert Loughry-Des Moines, 385th BG
Winston Lowe-Cedar Rapids, 94th BG, POW
Vern J Lowman-Ames, 491st BG, KIA
Tillman O Lowr-Des Moines, Unit Unk, KIA
Aaron Lowry-Iowa, 94th BG, POW
Paul J Lowry-Boone, 305th BG, KIA
Richard Lowry-Iowa, 398th BG, POW
Richard C Lufkin-Waterloo, 390th BG
Lloyd Lund-Cylinder, 305th BG
Wallace Lund-Rake, Unit Unk, KIA
Chester Lundquist-Winfield, 379th BG, KIA
Francis Lynam-Corning, 447th BG
Donald Lynam-Indianola, 493rd BG
Richard Lynch-Conrad, 44th BG
Robert Lynch-Fenton, 389th BG
Robert Lyon-Dennison, 447th BG
Bill Lyons-Marshalltown, 398th BG
Chester Lyons-Perry, 20th FG

-M-

Robert Mabie-Charles City, 4th FG
Glenn E Mace, Jr-Washington, 44th BG, KIA
Frank E Machen-Cedar Rapids, 452nd BG, KIA

Chapter Eighteen

George Mack-Davenport, 3rd CCRC
Norman Macloud-Sioux City, 388th BG, POW
Ronald MacKenzie-Ft Dodge, 379th BG, KIA
Derewood Macklin-Adel, 379th BG, POW
Earl Macksey-Oskaloosa, 305th BG, POW
Ervin Maden-Traer, 20th FG
Dallas Madland-Linwood, 446th BG, POW
Henry F Madsen, Mason City, 390th BG
Ray W Magin-Wheatland, 385th BG, KIA
Roger E Maillard-Mason City,, 34th BG, KIA
James Mairs-Marshalltown, 398th BG
George Maitland-Ottumwa, 479th FG
Joseph P Malloy-Gilmore City, 493rd BG, KIA
Delmar Malmquist-West Union, 95th BG
George Maly-Cedar Rapids, 94th BG
Robert Manahl-Evansdale, 384th BG
Norman W Mandelbaum-Des Moines, 384th BG, KIA
Robert Manderscheid-Boone, 390th BG
Orval Mans-Dubuque, 95th BG
Francis Marchan-Elberon, 20th FG
Charles Maring, Jr-Ewart, 388th BG
Morris R Marks-Lake Park, 95th BG, KIA
Donald Marner-Iowa City, 357th FG
Ray Marner-Iowa City, , 44th BG
Fred Marold-Waterloo, 44th BG
John Marthaler-Muscatine, 487th BG
Raleigh Martin-Ottumwa, 447th BG
William Martin-Beddford, 490th BG
Virgil L Massey-Oakland, 487th BG
William J Matteson-Sioux City, 390th BG
Harold Matz-Radcliffe, 96th BG, KIA
Allyn Matzen-Davenport, 467th BG
Donald Maule-Mondamin, 44th BG
Wallace Maxon-Marble Rock, 446th BG, POW
Charles McBride-Muscatine, 487th BG, POW
Glen McCabe-Mt Pleasant, 351st BG, E
Alva McCalley-Hazelton, 306th BG
Frank McCarne-Ft Madison, 95th BG
Richard D McCarthy-Ames, Unit Unk, KIA
Walter McCartie-Oskaloosa, 93rd BG, KIA
Harold McCarty-Donnellson, 388th BG, POW
James McClain-Waterloo, 389th BG

George McCord-Council Bluffs, 466th BG, KIA
William McCoy-Indianola, 447th BG
Robert K McCune-Clinton, 387th BG, KIA
James W McDowell-Lake Park, 390th BG
Rex McDowell-Waterloo, 44th BG
William McElhanney-Iowa City, 479th FG
Thomas McElherne-Ames,388th BG, POW
Robert McElree-Oelwein, 351st BG
Howard McElvis-Ddows, 359th FG
Roland McGee-Council Bluffs, 94th BG, POW
William McGinnis-Iowa City, 379th BG, KIA
Fred McGowan-Sioux City, 34th BG
Frank McGowen-Waterloo, 95th BG, E
Robert McGreevy-Ackley, 381st BG, POW
Roscoe McGregor-Grand Junction, 20th FG
W E McGrew-Varina, 447th BG
Thomas McGuire-Muscatine, 490th BG
Audrey McIntosh-Deep River, 490th BG
Oscar McKeever-Ft Madison, 445th BG
Bruce McKern-Mystic, TCS, KIA
Virgil McKesson-Cedar Rapids, 479th FG
Dale McLaughlin-Minburn, 93rd BG
Donald McLean-Dunlap, 306th BG
Joseph F McMahon-Dubuque, Unit Unk
Robert F McMaines-Des Moines, 493rd BG
George McMullin-Casey, 100th BG,POW
Harold McMurray-Des Moines, 91st BG, POW
Charles A McWilliams-Bloomfield, 487th BG, KIA
Gerald C Mead-Nasahua, 487th BG
Robert E Means-Manilla, 96th BG, KIA
Robert Megchelsen-Washington, 91st BG
William Mehegan-Cedar Rapids, 453rd BG, POW
Leon Mehring-Cedar Rapids, 305th BG
Robert Meline-Des Moines, 93rd BG, KIA
Robert Melville-Sidney, 389th BG
Freddie Menefee-Sioux Rapids, 94th BG, KIA
Derald W Melton-Council Bluffs, 384th BG, KIA
George W Mercer,-Muscatine,

Unit Unk, KIA
Ellsworth Meredith-Keokuk, 487th BG
Louis L Merfeld-Greene, Unit Unk, KIA
Charles Merril-Des Moines, 93rd BG
Thomas Merrill-Ft Dodge, 358th FG
Charles Messeri-Council Bluffs, 448th BG, POW
Julian Messerly-Ft Dodge, 487th BG, KIA
Robert Messerly-Janesville, 486th BG
Warren R Messmer-Burlington, 95th BG, KIA
Donald Meston-Council Bluffs, 100th BG, POW
Eugene Mettler-Des Moines, 467th BG, POW
William Metz-Sioux City, 388th BG, POW
Clarence Meyer-Aplington, 490th BG
Gregory C Meyer-Dubuque, 303rd BG, KIA
James Meyer-Sioux City, 445th BG, POW
Jerome Meyer-Dubuque, Unit Unk
John Meyer-Waverly, 466th BG
Leslie W Meyer-Blue Grass, 92nd BG
Vincent Meyer-Waukee, 385th BG
Darwin F Michaelson-Clinton, 390th BG, KIA
James Mileham-Webb, 20th FG
Albert Miller-Missouri Valley, 458th BG, POW
Dean Miller-Ackley, 458th BG
Dewitt Miller-Council Bluffs, 398th BG, POW
Donald Miller-Manilla, 490th BG
Francis D Miller-Carlisle, 487th BG
Fred Miller-Iowa City, 389th BG
Frederic L Miller-Des Moines, 390th BG
Frederick Miller-Des Moines, 458th BG
Gerard Miller-Des Moines, 458th BG, E
Gregory Miller-Dubuque, 303rd BG, KIA
Harvey Miller-Clarksville, 486th B
Homer Miller-Yale, 447th BG, POW
Maurice Miller-Humeston, 490th BG
Ray E Miller-Kalona, 44th BG, POW
Thomas W Miller-Sioux City, 493rd BG
Walter Miller-Ames, 55th FG
Willard Miller-Iowa, 100th BG, POW
Robert Millhollin-Perry, 493rd BG
John Milliken-Corning, 448th BG, I
Fred Mincks-Chariton, 446th BG, KIA
Earl Misel, Marengo, Unit Unk.
James L Mitchell-Crawfordsville, 306th BG, KIA
Joe E Mitchell-Marshalltown, 492nd BG, KIA

Iowans of the Mighty Eighth

Joseph A Mitchell-Buckingham, 93rd BG
Harold Mix-Mason City, 94th BG
Wilbur Mock-Onawa, 479th FG
Jack Modlin, Dawson, 95th BG
Charles J Moeller-Davenport, Unit Unk, KIA
Edward A Moen-Lake Mills, 487th BG
Donald S Mohr-North English, 379th BG, E
Leroy Mohr-Creston, 91st BG, KIA
Albert P Moline-Des Moines, 305th BG, KIA
William W Moller-Mapleton, 389th BG
William L Monroe-Estherville, 452nd BG, KIA
Marlin Monson-Forest City, 452nd BG, POW
Thomas N Montag-West Bend, Unit Unk, KIA
Douglas Moore-Council Bluffs, 359th FG
James Moore-Des Moines, Unit Unk
James Moorhead-Winterset, 381st BG, POW
Donald E Morgart-Melbourne, 2055th EFF, KIA
Alvin Mormon-Coon Rapids, 390th BG, KIA
Glenn W Morris, JR-Waterloo, 466th BG, KIA
James Morris-Waukee, 95th BG
Warren N Morris-Keokuk, Unit Unk, KIA
Frederick Morrison-Cedar Rapids, 379th BG
James Morrison-Grinnell, 401st BG, POW
Harold Morriss-Jefferson, 389th BG
Max Morrow-Seymour, 457th BG, POW
Kenneth Morse-Eagle Grove, 44th BG, POW
Loyd Morse-Ft Dodge, 448th BG, I, E
John Morton-Denison, 351st BG, KIA
Richard Moses-Storm Lake, 458th BG, KIA
Russell H Mott-Des Moines, 493rd BG
Robert C Mount-Lost Nation, 448th BG
Duane Mowry-Audubon, 452nd BG, POW
Kenneth Moye-Reinbeck, 305th BG
Kenneth L Mueller-Cedar Falls, 487th BG
James Mulder-Orange City, 388th BG, POW
Joseph Mulhern-Sheldon, 490th BG
Gerald Mulvaney-Cedar Rapids, 479th FG
Burl W Murdock-Mondamin, 390th BG
Phillip M Murillo-Cedar Rapids, 457th BG, KIA
Dennis Murphy-Ft Dodge, 303rd BG, KIA
James C Murphy-Sioux City, 306th BG, KIA
Raymond Murphy-Des Moines, 91st BG, E
Francis A Murray-Dubuque, Unit Unk
Ralph C Murray-Arnolds Park, 95th BG, KIA
Ed Musil-Chester, 95th BG
Norman Mutchler-Waverly, 486th BG
Earl Myers-Des Moines, 3rd CCRC
Edward P Myers-North Liberty, 91st BG, KIA
Orville Myers, Urbandale, Unit Unk.
Robert Myers-Tiffin, BAD2

-N-

George Nacos Dubuque, 453rd BG, POW, E
Charles Naden-Webster City, Unit Unk, KIA
Donald Nagel-Davenport, 490th BG, I
Fred F Nagle-Ames, 398th BG, KIA
Vernon Nappier-Bedford, 44th BG, KIA
Charles W Narvis-Muscatine, Unit Unk, KIA
Charles E Nason-Ottumwa, 390th BG
James Naugen-Soldier, 466th BG
Dean Naven-Ft Dodge, 305th BG
Glen Naze-Osage, 389th BG
Albert Neal-Albia, 78th FG
Charles Neal-Council Bluffs, 447th BG
Ernest Neal-Aredale, 489th BG
John Neal-Sioux City, 95th BG
Wilfred Neale-Collins, 447th BG
Alfred Nelson-Marshalltown, 466th BG
Earl B Nelson, Webster City, 381st BG, KIA
Hal Nelson, Iowa City, 452nd BG, E
Robert Nelson, Sioux City, 94th BG
Robert R Nelson, Jewell, Unit Unk, KIA
Ronald Nelson, Cherokee, 93rd BG
Rudolph Nelson, Marion, 95th BG
Arlon Nessa, Hubbard, 91st BG
Donald Nessa, Lake Mills, 487th BG
Kermit Neubauer-Iowa Falls, 94th BG
Lawrence Neuhauser-Clarksville, 306th BG, POW
Kenneth Newbrough-Alta, 398th BG
Leroy Newby-Webster Ccity, 353rd FG
Charles Newell-Audubon, 305th BG, POW
James Newell-Altoona, 389th BG
Ken Newson-Des Moines, 486th BG
Emmet Newton-Anita, 78th FG
Albert Nichols-Des Moines, 452nd BG
Charles Nichols-Des Moines, 389th BG
Robert R Nichols-FT Madison, 489th BG, POW
Ronald M Nichols, Colfax, Unit Unk, KIA
Fred Nicklas-Washington, 351st BG, POW
Floyd Nielson-Pocahontas, 25th BG
Tage R Nielson-Newell, Unit Unk, KIA
Niels Nissen-Cedar Rapids, 339th FG
Milo Noble-Aurelia, 466th BG
Lloyd Nodstrom-Davenport, 388th BG, POW
Ernest Nonneman-Hartley, 96th BG, POW
Carl A Nord, Atlantic, 493rd BG, KIA
Grover Nordman-Des Moines, 91st BG, E
Henry A Norgaard-Council Bluffs, 493rd BG, POW
Alvin J Norman-Coon Rapids, 390th BG, KIA
Lyle A Norquist-Mason City, 351st BG, KIA
Harold Norris-Russell, 94th BG
Donald Norvet-Forest City, 95th BG, POW
Robert L Novak-Cedar Rapids, 493rd BG
William H Nowels-Des Moines, 95th BG, KIA
Allen Nye-Ida Grove, HQ2AD
Arvest Nye-Keokuk, 490th BG
Vernon D Nyhus, Forest City, 390th BG

-O-

Donald E O'Brien-Sioux City, 390th BG
James T O'Brien-Dubuque, 390th BG
John O'Brien-Des Moines, 93rd BG, KIA
N T O'Brien-Strawberry Point, 93rd BG
Martin G O'Connell, JR-Beaconsfield, 78th FG, KIA
James O'Connor-Iowa, 379th BG, KIA
James E O'Connor-Conrad, Unit Unk, KIA
James E O'Connor-Peostsa, 388th BG,
Richard J O'Connor-Lockport, 364th FG, KIA
Wendell Oge-Burlington, 390th BG, E
Floyd C Oglesby-Luverne, 445th BG
Eugene O'Hearn-Spencer, 34th BG
Carl Olbertz-Milford, 95th BG
Clifford Olson-Newhall, 95th BG
Irvin Olson-Postville, 100th BG, POW
Julian M Olson-Moville, 390th BG
Lloyd K Olson-Selma, 305th BG, KIA
Oscar Olson-Forest City, 78th FG
Robert Olson-Sioux City, 94th BG

Chapter Eighteen

Albert C Omar-Grinnell, Unit Unk
Young Omer-Hazelton, 379th BG, KIA
Phillip Ong-Maason City, 100th BG, POW
Riley E Orr-Onawa, 467th BG, KIA
Owen O Osburn, Sioux City, 390th BG
Kenneth Oseth-Cedar Rapids, 94th BG
Charles Osman-Des Moines, 20th FG
William L Otterbeck-St Olaf, 493rd BG
William L Otterbeck-Farmersburg, 390th BG
Bernhard Ove-Cedar Falls, 452nd BG
Carl E Owens-Marshalltown, 390th BG
Herbert S Owens-Mapleton, 94th BG, KIA

-P-

Paul Pace-Marshalltown, 389th BG
Allen Packer-Marshalltown, 78th FG
John Padget-Waterloo, 94th BG, KIA
Thomas Page-Osceola, 94th BG
Willis Palmer-Hawkeye, 389th BG
Bernie Palmquist-Red Oak, 100th BG
Clarence F Parizek-Dysart, 95th BG, KIA
Robert Parmele-Davenport, 487th BG
Russell Parker-Mitchellville, 392nd BG
Charles Parkhill,-Iowa, 452nd BG, POW
Neil Parks, Waterloo, 447th BG
Jack Parsons, Sioux City, 95th BG
Charles Passica-Ft Dodge, 453rd BG, POW
Edward Patterson,-Iowa City, 389th BG, POW
Jesse L Patterson-Winfield, Unit Unk, KIA
Stanley Patterson, Masaon City, 305th BG
Norace B Patton-Fairfield, 390th BG
Lester E Paup-Scranton, 388th BG, KIA
Donald R Peacock-Shellsburg, 457th BG, KIA
Gene E Pearson-Des Moines, 390th BG
Warren J Pease-Farragut, 385th BG, KIA
Jack A Peck-Marshalltown, 92nd BG, KIA
John Peck-Bloomfield, 34th BG
Lawrence K Pedersen-Dow City, 487th BG
Leslie Pederson-West Branch, 479th FG
Chester Peek-Paullina, 95th BG
Ralph Peeters-Remsen, 447th BG
Ralph Pender-Cedar Falls, 388th BG
Ray Penticoff-Hampton, 55th FG
Marvin W Pepples-Waterloo, 390th BG
Dean Peppmeir-Truro, 446th BG, POW
Chester Perkins-Mt Pleasant, 489th BG
Jack Perrin-Cherokee, 390th BG
Gilbert Perry Dakota City, 384th BG, POW
Ivan Perry-Spencer, 96th BG
Eugene Person-Manson, 466th BG
Charles J Pessica-Ft Dodge, Unit Unk, KIA
Ed Peters-Estherville, 351st BG
Gale Peters-Oxford Junctin, 487th BG
Lavern Peters-Bedford, 389th BG
Milford F Peters, Dows, Unit Unk, KIA
Orville Peters-Storm Lake, 305th BG
Raymond Peters-Monticello, 458th BG
Robert Peters-Grinnell, 445th BG
Arthur Petersen-Mason City, 305th BG
Donald Peterson-Keokuk, 487th BG
Lee M Peterson-Gowrie, 92nd BG
Temen Peterson-Cresco, 447th BG
Richard M Petrus-Council Bluffs, 446th BG, KIA
Ralph I Pettit-Logan, 390th BG
Lee Petz-Sioux City, 4th FG
Joseph Pfiffner-Waterloo, 458th BG
Raymond G Phillips-Newton, 352nd FG, KIA
William Phillips-Altoona, Unit Unk
Richard Phipps-Ogden,379th BG
James B Piatt-Clinton, 491st BG, KIA
Roy Picht-Ames, 458th BG
John Piekielko-Des Moines, 457th BG
James Pierce-Grinnell, 303rd BG
Kelvin Pierce-Storm Lake, 487th BG, POW
Robert Pike-Ft Dodge, 493rd BG, POW
Donald Pilcher-Anamosa, 91st BG, POW
Herbert Pine-Knoxville, 389th BG
Eldon Pingrose-Afton, 389th BG
James Pippinger-Cedar Rapids, 467th BG
Elmer Pitsenbarger-Linden, 492nd BG, KIA
George Pogge-Council Bluffs, Unit Unk, KIA
Dwayne Pohl-Boone, 447th BG
Earnest Pohle-Marshalltown, 389th BG
Phillip Poland-Winterset, 95th BG
Warren Polking-Breda, 392nd BG
Theodore Pollard-Boone, 306th BG, POW
Vernise Polly-Sioux City, 490th BG, POW
Lehr E Pope-Rose Hill, 92nd BG
George Popelka-Cedar Rapids, 390th BG
James Porter-Cedar Falls, 94th BG
Les Portwood-Boone, 04SD
Stanley Potter-Marion, 385th BG
Clarence J Powell-Humeston, 8th TCS, KIA
Cy Powers-Waterloo, 91st BG
John Powers-Delmar, 448th BG, POW
Leslie Pratt-Cedar Rapids, 303rd BG
Richard A Pratt, Lohrville, 352nd FG, KIA
Robert Preis-Burlington, 493rd BG, I
Dave Preisser-Cedar Rapids, 96th BG
Francis Prendergast-Ft Dodge, 447th BG
John B Price-Des Moines, 303rd BG, KIA
Virgil V Prior-Cedar Rapids, 448th BG, KIA
Raymond Pritchard-Des Moines, 384th BG
Wendel Pritle-Fairfield, 467th BG
Robert J Prudhon-Iowa Falls, Unit Unk, KIA
Elmer Prusha-Tama, 303rd BG
Russell Pulis-Ottumwa, 447th BG
Leroy Puls-Davenport, 447th BG
Frank Purcell-Sioux City, 305th BG
John F Purdue-Ottumwa, 390th BG
Marino Pusateri-Vinton, 942nd

-Q-

Harold Quee-Milford, 95th BG

-R-

John Rabenold-Ottumwa, Unit Unk, POW
Robert Raecker-Meservey, 486th BG
Robert Raeside-Sioux City, 447th BG
Mile Raim-Cedar Rapids, 385th BG, POW
Gerald Ralston-Des Moines, 392nd BG, POW
James E Ralston-Cedar Rapids, Unit Unk, KIA
Robert Randall-Iowa City, 94th BG
Clyde Rames-Centerville, 78th FG
John Rames-Perry, 490th BG
Kenneth Ranson-Cedar Rapids, 96th BG
Oliver Rapps-Vinton, 385th BG, KIA
John Rasko-Blockton, 351st BG, POW
Gerald Raasmussen-Calamus, 303rd BG
Robert Rasmussen-Sioux City, 398th BG, POW
Leonard L Raspotnik-Des Moines, Unit Unk, KIA
Vernon Rathbun-Waterloo, 94th BG, POW
Leon Rathouz-Moorland, 353rd FG
Jean Ray-Newton, 100th BG, POW

Iowans of the Mighty Eighth

Harold Raynie-Hawarden, 389th BG, KIA
Al Razor-Collins, 2457th QMTC
Dale Rector-Tabor, 447th BG
Ronald Reed-Ringstead, 493rd BG, E
William Rees-Davenport, 479th FG
Earl Reese-Des Moines, 91st BG
Delbert Reeve-Tipton, 100th BG, KIA
Robert Reeves-Waterloo, 91st BG
Robert Reinartson-Ft Dodge, 447th BG, KIA
Russell Reindal-Scarville, 448th BG
Herbert Reis-Early, 453rd BG
Cloyde Remme-Independence, 490th BG
Burl Renolds-Tingley, 100th BG, POW
Gumencindo Rerumez-Waterloo, 447th BG
Vincent J Reuter-Jesup, 390th BG
Mark Reynolds-Shellsburg, 379th BG, KIA
Kenneth Rhodes-Bettendorf, 34th BG
Donald F Rice-Deloit, 701st MP, KIA
William Rich-Clear Lake, 487th BG
Donald Richards-Waterloo, 2006th Ord
Earl Richardson-Albia, 100th BG, POW
Eugene Richardson-Davenport, 447th BG
Leon Richardson-Ottumwa, 479th FG
Paul Richardson-Albia, 457th BG, POW
Elwood Richter-Akron, 466th BG
William Rickert-Selma, 458th BG, KIA
Theodore J Rickegl-Story City, 306th BG, KIA
Roger S Rickey-Ft Dodge, 487th BG
Haraley Reisgaard-Exira, 452nd BG
Clyde Rine-Carter Lake, 448th BG
Bruce M Rinisland-Muscatine, 384th BG, KIA
Joe Ritchey-Cedar Falls, 379th BG, KIA
Edward Ritts-Keokuk, 466th BG
Edward E Robb-Red Oak, 493rd BG
Darrah Roberts-Iowa Falls, 359th FG
James Roberts-Denver, 93rd BG, KIA
Lloyd Roberts-Oskaloosa, 445th BG, POW
William Roberts-Vinton, 479th FG
Glenn Robinson,-Des Moines, 491st BG
Maurice Robinson-Collins, 20th FG
Paul Dale Robinson-Albia, 401st BG
Roger Robinson,-Davenport, 31st FG
Vernon D Robinson-Oakland, 487th BG
Walter Robinson-Des Moines, 467th BG
Robert Rockdaschal-Onawa, 384th BG
Ralph Rodgers-Burlington, 447th BG
Walter Roelfs-Lake View, 389th BG
George Roepke-Oelwin, 357th FG
John Roesger-McCausland, 95th BG
Virgil Roethler-Algona, 445th BG
Edwin Rogers-salem, 492nd BG, KIA
Olaf Rogness-Cedaar Rapids, 466th BG
Edmund W Rohde-Lemars, 100th BG, KIA
Donald D Rohloff-Delta, 388th BG, KIA
Walter Rolfe-Council Bluffs, 458th BG, POW
Paul D Roland-Bode, Unit Unk, KIA
Douglas O Roll, Jr-St Ansgar, 390th BG
Richard Ronk-Council Bluffs, 490th BG
Loren Roorda-Montezuma, 93rd BG
Blair Rossow-Panora, 34th BG
Arne Rostad-Sioux City, 78th FG
Arthur Roth, Jr-Dubuque, Unit Unk
Paul Roth-Cedar Rapids, 490th BG
Lowell Rothbart-Dewitt, 20th FG
Aubrey Rothchild-Des Moines, 467th BG
Clair Rowe-Cedar Falls, 448th BG
Edwin Rowe-Beaman, 4th FG
John C Rowe-Promise City, 448th BG
Clarence Rowlison-LeGrand, 351st BG, KIA
Werner Rueschenberg-Westphalia, 359th FG
Donald Ruggles-Scranton, 100th BG
Herbert Ruggles-Hedrick, 447th BG, POW
Dale Rummens-Estherville, 448th BG
Harold Ruppert-Cedar Rapids, 490th BG
John J Ruppert-Iowa City, 447th BG
Louis Rush-Des Moines, 401st BG, KIA
Ray A Rush-Des Moines, 357th FG, KIA
Robert Russell-Bagley, 389th BG
Bruce Rust-Sheffield, 94th BG
Rudolph Rust-Burlington, 379th BG, POW
Richard Ruth-Shenandoah, Unit Unk.
Donald Rutt-Casey, 303rd BG, KIA
Donald H Rutt-Mason City, 390th BG
Warren Ryan-Grinnell, 96th BG
Elmer Rydberg-Des Moines, 357th FG, KIA

-S-

Myron Sabotka-Davenport, 490th BG
Floyd L Sackett-Arlington, 489th BG, KIA
Marion Saffell-Des Moines, 93rd BG, POW
Frank Sage-Colfax, 452nd BG, POW
Lloyd Saltzman-Sioux Center, 447th BG
Lloyd J.Saltzman-State Center, 94th BG
L E Salveson-Newton, 34th BG
Norman Sampson-Mason City, 303rd BG
Walter F Sampson-Cedar Rapids, 390th BG
Walter Sanders-Indianola, 34th BG
Everett Sandersfeld-S. Amana, 388th BG
George M Sanderson-Sioux City, Unit Unk, KIA
Keith Sandholm-Red Oak, 34th BG
Alvin Sands-Anton, 95th BG
Stanley Sands-Algona, 20th FG
Marvin E Sandven-Humboldt, 493rd BG
William Sanford-Sioux City, 352nd FG
Paul Santillan-Audubon, 96th BG, KIA
Herman A Sanneman-Creston, 44th BG, KIA
Frank Saunders-Dubuque, 303rd BG, POW
Emil A Schaeffer-Davenport, 487th BG
James W Schaen-Des Moines, 445th BG, KIA
Carl Scharf-Ft Dodge, 392nd BG
Paul Scharff-Aurora, 401st BG, KIA
William Scharnhorst-Iowa, 457th BG
Dale J Schaupp-Dunlap, 398th BG, KIA
Paul Scherb-Waverly, 18th WS
Paul J Scherranan-Farley, 381st BG, KIA
Edwin C Scherz-Davenport, Unit Unk, KIA
J J Schiacitano-Des Moines, 93rd BG
Arthur W Schinker-Norway, 303rd BG, POW
Loren Schipull-Eagle Grove, 398th BG
Ray Schleihs-Johnston, 390th BG
Ray Schmelzer-Postville, 479th FG
John Schmidt-Council Bluffs, 93rd BG, POW
Neil Schmitz-LaPorte City, 389th BG
Arthur Schneider-Keystone, 453rd BG
Marvin D Schneider-Ashton, 446th BG, KIA
Robert Schnieder-Remsen, 94th BG
Jerome Schnitker-Neola, 96th BG
John Schobert-Waukon, 355th FG
Harold Schoelerman-Moneta, 392nd BG, KIA
Donald W Schoen-Sioux City, 353rd FG
Val Schoenthal-Des Moines, Unit Unk
Walter Schoer-Holstein, 44th BG, KIA
Arthur Schonker-Norway, 303rd BG
Clarence Schramm-Charter Oak, 357th FG
Robert Schreiner-Waterloo, 493rd BG
Kenneth J Schriber-Ottosen, 390th BG
Wayne Schrum-Manning, 467th BG
Clarence Schuchmann-Hawkeye, 457th BG
Ralph Schuls-Burlington, 359th FG
James Schulte-Davenport, 93rd BG

Chapter Eighteen

Robert Schultz-Ackley, 322MBG
Russell Schultz-Ft Dodge, 384th BG, POW
Albert Schwab-Keokuk, 457th BG
Carl Schwaderer-Guthrie Center, 379th BG
Carl Schwartz-Essex, 95th BG
Willis Schwartz-Burlington, 94th BG
Victor Schweer-West Liberty, 100th BG
Clayton Scott-Osceola, 381st BG
Dale Scott-Sidney, 401st BG, POW
Frank Scott-Storm Lake, 487th BG, POW
Thomas W Scott-Clearfield, 93rd BG
Albert Seaquist-Bradgate, 390th BG, KIA
Laverne Sedore-Fairfield, 493rd BG
Leroy E Seeger-Glenwood, Unit Unk, KIA
Seegmiller-Decorah, 507th FG
John J Seerley-Burlington, Unit Unk, KIA
Myron Seiberling-Mitchellville, 351st BG, POW
Richard Seiberling-Burlington, 389th BG
Joel I Seidman-Iowa City, 493rd BG
Frederick W Selk-Dysart, 462nd BG, KIA
Emmett Sennett-Honey Creek, 447th BG
Paul W Septer-North English, 487th BG
Jack Serbert-Sioux City, 3rd CCRC
Charles Session-Cedar Rapids, 490th BG
Oscar Severson-Storm Lake, 78th FG
Arthur Sexton-Newton, 351st BG
George Seyfer-Cedar Rapids, 353rd FG
Mex L Shadle-Jefferson, 493rd BG
George R Shaeffer-Fraser, 801st BG, KIA
John M Shafer-Ottumwa, 390th BG
Claude Shaffer-Estherville, 78th FG
Milo Shaner-Williams, 389th BG
Robert Shannon-Washington, 93rd BG, KIA
Harold S Sharp-Dow City, Unit Unk, KIA
Walter Sharum-Bronson, 95th BG
James Shaw-Estherville, 305th BG, KIA
Lyle H Shaw-Estherville, 390th BG
Joseph Shea-Creston, 357th FG
William Sheets,-Des Moines, 94th BG
Chester M Sheley-Milford, 390th BG
Devere Shelton-Calamus, 94th BG
Everette Shelton, Oskaloosa, 94th BG
Morris Shendelman-Bettendorf, 479th FG
Dick Shepard-Janesville, 491st BG

Russell E Sheppard-Delhi, 351st BG, KIA
John Sherrets-Quasqueton, 92nd BG, POW
Ellsworth Shields-Waverly, 458th BG
Wildo W Shira-Garden Grove, 390th BG
Keith Shirk-Grundy Center, 389th BG
Alexander Shkerich-Sioux City, 390th BG
Gilbert H Shoecraft-Siux City, 390th BG
Robert Shuler-Des Moines, 20th FG
Charles Sickels-Ft Madison, 447th BG
Glade Sickels, Clearfield, 92nd BG
Vern Siebels-Anamosa, 96th BG
John Siefker-Melrose, 95th BG
Charles Siemsere-Audubon, 55th FG
Robert L Sill-Ft Dodge, 55th FG, KIA
George Simkins, JR-Mason City, 467th BG
Kenneth Simmons-Newell, 389th BG, POW
Vernon R Simmons-Winterset, 387th BG, KIA
Bernard A Simonsma-Inwood, 487th BG
Willard Simpson-Des Moines, 91st BG, KIA
George R Singer-Newton, 384th BG, KIA
William Singer-Newton, 384th BG, POW
W W Sissons-Greenfield, 466th BG
Carroll Skalberg-Shenandoah, 353rd FG
Joseph J Skubal-Riverside, 202rd BG, KIA
Eldon Slager-Marengo, 446th BG, KIA
Charles Sloca-Fairfield, 301st BG
Winford Smalley-Des Moines, 384th BG, KIA
Eldon Smeltzer-Creston, 445th BG, KIA
Arnold Smith-Marshalltown, 490th BG
Beryl J Smith-Ottumwa, 388th BG, KIA
Cecil Smith-Nemaha, 487th BG, KIA
Dalton Smith-Farmington, 31st FG
Donald L Smith-Mason City, Unit Unk, KIA
Floyd S Smith, Jr-Edgewood, 487th BG
George W Smith-Bronson, 390th BG
Howard M Smith-Atlantic, 448th BG, KIA
Jimmie R Smith-Wesley, 303rd BG, KIA
Justus C Smith-Davenport, 493rd BG
Loren Smith-Ottumwa, 392nd BG, POW
Martin Smith, JR-Davenport, 78th FG, KIA
Maynard Smith-Okoboji, 447th BG
Ralph J Smith-Des Moines, 379th BG, KIA

Richard Smith-Council Bluffs, 381st BG
Roger Smith-Monticello, Unit Unk
Raymond L Snodgrass-Des Moines, 36th BG, KIA
Emary Snyder-Cedar Rapids, 95th BG
James Soesbe-Clinton, 458th BG, KIA
John D Somsky-Granger, 493rd BG
Walter Sondag-Harper, 44th BG, KIA
Myron Sorden-Indianola, 306th BG, POW
Donald J Sorensen-Story City, 92nd BG
Herbert Sorensen-West Branch, 95th BG
Robert M Sorenson-Clinton, 390th BG
Donald Soseman-Nevada, 305th BG, POW
Edwin Sowles-Iowa, 458th BG, KIA
Willard Spangler-Everly, 388th BG, POW
Robert Sparks-Oakland, 93rd BG
John Spear-Churdan, 95th BG
Melvin Spencer-Mason City, 95th BG, POW
Robert Spicer-Rad Oak, 390th BG, KIA
John Springer-Wapello, 389th BG, KIA
Richard A Sporrey-Davenport, 3 92nd BG, KIA
Robert L Sprout-Rodman, 92nd BG, KIA
Jack H Srout-Fairfield, Unit Unk, KIA
Robert Stacey-Hampton, 78th FG
Robert Stafford-Ames, 94th BG
Perle D Stainbrook-Brandon, Unit Unk, KIA
Harold R Staley-Nashua, 390th BG
Ed Stamer-Davenport, 479th FG
Ervin Stamp-Holstein, 306th BG/20th FG
Carl P Stark-Colo, 487th BG
Henry Starr-Tabor, 447th BG
Arthur Staton-Audubon, 452nd BG, POW
Benjamin P Steckel-Davenport, 390th BG
Richard Steelman-Ft Dodge, 93rd BG
Loran A Steen-Des Moines, 390th BG, KIA
Morris Steffen-Cumberland, 351st BG
Edward Stein-Toledo, 447th BG
Harold Steiner-Wellman, 93rd BG
Mahlon T Stelle-Burlington, Unit Unk, KIA
Wayne Stellish-Aurelia, 306th BG
Hjalmer Stenseth-Des Moines, 96th BG
Alonzo Stephens-Des Moines, 490th BG
Eugene Stephens-Waterloo, 453rd BG, POW
Clarence M Stephenson-Spirit Lake, 390th BG
George Sterler, Ashton, 96th BG, POW
Jay R Sterling, Sioux City,

Iowans of the Mighty Eighth

303rd BG, KIA
Gerald Steussy-Algona, 100th BG, POW
Elmer Steven-Spencer, 339th FG
Raymond Steven-Algona, 25th BG
Laurel C Stevens-Monroe, Unit Unk, KIA
Lowell Stevenson-Des Moines, 303rd BG, POW
George Stewart-Chester, 303rd BG, POW
Eugene Stientjes-Pella, 93rd BG
Dale Stillwell-Ocheyden, 447th BG
Robert Stine-Monroe, 364th FG
Eugene Stock-Sac County, 92nd BG
Kenneth H Stockman-Council Bluffs, 303rd BG KIA
Milton P Stoll-Blairstown, Unit Unk, KIA
Edward S Stone-Des Moines, 351st BG, KIA
James Stone-Cedar Rapids, 94th BG
Parker Stone-Ames, 95th BG
Theron J Stookesberry-Monroe, 100th BG, KIA
James Stopulos-Davenport, 94th BG
Merton Straub-Spencer, Unit Unk, KIA
Ray Stringer-Ft Dodge, 94th BG
Elmer J Stromblad-Sibley, 487th BG
Norman Struchen-Webster City, 96th BG
Lyle D Stufflebeam-Bloomfield, 390th BG
Richard Stulman-Ft Dodge, 95th BG
Max Struve-Audubon, 94th BG
Cleo C Struble-Turin, 91st BG, KIA
Norman Stuckey-Udell, 91st BG, POW
Max E Stump-DeSoto, 453rd BG, KIA
George Sturtz-Boone, 91st BG
Robert Suckow-Newton, 445th BG
George M Sullivan-Corning, Unit Unk, KIA
Raymond Sumpter-Cincinnati, 55th FG, KIA
John Sunberg-Red Oak, 447th BG, KIA
Henry D Surber-Moravia, 493rd BG
Maurice Swan-Winfield, 453rd BG, KIA
Gerald Swanger-Cromwell, 92nd BG, POW
Dean Swank-Anton, 390th BG
Elvin Swanson-Swea City, 97th BG
Carroll D Swartzendruber-Wellman, 384th BG, KIA
Curtis Sweeny-Council Bluffs, 78th FG,
Duane G H Sweeny-Council Bluffs, 390th BG
Harold Swett-Ames, 94th BG
John Swift-Manchester, 94th BG
Donald Symonos-Decorah, 34th BG
Wilbur Symonds-Muscatine, 78th FG

-T-

Wayne Tabor-Newton, 446th BG
Emil Tagtmeyer-Cedar Rapids, 490th BG
Ellard V Tangen-Blue Grass, 487th BG
Robert Talbott-Douds, 34th BG
Edward Tarr-Des Moines, 467th BG
Chester Taylor-Spencer, Unit Unk
Don Taylor, Lemars, 336th FG
Francis Taylor-Des Moines, 78th FG
George F Taylor-Sioux City, 379th BG, KIA
Lauren Taylor-Boone, 20th FG, KIA
Richard Taylor-Cedar Rapids, 388th BG
Robert Teeter-LaPorte City, 357th FG
Gerald Terlouw-Pella, 78th FG
Winston Teter-Coon Rapids, 303rd BG, KIA
Richard O Thacker-Emmetsburg, 357th FG
Robert Thacker-Sioux City, 359th FG
John Thatcher-Kalona, 78th FG
Gaylord Thayer-Iowa Falls, 458th BG
Wendall Thieman-Waterloo, 95th BG, POW
Blaine Thomas-Council Bluffs, 303rd BG, POW
Frederick Thomas-Dayton, 452nd BG, KIA
Ralph Thomas-Fayette, 381st BG, KIA
Richard Thomas-Des Moines, 447th BG, POW
Richard Thomas-Nevada, 447th BG
Robert Thomas-Washington, 379th BG
Roland E Thomas-Hopkinton, 390th BG
Theodore Thomas-Mason City, 95th BG
Winfred Thomasson-Des Moines, 447th BG
Merele Thomkins, Waterloo, 452nd BG
Donald Thompson-Marion, 384th BG
Duane Thompson-Postville, 487th BG
Fred Thompson-Cedar Rapids, 447th BG
Gerald Thompson-W.Des Moines, 91st BG
Richard G Thompson-Davenport, 487th BG
Robert Thompson-Algona, 448th BG, KIA
Robert Thompson-Clare, 389th BG, KIA
Robert Thompson-Sioux City, 95th BG
Wilford Thompson-Lovilia, 490th BG
Elden Thomsen-Rolfe, 3rd CCRC
Wayne C Thulin-Cedar Rapids, 305th BG, KIA
Carroll Tiegland-Ames, 92nd BG, POW

Bennie Tillotson-Ottumwa, 446th BG, KIA
Francis Tilton-Cherokee, Unit Unk
Jack Timmins-Des Moines, 303rd BG, POW
John T Toher-Davenport, 487th BG
William Tomasek-Waucoma, 388th BG
John Tomke-Clarion, 306th BG, POW
Harry N Tomlin-Cedar Rapids, 306th BG, KIA
Frank Tomlinson-Packwood, 92nd BG, KIA
Joseph Toms-Central City, 490th BG
Vernon Torreson-Wallingford, 452nd BG
Richard E Touet, Osceola, 390th BG
Karl Treanor-Dubuque, 100th BG
Walter Trettin-Rockford, 447th BG, KIA
Robert Tripe-Des Moines, 389th BG
Robert Tritle, JR-Des Moines, 389th BG
Ralph Trout-Logan, 398th BG
Leon Tucker-Des Moines, 95th BG
Charles W Turner-Waterloo, 390th BG, POW
Harlyn Turner-Dubuque, 446th BG
Robert Turner-Redfield, 92nd BG, KIA
Marion Turnipseed-Des Moines, 491st BG
Howard A Turnquist-Swan, 487th BG, KIA
Lyle Turnquist-Sioux Rapids, 94th BG
Joe Tursi-Des Moines, 447th BG
Francis Tuttle-Corydon, 398th BG, KIA
Melvin Tyner-Randolph, 490th BG

-U-

Duane Ulstad-Ft Dodge, 398th BG
Glenn Underwood-Shenandoah, 447th BG, POW

-V-

Edaard B Vaderweid-Sioux Center, 44th BG, I
Nathan Van Alstine-Ft Dodge, 392nd BG, KIA
Charles E Van Ausdall-Keokuk, 91st BG, KIA
Lee Van Baale-Monroe, 8th AFHQ
Dale Vance-Floyd, 457th BG
William Vance-Des Moines, 381st BG
Doyle Vandamanet-Sigourney, 490th BG
Lowell Vander Hamm-Lawton, 490th BG
Clair Vander Schaaf-Hull, 801st BG, KIA
Gerritt Vander Schaaf-Hull, 305th BG

Chapter Eighteen

Rene Van De Voorde-Fairfield, 389th BG, KIA
Dick Vanduyn-Iowa City, BAD2
Roy Van Dyke-Jefferson 91st BG
Warren Vaneschen-Ackley, 94th BG, POW
James Van Ginkel-Atlantic, 466th BG
James Van Ginkel-Prairie CIty, 446th BG
Carl H Van Houten-Cedar Rapids, 487th BG
Laverne Varenhorst-Lemars, 447th BG
Harry Vasconcellos-Des Moines, 392nd BG
Charles Vavra-Ferguson, 392nd BG, KIA
Charles Vejda-Cedar Rapids, 466th BG, E
Floyd M Vevle-Ft Dodge, 390th BG, KIA
Lloyd O Velve-Ft Dodge, 384th BG, KIA
Layton P Verme-Des Moines, 390th BG
Bernard M Vermeer-Sioux Center, 305th BG, KIA
David Vermeer-Sioux Center, 401st BG, KIA
William Vint-Beaman, 96th BG
Clarence Vinton-Union, 447th BG
Raymond Vogel-Clinton, 467th BG, POW
Wilbur J.Vogel-Dubuque, 448th BG, POW
Wilbur Volz-Edwardsville, 447th BG, E
George Von Hagel-Akron, 389th BG
Roy Voorhees-Washington, 386th BG
Frank Vrathny-Lehigh, 487th BG, POW

-W-

Walter Waechter-Sigourney, 94th BG
Edwin D Waggoner-Des Moines, 457th BG, KIA
Ernest Wagner-Waterloo, 379th BG
Harold Wagner-Burlington, 93rd BG
William Wagner-Cedar Falls, 447th BG
Harold D Wagoner-Waterloo, 384th BG, KIA
Arthur Walker-Primghar, 93rd BG
Billy Walker-Des Moines 384th BG, POW
Floyd Walker-Des Moines, 491st BG, KIA
John Walker-Gravity, 34th BG
Chester Wall-Adel, 4th FG
Wayne Walrath-Keokuk, 490th BG
H Ben Walsh-Hampton, 458th BG
Howard Walsh-Des Moines, 94th BG
Howard Walsh, Hampton, 389th BG
Ramond Walton-Clinton, 392nd BG, POW
Kenneth P Ward-Burlington, 44th BG, KIA
Robert Ward-Boone, 91st BG, POW
Robert Ward-Toledo, 361st FG
Walter Ward-Vinton, 94th BG, POW
Willard Ward-Corydon, 94th BG, KIA
Robert H Warren-Ames, 388th BG, KIA
Edgar Warrington-Marion, 490th BG
Richard Waterman-Davenport, 78th FG
Joseph Waters-Carroll, 392nd BG, POW
Dale R Watson-Belknap, 445th BG, POW
John Watson-Glidden, 351st BG, POW
Donald E Watts-Ionia, 445th BG, POW
Frank K Watt-Lamoni, 452nd BG, KIA
Dale Watterson-Cedar Rapids, 100th BG, KIA
Robert Weander-Sioux City, 93rd BG, KIA
Loren Weaverling-Maason City, 352nd FG
Neil Webster-Guttenberg, 55th FG
William F Weck-Davenport, 491st BG, KIA
Harold D Weede-Bloomfield, 322 BG, KIA
Theodore Welch-Albia, 78th FG
Jens T Weiby, JR-Armstrong, 91st BG, KIA
Dennis Weideman-Ft Dodge, 384th BG
Ollie J Weigel-Guthrie center, 493rd BG
Donald L Weiss-Denison, 386th BG, KIA
John Wells-Sioux City, 92nd BG, POW
John E Wells-Storm Lake, 92nd BG, KIA
Richard Wells-Des Moines, Unit Unk
Vernon Wells-Oskaloosa, 389th BG
Fred C Weltz-Cedar Falls, Unit Unk, KIA
Emil Wente-Waverly, 305th BG, KIA
William F Wentz-Waterloo, 466th BG, KIA
Bill Werener, Muscatine, 1SAD
Donald J Wessar-Fort Dodge, 390th BG
Delmar Wessel-Dow City, 78th FG
Keith I Wessling-Paton, 493rd BG
Ernest West-Burlington, 96th BG
Lewis West-Des Moines, 479th FG
Hartley Westbrook-Coon Rapids, 44th BG, POW
David T Westell-Pocahontas, 390th BG, POW
Theodore J Westerhof-Davenport, 487th BG
Joseph S Westvold-Huxley, 487th BG
Eugene H Whalen-Davenport, 457th BG, KIA
George R Wharton, JR-Aurelia, 447th BG
Jack M Wheeler-Des Moines, 306th BG, KIA
Okley Wheeler-Burlington, 447th BG
Charles E Whitacre-Dallas Center, 467th BG, POW
Orville Whitcanack-Cantril, 493rd BG
Robert White-Burlington, 493rd BG
Robert E Whitehand-Iowa City, Unit Unk, KIA
Erwin E Wiese-Davenport, 487th BG
Myrick Whiting-Whiting, 457th BG
Gene White-Pleasant Valley, 93rd BG, KIA
Frank Whitehead-Marshalltown, 390th BG, POW
John Whitney-Des Moines, 91st BG, E
Jack Whiton-Panora, 388th BG
Frank Whittington-Dubuque, 486th BG, POW
Charles Whitacre-Dallas Center, 467th BG
Richard Wigim-West Liberty, 490th BG
Blaine Wilcox-Glenwood, 401st BG, KIA
Eugene Wilcox-Moravia, 96th BG, KIA
Steward Wilcox-Glenwood, 401st BG, KIA
Melvin Wile-Marathon, 389th BG, POW
Galen Wiley-Boone, 305th BG
Lanson Wilkerson, Perry, Unit Unk.
John J Williams-Dubuque, 91st BG, KIA
Norman E Williams, Mechanicsville, 25th BG
Roger Williams-Keokuk, 389th BG
Cecil W Wills-Osceola, 390th BG
Louis Willson-Ames, 303rd BG, KIA
Billy J Wilson-Knoxville, 398th BG, KIA
Donald Wilson-Eldora, 91st BG
James Wilson-Waterloo, 379th BG, E
John Wilson-Des Moines, 91st BG, KIA
Norris Wilson-Belmond, 93rd BG
Woodrow H Wilson-Ottumwa, 390th BG
Robert Wims-Belle Plaine, 95th BG
Herbert T Winter,Jr-Swea City, 55th FG, KIA
Everett Wirtz-Boone, 94th BG
William Wixon-Keokuk, 100th BG
James J Wolfe-Danville, 447th BG, KIA
Joseph Wolfe_Ossian, 361st FG, KIA
Donald Wombacher-Iowa City, 490th BG
Ralph Wombacher-Hills, 489th BG
Cleon Wood-Cedar Falls, 452nd BG
Leon Wood-Center Point, 447th BG
Johnnie Wooden-Shenandoah, 490th BG
Ross Woods-Red Oak, 389th BG
Edward Woolums-Ottumwa, 04SD

Iowans of the Mighty Eighth

John Woolway-Des Moines, 453rd BG
Eldon Wrighe-Sergeant Bluff, 447th BG
James G Wright-Mediapolis, 390th BG
Thomas Wright-Des Moines, 453rd BG
Edwin C Wulfekuhle-N. Buena Vista, 96th BG, KIA
Marvin Wunschel-Ida Grove, 493rd BG
Stephen Wurtz-Underwood, 305th BG, POW
Carmen Wymore-Gibson, 389th BG

-X-

-Y-

Allen Yashack-Diagonal, 306th BG

Charles W Yeager, Jr-Colo, 92nd BG
Donald W Yeager-Agency, 390th BG
William Yenerich-Ames, 305th BG
Gerald Yoder-Woolstock, 453rd BG, KIA
Adelbert Young-Nora Springs, 487th BG
Horace Young-Winterset, 507th FG
Omer Young-Cedar Rapids, 379th BG, KIA
Robert Young-Estherville, 457th BG
Edward Youngers-Dewitt, 96th BG

-Z-

Leroy M Zach-Swisher, 466th BG

William Zachar-Davenport, 303rd BG
Wayne Zeigler-Iowa Falls, 384th BG
Clarence Ziebell-Charles City, 801st BG
Ray Ziegenmeyer-Grinnell, 93rd BG
Floyd H Zimmer-Russell, 44th BG, KIA

Chapter Nineteen

KILLED IN ACTION

The persons pictured in this section were Iowans assigned or attached to the Eighth Air Force in England during World War II and killed in action in the air war over Europe. Over one-quarter million men and women served in the Eighth Air Force from 1942-45. Nearly 26,000, one-tenth of all Americans killed during the war, were members of the Eighth Air Force.

With written permission of the State Historical Society of Iowa at Des Moines, names and photographs for this publication only, were retrieved from World War II Casualty files. Data and photographs contained in the files were contributed by relatives of those killed in action for historical purposes.

It is possible all Iowans of the "Mighty Eighth", killed in action, are not listed or pictured. Information identifying the specific unit to which an individual was assigned was sometimes incomplete and lacking in supportive data. Records indicating only that the individual was based with the Eighth Air Force with no other identifying information were recorded as "Unit Unknown". Other Army Air Corps units were also based in England at various times. Individuals whose unit designation could not be identified with the Eighth were not listed.

Reviewing files to determine those who were killed in the Eighth Air Force I learned not only how each met their death, but also those in other branches of the military. Tragically the files were voluminous. They were fine young men who gave the best years of their lives, their tomorrows for our todays, in one of civilizations greatest struggles for survival. Soldier, sailor, Marine, merchant marine, air men, in far away, lonely places, met their death in prison camps, Pacific islands; went down with their ships; were shot by snipers; blown apart by hand grenades or artillery; or shot out of the air. Each file detailed how those who fought for freedom and human dignity, perished and now rest at the bottom of the seas, in cemeteries at home and foreign countries, or remain unknown or their bodies never recovered. Without their sacrifice and the efforts of those who survived, the world as we know it would be totally different. May they all rest in peace. While those pictured on the following pages were in the Eighth Air Force, they stand for all those who lost their lives in World War II regardless of branch of service. May all the young men who sacrificed their lives and those who put their lives in harm's way and survived so that we may live in a free, more decent and humane world not have been in vain.

Iowans of the Mighty Eighth

Adolph Abraham
Cedar Rapids, 448th BG

Billy Adam
Sigourney, Unit Unk

Carl Adams
Washington, 490th BG

Donald Ahlwardt
Danbury, 44th BG

Norbert Allen
Des Moines, 44th BG

Donald Alvestad
Roland, 390th BG

Dale Anderson
Des Moines, 52nd FG

Ernest Anderson
Lake Mills, 52nd FG

Richard Anderson
West Bend 100th BG

Chapter Nineteen

Robert Anderson
Mason City, Unit Unk

John Arihood
Grandview, 96th BG

Harold Aucker
Mason City, 448th BG

Herbert Autenreith
Creston, 493rd BG

Jay Baas
Oskaloosa, 305th BG

Edwin Bachman
Montezuma, 95th BG

Charles Bagley
Audubon, 398th BG

John Baker
Villisca, 82nd FG

Lowell Baker
Sharpsburg, 457th BG

Iowans of the Mighty Eighth

Warren Ball
Cummings, 303rd BG

Anthny Bamburg
Lemars, 487th BG

Thomas Barnett
Farley, 3035th BG

Benjamin Barron
Corydon, 56th FG

Harold Barton
Sioux City, 392nd BG

John Baxter
Chariton, 100th BG

John Becker
Waterloo, 392nd BG

John Beckman
Burlington, 355th FG

Francis Beedle
Sioux City, 100th BG

Chapter Nineteen

George Benedict
Davis City, 452nd BG

Norbert Bengford
Odebolt, 389th BG

Kenneth Bennett
Iowa City, 303rd BG

Raymond Benton
Guthrie Center, 305th BG

Robert Benz
Des Moines, 392nd BG

Bernard Bernstein
Des Moines, 306th BG

Harry Bernstein
Brooklyn, 457th BG

Carl Bishop
Des Moines, 91st BG

Edwin Bishop
Red Oak, 34th BG

Iowans of the Mighty Eighth

Guilford Black
Ottumwa, 385th BG

John Blaylock
Council Bluffs, 351st BG

David Blue
Chariton, 388th BG

Laurence Bockeloo
Clinton, 490th BG

William Boone
Delaware, 389th BG

Robert Bottorff
Ottumwa, 92nd BG

Arthur Boyd
West Des Moines, 388th BG

Raymond Bradley
Creston, 388th BG

Lawrence Brandenburg
Lemars, Unit Unk

Chapter Nineteen

Leslie Brandenburg
Strawberry Point, 457th BG

Raymond Brecht
Watkins, 36th BS, RCS

Albert Bricker
Greenfield, 303rd BG

Max P Brim
Osceola, 100th BG

William Brinkman
Pocahontaas, 379th BG

Arthur Brody
Des Moines, Unit Unk

Howard K Brooks
Otho, 390th BG

Lambert R Brostrom
Sioux City, 91st BG

Dale S Brown
Bonaparte, 100th BG

Iowans of the Mighty Eighth

Lynn R Brown, Jr
Independence, 447th BG

Robert P Buchanan
Tipton, 492nd BG

Lowell C Buchmiller
Jefferson, 56th FG

Robert D Buckley
Ogden, Unit Unk

Gerld J Budrevich
Des Moines, 13th Photo

Donald T Burke
Charlotte, 491st BG

Vernon Burke
Audubon, 385th BG

William R Burkett
Jefferson, 353rd FG

Edward W Bush
Galva, 389th BG

Chapter Nineteen

James A Bussey
Bussey, 364th FG

Ellsworth L Campbell
Oelwein, 95th BG

James A Campbell
Keokuk, 447th BG

Thomas J Campbell
Mason City, Unit Unk

Gerald R Carris
Keota, 452nd BG

Stanley P Carson
Woodburn, 100th BG

Charles G Cassaday
Denison, 27th Photo

Harold R Christensen
Eagle Grove, 91st BG

Donald E Chrissinger
Mt Pleasant, 20th FG

Iowans of the Mighty Eighth

James Clark
Chariton, 388th BG

Franklin Clemons
Bettendorf, 306th BG

James W Cline
Perry, 96th BG

William J Cochran
Elmira, 487th BG

Irving Cohen
Council Bluffs, 452nd BG

Homer Comegys
Des Moines, 385th BG

Craig T Conley
McCallsburg, 305th BG

Dick D Connelly
Ottumwa, 359th FG

Edward F Connolly
Dubuque, 379th BG

Chapter Nineteen

Mervin W Cook
Des Moines, 94th BG

Francis E Cooke
Fonda, 401st BG

Robert P Cooper
Stuart, 351st BG

Blaine Corbin
Nevada, 91st BG

Willis B Core
Indianola, 389th BG

Ray L Cornick
Davenport, 352nd FG

Dallas G Couchman
Sewal, 490th BG

Louis M Cowley
Sioux City, 303rd BG

Leroy A Coy
Randolph, 388th BG

Iowans of the Mighty Eighth

Clayton M Croft
Shenandoah, 390th BG

Dale D Croft
Ft Dodge, 100th BG

Roy D Cruse
Terril, 351st BG

William K Cutting
Des Moines 381st BG

Kermit O Dahlen
Thompson, 4th FG

Max E Dailey
Des Moines, 93rd BG

Wendell L Daily
Waterloo, 389th BG

Charles S Daskam
Cresco, 458th BG

Prosdocimo Della Betta
Chariton, Unit Unk

Chapter Nineteen

Robert F Demery
Ft Dodge, 392nd BG

John N Dennison
Bellevue, 306th BG

James Denny
Cedar Falls, 390th BG

Camille F Devaney
Cascade, 351st BG

Donald C Dewey
Spring Hill, 495th BG

Felix Diaz
Osage, 446th BG

Darrel R Dickerson
Union, Unit Unk

Robert W Dideriksen
Shenandoah, 14th Photo

Don S Differding
Walker, 385th BG

Iowans of the Mighty Eighth

Marvin E Dille
Belle Plaine, Unit Unk

Robert L Dittmer
Elkader, 490th BG

Victor E Doorley
Cedar Falls, Unit Unk

George J Douroumes
Boone, 458th BG

Gerald J Duffy
Davenport, 379th BG

Charles L Dulin
Cedar Rapids, 94th BG

Maynard L Dunker
Muscatine, 92nd BG

Stanley E Durrett
Burlington, 34th BG

Wayne R Dutler
Des Moines, 94th BG

Chapter Nineteen

Floyd D Eckrosh
Des Moines, 498th BG

Clair B Edel
Mason City, Unit Unk

Stephen L Edgington
Muscatine, 398th BG

Lyle R Edmondson
Washington, 379th BG

Hubert I Egenes
Story City, 357th FG

Nellins Egge
Inwood, 303rd BG

Charles W Emerson
Council Bluffs, 100th BG

James F Emerson
Volga, 453rd BG

Virgil L Emerson
Cambridge, 96th BG

Iowans of the Mighty Eighth

Ernest F Engeman
Ft Madison, 395th BG

Jack B Eppler
Des Moines, 306th BG

Roland H Erdman
Renwick, 466th BG

Dale R Estle
Ledyard, 466th BG

Leland J Evers
Council Bluffs, 452nd BG

Robert Feese
Albia, 388th BG

Byron J Fisher
Danbury, 56th FG

John G Fitch
Des Moines, 384th BG

William M Fitch
Cedar Rapids, 160th Tac Recon

Chapter Nineteen

Harold E Flaugh
Winterset, 44th BG

John F Fleege
Beresford, 392nd BG

Theodore M Fluegel
Cedar Rapids, 94th BG

William J Focht
Des Moines, 487th BG

Russell G Ford
Marion, 96th BG

Anthony J Forte
Des Moines, 390th BG

Howard E Found
Keokuk, 458th BG

Raymond Friedmann
Alton, 96th BG

James J Friend
Council Bluffs, 385th BG

Iowans of the Mighty Eighth

Eugene M Gallup
Logan, 392nd BG

Robert J Gamble
Mason City, 452nd BG

Helmer W Gangstad
Webster City, 447th BG

Darwin D Gant
Dana, Unit Unk

Richard A Gee
Knoxville, 55th FG

John E Gilligan
Sioux City 453rd BG

Edward J Gillmeier
Des Moines, 388th BG

Arthur R Ginder
Des Moines, 91st BG

Carroll J Gjerde
Radcliffe, 452nd BG

Chapter Nineteen

Kenneth J Glasscock
Stuart, 44th BG

James Golbski
Bettendorf, 453rd BG

Glenn E Gommela
Manson, 489th BG

Robert S Gorman
Waverly, 384th BG

William C Grady
Cedar Rapids, 453rd BG

Melvin H Graper
Ames, 392nd BG

Orland R Graper
Rockford, 445th BG

Robert G Green
Osage, 306th BG

Franklin M Grigg
Bronson, 401st BG

Iowans of the Mighty Eighth

Richard Grow
Mason City, 352nd FG

Max G Gunsolley
Burlington, Unit Unk

George F Hall, Jr
Des Moines, Unit Unk

Lloyd G Hally
Huxley, 353rd FG

Paul E Hammond
Mason City, 379th BG

Warren J Handley
Des Moines, 384th BG

James E Harl
Bloomfield, Unit Unk

Albertus Harrenstein
Grundy Center, 388th BG

Paul Hartkoph
Atlantic, 490th BG

Chapter Nineteen

Roger W Hayes
Mason City, 93rd BG

Robert H Hegg
Waverly, 306th BG

Carl W Heline
Marcus, Unit Unk

Kenneth J Herman
Traer, Unit Unk

Donald W Hess
Sioux City, 333392nd BG

Hugh Y Hilton
Ottumwa, Unit Unk

Stanley E Histed
Keokuk, 388th BG

Robert L Hodson
Eldon, 96th BG

Albert H Holiday
Glenwood, Unit Unk

Iowans of the Mighty Eighth

Dewey H Hollis
Waterloo, 479th BG

Lester W Hovden
Ridgeway, 359th FG

Glenn C Hovey
Fairfield, 44th BG

Charles J Howard
Council Bluffs, 17th BG

Dwayne H Huebner
Postville, 389th BG

Milton H Huebner
Sumner, 356th FG

Hayden T Hughes
Washington, 447th BG

David A Humke
Dubuque, Unit Unk

Howard C Humphrey
Postville, 44th BG

Chapter Nineteen

Gail R. Hunter
Atlantic, 387th BG

James S Huston
Olds, 93rd BG

Ernest H Hutton
Ollie, 445th BG

John F Inman
Grinnell, 95th BG

Myron G Jacobs
Muscatine, 44th BG

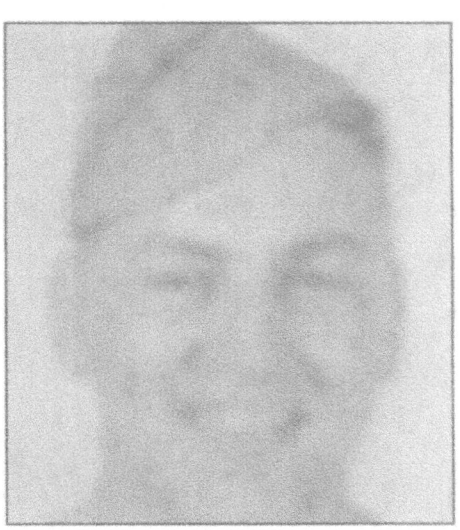
Alan R Jacobson
Britt, 78th FG

Alfred H Janss
Atlantic, 467th BG

Donald W Jeffrey
Des Moines, 384th BG

George L Johnson
New Sharon, 91st BG

Iowans of the Mighty Eighth

Guy W Johnson
Parkersburg, 44th BG

Harry B Johnson
Davenport, 386th BG

Olin D Johnson
Rockwell City, 445th BG

Carl H Jorgensen
Des Moines, 303rd BG

Jesse Joyce, Jr
Zearing, 303rd BG

Thomas J Keefe, Jr
Charles City, 96th BG

Harry A Kelley, Jr
Blencoe, 351st BG

Joseph Kelley
Delta, 491st BG

Oren H Kelley
Atlantic, 315th TCG

Chapter Nineteen

Gilbert O Kemmann
Lowden, 385th BG

Edward J Kempker
Lemars, 392nd BG

Michael G Kennedy
Storm Lake, 93rd BG

Dale C Killion
Denison, 379th BG

Clifford N Kirkpatrick
Grand River, 91st BG

Edmund B Knoll
Garner, 466th BG

Robert W Knutson
Davenport, 401st BG

Thomas K Kohlhaas
Algona, 3384th BG

Norbert D Koll
Mapleton, 91 BG

Iowans of the Mighty Eighth

Karle E Kolmerer
Muscatine, 390th BG

Lawrence Kooima
Rock Valley, 306th BG

Donald G Kopf
Muscatine, 351st BG

William E Kopf
Des Moines, 384th BG

Robert E Kraft
Mapleton, Unit Unk

Svend A Krogh
Hampton, 392nd BG

Norman C Kropf
Cedar Rapids, 392nd BG

Robert W Kudej
West Des Moines, 92nd BG

Theodore F Kuhlmeier
Ft Madison, 492nd BG

Chapter Nineteen

Edward W Kussman
Council Bluffs, 492nd BG

Joseph J Lamansky
East Pleasant Plain, 447th BG

Robert H Landen
Ida Grove, 94th BG

George N Larsen
Grinnell, 44th BG

Glenn N Larson
Badger, 490th BG

Robert W Larson
Thompson, 353rd FG

Robert L Laucamp
Tipton, 44th BG

Tillman O Lawr
Des Moines, Unit Unk

Dale B Leaf
Marshalltown, 4th FG

Iowans of the Mighty Eighth

Leonard D Leeds
Cherokee, 379th BG

David M Lesher
Waterloo, 401st BG

Joseph W Lewis
West Branch, 390th BG

Robert W Lewis
Mason City, 96th BG

Thomas W Lewis
Indianola, 93rd BG

Phil A Lichty
Mason City, 305th BG

Lowell A Lindbloom
Iowa, 379th BG

Charles E Lindquist
Burlington, 457th BG

Vern J Lowman
Ames, 491st BG

Chapter Nineteen

Paul J Lowry
Boone, 305th BG

Wallace D Lund
Rake, Unit Unk

Chester H Lundquist
Winfield, 379th BG

Richard D McCarthy
Ames, Unit Unk

George McCord
Council Bluffs, 466th BG

Robert K McCune
Clinton, 387th BG

William R McGinnis
Iowa City, 379th BG

Bruce A McKern
Mystic, Troop Car. Sdn.

Charles A McWilliams
Bloomfield, 487th BG

Iowans of the Mighty Eighth

Glenn E Mace, Jr
Washington, 44th BG

Frank E Machen
Cedar Rapids, 452nd BG

Ronald M MacKenzie
Ft Dodge, 379th BG

Ray W Magin
Wheatland, 385th BG

Roger E Maillard
Mason Cityh, 34th BG

Joseph P Malloy
Gilmore City, 493rd BG

Norman W Mandelbaum
Des Moines, 384th BG

Charles E Maring
Grinnell, 388th BG

Morris R Marks
Lake Park, 95th BG

Chapter Nineteen

Harold D Matz
Radcliffe, 96th BG

Robert E Means
Manilla, 96th BG

Robert C Meline
Des Moines, 93rd BG

Dearld W Melton
Council Bluffs, 3384th BG

Fereddie O Menefee
Sioux Rapids, 94th BG

George W Mercer
Muscatine, Unit Unk

Louis L Merfeld
Greene, Unit Unk

Julian W Messerly
Ft Dodge, 487th BG

Warren R Messmer
Burlington, 95th BG

Iowans of the Mighty Eighth

Gregory C Meyer
Dubuque, 303rd BG

Darwin F Michaelsen
Clinton, 390th BG

Fred E Mincks
Chariton, 446th BG

James L Mitchell
Crawfordsville, 306th BG

Joe D Mitchell
Marshalltown, 492nd BG

Charles J Moeller
Davenport, Unit Unk

Leroy M Mohr
Cresco, 92nd BG

Albert R Moline
Des Moines, 305th BG

William L Monroe
Estherville, 452nd BG

Chapter Nineteen

Thomas N Montag
West Bend, Unit Unk

Donald E Morgart
Melbourne, 2025th Eng,

Alvin J Morman
Coon Rapids, 390th BG

Glenn W Morris, Jr
Waterloo, 466th BG

Warren N Morris
Keokuk, Unit Unk

John M Morton
Denison, 351st BG

Richard L Moses
Storm Lake, 458th BG

Phillip M Murillo
Cedar Rapids, 457th BG

Dennis J Murphy
Ft Dodge, 303rd BG

Iowans of the Mighty Eighth

Ralph C Murray
Arnolds Park, 95th BG

Edward P Myers
North Liberty, 91st BG

Charles K Naden
Webster City, Unit Unk

Fred F Nagle
Ames, 390th BG

Vernon D Nappier
Bedford, 44th BG

Earl B Nelson
Webster City, 381st BG

Robert R Nelson
Jewell, Unit Unk

Ronald M Nichols
Colfax, Unit Unk

Tage R Nielsen
Newell, Unit Unk

Chapter Nineteen

Carl A Nord
Atlantic, 493rd BG

Lyle A Norquist
Mason City, 351st BG

William H Nowels
Des Moines, 95th BG

Martin G O'Connell
Beaconsfield, 78th FG

James E O'Connor
Conrad, Unit Unk

Richard J O'Connor
Lockport, 364th FG

Lloyd K Olson, Selma
305th BG

Riley E Orr
Onawa, 467th BG

Herbert S Owens
Mapleton, 94th BG

Iowans of the Mighty Eighth

John W Padget
Waterloo, 94th BG

Clarence F Parizek
Dysart, 95th BG

Jesse L Patterson
Winfield, Unit Unk

Leseter E Paup
Scranton, 388th BG

Donald R Peacock
Shellsburg, 457th BG

Warren J Pease
Farragut, 385th BG

Jack A Peck
Marshalltown, 92nd BG

Charles J Pessica
Ft Dodge, Unit Unk

Richard M Petrus
Council Bluffs, 446th BG

Chapter Nineteen

Milford F Peters
Dows, Unit Unk

Raymond G Phillips
Newton, 352nd FG

James B Piatt
Clinton, 491st BG

Elmer D Pitsenburger
Linden, 492nd BG

George H Pogge
Council Bluffs, Unit Unk

Clarence J Powell
Humeston, 8th TCS

Richard A Pratt
Lohrville, 352nd FG

John B Price, Des Moines
303rd BG

Virgil V Prior
Cedar Rapids, 448th BG

Iowans of the Mighty Eighth

Robert J Prudhon
Iowa Falls, Unit Unk

James E Ralston
Cedar Rapids, Unit Unk

Oliver J Rapps
Vinton, 385th BG

Leonard L Raspotnik
Des Moines, Unit Unk

Harold T Raynie
Hawarden, 389th BG

Delbert D Reeve
Tipton, 100th BG

Robert C Reinartson
Ft Dodge, 447th BG

Mark R Reynolds, Jr
Shellsburg, 379th BG

Donald F Rice
Deloit, 701st MP

Chapter Nineteen

Theodore J Riekegl
Story ity, 306th BG

William F Rickert
Selma, 458th BG

Bruce M Rinisland
Muscatine, 3384th BG

Joseph R Ritchey
Cedar Falls, 379th BG

James V Roberts
Denver, 93rd BG

Edwin F Rogers
Salem, 492nd BG

Edmund W Rohde
Lemars, 100th BG

Donald D Rohloff
Delta, 388th BG

Paul O Roland
Bode, Unit Unk

Iowans of the Mighty Eighth

Clarence Rowlison
LeGRand, 351st BG

Louis S Rush
Des Moines 401st BG

Roy A Rush
Des Moines, 357th FG

Donald H Rutt
Casey, 303rd BG

Elmer D Rydberg
Des Moines, 357th FG

Floydd L Sackett
Arlington, 489th BG

George M Sanderson
Sioux City, Unit Unk

Hermn A Sanneman
Creston, 44th BG

Paul J Santillan
Audubon, 96th BG

Chapter Nineteen

James W Schaen
Des Moines, 445th BG

Paul F Scharff
Aurora, 401st BG

Dale J Schaupp
Dunlap, 398th BG

Paul J Scherrman
Farley, 381st BG

Edwin C Scherz
Davenport, Unit Unk

Marvin D Schneider
Ashton, 446th BG

Harold A Schoelerman
Moneta, 392nd BG

Walter B Schoer
Holstein, 44th BG

Albert Seaquist, Jr
Bradgate, 390th BG

233

Iowans of the Mighty Eighth

Leroy E Seeger
Glenwood, Unit Unk

John J Seerley
Burlington, Unit Unk

Frederick W Selk
Dysart, 462nd Sub Depot

George R Shaeffer
Fraser, 4th FG

Robert H Shannon
Washington, 93rd BG

Harold S Sharp
Dow City, Unit Unk

James V Shaw
Esterville, 305th BG

Russell E Sheppard
Delhi, 100th BG

Robert L Sill
Ft Dodge, 55th FG

Chapter Nineteen

Vernon R Simmons
Winterseet, 387th BG

Willard O Simpson
Des Moines 91st BG

Joseph J Skubal
Riverside, 303rd BG

Eldon A Slager
Marengo, 446th BG

Winford R Smalley
Des Moines, 384th BG

Eldon L Smeltzer
Creston, 445th BG

Beryl J Smith
Ottumwa, 388th BG

Cecil J Smith
Nemaha, 487th BG

Donald L Smith
Mason City, Unit Unk

Iowans of the Mighty Eighth

Howad M Smith
Atlantic, 448th BG

Jimmie R Smith
Wesley, 303rd BG

Martin Smith, Jr
Davenport, 78th FG

Ralph J Smith
Des Moines, 379th BG

Raymond L Snodgrass
Des Moines, 36th RCMS

James A Soesbe
Clinton, 458th BG

Willis Sondag
Harper, 44th BG

Edwin E Sowles
Iowa, 458th BG

Robert F Spicer
Red Oak 390th BG

Chapter Nineteen

Richard F Sporrey
Davenport, 392nd BG

John H Springer
Wapello, 389th BG

Robert L Sprout
Rodman, 92nd BG

Jack H Srout
Fairfield, Unit Unk

Loran A Steen
Des Moines, 390th BG

Mahlon T Stelle
Burlington, Unit Unk

Jay R Sterling
Sioux City, 303rd BG

Laurel C Stevens
Monroe, Unit Unk

Kenneth H Stockman
Council Bluffs, 303rd BG

Iowans of the Mighty Eighth

Milton P Stoll
Blairstown, Unit Unk

Edward S Stone
Des Moines, 385th BG

Theron J Stookesberry
Monroe, 100th BG

Merton G Straub
Spencer, Unit Unk

Cleo C Struble
Turin, 91st BG

Max E Stump
DeSoto, 453rd BG

George M Sullivan
Corning, Unit Unk

Raymond L Sumpter
Cincinnati, 55th FG

John L Sunberg
Red Oak, 487th BG

Chapter Nineteen

Maurice L Swan
Winfield, 453rd BG

Carroll D Swartzendruber
Wellman, 384th BG

George F Taylor
Sioux City, 379th BG

Lauren J Taylor
Boone, 20th FG

Winston C Teter
Coon Rapids, 303rd BG

Frederick W Thomas
Dayton, 452nd BG

Ralph A Thomas
Fayette, 381st BG

Robert E Thompson
Clare, 392nd BG

Robert W Thompson
Algona, 448th BG

Iowans of the Mighty Eighth

Wayne C Thulin
Cedar Rapids, 305th BG

Bennie F Tillotson
Ottumwa, 446th BG

Harry W Tomlin
Des Moines, 306th BG

Frank E Tomlinson
Packwood, 92nd BG

Walter W Trettin
Rockford, 447th BG

Robert G Turner
Redfield, 92nd BG

Howard A Turnquist
Swan 487th BG

Francis M Tuttle
Corydon, 398th BG

Nathan G Van Alstine
Ft Dodge, 392nd BG

Chapter Nineteen

Charles E Van Ausdall
Keokuk, 91st BG

Clair D Vander Schaaf
Hull, 801st BG

Rene G Van De Voorde
Fairfield, 389th BG

Charles E Vavra
Ferguson, 392nd BG

Bernard M Vermeer
Sioux Center, 305th BG

David E Vermeer
Sioux Center, 401st BG

Floyd M Vevle
Ft Dodge, 390th BG

Lloyd O Vevle
Ft Dodge, 384th BG

Edwin D Waggoner
Des Moines, 457th BG

Iowans of the Mighty Eighth

Erwalt D Wagner
Waterloo, 379th BG

Harold D Wagoner
Waterloo, 387th BG

Floyd A Walker, Jr
Des Moines, 491st BG

Kenneth P Ward
Burlington, 44th BG

Willard E Ward
Corydon, 94th BG

Robert H Warren
Ames, 388th BG

Frank K Watt
Lamoni, 452nd BG

Dale F Watterson
Cedar Rapids, 100th BG

Robert A Weander
Sioux City, 93rd BG

Chapter Nineteen

William F Weck
Davenport, 491st BG

Harold D Weede
Bloomfield, 333rd BG

Jens T Weiby, Jr,
Armstrong, 91st BG

Donald I Weiss
Denison, 386th BG

John E Wells
Storm Lake, 92nd BG

Fred C Weltz
Cedar Falls, Unit Unk

Emil G Wente
Waverly, 305th BG

William F Wentz
Waterloo, 466th BG

Eugene H Whalen
Davenport, 457th BG

Iowans of the Mighty Eighth

Jack M Wheeler
Des Moines, 306th BG

Robert E Whitehand
Iowa City, Unit Unk

Blaine B Wilcox
Glenwood, 401st BG

Eugene Wilcox, Jr
Moravia, 96th BG

Stewart L Wilcox
Glenwood, 401st BG

Louis H Willson
Ames, 303rd BG

Billie J Wilson
Knoxville, 398th BG

John W Wilson
Des Moines 91st BG

Herbert T Winter, Jr
Swea City, 55th FG

Chapter Nineteen

James J Wolfe
Danville, 447th BG

Joseph B Wolfe
Ossian, 361st FG

Edwin C Wulfekuhle
N. Buena Vista, 96th BG

Gerald B Yoder
Woodstock, 453rd BG

Omer L Young
Cedar Rapids, 379th BG

Floyd H Zimmer
Russell, 44th BG

Not Pictured

Lawrence L Barnett - Lamoni   490 BG
James A Bettis – Burlington   91 BG
Norman J. Bruning – Breda, Unit Unk.
James E. Buker – Waterloo, Unit Unk.
John E. Burke – Clinton, Unit Unk.
William J. Caldwell – Cedar Rapids, Unit Unk.
William E. Callaway – Des Moines, Unit Unk.
Herbert R. Chickering – Winterset, Unit Unk.
Roy F. Davis – Clarinda, Unit Unk.
Heinz Deetlefon – Ft Dodge Unit Unk.
Fred R Douglas – Dubuque   452 BG
Robert J Galbraith – Kellerton   93 BG
George Grimes – Albia   44 BG
Gaylord Hubbard – Blockton   44 BG
James C Murphy – Sioux City   306 BG
Charles W Narvis – Muscatine   361 FG
John J Williams – Dubuque   91 BG

Missing in Action

Charles F. Bragdon
Arthur L Sonneborn
Lyle W Stepanek
Donald W Storm
Thomas A Stricker
Duane G H Sweeny
Robert L Terrell
Mearl L Toerber
Dale L Vance
Howard D Versteegh
Robert D Wenstrand
Paul Wilson Wolfe

Iowans of the Mighty Eighth

Iowans of the Eighth Air Force

KILLED IN ACTION

4th FG
Kermit O Dahlen-Thompson
Dale B Leaf-Marshalltown
George R Shaeffer-Fraser

8th Troop Carrier Squadron
Clarence J Powell-Humeston

14th Photo Recon
Robert W Dideriksen-Shenandoah

17th BG
Charles J Howard-Council Bluffs

20th FG
Donald E Chrissinger-Mt Pleasant
Richard A Gee-Knoxville
Lauren J Taylor-Boone

27th Photo Recon
Charles G Cassaday-Denison

34th BG
Edwin Bailey-Red Oak
Stanley Durrett-Burlington
Roger E Maillard-Mason City

36th BG
Raymond L Snodgrass-Des Moines

44th BG
Norbert Allen-Des Moines
Harold Flaugh-Winterset
Kenneth Glasscock-Stuart
George Grimes-Albia
Glenn C Hovey-Fairfield
Gaylord T Hubbard-Blockton
Myron G Jacobs-Muscatine
Guy W Johnson-Parkersburg
George N Larson-Grinnell
Robert L Laucamp-Tipton
Glenn E Mose, Jr-Washington
Vernon D Nappier-Bedford
Herman R Sanneman-Creston
Walterr B Schoer-Holstein
Willis Sondag-Harper
Kenneth P Ward-Burlington
Floyd H Zimmer-Russell

52nd FG
Dale Anderson-Des Moines
Ernest L Anderson-Lake Mills

55th FS
Richard Gee-Knoxville
Robert L Sill-Ft Dodge
Herbert T Winter-Swea City
Raymond Sumpter-Cincinnati

56th Fighter Group
Benjamin C Barron-Corydon
Lowell C Buchmiller-Jefferson
Byron Fisher-Danbury

78th Fighter Group
Alan R Jacobson-Britt
Martin G O'Connell, Jr-Beaconsfield
Martin Smith-Davenport

82nd FG
John L Baker-Villisca

91st BG
John Arihood-Grandview
James A Bettis-Burlington
Lambert P Brostrom-Sioux City
Harold R Christensen-Eagle Grove
Arthur Ginder-Des Moines
George L Johnson-New Sharon
Clifford N Kirkpatrick-Grand River
Norbert D Kill-Mapleton
Edward P Myers-North Liberty
Willard Simpson-Des Moines
Cleo C Stuble-Turin
Charles E Van Ausdall-Keokuk
Jens T Weiby-Armstrong
John J Williams-Dubuque
John Wilson-Des Moines

92nd BG
Robert T Bottorff-Ottumwa
Maynard Dinker-Muscatine
Robert W Kudej-West Des Moines
Leroy Mohr-Cresco
Jack A Peck-Marshalltown
Robert L Sprout-Rodman
Frank E Tomlinson-Packwood
Robert G Turner-Redfield
John E Wells-Storm Lake

93rd BG
Robert Brown-Cedar Falls
Benjamin Caplan-Des Moines
Blaine Corbin-Nevada
Max Dailey-Des Moines/Cedar Rapids
Robert Galbraith-Kellerton
Roger W Hayes-Mason City
James S Huston-Olds
Michael Kennedy-Storm Lake
Thomas W Lewis-Indianola
Walter McCartie-Oskaloosa
Robert C Meline-Des Moines
John O'Brien-Des Moines
James W Roberts-Denver
Robert Shannon-Washington
Robert Weander-Sioux City
Gene White-Pleasant Valley

94th BG
Donald Ahlwardt-Danbury
Mervin W Cook-Des Moines

Chapter Nineteen

Charles Dulin-Cedar Rapids
Wayne Dulter-Des Moines
Theordore Fluegel-Cedar Rapids
Howard C Humphrey-Postville
Freddie O Menefee-Sioux Rapids
Herbert S Owens-Mapleton
John W Padget-Waterloo
Willard E Ward-Corydon

95th BG
Donald Ahlwardt-Danbury
Edwin Bachman-Montezuma
Ellsworth Campbell-Oelwein
John F Inman-Grinnell
Morris P Marks-Lake Park
Warren R Messmer-Burlington
Ralph C Murray-Arnolds Park
William H Nowels-Des Moines
Clarence F Parizek-Dysart

96th BG
James W Cline-Perry
Virgil Emerson-Cambridge
Russell Ford-Marion
Raymond Friedmann-Alton
Robert L Hovson-Eldon
Thomas J Keefe, Jr-Charles City
Robert W Lewis-Mason City
Harold Matz-Radcliffe
Robert E Means-Manilla
Paul J Santillan-Sioux City
Eugene Wilcox, Jr-Moravia,
Edwin C Wulfekuhle-N Buena Vista

100th BG
Richard K Anderegg-West Bend
John E Baxter-Chariton
Francis G Beedle-Sioux City
Max P Brim-Osceola
Lynn R Brown, Jr-Bonaparte
Stanley P Carson-Woodburn
Dale D Croft-Ft Dodge
Charles Emerson-Council Bluffs
Delbert D Reeve-Tipton
Edmund W Rohde-LeMars
Theron J Stookesberry-Monroe
Dale F Watterson-Cedar Rapids

160th Tactical Recon Squadron
William Fitch-Cedar Rapids

303rd BG
Warren G Ball-Cummings

Kenneth A Bennett-Iowa City
Albert Bricker-Greenfield
Thomas J Campbell-Mason City
Louis M Cowley-Sioux City
Nellins Egge-Inwood
Carl H Jorgensen-Des Moines
Jesse Joycer, Jr-Zearing
Gregory C Meyer-Dubuque
Dennis J Murphy-Ft Dodge
John B Price-Des Moines
Donald H Rutt-Casey
Joseph J Skubal-Riverside
Jimmie R Smith-Wessley
Jay R Sterling-Sioux City
Kenneth H Stockman-Council Bluffs
Winston C Teter-Coon Rapids
Louis H Willson-Ames

305th BG
Jay S Baas-Oskaloosa
Thomas Barnett-Farley
Raymond J Benton-Guthrie Center
Craig T Conley-McCallsburg
Phil A Lichty-Mason City
Paul J Lowry-Boone
Albert P Moline-Des Moines
Lloyd K Olson-Selma
James V Shaw-Estherville
Wayne C Thulin-Cedar Rapids
Bernard M Vermeer-Sioux Center
Emil G Wente-Waverly

306th BG
Bernard A Bernstein-Des Moines
Franklin Clemons-Bettendorf
John N Dennison-Bellevue
Jack Epplen-Des Moines
Robert Green-Osage
Robert Hegg-Waverly
Lawrence W Kooima-Rock Valley
James L Mitchell-Crawfordsville
James C Murphy-Sioux City
Theodore J Rickerl-Story City
Harry N Tomlin-Des Moines
Jack M Wheeler-Des Moines

333rd BG
Harold D Weede-Bloomfield

351s BG
John E Blaylock-Council Bluffs
Roy D Cruse-Terril
Camille F Devaney-Cascade

Robert P Cooper-Stuart
Harry A Kelley, Jr-Blencoe
John M Morton-Denison
Lyle A Norquist-Mason City
Clarence Rowlison-LeGrand
Elmer D Rydberg-Des Moines
Russell E Sheppard-Delhi

352nd FG
Ray L Cornick-Davenport
Richard Grow-Mason City
Raymond G Phillips-Newton
Richard A Pratt-Lohrville

353rd FG
William Burkett
Lloyd Hally-Huxley
Robert W Larson-Thompson

355th FG
Jack M Beckman-Burlington

356th FG
Milten H Huebner-Sumner

357th FG
Ray A Rush-Des Moines
Elmer D Rydberg-Des Moines

359th FG
Dick D Connelly-Ottumwa
Lester W Hovden-Ridgeway

361st FG
Charles W Narvis-Muscatine
Joseph B Wolfe-Ossian

364th FG
James A Bussey-Bussey
Richard J O'Connor-Lockport

379th BG
William Brinkman-Pocahontas
Edward Connolly-Dubuque
Gerald J Duffy-Davenport
Lyle Edmondson-Washington
Paul Hammond-Mason City
Dale C Killion-Denison
Leonard D Leeds-Cherokee
Lowell Lindbloom-Iowa
Chester Lundquist-Winfield
Ronald MacKenzie-Ft Dodge
William McGinnis-Iowa City
James E O'Connor-Iowa

Iowans of the Mighty Eighth

Young Omer-Hazelton
Mark R Reynolds, Jr-Shellsburg
Joe R Ritchey-Cedar Falls
Ralph J Smith-Des Moines
George F Taylor-Sioux City
Erwalt D Wagner-Waterloo
Omer L Young-Cedar Rapids

381st BG
William K Cutting-Des Moines
Harry B Johnson-Davenport
Earl B Nelson-Webster City
Paul J Scherranan-Farley
Ralph A Thomas-Fayette

384th BG
John Fitch-Des Moines
Robert Gorman-Waverly
Warren Handley-Des Moines
Donald W Jeffrey-Des Moines
Thomas K Kohlhaas-Algona
William E Kopf-Des Moines
Norman W Mandelbaum-Des Moines
Derald W Melton-Council Bluffs
Bruce M Rinisland-Muscatine
Winford R Smalley-Des Moines
Carroll D Swartzendruber-Wellman
Lloyd D Velve-Ft Dodge

385th BG
Guilford N Black-Ottumwa
Vernon Burke-Audubon
Homer C Comeggs-Des Moines
Don S Differding-Walker
James Friend-Council Bluffs
Edward W Kussman-Council Bluffs
Ray W Maew-Wheatland
Warren J Pease-Farragut
Oliver J Rapps-Vinton
Edward S Stone-Des Moines
Harold D Wagoner-Waterloo

386th BG
David L Blue-Chariton
Leroy A Coy-Randolph
Albertus Harrenstein-Grundy Center
Don L Weiss-Denison

387th BG
Gail R Hunter-Atlantic
Robert K McCune-Clinton
Vernon R Simmons-Winterset

388th BG
David Blue-Chariton
Arthur S Boyd-West Des Moines
Raymond E Bradley-Creston
James O Clark-Chariton
Leroy A Coy-Randolph
Robert Feese-Albia
Edward Gillmeier-Des Moines
Albertus Harrenstein-Grundy Center
Stanley E Histed
Charles Maring, Jr-Grinnell
Lester E Paup-Scranton
Donald D Rohloff-Delta
Beryl J Smith-Ottumwa
Robert H Warren-Ames

389th BG
Norbert B Bengford-Odebolt
William E Boone-Delaware
Edward W Bush-Galva
Willis B Core-Indianola
Wendell L Daily-Waterloo
Dwayne Huebner-Postville
Harold T Raynie-Hawarden
John H Springer-Wapello
Rene Van De Voorde-Fairfield

390th BG
Donald E Alvestad-Roland
Howard K Brooks-Otho
Clayton Croft-Shenandoah
James Denny-Cedar Falls
Anthony Forte-Des Moines
Karle E Kolmerer-Muscatine
Joseph W Lewis-West Branch
Darwin F Michaelson
Fred F Nagle-Ames
Alvin Mormon-Coon Rapids
Albert Seaquist, Jr-Bradgate
Robert F Spicer-Red Oak
Loran A Steen-Des Moines
Floyd M Vevle-Ft Dodge

392nd BG
Harold T Barton-Sioux City
John L Becker-Waterloo
Robert F Benz-Des Moines
Roy W Bettis-Iowa
Robert E Demery-Ft Dodge
John Fleege-Beresford
Eugene Gallup-Logan
Melvin Graper-Ames
Donald Hess-Sioux City
Edward J Kempker-Lemars
Norman C Krapf-Cedar Rapids
Swend A Krogh-Hampton
Robert W Kudij-W Des Moines
Harold A Schoedlerman-Moneta
Richard A Sporrey
Robert E Thompson-Clare
Nathan G Van Alstine-Ft Dodge
Charles E Vavra-Ferguson

398th BG
Charles P Bagley-Audubon
Stephen Edgington-Muscatine
Ernest Engeman-Ft Madison
Dale J Schaupp-Dubuque
Francis M Tuttle-Corydon
Billie J Wilson-Knoxville

401st BG
Francis E Cooke-Fonda
Robert W Knutson-Davenport
David M Lesher-Waterloo
Louis S Rush-Des Moines
Paid F Scharff-Aurora
David E Vermeer-Sioux Center
Blaine B Wilcox-Glenwood
Stewart Wilcox-Glenwood

445th BG
Donald C Dewey-Spring Hill
Orland Graper-Rockford
Ernest W Hutton-Ollie
Olin D Johnson-Rockwell City
James W Schaen-Des Moines
Eldon L Smeltzer-Creston

446th BG
Felix Diaz-Osage
Fred E Mincks-Chariton
Richard M Petrus-Council Bluffs
Marvin D Schneider-Ashton
Eldon Slager-Marengo
Bennie Tillotson-Ottumwa

447th BG
Lynn R Brown, Jr-Independence
James A Campbell-Keokuk
Helmer Gangstad-Webster City
Hayden T Hughes-Washington
Joseph J Lamansky-E Pleasant Plain
Robert C Reinartson-Ft Dodge

Chapter Nineteen

Walker W Trettin-Rockford
James J Wolfe-Danville

448th BG
Adolph Abraham-Cedar Rapids
Harold L Aucker-Mason City
Floyd Ecknosh-Des Moines
Virgle V Prior-Cedar Rapids
Howard M Smith-Atlantic
Robert W Thompson-Algona

452nd BG
George J Benedict-Davis City
Gerald R Carris-Keota
Irving Cohen-Council Bluffs
Fred R Douglas-Dubuque
Leland Evers-Council Bluffs
Robert Gamble-Mason City
Carroll Gjerke-Radcliffe
Frank E Macher-Cedar Rapids
William L Monroe-Estherville
Frederick W Thomas-Dayton
Frank K Watt-Lamoni

453rd BG
James Emerson-Volga
John Gilligan-Sioux City
James Golbski-Bettendorf
William Grady-Cedar Rapids
Max E Stump-DeSoto
Maurice L Swan-Winfield
Gerald B Yoder-Woolstock

457th BG
Lowell D Baker-Sharpsburg
Harry Bernstein-Brooklyn
Leslie E Brandenburg-Strawberry Point
Charles E Lindquist-Burlington
Phillip M Murillo-Cedar Rapids
Donald R Peacock-Shellsburg
Edwin D Waggoner-Des Moines
Eugene H Whalen-Davenport

458th BG
Charles S Daskam-Cresco
George J Douroumes-Boone
Howard Found-Keokuk
Richard L Moses-Storm Lake
William F Rickert-Selma
James A Soesbe-Clinton
Edwin E Sowles-Iowa

462nd Sub-Depot, 832nd Air Eng Sdn
Frederick W Selk-Dysart

466th BG
Roland Erdman-Renwick
Dale Estle-Ledyard
Edmund B Knoll-Garner
George McCord-Council Bluffs
Glenn W Morris, Jr-Waterloo
William F Wente-Waterloo

467th BG
Alfred H Janss-Atlantic
Riley E Orr-Onawa

479th FG
Dewey H Hollis-Waterloo

487th BG
Anthony O Bamburg-Lemars
William J Cochran-Elmira
William Focht-Des Moines
Charles A McWilliam-Bloomfield
Julian W Messerly-Ft Dodge
Cecil J Smith-Nemaha
John L Sunberg-Red Oak
Howard A Turnquist-Corydon

489th BG
Glenn Gammela-Manson
Floyd L Sackett-Arlington

490th BG
Carl R Adams-Washington
Laurence L Barnett-Lamoni
Laurence L Bockeloo-Clinton
Dallas G Couchman-Sewal
Robert L Dittmer-Elkader
Paul Hartkoph-Atlantic
Glenn N Larsen-Badger

491st BG
Donald T Burks-Charlotte
Jasper L Kelley-Delta
Vern J Lowman-Ames
James B Piatt-Clinton
Floyd A Walker, Jr-Des Moines
William F Weck-Davenport

492nd BG
Theordore F Kuhlmeier-Ft Dodge

Edward W Kussman-Council Bluffs
Joe D Mitchell-Marshalltown
Elmer D Pitsenbarger-Linden
Edwin F Rogers-Salem

493rd BG
Hubert D Autenreith-Creston
Joseph P Mallory-Gilmore City
Carl A Nord-Atlantic

701st MP, 700 Squadron
Donald F Rice-Shellsburg

801st BG
Clair D Vander Schaaf-Hull

2025th Engineers, Firefighters
Donald E Morgart-Melbourne

Special Operations-Carpetbaggers
Robert P Buchanan-Tipton

Troop Carrier Squadron
Bruce A McKern-Mystic

Unknown Unit
William Adams-Waterloo
William "Billy" Adams-Sigourney
Robert H Anderson-Mason City
Willard K Benson-Kellogg
Carl S Bishop-Des Moines
Charles F. Bragdon
Lawrence J Brandenburg-Lemars
Raymond P Brecht-Watkins
Arthur D Brody-Des Moines
Lynn R Brown Jr-Independence
Norman J Bruning – Breda
James E Buker – Waterloo
Robert D Buckley-Ogden
John E Burke – Clinton
William J Caldwell – Cedar Rapids
William E Callaway – Des Moines
Thomas J Campbell-Mason City
Robert Carmen-Montrose
Prosdocimo J DellaBetta-Chariton
Herbert R Chickering – Winterset
Roy F Davis – Clarinda
Heinz Detlefon-Ft Dodge
Darrel R Dickenson-Union
Marvin E Dille-Belle Plaine
Victor E Doorley-Cedar Falls
Clair Edel-Mason City
Herbert Egenes-Story City

Iowans of the Mighty Eighth

- Darwin Gant-Dana
- Max Gunsolley-Burlington
- George Hall, Jr-Des Moines
- James Harl-Bloomfield
- Carl Heline-Marcus
- Kenneth Herman-Traer
- Hugh Hilton-Ottumwa
- Albert H Holiday-Glenwood
- David A Humke-Des Moines
- Robert E Kraft-Mapleton
- Tillman O Lawr-Des Moines
- Wallace D Lund-Rake
- Richard D McCarthy-Ames
- George W Mercer-Muscatine
- Louis L Merfeld-Greene
- Charles J Moeller-Davenport
- Thomas N Montag-West Bend
- Warren N Morris-Keokuk
- Charles K Naden-Webster City
- Robert R Nelson-Jewell
- Ronald M Nichols-Colfax
- Tage R Nielson-Newell
- James E O'Connor-Conrad
- Jesse L Patterson-Winfield
- Charles J Pessica-Ft Dodge
- Milford F Peters-Dows
- George Pogge-Council Bluffs
- Robert J Prudhon-Iowa Falls
- James E Ralston-Cedar Rapids
- Leonard L Raspotnik-Des Moines
- Paul D Rolland-Bode
- George M Sanderson-Sioux City
- Edwin C Scherz-Davenport
- Leroy E Seeger-Glenwood
- Harold S Sharp-Dow City
- Donald L Smith-Mason City
- Jack H Srout-Fairfield
- Perle D Stainbrook-Brandon
- Mahlon T Stelle-Burlington
- Laurel C Stevens-Monroe
- Milton P Stoll-Blairstown
- Merton G Straub-Spencer
- George M Sullivan-Corning
- Fred C Weltz-Cedar Falls
- Robert E Whitehand-Iowa City

Chapter Twenty

DECEASED

Of five hundred members of the Eighth Air Force Historical Society slated for interview, the following members were deceased. Photographs and unit information were supplied by family members or obtained from other sources.

Iowans of the Mighty Eighth

Max Adkins, Marshalltown, 398th BG

Glenn Allen Panora, Automotive Equipment Mechanic, Det 1, HQ&HQ Sdn, BA ASC USSTAF

Robert Arn, Iowa City, 385th BG

James Avit, Ankeny, Navigator, 306th BG, Thurleigh, England

Chapter Twenty

George Armington, Sioux Center, Engineer and Top Turret Gunner, 379th BG, Kimbolton, England. 25 missions

George and his crew at Kimbolton, George is back row, left.

Bruce Bavender, Marshalltown, Navigator, 487th BG, Lavenham, England

Duane Bredensteiner, Shenandoah, 487th BG, Lavenham

  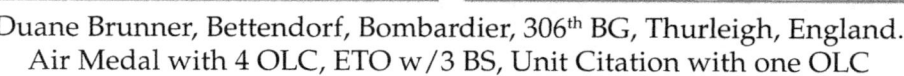

Duane Brunner, Bettendorf, Bombardier, 306th BG, Thurleigh, England. Air Medal with 4 OLC, ETO w/3 BS, Unit Citation with one OLC

Gerald Beaman, Cedar Rapids, 14th Sdn, 7th Photo Recon Group, Mt Farm, England

Chapter Twenty

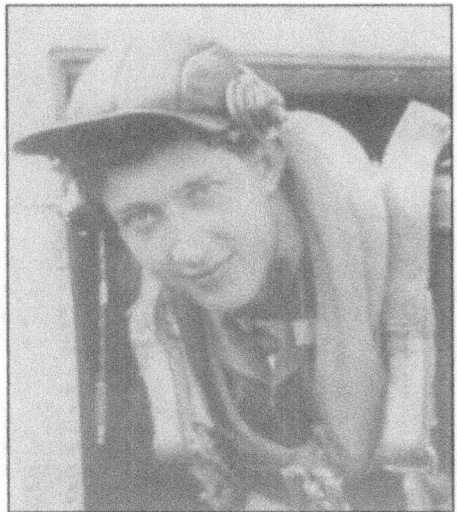 

Howard Burmeister, Davenport, waist gunner, 385th BG, Great Ashfield, England. Awarded three Purple Heart Medals. Wounded on three separate missions including o ne mission when his aircraft was cut in half and he was blown out of the plane. Also awarded the Air Medal with 4 Oak Leaf Clusters, ETO Ribbon with 4 Battle Stars. Was Past Iowa Commander of the Disabled American Veterans and Iowa Commander of the Military Order of the Purple Heart

Willard Burns, Council Bluffs, 1053rd QM Company, 94 th BG, Bury St Edmunds, England.

Tom Burris, What Cheer, Pilot, 305th BG, Chelveston, England.

Tom Burris and his crew at 305th BG. Tom, Pilot, is back row, left.

Franklin Busesman, Kanawha, 495th Fighter Group, Atcham, England

Chapter Twenty

Leonard "Kit" Carson, Clear Lake, Pilot, 357th FG, Leiston, England. Carson was one of the top aces in the Eighth Air Force in World War II. Flying a P-51 Mustang he was credited with 18 _ aerial victories and 3 _ enemy planes destroyed on the ground. On November 27, 1944, he shot down five German FW-190 aircraft during a single mission.

Lloyd Byam, Vinton, Hangar Chief, 392nd BG, Wendling, England

John B Carder, Red Oak, Pilot, 357th Fighter Group, Leiston, England. Became an Ace before he crashed in enemy territory and waas taken prisoner of war. He later escaped and returned to Allied control.

Chapter Twenty

William Campbell, Indianola, Crew Chief, 452nd BG, Deopham Green, England

Frank Cardamon, Des Moines, Ball Turret Gunner, 96th BG, Snetterton Heath, England

Russell Carlson, Des Moines, Pilot, 384th BG, Grafton Underwood, England.

Crew of Russell Carlson at 384th BG. Russell, Pilot, is back row, right.

Chapter Twenty

F. Ray Carter, Hedrick, Aerial Gunner, 390th BG, Framlingham, England. Awarded the Distinguished Flying Cross and Air Medal. Flew 35 missions.

Ray and his crew at 390th BG. Ray, Aerial Gunner, is back row, left. Fellow Iowan, George Popelka, Bombardier from Cedar Rapids, is front row, right.

Iowans of the Mighty Eighth

Loren Clark, Lake City, Crew Chief, 357th FG, Leiston, England

Robert Clark Cedar Rapids, 91st BG, Bassingbourn, England

Loren Clark, Crew Chief at 357th FG, Leiston, England. Loren is second from left.

William Cregar, Newhall, Navigator/Radar Observer

Chapter Twenty

Robert Croker, Bode, 339th Fighter Group, Fowlmere, England

Gerald Cunningham, Waterloo, Intelligence Officer, 13th Sdn, 7th Photo Recon Group, Mt Farm, England

Gale Daudel, Harpers Ferry, 1826th Orddnance, S&M Company, 445th BG, Tibenham, England

Daryl Dennis Conrad, 486th BG, Sudbury, England

Ray Dombrowski, Mason City, Unit Unk.

John Duff, Des Moines, tail gunner, 398th BG, Nuthampstead, England

John Duff and his crew at Nuthampstead, John is front row, second from right.

Chapter Twenty

John Earnest, Washington, formerly of Wayland, IA. Aircraft mechanic, 339th FG, Fowlmere, England. Awarded Bronze Star Medal for meritorious conduct in performance of outstanding service

Ray Edens, Clinton, 303rd BG, Molesworth, England

Norman Erbe, Des Moines, 457th BG, Glatton, England. Norm would later become Governor of Iowa.

Laverne Edgeton, Grinnell, Aircraft Propeller Specialist, 303rd BG, Molesworth, England

Dale Farnham, Algona, Unit Unk

John Erbes, Radcliffe, 385th BG, Great ashfield, England. Awarded Distinguished Flying Cross, Air Medal with 4 OLC, ETO Ribbon w/ 3 Battle stars.

Robert Finkle, Marshalltown, Aerial Gunner, 491st BG, Norrh Pickenham, England

Chapter Twenty

Donald Floden, Des Moines, Pilot, 351st BG, Polebrook, England. 33 missions, Distinguished Flying Cross, Air Medal with OLCs

Donald and part of his crew at 351st BG. Donald is in center.

Donald Florine, Sutherland, Pilot, 7th Photo Recon Group. Donald flew unarmed P-38s and P-51 fithrers on reconnaissance missions.

Victor Foster, Cedar Falls, Technical Supply Officer and Test Pilot, BAD 2, Wharton, England.

Chapter Twenty

Verlin Gale, Maxwell, Waist Gunner, 384th BG, Grafton Underwood, England

Gerard Glaza, Cedar Rapids, Spitfire and P-51 Pilot, 7th Photo Recon Group, Mt Farm, England. Evaded capture behind enemy lines after being shot down on low-level, unarmed photographic recon mission

Gerard by his Spitfire with Vernon Grubb, Crew Chief from Kingsley, Iowa. Gerard sits atop his Spitfire

Iowans of the Mighty Eighth

Doduglas Granzow, Iowa Falls, 30 missions, Distinguished Flying Cross and air Medal with Oak Leaf Clusters

Willard Gray, Washington, 456th Fighter Group

Hank Hagedorn and his crew at 358th BG

Forest "Hank" Hagedorn Spirit Lake, Flight Engineer, 358th BG, Nuthampstead, England

Chapter Twenty

Billy Hancock, Perry, Aerial Gunner, 379th BG, Kimbolton, England, 30 missions, Distinguished Flying Cross, Air Medal with 3 OLC, ETO Ribbon with 3 Battle Stars

Billy and enlisted men of his crew o n R&R in London. Billy is on the right, behind cab driver.

Billy and his crew at 379th BG. Bill is in second row, second from right.

Leon Hanna, Havelock, Navigator, 392nd BG, Wendling, England. Served two terms in Iowa Legislature. Owned and flew 22 airplanes in his lifetime.

Erwin Hebbeln, Davenport, Waist Gunner, 96th BG, Snetterton Heath, England. 29 missions. Distingujished Flying Cross, Air Medal w/ 4OLC, ETO Ribbon w/3 Battle Stars

Ervin Hansen, Griswold, Crew Chief, 446th BG, Bungay, England

Erwin Hebbeln's crew at Snetterton Heath. Aerial Gunner Erwin is front row second from left.

O.K. Hill, Vinton, 44th BG, Shipdham, England

Chapter Twenty

Kenneth Hoff, Ft Dodge, 94th BG, Bury St Edmunds, England

Robert Holscher, Dubuque, 35 missions, bomardier/ navigator, 306th BG, Thurleigh, England

Roberly Howe, Central City, Ball Turret Gunner, 100th BG, Thorpe Abbotts, England. Wounded when shot down on his last mission. Bailed out of his aircraft over England.

Crew of Roberly Howe, Central City. Aerial Gunner, 100th BG. Roberly is back row, second from left.

John Hurley's crew, 448th BG. John is in back row, second from left.

Chapter Twenty

Harold Hutchcroft, Middletown, 392nd BG, Wendling, England. Flew 34 missions. On 35th mission was involved in mid-air collision with an aircraft of another squadron. Harold parachuted to safety. Only two crewmen from each plane survived.

Iowans of the Mighty Eighth

Paul Ingvolstad, Ames, Navigator, 323BG (M), on B-26 "Klank's Tank" at Earls Colne, England.

D J Ibeling, Mt Vernon, 398th BG, Nuthampstead, England

Donald Janss, Belle Plaine, Navigator on B-24 named "Leading Lady", 93rd BG, Hardwick, England.

Bernard Kajewski, Waterloo, Toggelier, 35 missions, 91st BG, Bassingbourn, England

Chapter Twenty

Donald Klosterman, Sibley, 33 missions, tail gunner, 385th BG, Great Ashfield

Ken Kinyon, Iowa, 457th BG, Glatton, England

Glenn L. Kilbourn, Waterloo. Served in both WWII and in the Korean War. Unit Unk

Lloyd Koehler, Rockford, Aircraft Mechanic, 7th Photo Recon Group, Mt Farm, England

Herb Konrad, Flight Engineer, Lacona, back row, left, in front of B-17 named "Chief Oshkosh".

Iowans of the Mighty Eighth

Robert LeClere, Coggon, Ball Turret Gunner, 388th BG, Knettishall, England. Shot down on 17th Mission and taken Prisoner of War. He was blown out of his aircraft when it exploded from "flak". Knocked unconscious he awoke when falling to earth, pulled ripcord to his parachute and landed safely. Only four members of his crew survived.

Carl Larsen, Fertile, 7th Photo Recon Group, Mt Farm, England

Robert LeClere's crew at Knettishall, England. Robert is front row, third from left.

Chapter Twenty

Robert Loughry, Des Moines, 385th BG

Al Lichter, Algona, Fighter Pilot, 357th Fighter Group, Leiston, England

Bill Lyons, Mason City, Aerial Photographer/ Gunner, 398th BG, Nuthampstead, England.

Dr. Robert Manderscheid, Boone, Radio Operator/aerial Gunner, 390th BG, Framlingham, England, 32 missions

Donald Maule, Mondamin, 44th BG, Shipdham, England

Alva McCalley, Hazelton, Pilot, 306th BG, Thurleigh, England, 35 missions

Chapter Twenty

Alva McCalley and his crew, 306th BG. Alva, Pilot, is front row, second from left.

Roland McGee, Mason City, 94th BG, Bury St Edmunds, England

Robert McCreevy, Ackley, Aerial Gunner, 381st BG, Ridgewell, England.

Robert McGreevy and his crew, 381st BG. Robert, aerial gunner is front row, center.

Chapter Twenty

Leslie Meyer, Blue Grass, Ball Turret Gunner, 92nd BG, Podington, England. 30 missions, Air Medal w/4OLC and ETO Ribbon w/2 Battle Stars

James Mileham, Webb, Aircraft Mechanic, 20th Fighter Group, Kings Cliffe, England

James Moore, Des Moines, Aircraft Mechanic, Base air Depot #2, Wharton, England

Kenneth Moy, Reinbeck, Radio Operator/ Aerial Gunner, 305th BG, Chelveston, England

Chapter Twenty

Kenneth Newbrough, Storm Lake. 31 missions, B-17 named "Betsy Ross". Awarded Distinguished Flying Cross and Air Medal.

Kenneth Newbrough and crew at 398th BG. Ken is front row, right.

Bernhard Ove, Cedar Falls, 452nd BG, Deopham Green, England

Edmund Peters, Estherville, 351st BG, Polebrook, England. On June 12, 1944, he was wounded when his aircraft was shot down. He and his crew had to make a water landing in the English Channel.

Leslie Pratt, Cedar Rapids, Armorer/Ball Turret Gunner, 303rd BG, Molesworth, England

Leroy Puls, Davenport, Ball Turret Gunner, 447th Bg, Rattlesden, England, 35 missions

Chapter Twenty

Crew of Leroy Puls, 447th BG, Leroy, Ball Turret Gunner is front row, center.

Marino Pusateri, Cedar Rapids, 942nd Topographics Engineers, U.S. Army, attached to Eighth Air Force.

Robert Raecker, Meservey, 486th Bomb Group, Sudbury, England

John Schobert, Waukon, Armorer/Elec. Specialist, 355th Fighter Group, Steeple Morden, England

James Schulte, Davenport, Finance Officer, 93rd BG, Hardwick, England

Chapter Twenty

Robert Schultz, Ackley, B-26 Pilot, 322 BG (M), Andrews Field, England.

Robert Schultz in center, aboard P-38. In addition to 322nd BG. Robert served as fighter pilot with 474th

Ray Schmelzer, Postville, Crew Chief, 479th Fighter Group, Wattisham, England

George Seyfer, Cedar Rapids, 353rd Fighter Group, Metfield and Raydon, England. Star athlete in college after war. Inducted in Cedar Rapids Washington Athletic Hall of Fame. Clearfield, 92nd BG, Podington, England

Vern Siebels, Anamosa, 96th BG, Snetterton Heath, England

Glade Sickels, Clearfield, 92nd BG, Podington, England

Chapter Twenty

Glade Sickels and crew, 92nd BG. Glade, aerial gunner, is fourth from left

Myron Sorden, Indianola, Navigator, 306th BG, Thurleigh, England. Shot down on first mission over Bremen, Germany, 8 October 1943. Taken Prisoner of War, Stalag Luft III. Survived winter death march to new prison location. Liberated by US Army forces of General Patton, April, 1945

H.D. Stenseth, Des Moines, 96th BG, Snetterton Heath, England

Robert Stine, Des Moines, Radio Mechanic, 364th Fighter Group, Honington, England.

Norm Struchen, Webster City, Waist Gunner, 96th Bomb Group, Snetterton Heath, England

Norm and his crew, 96th BG. Norm, Aerial Gunner, is front row, left.

Chapter Twenty

Donald Thompson, Marion, 384th BG, Grafton Underwood, England

Francis Tilton, Cherokee, Airfraft Mechanic

Duane Ulstad, Fort Dodge, 398th BG, Nuthampstead, England

Roy Van Dyke, Jefferson, 91st BG, Bassingbourn, England

Frank Vrathny, Lehigh, 487th BG, Lavenham, England

Iowans of the Mighty Eighth

George Wharton, Aurelia, Medical Corps Technician, 447th BG, Rattlesden, England

George, fourth from right, at the door, assisting in removal of wounded at 447th BG, Rattlesden, after return of aircraft from a mission.

Chapter Twenty

Jack Whiton Perry, Aerial Gunner/Toggelier, 388th BG, Knettishall, England

Crew of Jeff Wombacher at 489th BG, Halesworth. Jeff is back row, right

Everett Wirtz, Boone, 94th BG, Bury St Edmunds, England

Ralph "Jeff" Wombacher, Iowa City, Navigator, 35 missions, 489th Bomb Group, Halesworth, England

Edward Woolums, Ottumma, 045DV

Chapter Twenty-One

ALTON GLENN MILLER, Major, U.S. Army Air Corps, born March 1, 1904, Clarinda, Iowa. Probably the most popular dance band leader who ever lived, he broke up his band at the height of its popularity in September, 1942, to enlist in the Army Specialist Corps. He was transferred to the Army Air Corps and placed in charge of forming bands.

In 1944, he took an all-star Army Air Force band to England where they entertained troops, including those at many Eighth Air Force bases, and broadcast music over the BBC and AEF radio networks. On December 15, 1944, he was given permission to take his band to France. Major Miller decided to fly to Paris ahead of his band. He and his pilot took off in dense fog in a Norseman C-64, a single-engine plane with a one-way radio receiving set and fixed landing gear. They were never heard from again. His disappearance remains a mystery and the subject of much speculation as to what happened. Ten days later he was declared officially dead.

There never was a band that exercised such a powerful romantic effect upon its listeners. Miller's style of music has endured to this day with fan clubs in America, Great Britain and many other countries. In June of every year Clarinda, Iowa, hosts the Glenn Miller Festival with guest bands from many countries and the Glenn Miller Band playing the many dance numbers he made famous, particularly the greatest big band theme of them all, "Moonlight Serenade."

Chapter Twenty-One
MEDALS

Military Medals and Awards Earned by Members of the Eighth Air Force in World War II, Including Numbers Awarded to Total Eighth Air Force Complement

Chapter Twenty-One

The Congressional Medal of Honor, the highest award the United States bestows "for conspicuous gallantry and intrepidity at the risk of life above and beyond the call of duty". During World War II seventeen Medals Of Honor were awarded to members of the Eighth Air Force.

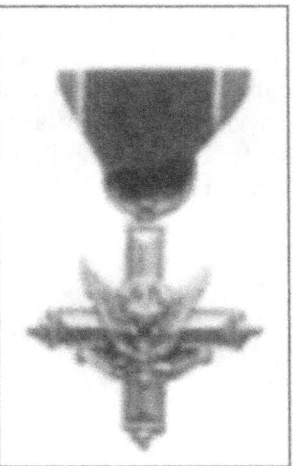

The Distinguished Service Cross is awarded to a person who distinguishes themselves by extraordinary heroism not justifying the Congressional Medal of Honor, while engaged in an action against an enemy of the United States, The acts of heroism must have been so notable and have involved risk of life, so extraordinary as to set the individual apart from his or her comrades. Two Hundred twenty DSCs were awarded to members of the Eighth Air Force in World War II with six oak leaf clusters, denoting the medal was awarded to six individuals twice.

The Distinguished Service Medal, is awarded to a person who, while serving in any capacity with the U.S. Army has distinguished themselves by exceptionally meritorious service to the Government in a duty of great responsibility. The performance must be such as to merit recognition for service which is clearly exceptional. Eleven DSMs were awarded to members of the Eighth Air Force in World War II.

The Silver Star is awarded to a person who, while serving in any capacity with the U.S. Army, is cited for gallantry in action. Eight hundred seventeen Silver Stars with 47 oak leaf clusters were awarded to members of the Eighth Air Force in World War II.

The Legion of Merit is awarded to any member of the Armed Forces of the United States or a friendly foreign nation who has distinguished themselves by exceptionally meritorious conduct in the performance of outstanding service and achievement. 207 were awarded to members of the Eighth Air Force in World War II.

Chapter Twenty-One

The Distinguished Flying Cross is awarded to any person of the Armed Forces of the United States who distinguishes themselves by heroism or extraordinary achievement while participating in aerial flight. The act of heroism must be evidenced by voluntary action above and beyond the call of duty. The extraordinary achievement must have resulted in an accomplishment so exceptional and outstanding as to clearly set the individual apart from his or her comrades or from other persons in similar circumstances. 41,497 DFCs were awarded to members of the Eighth Air Force in World War II with 4,480 oak leaf clusters.

The Soldier's Medal is awarded to any member of the Armed Forces of the United States who distinguishes himself by heroism not involving actual conflict with an enemy. The performance must have involved personal hazard or danger and the voluntary risk of life under conditions not involving conflict with an armed enemy. 478 Soldier's Medals with two oak leaf clusters were awarded to members of the Eighth Air Force in World War II.

Iowans of the Mighty Eighth

The Bronze Star is awarded to any person who, while serving in any capacity in or with the Army of the United States, distinguishes himself or herself by heroic or meritorious achievement or service, not involving participation in aerial flight, in connection with military operations against an armed enemy. Members of the Eighth Air Force were awarded 2,972 Bronze Stars with twelve oak leaf clusters.

The Purple Heart differs from all other decorations in that the individual is not "recommended" for the decoration, rather is entitled to it. It is awarded to members of the Armed Forces or any civilian national of the United States, wounded, or who has died or may hereafter die after being wounded in any action against an enemy of the United States. 6,845 Purple Hearts were awarded members of the Eighth Air Force in World War II, with 188 oak leaf clusters. An oak leaf cluster is awarded an individual in lieu of a second Purple Heart.

Chapter Twenty-One

The Air Medal is awarded to those who have distinguished themselves by meritorious achievement while participating in aerial flight, or for acts of heroism in connection with military operations against an armed enemy. In World War II members of the Eighth Air Force were awarded 122,705 Air Medals plus 319,595 oak leafs clusters. At that time air crewmen were awarded an Air Medal after completing five combat missions. An Oak Leaf Clusters for every five missions thereafter was awarded in lieu of another Air Medal.

The Europe-African-Middle East Campaign Medal was awarded for participation in armed conflict against an opposing enemy force in that part of the world. A bronze star was added to the ribbon for participation in campaigns or operations. A silver star was added to the ribbon in lieu of five bronze stars.

The World War II Victory Medal commemorates military service during the Second World War.

The Presidential Unit Citation was awarded for service in a unit in the name of the President for extraordinary heroism in action. Bomber and Fighter Groups of the Eighth Air Force in World War II were given Distinguished Unit Citations after completion of exceptionally hazardous missions or operations against the enemy.

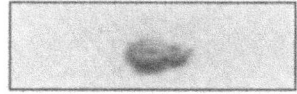

The Bronze Oak Leaf Cluster on a medal or ribbon represents a subsequent award of the same medal. Up to four oak leaf clusters can be worn on a ribbon. The bronze cluster is replaced by a Silver Oak Leaf Cluster for the fifth award of the same medal.

A star added to military ribbons represents participation in campaigns or operations. A bronze ribbon star was awarded for each campaign or operation. A silver ribbon star was worn in lieu of five bronze ribbon stars.

Chapter Twenty-Two

BIOGRAPHIES

The following section contains biographies and experiences of Iowa veterans of the Eighth Air Force in World War II who belong to the Eighth Air Force Historical Society. A listing of 500 members to interview was obtained from membership rosters of the Society for the most recent ten-year period. Some intended for interview were deceased and some had moved out of state. Each interview contains a photograph taken of them at the time of interview and placed next to a photograph taken of them during World War II. Crew photographs and candid snapshots obtained during the course of each interview are also included. Next of kin provided photographs of those members who were deceased.

Interviews were restricted to members of the Eighth Air Force Historical Society. Names of additional persons who had possibly served with the Eighth Air Force in World War II were obtained during interviews. It was the decision of the author to continue interviewing only Historical Society members to maintain a parameter with which to bring this project to a conclusion.

Attempts were made to obtain a listing of all Iowans who served in the Eighth during World War II, but was impossible due to incomplete records at that period of time. Chapter Eighteen is an alphabetical and unit listing of over 2,000 names of Iowans who served in the Eighth Air Force and as explained in the introduction to the listing, may only scratch the surface of Iowans who actually served.

Over fifty plus years has passed since these men served their country during the largest global conflict in history. For some, memories were as vivid as the day they occurred. For others, specifics as to dates, places and events have faded with aging and deteriorating health. What hasn't faded was pride in their unit, the "Mighty Eighth" and pride they were participants in civilization's greatest struggle for survival. Deeply patriotic, to a man they were modest regarding their contribution to victory in World War II and hero status placed on them. To each, the real heroes of World War II "were the ones that didn't come back".

Iowans of the Mighty Eighth

ROBERT W. ABERNATHY, MASON CITY, IA, was originally from Pulaski, Tennessee. He enlisted in the Army Air Corps in 1942 and was sent to a clerical school in Louisiana. The Air Corps, in need of pilots, lowered requirements for entry into the Aviation Cadet Program. "Ab" meet the new requirements, applied, and was accepted.

"Ab" completed Pre-flight training at Santa Ana, California, consisting of classroom training in various courses including cloud formations and aircraft identification. Primary Flight Training was taken at Ontario, CA; Basic Flight at Tucson, Arizona and Advanced Single Engine Pilot's School at Luke Field, Phoenix, AZ. He received his wings and commission as a Second Lieutenant on February 8, 1944.

Flight training in the P-47 Thunderbolt was taken at Baton Rouge, Louisiana, practicing over water flying. "Its totally different flying over water, you have no reference points like you do on land." "Ab" completed additional training at Long Beach, California, before he boarded the "Queen Mary" for Scotland and eventually, the 353rd Fighter Group at Raydon, England.

"Ab" would fly seventy-two combat missions, twenty four of which were in the P-47. The 353rd changed to the P-51 late in 1944. "Ab" flew his last forty-eight missions in a Mustang named "Lady Gwen".

"Escorting Bomber Groups was our primary duty. We would stay away while they were on the bomb run. I don't see how they made it through the "flak" that was thrown up at them. We didn't want to be part of that. When they finished the bomb run we would pick them up and escort them back to England. If we had time and fuel we would attack any target of opportunity, such as bridges, tanks, convoys, and trains. The Germans sometimes released barrage balloons with nets stretched between them to snare strafers so you had to be careful."

"Ab" got his first aerial victory flying a P-47 when he downed an ME-109 over Arnheim on September 23, 1944. Flying in his P-51 he claimed his second victory over Merseburg on November 2, 1944, another ME-109. After receiving credit for damaging 1 _ planes on the ground he damaged a FW-190 in the air. Over Coblenz on December 24, 1944, "Ab" shot down two ME-109s, his third and fourth victories. At that stage of the war opportunities to combat the Luftwaffe were declining. When they could muster enough fighters to attack they weren't in formation, but "like a flock of blackbirds". "You could always tell the experienced pilots from those that weren't. The experienced pilots were flight leaders who would always hang around looking for a dogfight. You could sense the inexperienced by the way they flew. They only had one-way radios, so no one could communicate with the flight leader to tell him what was going on. He was doing all the talking."

On April 10, 1945, "Ab" earned the title Fighter Pilot Ace. On an escort mission over Dessau, Germany, a new German jet, the ME-262 made a pass on the Bomb Group the 353rd was escorting. Although able to fly at least 100 miles per hour faster than the P-51, "Ab" took chase. "He was just a speck in the sky ahead of me. I kept my eyes glued on him because if I looked away and then back I would never find him. You become sort of snow blinded in the sky after so long if you don't wear colored lens in your goggles. Suddenly he started to make a wide left turn as if he was turning around and going to make another pass at the bombers. I cut him off so that when he completed his 180 degree turn we were coming right at each other at a closing rate of about 900 miles an hour. I don't know if he saw me or not, but I got off the first shots and he flamed right away. He tried to bail out but got hit by my wingman firing at the plane. The 262 started a slow spiral to the ground. I followed it all the way down until it exploded in some woods." This was but one of very few aerial victories by propeller aircraft against the German jet.

"Ab" believed his most memorable missions were his first and his last. On the first "I realized this wasn't training anymore and they shoot back at you" after a foot and half section of one of his wings was blown off by a shell. He was still able to fly the aircraft and return safely to base. Returning to base at the conclusion of his last mission "Ab" felt as if a big weight had been lifted off him. As was customary on last missions, he buzzed the base control tower then came too close to the runway. His propellers hit the concrete sawing about four inches off each blade. He was able to control the aircraft and land safely.

On April 23, 1945, "Ab" returned to the United States aboard the "Ile de France" ocean liner. Eligible for discharge, he volunteered to stay in the Air Corps and fly combat in the Pacific Theater of Operations. He was in Long Beach, California, when the war ended precluding further military service. "Ab" received his discharge at Maxwell Field, Alabama. He had been awarded, among other medals, the Distinguished Flying Cross, the Air Medal with twelve oak leaf clusters and the ETO Ribbon with three battle stars.

While in training at Long Beach in early 1944 "Ab" had met a girl from Algona, Iowa, working for a CPA firm. They continued to correspond while he was in Europe. Now that the war was over they married and the couple settled in Tennessee where "Ab" was employed as an installer for Bell South Telephone Company. He transferred to Mason City, Iowa, in 1955 with Northwestern Bell and has subsequently retired. For twenty-eight years "Ab" was a member of the River City Barbershop Chorus.

Right -"Ab" prepares to takeoff for an escort mission. Above- "Ab" stands in front of his P-51 "Lady Gwen". He scored five aerial victories making him an "Ace". The last victory was over the new German jet, an ME-262.

FRED ABIGT, CEDAR RAPIDS, IA, was a riveter building the P-47 Thunderbolt in Evansville, Indiana, when he was inducted into the Army Air Corps in April, 1943.

Fred was sent to Greensboro and Goldsboro, North Carolina, for Basic Training. Following a "snafu" where he was almost assigned to a combat engineer unit training at Lansing, Michigan, he eventually reported to McDill Field, Tampa, Florida, for Aerial Gunnery School. Fred had never fired a weapon before other than a BB gun and a .22 caliber rifle. Upon completion of training he was assigned to an aircrew and took Phase Training with the crew at McDill in preparation for deployment overseas.

Fred reported to Camp Kilmer, New Jersey, and was allowed a three day pass before he had to board a ship for Europe. It was while he was in Times Square that he learned from the famous news board that Allied forces had landed on the French coast at Normandy.

Fred sailed to Liverpool, England aboard the ship "William Mitchell". "Hammocks in the hold of the ship were stacked seven high." The large convoy encountered heavy seas in route with many aboard getting seasick except for air corps personnel who were used to motion.

Fred was assigned to the 388th Bomb Group at Nettishall, England. His sixth mission, on November 9, 1944, was to bomb a chemical plant at Saarbrucken, Germany, which made substances for jet fuel. His aircraft was hit by flak on the bomb run while the bomb bay doors were open. His bombardier and navigator were killed from the direct hit. Fred, as waist gunner, was knocked to the floor of the airplane. He was hit by shrapnel in the eye and lines to his oxygen mask and heated suit were severed. Hazy from lack of oxygen he managed to exit his aircraft with the other remaining crewmembers. When his parachute opened it separated him from his flight boots. On landing his parachute draped over the top of a large pine tree. He managed to get out of the parachute and drop to the ground in a snow bank. Wearing only wool stockings on his feet, Fred began walking and after what seemed several hours, wound up back at the tall pine tree.

A member of the German Home Guard on a motorcycle took Fred to a house where an elderly German woman dressed his wounds and bathed his frozen feet. Later a German soldier took him by car to a stone building and gave him coffee and bread. He later went by ambulance with his Co-Pilot to a hospital for medical attention. He remained there for fifteen days before being transported by truck to Magdeburg, Germany, for interrogation.

Fred's interrogator was a U.S. citizen, a surgeon from Chicago who had returned to Germany to take two families with him back to Chicago to live. The night before they were supposed to leave for America, Hitler closed Germany's borders and he was trapped with the Third Reich.

Fred was transported to Stalag Luft IV near Stargard, Germany. The prison camp was comprised of four compounds, three of which housed American POWs. Each compound held about 2,500 prisoners of war. He described the guards as farmers, the Commandant a military man, but not a Nazi, and believed this was why the POWs received humane treatment.

On February 6, 1945, the Commandant advised the POWs the Russian Army was nearing the prison. The Germans were leaving and the POWs were free to stay at the camp and be liberated or leave with the Germans. Nearly everyone chose to leave.

The POWs started walking toward the Baltic Sea and Schwinemunde. "Farmers fed us along the way. We split up into small groups and slept in barns." After eighty-six days on the road the POWs were turned over to elements of the British Second Army. British and American aircraft arrived to airlift them to Allied control. Fred went to Brussells, Belgium then later to Camp Lucky Strike, near Le Havre, France. It was at Le Havre that Fred was assigned to board an old Italian ocean liner for the voyage home to America.

Fred received his discharge from military service on October 12, 1945. He had been awarded the Purple Heart for battle wounds, World War II Victory Medal and the ETO Ribbon.

Fred re-enlisted in the Aviation Cadet Program of the Army Air Corps in May, 1947, to become a fighter pilot. Eyesight problems prevented him from completing the program. He joined Collins Radio Company in Cedar Rapids in 1959 and retired from them as an Engineering Laboratory Technician.

WALLACE ALBERT, MARENGO, IA, was working on the family farm after he graduated from high school. He attended night school at Perry, Iowa, to supplement his education in hopes of becoming a pilot in the Army Air Corps. He failed their physical when a spot was discovered on his lung preventing him from flying. He was subsequently drafted into military service,

passed the physical examination and assigned to the Army Air Corps.

Wallace took Basic Training at Wichita Falls, TX, then proceeded to Aero Mechanics School. He was almost finished with that training when a call was issued for volunteers to become aerial gunners. He applied, was accepted and sent to Panama City, FL, for training. Upon graduation he was assigned to a flight crew at Salt Lake City, UT. Wallace and his crew trained at Blythe, CA, and flew many practice missions including some at night.

The crew was then sent to Hamilton Field, CA, for their aircraft. Wallace had received training in recognition of Japanese aircraft and appeared destined for the Pacific Theater of Operations. Aircraft at Hamilton Field was not ready for them and they were sent to Camp Kilmer, New Jersey. Wallace then had to receive training in recognition of German aircraft and left for Europe on January 1, 1943, aboard the Victory ship, "Sir Walter Raleigh" for Glasgow, Scotland.

Wallace finally arrived at Wendling, England, home of the 392nd Bomb Group, a B-24 Liberator base. He had been trained as a ball turret gunner however the B-24s at Wendling had the ball turret removed to accommodate a bigger bomb load so he was assigned as a tail gunner.

In the next twenty-one months Wallace would fly 35 combat missions against oil refineries, factories, submarine pens and other strategic targets located at Frankfurt, Koblenz, Munich, Hamburg and Schweinfurt. He participated in an Eighth Air Force raid against the Rumanian oil refinery at Ploesti on August 1, 1943. Of the 177 aircraft dispatched, 122 made it to the target. Forty-two airplanes crashed or were shot down.

Three missions were flown on D-Day, June 6, 1944 in support of the invasion of Europe. The first raid Wallace could see ships leaving the English ports. The second mission they were midway and the third mission there were so many ships in the English Channel "you could walk across the Channel on their decks". A subsequent mission in support of Allied ground forces was against a timbered area allegedly containing German troops. The target area was supposed to be outlined by four fires, one at each corner of the target. Nearing the target area, fires were lit at the last possible moment, outlining the target, and the bombs were dropped.

Wallace experienced only one enemy raid on his base at Wendling by German forces. Late one afternoon a German fighter strafed the airfield causing no injuries or damage. No buzz bomb attacks occurred at the base. He did experience them while in London on pass. "They made a funny sound. When the engines stopped you had about ten seconds before they hit the ground and exploded." A lot of buzz bombs failed to make it to London, hitting barrage balloons or their cables. Spitfire pilots would fly alongside the rockets and with their wings tip the buzz bomb causing it to divert from its line of travel and fall harmlessly in the countryside.

Of Wallaces' thirty-five mission only four or five were flown without fighter escort at least some of the distance to and from the target. Although flak caused damage to his aircraft on many missions, not one crew member was wounded. Flak was their greatest concern particularly on the bomb run. "You didn't have to worry about enemy fighters, but you had to fly straight and level and the Germans would throw up everything they had." He was credited with shooting down three German ME-109s.

"When I reached the required twenty-five missions they changed it to 30. When I got to 28 they changed it to 35 missions." Wallace returned to the United States after completing his required number of missions in October, 1944. Sailing on an old German luxury liner, the trip took twenty-one days to make it to New York by a southern route.

He was discharged from military service at Jefferson Barracks, St. Louis, MO, having been awarded among other decorations, the Distinguished Flying Cross and the Air Medal with six Oak Leaf Clusters.

Wallace farmed for awhile, then operated a service station but for the next thirty years operated dairy farms in Woodward, Iowa City and Marengo, IA.

Right - Wallace and his crew at 392nd BG, Wendling, England. Wallace, Aerial Gunner is in the middle of the back row.

DAVID ALFREY, WATERLOO, IA joined the Air Corps Reserve in the summer of 1942 while still in high school. After graduation he was called to active duty on June 1, 1943 and sent to Sheppard Field, Wichita Falls, Texas, for Basic Training. Enrolled in the Aviation Cadet Program he attended Utah State Agricultural College at Logan, Utah, for twelve weeks prior to

Pre-Flight training at Santa Ana, CA. He opted out of the Cadet Program to attend Mechanics School at Amarillo, Texas and Aerial Gunnery School in Wyoming.

David was assigned to an air crew at Lincoln, Nebraska, and sent to Alexandria, Louisiana, for overseas training. The crew picked up a new B-17 at Lincoln, Nebraska, in September, 1944, for their flight to England and assignment with the 487th Bomb Group at Lavenham.

More training was required at Lavenham before David flew the first of his thirty-five combat missions on November 16, 1944, as Flight Engineer and Top Turret Gunner. The most memorable mission came on December 24 when all Eighth Air Force groups made a maximum effort in support of the Battle of the Bulge.

Arriving over the European Coast, German fighters attacked the 487th BG leading the mission shooting down four B-17s and causing five more to abandon the mission and seek emergency landing fields. Included in those shot down was General Frederick Castle, Commanding Officer of the Fourth Combat Wing. General Castle was awarded the Congressional Medal of Honor posthumously. The aircraft he was in developed engine trouble and was set on fire by German fighter aircraft. While six of the crew bailed out the General took control of the airplane. He refused to jettison the bomb load for fear of hitting Allied troops. When attacked a second time by fighters the plane broke up and spiraled into the ground killing the General.

On another mission David's aircraft hit an air pocket at 25,000 feet causing doors of his aircraft to pop open including the bomb bay doors. The airplane went into a diving spin. David recalled seeing the Pilot and Co-Pilot with their feet on the instrument panel as leverage attempting to pull the airplane out of the dive. All other crew members were pinned against the sides of the plane by centrifugal force. The pilot was able to pull the airplane out of the dive at about 10,000 feet.

During the thirty-five missions only one casualty occurred to his crew. The radio operator was hit by flak in the upper body and legs. David and others gave him an injection of morphine and patched him up the best they could. Air crews had limited first aid training. Serious casualties that occurred during missions were up to six hours away from qualified medical assistance.

David's last mission was on March 19, 1945. He returned to the United States aboard a troop ship on May 1, 1945, having been awarded the Air Medal with five oak leaf clusters among other medals. After discharge from military service in November, 1945, David entered the University of Nebraska. Following graduation he taught school for a short time before returning for his Masters degree in Education. He then taught school in the Beatrice, Nebraska and Waterloo, Iowa, school systems until retirement in 1989.

Right - David and his crew, 487th Bomb Group, Lavenham, England. David, Flight Engineer and Top Turret Gunner is back row, left.

GERHARD AUSBORN, SAC CITY, IA, enlisted in the Army Air Corps in December, 1940, one year before America's entry into World War II. He attended Armaments School at Lowry Field, Colorado, before being assigned to the 31st Fighter Group which had been activated at Selfridge Field, Michigan, and in training flying the P-39.

After the Japanese attack on Pearl

Harbor and other military bases in the Hawaiian Islands on December 7, 1941, Gerhard was sent to Spokane, Washington, where his 41st Pursuit Squadron was split and re-designated the 309th Fighter Squadron. Some members were sent to the Pacific while Gerhard remained at Spokane and worked on P-39s getting them ready for combat. "Ammunition chutes and guns didn't work on the planes. The guns that did work were completely out of line and had to be calibrated."

In June, 1942, he sailed on the "Queen Elizabeth" to Scotland. His squadron was based at High Ercall, England, flying the British Spitfire and later moved to Westhampnett. On September 1, 1942, Gerhard was one of sixteen men chosen for a special mission that later became known as a "war time vacation". Twelve aircraft mechanics, two radio men and two armament men, including Gerhard were sent to Scotland where they boarded the "Queen Elizabeth" and sailed for the United States. They had no idea why they were being sent home and took with them only their personal belongings.

What they didn't know is that they were chosen to be part of the invasion troops that would land in North Africa as part of "Operation Torch". It was planned that after an enemy airstrip was taken by ground troops, the sixteen would remain at the airbase to maintain Spitfire aircraft flown in for support of the ground action. Planners of the special mission forgot to have the men take their tools with them. When the error was realized special tool kits were assembled and flown to them in America. The "special" tool kits consisted only of a pliers, a long-nosed pliers, screwdrivers and tools to remove the cowling from a Spitfire. They additionally received a "Tommy" gun, ammunition, gas mask, helmet, fatigue clothes and new uniform.

After boarding a Liberty ship at part of the invasion convoy Gerhard and his men were briefed on their special mission. They were to invade the beaches of North Africa with regular Army troops. They practiced climbing down netting into landing barges before the convoy set sail. Gerhard's assignment was an airfield at Port Lyauty, Africa, north of Casablanca.

On November 9, 1942, Gerhard went over the side of the ship into a landing barge with artillery shells screaming overhead. When the ramp on the barge dropped to unload the troops Gerhard stepped into water up to his arm pits with enemy shells bursting too close for comfort. After spending a cold night on the beach in wet clothing Gerhard was able to advance five miles to the captured airbase. The Spitfires that were to arrive there were operating from Gibraltar and would not be coming to the captured airstrip. Gerhard was then transferred to a quartermaster unit where he spent the rest of his detached service time loading, unloading and stacking ammunition and supplies. Two weeks later he was flown to Oran and rejoined his Squadron at LeSenia, North Africa, as part of the 12th Air Force.

Gerhard would also become part of the invasion forces at Sicily and Salerno, Italy, for the purpose of aircraft maintenance once airstrips were captured from the enemy. He then became part of the 15th Air Force based at Foggia, Italy. His duties included cleaning, repair and maintenance of fighter aircraft guns, replacement of defective or damaged weapons, loading bombs attached to the fighters and ensuring wing guns converged at the proper distance for maximum impact on targets.

After his return to the United States in May, 1945, Gerhard was assigned to a P-40 unit training at Ft Sumner, New Mexico. After discharge from military service he returned to Iowa to resume farming, having been awarded the ETO Ribbon, World War II Victory Medal and Presidential Unit Citation. He retired from the State of Iowa as a tax auditor.

CLELE BAKER, WAVERLY, IA, entered the Army Air Corps on January 3, 1943. Assigned to the Eighth Air Force he was sent to England aboard the "Queen Elizabeth" with 15,000 other American soldiers. Clele was assigned to the headquarters of the Commanding General of the Eighth Air Force, James Doolittle, and worked as a clerk-typist in Headquarters and Headquarters Squadron at High Wycombe.

Clele's duties included clerical work for the General and members of his staff. He typed orders and letters dictated to him although he had received no shorthand training. Eighteen months later Clele was assigned to a Special Services Unit. He assisted in organizing and planning for visits from celebrities such as Bob Hope and his USO Tour and singer Frances Langford. He attended functions attended by the King and Queen of England and the Kings of Norway and Yugoslavia.

Being part of special services did not rate special privileges. Breakfast still consisted of powdered eggs and powdered milk. Occasionally tomatoes and bacon were added to the eggs. Spam, the All-American luncheon meat at the time, was readily available for sandwiches. When a can of ground beef could be "requisitioned", hamburgers were made and grilled on their barracks stove.

After the war Clele sailed for home aboard the Queen Mary and eventually was discharged in December, 1945. He had been awarded the European Theater of Operations and Good Conduct Medals.

WILLIAM BALTISBERGER, MARSHALLTOWN, IA, enlisted in the Aviation Cadet Program of the Army Air Corps on August 20, 1942. Cadet Training began at San Antonio, Texas to become either a Pilot, Co-Pilot, Navigator or Bombardier. After Pre-flight trainng at Ellington Field, Texas, Bill attended Navigation School at Hondo, Texas and Aerial Gunnery School at Harlingen, TX.

After being assigned to a flight crew overseas training had to be completed to mold themselves into a combat crew. While flying a practice mission at night in Kansas, Bill's pilot spotted a train below them. He dropped the plane down to ground level and came at the train with one wing light on. It was never discovered who the aircrew was that caused the railroad engineer to slam on his brakes and practically melt the wheels of the locomotive. "We were only 19, 20 years old. If we were older we wouldn't have done that."

Bill and his crew picked up a new B-17 bomber at Kearney, NE, and began their overseas flight to England. Their route took them from Presque Isle, ME to Scotland after stopping at Newfoundland for fuel. On arrival in Scotland their aircraft was taken from them for retro-fitting and they proceeded by train to Deopham Green, England, home of the 452nd Bomb Group.

"We slept in Quonset huts. There were eight officers. The thing that bothered me most when we got back from a mission and the other guys didn't, was seeing them clean out the other guy's stuff. You would be with them the night before. Went through this routine many times."

Bill flew 32 missions, twenty-five of which were as wing leader for the bombing formations. Lead aircraft crews went to a Pre-briefing meeting the night before missions. "We would walk into the Officer's and NCO Clubs at about 5:30 or 6:00 PM. That's when the balls went up over the bar. There was a red, white and a green ball. A white ball meant a raid was a "maybe". As soon as a mission was ordered the clubs would be called and they would change the balls. Green meant no mission the next day. Red meant a mission was on and the clubs closed all activities at the bar."

The Norden bombsight was placed in only four or five lead aircraft. All other planes on the raid released their bombs when the leaders dropped theirs. The Germans, aware of American bombing procedures, then concentrated fighter attacks on the lead airplanes to disrupt the formation and hopefully cause them to miss their target.

As lead aircraft Bill's Co-pilot took the place of the regular tail gunner. He also acted as observer calling out who in their formation dropped out when hit or aborted from the mission. The Command Pilot sat in the Co-Pilot's seat and made decisions for the Wing, whether to drop on target or chose a secondary target and was in contact with Eighth Air Force Headquarters and the rest of the planes on the raid.

The bombardier took pins out of the bombs, put them in his shirt pocket and had to turn them in at the end of the mission. If bombs "hung up" during a raid and didn't drop, someone had to go into the bomb bay area and manually get them out of the aircraft, often by kicking them out. "Had a guy in our Group fall out of the bomb bay with no parachute on when his aircraft hit an air pocket. In falling he caught hold of the catwalk. While dangling under the plane he was able to climb back into the bomb bay."

"The bombardier also had a blowup picture of the target propped up so he could see it. He had to know it by heart. From the Initial Point, 20 miles out, the bomb bay doors were opened. All aircraft had to hold their position and speed. The Command Pilot would be screaming to the aircraft in the formation to "Pull it in, pull it in tight", to get better bombing results. When the cross-hairs in the bombsight were on target the bombardier released the bombs."

Bill flew two shuttle missions to Poltava, Russia. Targets too distant to bomb and return to England were still bombed, but the Group would fly on to Russian bases. There they would be refueled, rearmed and targets bombed when they made their return to England.

Five missions were flown to Berlin. During one mission "the sound of flak hitting our plane scared the hell out of me, I peed in my heated flying suit shorting it. It burnt and I had to shut it down when it was forty degrees below zero. "

Bill's most memorable mission was a bombing raid on submarine pens at Bremen, Germany. Twenty feet of concrete protected submarines. "Bombs just bounced off. We got the hell shot out of us. Flak was the toughest I'd seen. I got hit by shrapnel in the leg. Our Pilot was killed and the Co-Pilot severely wounded." Bill and the tail gunner both had training as pilots. With guidance from the wounded Co-Pilot, Bill and the tail gunner were able to bring the stricken plane and its crew safely home. For their heroism they were awarded the Silver Star. "When you're over a target and get wounded its at least four hours before you can get medical attention. All we could do was give wounded a shot of morphine. If we had someone on board with medical training we could have saved a lot of boys from bleeding to death."

Other missions were flown in support D-Day ahead of American troops and to drop weapons and ammunition to Underground fighters. "We had two Underground people in our bomb bay, a man and a woman. After they pushed out the ammo they jumped out too."

In May, 1944, Bill's aircraft was attacked by German fighter planes. On fire and spiraling downward, the crew parachuted from the aircraft. They landed in the icy English Channel where they floated for thirty minutes before being rescued. It would not have taken much longer for them to have died from over-exposure.

After thirty-one missions Bill volunteered for one more. He and a pilot were to fly a B-17 intended for the scrap pile. The plane was loaded with explosives. They were to fly the aircraft causing it to crash into an important bridge behind enemy lines and bail out before the plane hit its target. French Resistance members were to pick them up and guide them back to safety. The target was hit but German troops reached them first and they were captured. After two weeks in captivity Bill and the pilot were to be moved to another location. During a lax moment they saw their chance to escape and ran for it. Hiding and moving west for two weeks they were aided by a farmer who contacted members of the resistance and returned them to American lines.

After the war ended in Europe Bill returned to America aboard the Queen Mary. After discharge from military service he entered Iowa State College under the GI Bill. He returned to service during the Korean War. Then was an agriculture teacher in the Columbus Junction School District until retirement.

Bill was awarded the Distinguished Flying Cross, Silver Star, Air Medal with oak leaf clusters and the Purple Heart.

Right - Bill and his crew, 452nd BG, Deopham Green, England. Bill is back row, right.

JOSEPH BARNES, MASON CITY, IA, had attended Cornell College, American Institute of Business and Drake University before he enlisted in the Army Air Corps. He had just come out of a movie theater in Des Moines when he learned of the Japanese attack on American military bases in the Hawaiian Islands on December 7, 1941. Joe wanted to join the Army Air Corps and

become a pilot. He learned Drake University and the Elks Club had combined to hold classes in Geometry, Trigonometry, English, History and Government at the Elks Club for those wishing to take a test qualifying them for pilot training. While working at a Des Moines bank he enlisted in the Army Air Corps, was put on reserve and attended classes at the Elk Club.

Joe was successful in passing the pilot's examination and was called to active duty in January, 1943. After Basic Training at Jefferson Barracks, St Louis, Missouri, he attended Central State Teachers College at Stevens Point, Wisconsin for one semester under the College Training Detachment Program. Joe then completed Pre-Flight Training at Santa Ana, California, but was washed out of pilot training during Primary Flight Training at Tucson, Arizona.

Sent back to Santa Ana for reclassification, he was selected to become a Navigator. Schools for navigators were full at the time so he was sent to Las Vegas, Nevada, for Aerial Gunnery training. He was then sent to Navigation School where he earned his wings and commission as a Second Lieutenant in May, 1944. After being assigned to an aircrew and training with them at Boise, Idaho, Joe and his crew were sent to the East Coast in August, 1944, where they boarded the ship "USAT Brazil" which was part of a convoy bound for the European Theater of Operations. "We got two meals a day. A chamber orchestra even played in the officer's mess during the evening meal."

Assigned to the 392nd Bomb Group at Wendling, England, it was not until September 25, 1944 that Joe flew the first of his thirty-five combat missions, a raid on targets at Koblenz, Germany. His last mission was to Schwandorf, Germany on April 20, 1945. There were numerous "stand down" times of up to eleven days when their Group did not fly, because there were no missions scheduled or because of weather.

"No one in our crew ever got so much as a scratch. The closest was when a piece of flak blew a circular slide rule out of my hand. We had a job to do and it was like going to the office, because no one in the crew got hurt and we never saw enemy fighters. We had the opportunity to reduce our required number of missions from thirty-five to thirty by being a lead crew but all of us in the crew voted to turn it down. In our crew we had an eighteen-year old tail gunner that completed thirty-five missions and an Engineer who was in his 30's.

Joe returned to the United States in May, 1945, aboard the ship "Ile de France". He was interviewed to become the personal navigator of a general stationed in the Pacific Theater of Operations. After he turned down the opportunity he reported to Houston, Texas, where he was separated from military service in October, 1945. Joe remained in the Air Force Reserve until 1952. He worked for Bankers Trust in Des Moines as Operations Manager of the Trust Department until 1962 when he moved to Mason City to join what would become First Interstate Bank as Senior Vice-President and Trust Officer until retirement.

Right – Joe's crew at 392nd BG, Wendling, England. Joe, Navigator, is back row, left.

BURL BEAM, MARTENSDALE, IA, enlisted in the Army Air Corps in August, 1942, but was not called to active duty until February, 1943, while in his senior year at Simpson College. He was sent to Jefferson Barracks, St Louis, Missouri, for Basic Training, Oshkosh, Wisconsin, under the College Training Detachment Program and then to San Antonio, Texas for classification.

Accepted as a candidate for pilot training, Burl reported to Thunderbird Field, Phoenix. Arizona for Primary Flight Training then took Basic Flight Training at Pecos, Texas. He remained at Pecos for twin engine training and upon completion in March, 1944, received his wings and commission as a Second Lieutenant.

B-17 Training was completed at Roswell, New Mexico. He then reported to Lincoln, Nebraska for crew assignment and trained with his crew at Alexandria, Louisiana in preparation for overseas deployment. After a brief assignment training air crews in radar at Langley Field, Virginia, Burl and his crew in October, 1944, flew through Bangor, Maine and Goose Bay, Labrador to England. They were assigned to the 398th Bomb Group at Nuthampstead.

The first three of Burl's thirty-five missions were flown to Merseburg, Germany, site of artificial oil refineries where soft coal was converted to petroleum products. He estimated that during twenty-five of his missions cloud cover obscured the target and radar was used to drop their bombs. His aircraft suffered only minimal damage from flak and they rarely encountered enemy fighters.

Returning to England from one mission their base was "socked in" due to weather with visibility reportedly down to one thousand feet. "Actually there was no visibility at all. We were down to low I saw a tree coming at us through the fog. I gave the engines full throttle and pulled up and away just in time to miss it. Our radio operator was able to get us to an auxiliary field.

Burl completed his thirty-five missions on March 10, 1945. He returned to the United States aboard the "USS Richardson". After furlough he reported to Santa Ana, California, where he was re-assigned to Bakersfield for advanced AT-6 Training. Burl then reported to Thunderbird Field, Phoenix where he ferried airplanes to nearby Williams Field. A bonus included ferrying aircraft with others to Ft Myers, Florida with many stops and side trips in route. The group returned to Phoenix by train via Chicago.

Burl was discharged from military service in August, 1945. He had been awarded the Air Medal with five oak leaf clusters, World War II Victory Medal and the ETO Ribbon, among others. He returned to school under the GI Bill at the University of Nebraska where he earned his Masters Degree in Music Education. After teaching music a short while and employment with the Iowa Bonus Board he returned to school in Mexico. Other employment included working as an administrator in building air bases in Greenland; on the administrative staff of the Iowa House of Representatives and farming from which he retired. Burl remains active in woodworking projects.

JOHN BECKMAN, ANKENY, IA, graduated from Dyersville, Iowa, High School and worked in a local grocery store until he was drafted into the Army Air Corps in September, 1943.

After John completed Basic Training at Shepard Field, Wichita Falls, Texas, he attended Aerial Gunnery School at Harlingen, Texas and Armaments School at Lowry Field, Colorado. He was then assigned to an aircrew at Lincoln, Nebraska, and trained with the crew at Davis Monthan Field, Tucson, Arizona, in preparation for overseas deployment.

In November, 1944, at Camp Miles Standish, Boston, Massachusetts, John boarded the "USS Wakefield" a troop transport for a voyage to Liverpool, England, that took seven days to reach. "I think I was seasick before I got out of Boston harbor. The seas were rough and everyone down below was sick."

John was assigned to the 490th Bomb Group was a waist gunner. On February 5, 1945, the first of twenty-eight missions was flown to bomb targets in Berlin. In addition to combat missions, two missions were flown to Holland as part of "Operation Chowhound". Food supplies were dropped to Dutch civilians who had subsisted on starvation diets under Nazi rule.

Iowans of the Mighty Eighth

Upon discharge from military service John had been awarded, among other medals, the Air Medal with oak leaf clusters, ETO Ribbon with battle stars and the World War II Victory Medal.

John retired from the Iowa Highway Patrol in 1980. He continued his career in law enforcement as a fraud investigator for banking establishments. John has attended all national reunions of the 490th Bomb Group and in 2001 met his pilot for the first time since the war ended.

Right - John and his crew at 490th BG, Eye, England. John, Aerial Gunner is front row, third from the left.

GEORGE BERRY, WINTERSET, IA, was helping on the family farm when he enlisted in the Army Air Corps in January, 1944. He took Basic Training at Keesler Field, Mississippi, and then was shipped to Las Vegas, Nevada, for Aerial Gunnery School. George was assigned to an aircrew and trained with them at Drew Field, Tampa, Florida, in preparation for overseas deployment.

George and his crew then picked up a new B-17 bomber at Savannah, Georgia, and flew to Iceland through Bangor, Maine, and Goose Bay, Labrador. In route to Iceland, the wings of their aircraft "iced up", "we got lost and our gas tanks were about down to zero. We had thrown out everything we could to lose weight including our radio equipment except for one when our radio operator finally got a hold of Iceland to direct us in. We had to stay there thirty-one days until the aircraft was repaired before we flew out. While there we only had four hours of daylight each day and the wind seemed like it blew a hundred miles an hour. We flew to Valley, Wales, then transferred to Stone, England, where we were assigned to the 447th Bomb Group at Rattlesden."

George flew twenty-three combat missions as waist gunner beginning in February, 1945. On one mission to bomb Berlin a plane flying off to the side of his in the formation took an anti-aircraft hit in engine number 3 and began leaking fuel. The propeller was "feathered" and engine number 4 was shut down. "The plane was off to the side and above us, he veered over the top of us spraying gasoline all over us and the rest of the formation behind us. It was lucky we and the whole formation didn't catch fire."

While on a mission to bomb German submarine pens at Kiel, a P-51 Mustang fighter plane flew along George's aircraft during the bomb run. "I looked at the pilot and we waved to each other. I then heard a "boom" and the next thing I knew he was gone. What used to be his airplane was a ball of fire and he was gone. He took a direct hit." Fighter planes usually stayed clear of the bomb run for safety and also to have some flak directed towards them and away from the bombers. "I knew them to sometime fly on the bomb run with us."

George's last mission was on April 16, 1945. The next scheduled mission all waist gunners from the 447th were ordered to "stand down' for some reason he had never found out. The balance of his crew flew the mission and was shot down by a German jet fighter, the ME-262, the only loss suffered by the bomb group that day. It is believed that aircraft, "Dead Man's Hand" was the last bomber shot down by enemy fighters in the war. George waited in vain for his aircraft and friends to return from the mission and recalled the sickening feeling he experienced when he had to accept they were killed in action. He later learned the crew had successfully bailed out of the aircraft and landed on the ground safely. The Co-Pilot, however, "got with some artillery people that were overrun by German troops and civilians got a hold of the Co-Pilot and killed him."

After the war ended in Europe, George remained behind at Rattlesden to help clean up and close the base for return to the Royal Air Force. "I was on the last truck to leave the base." He returned to the United States in August, 1945, and sent to the redistribution center at Santa Ana, California. He received his discharge from military service November 5, 1945, having been awarded among other medals, the Air Medal with oak leaf clusters, World War II Victory Medal and the ETO Ribbon with battle stars.

When George returned to civilian life he worked four years for an electrical contractor before accepting a position with the City of Winterset Municipal Utilities. He worked for the city for thirty-seven years and was Superintendent for twelve of those years before retiring in 1988.

JOHN BETTEN, KANAWHA, IA, was helping on the family farm at the outbreak of America's entry into World War II. He enlisted in the Army Air Corps in 1942 and sent to Utah for Basic Training after short stays in Bakersfield, California and in Arizona.

John was shipped to the European Theater of Operations in September, 1943 aboard the ocean liner "Queen Elizabeth" along with twenty thousand other American troops. The trip to Edinburgh, Scotland lasted only five days. From there he was sent to the 482nd Bomb Group at Alconbury, England, as a truck driver. His main duty consisted of loading bombs on B-17 bombers assigned to the Group. Sand bombs were also utilized to train bombardiers prior to combat missions. John also assisted medics in recovery of wounded from aircraft that returned from missions.

He will never forget D-Day morning, June 6, 1944, when the skies were filled with aircraft on their way to support the invasion of Normandy. "They took off right over our barracks. The sight and sound was unbelievable."

John loaded ordnance until the war was over in Europe and returned to the United States July 4, 1945. He was sent to Bakersfield, California, to train for deployment to the Pacific Theater of Operations when, during a physical, a spot was discovered on his lung. After hospital stays at Ft. Fitzsimmons, Colorado, where he was tested for tuberculosis, he was sent to Ft Lowry, Colorado for further medical testing. It was discovered he suffered from an ailment he had contracted at Bakersfield upon initial entry into military service. John received a medical discharge in April, 1946, returned to Iowa, and resumed farming until retirement in 1986.

LOWELL BLIZZARD, OSKALOOSA, IA, was a B-17 Mechanic and Crew Chief with the 96th Bomb Group at Snetterton Heath, England. He was deployed to England on a troop ship "packed in so as to make a sardine can look roomy". "I stayed below deck for twenty-four hours and above deck for twenty-four hours."

Lowell died in 1995. During World War II he wrote letters home describing what a "thrill it was to watch the Bomb Group's bombers sent out day after day and await their return in the day. You watch them across the field in perfect formation and peel off to land. They taxi into the dispersal area and me and my crew go to work getting the planes ready for the next mission." "We're pretty proud of our Forts. To us they are the greatest airplanes ever built."

On leave in Edinburgh, Scotland, on V-E Day he took part in the celebration with people singing and dancing in the streets. As was the custom, air crews took their ground crew personnel on flights over territories bombed by them. Lowell witnessed firsthand the destruction inflicted on Axis targets. One flight was to Linz, Austria to pick up repatriated French prisoners of war some of whom had been incarcerated in concentration camps. He also participated in food drops to the Dutch who had been starved under Nazi rule. To see the Dutch people waving and rushing to the food parcels as they were dropped was extremely heartwarming.

CARROLL BOGARD, MASON CITY, IA, graduated from high school in 1939 and attended Eagle Grove Junior College and the American Institute of Business until he secured employment with the Office of Price Administration in Washington, DC, as a statistical typist. He tried to enlist in Naval Aviation and the Army Air Corps but failed the eye color chart. Carroll returned to Iowa and joined the Civilian Pilot Training program. A different eye test was administered and he passed. The first time he had ever been in an airplane was to take his first lesson. He completed primary training and had forty-two hours flight time when, in July 1943, the program was eliminated and trainees were notified they would be going to Basic Training in the Army Air Corps.

After induction into military service, Carroll completed Basic Training at Sheppard Field, Wichita Falls, TX and was then assigned to work in the base Flight Engineer's office. He subsequently requested to be put in a flying status. He request was granted and Carroll was sent to Aerial Gunnery School at Harlingen, TX. He was then assigned to an aircrew at the Salt Lake City, UT, re-assignment center, and trained with his crew at Pueblo, CO, in preparation for deployment to the European Theater of Operations. The crew then boarded the "Queen Elizabeth" for a five and a half day voyage to Grenock, Scotland. Following additional training in Ireland, Carroll and his crew were assigned to the 466th Bomb Group at Attlebridge, England.

Carroll flew nine missions as ball turret gunner but only got credit for six missions flown. On several of the missions his crew returned to Attlebridge on two engines, the rest having been put out of action by German flak batteries. One instance when they were unable to drop their bombs on target they flew back to base with three, 2000 pound bombs in the bomb bay. They were denied permission to salvo the bombs in the English Channel. When the pilot landed the plane the front nose wheel collapsed and the aircraft skidded down the runway on its nose. Needless to say when the airplane came to a stop the crew made a hurried exit in case the bombs would detonate.

On August 8, 1944, Carroll's crew was not scheduled to fly while other aircrews from his Group were scheduled to bomb a target at Hamburg, Germany. The mission was "on" then was "scrubbed", then on and scrubbed a second time. Then Carroll and his crew received notice to report to their aircraft. With no breakfast, no briefing, and no escape kits they were met at their airplane by ground crew who handed them their parachutes. They took off and "formed up" for their flight to Germany.

"We didn't encounter any enemy fighters and we had no flak being shot at us all the way to the target. Right after "bombs away" we took a direct hit from flak in the bomb bay. Fuel poured from our plane and soaked all of us in the back of the aircraft. The pilot was able to close the bomb bay doors. We had to leave formation and dropped down to about ten to twelve thousand feet in altitude to be off oxygen. Our hydraulics and intercom systems were inoperable. The plane went into a diving spin but the pilot got it straightened out. He told us that if it happened again to bail out. Well, it happened again and we jumped while still over enemy territory. When I first bailed out I was flopping all over then I learned to straighten out and pulled my ripcord. It was quiet floating down. Its unbelievable what you can hear. I remember I talked to myself all the way down. I floated by two towns hoping I could continue and land in Allied territory. I landed about fifty feet from a high line wire near a forest. In the forest was a German flak gun camp. About twenty-five "Krauts" surrounded me pointing their guns at me. I told them I was an American. They made me pickup my parachute and carry it in front of me. Trying to hold onto a big bundle of silk was difficult. They took me to a building in the woods and locked me in a room. Then I heard shooting again which lasted about fifteen minutes."

Carroll was put in a touring car with two other members of his crew that were captured and taken to another building that held more prisoners of war. "I was taken to Lille, France where they attempted to interrogate me for three days, then to Brussells, Belgium where we were put in an old jail that had water on the floor and we had to sleep on straw tick mattresses. For four days hey attempted to interrogate us before sending us to Frankfurt, Germany for further interrogation. Once a day I got a jelly sandwich. It was the first food I had eaten in a week. At Wetzler, Germany, a transit camp for prisoners of war (POW), I got a Red Cross parcel."

Carroll was sent to Stalag Luft VI at St. Wendel, Germany. Stalag Luft VI was originally at Hydekrug in East Prussia. The camp was closed and the new camp at St. Wendel was given its Stalag Luft number.

"After about six weeks Patton's Army was closing in so they moved all of us out of the camp, There was about 2500 British and 7500 Americans. We were loaded into 40X8 railroad boxcars and sent to Stalag Luft IV at Gross Tychow in Northern Germany. We spent five and a half days in the cattle cars with no sanitary facilities and no food the whole trip. Twice American planes bombed railroad yards we were at. The Germans ran for cover and left us locked in the cars. When we got to Stalag Luft IV they ran us from the train station to the prison camp. They put eight of us in a smaller building, much like a hog house. We were each given a blanket, not much with winter coming. After a new compound was built at the camp we got assigned to a barracks."

"There were eight barracks to a compound and a mess hall at the end. We had twenty-five of us sleeping in a room. We were each supposed to get a Red Cross parcel once a week but it wound up being one parcel for four of us to share. German rations amounted to a cup of boiled potatoes a day. Once in awhile we could get some horse meat. We also had what we called "ball bearing soup" made of hard peas or a dehydrated cabbage soup that gave everyone diarrhea. We only had an outdoor "privy" with sixteen holes. After the cabbage soup the line to the privy was a half block long.

"Appel" or roll call was at 8:00 AM and 5:00PM. We were locked in our barracks each evening at 5:00 o'clock. On Christmas Eve, 1944, the prison Commandant turned on all the lights in the prison camp and let us out of the barracks until midnight. We could even go to other barracks. It was like going to Las Vegas – the little bit of freedom. It's the little things we missed."

"After Christmas and all through January we started hearing guns. It was the Russians and Germans fighting. On February 5 we were told we would evacuate the camp the next day. I made a backpack out of a shirt to carry my things. We were each given a Red Cross parcel. From February 6 to May 4, 1945, we walked across Northern Poland and Germany and stayed on the road until we were liberated by the British Seventh Army at Lauenburg near the Elbe River, Southeast of Hamburg."

"During the march we had no food except a piece of bread every three weeks. I would find raw potatoes deep in manure piles near barns where they were stored. I would brush them off as best I could before eating. I remember we walked twenty-five miles on Valentine's Day, 1945. We slept outside and I had one cup of a millet soup. We slept in barns as much as possible. For four days we stayed in a gymnasium. The floor was covered with guys. Everyone had dysentery. I went through three sets of clothes. I once sneaked away and visited a slave labor camp. I opened the door to a barracks. The stench was unbearable. Men were lying in bunks with a blank stare in their eyes. I'll never forget it. Another place I visited was a British POW camp. They were cutting up horse meat and throwing the bones in a mud pile. I saw two Russian laborers sneaking around with a crazed look in their eyes. They dove into the mud to get the bones. One Russian hit the other one over the head with a bone and began eating at what meat was left on the bone. The one that got hit then dove into the mud and got a bone. They ate like animals looking at each other like dogs protecting their food and watching out for anyone else."

When Carroll was liberated he was sent to Camp Lucky Strike for food, medical attention, showers, clothing, de-lousing, back pay and processing. He boarded the "USS Gideon Wells" for the United States and worked as a cook on the boat ride home ensuring himself plenty to eat. "It took about three to five years to eat a good meal without feeling nauseated."

After a ninety day furlough during which Carroll got married, he reported to San Antonio, TX where he received his discharge from military service. He entered Oklahoma City College under the G.I. Bill of Rights and graduated with a Bachelor's Degree in Economics in 1948.

Carroll taught and coached baseball and basketball in the Inwood, Iowa school system for three years and twelve years as Principal and Superintendent of Schools at Armstrong, Iowa. He earned his Master's Degree from Drake University in 1952 and PHD at Iowa State University in 1972. He retired in 1989 after serving in the Mason City, Iowa school system as Assistant Principal and Principal.

ROBERT BOICE, WATERLOO, IA, was working at Douglas Aircraft Company when he was drafted into military service in March, 1943. Sent to Wichita Falls, Texas, for Basic Training, Bob was then sent to Sioux Falls, South Dakota for Radio School and Yuma, Arizona for Aerial Gunnery/Radio School. After crew assignment at Salt Lake City, Utah, overseas training took place at Rattlesnake Army Air Field at Pyote, Texas.

In June, 1944, Bob and his crew picked up a new B-17 bomber at Kearney, Nebraska and flew to Valley, Wales, where their aircraft was taken from them for combat retro-fit. Assigned to the 91st Bomb Group at Bassingbourn as a Radio Operator/Waist Gunner, Bob flew thirty-five combat missions aboard aircraft named "Red Alert" and "Dear Becky". He was also responsible for dropping "chaf" from their aircraft to confuse German radar and anti-aircraft batteries. A bunk mate in his barracks at Bassingbourne was Don Connell also of Waterloo.

Bob's most memorable mission was when their squadron was attacked by at least thirty German ME-109 fighters at the beginning of their bomb run. "We had seven or eight of our planes go down. They shot the hell out of the rest of us. We had one hundred-thirty holes in our plane. We lost one engine and had to salvo our bomb load to keep up with the rest of our formation. We had a runaway propeller on one engine all the way back to base. We radioed an emergency to our base. The pilot was wounded and the co-pilot landed the plane OK."

Bob returned to the United States in November, 1944 aboard the ship "West Point". He was re-assigned to the China/Burma Theater where he was part of a crew hauling gasoline in B-24 Liberator bombers between China and India. Bob made ninety trips over "the Hump". He was then put on a DC-4 crew evacuating troops from the CBI Theater to Calcutta. On one flight during a monsoon and with one engine lost from malfunction, their aircraft ran out of fuel on approach to their runway. Bob was successful in bailing out into a jungle but the pilot and co-pilot were lost with the plane.

Bob was discharged from military service after a twenty-one day voyage home through the Suez Canal. He had been awarded, among other medals, the Distinguished Flying Cross and the Air Medal with three oak leaf clusters.

In 1947 Bob joined Bell Telephone Company. He retired from them after a thirty year career in equipment maintenance and repair.

Right - Bob and his crew at 91st BG, Bassingbourn, England. Bob, Radio Operator/Aerial Gunner is back row, third from left.

JAMES BOTTENFIELD, DES MOINES, IA, graduated from high school and was unsuccessful in finding meaningful employment because he was not classified as "4F" by his local Draft Board. Employers were reluctant to hire able bodied men and spend time and money in training them when it was obvious they would be drafted into military service.

In January, 1941, almost a year before the Japanese surprise attack on Pearl Harbor, James enlisted in the Army Air Corps. He was sent to Chanute Field, Illinois, with the intention of taking courses in welding. Instead he was detailed to a Mess Squadron and made permanent kitchen police. He was sent to Sheppard Field, Wichita Falls, Texas, and Amarillo, Texas, in the same duty assignment while the bases were expanded or built. It was while he was at Sheppard Field the attack on Pearl Harbor cast America into World War II.

James took and passed examinations for the Aviation Cadet Program. He was sent to Iowa Wesleyan College, Mount Pleasant, Iowa, under the Cadet Training Detachment program where they "crammed two years of college into us in about eight weeks". Next came Pre-Flight Training at Santa Ana, California; Primary Flight Training at Oxnard, California, and Basic Flight Training at Mirana Field, Arizona. After completing Advanced Flight Training at Douglas, Arizona, James was awarded his pilot's wings and commission as a Second Lieutenant.

He was assigned an aircrew at Lincoln, Nebraska, and trained with them at Rapid City, South Dakota, in preparation for overseas deployment. "When we graduated they held a base party. Near the end of the party those graduating threw their drinking glasses into a stone fireplace. Everyone got into the act. When we went to the club to get a drink the next day they told us they couldn't serve any drinks because they didn't have any glasses."

In January, 1945, James sailed aboard the ocean liner "Aquatania" for the European Theater of Operations and the 452nd Bomb Group at Deopham Green, England.

James flew eighteen combat missions before V-E Day(Victory in Europe). "We started off with a "milk run" mission. We thought "this isn't so bad". "Then things got rougher. We came back from one mission and the ground crews asked us if we had heard cracking sounds and the plane jump. We told them "yes". They said we were taking direct flak hits. Both wings were so shot up they had to replace them. When we heard the hits we didn't think much about it at the time."

On a mission to bomb targets at Frankfurt, Germany, "we lost one engine on the bomb run". "Another engine wasn't running to full power and we had to drop out of formation. Our wheels dropped and locked in the landing position causing more air drag. We found an airstrip in Germany and landed. It was a German airstrip that American ground forces had captured just twenty-four hours earlier. We were flown to Paris and then back to England."

On V-E Day we were told not to leave the base but we sneaked off anyway. They closed all the bars because of how we might celebrate. Some guys were shooting off flares in a Very Pistol and caught some English farmer's haystacks on fire. When some guys started shooting their .45 pistols in the air things were called to a halt."

James flew two "Chowhound" missions to Holland where food supplies were dropped to Dutch civilians that survived on starvation diets under Nazi rule. "They made targets in open fields for us to drop the supplies. On the second mission we flew over an area where they had spelled out "Thanks" in tulips for us." He also flew one mission to pickup American prisoners of war freed from a German POW camp and flew them back to England. We were told not to wear clean uniforms because they would be filthy and covered with lice. When we got them they were cleaner than us."

In July, 1945, James flew back to the United States. He got married and was in Chicago with his bride on their honeymoon when they received word the Japanese had surrendered ending World War II. James received his discharge from the military at Santa Ana, California, in September, 1945. He had been awarded the Air Medal with two oak leaf clusters, European Theater of Operations and World War II Victory Medals.

James entered Drake University at Des Moines after the war under the G.I. Bill of Rights and went on to earn his Bachelors, Masters, and a Specialist Degree in Education. He taught commercial business courses at Newkirk, Iowa, and served as Superintendent of Schools at Ledyard and Lone Tree, Iowa. He then finished his career with the State of Iowa, Department of Public Instruction where he worked for nearly twenty years before retirement.

Right - James' crew at the 452nd BG, Deopham Green, England. James, Pilot, is back row, right.

Right - Officers of James" aircrew at Deopham Green. James is second from the right.

CHARLES BOYER, FORT MADISON, IA, was a tool and die operator at Shaeffer Pen Company in Ft. Madison prior to World War II. He enlisted in the Army Air Corps, December 9, 1941, two days after the Japanese attack on Pearl Harbor.

After Basic Training Charles was sent to Las Vegas, NV for Aerial Gunnery School, Airplane Mechanic and Flight Engineer School at Wichita Falls, TX and worked at Consolidated Aircraft Company in San Diego for familiarization with the B-24 bomber.

Assigned to a flight crew and training at Topeka, KS, his aircraft caught fire during a training mission requiring the entire crew to parachute from the airplane. As a result of this, the Air Corps "split us up and put us on different crews, so we had to train again".

In February, 1943, Charles and his crew flew the northern route to England. Nearing their destination they lost one engine and had another engine going out. They landed in Ireland. It was three weeks before they reached their home, the 93rd Bomb Group at Hardwick.

In June, 1943, Charles and his crew were attached to the Ninth Air Force and trained in preparation for the low level raid on the Ploesti Oil Refineries in Romania. On August 1, 1943, enroute to Ploesti for the raid, fittings came loose on their gas tanks when they were halfway to the target. Losing fuel they returned to base. In view of the heavy losses sustained during this raid, this quirk of fate probably saved his life.

Charles flew twenty-five missions as Flight Engineer and Top Turret Gunner. Of the eleven original crews in his squadron, only two were left when re rotated back to the United States.

Charles felt like he flew no "milk runs". The most feared missions were those requiring they fly down the Ruhr Valley where German gunners were termed "The Ruhr Valley Squirrel Hunters". "When I finished my tour, the life of a crew was five missions. If you didn't volunteer for a second tour you were required to stay at the base for sixty days helping ground crews."

After rotating to the United States Charles was assigned to Boise, ID, as a Flight Instructor checking out crews. He received his discharge in September, 1945, having been awarded the Air Medal with three oak leaf cluster, the European Theater Medal and the Distinguished Flying Cross.

Charles returned to Shaeffer Pen Company and entered the Air Force Reserves. He was recalled to active duty for the Korean War as a Flight Engineer. Following his tour of duty, Charles worked for an atomic energy plant in Colorado as a Prototype Engineer.

WILLARD BRANCH, DAVENPORT, IA, entered the Army Air Corps at Camp Dodge, IA, in January, 1943. He was sent to Basic Training at Miami Beach, FL before attending Aerial Gunnery School at Buckley Field, CO and Armorer's School. Willard was accepted for the Aviation Cadet Program and sent to Grand Forks, ND, under the College Detachment Training Program.

In preparation to become either a Pilot, Co-Pilot, Bombardier or Navigator he was sent for ACP Training at Santa Ana; Flight School at King City and Basic Flight School at Merced, all in California. After being declined further pilot training Willard attended Aerial Gunnery refresher training at Las Vegas, NV, before being assigned to a flight crew at Lincoln, NE. The crew took their overseas training at Rapid City, SD before boarding the ship "Isle de France" as part of a convoy bound for England and the Eighth Air Force.

Assigned to the 401st Bomb Group at Deenethorpe as a gunner Willard flew twenty-eight combat missions beginning in February, 1945 until April 20, 1945. Most of his missions were flown in a B-17 named "Shark's Tooth" which survived the war only to be sold for scrap metal. His most memorable mission was when their formation was twice attacked by the new German jet, the ME-262. "No damage was sustained to our aircraft but the jets were successful in downing others. Other than flak we had to endure during bomb runs, little Luftwaffe intervention occurred because American long-range fighters were able to escort our bomb groups all the way to the target and back."

After V-E Day Willard flew back to the United States in a B-17 and landed in Connecticut. He reported to Santa Ana, CA, to begin training in the B-29 Super Fortress for deployment to the Pacific Theater. However the war ended after the Atomic Bomb was dropped on Hiroshima and Nagasaki precluding further war preparations. Willard received his military discharge October 15, 1945. He had been awarded among other decorations, the Air Medal with four oak leaf clusters.

Willard entered Iowa State College (now University) under the GI Bill majoring in Education. He was an Industrial Education teacher in the Davenport School System for thirty-eight years until retirement in 1989.

MAURICE BRANDENBURGER, DES MOINES, IA was married three weeks before the Japanese attack on Pearl Harbor, December 7, 1941. He entered on duty in the Army Air Corps in May, 1942 at East St. Louis, Missouri, and was sent to Jefferson Barracks, St Louis, Missouri, for Basic Training.

Poor eyesight at the time disqualified Maurice from flight assignments and he worked in supply at the basic training site. He was then transferred to Atlantic City, New Jersey, and billeted in the Ambassador Hotel that had been taken over by the military for use as a training and processing center. Maurice's wife joined him in New Jersey and they lived in an apartment near the Boardwalk. "Thousands went through there before going to military schools for training. In addition to supplying the recruits I had to escort some troops to their next duty assignment. If I left with thirty, I had better have thirty when we arrived at our destination."

When the military began reaching their complement in May, 1943, the processing center began "winding down". Maurice was deployed to the European Theater of Operations aboard the "Queen Mary" with twenty thousand other American troops. After landing at Glasgow, Scotland, Maurice reported to the 445th Bomb Group at Tibenham, England.

The base at Tibenham was not fully completed and aircraft from the bomb group had not arrived. A former Royal Air Force base, construction was in progress to lengthen the runway, complete hard stands, taxiways and Nissen huts to house base personnel. After completion the balance of 445th personnel and aircraft arrived to commence bombing operations. Maurice remained in supply to provide for the needs of twelve hundred service personnel. This included those in weather and photographic units, base PX, military police, cooks, station defense, medical and administrative personnel. "The squadrons of the 445th had their own supply personnel. I had three large supply tents full of equipment for which I was responsible."

Maurice recalled a 445th mission in September, 1944, when thirty of his bomb group's aircraft were lost. "Hardly any aircraft came back. Those that made it, most were so shot up they were no longer flyable. It was a tough night at the base with a lot of long faces. We didn't know any of the air crews and didn't want to know them because you didn't want a friend lost in action."

"After the war ended in Europe we were among the last of the Groups out. I was sent to Casablanca to be part of a force that was to get ready to go to the Far East.. We had absolutely nothing to do, so they sent us to Tunis where we did nothing. Then they sent us back to Casablanca where we were loaded on a C-54 cargo plane and flew us back to America. I was in Boston on V-J Day. What a night with the whole town celebrating the end of the war."

After a furlough Maurice was sent to Hamilton Field, California, where he managed a supply station for about a month and was then discharged from military service. He had been awarded the ETO Ribbon and World War II Victory medal.

In civilian life Maurice retired after forty years as an accountant with Williams Fertilizer Company in Des Moines.

Right - Maurice and Communications Crew at 445th Bomb Group, Tibenham, England. Maurice is front row, left.

HOWARD BRESON, DUBUQUE, IA, believed war was inevitable and enlisted in the Army Air Corps with his brother on October 16, 1941. Howard and his brother remained together throughout training, deployment to Europe and were in the same air corps squadron.

They were sent to Fort Sheridan, Illinois, for Basic Training and then Aircraft Mechanics School at Wichita Falls, Texas. They attended a Boeing Aircraft B-17 bomber school at Lawton, Washington, learning instruments, controls, engines and aerodynamics. "I learned more in those two weeks with Boeing than I did through all of the military schools. Upon completion of training Howard was sent to Tampa, Florida; Rapid City, South Dakota; Boise, Idaho and Pyote, Texas, performing flight line maintenance for aircrews in training.

He boarded the "Queen Elizabeth" at Camp Kilmer, New Jersey, in May, 1943, for England where he and his brother were assigned to the 413th Squadron of the 96th Bomb Group at Snetterton Heath.

Howard was a crew chief with other aircraft mechanics assigned to him to perform maintenance on one B-17 bomber. Prior to scheduled take-off engines would be pre-flighted. All engines would be started, run up and gauges checked for proper running. After shutdown fuel tanks would be "topped off". "When refilling the gas tanks you had to be careful of static electricity" to prevent an explosion or fire. When the aircraft returned from a mission the pilot would report to us any items needing repair or how the engines were running. We would make any repairs for which we were qualified, including engine change.

Later in the war the ball turret was taken out of the planes and a radar dome installed. Electronic equipment was placed in the radio compartment. This was an H2X blind bombing device called a "Mickey" and allowed a pathfinder aircraft to identify a target through overcast and the bomber formation to release their bombs on target. "We also maintained Pathfinder aircraft. We would fly the Pathfinder at our base to another unit set for mission, refuel it and recharge oxygen and then get a ride back to our base."

Howard was responsible for maintenance of "Kipling's Error III", a bomber crew made up of five members who came from East of the Mississippi River and five from West of the river. "The crew came back from their first mission in "Error I" so shot up the plane had to be scrapped. They named their next plane "Error II". When they got back from their first mission in it, the plane was so badly battle damaged it also had to be scrapped. They were able to finish their missions in their next plane "Error III". The plane later went down in the North Sea with another crew."

Howard was awarded the Bronze Star medal for meritorious service in maintaining an aircraft without an abort for mechanical malfunction.

On October 18, 1944, Howard was on the flight line directing two aircraft to their parking hardstands. The planes had just returned from a bombing mission to Kassel, Germany. In one of the bombers a ball turret gunner had a .50 caliber bullet jammed in his weapon and while trying to clear his guns, the bullet fired. It struck Howard in the right calf of his leg and "blew it off". Following hospitalization in England and Scotland Howard returned to the United States in December, 1944, aboard the ship "Ile de France". Following additional recuperation and fitting for an artificial leg at Brigham City, Utah, he was discharged from military service on August 9, 1945. He had been awarded, among other medals, the Bronze Star, European Theater of Operations and World War II Victory Medals.

Howard retired after thirty-three years with John Deere and Company at Dubuque, Iowa.

Right - Howard on left, and his aircraft mechanic crew by their assigned B-17, "Kipling's Error III"

EARL BRINDLEY, ATLANTIC, IA, was drafted into the U.S. Army in March, 1943. For five months he was in an anti-aircraft unit until he was transferred to the Army Air Corps. He was sent to radar and radio school at Sioux Falls, South Dakota and Aerial Gunnery School at Yuma, Arizona. Earl was then assigned to an aircrew at Rapid City, South Dakota where they trained for combat duty.

After picking up a new B-17 bomber at Lincoln, Nebraska, Earl and his crew flew to the 398th Bomb Group at Nuthampstead, England. Earl flew twenty-six combat missions. In that period of time he and his crew "went through" five aircraft.

On a January, 1945, raid on the German city of Schweinfurt the number two engine on his bomber was hit by flak. The engine could not be "feathered" and the propeller began to "windmill" out of control. They landed at an emergency landing strip in France behind Allied lines. The wind-milling propeller came off the engine and cut into the aircraft but not harming anyone aboard. Earl and his crew flew back to England the next day in another bomber that had previously been forced down and repaired.

Earl flew what he described as the RDX raid that "took out most of the 601st Squadron". "Bombs containing plastic explosives were stored in the Group's bomb dumps. They knew the war was about over and these explosive were very unstable. To get rid of them it was decided to drop them over Germany but the crews were ordered to drop them in a string, not all at once. Some guy salvoed all his bombs. As they fell they hit each other and exploded near where the 601st was flying and several bombers were blown apart. Shrapnel from the explosions punctured our transfer lines and leaked gas into our bomb bay. We crawled into the bomb bay and used rags tried to halt the flow of gas. The bomb bay doors were open and we couldn't close them for fear of sparks setting off the gas. We landed in Austria with the bomb bay doors open."

Returning from another mission "we were shot up pretty bad". We threw out everything from the aircraft to try and lighten the load and try to maintain altitude. England was fogged in and we were lost. We finally located an emergency landing strip but we had no brakes. The pilot set the plane down and we used all the runway before we finally stopped."

After V-E Day, Earl flew two missions to pick up Prisoners of War from a POW camp located near Barth, Germany. They had orders not to shut down their engines when they landed on a former German airstrip. POWs were waiting in plane load groups. As soon as each bomber landed and taxied to a POW group, they were herded aboard the aircraft and it took off for Camp Lucky Strike, a POW processing camp near Le Havre, France. Earl also flew on two aerial sightseeing trips over Europe taking ground personnel to see devastation inflicted by the Eighth Air Force on Nazi Germany.

Earl and his crew including their crew chief were to fly a battle weary B-17 bomber back to the United States. The crew chief was determined to include his tools aboard the aircraft. After takeoff one engine quit working and the propeller began to windmill out of control. They were able to make it to Iceland where the crew chief changed propellers with another bomber that was stranded there. They were able to take off the next day and flew home without further incident.

After furlough Earl reported to Tampa, Florida, "to change over to B-29s to go to the Pacific". After the Atomic Bomb was dropped I was shipped to Stuttgart, Arkansas where I received my discharge in September, 1945." Earl had been awarded the Air Medal with four oak leaf clusters, ETO ribbon with battle stars and the World War II Victory Medal. After returning to Iowa, Earl spent nine years in the Iowa National Guard. He operated an auto body business for thirty-eight years and retired n 1982.

REUBEN 'WARD' BRITSON, RADCLIFFE, IA, was working on a farm in the Radcliffe area as a hired man prior to World War II. He enlisted in the Army Air Corps January 25, 1944 at Ft. Des Moines, Iowa, and was sent to Biloxi, MS for Basic Training.

Ward attended Aerial Gunnery School at Laredo, TX, before being shipped to Westover, MA, for crew assignment and training. In the middle of September, 1944, he and his aircrew picked up a new B-24 bomber at Mitchell Field, NY and headed overseas to Europe from New Hampshire. Their route was to take them to Goose Bay, Labrador and Iceland with a final stop at Prestwick, Scotland. Their aircraft carried extra fuel in wing tanks for the long journey. Nearing Iceland they found their transfer pumps allowing extra fuel to enter the engines didn't work. They were forced to turn back only to find the nearest base, Greenland, was "socked in" due to weather. With only fifteen minutes of fuel remaining and one hour from Labrador their transfer pumps began working. They landed safely only to be held in Labrador for five days because of a snow storm. When the weather cleared they resumed their flight to Scotland where their aircraft was taken from them and they boarded a train to the 93rd Bomb Group at Hardwick, England.

Ward flew twenty-two combat missions. Trained as a ball turret gunner he flew three missions as tail gunner and the remaining as a nose gunner. His first mission was the most memorable. Their tail gunner was ill and Ward took his position. After takeoff and forming into formation Ward tested his guns while over the English Channel. They didn't work. He took the guns apart and put them back together in time to re-test them while over Belgium. This time they worked. From the tail position he could see endless formations of American bombers strung out behind him in route to their target.

Although he didn't experience much German fighter opposition because of American long-range fighter escort, flak from German anti-aircraft guns was intense and accurate. A measure of revenge was gained when their Group bombed a German .88 shell loading plant scoring direct hits. Concussion from the ground explosions could be felt in their aircraft.

Following V-E Day Ward flew back to the United States in early July, 1945, with the 90th Bomb Group. Getting to and from England seemed to be a problem. Going over the problem was transfer fuel pumps and snow storms. Returning home their route was from Scotland through the Azores and Newfoundland to Massachusetts. Landing in the Azores a fuel tank leak was discovered requiring a delay in getting it repaired. In the meantime, their pilot, a second lieutenant with thirty-nine missions to his credit began celebrating their return to America a little too early. He got into trouble with local military authorities. It was another five days before the matter was cleared or forgotten and they resumed their flight.

After stints at Jefferson Barracks, MO, Sioux Falls, SD, and Alamagordo, NM, Ward received his discharge from military service December 14, 1945 at Lowry Field, CO.

He had been awarded, among other decorations, the Air Medal with three oak leaf clusters, ETO ribbon and WWII Victory Medal.

DONALD BROADBENT, DES MOINES, IA, was a Des Moines Register carrier salesman prior to America's entry into World War II. He had attended Mason City Junior College for a semester and then entered on duty with the Army Air Corps in February, 1943.

After Basic Training at Jefferson Barracks, St. Louis, Missouri, Donald was accepted into the Aviation Cadet Program and sent to Stevens Point, Wisconsin, to attend college under the College Training Detachment Program. Donald then reported to Bakersfield, California, to begin Basic Flight Training. Next came Primary Flight Training at Tucson, Arizona and Advanced Flight Training at Santa Ana, California. He "washed out" of flight training and was sent to Bombardier's School at Victorville, California.

After graduation from Bombardier School, Donald was awarded his wings and commission as a Second Lieutenant and assigned to an aircrew. The crew took overseas training at Kearney, Nebraska. Seven days before completion of training and deployment to the European Theater of Operations Donald married the girl he had known since sixth grade. While restricted to his base at the time, Donald managed to sneak into town and spend two nights with his bride by hiding in the trunk of a car driven by a solider with pass privileges.

In July, 1944, Donald and his crew flew a new B-24 bomber to Nuts Corner, Ireland through Bangor, Maine; Goose Bay, Labrador and Iceland. Their aircraft was taken from them for installation of additional equipment and Donald proceeded to England by boat and then was transported to the 487th Bomb Group at Lavenham.

Donald flew thirty-five combat missions beginning August 9, 1944, to Nurnberg. Missions included bombing German troop concentrations at Aachen in support of Allied ground forces, and four missions to Merseberg to bomb oil refineries. Only one crew member was injured during the thirty-five missions. Donald's tail gunner was hit by a piece of German flak that tore off his thumb. Their aircraft was hit by flak which disabled one engine that had to be "feathered". While on the bomb run with the bomb bay doors open, a German .88 shell went through the bomb bay without striking any of the bombs and exited through the top of the aircraft. Hydraulics to the bomb bay doors was severed and the doors had to be hand-cranked shut after "bombs away".

Following completion of his missions Donald remained in England until February, 1945, when he flew from Prestwick, Scotland to Washington, D.C. He received his discharge from military service in September, 1945, and had been awarded the Air Medal with four oak leaf clusters, ETO Ribbon with battle stars and World War II Victory Medal.

After military service Donald was a distributor for Wynn's Friction Oil until he started his own auto products company, BG Products, at Wichita, Kansas.

Right - Donald, second from right, front row, during Primary Flight Training at Tucson, Arizona. George Brown, also from Mason City, is front row, right.

Right - Donald and crew flew a war-weary B-24 home to the United States from Scotland in February, 1945.

HAROLD BROOKHISER, WEVER, IA, was employed spreading agricultural lime and as a power shovel operator. He had received a one year deferment from the Selective Service System until being drafted on November 19, 1943.

He was sent to Basic Training at Amarillo, TX, and Aerial Gunnery School at Las Vegas, NV. After assignment to an air crew Harold trained for three months with his crew at Alexandria, LA, before being deployed to England on March 4, 1945. They flew the northern route and landed at Labrador to refuel where "the snow was stacked thirty feet high on both sides of the runway". After they reached England, Harold and his crew were assigned to the 92nd Bomb Group at Podington.

Harold flew six combat missions as toggelier. On one mission to Dresden, Germany, it was decided not to drop their bombs on the first bomb run. Instead "chaff" was thrown out in an attempt to confuse anti-aircraft batteries and German radar operators. The formation made another bomb run and released their bombs on target. "They say we killed 300,000 people in the raid." Harold's plane received flak in the wing. "The hole was so large you could have jumped through it". An .88 shell went through the bottom of the plane and out the top without exploding. "It came through right behind the pilot's seat. I got hit by a piece of flak in the chest. I was wearing my flak vest that protected me. It felt like someone hit me with a hammer."

Upon return from the mission they attempted to land at their base when they realized their flaps wouldn't lower. They got out of the landing pattern, fixed the problem and attempted a second landing. This time the wheels wouldn't come down. They aborted the landing to manually crank the wheels down. They were successful in landing the third time.

After the war ended in Europe, it was determined Harold didn't have enough points for discharge. He was assigned to an engineer company at Marseilles, France, for two weeks prior to returning to the United States on the "Queen Mary". He was assigned to San Antonio, TX for one month before reporting to Lincoln, NE, and re-assignment to the Pacific Theater. While at Lincoln it was determined he had enough points for discharge and was sent to Jefferson Barracks, St Louis, MO. Harold was discharged on April 7, 1946, and had received among other medals the European Theater of Operations medal with two battle stars.

After the war Harold farmed and operated a trucking firm. The firm expanded into a fleet which hauled corn syrup.

Right - Harold and crew at 92nd BG, Podington, England. Harold is on the far right.

ROBERT BROWN, FORT DODGE, IA, had attended Kemper Military School in Missouri and one semester at Texas A&M University when America entered World War II. Bob went to Dallas and enlisted in the Army Air Corps in March, 1943.

Selected for the Aviation Cadet Program, Bob reported to a classificaton center at Santa Ana and was sent to Oxnard, California for training. After having "washed out" of pilot training he attended Aerial Gunnery School at Las Vegas, Nevada. After completion of training he was sent to another classification center at Salt Lake City, Utah, for assignment to an air crew. Bob and his crew trained together at Kearns, Utah and Ardmore, Oklahoma, in preparation for deployment overseas.

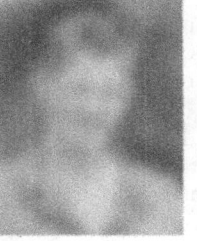

In March, 1944, Bob and his crew picked up a new B-17 aircraft at Grand Island, Nebraska, and flew through Goose Bay, Labrador and Iceland to England. Bob was assigned to the 95th Bomb Group at Horham as a left waist gunner. One week of final gunnery practice took place in "The Wash" area of England before he flew his first of thirty missions.

Bob's first mission came on April 18, 1944, a bombing raid on Berlin. He would fly two other missions to Berlin, including his next to last mission, before his tour ended on October 7, 1944, with a bombing raid on Leipzig, Germany.

On Bob's twenty-eighth mission, a bombing raid on Merseburg, Germany, enemy anti-aircraft batteries defending the city was "intense and damned accurate". A piece of shrapnel ("flak") penetrated Bob's aircraft and struck his navigator between the eyes killing him instantly. Two engines of his aircraft were disabled but they were able to make it back to England safely.

On one mission to Berlin all Bomb Groups were ordered to abort their mission while over Germany. "For some reason, our Group didn't get the message and we were the only Group to continue on to the target and bomb it. For that we got a Unit Citation."

Although the tour requirement was thirty-five missions for rotation back to the United States, Bob flew in the Group's lead crew thereby reducing his missions to thirty. Bob returned to America aboard the ocean liner "Mauritania". He applied for Navigation School and after spending three months at San Antonio, Texas, and other assignments he received his discharge from military service October 27, 1945 at Scott Field, Illinois.

Bob attended the University of Iowa under the G I Bill of Rights and graduated in 1947. He farmed until retirement in 1985. He had been awarded, among other medals, the Distinguished Flying Cross, Air Medal with oak leaf clusters, ETO Ribbon with battle stars and the World War II Victory Medal.

Bob's father, DeWayne, had been an Army officer in World War I. He re-entered military service in World War II and rose to the rank of full Colonel, having had his "birds" pinned on him by General Omar Bradley. Bob was able to meet his father in England during the war.

Right - Bob's crew at 95th BG, Horham, England. Bob, Waist Gunner, is back row, second from the left.

GEORGE BROWN, WATERLOO, IA, was attending Mason City Junior College when he enlisted in the Army Air Corps in December, 1942. He was called to active duty in February, 1943, and sent to Jefferson Barracks, St Louis, Missouri for Basic Training.

He volunteered for the Aviation Cadet Program and was sent to Santa Ana, California for Pre-Flight Training. Primary Flight Training took place at Tucson, Arizona, where he flew the Ryan PT-22. Basic Flight Training was at Bakersfield, California, flying the AT-6 where no one in his class was "washed out". Upon graduation cadets were then assigned to Advanced Training in either twin-engine, multi-engine or fighter aircraft.

George was selected for Advanced Fighter Pilot Training and sent to Luke Air Base flying the Curtiss P-40. The day he was to solo "I sat in the cockpit for what seemed hours, studying the instrument panel and rehearsing every movement of takeoff under the watchful eye of an instructor." His aircraft was then towed to the end of the runway for startup and takeoff. "At that time I looked at the panel as if I'd never seen it before. I was scared stiff. An old Master Sergeant climbed up to the cockpit and very calmly told me what I was to do first and from then on I had no trouble, I was on track."

George was then sent to Hamilton Field, California, where he was assigned to the 398th Squadron of the 369th Fighter Training Group being formed there. During the Winter of 1944 the Group was transferred to DeRidder, Louisiana, for combat training, however in the Spring of 1945 they were transferred again. This time to Meridian, Mississippi, where they were outfitted with the P-51 Mustang. "What a smooth, great airplane, especially with the Rolls Royce engine." The war ended before George could be deployed overseas. He had logged over 900 hours flying time in the two aircraft. "Fighter pilots were virtually wiped out of the service" and George received his discharge in time to enter the University of Iowa for the Fall semester of 1945.

George received his Bachelor's degree in Business Administration in 1948. He would remain in the Air Force Reserve and reach the rank of Major before military retirement in 1984. In civilian life he become Assistant Manager of the Waterloo Airport, Chief of Operations at the Salt Lake City, Utah Airport and then return to his hometown of Mason City to become the Airport General Manager. He retired in 1986. George keeps in excellent physical condition through almost daily bicycling and is an avid HO gauge model railroader.

JAMES BROWN, MASON CITY, IA, had graduated from the University of Iowa Law School and passed the bar examination to practice law when he enlisted in the Army Air Corps in 1942. While at the University he also obtained a private pilot's license under the Civilian Pilot Training Program.

Jim was sent to Santa Ana, California, for Pre-Flight Training. He completed

Primary Flight Training at Glendale, Arizona; Basic Flight at Pecos, Texas and Advanced Flight Training at Douglas, Arizona. He earned his wings and commission as a Second Lieutenant during the Fall of 1943.

During B-17 flight training at Hobbs, New Mexico, he was on a cross-country practice mission to Spokane, Washington, when the wings of his aircraft "iced up" and the engines quit. All aboard the aircraft were forced to parachute out of the airplane over a mountainous region of Idaho. "The crew was strung out over miles. I landed in a tree and walked for two days before reaching a logging camp."

After being assigned an aircrew, Jim trained with them at Dyersburg, Tennessee, in preparation for overseas combat duty. After completion of training they picked up a new B-17 bomber at Kearney, Nebraska and flew to Scotland through New Hampshire, Labrador and Iceland. They were assigned to the 305th Bomb Group at Chelveston, England.

Jim and his crew however were to fly for a Composite Squadron of the 305th at Cheddington, England. They flew only at night, in a black B-17 bomber dropping propaganda leaflets over Nazi –occupied Europe and weapons and supplies to Underground forces on the continent. Blackout conditions in all of England required they take off and land in total darkness. Pinpoint lights along the runway allowed Jim to take off from his base runway. Other pinpoint lights, visible from only one direction at low altitude allowed him to find their runway at night and land. The lights, along the beginning of the runway, were different colors at various distances that allowed him to identify whether he was landing too high, too low, or was at the right altitude to land.

Jim flew twelve combat missions. During his thirteenth mission, a German night fighter attacked Jim's plane. His crew returned fire and shot down the German fighter, but not before its bullets set his left wing and left inboard engine afire. Jim and his crew were forced to parachute from their aircraft while over Holland. Jim landed in a small town outside of Rotterdam near a German Army Headquarters. He escaped notice and walked between two German outposts. Jim began knocking on doors of Dutch civilians to ask for help. "People were afraid to help. They would be shot if they did. Finally some people took me in and a man went out to contact the Dutch Underground. I was told to put on a suit of the man who left. I was taken to the home of a dentist who was head of the resistance movement in the area. I made it back as far as Antwerp, Belgium, by bicycling and walking. The Underground had made me a forged passport. I showed them the photo I carried of myself to be used for a forged passport if I was captured. They just laughed pointing out that all of the American flyers wore the same suit coat when they had their pictures taken."

"After a month of hiding from the Germans a Belgian man and woman and a Dutch woman working for the Germans came and got me from a shop where I was staying. I didn't know it but they were working for the Germans. I was to meet a man at a park who would help me. A man approached me and asked "Are you worried?" I replied that I was. He said "your worries are over" and led me to a house. After I entered the house the door slammed shut and I was suddenly in the custody of German soldiers. They told me they could shoot me as a spy because I was in civilian clothes."

Jim was taken to Frankfurt, Germany, for attempted interrogation and then transported to Stalag Luft III at Sagan, Poland. "There were only officers in my compound. Food was soup that had worms in it but we ate it anyway. Bread was like sawdust with rodent holes in it. We were supposed to get a Red Cross parcel once a week but that didn't happen. Packages and letters sent from home never reached me either."

In the winter of 1944 as Russian ground forces began to advance on the POW camp, the Germans decided to move the prisoners to Spremberg, Germany. Guarded mainly by older German troops the POWs began a forced march in below zero weather with only what clothing and blankets they had in camp. Food had to be foraged from the land or bartered from farmers along the route. At one time Jim passed out during the march but was assisted by his fellow POWs. Sleds were made to pull their belongings in the snow. One night they were able to gain some means of shelter from the weather by staying in a pottery factory.

From Spremberg the POWs were loaded in railroad boxcars and shipped to Nurnberg. Later as American troops advanced further into Germany the POWs were forced to march again, this time to Moosburg. On April 29, 1945, American tanks could be seen on the hilltops surrounding the prison camp. It wasn't long before General George Patton's tank crashed through the prison gates liberating the prisoners.

The prisoners remained at the camp until transportation could be arranged for them. Jim was flown to Camp Lucky Strike at Le Havre, France, used as a POW processing center. After delousing, new clothes, shaves, showers, food, medical treatment and pay, Jim boarded a Victory ship for the United States. Instead of the usual bunk or hammock in the hold of the ship to sleep in, Jim found an empty bunk in the hospital ward and slept there the entire return trip. He learned the war ended in Europe while at sea.

Jim received his separation from military service during September, 1945. He had been awarded, among other medals, the Air Medal, ETO and World War II Victory Medals. He practiced law in Mason City for fifty years. During that span he also served as County Attorney for three terms.

In 2002 Jim and his wife returned to the small town in Holland where he landed when he parachuted from his flaming aircraft. He met persons who had assisted him in 1944 by hiding him from German forces. He was presented with a headlight from his crashed B-17 bomber and a piece of metal from the crashed German night fighter that shot down his aircraft.

He learned that the Belgian man who turned him in to the Germans in 1944 was shot, his wife committed suicide and the Dutch woman spent twenty years in prison.

MERLIN BRUNING, CARROLL, IA, was originally from the small Iowa town of Breda. He was still in high school when America entered World War II. While only seventeen he was able to join the Air Corps Reserve and was called to active duty when he turned eighteen in February, 1944.

He attended Aerial Gunnery School in Kingman, Arizona, and was then assigned to an air crew for overseas training at Rapid City, South Dakota. In January, 1945, Merlin and his crew picked up a new B-17 bomber at Lincoln, Nebraska and flew to the European Theater of Operations.

Merlin flew seven combat missions as aerial gunner. On his fifth mission flak knocked out one engine starting a fire. Extinguishers and feathering the propeller failed to put out the fire. Then two other engines failed. Merlin's pilot was successful in landing the aircraft in a field behind American lines in France. On landing, a wind-milling propeller broke off the engine tearing a six foot section off a wing. The French advised them another B-17 was nearby and the only thing wrong with it was the wheels wouldn't retract. Merlin and his crew flew it back to England, landing at an RAF base. Two more missions were flown before the war ended in Europe.

Merlin returned to the United States in June, 1945 and began training on the B-29 bomber for what was intended to be re-deployment to the Pacific. The Japanese surrender precluded further training. Rather than be discharged from the military, Merlin re-enlisted in the Army and spent five years in Germany after World War II as a First Sergeant of an Anti-Aircraft battery. He was able to see first hand the destruction of cities by aerial bombardment.

Merlin volunteered for airborne forces and completed training at Ft. Benning, Georgia, as a Master Sergeant. He served a year in Korea during the war there. When the fighting broke out in Viet Nam, Merlin volunteered for Special Forces training, became a Green Beret, and served a short time in Viet Nam. He retired from military service in 1965 having served in three wars. He had been awarded the Air Medal, World War II Victory Medal, ETO Ribbon with two battle stars and medals associated with service in both Korea and Viet Nam.

After return to civilian life Merlin worked for twenty years with a facsimile company during which time he became the company's vice-president.

Iowans of the Mighty Eighth

Right - Merlin's crew at 34th BG, Mendelsham, England. Merlin, Aerial Gunner, is back row, fourth from left, kneeling.

CHARLES BUCKLEY, IOWA CITY, IA, graduated from high school in 1943 when he was seventeen years old. He enlisted in the Army Air Corps but wasn't accepted until January, 1944, when he turned eighteen. Accepted for the Aviation Cadet Program at a time when there was a surplus of pilots, navigators and bombardiers and when the Program was being eliminated, he was   then sent to Miami, FL, for Basic Training. This was followed by Aerial Gunnery School at Laredo, TX, and assignment to a crew at Lincoln, NE. However, replacement crews, particularly gunners, were needed at Casper, WY and he was sent there. Trained as a B-24 nose gunner Charles was made a tail gunner and given only two weeks training before deployment to the Eighth Air Force.

In July, 1944, Charles and his crew picked up a B-24 bomber at Topeka, KS, and flew the northern route to England through New Hampshire; Goose Bay, Labrador and Iceland. They reported to the 392nd Bomb Group at Wendling.

Charles flew thirty combat missions, down five from the required amount because he and his crew were shot down, not once, but twice. The first time came on his nineteenth birthday, January 16, 1945. Coming back from a raid on Lauta, Germany and after taking numerous "flak" hits, the Flight Engineer advised the pilot they only had fifteen minutes of fuel remaining. The pilot believed they could still make England or at least get back over Allied lines. After fifteen minutes the engines quit while they were Northeast of Paris. They bailed out and the airplane went down taking the nose gunner and navigator with it. Why they hadn't bailed out remains a mystery unless they didn't hear the alarm bell to bail out or the bell was not activated. The rest of the crew were safe in American hands and were taken to Paris for transport back to their base.

The second time they had to bail out of their aircraft was exactly a month later after a bombing raid on a Salzburg fuel plant. Returning to their base the top turret gunner noticed another B-24 above them with its bomb bay doors open. The aircraft had not dropped its bomb load. The bombs were released while over Charles's airplane. One bomb struck his plane a foot and a half away from Charles knocking out the left tail and stabilizer. They were headed in a westerly direction toward England. Weather in England had deteriorated to the extent landing back at their base was impossible. All aircraft in the formation were ordered to turn around and land at the nearest friendly air base in France. Because of damage Charles's pilot could not turn their aircraft back to France nor land in England because of weather. It was decided to abandon their airplane while at ten thousand feet. After the crew bailed out the airplane went into a steep dive and then exploded when it was at about two thousand feet. The crew believed the pilot had stayed with the airplane and was killed. When the pilot let loose of the controls the airplane went into its dive pinning him in the top turret area by centrifugal force. When it exploded the force of the blast propelled him out the bomb bay area. He was still able to pull the rip cord on his parachute and land safely. He suffered only a black eye.

Other missions included a low-level mission in support of Operation Market Garden, the airborne invasion of Holland, supplying paratroopers on the ground. While pushing supplies out the bomb bay "flak" tore through Charles's airplane near where he was located. He instinctively ducked behind a crate only to realize the crate he was hiding behind was loaded with hand grenades.

Flying daily missions in support of Allied forces during the Battle of the Bulge they were required to fly in weather that prevented visual bombing. They were unable to see beyond their wing tips in formation or see the runway in taking off and landing. Ordered to take off or crash trying because of the desperate situation of the ground forces, Charles and his crew roared down the runway. A vacuum pump went out causing them to lose readings on all instruments. Trying to lift off when it was believed ready, their aircraft went off the end of the runway, through mud and dirt and a barbed wire fence. They hit a perimeter road around the airfield that bounced them into the air with enough force they were able to get airborne. The vacuum pump was fixed and they continued with their mission. A couple days after the mission Charles was getting a haircut. In the barber chair ahead of him was an M.P. that appeared visibly shaken. The barber asked him what was wrong. The M.P. replied, "The other day a bomber tried to run over me". The M.P. had been stationed at the end of the runway.

Charles returned to United States in April, 1945, aboard a troop ship. He and 2,700 other gunners, because of the shortage of men, were eventually sent to the West Coast to help battle forest fires. He was discharged from military service in September, 1945, having been awarded the Air Medal with four oak leaf clusters and the European Theater of Operations medal with four battle stars. He re-enlisted in the Air Force in 1958 as an electronic warfare maintenance specialist until retirement in 1977.

Right - Charles and his crew at 392nd BG, Wendling, England. Charles is front row, second from left.

Right - Charles and crew celebrate after successfully bailing out of their stricken aircraft. Charles is back row, hand on chin.

JOHN R. BUTLER, WASHINGTON, IA, was a B-17 Bombardier with the 490th Bomb Group stationed at Eye, England. On July 20, 1944, John flew his thirteenth mission, a raid on a German airfield north of Leipzig. Among John's crew was a Flight Engineer on his thirty-fifth and final mission required for rotation back to the United States and a newlywed Navigator flying his first combat mission.

When attacked by enemy fighters John's aircraft was hit. The tail gunner called out that there was a fire on board the airplane. John left his bombardier's position in the nose of the airplane and grabbed a fire extinguisher. Meanwhile .20 mm shells from a German fighter hit their bomber and exploded in the nose of the airplane riddling it with holes. Uncertain what happened next John remembered being mashed against the escape hatch. "I reached for the emergency release handle. After a couple pulls, the door was gone. I must have been dazed because I didn't remember when it opened. All I knew was that I was hanging half out of the plane. I couldn't get out nor could I get back in. We were roaring down in a tight spin. All of a sudden, I was fully conscious of what was happening but was helpless to do anything. It's funny – I wasn't a bit terrified. I knew we would crash and that in my position I wouldn't have a chance. I prayed and couldn't remember when I had started to pray. All I knew was that there was that terrible roaring of the motors and the sensation of being swung about. I couldn't feel any power in my legs to push my body out of the plane. I gave up and waited and prayed."

"The next thing I knew was that it was still as death. There wasn't any noise at all. I was on my back and falling free. I had my left hand on the ripcord and just pulled it. I remember groaning once with intense relief when I felt the jerk of the chute opening. I looked up to see the chute in one piece and in good shape."

John landed on the roof of a house in a small German town. After he climbed down from the roof he was met by the town's chief of police who kicked at his feet. Someone else clubbed him in a back of the head with a stick. He was marched to the middle of the street with a crowd following. "The chief kept kicking me in the pants all the way to the police station where he slammed me against a wall and started shaking his fist at me and spit in my face."

John learned that of his nine man crew, three were unhurt, three were seriously hurt but survived and three men perished including the Flight Engineer on his last mission and the Navigator on his first mission.

He was sent to temporary prisoner of war camps before finally reaching his destination, Stalag Luft 1 near Barth, Germany. At the temporary camps the food was described as "lousy" consisting of bread with syrup on it and a green soup. Living conditions was "primitive" with straw filled pallets for mattresses in cells full of fleas, chiggers and filth.

At Barth, food was scarce. Food parcels sent by the Red Cross kept them from starving to death. German rations consisted of black barley bread often filled with glass or metal pieces, potatoes, and once in awhile a little oleomargarine and sugar.

With nothing to do but sit out the war boredom became a major problem. For release prisoners played softball, football, cards and exercised. Chess sets were carved from soap. John kept a diary of his ten month prisoner of war experience on a roll of toilet paper which filled 53 sheets of normal typing paper when transcribed.

As Spring of 1945 arrived the prisoners learned from German guards how bad the war was going for the Third Reich. American and Russian forces were closing in on them. Germans began sabotaging their own equipment to prevent it from falling into Allied hands. Senior American officers were advised by the German Commandant their guards would leave when the Russians got within twenty miles of the prison camp. In late April German guards were seen leaving their watch towers and the camp. Senior officers advised their fellow prisoners not to leave the camp for fear of being inadvertently shot by Russian troops and to wait for American airplanes to pick them up.

After waiting several days, John and others decided to leave on their own. Finding a map of Germany they left camp. Four days later, May 9, John reached American lines, the day the war ended in Europe.

Following the war, John bought a general store in Lytton, Iowa. He later became a banker when he purchased the West Chester, Iowa, Savings Bank. John retired in 1985.

HUBERT CAMPNEY, EMMETSBURG, IA, was a dairy herd improvement supervisor at Iowa State College when he enlisted in the Army Air Corps on September 25, 1942. He was sent to the Army Air Corps Cadet College at Stevens Point, WI; Santa Ana, CA Army Air Base; Armorer Training at Lowry Field, CO; and Aerial Gunnery School at Las Vegas, NV before being assigned to a combat crew at Salt Lake City, UT.

Hubert was deployed to England in March, 1944, as a ball turret gunner with the 452nd Bomb Group at Deopham Green. He would fly seventeen combat missions including one to Berlin when his aircraft was flying deputy lead and they were attacked by German fighters before they began their bomb run. During the bomb run "the flak was so heavy you could walk on it". Despite later being shot down and taken prisoner of war Hubert believed his most memorable mission was when the German jet, the ME-262 made its first appearance. "It was impossible to track them with our guns, they were so fast. It was a hot topic of discussion in the post-mission briefing room."

A mission on D-Day, June 6, 1944, allowed him to see the vast armada of the invasion fleet spread out below. Another mission, to St. Lo, in support of the invasion was described as uneventful until they returned to base. "The whole squadron was called on to report on the mission and we were really interrogated." Smoke marking the target area to be bombed had shifted due to winds and bombs were dropped on American ground troops killing many soldiers including General McNair. From his ball turret position Hubert could clearly see the bombs from his squadron hit its intended target.

On his seventeenth mission, a bombing raid on Mannheim to knock out generators supplying electricity to Southeast Germany, Hubert's plane was hit by flak knocking out two engines and all controls to the airplane. The controls were locked in an upward climb position and the pilot gave the order for all crewmen to bail out. It was all the pilot could do to avoid collision with other planes in the formation. Due to the high altitude, and lack of oxygen, the crew had to free fall until their faces felt warmth, then they could open their parachutes. Before bailing out, Hubert's ball turret, unable to work without electricity had to be opened by crank. Climbing out of the ball he could not find his parachute until he noticed it on the floor of the plane bouncing around near an open door where others were bailing out. He was able to reach the chute just before it would have fallen out the door, put it on and exited the airplane. "When the parachute opened it was like jumping back up in the air." Hubert's flight engineer landed one half mile from him and was never seen or heard of again, believed killed and buried by German civilians. Hubert was taken prisoner of war and transported to Frankfurt, Germany, where he was placed in solitary confinement and attempted to be interrogated. He gave only his name, rank and serial number.

Hubert was shipped by train to Stalag Luft VI in the Alsace Lorraine region of Eastern France. When it appeared invading American troops would soon overrun the area the prisoners were evacuated and loaded on a train for shipment to Stalag Luft IV near the Baltic Sea. Boxcars were crowded with prisoners with no room to sit or lay down. They were given little food and water during the trip and had only a pail in each boxcar for a latrine. Vomit, urine and excrement filled the boxcar floor and clothing was soiled from trying to sit or lay down to rest. "The stench was terrible." In February, 1945, with Russian troops closing in on the camp, the prisoners were evacuated and forced to march for eighty-two days without food and water except what could be foraged from the land or traded with farmers. Their destination was Moosberg, Germany, where they remained until American troops liberated the prison camp on April 29, 1945.

Hubert flew out of the prison camp in a B-17 to Camp Lucky Strike for food, clothing, and delousing. He returned to the United States by ship and eventually reported to Jefferson Barracks, St. Louis, Missouri where he received his discharge from military service on September 20, 1945. He had been awarded, among other medals, the Purple Heart, Air Medal with three oak leaf clusters, ETO Ribbon and World War II Victory Medal.

Back pay he received from being a prisoner of war allowed him to purchase farm equipment necessary for him to start farming. He farmed in the Emmetsburg area until retirement.

An amusing incident (not at the time) took place prior to a mission to Berlin in June, 1944. While preparing for the mission Hubert test fired his machine guns as instructed, but several rounds struck the tail of a nearby B-17. His crewmembers believed they were being strafed by German fighters. Hubert was arrested by military police. Two planes needed for the mission were now grounded. He was allowed to continue flying missions until his scheduled court martial. Investigation disclosed a spring in the hold back pin for the ammunition belt had not been replaced in the seventy missions his plane had flown and the charges against him were dismissed.

Right - Hubert and his crew in January, 1944, just before going overseas and assignment with the 452nd BG, Deopham Gree, England. Hubert is back row, third from the left.

RAYMOND CARLSON, WALCOTT, IA, had attended the University of Nebraska, participated in Civilian Pilot Training and was working at Rock Island Arsenal at the time of America's entry into World War II. He enlisted in the Army Air Corps in September, 1942, and was chosen for the Aviation Cadet Program in April, 1943.

After Basic Training at Sheppard Field, Texas, Raymond was tested at the San Antonio, Texas Classification Center to determine his flight crew qualifications. He was then sent to Wittenburg College in Springfield, Ohio as part of the College Training Detachment Program before attending Navigation School.

Raymond received his wings and commission as a Second Lieutenant April 22, 1944. After assignment to a crew at Fresno, California, and overseas training at Tonapah, Nevada, Raymond and his crew picked up a new B-24 Liberator Bomber at Hamilton Field, CA. They flew to Nutts Corner, Ireland, through Manchester, New Hampshire. On arrival in Ireland their aircraft was taken from them for retrofitting and they were flown on to England.

Assigned as a Navigator with the 466th Bomb Group at Attlebridge, Raymond and his crew went through a period of transition training prior to their first combat mission. They also flew their B-24 loaded with gasoline on low-level flights to France in support of Patton's Armored Forces after the Normandy breakout. Flying at only 200 feet they landed at captured airfields. Raymond recalls troops "swarming all over our plane to unload the fuel the instant we stopped." They received no credit for missions on these flights.

Raymond flew the first of his thirty-five combat missions on October 15, 1944. His eighth mission required an eight hour flight to and from the marshalling yards at Bebra, Germany. After the bomb run they encountered problems with their number three engine and lost radio communications. Falling behind their Group, alone and unable to communicate their problems they were able to land at a recently captured airstrip in Belgium. Three days later their aircraft "Slick Chick" was repaired, refueled and they returned to Attlebridge to cheers from ground crew personnel. Raymond and his crew had been about to be reported as missing in action.

Mission number 12a (thirteen is rarely used by flight crews) was to destroy the bridge over the Rhine River at Remagen. Fortunately the bridge was not totally destroyed allowing American forces under General Patton to cross the river in pursuit of German troops.

On March 4, 1945, Mission number 28 was scheduled to bomb a German jet airfield at Kitzingen, Germany. Thick overcast prevented bombers of the 466th from gathering into formation. They proceeded singly to Northern France where they formed for the remaining flight to the target. "We found our formation flying through clouds so dense, we could barely see our wing man. At that time a group of B-17s flew through our formation from the right. The next five to ten minutes was spent in doing evasive action to prevent mid-air collisions. As a result, our formation was completely scattered and we abandoned the mission. Approximately eight or nine of us that were still in reasonable formation formed on a lead plane and started home together."

The lead plane radioed that through a break in the clouds they had identified a city below them as Freiburg, Germany. It was considered a target of opportunity. The nine aircraft were told by the lead aircraft they would make a bomb run on the rail yards. Other navigators suspected the town not to be Freiburg but Basel, Switzerland, a neutral country in the war. After "bombs away" it was determined the lead aircraft had incorrectly identified the city below. Freiburg was twenty-five miles away and they had indeed bombed Basel, Switzerland. Six aircraft from another Bomb Group had also incorrectly identified a city below them as Freiburg and had bombed Zurich, Switzerland. Heavy damage occurred in both Swiss cities. An investigation into the incidents possibly resulted in monetary reparations to the Swiss government.

On March 18, 1945, Raymond's thirty-second mission was to bomb an ordinance plant at Berlin, Germany. "We were the last group into the target and had to stay under the contrails of the flights before us in order to bomb visual at 18,000 feet. After three near mid-air collisions bombs in Raymond's aircraft "hung up" in the bomb bay and were not released on the target. On the return flight to their base it was decided to kick the bombs loose on a Northern Germany farm field. The explosions created a huge crater in the field.

Raymond's thirty-fifth and last mission was on March 25, 1945. He sailed for the United States and was at sea when President Roosevelt died on April 12, 1945. He was sent to a personal affairs school in New York City and then assigned to Mayo General Hospital in Galesburg, Illinois, as Air Force Liaison Officer before his discharge in October, 1945, having been awarded the Air Medal with five oak leaf clusters and the European Theater of Operation Ribbon with battle stars.

Raymond retired in 1983 as Classified Advertising Manager of the Quad City Times newspaper where he was employed for thirty-seven years. He has a Heidelberg printing press in his basement and free lances as a die cutter and printer. While employed at the "Times", a young German typesetter was hired in his department. Raymond and he became good friends and regular golfing partners. Raymond eventually learned the German farm on which his aircraft dropped their bombs on March 18, 1945, belonged to his typesetter's father. The crater created by the bombs filled with rain and was used to water cattle.

Right - Ray and his crew at 466th BG, Attlebridge, England. Ray, Navigator, is front row, left.

WILLIAM J. CARTER, AMES, IA, was a first year college student when he entered military service at Camp Dodge, Iowa. He was sent to Basic Training at Sheppard Field, Wichita Falls, Texas; Aerial Gunnery School at Las Vegas, Nevada and completed overseas training with his newly assigned crew at Drew Field, Tampa, Florida.

Bill was assigned with the 303rd Bomb Group at Molesworth, England, in December, 1944, as a ball turret gunner and flew thirty-five combat missions. His third mission, January 8, 1945, was a raid on Koblenz, Germany. Once over the target, flak knocked out two of their aircraft's engines. Then their armed bombs "hung up" in the bomb bay requiring a crew member climb into the open bomb bay area and manually release them. Bill's pilot took a wrong direction heading after being hit by flak which caused a fire within the aircraft. Loss of fuel caused Bill and his crew to make a crash landing near Tournier, France, in the Normandy area of the country. It took two and a half to three weeks for them to be returned to their base in England.

On his thirty-fifth mission, the required number of missions for rotation back to the United States, the target was Pilsen, Czechoslovakia. Tempting fate with falk on one bomb run was bad enough, but on this mission three passes were made over the target before "Bombs Away".

Bill was discharged from military service October 23, 1945, at Sioux City, Iowa. He had been awarded, among other medals, the Air Medal with five Oak Leaf Clusters, ETO Ribbon with four battle stars and the World War II Victory Medal.

After the war Bill was an agriculturist, banker, in sales, and active in the Iowa Chapter of the Eighth Air Force Historical Society.

JOSEPH J. CECIL, SPIRIT LAKE, IA, was working at Douglas Aircraft, Long Beach, California before World War II broke. He enlisted into military service in 1942, and began his pilot training at Santa Ana, CA in February, 1943.

Dr. Cecil was deployed to Norwich, England as a B-24 pilot in April, 1944, with the 466th Bomb Group.

He flew thirty-five combat missions. As the German Luftwaffe was being reduced or eliminated as a fighter force in the air, flak from anti-aircraft batteries appeared more intense near major targets. The concern with flak became a strain on bomber crews. The Luftwaffe did make appearances. On a bombing mission to Weisbaden. Dr. Cecil's Group was attacked by German fighters. Nine enemy fighters were shot down and two probably destroyed during the attack.

Dr. Cecil's most memorable mission was in support of D-Day on June 6, 1944, when the 466th flew raids against bridges, rail and road junctions, German airfields and villages that gave access to roads leading to the invasion beach. The Luftwaffe was notably absent as a defensive force on that historic day.

J.J. received his discharge from military service on November 13, 1945. He had received the Distinguished Flying Cross, Air Medal with two oak leaf clusters, ETO Ribbon and WWII Victory Medal. He resumed employment at Douglas Aircraft at Long Beach, CA, until he returned to college to obtain a Doctor of Veterinary Medicine Degree.

GEORGE CHIPMAN, ESTHERVILLE, IA, had graduated from River Falls State Teachers College at Eau Claire, Wisconsin, when he enlisted in the Army Air Corps in August, 1942. He was called to active duty in December, 1942, and sent to Valley Forge Military Academy for Basic Training. In May, 1943 he completed technical training in armaments at Yale University, New Haven, Connecticut and was awarded a commission as a Second Lieutenant.

George was assigned to the 453rd Bomb Group being formed at Pocatello, Idaho. The Group subsequently moved to Riverside, California where they finished training in preparation for deployment to the European Theater of Operations. In December, 1943, George sailed aboard the ocean liner "Queen Elizabeth" with twenty-one thousand other American troops to Scotland. "There was bunk space for only thirteen thousand on the ship. Every other night you had a bunk. The other night you slept wherever you could."

George was an Ordnance Officer assigned to the 453rd Bomb Group at Old Buckenham, England. Forty armorers were under his charge, two to each aircraft, to clean and oil machine guns after missions, make gun repairs, and ensure gun turrets, auto pilots, and bombsights were in proper working order. Of the original sixteen crews in his squadron, only one crew survived the required number of missions. A mid-air collision over his base caused one aircraft to spin tailless down to earth. One crewman's parachute got caught on a wing and was killed when he was dragged by the aircraft to earth.

In January, 1945, special racks were devised on the Group's aircraft to hold four 2,000 pound bombs to be used in support of American ground troops during the Battle of the Bulge. After inspecting an airplane George came from under the aircraft to see a bomber taking off, fail to make altitude and come directly at him. He thought he had "bought the farm". George "hit the dirt". The bomber hit the tops of two other aircraft including the one George had just exited, then crashed into a tree killing all aboard. George was unhurt.

After V-E Day George boarded an Italian ship for return to the United States. He was separated from military service in December, 1945 at Madison, Wisconsin. In 1946 George was employed by the Soil Conservation Service of the Department of Agriculture. In 1950 was re-called to active duty during the Korean War and served in Japan as an Assistant Wing Adjutant. Following active duty he remained in the Reserves until he accumulated a total of twenty-two years service. He resumed his employment with the Department of Agriculture until retirement with thirty years service. George continues to farm and is an area seed corn dealer.

ROBERT CHRISJOHN, ALDEN, IA, worked on a farm until he joined the Army Air Corps in January, 1941, nearly a year before America entered World War II. He became an aerial gunnery instructor at Las Vegas, Nevada, and was kept in that position despite numerous requests for pilot training. Robert was finally given the chance to fly and completed Pre-Flight   Training at Santa Ana, California; Primary Flight at King City, California; Basic Flight at Chico, California and Advanced Flight Training at Douglas, Arizona. Upon graduation during January, 1944, he was awarded his wings and commission as a Second Lieutenant. B-17 bomber training was then completed at Hobbs, New Mexico.

Robert was then assigned an air crew and completed combat training with them at Alexandria, Louisiana, before boarding the ship "George Washington" to sail in a convoy to Scotland. At Stone, England, he was assigned to the 306th Bomb Group at Thurleigh.

Robert would fly thirty-five combat mission beginning July 24, 1944 with a raid on fuel production facilities at Merseburg, Germany. "The flak was unbelievable. Merseburg was a heavily defended area."

On September 12, 1944, during a mission to Ruhland, Germany, Robert's Group got out of the "bomber stream". "German fighters hit us hard. One German pilot brought his fighter up from below and just missed hitting our wing. As he flew by he saluted us. We lost nine planes that day to fighters."

"After five or six missions my top turret gunner had to be replaced. He came to me and said "you can't make me go again". They gave him a desk job somewhere as a clerk."

Robert's last mission required for rotation back to the United States was on Christmas Eve, 1944. He then flew a war-weary B-17 back to the United States and landed at Washington, D.C. National Airport. He was assigned to Columbus, Ohio as a B-17 instructor before attending Officer's Armament School at Buckley Field, Colorado.

After World War II ended Robert remained in the Air Force and returned to Germany during 1946. He served a three-year tour at Weisbaden as Commander of a Headquarters Squadron. On weekends he flew coal and food supplies to Berlin during the Berlin Airlift. "We had to fly strictly within a certain corridor. You couldn't stray despite a lot of bad weather. The planes flew round-the-clock and took off in three-minute intervals. As soon as we rolled to a stop it was off-loaded and we took off again."

Robert returned to the United States in 1950 and off active duty status. While working as a banker at Alden, Iowa, he joined the Iowa National Guard. After three years he became a full-time employee of the Guard as Chief of Maintenance. He was promoted through the ranks to Deputy Commanding Officer and Assistant Adjutant General in Iowa's State Headquarters. After twenty years Robert retired as a one-star general. He had been awarded the Distinguished Flying Cross and Air Medal with oak leaf clusters during World War II.

Right - Robert's crew at 306th BG, Thurleigh, England. Robert, Pilot, is front row, left.

FREDERICK CLARK, MACEDONIA, IA, was originally from the Philadelphia area of Pennsylvania. He was attending Harvard University when, in the summer of 1941 he was able to obtain a private pilot's license. After graduation in 1942 Fred attempted to enlist in the U S Navy but was turned down due to a collapsed lung and con-   cussion suffered in a mountain climbing fall. He was rejected by the Army as underweight until a crash diet allowed him to fulfill physical requirements. He was inducted into the Army on October 18, 1942, and sent to an army classification center where a Harvard classmate was the reviewing clerk. Fred was assigned to the Army Air Corps and sent to Keesler Field, Biloxi, Mississippi for Basic Training.

Additional training included Pre-Flight at Maxwell Field, Alabama; Primary Flight at Jackson, Mississippi; Basic Flight at Walnut Ridge Field, Arkansas and Advanced Flight Training at Blytheville, Arkansas where he earned his wings and commission as a Second Lieutenant in February, 1944.

More training was in Fred's future. He completed a B-17

pilot training course at Columbus, Ohio in June, 1944, and was then re-assigned to a B-17 gunnery school in Florida that had no aircraft available for training. He passed time flying the B-24 Liberator bomber at a nearby base until B-17s could arrive and gunnery school resumed. This consisted of flying aerial gunners that would shoot at targets being towed by other aircraft.

In October, 1944, Fred was assigned to the Air Transport Command at Lincoln, Nebraska, as a ferry pilot shuttling aircraft between various bases. In November he was assigned to an aircrew and began training with them at Biggs Field, El Paso, Texas, in preparation for overseas combat duty. In March, 1945, Fred and his crew boarded the Liberty ship "Marine Fox" for an Atlantic Ocean crossing to the 401st Bomb Group at Deenethorpe, England.

Fred's first mission came on March, 28, 1945, to bomb Templehof Airdrome at Berlin, Germany. In route to the target and after the bomb run, his Group was attacked by German fighter aircraft that attacked them head-on. Bullets rained through Fred's aircraft

"Dynamite John", including the cockpit, but caused no serious damage to the aircraft or injuries to his crew. He would encounter a different fighter on his second mission, the German jet, ME-262, which fired cannon from its wings and carried rockets under the wings to decimate American bomber formations.

Fred's worst mission came on April 10, 1945. Their target was railroad marshalling yards north of Berlin at Oranienburg. Just after "bombs away" an explosion beneath Fred's aircraft threw his aircraft straight up several hundred feet. German anti-aircraft guns used a new aerial bomb filled with burning magnesium. All four of his engines instantly went dead. The two inboard engines were completely burned out. Fires started within the aircraft on ceilings, walls and floors in every compartment. Their seats, wiring and cartridge cases caught fire and exploding ammunition sent lead in every direction. Trapped in a dead airplane with fires all around, they could not bail out of the plane, their parachutes had been destroyed in the fire. The crews' practice in emergency procedures paid off when fuel supplies were cut off to the engines, the engines were "feathered" and fire extinguishers employed to put out fires including clothing of crewmembers. Luckily their oxygen system did not catch fire and they were not attacked by enemy fighters.

Fred put the aircraft in a northerly glide while the crew threw everything out of the plane that "wasn't nailed down" to lighten their load. From 33,000 feet they glided silently down to 3,000 feet where they reached the English Channel and Fred turned the aircraft west toward their base. As they soared toward England it was apparent they would not have enough altitude to clear the cliffs on the east coast. As they made preparations for a water landing, the flight engineer suggested Fred try to start their two outboard engines. To their surprise, the engines started and began to run normally. The superchargers had been damaged but the engines would operate at a low altitude. They slowly reached cruising power and were able to make Deenethorpe, "landing with clanks and bangs on the runway from falling pieces of our ship loosened by the magnesium bomb".

On Fred's eleventh mission a bombing raid on submarine pens at Kiel, Germany, German jets attacked the bomber formation on the way to the target. "One jet dove through our Group so close it grazed our right wing and crashed into a B-17 bomber below us." After "bombs away" it was discovered the bomb bay doors had stuck in a half-open position and the bombs were piled on the doors. In order to free the bombs Fred and another crewman laid down on the narrow catwalk of the bomb bay area. With others holding their ankles, they grabbed the ankles of their radio operator and lowered him into the bomb bay area. With numbing cold limiting their endurance to hold the radio operator he was able to push the doors open freeing their bombs. When Fred returned to his pilot's position they were again attacked by German jets. His gunners were able to track the enemy fighters. One jet exploded when hit and another disappeared trailing smoke.

An amusing incident that could have been disastrous occurred on the base at Deenethorpe. A German V-2 rocket carrying a ton of explosives landed near Fred's barracks and exploded creating a large crater. Shrapnel created by the explosion banged against his barracks but didn't penetrate the walls. A wall of the latrine next door to his barracks was damaged but never repaired. Thereafter a little uncleanliness was preferred to freezing in the shower.

Fred flew two mercy missions to Dutch towns dropping food, medical supplies and clothing before he and his crew left England after V-E Day for the United States. They arrived back on June 6, 1945. Fred was re-assigned to Sioux Falls, South Dakota and Roswell, New Mexico for B-29 training in preparation for possible deployment to the Pacific Theater of Operations. When the war ended Fred remained at Roswell until separation from military service in November, 1945. He had been awarded the Air Medal, ETO Ribbon and World War II Victory Medal, among others.

In civilian life Fred purchased his own airplane and continued to fly. He earned his Master Degree in Business Administration from the University of Nebraska and then worked as an investment banker in New York City for ten years. He became Senior Vice-President and head of the Trust Department of the First National Bank in Palm Beach, Florida. After twenty years at that position he retired from banking and moved with his wife to her family farm in Iowa.

Right - Fred's crew at 401st BG, Deenethorpe, England. Fred, Pilot, is back row, left.

GEORGE FORREST CLARK, AMES, IA, grew up on an Iowa farm and attended the then Iowa State College at Ames. He enlisted in the Army on September 10, 1942, and was sent to Camp Crowder, Missouri, for Basic Training. He received other training at Buckley/Lowry Fields, Colorado; Harlingen/Laredo, Texas; Salt Lake City, Utah; Pueblo, Colorado and Westover, Massachusetts.

George was deployed to the European Theater of Operations as a B-24 tail gunner with the 567th Squadron, 398th Bomb Group at Hethel, England. On his nineteenth combat mission, July 24, 1944, over St. Lo, France, his plane was hit by flak and was unable to continue in the air. The crew bailed out and landed near the front lines but behind enemy lines. George was captured by German SS Troops.

The next several days George was transferred and shuttled to different locations often by forced march or transported by truck. On August 5, 1944, he was loaded on a train destined for a prisoner of war camp. Three days later he and six other Americans escaped from the moving train east of Chateau Thierry, France. Re-capture was now their biggest fear. Travelling by foot, cross-country, they came upon a French farmer, who at the risk of his own life, hid them from the Germans and fed them until the area was taken by the American Army on August 28, 1944.

George was sent back to England and returned to the United States where he finished his military service at Sioux City Air Base as a gunnery instructor. George was discharged on October 4, 1945, at the rank of Staff Sergeant. He had been awarded the Purple Heart, Air Medal with two oak leaf clusters, ETO Ribbon and World War II Victory Medal.

George married Gaynell Gabrielson in June, 1945, and they had four children. George farmed until his death on August 16, 1978.

ROBERT CLARK, NEVADA, IA, worked at the Iowa Ordnance Plant, Ankeny, Iowa, until he entered military service January 28, 1943 at Camp Dodge, Iowa. He was sent to Clearwater, Florida, for Basic Training and then to Camp Crowder, Missouri, for Signal Corps Training.

The Commanding Officer at Crowder, learned from Bob's personnel file that he was a ventriloquist and wanted him to put on a show during a base dance. At the same time the base was experiencing a food shortage. Everyone on the base, except the commanding officer's staff, knew the mess sergeant was stealing food for the black market or for special favors from female friends. Bob built a dummy and put on a show during the dance as promised. He jokingly used the dummy to make the Commanding Officer aware of why there was a shortage of food for the soldiers. The mess sergeant was soon transferred out of Crowder.

While attending Signal Corps School Bob applied for the Aviation Cadet Program. He was accepted and sent to the University of Missouri to take college courses applicable to the Air Corps under the College Detachment Training Program. Before graduation all applicants were "washed out" of the program due to a glut in officer candidates. Bob was then re-assigned to Aerial Gunnery School at Yuma, Arizona.

In August, 1944, Bob attended Radio School at Sioux Falls, South Dakota, where he was able to master thirty words a minute sending and receiving in Morse Code. Upon graduation he was assigned to an aircrew and completed training with the crew at Biggs Field, El Paso, Texas, in preparation for overseas deployment.

In February, 1944, Bob and his crew picked up a new B-17 bomber at Lincoln, Nebraska, and flew to England through Greenland and Iceland. At Stone, England, he was assigned to the 34th Bomb Group at Mendelsham.

He was able to fly six missions before V-E Day. Following a bombing mission to Kiel, Germany, on April 4, 1945, to bomb submarine pens, he was scheduled the next day for a mission to bomb targets at Nuremberg. Bob and his crew took off in heavy overcast. While trying to assemble over France for the flight to Nuremberg "it appeared everyone was lost and in a panic. I saw a B-17 fly right across the top of us going in a different direction." "Instruments to fly by when there was no visibility were not working properly. Our wings were icing up and shorted out any communications we had. When the pilot tipped our plane to try and see through the overcast, the aircraft went into a flat spin. Our ball turret gunner pulled the pins to release the side escape hatch so we could bail out but the pilot was able to regain control of the aircraft and we had to land at an American airstrip in France. We later flew back to our base."

The next day Bob and his crew along with several other aircraft were scheduled to fly a practice mission over England. Ground crews had replaced the door of their aircraft but secured it with over-sized pins that they had to hammer in place. "When we finished the mission and we were descending in preparation for landing in another heavy overcast, the plane again went into a flat spin. I tried to pull the pins on the escape hatch but couldn't budge them because they were oversized. Then centrifugal force took over. I recall my mouth was open and I couldn't close it. Rivets began popping on the wings and in the radio compartment. The pilot then seemed to temporarily gain control the plane and I managed to pull the escape hatch pins. I pushed the door out and went with it but was swept back to the right stabilizer after hitting my head on the tail of the plane. I lost consciousness for only a short time and came to bent over the stabilizer. The plane was in a spin again and I couldn't push away from the plane. I managed to crawl over the top of the stabilizer because the force of the spin kept me glued to the plane. I managed to reach one of the tail gunner's guns, grabbed a hold of it and then pushed myself away from the plane. I free fell for a few seconds before opening my parachute. I came down to earth in a snow storm with other members of my crew that bailed out. English farmers armed with pitchforks came after us thinking we were Germans. Luckily they saw the patches on one guy's uniform and we were alright."

Right - Bob demonstrates where he was pinned by centrifugal force on the right stabilizer after attempting to bail out of his aircraft.

Bob flew "Revival Missions" to Czechoslovakia to pick up French prisoners of war and return them to France. He also participated in several "Chowhound" missions to Holland where food parcels were dropped to starving Dutch civilians who had spent years under Nazi rule. "At the end of our food drop run over a soccer field the Dutch used white sheets to spell out "Thanks Yanks".

Bob returned to the United States on July 4, 1945. After a thirty day leave he was scheduled to transfer to the Pacific Theater of Operations at Okinawa to begin the bombing of Japan. This was cancelled after atomic bombs were dropped on Hiroshima and Nagasaki, Japan, and ended World War II.

Bob returned to college and attended Iowa State College before transferring to the University of Iowa. After graduation he entered U.S. Government service as a radio and television writer for dramatic and documentary productions in New York and Hollywood with screen personalities.

Right - Bob, on left, and his tail gunner in front of a coast artillery gun on the English coast at Clacton-On Sea, Essex

WILLIAM CLARK, AMES, IA, graduated from Iowa State College at Ames, Iowa, and was employed as an engineer with a company in Moline, Illinois, when the Japanese attacked Pearl Harbor on December 7, 1941 casting America into World War II. Although he had deferment from military service based on testing and inspection of products sold by his company to the military, Bill asked to be released from the deferment. He was drafted

Chapter Twenty-Two

into the Army Air Corps on March 21, 1943, at Chicago, Illinois and sent to St. Petersburg, Florida, for Basic Training.

"We lived in tents. We had an open-air mess hall with a canvas canopy. Fifty yards away were slit trenches for latrines. Flies were everywhere and a lot of guys got sick. You had to keep your hand waving to ward off the flies while you ate. They would come down onto your food in hordes. They finally moved us to hotels after two weeks."

Bill then attended the American school of Aircraft Instruments near Los Angeles to learn maintenance and repair of the aircraft compass, horizon, trim and bank and auto pilot instruments. "We had to take them apart, clean them and put them back together."

After a short duty stint at Kelly Field, Texas, Bill was sent to Camp Kilmer, New Jersey, where, in the Fall of 1943, he boarded the ship "A. B. Alexander" for England. "We spent sixteen days in a convoy. Our ship was eighteen thousand tons. We hit a sleet storm in the North Atlantic. There were two Victory ships ahead of us that would go over a wave and go down a trough where other waves would wash over the bow of the ships. At times the rear "screws" would be out of the water. I was in G Deck. The only thing below me was the hold of the ship. Bunks were stacked five high and I was in the top bunk. We took turns in the bunks. For twenty-four hours we were down below and the next twenty-four hours we were on deck where we slept. Each time we moved we had to take our gear with us. During the storm water in the latrines would wash all over the deck where we were. Guys got seasick and it was a mess."

When he arrived in England Bill helped lay concrete for runways and sidewalks at an airbase in progress of being built. "The day after we finished the Germans came over and bombed the runways."

Bill was assigned to the 89th Depot Repair Squadron at Strategic Air Depot 3, Watton, England, later name changed to Neaton after the local parish. "For awhile I replaced spark plugs on B-24 bombers. Each engine had two spark plugs for each of its sixteen cylinders. To replace all of the spark plugs on one aircraft took 144 plugs." He was then assigned to take additional training on the Isle of Man at an Advanced Navigation and Bomb Aimer's School. On his return Bill began duties for which he had been trained.

Strategic Air Depots were established for advanced supply to airbases, repair aircraft, perform major overhauls and salvage operations, They also maintained workshops for repair and testing of many aircraft technical items including the instruments and manufacture of special equipment or component parts and a propeller shop. Bill repaired damaged instruments. "I just repaired them and put them on the shelf in case they would be needed." But he also had to make local flights to test instrument reliability. "Some instruments required adjustment every fifteen minutes during a mission."

Right - Workshop

Right - Instrument workshops at Neaton Strategic Air Depot. Bill's work station overlooked other personnel in photo on the right.

After V-E Day (Victory in Europe) Bill was treated to an aerial sightseeing trip of Germany to view bomb damage inflicted by the Eighth Air Force. In August, 1945, he boarded the "Queen Elizabeth" to sail to New York. He was at sea when he learned the Atomic bomb had been dropped on Japan. He made it home to Chicago where he learned of the Japanese surrender ending World War II.

Bill received his discharge from military service at Patterson Field, Ohio, on November 17, 1945. He had been awarded, among others, the European Theater of Operations and World War II Victory Medals.

Bill returned to Iowa State College where he earned another degree in engineering, but bought a local drug store that he operated until his retirement in 1970.

CHARLES CLAUDE, CORWITH, IA, was an auto mechanic and farmer when he enlisted in the Army Air Corps October 30, 1942. He was sent to Jefferson Barracks, St. Louis, Missouri for Basic Training. Although he only had a year and a half of high school he passed examinations required to become an Aviation Cadet. After classification at San Antonio, Texas, to determine what flight crew position he would be most suitable for, he was chosen for pilot training.

After Pre-flight Training at San Antonio Charles completed Primary Flight Training at Bonham, Texas; Basic Flight Training at Greenville, Texas and Advanced Flight Training at Ellington Field, Houston, Texas. He was awarded his wings and commission as a Second Lieutenant on June 27, 1944.

Charles attended Instructor School at Randolph Field, Texas and served as instructor at Denison, Texas before being assigned to an aircrew and trained with them at Gulfport, Mississippi. Charles and his crew picked up a new B-17 bomber at Savannah, Georgia and flew to Valley, Wales where their aircraft was taken from them and they proceeded to the 398th Bomb Group at Nuthampstead, England.

Beginning in January, 1945, Charles flew twenty combat missions in a B-17 named "Out of this World". On his ninth mission, a bombing raid on targets at Dresden, Germany, "we got shot up pretty bad by flak. Coming off the bomb run we were leaving a vapor trail behind number three engine from fuel leaks. Number four engine was smoking bad so we transferred fuel from it. We were south of Berlin and had to break formation. Two P-51 Mustang fighters flew along side as escort. We were losing gas fast and knew we couldn't make it back to England. We found an emergency field in France behind American lines and landed there. We were later flown back to our base."

After the war was won in Europe, Charles flew one low-level mission to Holland and dropped food supplies to the Dutch who had been starved under Nazi rule. Ex-prisoners of war were flown from Bordeaux, France and "rubberneck" tours, (flights of ground personnel to view the damage inflicted on the Third Reich and its allies), were made before Charles returned to the United

States in June, 1945. He spent six months in Florida at a rest camp and received his separation from military service in 1946. He remained in the Air Force Reserve until 1958. He had been awarded, among other medals, the Air Medal with three oak leaf clusters, ETO Ribbon with three battle stars, World War II Victory Medal and a Unit Citation.

Charles was an electrician for the city of Corwith for twenty-two years and owned his own plumbing and heating company before retirement.

Right - Charles and crew at 398th BG, Nuthampstead, England. Charles, Pilot, is front row, right.

RUSSELL CLINGAN, DES MOINES, IA, graduated from high school in 1941. He attended Gates Business College, Waterloo, Iowa, until he was old enough to enlist in the Army Air Corps.

He was accepted into the Aviation Cadet Program and sent to Hobbs, New Mexico for pilot training. Due to an excess of pilots slated for training Russell was sent to Aerial Gunnery

School and deployed to England with the 100th Bomb Group at Thorpe Abbotts, England as a ball turret gunner. Russell flew twenty-five combat missions. He remained in England to fly food missions to civilians in countries that had virtually starved under Nazi rule.

After military service Russell obtained a journalism degree from Drake University and worked in the advertising department of the "Des Moines Register and Tribune" Newspaper. He left to start his own paper, the "Lee Town News" which he published for twenty-five years. After he sold the paper he served as Chairman on the Polk County Conservation Board and was active in the Eighth Air Force Historical Society until his death from cancer in 1997.

Right - Russell beside his B-17, Thorpe Abotts, England

Right - Russell's crew at the 100th Bomb Group, Thorpe Abbotts, England. Russell, ball turret gunner is back row, second from the right.

HOWARD F. COLEMAN, TOLEDO, IA, was a printer/linotype operator until he was drafted into the U.S. Army in December of 1942. After Basic Training and Clerical Training at Louisiana State University he was assigned to Detachment A of the 1073rd Quartermaster Company.

He boarded the "Queen Mary" in November of 1943 and sailed to the European

Theater of Operations where his unit was attached to the 361st Fighter Group at Little Walden, England.

During the Battle of the Bulge his Group was loaned to the Ninth Air Force and in January, 1945, moved to St. Dizier, France. In February, 1945, the entire group moved to Chievres, Belgium, to assist ground forces until April, 1945, when they returned to Little Walden.

Howard was a Supply Sergeant and assisted in procuring and distributing solid and liquid fuel for their fighter aircraft. After V-E Day in May, 1945, he was transferred to the 96th Bomb Group at Snetterton Heath.

Howard returned to the United States in December, 1945 and received his discharge from military service on Christmas Day, 1945.

After the war Howard resumed his career as a printer, worked for Borden's milk and later became the Assistant County Assessor for Tama County.

Right - Howard gets tourist photo taken while on furlough at Aberdeen, Scotland.

CLAUDE CONKLIN, BELLE PLAINE, IA, was in high school at the outbreak of World War II. Upon graduation and eligible for military service he enlisted September 6, 1943 at Camp Dodge, Iowa.

Claude attended CRTD School at Arkadelphia, Arkansas; Gunnery School at Harlingen, Texas and RTU School at Walla Walla, Washington. Upon comple-

tion of crew training he was assigned as a ball turret/waist gunner with the 34th Bomb Group at Mendlesham, England. On November 15, 1944, Claude along with 22 replacement crews and ground personnel sailed for England aboard the *Aquitania*. The ship sailed alone. Although armed with eight inch guns it was susceptible to attack from enemy submarines and proceeded on a zig-zag course. The ship arrived without incident except for many cases of seasickness affecting most of the ground support personnel aboard.

Claude flew six missions as ball turret gunner and the balance of his missions as waist gunner until war's end. His most memorable mission was a bombing raid on Dresden, Germany, when their formation was hit hard by anti-aircraft fire and attacked by Luftwaffe fighters causing the loss of many planes. Suspended under the belly of the B-17 in the ball turret Claude soon found that if he lined the bottom of the turret with flak suits it afforded him some measure of protection from the flak fragments exploding around him. He was still small enough and had plenty of room to maneuver and his visibility was not affected.

His most enduring memory is that of an English family with whom he has had a lifelong association since the war. His favorite pub in Mendlesham was "The Oak", a two-story home with the ground floor converted to a pub. It was better known to Claude and his crew as "Charlie's", after Charlie Huggins, the owner who lived with his family on the second floor. Many an hour was spent at Charlie's sharing provisions "requisitioned" from the base mess hall sergeant particularly butter and ground beef. At Charlie's they made hamburgers. He recalls when a crew member received a package of popcorn kernels from home. Of course this was taken to Charlie's and popped on the stove. The English, unfamiliar with popcorn, delighted in watching the sudden transformation from kernel to fluffy edible.

Claude was discharged from the Army Air Corps, November 23, 1945, at Sioux Falls, South Dakota. He had been awarded the Air Medal, ETO Ribbon and World War II Victory Medal. He was recalled during the Korean War and flew thirty-four missions as a B-29 top turret gunner.

The Conklins' have kept in constant touch with the Huggins family since the war, exchanging Christmas cards and family photos. Beginning in 1990, Claude and his wife have returned to Mendlesham on alternate years and the two families have been able to see each other's children grow as well as their children's children.

Claude returned to civilian life as a telephone installer/repairman for his area telephone company. He retired in 1988 and remains active in the American Legion, as a Board member of the 34th Bomb Group Association, the oldest Bomb Group in the Eighth Air Force, and helped restore an historic Skelly Service Station near Belle Plaine.

DONALD CONNELL, WATERLOO, IA, graduated from high school and enlisted in the Army Air Corps in November, 1942. After Basic Training at St Petersburg, Florida, where he was billeted in the Wigwam Hotel, Donald was sent to Aerial Gunnery School at Harlingen, Texas. He then graduated from Aircraft Mechanics School at Amarillo, Texas.

Donald had applied for pilot training under the Aviation Cadet Program and was to be sent to Sheppard Field, Wichita Falls, Texas. All Cadet's were automatically washed out of the program at that time and he was sent to Salt Lake City, Utah, for crew assignment. Donald trained with his crew at Rattlesnake Army Air Field, Pyote, Texas, before they picked up a new B-17 bomber in June, 1944, and flew to Valley, Wales.

Donald flew thirty-five combat missions in just forty-five days with the 91st Bomb Group as Flight Engineer and Top Turret Gunner aboard a B-17 named the "Yankee Belle". His first mission was on July 1, 1944. On numerous missions his aircraft returned to base on just three engines with numerous flak holes in the aircraft. On one mission two engines had been shot out and a third engine was not running properly. Hit at a high altitude they were able to drift back to England although they lost altitude steadily. Their brake system had also been shot out. Don's pilot made a landing at an emergency landing strip and stopped only after the airplane rolled off the end of the runway. No one was injured. Donald was on the same mission as his bunk mate, Bob Boice, also of Waterloo, when enemy fighters attacked their squadron and shot down seven or eight aircraft and riddled the remaining aircraft with machine gun and cannon fire. Don's aircraft had eighty-five holes in it but no casualties.

Donald's last mission was on October 15, 1944. He returned to the United States and attended a Gunnery Instructor's Course at Laredo, Texas. After reassignment to Sioux City, Iowa, he was then transferred to Pueblo, CO, for overseas training as part of a B-29 crew. The war ended and Donald returned to Sioux City for discharge from military service on September 15, 1945. He had been awarded, among other medals, the Distinguished Flying Cross and Air Medal with five oak leaf clusters.

Donald retired from Ruan Trucking Company as a Field Maintenance Manager.

CECIL E. COOPER, OTTUMWA, IA, graduated from Albia High School in May, 1942. He volunteered for the draft provided he would be assigned to the Army Air Corps. This was accepted and he was inducted and sent to Jefferson Barracks, MO where he said about all they did was march and drill. He subsequently wound up at Harlingen, TX for Aerial Gunnery School.

Cecil was deployed to England from Camp Kilmer, NJ aboard a Kaiser Victory ship and crossed the North Atlantic in a convoy of ships. He recalls the sea never seemed to be calm and the boat listed from to side and heaved from bow to stern causing most of those on board to become seasick. "Ropes were tied along walkways for grabbing onto to prevent being swept overboard. The only good part of the voyage was a contingent of Army nurses also aboard."

On arrival in England Cecil was assigned to the 392nd BG at Wendling. He flew five combat missions before being hit in the head by a piece of flak. Fortunately he was wearing a flak helmet but the concussion caused damage to his eyes which prevented him from further missions. The war was ending at this point and he was assigned to the 25th Communications Squadron and sent to Weisbaden, Germany, where he served as a courier escort and delivered classified documents.

Cecil met and married a German girl in June, 1948. He flew back to America on a B-24 through Iceland and Greenland sitting on a box in the bomb bay of the aircraft. After discharge from the military he joined the Air Force Reserve and secured a job with the Dexter Washing Machine Company at Fairfield, IA.

When the Korean War broke out Cecil received orders to report immediately to Champagne, IL for active duty. He had just settled into a new job and his wife was new to the United States. After spending one week in Champagne the need for recall to active duty was dismissed as unnecessary and he was able to return to civilian life in Fairfield. Cecil later worked for Morrell Meat Packing Company in Ottumwa until it closed in 1973 then became a foreman for a company rebuilding automobile air conditioners from which he retired.

DELMAR CORDERMAN, SAC CITY, IA, was farming prior to Japan's attack on Pearl Harbor, December 7, 1941. He enlisted in military service in January, 1942. After training at Sheppard Field, Texas, Delmar was sent to Wendover Field, Utah, for group assignment and staging prior to deployment overseas in August, 1942.

Delmar served as crew chief with the 368th Squadron of the 306th Bomb Group at Thurleigh, England.

As crew chief, Delmar was responsible that the plane(s)

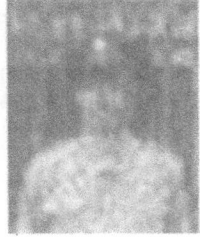

to which he was assigned were repaired after return from a mission, from bullet and flak holes to instruments, engines and all parts of the airplane's structure and operational needs. This meant he often had to work far into the night to ensure his airplane was ready for a mission the next day. Other aircraft too damaged for repair were scavenged for parts to fill needs of his aircraft. The air war couldn't have been waged without crew chiefs and ground personnel to keep the aircraft in a state of readiness. Flight crews couldn't fly a mission without them.

In September, 1945, at Ft. Sheridan, Illinois, Delmar received his discharge from the military but he continued his skills both as a mechanic and farmer in civilian life and eventually retired from both

Right - Delmar in center, waiting for mission aircraft to return to base.

MAURICE COX, DES MOINES, IA, enlisted in the Army Air Corps in October, 1942. He was sent to Randolph Field, San Antonio, Texas, to become an aircraft mechanic. He applied for the Aviation Cadet Program but failed the physical examination due to a stiff neck. He re-applied, passed the physical and attended college at Logan, Utah, under the College Training Detachment Program.

Maurice was sent to Santa Ana, California, for Pre-flight Training and Blythe, California, for Primary Flight Training. After Basic Flight Training he completed Advanced Flight Training at Pecos, Texas, and was awarded his pilot's wings and commission as a Second Lieutenant.

He did not receive Transition Flight Training to four engine aircraft and after reporting to Rapid City, South Dakota, for training with his newly assigned aircrew, Maurice had to learn to fly the B-17.

In 1944 Maurice and his crew flew the northern route to England and assignment with the 384th Bomb Group at Grafton Underwood. Maurice flew thirteen combat missions. The first two were as Co-pilot but switched positions with his pilot when the pilot suffered from vertigo.

During one mission to bomb targets at Munich, Germany, "the scariest moments were when the bomb bay doors were open". "I was always afraid of "flak" being shot at us hitting our bombs. We lost two engines due to "flak" and had to drop out of formation and try and get back to England. We threw everything we could out of the plane and got right down to ground level. We made it back to our base with both engines out on the right wing."

Maurice had high praise for the weather forecasters. "They were experts, never missed a prediction on missions I flew."

He flew his crew to Scotland for a three-day pass. "The wind was so bad at the airstrip I had to make three passes before I could land. General Eisenhower was at the airstrip in a C-47 and saw us landing. He said "I want to meet the pilot that landed that plane." When I got out of the plane he came up to me with congratulations and shook my hand. What a thrill."

After V-E Day, Maurice flew a General to Germany for an overnight trip. His B-17 was loaded with three kegs of beer which were brought back to his base. One keg was setup in his barracks. In another instance unlimited quantities of "free booze" was given to his crew. Two parachute bags were loaded with all they could hold and flown back to base. It was quickly consumed.

Maurice was sent to the 94th Bomb Group along with nine other planes manned with skeleton crews. They were to fly back to the United States in the aircraft. After spending the night at a local hotel they reported back to the base to find their aircraft was gone. They were told they would then become part of the occupation forces in Germany but instead returned to the United States.

He received his discharge from military service at Camp McCoy, Wisconsin in November, 1945, and had been awarded, among other medals, the Air Medal with one oak leaf cluster, European Theater of Operations and World War II Victory Medals.

Maurice was recalled to active duty during the Korean War from 1951 to 1953, and served at Bangor, Maine. He was one of the first seven officers in the newly formed Iowa Air National Guard and flew the C-47 cargo plane. He retired from Abild Construction Company in Des Moines as their General Superintendent after thirty-one years with the firm.

ROGER COX, DES MOINES, IA, worked as a teller in a St. Louis, Missouri, bank before America's entry into World War II. He then worked in a small arms defense plant until he was drafted into the Army Air Corps in August, 1942. Roger was sent to Jefferson Barracks, St. Louis, for Basic Training and then to Radio School at Madison, Wisconsin, where he learned maintenance of radio equipment.

Roger was then sent to Radar School at Boca Raton, Florida, before spending nine months at Columbia, South Carolina, on the IFF (Identification Friend or Foe) Box. In 1944, sometime after D-Day, he was deployed overseas from Boston, Massachusetts, to Liverpool, England. "We sailed on a converted cruise ship that followed a zig-zag course and made it to England in just a few days. It could outrun submarines. We were billeted down below on the ship with bunks seven high."

Roger was attached to Royal Air Force where he installed radar in their airplanes. The radar was supposed to divert V-2 rockets fired from Germany. "The rocket had four fins on the back. They were fired toward London. The RAF would take to the air and manipulate the radar to flip the fins, send them off course and hopefully into the English Channel."

He was then sent to the 453rd Bomb Group at Old Buckenham, England. Movie star, Jimmy Stewart was our Executive Officer. "I loaded "chaff" in airplanes. These were thousands of aluminum strips dropped from aircraft before the bomb run to confuse German radar operators. I also performed maintenance on aircraft radios that mal-functioned or had received battle damage."

Roger returned to the United States and was home on V-E Day, Victory in Europe.

After another duty assignment at Love Field, Dallas, he was sent to Scott Field, Illinois where he received his discharge from military service on October 26, 1945. He had been awarded the

European Theater of Operations and World War II Victory Medals, among others.

In civilian life, Roger owned and operated Cox Neon Signs before retirement.

Right - Roger in fatigues at 453rd BG

Right - Roger and his truck on the road to install radar in RAF aircraft.

EUGENE P. CRAWFORD, WINFIELD, IA, was married, had one child and farmed in the Winfield area until he was drafted into the Army Air Corps in May, 1945.

Following basic training, he was sent to Aviation Mechanics School in Amarillo, TX. Upon graduation he boarded a Liberty Ship for Europe. Phil was part of the occupation forces in Lechfeld, Germany where the 305th Bomb Group was involved in "Operation Casey Jones" conducting aerial photography of Europe and North Africa.

Phil was utilized as a mechanic and performed maintenance of facilities at a former Luftwaffe air base. Ground forces were utilized to protect the facilities and restore them to usable condition. As such he performed mechanical and carpenter duties, fulfilling needs of the base during occupation and in support of air crews. He was even utilized as a base bartender.

He returned to the United States in October, 1946, as a B-29 Super Fortress Mechanic until his discharge from military service.

HOWARD CRONER, ESTHERVILLE, IA, was in high school at the outbreak of World War II. He entered military service February 17, 1943, at Camp Dodge, Des Moines, Iowa.

After Basic Training at Miami Beach, Florida, Howard attended Aerial Gunnery School at Tindal Field, Panama City, Florida, Airplane Mechanics School at Sheppard Field, Wichita Falls, Texas, and Crew Training at Sioux City, Iowa.

In April, 1944, Howard was deployed to the 452nd Bomb Group at Deopham Green, England as Flight Engineer and top turret gunner. He flew thirty-four combat missions. In the Spring of 1944, with the Allies gaining air supremacy, planners turned their attention to bombing German oil producing plants which were numerous and widely dispersed. The goal was to deny oil to the German war machine and put their economy in chaos. During one such mission, a raid on Brux, Czechoslovakia, on May 12, 1944, ten of the fourteen B-17s in Howard's squadron were lost to enemy action. Their Group shot down thirty-nine of 100 enemy aircraft sent in the air against them. Howard was credited with one ME-109 destroyed.

On D-Day, June 6, 1944, as Howard flew in route to a target in France in support of the invasion, "I'll never forget the sight of thousands of navy shjips in the English Channel while we passed over them." Another mission, on June 26, 1944, in connection with Operation Frantic, Howard's Group was to bomb Ruhland, seventy-five miles south of Berlin. The distance back to their English base was too great to make with their fuel supply. Arrangements had been made with the Russians for Allied planes to land on their air bases near Kiev. Howard's Group was to fly on to Poltava, Russia. Unknown to them, a German plane shadowed the Group to their destination. Seventy-one bombers landed at Poltava and parked in the open around the air field. Just after ll:30 P.M., the Russians were notified German aircraft were en route toward Poltava. Air raid sirens wailed and the crews ran for the safety of slit trenches. At about midnight the German aircraft arrived and for one hour bombed and strafed the airfield with impunity. Very little anti-aircraft fire was directed at the German aircraft from the Russians. Russian night fighters took off to meet the Germans but no contact was ever made with them. After the raid it was found that forty-seven B-17s had been destroyed. Four hundred thousand gallons of fuel had gone up in flames and two Americans had been killed and six wounded. "No one who was there will ever forget that night on the Russian airfield."

On July 14, 1944, a mission called for dropping food and supplies to Freedom French Marquis who were assisting U.S. troops in Operation Anvil, the invasion of Southern France.

Howard received his discharge from military service on February 21, 1945. He had been awarded, among other medals, the Distinguished Flying Cross, Air Medal with two bronze stars and five oak leaf clusters, ETO Ribbon and World War II Victory Medal. In 1997 he received the Gold Medal from the French Embassy, Freedom Medallion from the French military and Russian Medal commemorating the Poltava affair.

Subsequent to World War II, Howard was a super market manager and professional salesman.

Right - Howard in flight gear

Right - Enlisted men of Howard's "Sack Tim Sioux" crew, 452nd BG, Deopham Green, England. Howard is top person in picture.

HOWARD CROPP, CEDAR RAPIDS, IA, was an Engineer for Iowa Manufacturing Company in Cedar Rapids and a member of the Air Corps Reserve prior to World War II. He was called to active duty February 3, 1942 and sent to Jefferson Barracks, St. Louis, Missouri, for Basic Training. Under the College Training Detachment Program he attended Beloit College in Wisconsin to take aviation related courses. He missed by one person from being sent to his native Cedar Rapids and Coe College for the training.

Howard was classified for pilot training at Santa Ana, California. He received his wings and commission as a Second Lieutenant in single pursuit aircraft at Luke Army Air Base, Arizona. He was then ordered to Randolph Field, Texas, as an instructor. He subsequently volunteered for co-pilot training and sent back to Luke Air Base. Howard was made an Intelligence Officer until re-assignment to Yuma, Arizona, for co-pilot training in C-46 cargo aircraft. He became a close friend of actor Gene Raymond, married to singer Jeanette McDonald who he met on several occasions.

Howard volunteered to fly the P-39 and P-63 fighters in simulated attacks on B-17 bomber crews in training. He was then sent to Biloxi, MS, where he was assigned to an aircrew and completed overseas training. Nearing the end of 1944 Howard and his crew were assigned a new B-17 bomber at Savannah, GA, and began their flight via Labrador and Iceland to Valley, Wales. Their aircraft was left there and Howard and his crew were trucked to the 401st Bomb Group at Deenethorpe, England.

Early in January, 1945, Howard flew his first combat mission, a bombing raid on Rouen, France. His thirty-fifth and last mission would also be to Rouen. He flew nineteen missions as Co-pilot before he took over as Pilot for his last sixteen missions. One raid was on Easter Sunday, 1945. The weather was cold and temperatures inside the aircraft required he talk to each crew member every fifteen minutes to make sure their oxygen masks had not frozen and they were still breathing normally. As they neared their target, the mission as cancelled at the last minute because of the religious holiday. The entire formation of bombers returned to their bases after their bomb loads were salvoed in the area of Great Britain known as "The Wash".

On occasion Howard saw white columns of smoke rising in the air from the direction of Germany. V-2 rockets had been launched toward England. While on a visit to London, Howard and some friends went shopping at a department store. They spent the night in a nearby hotel. Early the next morning a tremendous explosion rocked them from their beds. A V-2 rocket had hit the department store and "wiped out" the entire city block.

After V-E Day (Victory in Europe) Howard flew his ground crew on a tour of Germany and France to show them effects of Eighth Air Force bombing on Nazi occupied Europe. Another mission was flown to Linz, Austria, to bring English prisoners of war back to England.

Howard and his crew flew back to the United States via Iceland and Labrador to Boston. Howard reported to Jefferson Barracks, Missouri, and was transferred to Sioux Falls, South Dakota. He was then transferred to Long Beach, California, where he flew C-47 cargo aircraft in the Air Transport Command. His main duty was to give instrument checks to pilots. In November, 1945, he was transferred to Truax Field, Wisconsin for discharge. Howard had been awarded, among other medals, the Air Medal with oak leaf clusters, the ETO Ribbon with three battle stars and the World War II Victory Medal.

Howard returned to Iowa Manufacturing in Cedar Rapids and retired in 1982 after forty-one years service with the firm. He remained in the Air Force Reserve and retired twenty-six years later as a Lieutenant Colonel.

Right - Howard and crew at 401st BG, Deenethorpe, England. Howard, Pilot, is back row, third from the left.

WINFIELD DAHLGRAN, IOWA CITY, IA, worked for General Mills in Bemidji, MN, prior to World War II. He enlisted in the Army Air Corps in February, 1942, but wasn't ordered to report for duty until February, 1943. In the meantime he obtained his civilian pilot's license.

After flight training at Cuero, Waco and San Antonio, TX, Winfield received his wings and commission as a Second Lieutenant. He was assigned a crew at Salt Lake City, UT, and sent with the crew to Rattlesnake Air Base, Peyote, Texas where they trained in preparation for overseas deployment. They picked up a new B-17 at Grand Island, NE, and flew the northern route to Europe via Exeter, NH, Goose Bay, Labrador, and Nuts Corner, Ireland.

Assigned to the 447th Bomb Group at Rattlesden, England, Winfield flew thirty combat missions. Nearly half of those missions were flown as Lead Pilot for the Bomb Group and the majority of his missions were flown in a B-17 named "Old Scrap Iron".

His most memorable mission was a raid on the oil refinery at Hanover, Germany, where anti-aircraft fire was extremely intense. On the bomb run, the formation had to maintain a constant course and speed without evasive action. A "box barrage" thrown up by German guns required the Group fly directly through the barrage which made them extremely vulnerable to deadly "flak". The lead aircraft are especially targeted since all other bombers dropped their bombs when the leaders released theirs.

Winfield's missions included two to Berlin, two missions on D-Day in support of ground troops and a low-level mission in support of General Patton to bomb enemy troops and targets ahead of him. He was promoted to Captain in December, 1944.

Winfield returned to the United States aboard the "Queen Elizabeth" just before V-E Day. He received his military discharge at Miami, FL, having been awarded the Distinguished Flying Cross and the Air Medal with five oak leaf clusters. He returned to employment at General Mills from which he retired and subsequently moved to Iowa to be near his daughter.

He recalled an incident where his tail gunner fifty years after World War II passed out while driving a car. Taken to a hospital doctors discovered the cause to be a piece of shrapnel in his skull taken from "flak" during one of the missions fifty years earlier. He did not know at the time he was even wounded.

Right - Winfield and his crew at 447th BG, Rattlesden, England. Winfield is front row, left.

LOREN DARLING, WATERLOO, IA, worked as a farmer's hired hand at the time of America's entry into World War II. His mother died when he was nine years old. His father then abandoned Loren and four other siblings. Farm families in the Sac City, Iowa, area where they lived, took in the children and raised them as their own.

Loren enlisted in the Army Air Corps July 6, 1942, and was sent to Jefferson Barracks, St Louis, Missouri, for Basic Training. Additional training followed at Lin-

coln, NE, for Aircraft Mechanics; In-line Engines at Burbank, CA; Aerial Gunnery at Kingman, AZ, and Pyote, TX. He was assigned to an air crew as a waist gunner. His pilot, Robert Rosenthal, would fly fifty-two combat missions and become legendary in the annals of the Eighth Air Force. Their overseas training took place at Dyersburg, TN, where Loren met a girl who would eventually become his wife of fifty-four years.

Loren's crew was assigned a new B-17 bomber in October, 1943, and flew a northern route through Bangor, Maine; Greenland and Iceland to their eventual destination of Thorpe Abbotts, England and the 418th Squadron of the 100th Bomb Group. After a bombing mission to Bremen, Germany, where heavy losses were sustained by Allied bombers, and a lenghty mission to Marienburg in East Prussia, Loren's third mission came on October 10, 1943. The target was railroad marshalling yards at Munster, Germany. Over two hundred-fifty bombers were sent on the mission. Thirteen bombers were in Loren's squadron. Only one, his, would survive the mission. The other twelve would be shot down by enemy fighters.

As they neared their run on the target the bomber formations were attacked by over two hundred enemy fighters which shot rockets, cannon and machine gun fire at the bombers. The sky was filled with bombers on fire and falling to earth. Once over the target anti-aircraft flak also filled the sky with shrapnel that shredded bombers. A flak burst on the left side of Loren's aircraft wounded the left waist gunner with over eighty pieces of metal splinters. Loren as right waist gunner was thrown against the side of his aircraft by the explosion and had his jaw broken. He was also wounded in the head with over eighty metal fragments from the shell. Unknown to him at the time, his left hand also sustained a severe wound. Despite his injuries Loren continued to man his post firing at enemy fighters after the bomb run until the fighters broke off the action. The remaining planes of the 418th Squadron were also in danger of not making it back to their base. Two engines were shot out, they lost altitude and leaked fuel from flak hits in the wing. Loren received an emergency shot of morphine for his wounds and assisted other crew members in throwing out all equipment they could to reduce the weight of their aircraft. As they skimmed across the English Channel at water level they needed to regain altitude to avoid crashing into the White Cliffs of Dover. They were barely able to clear the Cliffs. As they did their aircraft brushed the tops of trees at cliff's edge. Heavy mists had settled in over the English countryside. Loren, now in the Co-Pilots seat assisted the Pilot in locating their base where they made a successful landing.

Loren's left gunner's mitten was filled with blood and he bled from head wounds. Both waist gunners were rushed to the base hospital for medical treatment. When the left mitten was taken off his hand, his thumb came with it. Doctors re-attached his thumb in what would prove to be a successful operation with full flexibility although limited gripping power. Metal fragments from the exploding shell were not totally removed from his head wounds. During rehabilitation Loren wore a magnetic cap that successfully drew out other metal splinters still imbedded in his head. His broken jaw was wired shut after four teeth on one side of his mouth were removed to allow him to be fed. For his actions in manning his guns while wounded and for helping the pilot Rosenthal locate their base in heavy fog, Loren was awarded the Purple Heart and Silver Star Medals. The Silver Star was pinned on him by Eighth Air Force Commanding General Curtis LeMay.

Loren returned to combat status two months later. His next mission came in December, 1943, a bombing raid on Bordeaux, France. In route to the target at high altitude and while the inside temperature of the aircraft was sixty degrees below zero, Loren's heated flight suit shorted out. He had only two choices, either bail out over enemy territory and be captured or stick with the aircraft and try to keep from freezing to death. He decided to remain with the aircraft. On return to base his legs were frozen. While in the base hospital gangrene began to set in and it was feared his legs would have to be amputated. A doctor assigned five nurses to rub Loren's legs with a medical salve on a 24-hour basis. Eventually color returned to his legs and he fully recovered. He could not wear Air Corps issued shoes because of the frostbite. He was given written permission to wear his flight boots for all occasions. Loren was awarded his second Purple Heart Medal. He no longer flew missions but remained at Thorpe Abbotts as a gunnery and mechanics instructor and taught aerial gunnery to RAF aircrews that were flying the B-17.

Loren returned to the United States aboard the "Queen Elizabeth" with an estimated 40,000 other American troops. He was sent to a military hospital in Florida for treatment of nightmares from combat. Upon discharge from military service he married the girl from Dyersburg, Tennessee, he had met during training there and who faithfully wrote him letters during his overseas tour.

Loren secured employment in Waterloo as a dock foreman for a motor freight company. He later purchased a freight line that picked up and delivered less than truck load shipments for other motor freight companies. Loren retired after twenty-eight years in that business. He was especially complimentary regarding the doctors and nurses of the 100th BG Medical Detachment and his pilot Robert Rosenthal. "They were the greatest".

Right - Loren and his crew at 100th BG, Thorpe Abbotts, England. They were the sole survivors from their Group from a 10/10/43 raid on Munster, Germany. Loren, waist gunner, back row, left, was seriously wounded on that raid. His pilot. Robert Rosenthal, front row, second from left, flew over 50 combat missions.

STANLEY V. DAVIDSON, AMES, IA, entered military service October 1, 1942. He was sent to Jefferson Barracks and Columbia, Missouri for induction training, then to San Antonio, Texas, for pre-flight training. Primary Flight Training was at Grider Field, Pine Bluff, Arkansas; Basic Flight Training, at Independence Army Air Field, Independence, Kansas and Advanced Twin Engine Training at Ellington Field, Houston, Texas. Overseas training and staging was at Rapid City Army Air Base, Rapid City, South Dakota.

Stan was deployed overseas on July 19, 1944, as a Co-pilot, with the 358th Bomb Squadron of the 303rd Bomb Group at Molesworth, England. After several weeks of additional flight training and ground instruction to prepare them for flight over enemy territory, Stan and his crew were assigned their first mission. Stan was left on the ground to allow an experienced pilot accompany the crew. From then on Stan would be one mission behind his crew.

On September 13, 1944, his fourth mission, was a bomb raid on synthetic oil plants near Meresberg, Germany, an important source of lubricants for the German armed forces. The industrial area was ringed with anti-aircraft guns equipped to determine Allied bomber's flight pattern and altitude with accuracy. Flak hit Stan's plane at 31,000 feet. Two engines were "knocked out" and controls cut to a third engine. As their aircraft lost altitude the crew stayed with the aircraft until they reached 3,000 feet near Oberhof, Germany. After the order was given to "bail out" only Stan and the First Pilot remained aboard. Then they bailed out. Stan does not recall seeing his pilot's chute open nor any other members of his crew descend in chutes.

Stan landed in a forested area. He quickly buried his parachute, pistol and other items he didn't want on himself if captured. He found a place to hide for the rest of the day and walked through the forest toward where he thought U.S. troops might be. At dawn he found another place to hide. That night, he walked west and came to a small village. He attempted to walk through the village but a night watchman stopped him and took him into custody. Stan spent the night in the village lockup. The next day German soldiers took him to an interrogation center where he was threatened with execution as a spy if he didn't answer their questions. After ten days of repeated questions wherein he gave only name, rank and serial number one interrogator told him "It makes no difference to us whether you answer our questions, we already know about you and your crew members." The man opened a book and proceeded to read the names of his crew members, where they were from, where they had been trained and the base to which they were assigned.

Stan was to learn that all his crew members had survived and taken prisoner of war except his First Pilot who died when his parachute failed to open.

Stan was sent by passenger train with two others of his crew to Stalag-Luft I, a Prisoner of War camp located near the town of Barth, Germany on a peninsula that stuck out into the Baltic Sea. The camp was divided into four compounds for prisoners, eight barracks to a compound. Each barrack was of rough lumber construction with no insulation, divided into several rooms with sixteen men to a room. The barracks were elevated off the ground two or three feet to permit guards and their dogs to check for attempts by prisoners to dig escape tunnels.

Their compound was surrounded by a double row of barbed wire fence twelve feet high with a space of 15-20 feet between the fences. Twenty-four tall guard towers surrounded the entire camp manned by guards armed with machine guns. Search lights were played over the camp during the night hours.

Stan's room was furnished with bunks, stacked three high, with wood slat bottoms and pads stuffed with straw for mattresses. He was issued two blankets but found it necessary to sleep in his clothes including shoes and socks to keep warm. Each room had a so-called stove made of bricks and a small ration of coal was given them each day.

One building in the compound housed the latrines and wash basins. Only cold water was available for washing and a limited amount of soap provided. Every three to four weeks prisoners in Stan's compound were marched to another compound for a warm water shower. Shaving with poor quality razors was an ordeal and many men didn't shave at all.

Food provided by the Germans consisted of potatoes, cabbage, ruabagas, black bread containing saw dust, imitation coffee and about once every two weeks a small amount of horse meat. Until late December, 1944, the prisoners received a Red Cross food parcel, one parcel for two men each week or ten days. These parcels contained foods of high nutrient value including canned Spam, canned dried milk, chocolate, oleo, jam, dried fruit, crackers and sometimes a can of coffee. The parcels saved many an Airman's life from the starvation diet provided by the Germans.

Monotony was a problem eased by books and a few musical instruments sent by the YMCA. Men who knew how to play the instruments gave programs for the camp. Prisoners with a college education conducted classes on a variety of subjects. From radios ingeniously assembled the prisoners were able to listen to news on progress of the war. By late April, 1945, guns of the Russian army could be heard in the distance. It wasn't long before the German guards disappeared and Russian troops arrived to liberate the camp.

On May 11, 1945, bombers and transport planes arrived to move the entire camp to France for medical and record processing, decent food, delousing, hot showers and new clothing. Stan was down to 115 pounds. On June 16, 1945, he boarded a Liberty Ship for the trip to America. After thirty days leave he reported to Miami Beach, Florida for more rest and recreation. While there Stan learned the war in the Pacific had ended. He received his discharge from military service on November 12, 1945, at Camp Blanding, Florida. He had been awarded the World War II Victory Medal, Northern France, Rhineland, Central Europe ribbon with three bronze stars and the ETO Ribbon.

Stan returned to Iowa to work at Iowa State University in their Cooperative Extension Service. He became a Central Staff member and retired in 1986 as an Associate Professor.

WARREN DEDRICKSON, CLARINDA, IA, worked as a hired farmhand before World War II. He enlisted in the Army Air Corps September 9, 1942 at Omaha, Nebraska.

Warren's training included stints at Lowry Field, Colorado; Sheppard Field, Texas; Tucson, Arizona; Alamorgordo, New Mexico and Aerial Gunnery School at Las Vegas, Nevada.

He was sent to the European Theater of Operations on February 10, 1944, as a tail gunner with the 466th Bomb Group at Attlebridge, England.

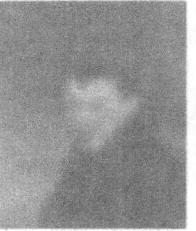 

Warren flew thirty-three combat missions beginning on March 22, 1944, with a bombing raid on Berlin. His twenty-third mission was on June 6, 1944, in support of the Allied invasion at Normandy, France. He was awestruck to see the largest invasion fleet ever assembled below him. "It was quite a sight to see."

His most memorable mission, was his last because it meant he would be rotated back to the United States. It was his tenth mission in a span of twenty-two days aboard the "Galloping Ghost", the name of his B-24 bomber.

Warren was discharged in October, 1945, at Denver, Colorado. He had been awarded, among other medals, the Distinguished Flying Cross and Air Medal with three oak leaf clusters. In civilian life Warren was employed for over twenty years as a rural mail carrier with the U.S. Postal Service.

EARNEST DEGAN, DES MOINES, IA, graduated from North High School in Des Moines in 1941. He enlisted in the Naval Air

Chapter Twenty-Two

 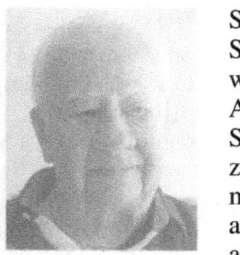

Corps and passed tests to become a Naval Cadet. He was sent to Cornell College, Mt. Vernon, Iowa, as part of the College Training Detachment Program but was later discharged from the Navy when he was disqualified from becoming a pilot. The Navy policy at the time was not re-assignment to another position but discharge from service.

Earnest tried to enlist in the Army Air Corps and was told "we don't need anybody but wait to be drafted". He was drafted in the Army Air Corps in November, 1943, and sent to Sheppard Field, Wichita Falls, Texas, for Basic Training. He then completed Aerial Gunnery School at Las Vegas, Nevada. Earnest was assigned to an aircrew and trained with them as a waist gunner at Rapid City, South Dakota, as a waist gunner. They then flew to Valley, Wales and eventual assignment with the 487t⁴ Bomb Group at Lavenham, England.

On November 14, 1944 Earnest flew the first of thirty-three combat mission to Koblenz, Germany. Missions were flown four straight days starting on December 18, 1944. His last mission was flown March 17, 1945. During a mission to Babenhausen, Germany, on Christmas Eve, 1944, his Bomb Group lost one whole squadron to enemy fighters. "An FW-190 German fighter flew alongside our plane. I fired bullets into him and it didn't seem to do any harm. He tipped the plane on its side exposing his underside and I kept firing but it still didn't' do anything. He just flew away. I can't explain it unless he had some special armor on the aircraft."

During one mission "we lost an engine from flak and it was on fire. Our tail gunner lost control and I had to wrestle him to the floor to keep him from jumping. We got the fire out by feathering the engine. Three bombs hung up in the bomb bay and I had to go into the bomb bay area and kick them free. I watched the bombs go down. It just happened that we were over a little German town and the bombs hit three houses in a row. I always wondered about what happened to the people in them."

"A German jet, the ME-262 once flew alongside our plane. We didn't know what it was. It didn't have a propeller. We never heard of jets. The pilot waved to us and flew off."

"Our crew was the only crew in our hut that made all their missions. We never got acquainted with other crews, never made friends with them, because we didn't want to lose friends. There was such a turnover in air crews."

After completion of his tour Earnest returned to the United States and was discharged from military service in October, 1945. He had been awarded the Air Medal with four oak leaf clusters, ETO Ribbon with one battle star and the World War II Victory Medal.

Earnest worked as a printer for Wallace Homestead and ended his career in sales with the firm. Wallace was purchased by American Broadcasting Company (ABC) which in turn was sold to Disney.

JOHN DELORBE, WATERLOO, IA, attended Loras College in Dubuque, Iowa, prior to America's entry into World War II. He dropped out of school and enlisted in the Army Air Corps in the early part of 1942. He had applied for the Aviation Cadet Program and was sent to San Antonio, Texas, for training. He washed out in Primary Flight Training and re-assigned to Radio School at Sioux Falls, South Dakota. This was followed by Aerial Gunnery School at Yuma, Arizona; crew assignment at Lincoln, NE, and overseas training at Dyersburg, TN.

In September, 1944, John and his crew picked up a new B-17 at Kearney, NE, and flew the northern route to England. Assigned to the 96th Bomb Group at Snetterton Heath, John flew thirty missions as Radio Operator. He maintained a log of all radio transmissions during missions and served as spotter. In his flight crew was a Flight Engineer/Top Turret Gunner who had flown fifty missions with the Ninth and Fifteenth Air Forces and volunteered for another thirty missions with the Eighth.

During one mission the hydraulic system on John's aircraft caught fire while over the North Sea. Although John couldn't swim he put on his parachute and entered the bomb bay area in preparation to abandon ship. He had not smelled anything on board the aircraft but when the bomb bay doors were opened the plane filled with smoke. The Flight Engineer was able to put out the fire and they returned to their base landing last because of no brakes.

On another mission, while on the bomb run, John looked out the window above him to see another B-17 out of formation and directly above them with the bomb bay doors open. Its whole salvo of bombs dropped between the front and rear wings of John's aircraft without striking them.

During a practice mission a P-51 pilot volunteered to make simulated attacks on their formation. When the pilot dove toward the bombers it clipped a B-17 tearing off one of the fighter's wings. It cart-wheeled to the ground killing the pilot

John returned to the United States in May, 1945, aboard a Victory Ship. The voyage was highlighted by a storm with deep wave troughs that would lift the rear of the ship out of the water. The ship's propellers would cause the ship to shudder each time they spun in open air. Nearly everyone on board was seasick.

John was awarded, among other medals, the Air Medal with four oak leaf clusters, ETO Ribbon and the World War II Victory Medal. After discharge from military service he returned to Waterloo to enter his families' clothing store business. He retired in 1985 turning the business over to his son.

EVERETT DEXTER, MARSHALLTOWN, IA, was still in high school when he enlisted in the Army Air Corps for the aviation Cadet Program. He was not called to active duty until he turned eighteen years old in the summer of 1944.

Everett was sent to Keesler Field, Mississippi. Because he lacked the education requirements for the Cadet Program and

there was an urgent need for aerial gunners, he was sent to Laredo, Texas, for Aerial Gunnery School. After training he was sent to Westover, MA, for crew assignment and overseas training at Savannah, GA. On October 16, 1944, Everett and his crew picked up a new B-24 Liberator bomber at Mitchell Field, NY. They flew from Bangor, ME, to Stone, England through Goose Bay,

Iowans of the Mighty Eighth

Labrador, and Iceland. At Stone their aircraft was taken from them and they proceeded by train to Cheddington, home of the 406th Squadron.

The 406th was a Night Leaflet Squadron that flew older B-17 and B-24 model bombers filled with propaganda leaflets. Each of twelve aircraft assigned to the Squadron flew alone at night over Axis territory and dropped the leaflets at assigned locations. The leaflets were worded to try and convince enemy troops to surrender. In return the soldiers were promised humane treatment.

Everett flew forty-one missions. He could not recall being attacked by enemy fighters or fired upon by anti-aircraft batteries. Rarely would the Luftwaffe be scrambled to attack a single aircraft, particularly at night. When they left their base at dusk Everett and his crew would reach the European coast at night. On three consecutive missions engine malfunctions required they make emergency landings at other allied airstrips. On another mission two engines were lost due to malfunction. Their B-24 was too heavy to maintain altitude and they landed at Lille, France, now in Allied hands. They were billeted at a local hotel, complete with their own dining room until their aircraft was repaired. During the Battle of the Bulge, Everett flew missions on seven consecutive nights.

One night in route to a target over Germany, Everett's pilot suddenly found his aircraft in the middle of a British formation flying to their target. To avoid mid-air collision, the pilot turned on all of his aircraft's lights and made his way out of the formation.

The night leaflet squadron dropped nearly 1.5 million pounds of leaflets over Axis territory during 2,300 sorties. They lost three aircraft to enemy action and was credited with three enemy aircraft shot down. During a single mission each aircraft may be designated to drop leaflets at as many as five different locations.

Two hundred-fifty hours were required for a tour of duty. Everett's last mission was flown March 10, 1945. He sailed back to America aboard a hospital ship and assisted the medical staff tend to wounded GIs aboard. While on furlough the war in Europe ended. Everett was sent to Fort Myers, FL, for B-29 training and while there the war ended in the Pacific.

Everett received his discharge from military service in October, 1945. He had been awarded the Air Medal with oak leaf clusters, ETO Ribbon and WWII Victory Medal.

After the war he farmed in the Marshalltown area until retirement.

Right - Everett and his crew at the 406th Night Leaflet Squadron, one of the Mighty Eighth's Secret Squadrons, Cheddington, England. Everett is back row, second from left.

LYLE DIRKS, OCHEYEDEN, IA, quit school when he was fourteen years old to help on the family farm. He was drafted into the U.S. Army in July, 1942 and completed Basic Training with a Heavy Weapons outfit. Due to the need for pilots in the Army Air Corps he successfully passed examinations to enter the Aviation Cadet Program. He completed Pre-Flight Training at Santa Ana, California, Primary Flight Training at Thunderbird II Air Base near Phoenix, Arizona and Basic Flight Training at Marana, Arizona. Upon completion of Advanced Flight Training

at Douglas, Arizona, on August 30, 1943, Lyle was awarded his pilot's wings and commission as a Second Lieutenant. Transition Flight training to four engine aircraft was taken at Roswell, New Mexico.

Lyle was then sent to Salt Lake City, Utah, where he was assigned an air crew and trained with them at Sioux City, Iowa, in preparation for overseas deployment. Lyle and his crew picked up a new aircraft at Kearney, Nebraska and flew to Prestwick, Scotland where the airplane was taken from them. They were transported to Stone, England, a replacement center where they were assigned to the 379th Bomb Group at Kimbollton, England.

Lyle flew thirty combat missions in a very short time span. His first mission was on April 10, 1944, to bomb a Nazi airstrip at Brussells, Belgium. His final mission was to Bremen, Germany, on June 21, 1944. "Every mission was an easy one, if you get home alive." During one mission he flew a bomber usually reserved for his commanding officer. Plexi-glass windows in the front of the aircraft were of abnormal thickness for protection. During the mission a piece of shrapnel from "flak" struck the windshield in front of Lyle and failed to enter the aircraft. "Normal plexi-glass would have been broken and I wouldn't be here now."

During a May 13, 1944 mission to Settin, Germany, his thirteenth mission, "we got attacked by 80-100 German fighters. We lost three out of twenty aircraft but our Group's gunners shot down several Germans. We bombed the target with PFF Equipment (radar).

At the completion of his tour Lyle returned to the United States by flying home a war-weary B-17 bomber. He was assigned to Gulfport, Mississippi as a Combat Crew Pilot Instructor until the end of the war. He was also "checked out" on the newer B-29 bomber as an instructor. In September, 1945, Lyle received his discharge from military service at Jefferson Barracks, St. Louis, Missouri. He had been awarded the Distinguished Flying Cross, Air Medal with four oak leaf clusters, the European Theater of Operations Medal with two battle stars, and the World War II Victory Medal.

Lyle served in the Iowa Air National Guard and farmed for eight years before entering the carpentry business from which he has retired.

ROBERT DOUGHERTY, FORT MADISON, IA, graduated from high school in 1942 and worked at Shaeffer Pen Company in Fort Madison until he enlisted in the Aviation Cadet Program(ACP) of the Army Air Corps. During his enlistment physical examination at Camp Dodge, Iowa, it was discovered his eyesight was not 20/20 and disqualified him from Pilot, Navigator or Bombardier training. He was told there was a newly established ground cadet program for which he was qualified and was entered in that program. He first completed Basic Training at Kerns, Utah.

Chapter Twenty-Two

Robert was sent to Lincoln, Nebraska, where he was assigned to attend the University of Iowa at Iowa City, Iowa. and take courses in meteorology. He remained at the University for one year. He learned eyesight requirements in the Aviation Cadet Program had been lowered and he re-applied. At Jefferson Barracks, St. Louis, Missouri, he passed physical and written examinations for the ACP and was scheduled to go before the Cadet Board when he received shipping orders for Aerial Gunnery School at Las Vegas, Nevada.

While at gunnery school he went before the Cadet Board and was told aerial gunnery was a pre-requisite to become either a Navigator or Bombardier. After he completed training he was sent to Salt Lake City, Utah for crew assignment. While there he again inquired regarding his application for the ACP. "This time they listened." Robert was sent to Buckley Field, Colorado to re-test for the ACP. During testing a telegram arrived at the airfield that all applicants for the ACP from technical schools were to be eliminated from consideration. Robert then attended Armaments School at Lowry Field, Colorado. Upon completion of training he was assigned to an aircrew at Ardmore, Oklahoma and trained with them there in preparation for overseas deployment.

In June, 1944, Robert was sent by troop train to Camp Kilmer, New Jersey where he boarded the ship "Mauritania" for a seven day voyage to Liverpool, England. "There was fifteen thousand of us on board ship. When I went on board I was carrying my trombone in its case with all my military gear. A guy stopped me and asked if that was a trombone I was carrying. As it turned out there were USO entertainers on board ship to entertain the troops. They needed a band to accompany them with their music. We made up a band from guys on board and played all the way over to England in the officer's lounge of the ship. The good part was we could eat meals at any time instead of the two meals a day for everyone else."

At Stone, England, Robert was assigned to the 92nd Bomb Group at Podington, England. "My first night at the base I filled in with the base band "The Skyliners" for a trombone player who had gotten sick." Robert flew thirty-five combat missions as a ball turret gunner. When not flying missions he was a regular member of the "Skyliners" playing at local and area dances.

Robert's most memorable mission was to bomb targets at Bremen, Germany. "Flak" knocked out our number three engine. We lost speed and altitude and dropped out of formation. Then "flak" got our number four engine. We lost more altitude and speed and were all alone. Four German Focke-Wolfe fighters flew alongside us just out of machine gun range evidently looking over their "sitting duck". To make things worse none of our machine guns worked. They were froze probably because we lost altitude so fast condensation on the guns froze. We tracked them with our guns anyway. When all hope for survival seemed to be lost, suddenly, ten American P-51 fighters appeared and drove the enemy fighters away."

Robert flew his last combat mission on February 1, 1945. His commanding officer was able to convince Robert to stay on at the base and play in the band for morale building purposes. "We played all over England, France, and North Africa. I didn't get to come home until November 1, 1945, and that was aboard the "Lake Champlain" an aircraft carrier converted into a transport ship. There were only fifteen hundred of us on the trip home."

Robert received his discharge in November, 1945, at Jefferson Barracks, Missouri. He had been awarded the Air Medal with three oak leaf clusters, European Theater of Operations Medal with four battle stars and the World War II Victory Medal, among others. In civilian life Robert retired after forty years as an auto parts manager.

Right - Robert and "The Skyliners", 92nd BG, Podington. Robert is trombone player in back, second from left.

Right - Robert, second from right, front row, at 92nd BG, Podington

GILBERT DOUGLASS, STORM LAKE, IA, enlisted in the Army Air Corps in January, 1942. He had completed civilian pilot training prior to entry into military service and had earned his private pilot's license.

After Basic Training, Aircraft Engine School at Sacramento, California, and Armaments School at Lowry Field, Colorado, he was assigned to Martin Aircraft Company at Baltimore, Maryland, where he performed flight testing on the B-26 Marauder bomber. "We would lose about a plane a day." The B-26 became known as "The Widow Maker" due to its high rate of crashes. "A design problem was found in the flaps. The plane had to come in to land "hot" and couldn't be slowed down like normal aircraft."

In early 1943 Gilbert was sent to the European Theater of Operations assigned to Base Air Depot #2 at Burtonwood, England. "We furnished 90 per cent of all engines to the Eighth Air Force. We had a nine cylinder and an eighteen cyclinder line doing overhauls on engines. I worked on the eighteen cylinder line."

After the end of World War II, Gilbert returned to work in the families' clothing store at Storm Lake which had been in business locally for seventy-two years.

MERLIN DYVIG, HUMBOLDT, IA, graduated from high school in the Spring of 1942. He enlisted in the Army Air Corps in 1943 and sent to Jefferson Barracks, St. Louis, Missouri for Basic Training. He applied for and was accepted for the Aviation Cadet Program but was withdrawn from training because of excessive numbers of cadets already in training and Air Corps demands for other operational needs.

Merlin was sent to Las Vegas, Nevada, for Aerial Gunnery School. Upon completion of training he was assigned to an aircrew at Lincoln, Nebraska, and trained with them at Sioux City, Iowa, for overseas deployment.

In July, 1944, Merlin and his crew picked up a new B-17 bomber at Lincoln, Nebraska and flew to Nutts Corner, Ireland where they received additional training before they reported to the 95th Bomb Group at Horham, England.

Merlin flew ten combat missions as aerial gunner. His ninth mission was on November 2, 1944, a raid on Merseburg, Germany's synthetic fuel plants. "We got back all shot up". Three days later, his tenth mission, the target was Wilhelmshaven, Germany. "We took two direct hits in the left wing and one in the right wing. We were trying to make it to France, but we were leaking fuel and one engine caught on fire. All of us except the Pilot and Navigator bailed out. The engine that was on fire I learned later fell off the aircraft and the pilot and navigator were able to make a forced landing behind Allied lines."

Merlin bailed out of the stricken bomber at twenty-six thousand feet and free fell "for what seemed a half a day" before he pulled the ripcord on his parachute. He remembers "it was quiet, peaceful. You don't realize you are falling until you see the ground coming up at you." When the parachute opened "it was like hitting a brick wall." He lit in the middle of a German anti-aircraft battery and immediately taken prisoner of war. Other crew members were not so fortunate. Merlin learned his Co-Pilot was hung by German civilians who were also about to hang one of his other crewmembers when he was rescued by German military. Crewmembers suffered beatings at the hands of civilians until they also, were rescued by German soldiers.

"The Germans that took me prisoner were very hostile. Fortunately an American P-51 fighter followed me down and circled a few times. The Germans were terrified of that airplane. He finally waggled his wings on a pass and flew off. I always carried six packages of cigarettes with me. I took them out and passed them around to the German troops and things got better."

Merlin was taken to Frankfurt, Germany for interrogation. "They knew all about me and our bomb group. We arrived in the middle of an air raid. A guard took four of us into a bomb shelter. He kicked out some civilians so we could lay down. The civilians were going to attack us so the guard gave us a gun to protect ourselves. Our radio operator spoke a little German and he kept us aware of what was going on and what the civilians were saying. In fact he told me I might be in trouble because they though I was Jewish. After the air raid the guard took us to a restaurant and bought us sausage sandwiches and beer."

Merlin was loaded into a 40 and 8 railroad box car with other prisoners of war for shipment to Stalag Luft IV. "The trip seemed like it took an eternity because of Allied bombings and strafings." The camp consisted of compounds. Each compound had ten barracks. Each barracks had ten rooms. Each room housed as many as twenty-four to fifty prisoners. "I slept in a German burial bag filled with shredded paper. Each POW had two blankets, one German and one American. Each prisoner had a bowl buddy. Two men would share one bowl of food. We had one knife and two spoons between us. Food was usually soup of either beans, turnips or potatoes that were all filled with worms. We would let the soup settle and the worms would float to the top so we could skim them off. After awhile we realized we were missing nutrients so we started eating the worms too. What meat there was, was dog meat. It came already butchered. We got a pitcher of hot water each day. If it hadn't been for the Red Cross parcels a lot of us wouldn't have made it. I got trench mouth and lost my teeth."

In the middle of winter, 1944, Russian troops advanced on the German Army and were within miles of the prison camp. The Germans, to avoid capture by the Russians, evacuated the camp and forced the prisoners to go with them. The result was a forced march of eighty-two days with only food that could be foraged or bartered from farmers on the route.

Merlin was evacuated in advance of that march. He and others were marched for a week to reach a train that was to take them to Nurnberg. They were herded into box cars and rode for fifteen days without food and only a half cup of water a day. The trip lasted longer than normal because Allied aircraft bombed railroad tracks ahead and behind them. At one stop, in the rain, a trainload of Russian women prisoners brought them water.

"In the Spring they marched us from Nurnberg to Moosburg. Everyone had frozen feet. The Americans were closing in and then on April 29, 1945, General Patton's tank broke down the front gate to the camp and entered the compound. We were free. A skinny guy climbed the flag pole at the camp and tore down the German swastika flag and put up an American flag. There wasn't a dry eye in the place. We waited around for eight days for American troops to arrive. We opened a warehouse and found Red Cross parcels being stored there by the Germans that they didn't distribute to us. Then C-47s flew in and took us to Brussels, Belgium."

Merlin then rode a train to Camp Lucky Strike near Le Havre, France. "When I was captured I weighed 185 pounds. When liberated I was down to 127 pounds." On June 10, 1945, Merlin arrived back in the United States. After a ninety-day furlough he received his discharge from military service at San Antonio in November, 1945. He had been awarded the Air Medal with oak leaf cluster, ETO Ribbon and the World War II Victory Medal, among others. Merlin returned to Iowa and farmed until his retirement.

An unusual story occurred regarding a Hamilton wrist watch given him by his parents when he graduated from high school. When he was taken prisoner of war, a German soldier took the watch from him. When riding in a car with a German officer to his next detention point the officer inquired if he had been treated right and if the soldiers had taken anything from him. He mentioned the watch whereupon the officer turned the car around, returned to the German troops and recovered his watch for him. Later, at the POW camp the watch was again taken from him but returned after two weeks. His bowl buddy traded his own watch for food on the march but wouldn't let Merlin do the same because it was a gift from his parents.

"The best thing that ever happened to me was being captured and in a prisoner of war camp. No matter had bad things may get in life it will never be as bad as that."

DONALD EASTWOOD, RED OAK, IA, helped on the family farm until he was drafted into the Army Air Corps on August 27, 1942. After Basic Training at Jefferson Barracks, St. Louis, Missouri, Don attended a technical school on aircraft mechanics at Lincoln, Nebraska before he was sent to Boeing Aircraft Factory at Seattle, Washington for schooling on the B-17 bomber.

After assignment to a bomb group at Salt Lake City, Utah, Don worked on the flight line where he maintained aircraft at Walla Walla, Washington, and Rapid City, South Dakota, for aircrews in overseas combat training.

Don boarded the ocean liner "Queen Elizabeth" on January 1, 1944 along with fifteen thousand other American troops for

Glasgow, Scotland. "We slept on the deck of the ship because all other space was filled." From Glasgow Don took a train to Deopham Green, England and the 452nd Bomb Group.

Although never officially given the title, Don served as a crew chief with two mechanics under his supervision. He was assigned to maintain one aircraft in combat readiness. This included the aircraft's engines, oxygen and hydraulics systems, some structural repair, gas tanks, and tires. During his tour Don went through five aircrews and aircraft that either finished their required number of missions or failed to return from missions. Although considered major structural repair and normally performed by other specialists, Don and his crew did change one wing on one of his aircraft that crashed on takeoff due to a faulty pulley.

Don was awarded a meritorious citation for having aircraft under his maintenance control fly fifty-eight straight missions without a mechanical abort. One aircraft assigned to him was a B-17 named "Johnny Reb" whose crew finished thirty missions. The plane was shot down when flown by another crew. The crew was captured and taken prisoner of war. The pilot recognized one of his captors, a German SS officer, as a person who frequented a New York ice cream parlor before the war. He tried to persuade the pilot to switch sides. The German told the pilot that when the war was over he would get back to New York sooner than the pilot. He did.

In July, 1945, Don flew back to the United States and after furlough reported to Sioux Falls, South Dakota for discharge from military service on September 20, 1945. Don returned to Iowa to farm for eleven years before he accepted employment with Iowa Department of Transportation maintenance at Red Oak. After twenty-seven years with the State, he retired in 1983 and resumed farming until he retired again.

LEROY EDWARDS, MOUNT PLEASANT, IA, farmed prior to World War II. He enlisted into military service after the Japanese attacked Pearl Harbor. Called to duty in January, 1942, at Fort Leavenworth, KS, he was sent to Miami Beach, FL for Basic Training and Aerial Gunnery at Harlingen, TX. Leroy was then sent to the College Training Detachment at Iowa Wesleyan College in Mount Pleasant.

From there he entered the Aviation Cadet Program at Santa Ana, CA, where the top ten per cent were slated for pilot training. Leroy was sent to Aviation Mechanics School at Amarillo, TX. Upon graduation he was sent to Drew Field, Tampa, FL for crew assignment and training.

On July 9, 1944 he boarded a troop ship at Camp Kilmer, NJ with fifteen thousand other soldiers for a ten day zig-zag trip to Scotland. Spike Jones and his City Slickers were aboard the ship and provided constant entertainment for the troops.

On July 28, 1944, Leroy arrived at Thorpe Abbotts and the 100th Bomb Group. He had originally been slated to be in the 94th Bomb Group but the 100th had lost so many aircrews he was re-assigned to them.

Leroy flew thirty-four combat missions as top turret gunner and made emergency repairs on wiring, fuel and hydraulic systems. One mission was an eleven hour flight. Storms were over their intended target of Bolin. Chemnitz, Germany, was their alternate target. " We got hit and lost one engine. Coming back we had to put down near Rochester, England. There were 300 to 500 foot hills in the area and we were skimming the tops of them. Trying to make a final approach we lost another engine. The pilot picked out a wheat field on slanted ground. We landed and slid on wet ground. The remaining gas didn't explode but the navigator was trapped in the airplane. We had to kick out the plexiglass nose of the plane to get him free. The prop from number three engine in landing had cut through the side of the plane and put a big gash in his head. We were put up in a hotel until our base personnel came to get us. Wearing only our grubby flight clothes we had free drinks at the hotel, free rooms and even went to a free dance."

On a February 3, 1945, raid on Berlin the bombers were to have five groups of P-51 Mustangs as escort. They were to expect heavy flak from an estimated 1700 anti-aircraft guns in the area. They went to the target on a jet stream at about 345 miles per hour. As a result German guns miscalculated and were firing barrages that exploded five hundred yards behind them. "But they caught up with us on the bomb run and the return trip when the wind reduced us to a ground speed of fifty miles per hour. Four planes in our squadron were shot down. One plane was hit in the wing and sheared it off. The wing buckled back over the plane. It slid downward below us. I doubt if anyone got out. There were airplanes all over the sky. We had all approached the target on about six or seven different angles. Each group was expected over the target just minutes apart, so we had to be on time. I was astonished to see so many planes. There were four other Bomb Groups with us. "Rosie's Riveters" plane was hit. They jumped. The pilot floated twenty-three miles in his parachute to land behind Russian lines. We discovered we had one bomb that didn't release. I went into the bomb bay area with no parachute, took off my oxygen mask and kicked it loose."

Leroy's last mission with the 100th was on March 4, 1945. He was on a boat sailing back to the United States when news came that President Roosevelt had died. He arrived in America on April 14, 1945, and was sent to Randolph Field, San Antonio, TX assigned as a crew chief over B-29 mechanics until he was discharged from the military September 30, 1945. Leroy earned the Air Medal with four oak leaf clusters, the World War II Victory and European Theater of Operations Medals.

BYRL ELLIOTT, CHEROKEE, IA, farmed with his father at the start of World War II. He entered military service in June, 1942, at Ft. Des Moines, IA.

Byrl was initially sent to Ft. Leavenworth, Kansas, in July, 1942 then on to Sheppard Field at Wichita Falls, Texas on July 26. After four months he was re-assigned to Chanute Field, Illinois, for further training before transfer to MacDill Field, Tampa, Florida on January 29, 1943. In August, 1943, he boarded the "Queen Elizabeth" ocean liner for Scotland. On arrival he went by train to East Wretham, a Royal Air Force heavy bomber base and repair depot. On September, 5, 1943, Byrl was re-assigned as an instrument specialist with the 356th Fighter Group at Martlesham Heath.

The Fighter Group was comprised of three squadron s of P-47 Thunderbolts that provided bomber escort and fighter sweep duties. As Allied bombing raids penetrated further into Germany, belly tanks on the planes increased in size to accompany the bombers as far as possible. As Axis fighters became less a threat, 1000 pound bombs were mounted under the belly of the P-47 or 500 pound bombs under the wings. Eventually rocket tubes were mounted under the wings for ground targets.

Shortly after Byrl's arrival at the base, the German Luftwaffe "welcomed" the new occupants of the base to a night incendiary bombing raid. Byrl and two friends had bicycled into the English town of Ipswich just three miles from the base. They started back to the base after the "all clear" had sounded. Shortly after they left town, they began to have trouble keeping their bicycles upright. The roadway was bumpier than when they had traveled down it in daylight. The closer they got to base the bumper the road got. Could it have been the warm English beer they had consumed? The explanation was clear as soon as the sun rose and clean-up from the raid began. The "bumps" they were riding over were anti-personnel bombs, about the size of a can of Prince Albert pipe tobacco. Every one they hit was a dud. American intelligence personnel theorized the bombs had been made in Occupied Europe by forced labor. After examination, the bombs were found to be missing the triggering device. Three very relieved, but shook-up Americans really enjoyed that English sunrise.

Buzz bomb and fighter attacks occurred frequently from June through November, 1944. Buzz bombs with rocket engines were launched from their German sites with only fuel sufficient to make it to England. The bombs were directed toward England and drifted to earth to explode when it ran out of fuel. While many exploded harmlessly in the English countryside, some found their way to London and other cities. Byrl recalled many directly over his base, sometimes only 50 feet off the ground. Many were shot down by fighter aircraft and anti-aircraft gunners. On October 18, 1944, Byrl noted that twenty-nine were shot down that day, but three got through unscathed. One landed near his base and damaged a hangar. Another, on October 25 exploded 300 yards from his Nissen hut, damaged other huts and knocked Byrl off the bicycle he was riding at the time. Nine men were hurt when another bomb exploded within the base.

Other unexplained explosions occurred on or near the base. German V-2 rockets launched from Peenemunde, Germany, made no noise until they hit the ground and caused a terrific explosion. If spotted in the air, fighter aircraft were not fast enough to shoot them down. One fighter, Byrl noted, was able to photograph a V-2 through his gun camera.

On November 5, 1944, the three fighter squadrons of the 356th changed from flying the P-47 to the P-51 Mustang. Soon, 120 P-51s would occupy the base. Shortly thereafter Byrl was transferred to the 305th Bomb Group at Chelveston and then to the 306th Bomb Group at Thurleigh as a B-17 waist gunner.

Byrl noted in a dairy entry dated September 3, 1944, that he felt the end of the war in Europe was getting close. It would still take eight month months before victory was won in Europe. In January, 1946, as a Staff Sergeant, Byrl received his military discharge at New York City. He had been awarded the World War II Victory Medal, ETO Ribbon and a Distinguished United Citation while with the 356th Fighter Group for their participation in Operation Market Garden, the airborne invasion near Arnhem, in The Netherlands.

After the war Byrl was employed with a commercial painting contractor until 1949 when he started his own painting business. He quit painting in 1960 and bought a farm just _ mile from where he grew up. Byrl retired in 1984 and died in 1997 after a short illness. Information for this biography and a portion of the chapter Base Life came from a World War II diary maintained by Byrl.

Right - Elliot at plane 03-P-47 "Angel" of the 356th FG, Martlesham, England. Byrl, Instrument Specialist, is on the left.

THOMAS J ESTES, AURELIA, IA, worked for his father in a furniture store in South Carolina. Prior to America's entry into World War II, he enlisted in the Royal Canadian Air Force at Toronto, Ontario, Canada. He took Primary Flight Training at Windsor, Ontario, and Advanced Flight Training in an AT-6 Texan aircraft at Aylmer, Ontario, with hopes of becoming a

fighter pilot. After the Japanese attack on Pearl Harbor, December 7, 1941, he returned to the United States and enlisted in the American Army Air Corps.

Tom was sent to Sumter, South Carolina, for Basic Flight Training and Turner Field, Albany, Georgia, for Twin-engine Training. Four-engine training on the B-17 Flying Fortress was completed at Hendricks Field, Sebring, Florida. His dreams of becoming a fighter pilot were ended. Tom would eventually fly every model of the B-17.

On October 9, 1942, Tom received his wings and commission as a Second Lieutenant. He was posted to Boise, Idaho, where he met his combat crew and began training for overseas deployment. The 384th Bombardment Group was activated at Boise with further training at Wendover, Utah and Sioux City, Iowa. In late May, 1943, Tom and his crew picked up a newly assigned B-17 at Kearney, Nebraska, and began their flight to England. His route took him through Bangor, Maine, and Goose Bay, Labrador, to Grafton Underwood, England.

The 384th Bomb Group flew their first combat mission on June 22, 1943, against industrial areas in Antwerp, Belgium. They would continue to fly 314 missions during the war including the last mission of World War II against airfields and other military installations in southeastern Germany and Czechoslovakia on April 25, 1945. The Group received two Distinguished Unit Citations for an air strikes against aircraft production plants in Germany on January 11, and April 24, 1944.

Tom's B-17 was named "Wearie Willie". The last week of July, 1943, known as Blitz Week, saw Eighth Air Force bombers on their heaviest raids of the war on Germany. The Royal Air Force had struck at Hamburg, Germany, the night of July 24 and dropped "chaff", aluminum foil strips, to confuse Nazi radar that controlled both anti-aircraft guns and night fighters. Americans were to strike Hamburg the next day, Tom's sixth trip into combat.

Six bomb groups were assigned the mission. Three Groups were to bomb the Blohm and Voss U-Boat Yards and three groups were assigned the Klockner airplane engine factory. In route to the target thirteen planes returned to base due to mechanical problems leaving a force of 112 bombers to finish the mission. Each plane carried 1,850 gallons of fuel and was loaded with ten-500 pound bombs if they flew in the high or lead position or sixteen 250-pound incendiaries if in the low position. Tom's Combat Wing was on time for take-off and assembly. The Wing destined for the Klockner factory was late and not assembled in proper formation.

Meanwhile a diversionary force of two Combat Wings (six bomb groups) bound for Warnemunde and Kiel, Germany, were supposedly forty minutes ahead of the Hamburg groups. One combat wing however, did not complete its assembly before it headed for Germany and the entire group returned to their bases. This left one Wing that was attacked by Luftwaffe fighters. One Nazi plane shot was claimed as shot down against no American losses. German fighters returned to their base, refueled and re-armed at the time the Hamburg-bound groups crossed the German coast. This afforded them an excellent opportunity to get through to their target without serious enemy fighter opposition. They knew the return trip home would be a different matter.

Anti-aircraft guns fired barrages as Tom's crew crossed the coast of Germany at Cuxhaven. Several B-17s were hit and began to lag in the formation or turn back to England. Messerschmitt ME 109s attacked them armed with 20 mm. cannon under their wings. Two attacks were made but failed to break up the bomber formation. Two B-17s were damaged and crashed.

Their IP (initial point) was the village of Hollenstadt from where they would commence the bomb run. It was then they saw Hamburg still burning with a huge pall of smoke from the RAF attack of the night before. Anti-aircraft batteries cut loose again, firing box barrages the B-17s had to fly through. "It was the densest flak we'd ever flown through" Tom recalled. Smoke covered the shipyard they were to bomb but the bombs were dropped as accurately as they could. They were over the target four minutes then veered to the East to avoid further flak. The Combat Wing late for the aircraft factory target caused the American bombing to last for twelve minutes, six minutes longer than planned and unnecessarily exposed them to heavier concentrations of enemy fire. The Germans were able to fire on each Wing individually rather than deal with both Wings at the same time.

Seventy-eight of the 109 airplanes that flew in formation over Hamburg suffered some sort of flak damage. Many had engines or vital control surfaces damaged and fell back out of formation. At the rally point twenty-five miles east of Hamburg the six bomb groups began their return to England. This is where the German fighters hit them with orders to pursue them as far as their fuel would allow. While they were over the North Sea a second attack was to be mounted by German twin-engine night fighters from Holland.

Eleven B-17s dropped out of formation. Ten were shot down, four being from Tom's squadron of seven. "Wearie Willie" was the next loss. Two gun positions were out of ammunition. The gunners remained at their posts and continued to track their attackers with empty guns. Two ME-109s and a Focke-Wulf-190 chased them sixty-five miles off the German coast. With three engines out and other major damage, Tom brought his B-17 onto a smooth surfaced North Sea. "I leveled off about 20 feet above the water and told the Good Lord that he had control and the Good Lord sure made a wonderful landing. It was not a very pleasant feeling, but there was a lot of personal satisfaction in the fact we had ditched and did not lose anyone."

The three German fighters left, probably low on fuel, and did not strafe the ten men now afloat in two life rafts. The crew drifted on the North Sea until Tuesday the 27th when they spotted a Danish fishing trawler, the "Ternan", fishing for flounder. The Americans were plucked out of the water and were able to convince the reluctant skipper of the boat to take them to England. They were spotted by an English Air/Sea Rescue airplane and a launch was dispatched to pick them up.

During de-briefing "I told the de-briefing officers that we had flown the mission as briefed", Those last two words "as briefed" would become the title to the official history book of the 384th Bomb Group.

On his eleventh mission Tom and his crew were the only survivors of his 544th Squadron of nine crews. Tom completed his twenty-fifth mission on February 4, 1944, against the marshalling yards at Frankfurt, Germany. This came at a time when few American bomber crews survived to reached that plateau.

Discharged from military service in October, 1945 at Fort Stewart, Florida at the rank of Captain, Tom had been awarded two Distinguished Flying Crosses, four Air Medals, and a Purple Heart for injuries sustained during attacks on "Wearie Willie". His last assignment was at McDill Field, Florida, to train pilots to fly the B-29 Superfortress.

After the war Tom married a girl from Storm Lake, Iowa. They came home to the Hawkeye State where Tom owned and managed the local grocery store in Aurelia for twenty-five years and worked in furniture sales until retirement in 1981.

DONALD FAGEN, KEOTA, IA, graduated from high school in 1942. In 1943 he turned eighteen and went to Des Moines to take tests for entry into the Army Air Corps. He was told to come back in thirty days. In the meantime his draft board called him. When he told them he had already taken tests for the Air Corps it didn't matter and he was drafted. He was still assigned to the Air Corps and sent to Denver University for schooling and Buckley Field, CO, for Basic Training.

When a call went out for volunteers to become aerial gunners Don volunteered, was accepted, and sent to Kingman, AZ, for training. He trained seven days a week except for two hours on Sundays which was allowed to attend church.

After he completed combat training with his assigned air crew at Salt Lake City, UT, Don boarded a train for New Jersey and eventual deployment to England. He arrived at Thorpe Abbotts, home of the 100th Bomb Group just after D-Day but in time to fly three missions as a tail gunner in support of invasion troops.

Don went on to fly thirty-three missions that included a food drop mission in Poland and a shuttle run to Russia carrying P-51 belly tanks in their aircraft. When they returned from Russia they bombed a town near Budapest, Hungary, and flew on to Foggia, Italy. When they flew back to England Don could see the effects of D-Day. "Gliders and parachutes littered the ground as far as the eye could see."

During another mission an airplane near his was hit by flak. From his tail gunner position Don saw an escape hatch fly past his windowed position followed by a crewman going down in a burning parachute.

On a mission to Berlin, the number four engine of Don's airplane was hit by flak on the bomb run. This caused them to leave the bomber formation. The back of the right wing was on fire. The Co-pilot put the B-17 into a steep dive. By the time he was able to pull out of the dive the fire had been extinguished but another engine had quit running. Now they were left with two engines and one of them was not running good. Unsure how long they could remain airborne, the crew voted whether to bail out or try to make it to Sweden or England. The vote was England. Crossing the English Channel on one engine and nearing the closest air base Don's pilot was advised by the control tower to "go around" and get in the landing pattern. He replied, "like Hell, we're coming in". They landed safely. Don flew the majority of his missions on B-17s named either "Our Gal Sal" or "Mason-Dixon". He missed a month of flying missions and felt it was a blessing. During that time the buildup of P-51 Mustang fighters increased fighter protection all the way to the target and back.

After discharge from military service Don returned to Keota where he began a farmer's elevator service which he still operates.

MACK FARMER, CLARINDA, IA, had attended Northwest Missouri State College and taken Civilian Pilot Training at college when he was drafted into the Army Air Corps in March, 1943. He was sent to Wichita Falls, Texas, for Basic Training and then Radio School at Chicago, Illinois. The school was closed at Chicago and all personnel transferred to Scott Field, near E. St. Louis, Missouri. Following graduation he then attended Aerial Gunnery School at Yuma, Arizona.

After assignment to an aircrew at Salt Lake City, Utah, Mack trained with the crew at Alexandria, Louisiana. The crew was then to pick up a new B-17 bomber at Kearney, Nebraska, however none were available and they were sent to the East Coast and shipped to England by boat.

Mack flew thirty-five combat missions as Radio Operator and waist gunner with the 306th Bomb Group at Thurleigh. On his thirty-second mission to bomb targets at Stuttgart, Germany, Mack's aircraft was flying as lead aircraft when a German anti-aircraft shell exploded outside his plane after the bomb run. A piece of flak hit him in the chest. Luckily he was wearing a flak vest, however the force twisted him off his chair, knocked him through a door of his compartment and he fell into the bomb bay area. Flak had also cut the hose of his oxygen mask and he passed out. A radar operator gave him artificial respiration and a portable oxygen bottle which saved his life. Oxygen was lost to the aircraft. The pilot dropped in altitude so no oxygen was required and they limped back to England. Mack never reported being hit but that night at his barracks he was awaken from sleep and taken to the base hospital where he was put on oxygen.

After he completed his required number of missions in January, 1945, Mack sailed on the ocean liner "New Amsterdam" for the United States. While he was on furlough, he got married and then reported to Liberal, Kansas Army Air Base where he finished the war. He was discharged from military service in September, 1945, and had been awarded, among other medals, two Distinguished Flying Crosses, the Air Medal with seven oak leaf clusters, World War II Victory Medal and the ETO Ribbon with battle stars. Mack is retired in the rural Clarinda area on a tree farm and is an accomplished woodworker.

DON FENNELL, MUSCATINE, IA, had graduated from high school and was working for the Rock Island Arsenal when he was drafted into the Army Air Corps in November, 1943. He was sent to Amarillo, Texas, for Basic Training and then to Taft, California, where worked he helped to pre-flight aircraft being used by pilots in training.

Don was then sent to Yuma, Arizona, for Aerial Gunnery School. Upon completion of training he was transferred to Lincoln, Nebraska, where he was assigned to an aircrew and began training with them at Sioux City, Iowa, for overseas deployment. Don and his crew then picked up a new bomber at Lincoln on December 7, 1944, and flew to Valley, Wales through Bangor, Maine, Goose Bay, Labrador and Iceland.

He was assigned to the 305th Bomb Group at Chelveston, England. Don flew thirty-two combat missions as a tail gunner. His first day on base at Chelveston, "the fog was so thick and planes were coming back from a mission". "I saw bombers crisscrossing the runway at low altitude and it's a wonder there wasn't any collisions". His first mission was on Christmas Eve, 1944, when "everything that could fly flew that day" in support of the Battle of the Bulge.

On a mission to bomb Dresden, "there were so many German refugees crowding into Dresden we had orders to bomb the city, no military target, just the city, to scatter the refugees and cause confusion and delays for the German Army."

During a mission to Dortmund, Germany, "we were in the last element". "Flak was bursting about a thousand feet below us. Then we had four bursts alongside our plane that knocked out our number one engine. Our plane dove down into the lower flak but the pilot feathered the engine, regained control of the plane and got us back into formation."

In route to bomb Berlin, Germany "three planes were in the element behind us". "One took a direct hit in the bomb bay area and went down. Another got hit and slide away out of formation. Our top turret gunner got wounded by flak. I looked toward the front of our plane. When I looked back out the tail, the third plane behind us was gone. A German jet had sneaked into our formation through our contrails and hit the bombers."

Don was still at Chelveston on both VE and VJ-Days. The 305th Bomb Group had moved to the European mainland and began flying missions to photograph the European Continent from the air. He returned to the United States aboard a troop ship and after furlough reported to Santa Ana, California where he received his discharge from military service. Don had been awarded, among other medals, the Air Medal with oak leaf clusters, World War II Victory Medal and the European Theater of Operations Medal with battle stars.

Don was employed by the Royal Typewriter Company until he left to enter his own typewriter and office supply business from which he has retired.

Right - Enlisted men of Don's aircrew

Right - Don outside his tail gunner position

MARION FERGUSON, WASHINGTON, IA, worked for an aircraft company in California before World War II. He returned to Iowa and entered military service at Camp Dodge, IA. After Basic Training Marion was sent to Scott Field, IL, for Radio School.

Marion was deployed to the 452nd Bomb Group at Deopham Green, England, as a radio operator/gunner. He flew thirty-one combat missions including a shuttle mission to Poltava, Russia.   On this mission their target was south of Berlin, too far from England to allow them to return on their remaining fuel. Arrangements had been made to fly on to a Russian base at Poltava, where they would be refueled and rearmed and attack another target on return to England.

A German fighter shadowed their formation after they bombed their target and reported where the Americans had landed. That night German fighters and bombers attacked the unprotected, parked aircraft and destroyed many of them without meaningful opposition from Russian guns. It was three weeks before Marion and the other bomber crews were able to make it back to England. Transport aircraft had to be deployed to pick them up and return them through North Africa.

After he completed his required number of missions Marion returned to the United States and began training on the B-29 bomber in preparation for continued service in the Pacific Theater when the war ended. When discharged from military service he had been awarded among other medals, the Distinguished Flying Cross, Air Medal with four oak leaf clusters and the European Theater of Operations Medal. He attended the University of Iowa, University of Chicago and received his Doctorate Degree from the then Iowa State College. After working for Goodyear Aerospace he retired as a professor of biological sciences at Kent State University.

Right - Marion's crew at 452nd BG, Deopham Green, England. Marion is back row, left.

JOHN 'JACK' FERNHOUT, DES MOINES, IA, was eighteen years old when he enlisted in the Aviation Cadet Program of the Army Air Corps in June, 1944. He was sent to Sheppard Field, Wichita Falls, Texas for Basic Training. During Basic he learned there was no further need for Pilots, Bombardiers or Navigator applicants. He chose to become an Aerial Gunner and was sent to Kingman, Arizona, for gunnery training.

Jack was assigned to an aircrew and trained with them for overseas deployment at Plant Park, Florida, near Tampa where aircrews were billeted under grandstands at the Park. In January, 1945, he boarded the "Queen Elizabeth" for England. After arrival Jack and his crew reported to the Replacement Center at Stone, England, where they received assignment to the 95th Bomb Group at Horham, England.

Practice missions were flown before they were to be sent into combat. During one such mission with Jack flying as tail gunner, three bombers including his own, flew into bad weather. The two other planes returned to base while Jack and his crew became lost. Through a break in the clouds they spotted a large city. Everyone thought they had flown over London until someone spotted the Eiffel Tower.

"I remember that there was a lot of bickering and low morale among aircrews. They were afraid they would not finish their tour of missions. After it was explained to them they were not expected to finish the required number of missions for rotation, that they would be shot down or killed first, they accepted their fate and their attitude became better."

The war ended in Europe before Jack could fly a combat mission. He volunteered to fly two "Chowhound" missions, food drops to starving Dutch citizens who had lived under Nazi rule. "We came in a low-level and pushed the bales of food out the bomb bay doors. They had a cross formed by muslin on a field as a target for us. We went on our own, there was no formation flown. From my tail position I threw out a large tin of English "bully beef". I watched the tin crash through the roof of a house. I can still see the red tiles on the roof explode when it hit. I hope no one was hurt. Some people were killed by the falling food parcels."

In August, 1945, Jack flew back to the United States in a B-17 that had been recovered from Sweden. The original crew had been forced down in the neutral country and interned for the duration of the war. Eighth Air Force air and ground crews were sent to Sweden and Switzerland to make necessary repairs to evacuate the aircraft after the war ended.

Jack was assigned to the Air Cadet Center at San Antonio, Texas as a Separation Classification Specialist. In March, 1946, he was sent to Kerns, Utah, then to Ft Sheridan, Illinois, and finally back to Sheppard Field were he received his discharge from military service. He had been awarded the European Theater of Operations and World War II Victory Medals.

In civilian life Jack used the G.I. Bill of Rights to earn his Bachelor's Degree at the University of Wisconsin. He was employed with Amoco Oil Company for thirty-eight years and before retirement was Operations Manager of the Amoco Credit Card Center at Des Moines.

Jack returned to Holland in 1990 and 1995 for observance of Operation Manna/Chowhound sponsored by the Dutch in appreciation of Allied food drops during the war. The dates of the food drops also coincided with the birthday of Holland's Queen.

Jack relates the story of a German visitor during the Observation who inquired of a Dutchman what the local celebration was all about. "We are celebrating our Queen's birthday and the end of World War II because we lost so many people." The German inquired "How many people did you lose?" The Dutchman replied, about "800,000". The German stated "We lost 9 million people." The Dutchman countered, "Yes, we celebrate that tomorrow."

Right - Jack's crew at 95th BG, Horham, England. Jack, tail gunner, is back row, right.

ELMER FERREL, IOWA CITY, IA, was employed as a mechanic working for an auto dealer prior to World War II. He entered military service February 26, 1944, and was sent to Kessler Field, Gulfport, MS for Basic Training.

Elmer attended Radio Mechanic's School at Truax Field, Madison, WI, from June to October, 1944, and then Electronics School at Chanute Field, IL, during October and November. After a stint at Radar School at Boca Raton, FL and waiting for overseas orders at Sheppard Field, TX, he was sent to Mobile, AL, as a messenger center clerk. Most of his duties involved

copying military orders and other clerical tasks with the 108th ACS Squadron of the Eighth Air Force and the 738th AAFBU.

On May 6, 1946 he received his separation from military service at Jefferson Barracks, St Louis, MO. Elmer returned to the Iowa City area and has lived and worked there since the end of World War II.

BENNETT FISCHER, VINTON, IA, was attending the University of Iowa before the onset of America's involvement in World War II. He was drafted into military service on June 11, 1943, and assigned to the Army Air Corps. His father had been a World War I pilot who did "barnstorming" after the war, so an aviation assignment for Bennett was a "natural" for him. Af-

ter initial phases of training and classification, Bennett went through a period of testing at Nashville, TN, where he was afforded the opportunity to choose his assignment. He chose to become a bombardier and was then sent to Santa Ana, CA, for Pre-Flight training and then Deming, NM, for Bombardier School.

After crew assignment and training Bennett was deployed on December 8, 1944, to the 91st Bomb Group at Bassingbourn, England. The full meaning of war and its consequences met Bennett on his arrival at Bassingbourn. Shown an empty barracks on base he was told the flight crews housed there had not returned from their mission. "This was the first time I realized that there was a war going on, everything else was just training. Now they would shoot at you."

Bennett flew twenty combat missions which included a February 3, 1945, 4,000 plane raid on military targets at Berlin and Dresden, Germany. It was on this mission that after 'bombs away" a B-17 flying alongside with a close friend in it took a direct hit from flak in the middle of the aircraft. The airplane separated into two sections then blew apart and tumbled in pieces to the ground. His friend, Robert Carpenter from Cedar Rapids, Iowa, tried to escape the stricken airplane and had inadvertently pulled the rip cord on his parachute within the airplane. Despite the inflated parachute he put it on but was knocked unconscious. Amazingly he woke up dangling from his parachute in a tree and was taken prisoner of war. When the airplane blew apart, his parachute, already open, inflated and he floated to earth. It was on this same mission two other bombers were seen to collide on the way to the target. Only one parachute was seen from the twenty men aboard.

Later, while he convalesced in a hospital with an infected foot, Bennett learned that one of his nurses was originally from Dresden and both her parents had been killed in the bombing of February 3. She bore no ill will. The lady realized why the war was being fought and knew civilians would die, particularly during night bombing raids by British formations that targeted civilian centers.

On another mission, Bennett escaped certain death when flak pierced the nose of his airplane where the bombardier sat. For some reason the bombardier's seat was missing that day from his aircraft and required he sit lower in the nose than normal. The flak passed over his head.

Bennett witnessed the appearance of the new German jet fighter when it attacked bomber formations. Because of their speed gunners were unable to track them. The wholesale destruction of allied bombers could have occurred had the jets been perfected earlier in the war.

When Bennett returned to the United States after V-E Day, he was stationed at Tampa, Florida to train on the B-29 Super Fortress and eventual deployment to the Pacific Theater. When the Atomic Bomb was dropped on Hiroshima and Nagasaki, the war ended precluding further training. Bennett was discharged from military service on his birthday, September 13, 1945 at St Louis, MO. He had been awarded, among other medals, the Air Medal with three oak leaf clusters, ETO Ribbon and World War II Victory Medal.

Bennett returned to the University of Iowa, obtained his law degree and established a law practice at Vinton, IA,

Right - Bennett and his crew at 91st BG, Bassingbourn, England. Bennett is second row, left.

ROBERT E FITZGERALD, MILFORD, IA, was in high school at the outbreak of World War II. He entered military service July 10, 1943 at Des Moines, Iowa and went to basic training at Jefferson Barracks, Missouri. Following college training at S.W. Missouri State Teachers College and classification at San Antonio, Texas, Robert attended preflight training at

Ellington Field, Texas, bombardier and navigator's school at Big Springs, Texas with Advanced Training at Ardmore, Oklahoma.

Robert was sent to Thorpe Abbotts, England in Mid-October, 1944 assigned to the "Bloody 100th" Bomb Group, 350th Squadron. He flew 32 combat missions, twenty-seven as a bombardier and five as navigator. During a February 3, 1945, raid on Berlin, Robert was wounded in the leg but never reported it for fear of falling behind in required missions for rotation back to the U.S.

On February 6, 1945 on a mission to Chemnitz, Germany, an engine of his airplane was shot out while flying over battlefield front lines. The engine's propeller would not feather (shut down). As a result their bomber lagged behind the rest of the formation. They continued on to their target alone lacking air speed and vulnerable to enemy fighter attack. While over Stuttgart, Germany, an ME-109 German fighter was shot down by their crew. Unable to make the return flight to England the pilot was forced to land their bomber at a French fighter airstrip at Dole, France. It took three days for the crew to "hitchhike" back to their base.

Robert was discharged at Camp McCoy, Wisconsin, September 23, 1945. He was awarded the Air Medal with four oak leaf clusters. A promised Distinguished Flying Cross was never received. The 100th BG received two Presidential Unit Citations. Robert returned to Iowa and was a live stock feed salesman for thirty years.

CHARLES FIX, SPIRIT LAKE, IA, graduated from Iowa Wesleyan College at Mt. Pleasant and attended seminary at Boston College. He was a minister of the Methodist Church in Collins, Iowa, when the Japanese attacked American military bases in the Hawaiian Island on December 7, 1941. He enlisted in the Army Air Corps the next day.

Charles was sent to Chaplain's School at Harvard Divinity School. On completion of training he was assigned to Hunter Army Air Base, Savannah, Georgia. While there he was successful in having country music entertainer Minnie Pearl entertain the troops and sing in his church. In July, 1942 he boarded the ocean liner "Queen Elizabeth" for a six day voyage to the European Theater of Operations. His stateroom designed to accommodate two persons was home to eleven other officers during the trip.

Charles was assigned to Stanstedt, England, a supply unit located twelve miles from Manchester. A year later he was transferred to the 344th Bomb Group of the Ninth Air Force and remained with them until the end of the war in Europe.

In addition to regularly scheduled church services, Charles was available for crew personnel at mission briefings and on the flight line for prayer prior to takeoff. He provided consultation on personal and emotional matters, and made regular hospital rounds to give aid and comfort to the sick and wounded. Charles was in Paris on V-E Day where "the streets were packed with people celebrating the end of the war in Europe.

Charles was separated from military service in 1945 but remained in the Air Force Reserve. He completed post-graduate work at Harvard University but was recalled to active duty during the Korean War in 1950 as a chaplain at Hunter Field, Savannah, Georgia. The unit to which he was assigned was shipped to Korea. Charles instead was re-assigned to England for a three year tour of duty.

After his return to the United States, Charles spent three years at Big Springs, Texas, before re-assignment to Korea for a year. He received his discharge from military service as a Lieutenant Colonel in 1964. He then accepted a ministry position at Plantation, Florida, where he served for sixteen years until retirement. Charles was married in 1948 while serving as minister at Van Meter, Iowa. The best man at his wedding was Hall of Fame Baseball pitcher, Bob Feller.

Right - Wedding photo of Chaplain Charles. Best man, Bob Feller, Hall of Fame Baseball Pitcher with the Cleveland Indians is on the left.

LEIGHTON FORD, MARION, IA, was a policeman prior to World War II. In February, 1942, he answered America's call to arms and entered military service at Des Moines, Iowa. He left behind a wife and two small children. After aircraft mechanics training he was deployed to Snetterton Heath, England with the 96th Bomb Group and assigned to the 339th Squadron.

Leighton and his crew members were responsible for "keeping them flying", changing engines, superchargers, gas tanks, oil coolers, spark plugs or whatever it took to keep a maximum effort in the air for missions. He and his crew received a commendation for keeping a B-17 over the target sixty-eight straight missions without a turn back for mechanical trouble.

According to Leighton, being a member of a ground crew was like "having a job only you never knew when the starting time was. It could be as early as midnight, one, two or three o'clock in the morning or even as late as four or five o'clock." The routine was a two to four a.m. wakeup, a short cup of coffee and then on to the flight line to check the aircraft, warm up the engines and top off the gas tanks that could hold 2780 gallons of 100 octane gas. They were then ready to turn the aircraft over to the flight crew and sweat out their return.

Leighton recalled one incident when a new flight crew was going through their pre-flight check in preparation for their first mission. Leighton was standing in front of the plane as fireguard. When the procedure called for the bombardier to close the bomb bay doors, the SALVO switch was thrown instead. Six 500 pound bombs suddenly dropped on the concrete hardstand between the wheels of the plane. Leighton didn't stick around to see what the air crew did, he went to breakfast. Leighton and other engine mechanics's were an integral part of the overall bomber offensive team. Without their untiring effort to keep the bombers and fighters airborne, the aircrew could not have done their job.

Overall losses within the 96th Bomb Group was 51 per cent which included 209 air crews mostly within the second and third months of combat assignment. This included Leighton's brother Russell who was lost in the North Sea returning to the 96th BG from a mission to Brunswick, Germany.

After Leighton attained enough points for rotation back to the States, he was re-assigned to Santa Ana Air Base, CA until the war ended with the dropping of Atomic Bombs on Japan. Leighton was discharged from the Air Corps September 20, 1945, and returned to a career in law enforcement. He rose to Chief of Police, a position he held for twenty-six years. After retirement from the Marion Police Department he worked as an investigator with the Department of Public Safety and as Safety Officer with the Cedar Rapids Airport.

Leighton and his wife Joyce have four grown children, the youngest of which, Paul, is an associate member of the 8th Air Force Historical Society.

Right - Crew Chiefs of the 339th Squadron, 96th BG, Snetterton Heath, England. Leighton is second from right in the back two rows.

MARVIN FORD, TIPTON, IA, was a truck driver at the outbreak of America's entry into World War II. Aware that he would be drafted into military service by 1943 he enlisted in the Army Air Corps November 19, 1942, just before his twentieth birthday.

Marvin was sent to Basic Training at Kearns, UT; Gunnery School at Las Vegas, NV and Mechanics School at Amarillo, TX. He applied for pilot's training but a heart murmur disqualified him for further consideration. Assigned to a flight crew Marvin and his crew trained at Pyote, TX before proceeding to Kearney, NE where they picked up a new B-17. Along with fifty-two other aircraft Marvin flew the northern route to Belfast, Ireland, through Goose Bay, Labrador. He had to spend ten days at Goose Bay because of bad weather. They flew into Goose Bay in heavy fog and broke out from the fog at just four hundred feet above ground. They found the runway lighted by smudge pots. "I've never been so scared", Marvin recalled. After more combat training at Belfast Marvin and his crew were assigned to the 381st Bomb Group at Ridgewell, England.

Marvin flew thirty-five combat missions as flight engineer and top turret gunner. His first mission was on July 8, 1944, a raid on Calais, France, just twenty miles from the coast of England. Intense anti-aircraft fire was directed on the bomber formation. A piece of shrapnel came through the side of Marvin's aircraft and struck the pilot killing him. The co-pilot took over control of the airplane for the balance of the mission.

Flying a B-17 named "Tomahawk Warriors" Marvin flew four missions on oil synthetic plants at Meresberg, Germany, and raids in support of Allied infantry during the battle for St. Lo, France. He felt a mission to Leipzig was the roughest when German ME-109 fighters attacked their formation in route to the target and on return to their base. "The Germans knew how far to stay out from the formation and fire their 20 mm cannons. Our 50 caliber machine guns couldn't reach them. It was sometimes hard to tell our P-51s apart from the ME-109."

The life and death struggle in the skies over Europe hit home when crews assigned to Marvin's quonset hut never returned from missions. An aircraft along his took a direct hit from anti-aircraft fire and exploded sending a propeller spinning over the top of his gun turret. On another occasion an airplane below them got caught in the "prop wash" of the bomber formation and uncontrollably flew directly below them when their bombs were released. A bomb struck the nose of the airplane killing the bombardier. The bomb became lodged in the nose, but didn't explode.

Following his tour of duty Marvin was assigned to Rantoul, IL, as a supervisor of maintenance. Training was taking place on the B-29 Super Fortress in preparation for duty in the Pacific Theater when the war ended.

Discharged from military service September 25, 1945, Marvin had been awarded the Distinguished Flying Cross, Air Medal with three oak leaf clusters and the European Theater of Operations Medal. He returned to Iowa, resumed trucking and eventually owned his own fleet that hauled livestock and liquid fertilizer for over thirty years.

Right - Marvin and his crew at 381st BG, Ridgewell, England. Marvin, Flight Engineer and Top Turret Gunner is back row, left.

NANCY JOBSON FOSTER, CEDAR FALLS, IA, although born in Brooklyn, NY, grew up in neighboring New Jersey. After the Japanese sneak attack on United States bases in the Hawaiian Island on December 7, 1941, Nancy got a job in the Security Department of a Sperry Gyroscope defense plant. At the time she was engaged to a pilot with the Army Air Corps. Marriage was placed on hold until he returned from his overseas tour of duty with the Eighth Air Force. Nancy's fiance was killed on his third mission flying as a replacement Co-Pilot.

She saw an article in "McCall's" magazine advertising for women volunteers for the American Red Cross. She applied, was accepted and reluctantly released from her employment with Sperry. After two weeks training in Washington, DC, she boarded the "Queen Elizabeth I" for Scotland. She arrived in London by train in time to experience a German buzz bomb attack on the city.

After temporary assignments at various American Army bases, Nancy was assigned to a Field Club at Base Air Depot 2 at Wharton, England. With other Red Cross volunteers she lived in a private home on the base. The Field Club was one of three on the base where airmen could play cards, billiards, or ping pong, attend scheduled parties and dances, or visit their snack bar for sandwiches, cookies, soft drinks or coffee or their library and reading room. Established for moral building purposes the Field Club offered a diversion and relaxation from the war from 11 A.M. to 11 P.M.

While at BAD2 Nancy met and after the war married Victor Foster of Waterloo, Iowa, a Technical Supply Officer and Test Pilot at the base. At the end of the war in Europe Nancy and Victor were married. Following his discharge from military service the couple made their home in Waterloo where they had four children and operated a lawn and garden business until retirement. Nancy has remained active in her church and in the Red Cross since 1944. One of her most prized possessions is an invitation to tea at Buckingham Palace with the King and Queen of England. She and other Red Cross members were honored for their volunteer work during the War.

Nancy's father published a book entitled "Letters Home From England" that contained, as the title indicates, transcripts of the letters she wrote while overseas. She is also in the planning stages of another book detailing her experiences with the Red Cross during World War II.

EARL FOUTS, MARSHALLTOWN, IA, was employed in a jewelry store prior to World War II. In April, 1944 he entered military service at Camp Dodge, Iowa and was sent to basic training at Denver, CO. From there Earl was sent to Gunnery School at Las Vegas, NV.

Earl was deployed to the 457th Bomb Group at Glatten, England on March 15, 1945 as a waist gunner. Earl flew four combat missions before the war ended. On the fourth mission Earl's Group had taken off, formed into formation for the flight to Germany and was heading across the English Channel with armed bombs when the raid on the target was "scrubbed". Earl climbed into the bomb bay area to re-install the

Chapter Twenty-Two

pins in the bombs disarming them before they could land back at Glatten.

Earl was awarded among other medals, the World War II Victory Medal, European Theater of Operations Medal and Meritorious Unit Award. He was discharged from military service on April 28, 1946, at Ft. Meade, MD.

LEBRON FOX, JAMAICA, IA, worked as an auto mechanic when he was "caught up in the first draft" before America entered World War II. After his physical at the induction center he was classified 4F. His father went to find out what was wrong with Lebron and was told there were no physical problems, he was too fat for the Army.

After the Japanese attack on Pearl Harbor, December 7, 1941, Lebron was re-classified 1A and inducted into the Army Air Corps in February, 1942. He recalled one boy had packed his ears with dirt so he would flunk the hearing portion of the physical, however the examiners caught it and removed the dirt with a syringe. He rode to Des Moines with another young man who cried all the way during the trip, not wanting to go to the military. "I wasn't anxious to go either, but it was something we had to do."

After Basic Training Lebron was sent to Mechanics School at Sheppard Field, Wichita Falls, Texas. "In 110 days we went through a course that normally took three years to complete. We didn't only learn engine mechanics, we learned about the whole aircraft."

Lebron then spent one month in San Diego at a B-24 School, worked on B-17s on the flight line at Spokane, Washington, while pilots trained and also worked on the flight line at Biggs AAB, Texas and Colorado Springs, Colorado.

In May, 1943 he boarded the "Queen Elizabeth" ocean liner to England and the 351st Bomb Group at Polebrook, England. Rather than become a crew chief, Lebron was able to convince his commanding officer to let him be a floater, help other mechanics with less experience and work on all the squadron's aircraft rather than to be responsible for just one.

He organized a cleanup crew of the newly constructed base, replaced aircraft tires and serviced oxygen and hydraulic systems. He became an electrical specialist and installed extra armaments beyond what was installed in the aircraft. He and another mechanic devised a way pilot and co-pilot's windows could be easily removed in case the aircraft had to ditch in water and allow them to escape the aircraft. "Several aircraft were flying with valves out and it took all the engine's horsepower and excessive fuel consumption to fly. Out of nine aircraft only three would run. We had no compression gauges. There were none in the whole Eighth Air Force. I made one out of an oxygen gauge, spark plug and some rubber hose. We finally got gauges."

Lebron recalled amusing incidents that happened during base life that included almost hitting the actor Clark Gable with his vehicle. Gable was not used to driving on the base and they almost collided.

Stands to hold engines under repair were extremely heavy and were in disarray on the base. A young assistant to Lebron came to him wanting something to do. Lebron told him to go down and organize the stands thinking he would take someone with him to help. Later, the assistant came back exhausted and white with perspiration. He had moved the stands by himself.

Lying in bed dozing, explosions suddenly were heard near the base and personnel started running for slit trench bomb shelters half full of water. They then learned the explosions were from blasting at a nearby rock quarry.

The base PA system announced an aircraft on the base loaded with bombs was on fire and personnel were to seek safety in bomb shelters. "The dry shelters were full of guys. When the plane exploded, those not in shelters dove into ditches half full of water"

Lebron recalled a former sugar salesman from Texas in his barracks. When the PA system announced an unidentified aircraft coming over the base, everyone just stayed in their barracks except the man from Texas. "Sugar Sam" ran from the barracks in his shorts, it was winter time, and dove into a bomb shelter where water in the bottom had frozen over."

Not all was amusing. Lebron's squadron dispatched nine planes on a Schweinfurt raid and only the commanding officer's aircraft returned. On another mission, of over fifty planes sent by the Group on the mission, only one returned to Polebrook, the others were either shot down or landed at other bases.

After Victory in Europe Lebron returned to the United States aboard the "Queen Elizabeth" with twenty-three thousand other troops. He was re-assigned to Sioux Falls, South Dakota and was pulling KP when it was announced the Japanese had surrendered in the Pacific and the war was over. Lebron was sent to Randolph Field, Texas, and discharged from military service September 26, 1945.

Lebron operated a fix-it shop in Jamaica after the war, then was employed by a Perry, Iowa, auto parts store before he gained employment with a construction company from which he retired.

JOHN FRAMPTON, REINBECK, IA, assisted his father as a painter prior to World War II. In December, 1943, he enlisted in military service at Camp Dodge, Iowa, and was sent to Amarillo, TX for Basic Training. After Aerial Gunnery School at Las Vegas, NV, John was sent to Tampa, FL for crew assignment and training.

On September 20, 1944, John and his crew picked up a B-17 in Georgia and headed for Scotland via Maine and Newfoundland. They left their airplane in Scotland for refitting and were trucked to their base at Bury St Edmunds with the 94th Bomb Group.

Trained as a tail gunner, John was grounded when air crews were reduced from ten to a nine man crew. He helped crew chiefs in aircraft maintenance for a month. Wanting flight status he was trained as a substitute toggelier and flew twelve missions until the end of the war in Europe.

John recalled one mission to Kiel, Germany, to bomb submarine pens. The planes were loaded with bombs designed to penetrate thick concrete protecting the submarines. "Ships filled the harbor area throwing up heavy flak. Chaf was dumped out of their airplanes in hopes of confusing German radar systems.

After V-E Day, John was sent to Germany on temporary duty to guard captured SS troops. He then returned to England as a clerk-typist in the Operations Office until January, 1946, when he sailed for the United States aboard a Liberty ship. He recalled bunks in the hold of the ship were stacked four high and everyone got seasick.

John was discharged from the military on January 30, 1946. He had been awarded the Air Medal with one oak leaf cluster.

DALE FRANK, WINTERSET, IA,

farmed prior to World War II. Within a week of the Japanese attack on Pearl Harbor, December 13, 1941, Dale entered the military at Ft Des Moines, IA.

He was sent to the Spartan School of Aeronautics, Tulsa, Oklahoma, until June 1942 when training continued at Lubbock Air Base, Texas. In February, 1943, he served as Flight Chief at Frederick Air Base, Oklahoma.

In December, 1943, Dale was deployed to England as a crew chief with the 475th Sub-Depot, at Mendelsham. Attached to the 34th Bomb Group as crew chief in the main hangar, he had the tremendous responsibility for major repair work on the 34th's planes. From bullet and flak holes which riddled the planes to major re-construction of tail sections, wings, stabilizers and fuselage. Pressure was on the Sub-Depot team to get the Group's planes back on line for more missions. Replacement aircraft was slow in coming from the States. Wrecked planes were cannibalized to repair others. Unsung heroes, the ground crews put air crews in the air for maximum effort at selected targets.

One memorable event was when German planes followed the 34th home to their base and shot down aircraft as they tried to land.

Dale received his discharge from the military at Jefferson Barracks, St. Louis, Missouri, on November 5, 1945, with the rank of Staff Sergeant. Dale married his wife Esther in 1946 and the couple had two children, a boy and a girl, and then six grandchildren. He retired from the Engineering Department of the US Department of Agriculture Soil Conservation Service and currently enjoys woodworking, his family and traveling.

WESLEY FRANKLIN, DES MOINES, IA,

was in the grocery business when America was cast into World War II. He enlisted in the Army Air Corps in February, 1942, at Des Moines and was sent directly to Aircraft Mechanics School at Sheppard Field, Wichita Falls, Texas. Upon completion of training Wes was assigned to a B-24

School at Consolidated Aircraft Company at San Diego, California.

Wes then joined the 34th Bomb Group at Spokane, Washington. The 34th at that time was a training unit of pilots, bombardiers, navigators, aerial gunners and radio men. He worked on the flight line performing maintenance of aircraft until constant bad flying weather forced the 34th to move to Euphrata, Washington. "The weather was worse there than at Spokane so they moved us to Blythe, California. We remained a training unit until the start of 1944 when we were transformed into a combat unit."

After training for overseas duty new B-24 bombers were picked up at Lincoln, Nebraska and the unit flew to their base at Mendelsham, England, through Palm Beach, Florida; Brazil, South America; Dakar, Africa and Marrakesh.

Wes served as a crew chief with two aircraft mechanics assigned to him responsible for mechanical maintenance of one bomber. Shortly after arrival his squadron converted to the B-17 bomber.

Mechanics on the flight line erected a tent city to be near their aircraft. The tents were heated by burning coke in stoves but in Wes's tent a stove was converted to burn 100 octane aviation fuel. Black smoking coming from the tents caused the mechanics quarters to be known as "Little Pittsburgh". Wes's pilot brought him a bunk from the officer's quarters to sleep on.

On mission days flight line personnel fueled their responsible aircraft and pre-flighted engines. They had to be on hand when the aircraft returned from their mission for repair of battle damage or mechanical problems to make their planes available for the next day in case a mission was scheduled. Intense pressure was placed not only on Command but on aircraft mechanics to ensure all available aircraft were ready for missions at all times.

For his actions Wes was awarded the Bronze Star Medal. His citation read in part: "For meritorious achievement in connection with military operations against the enemy from 23 May 1944 to 13 January, 1945. During this period, extensive battle damage was sustained by the aircraft assigned to him, but, despite the handicaps of working in the open air and frequent shortages of equipment, Sergeant Franklin expertly and efficiently supervised all repairs and quickly returned his aircraft to perfect operational conditions.....the aircraft he maintained completed fifty-one bombardment missions against the enemy without being forced to return because of mechanical difficulty or failure." Wes was quick to add, "also without the loss of a man". He then remembered an airplane that was landing and had been "shot up pretty bad". "A guy fueling an airplane at the end of the runway saw the landing bomber coming at him and unable to stop so he jumped off the plane and broke his leg."

After the war ended in Europe Wes flew back to the United States through Valley, Wales, Iceland and Newfoundland. He reported to Jefferson Barracks at St. Louis, Missouri, and was reassigned to Sioux Falls, South Dakota, then Alamagordo, New Mexico. In route to New Mexico he learned the war with Japan had ended. Wes was transferred to Sioux City, Iowa, where in November, 1945, he received his discharge from military service. He had been awarded, among other medals, the Bronze Star, European Theater of Operations and World War II Victory Medals.

In civilian life, Wes owned and operated a grocery store until retirement.

Right - Wes, on the right, with friend and B-24 at 34th BG, Mendelsham, England.

Right - Wes, on the right with aircrew and flight line mechanics assigned to "his" aircraft, 34th Bomb Grou, Mendelsham, England.

FRANCIS FROAH, NEWTON, IA,

was employed at the Rock Island Arsenal, Rock Island, Illinois. He entered military service with the Army Air Corps at Camp Dodge, Iowa, on February 16, 1944. He attended Flexible Gunnery School at Kingman, Arizona.

Francis was deployed to Rattlesden, England, on December 16, 1944, as a ball turret gunner and togglier assigned to the 708th Bomb Squadron of the 447th Bomb Group.

Francis flew nineteen combat missions. One of them was a bomb raid on Berlin, the heart of Hitler's Third Reich. This was a nine hour 35 minutes flight, the majority of which Francis had to spend locked within the ball turret located under the belly of the B-17. A cramped, confined space in a sitting position with his knees up to his chin, Francis had to be constantly on the alert for enemy aircraft and was exposed to "flak" from anti-aircraft fire.

Francis received his discharge from military service at Brooks Field, San Antonio, Texas. He had been awarded, among other medals, the Air Medal with two oak leaf clusters, ETO Ribbon and World War II Victory Medal.

Right - Francis and his crew at 447th BG, Rattlesden, England. Francis is back row, right.

JACK FROST, DES MOINES, IA, attended Ottumwa, Iowa, High School prior to America's entry into World War II. After graduation in 1943 he attended one semester at Parson College, Fairfield, Iowa, and then enlisted in the Army Air Corps on December 7, 1943, as part of the Aviation Cadet Program.

After Basic Training at Keesler Field,Biloxi, Mississippi, Jack qualified for pilot training. "So did about one hundred other guys so they started cutting the list by test scores. I survived about three cuts. They finally took only about ten out of the ones that qualified."

Jack was sent to Armaments School at Lowry Field, Colorado and Aerial Gunnery School at Kingman, Arizona. Additional gunnery training was taken at Yuma, Arizona before Jack was assigned to an air crew at Tampa, Florida in preparation for overseas deployment. "We were billeted under the grandstand of a race track." Overseas training was taken at Gulfport, Mississippi, during the Winter of 1944. "We had a tail gunner from Arkansas. One day we were flying a practice mission near Texarkana, Texas. The pilot found out the tail gunner's hometown and we buzzed the town at tree top level. The tail gunner got stacks of mail from the people in his town. They knew it had to be him in the plane."

After Jack and his crew picked up a new B-17 at Hunter Field, Savannah, Georgia, they flew to Valley, Wales through Bangor, Maine and Gander, Newfoundland. "We were stuck in Newfoundland two to three weeks because of snow, mountains of it." On arrival in Wales their aircraft was taken from them for installation of additional armor and equipment. Jack and his crew proceeded to an assignment center where they were assigned to the 306th Bomb Group at Thurleigh, England.

Jack flew two combat missions to destroy oil targets in Austria and Germany. At that time air crews were reduced to nine men with the elimination of a waist gunner. Jack was initially reassigned to base defense at Thurleigh but "I wound up in supply until the end of the war in Europe.' After a brief duty assignment in southern France, Jack was transferred to a former Luftwaffe airfield in Germany as part of American occupation forces.

Jack was in the last group of personnel from his Squadron to return to the United States after the war. He received his discharge from military service at Camp McCoy, Wisconsin on May 2, 1946. He had been awarded the ETO Ribbon and World War II Victory Medals.

Jack retired from Northwestern Bell Telephone Company after thirty-five years as a special services engineering supervisor.

Right - Jack sitting in jeep at 306th BG, Thurleight, England.

AVERY GAGE, DES MOINES, IA, had graduated from Beloit College and was working for Borg-Warner Corporation as a cost accountant when he was called for the "draft". His failed his pre-induction physical examination and was classified as "4F". With that classification and unable to get into military service he married his fiancee but soon afterward received another notice to report for another physical. This time he was classified "1A". To beat the draft and have a choice of military service Avery enlisted in the Army Air Corps under the Aviation Cadet Program. He was sent to Camp Grant, Illinois for testing to determine his best qualifications. He was not called to active duty until January, 1943, when he boarded a troop train at Chicago for a three day ride to Miami Beach, Florida for Basic Training. "They loaded us in old 1890 style railroad coaches. We couldn't sleep and the food was terrible. When we got to Miami they took us to a hotel to board us. The sergeant on duty asked what we were doing there. Evidently they weren't expecting us. So he had us drag old mattresses out of the basement to sleep on."

After Basic, Avery was sent to the University of West Virginia under the College Training Detachment Program. Since he already had graduated from college and the courses were of little benefit to him he was sent to Knoxville, Tennessee, for classification and slated for Bombardier School. Avery protested the assignment up the chain of command until he was assigned to what he had enlisted for, Navigation School.

He completed pre-Navigation school and was sent to Ft Myers, Florida, for Aerial Gunnery School before he reported to Navigation School at Monroe, Louisiana. During training he had bouts of air sickness in the smaller, lighter training bombers. A medic gave him medicine to take before training missions and he was able to successfully graduate in February, 1944. He was awarded his wings and commission as a Second Lieutenant.

Avery was assigned to an aircrew at Ardmore, Oklahoma and completed overseas training with his crew in April, 1944. They were to pick up a new B-17 bomber at Kearney, Nebraska and fly to the European Theater of Operations but Kearney at the time was in the midst of a major snowstorm. He and his crew with others, were put on a train and shipped to New York City where they boarded an old English meat ship for what turned out to be a twelve day voyage to Liverpool, England. "It was an old English meat ship. We had to hang hammocks on meat hooks to sleep in. Crossing the Atlantic in late April the ship was either sailing nose up in the air or nose down in the waves. We had two meals a day. A typical meal was a piece of fish with some vile sauce on it, a sausage that tasted like sawdust and a biscuit that was so hard no amount of soaking would soften it. We were all sea sick."

After arrival at Liverpool, Avery reported to the Combat Crew Replacement Center at Stone, England and assigned to the 91st Bomb Group at Bassingbourn, England. He flew his first mission on June 2, 1944 to Boulogne, France. By D-Day, June 6, 1944, he had flown missions on five straight days to bomb marshalling yards, bridges and airfields in advance of the invasion.

On D-Day after completing their bomb run "we discovered three bombs had not released and were hung up in the bomb bay. The bombardier went into the bomb bay to replace the safety pins in them. He was holding one bomb when one of the others fell loose, knocked the bomb out of the bombardiers arms. Both bombs fell through the doors but the fuse exploded on one knocking a big hole in the bottom of the plane. The remaining bomb then broke loose and fell. The sky had been overcast and cleared alittle at the time for us to just see ships from the invasion fleet below. We never found out if those three bombs hit anything or not."

On a June 8, 1944, mission to bomb Hamburg, Germany, "the flak was tremendous". "Planes were blowing up all around us, guys in parachutes and pieces of planes falling. We were just lucky."

A mission on July 20, 1944, to bomb targets at Leipzig, Germany, was his most memorable mission. We were hit by about one hundred German fighter that came through our formation six or seven times. What they didn't shoot down, "flak" got. Only one of our bombers remained in the high squadron and we were the only plane left in the low squadron. An FW-190 flew alongside us and was shooting at the bomber ahead of him. I opened fire and he blew up. No one saw me do it so I never got credit for downing him.

"The next day we were scheduled for another mission. I just felt that after the day before I couldn't do it anymore. Everyone else went to get ready and so did I. Once I got in the plane I was alright. When we took off assembly was to be at ten thousand feet, but it was foggy. We were sent to another point to assemble at twenty-five thousand feet and it was still foggy. When we broke into the clear we saw no one was around so we joined another bomb group and flew the mission with them. On return to our base we were low on gas and there was no visibility because of fog. We dropped as low as we could get, found an airfield and landed out of gas."

Avery's last mission was on August 12, 1944. He returned to the United States in September, 1944 and reported to Boca Raton, Florida where he became a radar/navigation instructor. His former pilot was then able to assign Avery as his squadron adjutant until discharge from military service on September 1, 1945. Avery had been awarded the Distinguished Flying Cross, Air Medal with three oak leaf clusters, World War II Victory Medal, ETO Ribbon with battle stars.

In civilian life, Avery re-joined Borg-Warner Corporation for eight years before joining J.L. Clark Manufacturing from which he retired in 1980 as their Corporate Secretary.

Right - Avery's crew at Bassingbourn. Avery, Navigator, is bottom row, third from left.

THOMAS GALLAGHER, CEDAR RAPIDS, IA, enlisted in the Army Air Corps on June 22, 1943. He became a Flight Engineer and Aerial Gunner assigned to the 100th Bomb Group at Thorpe Abbotts, England.

Tom flew fourteen combat missions. The fourteenth was a raid on Berlin March 18, 1945. In addition to heavy and accurate flak encountered over the target their Group was attacked by ME-262s, the new German jet which used the bomber's contrails as cover to approach them from the rear.

The number two and four engines of Tom's aircraft were hit. Control cables were knocked out on the rear stabilizer and a Tokyo gas tank exploded taking off eight feet of a wing. While they lost altitude rapidly the pilot maintained an East heading toward Poland. As they descended from 32,000 feet to 9,000 feet they made it over Allied lines but a burst of fire exploded between the number two engine and the fuselage. A piece of shrapnel passed behind the pilot and stopped inside Tom's uniform wounding him. At 3,000 feet the plane stopped losing altitude and a pasture was found on which to land. The crew evacuated the aircraft for fear of further explosions when oxygen lines were hissing.

Russian soldiers arrived in a truck and took them to the town on Koscian, Poland. Tom and his crew were later shipped by train to Poltava, Russia, where they remained for a month before being picked up by a B-17 crew based in Italy. They borrowed the aircraft to fly back to England and landed at their base at their usual hard stand as though they had just returned from a mission. This mission lasted nearly two months.

In his fourteen missions Tom was credited with downing three enemy aircraft. Among other medals he was awarded the Purple Heart. After a long illness Tom died in 1991.

Right - Tom and crew at 100th BG, Thorpe Abbotts, England. Engineer and Aerial Gunner Tom is on the right.

ALLEN GARTMAN, MAQUOKETA, IA, farmed with his father prior to World War II. He entered military service September 4, 1943 at Camp Dodge, Iowa and was sent to Jefferson Barracks, Missouri, for Basic Training.

In December, 1943, he was sent to Flight School at Kent, Ohio, then Aerial Gunnery School at Harlingen, TX. In August, 1944, Allen was assigned to an air crew and trained with them for overseas deployment at Boise, Idaho.

In December, 1944, Allen was deployed to the 34th Bomb Group at Mendolesham, England, as a tail gunner. The 34th Bomb Group was the oldest bomb group in the Eighth Air Force and the last Group assigned as a unit to the Eighth. They flew the B-24 Liberator until August, 1944 when the Group converted to the B-17 Flying Fortress. In addition to combat missions, in May, 1945, the 34th flew six Missions dropping food to the Dutch, who, under Nazi rule, subsisted on starvation rations. The Group also flew several missions to pick up liberated Prisoners of War.

Allen flew fifteen combat missions, one relay mission and twelve missions in which his Group was recalled to their base. In a relay mission an aircraft circled the North Sea and radioed back to Command results of the missions and resistance encountered. On his relay mission it was snowing when Allen and his crew left the base. On return the weather was a complete "white out". As they approached their base Allen looked out the window of his B-17 and thought "it won't be long now and we'll be on the ground". That thought was interrupted when the pilot gunned the airplane and gained altitude. "We weren't anywhere near the direction of the runway. The second time trying to land I looked out one side and going by was a hangar and on the other side there were trees and they were higher than we were. I thought "Oh, boy, this is it". On the third approach he made it, he couldn't see where we were going. That was strictly flying by the seat of your pants. You came in on a heading and hoped that when you got down far enough the runway was there."

The Bomb Group practiced landings and takeoffs at night. This was not without it's dangers. Allen was in the tail of his airplane with a light and kept flashing it so the airplane taking off behind them could maintain a safe distance and not run into them. "I knew everyone in the plane behind us. We were just a few seconds ahead of them. Suddenly there was a big flash of fire and that was it for them. It was just a big boom for no reason at all. We never knew what happened to make the plane explode."

When Allen returned from one mission his airplane had taken hits from anti-aircraft fire (flak) that caused loss of oxygen. They had to leave the safety of their Group formation and drop to a lower altitude where oxygen wasn't required. This also subjected them to possible German fighter attack. "When you were alone you were just a sitting duck. We called for assistance. It wasn't long until a "Little Friend", (American Fighter) flew alongside and escorted us to the English Channel." When they landed at their base, they counted seventy-two holes in their aircraft. Only one minor casualty resulted. The Co-pilot had been grazed on the back of his head by a piece of flak. An inch either way would have meant a miss or possible death.

Allen was discharged from military service on November 9, 1945 at Davis-Monthan Field, Tucson, AZ. He had been awarded, among other decorations, the Air Medal with three battle stars for the Battles of the Rhine, Bulge and Berlin. He returned to farming until retirement.

Right - Allen and his crew at 34th BG, Mendelsham, England. Allen, Tail Gunner, is front row, fourth from the left.

FRED GEITZ, DES MOINES, IA had enlisted in the Air Cadet program when he was seventeen. He entered on duty with the Army Air Corps in October, 1943, at Des Moines and was sent to Amarillo, Texas, for pilot training. Due to an inner ear problem he was transferred to Aerial Gunnery School at Las Vegas, Nevada. Upon completion of training he was assigned to an air crew and completed overseas training with his crew at Ardmore, Oklahoma.

In June, 1944, the crew flew a new B-17 bomber from Kearney, Nebraska to Ireland by way of Greenland. He was assigned to the 306th Bomb Group at Thurleigh, England, as a ball turret gunner. After a month's training on practice missions Fred flew the first of thirty-five combat missions on August 15, 1944, a bombing raid on targets at Frankfurt, Germany.

Fred was born in Germany and had come to the United States while very young. He had relatives in Germany near Dortmund who was aware that he was in the U.S. Army Air Corps. After the war he learned he had bombed Bielefeld, Germany, five days in a row, the city where his relatives lived.

Fred's most memorable mission was a raid on Merseburg, Germany. In route to the target their formation skirted Berlin to draw the German Luftwaffe to them. They had to fend off German fighters all the way to the target. Over Merseburg they experienced heavy concentrations of German anti-aircraft guns. Then on the return to England, German fighters attacked their formation again. "I think I saw about every type of German aircraft there was on my missions. The deeper our penetration into Germany the more we were attacked by German fighters. On missions that didn't go deep into Germany we hardly saw any German aircraft. On one mission we were all shot up and had to land at the first landing field over the White Cliffs of Dover. It just so happened that the King and Queen of England were making an inspection of that base that day and I got to meet them."

Fred claimed credit for one FW-190 German fighter shot down. "He came up towards us after he had attacked a lower bomb group. He then appeared to try and dive back toward the lower group. When he reached the top of his climb I opened fire and hit him. He went down on fire."

Fred's last mission was on February 1, 1945, to bomb targets at Leipzig. He returned to the United States and was assigned as a flight engineer at Carlsbad, New Mexico, until discharge from military service in August, 1945. He had been awarded the Air Medal with five oak leaf clusters, ETO Ribbon with five battle stars and the WWII Victory Medal.

Fred spent thirty-seven years as a high school teacher and athletic coach predominately at North High School in Des Moines.

Right - Fred's crew at 306th BG, Thurleigh, England. Fred, Aerial Gunner is front row, second from left.

Right - Fred on the right, beside his ball turret position.

PAUL GIDEL, LAKE CITY, IA, worked on the family farm until he enlisted in the Army Air Corps Aviation Cadet Program in September, 1942. He was not called to active duty until February 25, 1943, and began Pre-flight Training at San Antonio, Texas. Primary Flight Training was taken at Cimarron Field, Oklahoma, until one-third of his class was "washed out" of training due to a need for aerial gunners.

Paul was one of those "washed out" and he was sent to Laredo and Eagle Pass, Texas, for Aerial Gunnery School. Upon completion of training in October, 1943, he was assigned to a B-24 bomber crew at Salt Lake City, Utah. Paul and his crew began the first phase of crew training at Tucson, Arizona, and then completed phase two and three at Alamagordo, New Mexico in March, 1944.

"We were then sent to Herington, Kansas where we were assigned to a new B-24 Bomber Group, the 492nd. It was composed of four squadrons of 21 airplanes each. I was in the 858th Squadron. In April, 1944, we started our trip overseas by the southern route through South America and Africa to North Pickenham, England."

Paul flew thirteen combat missions as tail gunner beginning on May 11, 1944. On his third mission "we were hit by anti-aircraft fire and our co-pilot was killed". The shell entered the bottom of their plane between the legs of the Co-pilot and exited through the top of the aircraft and exploded above them. The shell however, cut the Co-pilot in half."It was a mess, blood everywhere". "The Flight Engineer took over as the Co-pilot for the balance of the mission. After landing back at our base the Flight Engineer and the Pilot were required to take off again and just fly around for a half hour to try and calm down the Pilot from the experience."

On Paul's thirteenth mission, a raid on Hamburg, Germany, "we took a direct hit by an anti-aircraft shell which knocked us out of formation and did a lot of damage. It cut some of the gas lines. The Flight Engineer took a .50 caliber shell and put it in the finger of a silk glove liner and stuck it in the fuel line to stop the fuel from leaking until he could transfer fuel to a gas tank that was not hit. We didn't have much fuel left and had to make a forced landing in Sweden." Landing in a neutral country usually meant internment for the duration of the war. "We were billeted in a large building at a sort of resort. Two men to a room and about twenty rooms in the building."

After the 492nd Bomb Group was re-organized to become a "Carpetbagger" unit: "one night about midnight, a B-24 landed in Stockholm loaded with ball bearings for the Swedes who sold them to the Germans who in turn allowed a plane load of internees to fly out." "We stood up in the plane packed with as many guys as it would hold and flew out for Scotland. That's how I got out of the internment camp." Paul was then sent back to the United States to finish the war as a B-29 gunnery instructor. He could not return to fly combat missions in case he would be shot down and taken prisoner of war. If that were to happen "I could have possibly been shot as a spy or escapee".

Paul received his discharge from military service in November, 1945, and had been awarded, among other medals, the Air Medal with two oak leaf clusters, World War II and European Theater of Operations Medals. He spent three years in the Air Force Reserves and was called back to active duty during the Korean War to serve as a gunnery instructor. Paul then returned to farming until retirement in 1988.

Right - Paul's crew, 492nd BG, North Pickenham, England. Paul, tail gunner, is front row, second from left.

MARLYN GILLESPIE, DES MOINES, IA, completed two years at the University of Iowa majoring in accounting. He then worked as a bookkeeper for a car dealer in Pocahontas, Iowa, until the Japanese attack on Pearl Harbor on December 7, 1941. Marlyn returned to Des Moines and worked at the Army Ordnance Plant making .30 and .50 caliber bullets until October, 1942 when he enlisted in the Army Air Corps Aviation Cadet Program. He was not called to active duty until January, 1943.

After Basic Training at Jefferson Barracks, St. Louis, Missouri, Marlyn attended the then Iowa State Teachers College at Cedar Falls, Iowa, under the College Training Detachment Program where he took college courses in mathematics and physics until there was an opening for flight training.

Marlyn completed Pre-flight Training at Santa Ana, California; Primary Flight Training at Thunderbird Field, Glendale, Arizona; and both Basic and Advanced Flight Training at Pecos, Texas. Upon completion of these phases of flight training in March, 1944, he was awarded his pilot's wings and commission as a Second Lieutenant.

Marlyn was assigned an aircrew and trained with them at Alexandria, Louisiana, in preparation for overseas deployment. Deployment was delayed until he completed radar training at Langley Field, Virginia. Training flights were made up and down the East Coast at night in search of German submarines.

In the Fall of 1944 Marlyn and his crew flew a new B-17 bomber to Valley, Wales, through Goose Bay, Labrador and Iceland. On arrival their aircraft was taken from them for installation of additional armament. They reported to the Replacement Crew Center at Stone, England, where they were assigned to the 305th Bomb Group at Chelveston, England.

Between October, 1944, and March, 1945, Marlyn flew thirty-five combat missions. His most memorable mission was on January 10, 1945, to Cologne, Germany. "We had to make three passes over the target before we could release our bombs. One pass you want to get out of there. Two passes is fatal. Three passes they obliterated our squadron. I lost my number one and two engines on the left wing to "flak". We dropped out of formation and threw out everything inside the plane we could in order to lose weight. We still lost altitude." As altitude ran out and in heavy overcast Marlyn and his crew knew they could not make the return flight to England. "The loss of two engines on the same wing made the B-17 hard to control. It was imperative the plane fly in a tilted position with the dead engines high and the good engines running in a lower position to prevent the aircraft from going into a spin."

"We had no instruments, they were all shot out. We didn't know where we were. As we neared the ground I saw a landing strip through a break in the overcast. I made one pass at the runway but I couldn't line the plane up because of wind and two engines on one wing. So I made another pass. We were so low we flew past a church steeple and as I was about to land I saw an American P-51 fighter on the runway with its propeller dead. To avoid hitting it I veered off to the side, missed the runway and ran off into the grass and mud. We had lost one of our crew killed by "flak" and had another one wounded. We had landed at a small town near the Belgian border. Allied ground forces had just captured the landing strip within the last twenty-four hours. After the war I went back to that landing strip and it is now home for a flying school."

"We went to Merseburg, Germany, to bomb synthetic fuel plants. They made fuel from coal. The area was heavily protected by "flak". We could never fully knock it out. The Germans had a prisoner of war camp across the road from the refinery and our bombs had to be right on target. Any slip would have killed the POWs. The Germans would also put hospitals and schools near important targets so they wouldn't get bombed."

Marlyn returned to the United States aboard a ship from Liverpool, England, to New York City. He was assigned as a B-17 instructor at an air base near Columbus, Ohio, and was there on V-E Day (Victory in Europe). He was reassigned as an instructor at Sebring, Florida, and was there on V-J Day (Victory over Japan). He remained an instructor until the Fall of 1945 when he received his discharge from military service. He had been awarded the Air Medal with five oak leaf clusters, European Theater of Operations Medal with battle stars and World War II Victory Medal, among others.

In civilian life Marlyn returned to school at the University of Iowa and earned his Bachelor's Degree in accounting. He became a Certified Public Accountant and worked for a firm that had offices in Des Moines and St. Louis. Marlyn was employed in St. Louis and subsequently left the firm to return to Des Moines and work for Delavan Manufacturing from which he retired.

Right - Marlyn's crew, 305th BG, Chelveston, England. Marlyn, Pilot, is front row, left.

LEE GINGERY, SHENANDOAH, IA, was a student, defense plant inspector and did farm work prior to America's entry into World War II. He was inducted into the Army, May 27, 1943, at Ft. Leavenworth, Kansas and sent to Camp Callen near San Diego, California, for Basic Training. While there he read a notice that indicated enlisted men could apply for the Aviation Cadet

Program upon successful completion of an examination. Lee took the test, passed, and was sent to Amarillo, Texas, for Pre-Flight Training. Because the school was filled he never got into training and was instead re-assigned to Radio School at Sioux Falls, South Dakota. Next came Aerial Gunnery School at Yuma, Arizona before being assignment to an air crew at Lincoln, Nebraska and training with them at Dyersburg, Tennessee in preparation for overseas deployment.

In January, 1945, Lee and his air crew sailed for Scotland aboard the ocean liner "Queen Elizabeth". From there he rode by train to Stone, England, where he was assigned to the 351st Bomb Group at Polebrook.

Lee flew twenty-six combat missions as radio operator. His job was to communicate with Division Headquarters in Morse Code and send "bombs away" and position reports, send emergency signals and assist the navigator in taking position fixes. He would also trigger automatic cameras in the planes belly just prior to bomb release, discharge metallic chaff once their aircraft was over the target, maintain a log on all flights and give barometric readings for their altimeter readings.

He flew his first mission on February 28, 1945, a bombing raid on railroad marshalling years at Soest, Germany. Three missions were flown to the heart of the German Reich, Berlin. During one mission a bomb "hung up" on the bomb racks. Lee had to climb into the open area of the bomb bay where the temperature was between 30 to 60 degrees below zero and while under intense anti-aircraft fire, release the bomb manually.

At one stretch of time Lee and his crew flew five missions in six days, nine missions in twelve days, and seven missions in eight days. Each mission, deep to the interior of Germany lasted nine to ten hours under intense antiaircraft fire and attacks by German fighter aircraft. During one mission German jets downed eighteen American bombers.

Lee received a weeks rest and relaxation. Shortly after his return to the base at Polebrook the war ended in Europe.

Lee flew as a crewmember on aerial sightseeing trips over Europe affording ground crew personnel a look at devastation that been inflicted on the German Reich. His most worthwhile and totally interesting experience of his military career was flying with a skeleton crew to Linz, Austria for the purpose of transporting Frenchmen back to France who had recently been released from Mauthausen Concentration Camp. Two to three hundred prisoners had been dying each day at the camp from exhaustion and malnutrition under Nazi rule. Lee made two such trips.

Lee arrived back in the United States on June 13, 1945. After furlough he reported to Ft. Leavenworth, Kansas, and was sent to Sioux Falls, South Dakota. He was re-assigned again, this time to March Field near Riverside, California where he eventually received his discharge from military service on November 14, 1945. He had been awarded, among other medals, the Air Medal with three Oak Leaf Clusters, the European Theater of Operations Medal with two bronze battle stars and World War II Victory Medal.

After the war Lee returned to college and earned his bachelor's degree in journalism. He eventually became part owner of Henry Fields, a major nursery and seed distributor in Shenandoah and also served as the company Advertising and Marketing Officer. After retirement Lee served as chairman of the Shenandoah Historical Preservation Commission which created the Iowa Walk of Fame on downtown sidewalks honoring famous Iowans.

*Summary of Lee's military experiences taken from "Nicknames, Wars and Corporate Games, A 20th Century Memoir by Lee Emerson Gingery, Copyright 1991, Park Publishing Company

Right - Lee and crew at 351st BG, Polebrook, England. Lee, radio operator is back row, fourth from the left. Fellow Iowan, Donald Sexton, Pilot, is front row, left.

HENRY GLOVER, SANBORN, IA, was originally from Oklahoma and had completed two years at Eastern Oklahoma A&M College when he enlisted in the Army Air Corps in December, 1941 after the Japanese attack on military bases in the Hawaiian Islands on December 7, 1941. He was not called to active duty until January 25, 1942.

Henry was sent to March Field, California for Basic Training. He was then assigned to a Quartermaster Truck unit at Stockton, California, as an auto parts specialist until re-assigned to Aerial Gunnery School at Yuma, Arizona. After completion of training he was deployed to England with the 1915th Quartermaster Truck Company attached to the Eighth Air Force at Little Staunton, England.

He applied for the Aviation Cadet Program while in England, was accepted and sent back to the United States for training. He reported to Biloxi, Mississippi where he was told there was no longer a need for pilots. He was re-assigned to Radar and Radio School at Sioux Falls, South Dakota. Following graduation he was assigned to an aircrew at Sioux City, Iowa, where they trained in preparation for combat duty overseas. Henry and his crew flew to England and assignment with the 379th Bomb Group at Kimbolton.

Henry flew thirty-three combat missions as radio operator. While on one mission his aircraft was hit by "flak" that caused them to crash land in France. The aircrew escaped their aircraft and ran. While German troops searched for them, Henry and his crew hid in haystacks, barn lofts and attics of French people's homes until they were returned to England by the French in a boat.

Anti-aircraft fire shot Henry and his crew down a second time. Unable to maintain flight his pilot crash-landed their bomber at a German fighter base that had only recently been taken by American ground troops.

After V-E Day, Henry and his crew flew missions to Holland to drop food and medical supplies to the Dutch who had been starved while under Nazi rule. He also participated in missions to liberate American prisoners of war from Germany. Henry received his discharge from military service in August, 1945. He had been awarded, among other medals, the Air Medal with three oak leaf clusters, ETO Ribbon with two battle stars and the World War II Victory Medal.

Henry returned to college at Ames, Iowa, where he earned his Bachelor's Degree. He went on to earn a Masters Degree in Industrial Education and teach vocational agriculture and industrial arts for thirty-three years.

JAMES GOFF, SIOUX CITY, IA, entered military service on June 5, 1939, at Chanute Field, Illinois, two and one-half years before America's entry into World War II. He attended aerial photography school at Lowry Field, Colorado, Bombardier School at Midland, Texas and Navigation School at Hondo, Texas.

On September 14, 1943, James was assigned to the 95th Bomb Group at Horham, England and flew twenty-five combat missions as navigator. Four of these missions were during Black Week, October 8 to 14, 1943, James's first four missions.

On his arrival at Horham, like all young men and gullible, James was itching to meet the enemy. His first mission was on October 8, 1943, as a replacement navigator to Bremen, a memorable and frightening experience. The Eighth Air Force on that day encountered the most intense and accurate anti-aircraft fire of the war. When they entered German air space his formation was attacked repeatedly by FW-190 and ME-109 fighters. James found himself firing a .50 caliber machine gun at a person for the first time in his life. As they neared the target on the bomb run, anti-aircraft guns put up a terrifying box barrage that seemed to be impenetrable. B-17s just ahead of him flew into that barrage. James was horrified to see two fortresses explode and disintegrate. The entire formation was swallowed up in a solid curtain of black smoke. He remembered thinking that his first mission would be his last. "How could any bomber fly into that hell and survive?" In a matter of seconds his plane was in it too. He saw the angry red bursts and ugly black smoke all around and could hear muffled explosions and the rattle of shrapnel striking his plane. Somehow they made it through, dumped their bombs and again were busy fending off continued attacks by the Luftwaffe as they headed home.

James had little time for sleep. The alert flag flew over squadron headquarters that indicated another mission was scheduled the following day. This time it was Marienburg, Poland, to bomb a Focke-Wulf plant. They would be in the air almost eleven hours. They saw no German fighters, only a German observation plane that shadowed the American bomber formation. They bombed the plant unmolested and headed for home expecting any minute to be jumped by fighters. As they flew out over the North Sea they relaxed and brought out peanut butter sandwiches and hot soup which had been sent along for the long flight. They never got to eat. The tail gunner called out that German fighters were approaching fast from their rear. The fighters stayed out of range of the formation's machine guns and fired rockets and 37 mm cannon. James's wingman took a rocket in the number three engine and the burning Fortress plunged earthward. Seven parachutes were seen to exit the aircraft, the last two parachutes were on fire. Air/Sea Rescue was alerted although it was believed hypothermia would claim the lives of the men before boats could reach them. James' good friend and bunkmate, Bob Wing, was the bombardier on that plane. He recalled a conversation with Bob the night before the mission. Bob's crew had not been scheduled for the mission but Bob was assigned as a replacement bombardier. He did not want to fly the mission because he just knew he would not come back. That night the bunk next to James was empty. The Eighth Air Force lost thirty bombers that day and was scheduled to fly again the next day, the third in a row.

October 10, 1943, the target was Munster, Germany and for the first time the Eighth Air Force would be bombing civilians in a "morale raid". The aiming point was the historic Munster Cathedral. Within the bomb pattern were hospitals and other churches. Despite serious reservations about the morality of striking a civilian target, command reasoned there were railroad yards in the target area and this was total war. Hitler had never hesitated to wage war against civilians and indiscriminate bombing of European cities.

The action that took place on this raid was rated by historians as the fiercest air battle in history. The Luftwaffee was committed to a maximum effort to bring an end to daylight bombing of the Eighth Air Force. Two hundred twenty-nine B-17s were to fly a diversion over the North Sea to split the German fighter force. The lead bomber developed electrical problems that knocked out their radio. All efforts of the lead crew to communicate the problem to the deputy leader failed. When the lead ship turned back to England everyone followed. German radar operators were then able to send all their squadrons to engage the main bomber force as it approached Munster. When they neared their bomb run, American escort fighters had reached the extent of their range and turned back to England. A second force of P-47 Thunderbolt fighters scheduled for escort duty with the bombers were still back in England unable to takeoff because of fog. It was then 300 Luftwaffe fighters began to attack in wave after wave. In the furious battle that followed burning planes and parachutes filled the air. Gunners stood ankle deep in shell casings while German fighters kept coming. They concentrated on the 100th Bomb Group flying low position and within minutes only one Fortress remained. They then turned to the 390th Bomb Group flying high position. In the next few minutes, nine bombers went down and five from the 95th were shot down. The American bombers were in danger of complete annihilation. Despite the vicious action, the lead bombardier put the bombs exactly on target. An urgent message was sent to England to request fighter support and report their desperate situation. After what seemed an eternity, fighter support arrived. The battle in the sky over Munster had lasted just twenty-five minutes. Forty-one bombers of the 13th Combat Wing made it to the target and twenty-seven had been shot down. The balance limped home in deteriorating weather and fading daylight. As weather closed in, many pilots, unable to land at home bases, set their aircraft down where ever they could find a field. James' plane landed with one engine knocked out and less than ten minutes fuel remaining.

Four days later, October 14, Black Thursday, their target was ball bearing plants at Schweinfurt, Germany, regarded as the greatest air battle in history. Three hundred twenty-three bombers of the First, Second and Third Divisions were scheduled for this mission. The entire Second Division of B-24s unable to assemble over England because of weather, aborted over the English Channel and returned to their bases. This reduced firepower by one-third. The Luftwaffe was ready and engaged the rest of the bombers in a running battle that lasted for four hours. Before the target was reached, sixty-two bombers were shot down or forced to turn back due to battle damage or wounded crewmembers. German fighters landed, refueled, took on more ammunition and continued the attack. After bombing the target, thirty-two more bombers were shot down during withdrawal. A plane on James's wing was hit and dropped back. James' pilot throttled back in an effort to help protect the crippled B-17, but German fighters still shot it down. James's aircraft rejoined the formation without further damage or casualties.

In all, ninety-four bombers were shot down, ditched, crash landed in England, or were so badly damaged they never flew again. Officially, sixty-two bombers were shot down over enemy territory. More that 183 bombers were lost during the four days of "Black Week".

When James started his combat tour, he had little hope of completing twenty-five missions. Only one crew in three completed their tour. On his twenty-fifth mission he was full of apprehension. A lot of veteran crews were shot down on their last mission. The target, Wilhelmshaven had moderate but accurate flak. The bombers were escorted by P-47 and P-51 fighters that kept enemy fighters away. After they turned off the target, the ball turret gunner began babbling incoherently on the intercom. The pilot realized the gunner had lost his oxygen and was losing consciousness. He left the formation and began a rapid descent through ice, sleet, snow and rain until they broke into clear weather at about 1000 feet and were off oxygen. As they came over their base the pilot buzzed the runway to signify that another flier, James, would be joining the "Lucky Bastard Club". He had finished his missions five ahead of the rest of his crew. Asked if he wanted to fly five more missions with the crew, it was no surprise that he declined.

James was discharged from military service on September 114, 1945 at Ft. Lewis, Washington. He had been awarded, among other medals, the Distinguished Flying Cross, Air Medal with three oak leaf clusters, ETO Ribbon and World War II Victory Medal. The 95th Bomb Group was awarded three Presidential Unit Citations in an eight month period.

James returned to college and after graduation became a high school art teacher.

Right - James's crew at 95th BG, Horham, England. James, Navigator is second from right in the front row.

HOWARD GREINER, ALBIA, IA, grew up on an Iowa farm and after the outbreak of hostilities in World War II, enlisted in the Army Air Corps October 12, 1942. He was called to active duty January 30, 1943. After Basic Training at Jefferson Barracks, St. Louis, Missouri, Howard processed through a classification center at San Antonio, Texas. He was assigned to pilot training and took all stages of flight training in Texas.

Primary Flight was taken at Stamford, Basic Flight at Sherman, Twin Engine Flight at Ellington Field and First Pilot Training at Ft. Worth, Texas. After he was assigned an air crew, they trained together at Casper, Wyoming in preparation for overseas deployment.

Howard and his crew were deployed to England by boat along with twenty other aircrews. He was assigned to the 785th Squadron of the 466th Bomb Group at Norwich. His second mission was on March 2, 1945, a bomb raid on targets at Magdeburg, Germany. His plane was hit by flak that caused loss of three engines, oxygen, radios, intercom and the hydraulic system. As they lost altitude it was discovered the plane was on fire. Howard ordered the crew to bail out of the aircraft and followed them. He broke a leg and ankle upon hitting the ground and was immediately taken prisoner by German soldiers.

No medical attention was given Howard's leg and he was forced to walk on it. This included an overnight march to a railway station for a trip to Frankfurt. From there he was taken by car to a small German town where a church had been converted to a hospital. He received appropriate medical attention from a captured Scottish doctor. While there the American Army began to close in on the area. The German medical staff stayed with the POWs rather than flee and surrendered when the town was captured.

After hospitalization in England and the United States, Howard was discharged from military service on October 31, 1945. He entered farming with his father until he started a very successful fertilizer and ammonia application business. He also imported cattle and expanded his farming operation. Howard married the love of his life who he met while in service and had six children from the union. He lost his wife in 1985. He currently owns a motel and restaurant in Albia.

Iowans of the Mighty Eighth

Howard is the author of "Flying High in Iowa", a book that tells of his life during the Depression era, World War II experiences, and ups and downs of his business operations. His picture, in uniform, is on the cover of the book. Excerpts were taken from his book for this biographical sketch.

VERNON GRUBB, KINGSLEY, IA, entered military service in February, 1942 at Ft. Dodge, Iowa. He was sent to Sheppard Field, Wichita Falls, Texas for Basic Training and Chanute Field, Illinois for Aircraft Mechanics School.

"The school was open twenty-four hours a day with different classes running all the time. So was the mess hall. You could get a meal even at midnite."

Vernon was then sent to Bell Aircraft Corporation School at Niagara Falls, New York, for instruction on the P-39 aircraft. Following graduation he served on the flight line servicing aircraft at Everett, Washington before reporting to Glendale, California, wherhe learned maintenance of the Lockheed P-38 Lightning fighter. After working on aircraft at Muroc, California, in the Mojave Desert in March, 1943, Vernon reported to New York City along with five other enlisted mechanics and two pilots. While there waiting assignment for transportation overseas, Vernon and the other mechanics were asked to repair P-38 fighters at Newark, New Jersey. "We went over there and found we could fix the airplanes, but the problem was, they didn't have any parts, so we went back to New York."

Vernon sailed to England on a British ship that encountered rough seas during the voyage. "Everyone was seasick. The smell everywhere was overpowering especially down in the hold of the ship where everyone slept."

Vernon was assigned to the 7th Photographic Reconnaissance Group at Mount Farm, England as a crew chief responsible for maintenance of one fighter aircraft. "We had three squadrons in our group. The other two squadrons flew P-38s but our squadron had the British Spitfire." During his tour, Vernon serviced aircraft assigned to two pilots. "Missions were flown unarmed. In place of machine guns, the aircraft were armed with cameras to take pre-mission and post-mission photographs of targets. My first pilot was shot down and eventually made his way back to England." Vernon's second pilot was a fellow Iowan, Lt. Gerald Glaza of Cedar Rapids who was also shot down, evaded capture by the Germans and was able to make the safety of Allied-held territory. "We had no losses because of a mechanic malfunction. During the latter stages of the war in Europe they brought in P-51 Mustang fighters to fly as escort for our photo planes and we moved to the airstrip at Chalgrove, England."

Vernon left England in September, 1945 aboard a Victory Ship and received his discharge from military service at Chicago, Illinois. He was been awarded the European Theater of Operations and World War II Victory Medals, among others. Following the war Vernon returned to farming from which he has retired.

Right - Vernon, in front, and friend at Mount Farm on the favorite means of transportation

Right - Vernon on the right, crew chief for Lt Gerald Glaza, Cedar Rapids, IA

JOSEPH GRUNDON, SAC CITY, IA, enlisted in the Army Air Corps in June, 1943 from Illinois. He completed Basic Training in Utah and Aerial Gunnery School at Las Vegas, Nevada before being assigned to an aircrew. Joe and his crew completed overseas training at Alexandria, Louisiana, before deployment to the European Theater of Operations.

Beginning June 18, 1944, Joe flew thirty-five combat missions as ball turret gunner with the 358th Squadron of the 303rd Bomb Group stationed at Molesworth, England. He completed his required number of missions in September, 1944, but remained at Molesworth as a gunnery instructor until December, 1944, when he boarded the "SS Washington" for return to the United States.

Joe received his discharge from military service in 1945 and had been awarded, among other medals, the Distinguished Flying Cross, Air Medal with four oak leaf clusters, European Theater of Operations Medal with battle stars, and the World War II Victory Medal.

In civilian life Joe was a crane operator for over twenty years until retirement.

Right - Joe's crew at 303rd BG, Molesworth, England. Joe, Ball Turret Gunner, is back row, third from left.

ELLSWORTH GUSTAFSON, DES MOINES, IA, enlisted in the Army Air corps at Des Moines and was sent to Lowry Field, Colorado for Basic Training. He then completed Aerial Gunnery School at Buckley, Field, Colorado. After assignment to an aircrew and training with them for overseas deployment, Gus was deployed to the 493rd Bomb Group at Debach, England, as a tail gunner.

At the time he had completed twenty-four missions, one shy for rotation back to the United States, the number of required missions was raised to thirty-five.

His last mission was a raid on a target in Germany. He noticed his co-pilot stow extra items in their aircraft before the mission that included a suitcase, some packages and a long package that was difficult to put in the plane. While over France at about thirty thousand feet flying "tail end Charley", Gus saw the packages fly past his window and a parachute inflate below him.

Later, Gus' pilot called on the intercom asking where the co-pilot was. He couldn't be found. The co-pilot simply abandoned the aircraft during the mission and parachuted from the airplane to avoid further flying in the war. "All he had to do was report his problems to his commanding officer and request ground duty." The co-pilot finished the war as a prisoner of war and after repatriation, was dishonorably discharged from the military.

Meanwhile Gus and his crew continued the mission and upon entering Germany received intense "flak" from German anti-aircraft guns. Their formation was attacked by a small German jet believed to be an ME-163 "Komet". "I saw the jet climb straight up and then dive down through our formation. He came back up at the tail of our aircraft and I think I could have shaken hands with him he was so close to us. My guns jammed and I didn't get a shot at him. When I bent down to try and clear my guns a "flak" burst sent shrapnel through my position where my head had been. Another piece of "flak" entered my compartment and went right between my legs and out the airplane. The nose of our plane had been hit and air was rushing through the plane. The other crewmembers were in the middle of the plane when we took the hit and the plane exploded. I was blown out of the plane and falling through space. I saw a big thunderhead cloud below me and when I fell through it, it caused me to tumble over and over. I pulled on the ripcord on my parachute and collapsed it when I got out of the clouds. When I tried to open it again, the lines were all tangled in my legs and the chute was wrapped around me. I saw the ground coming up at me and I managed to get it open. German soldiers were shooting at me and shot my GI shoes I was carrying out of my hand. I was headed for some high tension wires and managed to land in a bomb crater. I hit hard cause the parachute opened just in time to only break my fall. I dislocated my arm. A German machine gunner kept shooting at me. I managed to raise one arm in surrender. He came up to me and yelled "Heil Hitler". I asked him if he spoke English. He drew a knife and put it under my chin and asked "you English?" He knocked me down. I said "Nix, English. Americano" He didn't seem to understand what "Americano" meant and for some reason I yelled "Chicago". He asked again, "you Chicago?" I said yes. He came up to me gave me a big hug and patted me on the back like we were long lost brothers. I learned he had a brother in Chicago, loved Americans and from then on I could do no wrong."

Gus was sent to a German Stalag Luft prisoner of war camp. "We were treated ok. The food was bad but the German Army didn't have good food either. Worms in the food we just ate. I went down to one hundred-twenty pounds."

Following American capture of his prison camp Gus was sent for processing and recuperation at Camp Lucky Strike near Le Havre, France. He boarded a ship for the United States that ran into a bad storm on the voyage home. "Down below the air was intolerable. The storm was so bad no one was allowed on deck, but I went up there anyway. I just couldn't stand it any longer. The waves seemed a hundred feet high. I was barely able to hang onto stairway rails on deck and could have been swept overboard and no one would have known. I was barely able to make it back inside the ship."

On return to civilian life Gus earned his Bachelor's Degree from Drake University and was recommend to the Federal Bureau of Investigation by a Drake speech professor. Gus spent twenty-seven years as a Special Agent predominantly in the New York City area. He retired in 1977.

Chapter Twenty-Two

Right - Gus' crew, 493rd BG, Debach, England. Gus, a tail gunner is back row, right.

JAMES HAAS, PERRY, IA, had attended the University of Iowa for one year and was working for Standard Oil Company in Chicago on America's entry into World War II. Although he enlisted in the Army Air Corps in 1942 he was not called to active duty until May, 1943, and was sent to Jefferson Barracks, St Louis, Missouri for Basic Training.

Jim attended Morningside College, Sioux City, Iowa, in the College Training Detachment Program as an Aviation Cadet. While there he received ten hours flight training before being sent to the cadet center at San Antonio, Texas. He was assigned to Bombardier School at Houston, Texas. Upon graduation on December 24, 1943, he received his wings and commission as a second lieutenant. He also attended Aerial Gunnery School at Laredo, Texas, where training was completed in the morning hours to avoid afternoon heat.

After assignment to an air crew at Salt Lake City, Utah, Jim and his crew completed overseas training at Dalhart, Texas, before boarding a troop train for Camp Kilmer, New Jersey. He boarded the "S.S. Brazil" in May, 1944, which set sail for Liverpool, England as part of a convoy. "It was one of the greatest sights I've ever seen. We had aircraft carriers and all types of ships as far as the eye could see, it was quite a sight for a kid from Iowa."

He was sent to Stone, England, a classification center, where he and his crew were assigned to the 398th Bomb Group as one of its first replacement crews. On June 20, 1944, Jim flew the first of his thirty-six combat missions. His second mission was to bomb a target at Berlin. After "bombs away" it was realized one bomb had "hung up" and did not release from its shackles. Without a parachute Jim climbed into the bomb bay area and was successful in getting it to drop. "I was scared to death. Any sudden jolt or movement of the plane that would cause me to lose balance, I would have been a goner."

On July 6, 1944, a mission was scheduled to bomb targets at St. Nazaire, France, Jim's crew was assigned a brand new B-17 named "The Prowler" that had a black tomcat painted on the side of the nose. They intended to rename the aircraft "Hissanmoan" after their mission. After they crossed the French coast they were hit by "flak" which put their aircraft in a spin, but the pilot was able to level the airplane. Their number three engine was smoking. The fire stopped after they feathered the engine and pulled the fire extinguisher handle. Number four engine was unharmed but number two engine began wind milling. The cowling had been ripped away and revealed exploded cylinders which were dripping oil and fuel. Number one engine also began wind milling out of control. With these problems the pilot turned back toward England. The crew reported they were unharmed except no word came from the ball turret gunner. He was found unharmed, but in shock staring at a large hole in his turret only inches from his face that had been blown out by debris from the number two engine. He was pulled from the turret, wrapped in a blanket, his wrists and face massaged and given inhalants to which he responded.

Shrapnel had ripped through the bomb bay area and cut shackles holding their bombs. The bombs were released through the closed doors and in doing so, one door was ripped from the aircraft. They constantly lost altitude from only one working engine. Drag was created from wind milling engines and open bomb bay area. When they crossed the English coast they desperately searched for an emergency field to land. Their radio aids also went out when they were hit. Two English fighters flew menacingly alongside. Recognition signals are blinked to them, they respond favorably and the two fighters flew away. At 3,500 feet the air speed of their aircraft was near stalling speed. When they reached 1,900 feet the pilot ordered the crew to bail out but the co-pilot and engineer elect to stay with the pilot. Shortly after the crew bailed out an airstrip was spotted and the pilot was able to make a safe belly landing. "After I bailed out, the altitude wasn't much and I hit the ground hard. A farmer sitting on a fence holding a pitchfork came to help me after I was able to convince him I was an American."

On July 28, 1944 during a mission to Merseburg Jim's aircraft took thirty flak hits that were at least five inches in diameter. His tail gunner was hit by flak but was wearing his flak suit which saved his life. His top turret gunner was also hit by flak but was also saved when the shrapnel hit his parachute harness. The pilot's oxygen line was cut and he lost consciousness, but was revived by crewmembers while the Co-pilot flew the aircraft.

On Jim's twenty-fourth mission, a bombing raid on a chemical plant at Ludwigshaven, Germany, a B-17 next to his blew up from a flak direct hit during the bomb run. His own aircraft took a hit in its number three engine and caught on fire. Shrapnel came through the side of Jim's airplane, struck him in the leg and knockied him backwards about six feet. Lying wounded he was able to see aircraft above him release their bombs. Jim crawled back to his bombardier's position and released his bomb load. The pilot then put their aircraft into a dive in an attempt to stop the fire in their number three engine. "I thought the wings were going to drop off, but the fire blew out." After the mission Jim was sent to a hospital at Cambridge, England where he received medical treatment covering several weeks.

With eleven missions to go, Jim's original crew finished ahead of him and he was used as a replacement bombardier. In November, 1944, he returned to combat status. "Our squadron became separated from the Group during a raid on Nurnberg. We were attacked by German ME-109 fighters that slaughtered us. We lost nine of our twelve airplanes. The rest of us got together and flew into clouds to escape the fighters. We were really shot up. We successfully landed with two flat tires. When we examined our plane we had 150-200 cannon holes in our ship and no one had been hit."

Jim completed his missions in January, 1945. He boarded a ship for a ten day sail to the United States. Most of the trip was spent in a storm. "I got seasick and just wanted to die. I just got over flying my thirty-five missions. I couldn't eat or get my head off the pillow."

Before reporting for further duty Jim spent a thirty day furlough in Perry. "My parents had an apartment above a store in downtown Perry. There was a big fire that took almost the entire downtown area including all my personal effects. I was given another thirty days leave so I got married."

Jim received his military discharge in June, 1945, at Jefferson Barracks. He had been awarded the Distinguished Flying Cross, Purple Heart, Air Medal with five oak leaf clusters, the ETO Ribbon with battle stars and the World War II Victory Medal.

Jim retired from banking in 1987 after serving for forty years as a Senior Vice-President and Trust Officer.

Right - James and his crew at 398th BG, Nuthampstead, England. James, Bombardier, is front row, left.

JAMES HALVERSON, SPENCER, IA, was attending the University of South Dakota when he enlisted in the Army Air Corps in February, 1942. Accepted for the Aviation Cadet Program, Jim took the four stages of flight training in Texas. Pre-Flight Training was held at Randolph Field, Primary Flight Training at Coleman, Basic Flight Training at San Angelo and Advanced   Flight Training at McAllen, Texas where he received his wings and commission as a Second Lieutenant in October, 1942.

Transition training from the AT-6 to the P-47 Thunderbolt meant moving from an aircraft with 550 horsepower to one with 2000 horsepower and twice the speed. "None of the graduates had ever seen a Thunderbolt. After classroom training on the aircraft fifteen of us took off the next day on training flights. One crashed on takeoff and another landed at another field."

Upon completion of training Jim left Texas in ninety degree heat and reported to Westover, Massachusetts where the temperature was minus thirty degrees. It was intended the newly assigned P-47s would be flown to the European Theater of Operations but it was decided at the last minute to ship them by boat rather than risk any losses in route. He boarded an Italian ocean liner named "Orion" for a trip to England of only six days.

The 356th Fighter Group, assigned to an RAF base at Martlesham Heath lacked housing for the pilots. They were billeted in a restored castle four miles from the base that had been equipped with central heating. "It was strange to fly missions and be scared to death then return to the castle exhausted and be expected to be in dress uniform and tie for dinner."

Jim flew sixty combat missions mostly in the role of escort for bomber groups including missions to Berlin of six hundred miles. "We were told not to fly at full throttle all the time because we had just enough fuel to make it back to base if we conserved some of it."

In August, 1944, Jim returned to the United States and was assigned to Wilmington, North Carolina where pilots were in training for transfer to the Pacific Theater of Operations. He was offered an administrative position on the base in the ground-training department and remained there until the end of the war. He received his discharge from military service in July, 1945, having been awarded, among other medals, the Distinguished Flying Cross, Air Medal with oak leaf clusters, ETO Ribbon and World War II Victory Medal.

Jim had been orphaned and became self-sufficient since eighth grade. He returned to Spencer after the war and eventually owned three office supply stores, was part owner of a resort in the Iowa Great Lakes area and a leasing company. He served on a bank board of directors for twenty years and at one time was simultaneously president of the local Chamber of Commerce and Rotary Club.

Right - Jim receiving the Distinguished Flying Cross at 356th FG, Martlesham Heath, England.

Right - Jim's Squadron at 356th Fighter Group. Jim is back row, third from right.

DAVE HAMILTON, DES MOINES, IA,

was a student at Iowa State College at the outbreak of World War II. He entered military service August 25, 1943, at Camp Dodge, Iowa.

Dave attended Cadet Training Detachment at St Cloud, MN; Gunnery School at Yuma, AZ and Operational Training at Biggs Field, El Paso, TX.

He was deployed overseas on January 5, 1945, as a waist gunner first with the 652nd Bomb Squadron, 25th Bomb Group at Watton, England, then the 351st Bomb Squadron of the 100th Bomb Group at Thorpe Abbotts, England. He also served at Third Air Division Headquarters, Elveden Hall, England.

Dave flew four missions with the 652nd Heavy Weather Recon Bomb Squadron. Each mission required lengthy flight time over water to the Azores in B-17s that required added fuel tanks. Crews were reduced with only two gunners and a trained weather observer added. The crew Dave had originally trained with was lost on a mission without a trace. Even though Dave was not flying with them at that time, an 8th Air Force Museum publication lists him as being with the crew and killed in action (KIA). Dave has met with the author of the publication and assured him that he is alive.

Dave was discharged from military service on April 6, 1946, at Camp McCoy, Wisconsin. He then pursued a career as a civil engineer with cement companies.

JAMES HAMILTON, COUNCIL BLUFFS, IA,

had graduated from Iowa State College and spent a year teaching vocational agriculture at Earlham, Iowa when he joined the Iowa National Guard, 120th Observation Squadron. The unit was expected to be called to active duty but when it wasn't, Jim resigned from the Guard and enlisted in the Army Air Corps.

In February, 1943 Jim was called to active duty and sent to Jefferson Barracks, St. Louis, Missouri for Basic Training. Accepted in the Aviation Cadet Program he took Pre-Flight Training at Maxwell Field, Alabama; Primary Flight Training at Chanute Field, Illinois and Basic Flight Training at Malden, Missouri. Advanced Flight Training was completed at Fayetteville, Arkansas, in January, 1944, when he received his wings and commission as a Second Lieutenant.

After being assigned an air crew at Salt Lake City, Utah, Jim completed combat training with his crew at Delbert, Texas and Gulfport, Mississippi. Additional crew training with radar operators was completed at Langley Field, Virginia, in August, 1944, before they flew to the European Theater of Operations and the 95th Bomb Group at Horham, England.

Jim flew forty combat missions, five more than was required. On one mission to bomb a heavily defended ball bearing plant at Kassel, Germany, "we got shot up pretty bad on the bomb run. We lost two engines and a third one was running at only half power. We broke from the formation and began a gradual descent of about one hundred feet per minute. We had to hide in clouds from German fighters. We made it back to England and landed on an airstrip in East Anglia. Coming over the tops of trees I saw two runways. One had concrete obstructions on it to prevent anyone from landing on it. I gave what power the plane had left to make it to the second airstrip. I couldn't get the plane stopped and we ran off the end of the runway."

"On another mission we had a fire in the cockpit which we got out, but we had no hydraulics so when we came in to land at our base the wheels had to be cranked down. When we landed we couldn't stop until we ran off the runway, through a fence and into a kale patch. But everyone on the crew was okay. Getting up in the middle of the night, eating breakfast and going to briefings, we just wanted to get the mission over with."

Jim's last mission was on February 14, 1945, a bombing raid on Chemnitz, Germany. He returned to the United States in March, 1945 and after furlough reported to Long Beach, California, where he finished the war ferrying aircraft between airbases. In November, 1945 he was discharged from military service, having been awarded, among other medals, the Distinguished Flying Cross, Air Medal with five oak leaf clusters, ETO Ribbon with battle stars, and World War II Victory Medal.

When he returned to civilian life, Jim taught vocational agriculture in the Audubon, Iowa School System for twenty-two years. He was President of the National Organization of Vocational Agriculture Teachers, and helped pass legislation establishing community colleges in Iowa, including Iowa Western Community College, where he was employed for seventeen years until retirement.

Right - James's crew at 95th BG, Horham, England. James, Pilot, is back row, right.

KENNETH HANSEN, CEDAR RAPIDS, IA,

was an ambulance driver when he enlisted in the Army Air Corps. He was sent to Jefferson Barracks, St. Louis, Missouri, for Basic Training. Ken had applied for the Aviation Cadet Program and took courses at Michigan State University before he attended a Curtis-Wright Aircraft Mechanics Course at Glendale, California. After graduation he was sent to Kingman, Arizona, for Aerial Gunnery School. While there he volunteered for high altitude experimental testing.

Ken was assigned to an aircrew and trained for overseas deployment with the crew at Dyersburg, Tennessee. While on a practice mission over the Gulf of Mexico his crew flew into a thunderstorm which "knocked" their plane down to an altitude of five hundred feet before the pilot could regain control of the aircraft.

In December, 1944, Ken and his crew boarded the "USS America" for a six day voyage in rough seas to Southampton, England. From there they rode a train to Snetterton Heath and the 96th Bomb Group. He spent his first Christmas Eve away from home assembling bombs.

Ken flew thirty combat missions as Flight Engineer and Top Turret Gunner. Most of his missions were flown in a B-17 named "Conga Belle". During one mission their aircraft had been loaded with five hundred pound bombs. After "bombs away" one bomb failed to release from one hook and was left dangling in a downward position. The propeller on the bomb had fully spun out and was in danger of exploding at any moment. Ken entered the bomb bay area and was not able to dislodge the bomb. Tying one end of a rope around a part of the bomb bay and the other end around his parachute harness Ken climbed as high as he could in the bomb bay and jumped up and down on the bomb until it feel to earth. Ken fell through the bomb bay and was dangling by the rope under the aircraft, but was able to climb back into the airplane.

On a mission to Chemnitz, Germany, an area heavily defended by anti-aircraft guns, the number two engine on his plane was hit. The propeller wind milled and couldn't be shut down. Another engine began to run erratically and wouldn't shut down. A third engine had been running at full speed for two hours. They attempted to make an emergency landing at Brussells, Belgium, however dense fog prevented this. A P-51 Mustang appeared and escorted them to an airfield in France that was being repaired from bombings. When they landed the aircraft could not be stopped. The pilot was able to ground loop the aircraft and miss parked bombers. They wound up with their rear wheel in a bomb crater.

An amusing incident took place in Africa when Ken and his crew had to fly there. In order to protect their aircraft Ken and another crew member slept in the plane. An intruder attempted to enter the plane near a door where Ken lay. He stuck a pistol in the face of the Arab intruder who fell off the ladder leading to the plane and took off running.

Ken returned to the United States in August, 1945. When discharged from military service he had been awarded the Air Medal with five oak leaf clusters, the ETO Ribbon and World War II Victory Medal. After the war he worked as a telephone and electronic technician until retirement.

ROBERT HARKEN, ACKLEY, IA, was a butter maker until he enlisted in the Army Air Corps in July, 1942. He wasn't called to active duty until February, 1943, at Camp Dodge, Iowa, and was sent to San Antonio, Texas, where he entered the Aviation Cadet Training Program. Bob completed all his flight training in Texas. About nine weeks were spent in each phase of Pre-flight, Basic, two and four engine training.

Bob was sent to Murdock Lake, California, where he trained with his crew before they were sent to Camp Kilmer, New Jersey for overseas deployment. He boarded a British ship that sailed a zig-zag route to England in an effort to avoid enemy submarines. Further training took place in Ireland to get used to the British system of communications before eventual assignment to the 466th BG at Attlebridge.

Robert flew thirty combat missions. The last ten mission were flown as lead crew of their Group. As a result of being "lead", Robert flew five less missions than what was normally required. His first mission was flown on August 7, 1944, against targets in Ghent. His last mission was on January 22, 1945 against Dortmund, Germany.

On Christmas Day, 1944, and January 1, 1945, as well as three days in between Bob flew fuel missions hauling gasoline in support of General Patton's Third Army in the Battle of the Bulge and food drops to Dutch civilians starved from occupation by Nazi forces.

Despite being hit by flak and attacks from enemy fighters on every mission, Bob's bombardier was the only crewmember of his that was wounded. His tail gunner was lost on one mission when his oxygen system failed and he fell unconscious. They were flying alone and susceptible to enemy fighter attack. Bob secured escort from an American P-51 Mustang fighter and flew to the nearest air base in Allied hands to get aid for his gunner. They were shot at by both Germans and Americans before he was able to land at a British base in Belgium. It was too late for the tail gunner. He could not be revived and died.

Bob returned to the United States in March, 1945. He had been awarded the Air Medal with five oak leaf clusters, and the ETO and World War II Victory Medals. He remained in the Air Force reserve and flew with the Air Transport Command. After the war Bob returned to college at the University of Dubuque and Colorado State Teachers College. After graduation he taught school for twenty-two years before he left to enter the insurance business.

Right - Robert and his crew with two extra navigators in front of their B-24 bomber named "Jennie" at 466th BG, Attlebridge, England. Robert is back row, third from right.

GEORGE HARTZ, NEWHALL, IA, entered military service October 14, 1942 at Camp Dodge, Iowa. After Basic Training he was attended Mechanics School. While there George learned of an urgent need for aerial gunners. He volunteered and was accepted for training.

After aerial gunnery school was completed, George was assigned to a crew for training before being deployed to Polebrook, England, with the 351st Bomb Group as a tailgunner. George completed thirty-three missions. He was wounded in the leg from the explosion of a .20 mm shell that hit his B-17 named "Buckeye Babe". The plane had been named by the crew chief from Ohio who maintained and serviced the aircraft.

After the war in Europe was over George was returned to the United States and attended Flight Engineer School before he was once again deployed, this time to New Guinea. His duties there involved air/sea rescue, testing rebuilt airplanes damaged in combat, delivering troops and supplies and bringing wounded back from the front.

George was discharged from the military September 16, 1945, at the rank of Staff Sergeant and had been awarded the Purple Heart, Distinguished Flying Cross and Air Medal with five oak leaf clusters.

He returned to farming until 1976 when he entered the insurance business. George died in 1999.

WOODROW HEITLAND, ACKLEY, IA, was married and farmed until he was drafted into the Army Air Corps on May 18, 1942. After Basic Training at Jefferson Barracks, St. Louis, Missouri, he attended Aircraft Mechanics School at Chanute Field, Illinois and at the Boeing Aircraft factory, Seattle, Washington.

Woody volunteered for Aerial Gunnery School and was sent to Las Vegas for training. He was later assigned to an air crew at Salt Lake City, Utah, and trained with them at Blythe, California, as part of the 34th Bomb Group. He failed a final physical because of an eyesight depth perception problem and was re-assigned to provide aircraft maintenance for air crews training at Ephrata and Spokane, Washington and Rapid City, South Dakota.

In April, 1944, Woody boarded the "USS Manhattan" for Liverpool, England. He was assigned to the 398th Bomb Group at Nuthampstead as an aircraft mechanic responsible for maintenance of one aircraft. Woody conducted inspections on engines after every fifty hours of logged flight time before engines were changed at 300 or 500 hours. While Sub-Depots performed major structural repair to aircraft, Woody and his crew ensured all systems were operational on their aircraft and engines performed at maximum capacity. On mission days ground crews were awakened ahead of flight crews to perform final checks on aircraft and pre-flight the engines. After takeoff ground crews usually ate or returned to their barracks for sleep prior to the aircraft's return. The return was a period of "sweating out" whether their aircraft would return or not.

Woody went through three aircrews during his tour. The last six months of the war in Europe he was the Crew Chief over a team of mechanics. "It was hard to take" when his aircraft failed to return from a mission. As a result "we never got too close to the air crew, it made it that much harder" if a crew was lost. If they did return, the ground crew could spend the rest of the day and all night getting their plane ready for the next mission.

On May 26, 1945, Woody flew home to the United States. He reported to Jefferson Barracks at St. Louis and was assigned to Sioux Falls, South Dakota, for B-29 training in preparation for transfer to the Pacific Theater of Operations in the war against Japan. The war ended before Woody could be re-deployed and he received his discharge from military service October 14, 1945 at Sioux City, Iowa. Woody was awarded, among other medals, the ETO Ribbon with six battle stars and the World War II Victory Medal.

Woody returned to farming in the Ackley area until retirement in 1977. While he was overseas his wife worked at a factory making cartridge belts and then a hemp factory in Iowa Falls which made rope for the Navy.

Above - Woody and the Engineering Department with the 602nd Bomb Squadron, 398th Bomb Group, Nuthampstead, England. Woody is on the right between engines one and two with arrow pointed at him.

HJALMAR HELLBERG, JR, MARSHALLTOWN, IA, enlisted in the Army Air Corps while he was still in high school. He was inducted into military service June 14, 1943, after he received a sixty day deferment to finish school.

After Basic Training at Lincoln, Nebraska, Hjalmar attended Armament School at Lowry Field, Colorado, and Aerial Gunnery School at Tyndall Field, Florida. He was back at Lincoln for crew assignment where he learned of the D-Day invasion of Normandy. In January, 1945, Hjalmar and his crew trained at Rapid City, South Dakota, in preparation for overseas deployment. While at Rapid City he met Edna, a young lady who would later become his wife.

Hjalmar and his crew flew the northern route to England which required re-fueling at Goose Bay, Labrador. "I had never seen snow like they had at Labrador. Except for the runways, they rolled the snow to flatten it. It built up covering the buildings so you had to go downhill into the mess hall. While there, a fueling truck hit a wing of our airplane." This caused a delay in their travel plans but eventually Hjalmar arrived at Kimbolton, England, home of the 379th Bomb Group.

Hjalmar flew twenty-four combat missions as ball turret gunner. This included nine missions in eleven days. His first mission was on February 3, 1945, a raid on the Tempelhof marshalling yards in Berlin. Over a thousand bombers took part in this portion of the raid while other bombers attacked nearby targets. "When the lead plane dropped its bombs over Berlin the last planes in the raid hadn't left England yet."

Hjalmar's third mission was on marshalling yards in Nurnberg. "We received over a hundred holes in our plane from "flak". No injuries. A crew that was in our barracks took a direct hit. Their airplane exploded and was gone."

Hjalmar was involved in the last mission of the war in Europe by Eighth Air Force bombers, a raid on armament works in Pilsen, Czechoslovakia. He recalled that prior to the mission it was realized that this could be their last mission of the war. "Goodbye and good luck" was said to two friends flying in different aircraft. They would meet after the mission. Hjalmar was aware that two aircraft from his squadron went down during the mission, one of them on fire. Afterward he met one of his friends for the traditional congratulations. He went to his barracks and was lying on his bunk reading when he suddenly realized he hadn't seen the other friend. Hjalmar ran to the operations room and found out his other friend was on the aircraft that had been on fire. Several days later he was again lying on his bunk reading a magazine close to his face when he felt the presence of someone standing over him. It was his other friend who had parachuted from the burning aircraft and was eventually returned to the 379th.

Hjalmar received his discharge from military service on December 18, 1945. He had been awarded, among other medals, the Air Medal with three oak leaf clusters. He returned to Marshalltown to a jewelry business that has been in his family for five generations. He is an active member of the Eighth Air Force Historical Society, has served as President of the 379th Bomb Group Association and currently operates the Group's PX.

Right - Hjalmar's first crew at 379th Bomb Group. He is back row, left.

Right - Hjalmar's second crew. He is back row, left.

CLARENCE HENDERSON, CEDAR RAPIDS, IA, worked at Bishop's Cafeteria before World War II. He enlisted in the Army Air Corps on September 17, 1941. He was sent to Jefferson Barracks, St. Louis, Missouri, for Basic Training then Logan, Colorado, site of a military clerical school. While there the Japanese attacked American bases on the island of Oahu officially entering the United States into World War II.

Clarence was sent to Moffitt Field, California, a dirigible base under Navy control. After only a week he was transferred to Santa Ana, CA, where a new air base was being built. The base was not ready to handle the influx of servicemen and Clarence was sent to Williams Field, AZ. After the base at Santa Ana was completed Clarence returned there as part of the permanent staff supervising operations in a base mess hall. Thirty-five thousand airmen were at Santa Ana as part of the Aviation Cadet Program. After one year Clarence volunteered for air crew duty and sent to Aerial Gunnery School at Las Vegas, Nevada.

Clarence was assigned to an air crew at Lincoln, NE. They trained at Rapid City, South Dakota, in preparation for overseas deployment. In February, 1945, Clarence boarded the "USS West Point" at Boston harbor bound for England.

Assigned as a ball turret gunner with the 303rd BG at Molesworth, Clarence flew twenty-three combat missions. These included raids on an Ordnance Plant at Orianienburg and Berlin, Germany, as well as Headquarters of the German High Command at Zossen, Germany. During one stretch he flew missions on nine straight days bombing German airfields.

It was a mission on Bremen that was his most memorable. During the start of their bomb run the pilot had to urinate. He relieved himself in a fuse can, opened his window at the cockpit and emptied the can. The contents sprayed over the windows of the plane and froze. At that time they were hit by flak that knocked out the number two engine and set it afire. The propeller began wind milling out of control. From his ball turret position Clarence radioed the pilot oil was leaking from the engine and running down the side of the plane. Then gas began leaking threatening to ignite the plane with its full bomb load. Suddenly Clarence couldn't breathe. His oxygen line had been hit by flak and was broken. He was able to get out of the turret and was handed a walk around oxygen bottle by the radio operator. The aircraft was put into a dive to try and put out the engine fire. Pins were replaced in the bombs and fuel transferred from the number two engine. Down to 800 feet and still behind enemy lines, American P-51s were radioed for escort assistance. Their bomb load was released in the countryside and they returned to base without further incident.

In July, 1945, Clarence returned to America aboard the "SS George Davis". He was discharged from military service at Santa Ana, CA. He had been awarded, among other medals, the Air Medal with three oak leaf clusters, ETO Medal with three battle stars and a Presidential Unit Citation.

Clarence retired from FMC Corporation in Cedar Rapids.

Right - Clarence beside his ball turret gunner position

Right - Clarence and his crew, 303rd BG, Molesworth. Clarence is front row, third from left.

GAYLORD HENRYSON, STORY CITY, IA, was farming when the Japanese attacked American military bases in the Hawaiian Islands on December 7, 1941. He enlisted in the Army Air Corps January 15, 1942 and was sent to Shepard Field, Texas, for Basic Training. Next came Aircraft Mechanics School at Rantoul, Illinois and Engineering School at Seattle, Washington.

In June, 1942 additional training with air crews took place in Oregon and Walla Walla, Washington until September 1, 1942, when Gaylord was shipped to the East Coast.

On September 6, 1942, he boarded the "Queen Mary" for a six day voyage to Grenock, Scotland and eventual assignment as Crew Chief with the 91st BG at Bassingbourn, England.

Gaylord and his ground crew members were responsible for the maintenance and proper operation of aircraft assigned to them. This often required they change engines, fuel tanks, super chargers, wheels, rudders and even wings on aircraft. On mission day before the aircrews "took off" they would be on the flight line at midnight to pre-flight the aircraft and "top off" the fuel tanks while other crews loaded bombs, ammunition, and perform other specialty assignments.

During his tenure several aircraft assigned to Gaylord for maintenance never returned from their mission. Gaylord never got "too close" to any aircrew assigned his aircraft aware that they might not return from their mission. Toward the end of the war his ground crew took turns sleeping in the aircraft on the flight line for security purposes.

After the war ended in Europe, Gaylord flew back to the United States on June 7, 1945, as Co-Pilot aboard "Oh Happy Day", the last aircraft to which he had been assigned as crew chief. He reported to Sioux Falls, South Dakota where he was re-assigned to El Paso, Texas to train as a B-29 crew chief. The war ended and precluded further military service. Gaylord received his discharge in September, 1945 at Lincoln, Nebraska. He had been awarded the European Theater of Operations and World War II Victory Medals. During his three and a half years in the military he never received a furlough home.

Gaylord returned to farming in the Story City area from which he retired. Meanwhile he built a campground near his home which he operated for twenty-seven years.

Right - Gaylord, B-17 which he maintained and its crew at 91st Bomb Group, Bassingbourn, England. Gaylord, crew chief, is back row, left.

RONALD E. HIGDON, IOWA CITY, IA, was employed by Bank of America at Firebaugh, California, as a bookkeeping machine operator prior to World War II. He entered the Army Air Corps on December 31, 1942, at Monterey, California.

Ronald attended Airplane Mechanics School at Keesler Field, Mississippi, and Flexible Gunnery School, Laredo Field,

Texas. He was assigned to the 578th Squadron, 392nd Bomb Group, at Wendling, England on April 20, 1944, as a waist gunner and flight maintenance gunner on a B-24 bomber.

Ronald flew thirty-three combat missions. On August 14, 1944, on a bombing mission to Lyon-Bron Airfield, France, in support of the invasion of southern France, their bomb load could not be dropped because of an electrical malfunction. On the return trip to England with a full bomb load, the plane was hit by flak from anti-aircraft fire. A shell came through the catwalk in the bomb bay area and hit the shackle holding the top bomb in the racks. The shell failed to explode. The shackle kept the shell from going through oxygen tanks which would have destroyed the plane and crew. The pilot gave the crew the opportunity to bail out of the damaged plane but also told them he was going to try and take them home. No one bailed out and they returned to base safely.

Ronald was discharged from military service on September 23, 1945, at Wright-Patterson Field, Dayton, Ohio. He had been awarded the Distinguished Flying Cross, Air Medal with three oak leaf clusters, European Theater of Operations Medal with four battle stars and the World War II Victory medal.

Ronald returned to accounting, farming and serving as a bulk station agent.

Right - Brothers Higdon, both with the Eighth Air Force. Ronald on left was Aerial Gunner with 392nd BG, Wendling, England. Willard on right, was a Navigator with the 458th BG, Horsham St. Faith, England.

WILLARD HIGDON, LAYTON, UT, was a bookkeeping machine operator with the Department of the Army in Washington, D.C. at the start of World War II. He entered the Army Air Corps, July 24, 1943, and attended Advanced Navigator School at Selma Field, Louisiana.

Willard was deployed to England on January 17, 1944, as a Navigator with the

458th Bomb Group at Horsham-St. Faith, near Norwich, England. Getting there was an experience. He flew with his crew from San Francisco to Florida, Puerto Rico, Brazil and on to Dakar, Africa. Over Africa they flew into a dust storm. Compasses on the B-24 went crazy and they were lost. They landed, out of gas at Rio Del Oro, Africa. From England, the crew was reported as missing. They were taken by boat to the Canary Islands and then to Spain. After a bus trip to Gibraltar, they were flown to Horsham-St. Faith.

On his nineteenth combat mission in August, 1944, a bomb raid on Epinal, France, just before D-Day, Willard's aircraft lost two engines and was forced to land in Switzerland, a neutral nation. It was Switzerland's policy to intern all World War II combatants for the duration of the war who violated their air space. Willard, his pilot and a crewmember from another plane that was also interned, escaped the prison camp where they were held. They boarded a train and rode as far as their money would take them. Then they walked for three nights, slept in the day to avoid detection and crossed the mountains into eastern France at Grenoble. The French Underground picked them up and took them to U.S. forces and eventually they made it back to England.

Willard was discharged from military service September 9, 1945, at Jefferson Barracks, Missouri. He had been awarded the Air Medal with two oak leaf clusters, the European Theater of Operations medal with four bronze stars and the World War II Victory Medal. Willard returned to farming and later was employed at Hill Air Force Base, Utah. Willard died from pneumonia, September 17, 1999.

Right - Willard and his crew at 458th BG, Horsham St Faith, England. Willard is back row, left.

CLARENCE HIGHTSHOE, IOWA CITY, IA, was a junior at Iowa State Teachers College, Cedar Falls, IA, when he received his draft notice in 1942. He enlisted in the Army Air Corps. He was allowed to finish the academic quarter before he reported for duty in January, 1943 and was sent to Jefferson Barracks, St.

Iowans of the Mighty Eighth

Louis, MO, for Basic Training. He contracted a cold and severe sinus infection which caused him to fail a physical for the Aviation Cadet Program. He was assigned to work at the base hospital where he had recovered from his illness. The doctor he worked for "signed off" on his medical records that cleared him for flying status.

Clarence was sent to Albion College in Michigan as part of the College Detachment Training Program consisting of classroom instruction, physical fitness and fifteen hours of flying in a piper cub airplane. He was then sent to a Classification Center at San Antonio, TX, where a series of testing took place to determine each trainees best qualifications. Clarence qualified for all flying officer's positions and was given the choice of Pilot, Navigator or Bombardier. Based on his studies at college he chose Navigator.

Clarence was a star track athlete in high school and college. This was not lost on the military who entered him in four events at various military and college track meets around the United States instead of training. All good things had to come to an end and Clarence was slated for Navigation School at Ellington Field, Texas, in September, 1943. Married in 1942, Clarence's wife Alda accompanied him to each base he was assigned where she gained local employment. He was then assigned to Advanced Navigation School at Hondo Air Base, TX. Graduation brought him commission as a Second Lieutenant and his Navigator's wings.

Advanced crew training took place at Pyote, TX. Crew members honed their skills and became familiar with each other's positions in the aircraft, equipment aboard, practiced bomb runs, and night flying.

Following indoctrination at Hutchinson, KS, on what to expect in combat, Clarence reported to Camp Kilmer, NJ, for overseas deployment. It was there he learned his pilot had been killed in an automobile accident. The crew was assigned a new pilot who had volunteered for a second tour of combat duty. They boarded a troop ship for what would be a three-week sail to England.

Assigned to the 384th Bomb Group at Grafton Underwood, Clarence flew twenty-nine combat missions. He was re-assigned as an instructor which prevented him from flying his last mission. Thirty missions were required for rotation back to the United States.

Clarence's first mission, in what was supposed to be a "milk run", was completed with 127 "flak" holes taken in his aircraft. No one was injured or vital parts of the aircraft damaged.

During one of his early missions Clarence was in the nose of their aircraft with the navigator. "Suddenly right in front of us was a burst of flak. We were feeling pretty safe with our escort and had just removed our steel helmets. We were descending, as the French coast was almost directly below us. Flak suits were coming off along with our oxygen masks that we had worn for about five hours. I had just picked up my head set. It consisted of the intercom ears joined together by an adjustable steel band of about three quarters inch in width. I placed it on my head and had leaned over the bombardier to orient my position to the White Cliffs of Dover when the flak burst. A large piece of shrapnel came through the Plexiglas nose over the bombardier's shoulders. It sheared the steel band across my head. There was no tug, no anything, the headphones fell, one on each side of me. The flak then passed through the pilots instrument panel popping out most of the glass covers, proceeded on upward, and imbedded itself in a sheet of one half inch armor plating along side the co-pilots head." The shrapnel had sheared the steel band on his head without harming a hair on his head. "Thank the Lord that I was only 5'10 _" and not 5' 11" tall."

On September 4, 1944, Clarence's sixth mission was scheduled to be a raid on a chemical plant at Ludwigshaven, Germany, which produced poisonous gas. Just after "bombs away" his plane was hit by "flak" that knocked out the aircraft's electrical and hydraulic systems and one engine. Unable to stay with the rest of their Group and losing altitude they took five more direct hits from flak. The crew snapped on their parachutes but decided to stay with the airplane as long as they could. In descending altitude they broke through a cloud barrier to discover they were directly over marshalling yards at Mannheim. Anti-aircraft then shot out the ball turret and most of their left wing. "There was a great amount of noise, and it seemed that the plane was being buffeted about. I tried to get out of the plane, but with the flak suit on and the erratic movements caused by who knows what, I could not move. It seemed to me that we were frozen in space. There was no visible movement. We seemed to be suspended in the air and the red streaks(tracers) kept chasing us. I knew nothing about the crew, whether they were still on board or had abandoned ship. I became aware of something else, the ground was starting to move. It was like looking through a scope and zooming in on an object using a zoom lens. I watched it gather speed as it rushed towards me. I knew without a doubt that my time had come. I was fully conscious of what was about to happen. The experiences of others had made this a truism. Did you ever wonder what people think of under such similar situations? As this situation drew to a close, I experienced no fear. I experienced only a rather peaceful calmness as I accepted the inevitable."

"The plane hit the ground accompanied by a great amount of noise and then followed by seemingly silence. I jumped to my feet to quickly exit the aircraft when I observed it was on the ground but moving at a good rate of speed. It had made contact with the earth at one edge of a twenty-acre field and plowed its way to the other side stopping within seventy feet from the edge of a large timber."

After freeing the Co-pilot's foot tangled in some of the wreckage and setting off explosives rigged to secret equipment, the crew exited the airplane. They were shot at by rifle fire. "Man did we move out. We rushed into the timber and I can remember that as I raced that short distance it was as though my knees were up around my chest and it took all of my strength to force my legs and feet down to the ground. I am convinced that I set a world record reaching the safety of the trees."

They decided to split up. Each officer was to take an enlisted man and make a run for it in pairs or groups of three to try and reach Allied lines. Clarence and the ball turret gunner slept in hiding during the day and walked at night through the forest and brush. Around 3 a.m. they heard someone talking. They hid in a shell hole and covered themselves with branches. Later it started to rain and numerous German soldiers walked by them. American artillery and mortars started shelling the Germans causing the shells to rain down where Clarence and his ball turret gunner were hiding. When the firing ceased they headed in the direction where firing had been the least and came to a clearing. Entering the clearing they spotted a campfire. Not knowing if it was friend or foe they re-entered the forest and circled around the campfire. Near daylight they came to another clearing and walked into the open. Turning around they found they were in front of concrete bunkers that were part of the Maginot Line that only the day before had been evacuated by German troops.

They needed to find a hiding place and left the forest for what appeared to be farming country. Following a hedgerow to a high point on the ground they had a good view of the surrounding countryside. While resting there the ball turret gunner believed he had seen an American jeep. An hour later another jeep came down the road. "How do you give yourself up without getting shot by your own troops? We decided to go to the road and walk in the direction of Paris. When we did two men stepped out of the hedgerow with machine guns pointed at us. I shouted "We're Americans". The two soldiers were part of a patrol that had been on the front lines for a long time and starved for information. They had picked up three others of our crew the day before."

Had Clarence and his ball turret gunner hid during the day and walked at night in that area they would have been shot by American troops who had set up a cross-fire and would have shot anything that moved. Had they walked down the road which had been mined they probably would have been killed by stepping on one.

A field kitchen was set up by the American soldiers to feed Clarence and his gunner with scrambled eggs, fresh bread, brandy and liberated wine. They spent the night in a foxhole and were transported the next day to Metz, France, where they were debriefed. After that they were flown to Cherbourg, France and then to Number 10 Downing Street, London, for another debriefing.

Clarence and his crew were granted a period of rest and recreation in Scotland. Then they caught a train for their base at Grafton Underwood. When they arrived they discovered they were scheduled for a mission the next morning.

After another mission deep into Germany Clarence and his crew were returning to their base when it became evident they didn't have sufficient fuel to make it. They landed at a base about sixty miles from their own and took on a full load of fuel, 2700 gallons. "There happened to be a group of airmen at the base wanting to catch a ride north and asked if we could take them. We replied we could and took off for the short hop to our base. I'm practically asleep but I see a red flash on the aluminum paneling beside me. Over the loud speaker someone yelled, "Fire, the bomb bay is full of fire"." I grabbed my chute but saw we were too low to bail out. Seconds later we were touching down on the runway. Almost immediately the hitchhikers started to abandon the ship as it was slowing down. The plane stopped and the bombardier and myself went out the lower hatch. The props were still spinning as we hit the concrete, rolled under them and ran off a safe distance. I recall gasoline on fire and falling from the wing reminding me of a waterfall. Evidently we had a ruptured gas tank and the only thing that kept it from blowing up was the fact that we had filled all of the tanks to capacity. The plane was destroyed but everyone escaped without injury."

In late October, 1944, Clarence and another navigator were trained in a new method of dropping bombs based on radio beams. The GH Method. It meant that whatever Bomb Group in the Eighth would be leading a mission Clarence would fly in that lead airplane. The new method provided bombing accuracy in inclement weather particularly during the Battle of the Bulge when visual sighting was not possible. When Clarence completed his twenty-ninth mission the military changed his plans for going home. "The changed plan was that if he never flies his thirtieth mission we don't have to send him home." He was taken off combat duty and sent to the 305th BG at Chelveston to train navigators in the GH method of dropping bombs.

Chapter Twenty-Two

After the war ended in Europe Clarence eventually sailed from Liverpool to America aboard a Victory Ship. While aboard they learned that Japan had capitulated and the war was over. He was separated from service subject to recall. He had been awarded the Distinguished Flying Cross, the Air Medal with three oak leaf clusters, European Theater ribbon with five bronze stars and the World War II Victory Medal.

Clarence returned to Iowa State Teachers College for his senior year and competed in track winning four first place titles. He subsequently received his Masters of Science degree from the University of Iowa.

In 1959 Clarence received a letter informing him that he was still in the service, had seventeen years accrued to his record, and he must join a reserve unit or be discharged from military service. He joined a reserve unit and was appointed a liaison officer with the Air University in Montgomery, Alabama. Clarence was a go-between University and Cadet Training units at Iowa's schools. He stayed in the reserves until he had twenty-six years total service and retired as a Lieutenant Colonel. Clarence eventually became a building contractor in Iowa City building customized homes for an exclusive clientele.

Right - Clarence in front of his B-17 "Woosh Woosh"

Right - Clarence and crew at 398th BG, Nuthampstead, England. Clarence is front row, right.

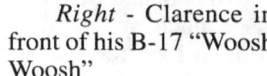

GLENN HILL, FAIRFIELD, IA, was originally from Missouri and worked for the Civilian Conservation Corps (CCC). He got a job with Louden's Machinery Company in Fairfield building overhead cranes. He was drafted into military service in December, 1943, and requested the Army Air Corps. He advised the medical personnel during induction he had been active in athletics and had a bad back and legs. They put him in the infantry. A Colonel at the induction center interceded and placed Glenn in the Air Corps.

Glenn was sent to Basic Training at Amarillo, TX. He put in for the Aviation Cadet Program but was "washed out" because of a bad eye and the Air Corps already had a surplus of ten thousand pilots. He was sent to Laredo, TX for Aerial Gunnery School where they trained seven days a week. He received crew assignment at Lincoln, NE, and departed for Boise, ID for crew training. The crew doubled-up on their training in order to have a seven day delay in route to the East coast before going overseas. They eventually boarded the "USS Brazilia" for a voyage that took eleven days to Great Britain.

Assigned to the 466th Bomb Group at Attlebridge, England, Glen flew thirty-five combat missions. The first mission was on October 6, 1944. The last mission was on April 5, 1945. He flew as gunner on his first three missions. When the Bombardier failed to perform satisfactorily Glenn took his place as Toggler. His main function was to release their bombs when the lead aircraft in the formation released theirs.

On his last mission flying in the "Parson's Chariot" a German .88 mm anti-aircraft shell hit their plane in engine number four. The shell lodged in the cowling surrounding the engine but failed to explode.

His most memorable mission was a mission to Germany that required they fly at a low altitude down the Ruhr Valley. "Flak guns opened up on us. It was like shooting ducks. A lot of planes were hit and went down. No parachutes were seen coming from them. We got hit in the bottom of the plane but we were still able to continue. The tail gunner's parachute had an .88mm shell go through it. If he needed it, it was worthless."

While at Attlebridge Glenn's aircraft "Dirty Gertie" was deemed battle weary and doomed to an aircraft graveyard in Scotland. A skeleton crew that included Glenn flew to Scotland to dispose of their airplane. "The weather was miserable, overcast, slush on the runway. But on the third try we got airborne. Flying to Scotland a Spitfire flew along side us. The pilot repeatedly made hand motions to us. Since we didn't have radio contact we didn't know until later what he was trying to tell us. The weather had "socked in" the airstrip in Scotland and he was trying to tell us to go back to our base. When we arrived in Scotland we made numerous attempts to land. We couldn't see much. We couldn't line up with the runway. The pilot told us to look for ground identification through the "soup". All at once I saw us heading for a church steeple and yelled at the pilot. He pulled up in time for one wing to go over the steeple. We were finally able to land."

Glenn returned to the United States in May, 1945, on a Liberty Ship which had been converted to a hospital ship for prisoners of war freed from German prison camps. Glenn and others volunteered to do work on the ship which otherwise would have to be done by the POWs. "They were thin, poor, just like animals, many got seasick- felt sorry for the poor devils."

Glenn was sent to Miami Beach for training in preparation for deployment to the Pacific Theater when the war ended. He then attended an Instructors School at Laredo, TX, until discharge from the military in October, 1945. He had been awarded, among other medals, the Air Medal with four oak leaf clusters and the ETO Medal with six battle stars.

Glenn returned to Louden Machinery from which he retired in 1983. He is a Life Member of the American Legion, Veterans of Foreign Wars, and the Eighth Air Force Historical Society.

Right - Glenn and his crew in front of their B-24 names "Whats Cookin Doc" at 466th BG, Attlebridge, England. Glen is back row, third from left.

Right - Glen in front of B-24 "Dirty Gerty" at 466th BG, Attlebridge.

FRANCIS 'FRANK' HINDS, MARION, IA, enlisted in the Army Air Corps on September 5, 1941. He had previously earned his pilot's license while in high school by working at a local airport and saving money from other after school hour employment.

Frank attended Aircraft Mechanics School at Boston, Massachusetts and Aerial Gunnery School at Spokane, Washington before he was deployed overseas with the 303rd Bomb Group at Molesworth, England.

Frank completed twenty-five missions as Flight Engineer and Top Turret Gunner.

His most memorable mission was on March 18, 1943, a bomb raid on a submarine construction yard at Vegesack, Germany. It was during this raid that Lt. Jack Mathis of San Angelo, Texas earned the Congressional Medal of Honor, awarded posthumously. As a bombardier, Mathis had his eye to the Norden bomb sight when within one minute of "Bombs Away" an anti-aircraft shell exploded near the nose of his plane shattering the plexiglass nose and hurling Mathis back nine feet from his bomb compartment. Although mortally wounded, his arm nearly severed and deep wounds in his side and abdomen, Mathis somehow managed to get back to his bombsight to release his bombs on time.

At this stage of the air war on Germany, fighters escorted the heavy bombers only as far as the English Channel. Frank recalls the buildup of bomber forces had only begun and at times during raids on enemy targets, only ten or twelve aircraft in their Group could be mustered for missions. Luftwaffe fighters were numerous and anti-aircraft flak was intense. During his second mission, while sporting a goatee, his oxygen mask froze. The goatee caused the mask to pull away from his mouth and he collapsed unconscious. Another crewman grabbed a portable oxygen tank and applied it to Frank reviving him and saving his life. Meanwhile a 20mm shell from a German fighter ripped through his top turret. Had he not collapsed he would have been killed by the shell.

During one mission the gunners on Frank's B-17, named "Sky Wolf", were credited with shooting down eight enemy fighters. Frank was credited with three, all of which exploded in mid-air when hit.

After being heavily attacked by the Luftwaffe during one mission, Frank and his crew crash landed at Essex, England, with both engines out on the right wing, part of the right wing missing, and a tire torn off the left wheel. All hands were safe.

Frank completed his twenty-fifth mission in August, 1943. He was discharged from the military at Lowry Field, Denver, Colorado after having been awarded the Distinguished Flying Cross, Bronze Star, and the Air Medal with four oak leaf clusters. His primary post-war occupation was as a production supervisor at Collins Radio, Cedar Rapids, IA

Right - Frank and his crew at 303rd BG, Molesworth, England. Frank, Flight Engineer and Top Turret Gunner is second from left in the second row.

HOWARD HOBBS, MORNING SUN, IA, worked for Lockheed Aircraft prior to World War II. He returned to Iowa and was inducted into military service November 11, 1942, at Camp Dodge, IA.

The following paragraphs are excerpts either quoted directly or summarized from a diary published by Howard entitled "Reflections" covering his military, combat and Prisoner of War experiences.

Chapter Twenty-Two

Assigned to the Army Air Corps he was sent to Miami Beach, FL for basic training consisting of KP (kitchen police) and marching. He was then sent to Gulfport, MS for five months training as an air plane mechanic and then to Long Beach, CA to attend a Douglas Aircraft Factory School to study the B-17 bomber. After a week at Camp Kearns, Utah for small arms fire training he was re-assigned to Las Vegas, NV for Aerial Gunnery School where he trained on .30 and .50 caliber machine guns. Howard met the personnel who would make up his bomber crew at Salt Lake City, UT. Over the next eight months crew training took place at Salt Lake, Ephrata and Walla Walla, WA and at Avon Park, Florida. The crew flew from Washington to their training site in Florida. They encountered engine trouble in route and had to land at Lubbock, Texas. They barely made it flying on two engines and nearly out of fuel. They had put out a "May Day" signal but got no response. They could not maintain altitude and had to land at night. They barely missed a freight train near the end of the airstrip but still ran off the end of the runway before stopping. The crew had to catch a train for Florida.

On September 1, 1943, Howard and his crew were assigned a new B-17 bomber and flew a thirteen day trip to Europe by way of Trinidad; Natal, Brazil; Dakar, Africa; Marrakech, French Morocco, and then to England. They were assigned to the 96th Bomb Group at Snetterton Heath, a small village between Attleboro and Norwich, 100 miles northwest of London.

Howard flew thirteen combat missions as Engineer and Top Turret Gunner. On his first mission, a crew that had gone through training with Howard was shot down and a friend killed. His third mission was to Berlin. One plane was lost when bombs were dropped on it from another B-17 above them. During a March 28, 1944, raid on a Luftwaffe air base near Chateaudon, France, the airplane directly in front of Howard's suddenly disappeared in a big flash when it received a direct hit in either the bomb bay area or fuel tanks.

On April 9, 1944, the target was an aircraft factory at Poznam, Poland, a thirteen hour flight. Terrible weather resulted in many planes being recalled. No fighter cover was provided for those that continued with the mission. Only three B-17s actually made it to the target.

April 11, 1944, weather prevented the primary target from being attacked. The secondary target, Rostock, was reached by only seven bombers. Eleven planes from the 96th failed to return to base. The 8th Air Force lost 64 planes that day.

April 13, 1944, the target was the aviation industry at Augsburg, Germany. Two hours into Germany a runaway propeller forced Howard's pilot to shut down one engine. With reduced speed their plane fell well behind the rest of the Group. As they continued on to the target they were hit by anti-aircraft fire that knocked out another engine just as they dropped their bombs. Howard was hit in the wrist by a piece of "flak", that broke his left forearm. The radio operator was also hit by flak, a minor wound in the head that caused severe bleeding. A third engine was running rough, they lost altitude and the pilot had difficulty in maintaining control of the plane. The pilot ordered the crew to bail out. Howard went first. On landing on the ground he was surrounded by civilians who determined he was not armed and took him to an inn until German soldiers arrived. He was taken by car to the town of Aalen. After a quick examination of his arm at a clinic he received a shot for the pain but no cast or splint was put on his arm. He was then locked in a closet for the night. The next day he rode by train to Frankfurt for interrogation. German interrogators were frustrated at getting only name, rank, and serial number from him and he was put back on a train. He was loaded in a cattle car that held twenty prisoners, had buckets for toilets, and a tub of soup for food. Two days later the train stopped in Krems, Austria, site of Stalag 17-B, his home for the next thirteen months. There he received competent medical attention from captured French doctors and assigned to a barracks with his crew members.

Stalag 17 was described by Howard as consisting of 20 barracks divided into five compounds. Thirteen barracks housed the prisoners, 300 to a barracks. Food consisted of a half loaf of bread for seven men and a tub of ersatz coffee. At noon a ration of boiled potatoes and a thin vegetable soup made of rutabagas, turnips, dried onions and a few pieces of poor quality meat. As the war progressed and German fortunes turned for the worse, so did the food supplied the prisoners. "It went from bad to worse and less frequent." So did the Red Cross parcels containing powdered milk, instant coffee, raisins, sugar, cheese, Spam, D bars, margarine and cigarettes. What was at one time one parcel per man per week, went to one parcel for five or six men and less frequent. The Red Cross also delivered sports equipment, playing cards and games.

The prisoners established a library, chapel, and classrooms for continuing education to keep mentally alert. Musical instruments were delivered through the Red Cross in sufficient variety to allow two bands to be formed. Among the prisoners were people of every occupation, vocation and talent. Religious needs were tended to by a Catholic priest who was a Des Moines native captured in Africa in early 1943. Each barracks had its own barracks chief, a person in charge of Red Cross food and one in charge of overseeing the German rations to the prisoners. One person in the camp was elected to be the official contact person with the Germans and had assistants to head up various departments such as kitchen, theater, education, Red Cross supplies and religious services. One resident in the camp was Ed Tryscinski who helped write and produce the stage play "Stalag 17" which was also turned into a movie starring William Holden.

On Christmas Eve, 1944, the Germans relaxed the rules and allowed the prisoners to visit other compounds and roam at will within the camp. "The public address system was turned over to the Americans and we heard for the first time Bing Crosby singing, "White Christmas". Mail from home usually took about six weeks to reach them. Howard got his first letter in July after his parents received word he was not missing in action but taken prisoner of war.

When Allied armies began closing in on the Germans they moved the prisoners out of the Stalag toward American lines. The Germans did not want themselves to be taken prisoner of war by the Russians. On April 8, 1945, every prisoner packed what he felt were essentials. Older German guards marched them for seventeen days until they reached Branau, Austria, Hitler's birthplace. The trek was made in every type of weather. They slept in the open and lived off the land. Food provided by the Germans was on a sporadic basis and limited Red Cross parcels were doled out to the prisoners. In a forest near Branau they built shelters out of logs and pine boughs and waited. One week later American tanks rumbled into their camp and they were free at last. In a little over a month Howard stepped off a train at Burlington, Iowa, where he was met by his brother.

On November 7, 1945, Howard received his discharge from the military service at Chanute Field, IL. He had been awarded the Purple Heart, Air Medal, ETO Ribbon, and World War II Victory Medal. Howard is a retired rural mail carrier.

Right - Howard and his crew at 96th BG, Snetterton Heath, England. Howard, Flight Engineer and Top Turret Gunner is back row, third from the right.

LEON HOEGH, ATLANTIC, IA, had worked on a farm and taken sheet metal classes to learn about aircraft before America's entry into World War II. He had tried to enlist in the Army Air Corps and the Navy but was rejected both times when he failed eye examinations. He then gained employment as an inspector with Aurora Aircraft Company at Chula Vista, California. After the Japanese attack on American military bases in the Hawaiian Islands on December 7, 1941, Leon was drafted into military service in June, 1942, and assigned to the Air Corps.

After Basic Training at Jefferson Barracks near St. Louis, Missouri, Leon was sent to Salt Lake City, Utah, a re-routing center where he was picked to become a cook and assigned to the 303rd Bomb Group in training at Alamagordo, New Mexico.

In September, 1942, Leon boarded the "Queen Mary" along with eighteen thousand other American troops and set sail for the European Theater of Operations. "The ship moved out at sunset and headed North on a zig-zag course to prevent submarine attack. "The ship's captain turned the ship wide open at night when diesel smoke couldn't be detected on the horizon. The back end of the ship shuddered from its powerful engines. There were sixteen of us staying in a room designed to accommodate two people. We got to sleep in the room every other night. The odd night we had to find our own place to sleep, on deck or on stairways. There was vomit everywhere from those that got seasick. We had one guy who was going to die because he was so sick he wouldn't eat. All we got to eat was bread that was sometimes moldy, some dried out cheese, old coffee and canned figs. I finally got the sick guy to eat and he started feeling better."

"At Molesworth there were sixteen hundred men on base. My mess hall was the smaller of two and served about four hundred twenty-five of the personnel. We were open twenty-four hours and had to have food available all the time, especially at night for ground crews and medics. We cooked food in sixty gallon pots heated by coke. Because we were handling food we had to have a physical examination every thirty days."

"We had mutton shipped in to us as carcasses. The smell of mutton was over-powering and a lot of guys couldn't handle it. As supplies became more plentiful and shipped in from the States regularly, we did away with mutton. There never seemed to be a problem with meat supplies. Steaks and hamburgers were shipped in frozen. Even chicken was sent frozen. It had not been gutted and with the feet were still on. We would take a meat clever to them. Why chicken was sent this way I don't know."

"All milk was supposed to go to the English children so we had powered milk or Pet milk. The Air Corps took over an ice cream factory so we had ice cream every Sunday made with the Pet or powdered milk.

The vegetables we got, potatoes, carrots and brussel sprouts, were wormy, but we cooked them anyway. Later in the war we got fresh eggs shipped in from the States. About sixty per cent of the fresh stuff that was shipped to us was spoiled by the time we got it. Our bread was made in England. It was whole wheat, unwrapped, and was good."

"We made coffee in the large pots, sixty gallons at a time. A guy who was on KP (kitchen police) during the day came back to the mess hall at night and somehow used one of the pots to do his laundry. He got by with it. Coffee was made in the pot the next day. When the pot was drained one of the guy's socks was found in the bottom. As far as I know no one got sick from the coffee."

After V-E Day, Leon flew on one of the aerial sightseeing trips over Holland, France and Germany to view the devastation inflicted by the Eighth Air Force on Nazi occupied Europe. "I went to stand behind the pilot when we landed back at our base. It was fortunate I did. I was behind and above him and saw another plane landing at the same time as us right below us. I yelled at the pilot and he avoided collision with the other aircraft. From his position he couldn't see the other plane."

Leon was flown to North Africa where he was in charge of a motor pool before being flown to the United States through South America. He received his discharge from military service in October, 1945, having been awarded the ETO Ribbon and World War II Victory Medal. Leon returned to Iowa and resumed farming in the Exira area.

GEORGE HOFFMAN, LEON, IA, enlisted in the Army Air Corps when he was seventeen years old. He was not called to active duty until he turned eighteen in 1943 and sent to Keesler Field for Basic Training. Following Basic, George was sent to Aerial Gunnery School at Las Vegas, Nevada and Plant Park, Florida where he was assigned to an air crew.

George and his crew trained for overseas deployment at Drew Field, Tampa, Florida. They boarded the "Ile de France" ocean liner at Camp Kilmer, New Jersey, for a five day, zig-zag voyage to Scotland in stormy seas. Nearly everyone got sea sick. From there he boarded a train for his destination, the 303rd Bomb Group at Molesworth, England.

George flew thirty-five combat missions as B-17 tail gunner. In December, 1944, his first mission was flown as a replacement tail gunner for another air crew to a target in the Ruhr Valley. His next mission was also flown as a replacement before he joined his regular crew for the remainder of their tour.

On one mission George spotted a new German jet, the ME-262 coming out of the sun to attack his aircraft from the rear. He fired a steady stream of bullets at the jet and saw it break up and plunge to earth after it passed under his aircraft. Superstitious that if he claimed credit for the kill he would be killed next, George did not report it. The 262 had put twenty-five bullet holes in the tail section around him. He had learned what fate could deal in war when bunk mates in his barracks were lost on their 34th and next to last mission.

During another mission, flak had blown the tail wheel off of his aircraft and sent it through the fuselage of the plane behind him and out the top of the aircraft. Although George flew three missions to Berlin and other important targets, a mission to Hamburg was his most memorable. German fighters "shot us up, we lost two engines and had to drop out of formation. One propeller was wind milling and we flew back across the English Channel at water level. When we arrived at our base it was discovered only one bolt was holding a damaged engine onto the wing".

Eight of his missions were flown aboard "Thunderbird", a B-17 that survived 112 missions with no injuries to any of its regular crew members.

After he completed his tour George returned to the United States by ship. He believed his ship was one of the first to arrive in New York following V-E Day (Victory in Europe). "The reception and partying taking place in New York harbor for the returnees was wild, to say the least." He boarded a train for Jefferson Barracks, St. Louis, Missouri, where he reported in before taking furlough.

George was then assigned to Santa Ana, California, for classification and taken off flight status. Given his choice of assignments George chose to be a Physical Education Instructor at Frederick, Oklahoma and then was a swimming instructor at Ardmore, Oklahoma teaching Survival Swimming School. He boarded a train to Kansas City in October, 1945, for discharge from military service. He had been awarded, among other medals, the Air Medal with six oak leaf clusters and the ETO Medal with four battle stars.

George entered Simpson College under the GI Bill. After graduation he entered the University of Iowa Law School and in June, 1950, began practicing law in the family law firm at Leon which has been in existence since the late 1800s.

Right - George and crew at 303rdd BG, Molesworth, England. George, tail gunner, is on the left. The B-17 "Thunderbird" survived over 100 missions.

DWIGHT HOHL, ARGYLE, IA, had attended Iowa State College, Ames, Iowa, for two years before he enlisted in the Army Air Corps. Accepted for the Aviation Cadet Program at San Antonio, Texas, Dwight took ground and various stages of flight training at Ft. Stockton, San Angelo and Tampa, TX before he received his wings and commission as a Second Lieutenant.

Dwight was assigned an air crew and trained with them at Mountain Home, ID, for overseas deployment. He and his crew picked up a new B-24 Liberator bomber at Topeka, KS, and began a flight to the 445th Bomb Group at Tibenham, England. They flew the northern route from America to England and encountered severe weather causing a delay of two weeks at Goose Bay, Labrador and a one week delay in Ireland.

Dwight, as pilot, flew thirteen combat missions. During one mission, a raid on a ball-bearing plant in the southwest corner of Berlin, flak from anti-aircraft batteries was intense. "Our wing man was shot down. We had our number three engine shot out after the bomb run and had to drop out of formation." As a straggler they were susceptible to enemy fighter attack to finish them off, but luck was with Dwight when American P-51 fighters flew alongside and escorted them back to their base.

On another mission, this time to attack submarine pens at Bordeaux, France, napalm bombs (jelly gasoline) was used. Conventional bombs had not been able to penetrate the thick concrete of the pens during other missions. Napalm was used to burn oxygen and suffocate German troops occupying the pens.

Oil refineries and synthetic fuel plants were targets favored by Allied planners to deny the German war machine of fuel to run its aircraft, tanks, and trucks. Transportation targets, such as railroad marshalling yards and bridges were also priority targets to deny German forces, food, ammunition and fuel. Dwight flew one mission to bomb railroad bridges on the rail line from Rumanian oil fields.

During the latter stage of the war horses and oxen pulled German planes to the end of their runways to conserve fuel. The Luftwaffe had become noticeably absent. American bombing raids became more destructive to the Third Reich. Allied bombers over any target began to number over a thousand.

After the war ended in Europe, Dwight flew ground crews on a tour of Germany to show them the effects of Allied bombing. He returned to the United States in August, 1945, and was scheduled to attend a B-29 bomber school at Sioux Falls, South Dakota. Japan's surrender after the atomic bomb was dropped on Hiroshima and Nagasaki ended World War II, and precluded his deployment to the Pacific Theater of Operations. When Dwight was separated from military service he had been awarded, among other decorations, the Air Medal, European Theater and World War II Victory Medals.

Dwight remained in the Air Force Reserve and was recalled to active duty for eighteen months during the Korean War. After training at Lowry Air Force Base in Denver, Colorado, he was sent to Warner Robins Air Force Base, Georgia, where he was placed in charge of the Office of Classification and Assignment to recall airmen from eleven southern states to active duty.

Following discharge from military service, Dwight returned to college. After he earned his degree he taught high school physics, chemistry and math for twenty-six years at Argyle, Iowa. The school later combined with three other schools to become Central Lee High School. Dwight retired in 1983. He and his wife Freda still reside in rural Argyle.

Long after World War II ended, Dwight attended an Eighth Air Force Reunion in Denver, Colorado. One speaker was a Dutch Air Force officer, who, as a ten year old boy during World War II, watched the sky turn black each morning and evening from Allied planes going to and from Germany on bombing missions. He was told "Don't be afraid, the Americans have come to save us".

Right - Dwight and his crew at 445th BG, Tibbenham, England. Dwight, Pilot, is in the middle of the back row.

ROBERT HOUSER, DES MOINES, IA, had attended the University of Iowa for two years and was working in the home office of Banker's Life Insurance Company when the Japanese attacked American bases in the Hawaiian Islands on December 7, 1941.

Bob enlisted in the Army Air Corps in 1942 and after Basic Training at Jefferson Barracks, St. Louis, Missouri, he was sent to Aerial Gunnery School at Ft. Myers, Fl. He finished first in his class despite never previously having fired a weapon.

He was chosen for the Aviation Cadet Program and attended College Training Detachment schooling at Arkadelphia, Arkansas, where college science courses were taken as they related   to aviation. Bob was then selected to attend Navigation School at Monroe, Louisiana. He graduated February 5, 1944, and was awarded his wings and commission as a Second Lieutenant.

Bob was then assigned to an air crew and trained with them at Rapid City, South Dakota, in preparation for overseas deployment. Upon completion of training he was sent to the East Coast where he boarded an English crewed ship to sail to Liverpool, England and the European Theater of Operations. "The ship was an old tramp. We bounced around on the rough seas. The food was terrible. We lived mostly off what we could buy in the PX."

On arrival in England Bob was assigned to the 306th Bomb Group at Thurleigh as a Navigator. He flew the first of twenty-seven missions on June 11, 1944, bombing enemy troop concentrations in support of Allied D-Day invasion forces. His other missions included bombing raids on Schweinfurt ball bearing plants, Berlin and Merseburg oil refineries where enemy fighters and heavy concentrations of German anti-aircraft fire was encountered. Despite numerous hits on his aircraft from German "flak", only his tail gunner was injured and he survived his wounds. Emergency medical attention was afforded the gunner by Bob and other crew members.

The original members of Bob's crew finished their tour of duty at different times and were essentially "split up". Bob was re-assigned to the Air Transport Command as a Navigator/Briefing Officer briefing crews arriving and departing England. He remained in this position until the end of the war in Europe and was able to fly to major cities in occupied Europe and North Africa. He was in Paris the evening of V-E Day(Victory in Europe) where "they were dancing in the streets" celebrating the end of the war.

His most memorable experience and one that nearly cost him his life was on a "shakedown flight" of a repaired B-17. The official report stated "fuel fumes were strong in the aircraft at take off and increased as they were flying. They decided to land. Flames came from #3 supercharger and engulfed the bomb bay area and spread rapidly. On landing the ship nosed over and swerved off the runway. The Flight Engineer suffered burns and a broken leg." The aircrew escaped from the burning aircraft and ran in case of explosion. Bob escaped out the front hatch and almost ran into the still rotating propellers. After taking one step in the wrong direction, he ran forward from under the aircraft. The plane was a total loss.

After V-E Day, Bob returned to the United States riding in a war-weary B-24 bomber from North Africa to Ft. Myers, Florida by way of South America. The aircraft was one that been interned in Switzerland for the duration of the war. Its tires were bad and could have blown out during any takeoff or landing. The engines were running "rough" and one engine was lost while flying across the Atlantic Ocean. They finished their flight on three engines and later discovered wiring within the engine was not correctly connected.

Bob was separated from military service in February, 1946. He returned to the University of Iowa and earned his B.A. Degree in Business Administration and took additional courses in Actuarial Science. He returned to employment with Banker's Life until he was recalled to active duty during the Korean War. Following his tour of duty he again returned to Banker's Life that eventually became the Principal Financial Group. He retired from the firm after attaining the top position of Chairman. He had worked himself from the mail room to the top.

Right - Bob's crew at 306th BG, Thurleigh, England. Bob, Navigator, is back row, third from the right.

Right - All the crew escaped the burning aircraft. Bob, went out a front escape hatch and barely missed running into the swirling propellers.

Below - Burned remains of B-17 that crashed on landing after shakedown flight.

JAMES HOY, ELDORA, IA, was originally from Owosso, Michigan and attending college at Kalamazoo when he enlisted in the Army Air Corps on August 29, 1942, as an Aviation Cadet. His status was changed to Aviation Student and he was called to active duty in February, 1943.

After Basic Training at Fresno, California, James attended the University   of Nevada at Reno under the College Training Detachment Program taking courses in geography, physics, weather, history and English. He failed to meet eyesight requirements for pilot training and was sent to Scott Field, Illinois, for Radio School and Photo Intelligence Training at Will Rogers Field, Oklahoma City, OK.

In March, 1944, James boarded the "Queen Mary" with 15,000 other servicemen for Grenock, Scotland. He was assigned to the 325th Photo Recon Wing at Eighth Army Air Force Headquarters, a former girl's school at High Wycombe, England. The Commanding General at the time was Jimmy Doolittle. "Everyone from Major on down lived in tents." Also based at High Wycombe was Elliott Roosevelt, the President's son, who was married to actress Faye Emerson.

Reconnaissance photographs were interpreted at the Headquarters and bomb damage reports typed, mimeographed and distributed to appropriate personnel. Models were made of proposed targets and Engineers made maps of enemy territory. An area of

Chapter Twenty-Two

High Wycombe known at Dawes Hill consisted of underground rooms at various levels to maintain security and secrecy of work performed.

In January, 1945, Jim was sent to Belgium to set up a photo laboratory to assist infantry units and the Ninth Air Force. He remained there until V-E Day (Victory in Europe) then returned to High Wycombe. As part of a program to defray costs incurred by the British Government in Lend Lease, Jim attended a school in Scotland for three weeks. He was then transferred to Headquarters of the Seventh Photo Group at Chalgrove, England until November, 1945, when he returned to the United States.

Jim received his discharge from military service at Indianapolis, Indiana, on January 30, 1946. He returned to college and received his Bachelor degree in Sociology at Western Michigan and Masters degree in Social Work at the University of Michigan. Jim was Superintendent of the Eldora, Iowa Training School for Boys from 1972 until retirement in 1986.

Right - Jim obtained Glenn Miller and Ray McKinley autographs on concern program

DELPH HRUSKA, FORT DODGE, IA, enlisted in the Army Air Corps in September, 1940, over a year before America was thrust into World War II by the Japanese attack on naval and air bases on the Hawaiian Islands in December, 1941. On Pearl Harbor Day he was in Salt Lake City, Utah, getting ready for deployment to the South Pacific. The sneak attack altered plans of military leaders. "One half of our men were sent to the Pacific and the other half, including me, stayed behind. I was sent to Mechanic's School at Yakima, Washington."

After he completed schooling Delph was assigned to the 389th Bomb Group activated at Davis-Monthan Army Air Base in Arizona. "They were starting to train pilots and I performed maintenance work on the aircraft. The second phase of training was at El Paso, Texas, and I worked on airplanes there for four to five months while pilots trained." Delph then was transferred along with the Group to Lowry Field, Colorado before being sent to Camp Kilmer, NJ for overseas deployment.

In July, 1943, Delph boarded the "Queen Elizabeth" ocean liner for a five day zig-zag voyage to Glasgow, Scotland. "There were 20,000 troops on board. We got two meals a day. We had a bunk to sleep in every other night, the odd nights we had to sleep wherever we could." After arrival Delph took a train to Hethel, England, home of the 389th.

Delph served at crew chief over four other mechanics that provided maintenance on one B-24 aircraft. They were responsible for routine maintenance and emergency repair. Sump pumps were checked for metal filings which meant an engine had to be replaced, often overnight in order to fly a mission the next day. "Generators were a problem, it seemed some burned out after every mission, so they had to be changed. When the aircraft came back from a mission we would check the engines. If everything was alright, the aircraft was fueled until it was given a pre-flight check the next day. We were usually up at 4:00 A.M. on mission days to pre-check the aircraft. After the aircraft left for a mission we had a lot of leisure time. We had a shack near our hardstand where we could sleep until the aircraft returned. We never got close to knowing the air crews because we went through five different planes that didn't return from missions."

Off-duty time was spent by many of the ground crew at a nearby English pub named "Old Oak". "American servicemen were treated well by the English at the pub. Getting back to base during blackout, a distance of about two miles was sometimes adventuresome. It was at a different social gathering Delph met an English girl named Nancy Foster who he married on October 8, 1944.

"After I had been there a long time, they started sending over replacement mechanics. I was transferred to a base at Halesworth. We didn't stay there long. Crews were unloading bombs at the bomb dump when the whole dump exploded. The crews were killed, and hangars and aircraft destroyed or damaged. We were sent to North Pickenham to help them out until the war in Europe ended."

Delph flew back to the United States in a war weary B-24 and was assigned to Tacoma, Washington, for eventual re-deployment to the Pacific Theater of Operations. After the Atomic Bombs were dropped on Japan and the war ended, Delph was transferred to Jefferson Barracks, St Louis, Missouri, where he received his discharge from military service in September, 1945.

In 1951 Delph gained employment with Hormel Packing in Fort Dodge. He remained with the firm until retirement when the plant closed in 1982.

RICHARD HUBBARD, COUNCIL BLUFFS, IA, graduated from high school and enlisted in the Army Air Corps in February, 1943. He was sent to St. Petersburg, Florida, for Basic Training, referred to an "tent city". He contracted ptomaine poisoning from food prepared at the facility. The camp was subsequently closed due to widespread food poisoning suffered by the recruits.

Richard had taken an air mechanics course while in school and based on test scores taken during Basic, was assigned to Aircraft Mechanics School at Lincoln, Nebraska. Upon completion of training he attended a B-17 School held by Lockheed Aircraft at Burbank, California

He then completed Aerial Gunnery School at Las Vegas, Nevada before reporting to Salt Lake City, Utah, for assignment as Flight Engineer to an aircrew. Richard and his crew then completed combat crew training at Rapid City, South Dakota, in April, 1944, and boarded a train for Camp Kilmer, New Jersey, for deployment to the European Theater of Operations.

Richard and his crew boarded an English ship which sailed in a convoy and took three weeks to cross the Atlantic Ocean to Liverpool, England. "We had a rolling ocean all the way. There was no air in the hold of the ship. Everyone was seasick and throwing up in the mess hall."

Richard reported to Stone, England, site of an Aircrew Replacement Center where they were assigned to the 379th Bomb Group at Kimbolton, England. His first of thirty-five combat missions was flown on June 6, 1944, D-Day. "We bombed at 9,000 feet. On our way back to base the sky was full, as far as the eye could see, with planes towing gliders full of paratroopers."

His most memorable mission was to drop anti-personnel bombs on rocket launching sites at Peenemunde, Germany. "We were trying to get the scientists and people sending V-1 and V-2 rockets over to England. We lost our #3 engine from lack of oil and couldn't

"feather" the props. The engine seized up and caused a vibration in our aircraft that I thought would tear it apart. We lost air speed and couldn't maintain altitude. A P-51 fighter was sent to escort us back to England. I didn't think we would make it. We got so low we could wave to sailors on board ships, but we cleared the cliffs on the coast and made it back to our base."

"One mission we flew we were supposed to bomb a forest at 7,000 feet. Photo reconnaissance flights had revealed German tanks hidden in the forest and we leveled the place."

Richard finished his thirty-five missions in only two months. Two missions a day were flown on many occasions. "As we neared the end of our tour they cut our crew down from ten men to nine. Our ball turret gunner was sent to another crew. When the crew failed to return from a mission we thought he had been killed. We found out later he had survived."

"My return to the United States was aboard an ocean liner from Liverpool to Boston. Instead of the three weeks it took to get to England, we sailed back in four days." After furlough Richard reported to San Francisco where he was assigned to Miami, Florida. He was then re-assigned as an Aircraft Mechanics instructor teaching propeller school at Amarillo, Texas. He met his former pilot from Kimbolton at Amarillo who was able to put Richard back on flying status. Planes repaired at sub-depots in the United States had to be flight tested before they were flown to an aircraft "bone yard" in Arizona.

Richard received his discharge from military service on October 6, 1945. He had been awarded, among other medals, the Distinguished Flying Cross, Air Medal with five oak leaf clusters, European Theater of Operations and World War II Victory Medals. He attended the University of Nebraska and upon graduation entered the motor freight business from which he retired as a Terminal Manager.

LEON HUGGARD, PLAINFIELD, IA, worked for Illinois Central Railroad prior to World War II. He enlisted in the Army Air Corps in January, 1943, and was sent to St Petersburg, FL for Basic Training. Leon attended Radio Operators School at Camp Crowder, MO, near Joplin and Gunnery School at Laredo, TX.

Following crew assignment and training at Peterson Field, Colorado Springs, CO, Leon and his crew picked up a new B-24 at Topeka, KS. They headed for the Eighth Air Force in England via a southern route. They were routed through Puerto Rico, Brazil, Africa, French Morocco and a final destination in Ireland. There their plane was taken from them for refitting. They sailed to Scotland and took a train to the 458th BG, at Horsham-St. Faith.

Leon flew thirty combat missions as Radio Operator. He was responsible for monitoring weather reports, sending bomb strike reports and changes in route back to Group. All messages were sent in code. He had received radio intercept training at Camp Crowder, Missouri and assumed the Germans were trained to do the same with Allied messages.

Leon also served as top turret gunner during bomb runs. During a raid on Metz and flying as lead aircraft for their Group, their airplane got caught in the prop wash of the Group flying ahead of them. This made their aircraft, and that of the deputy lead plane flying alongside, pitch up and down. Flying in close formation the wings of the two aircraft collided. The deputy lead plane was able to continue with the mission but Leon's plane lost ten feet of the right wing. The collision caused them to dive down to 15,000 feet altitude. Leon was pinned to the floor of the aircraft by the force of the dive and was unable to put on his chest pack parachute. When the pilot was able to level the aircraft they jettisoned their bomb load. The two right engines were put on climbing power but they were only able to maintain a speed five miles per hour over stalling by lowering the nose of the aircraft. The crew considered bailing out of the plane and were thankful when a P-51 Mustang fighter flew alongside to escort them as far as they could fly. They made it all the way to Horsham-St. Faith without further incident.

Several missions were flown hauling gasoline in support of General Patton's Army and his drive across France. The crew received no mission credit for these trips. Other missions were flown testing the Azon Bomb, a radio-controlled bomb controlled by the Bombardier who could direct the bomb left and right.

Leon returned to the United States in March, 1945. He was discharged from the military in September, 1945, and had been awarded the Air Medal with five oak leaf clusters, ETO and World War II Victory medals, among others. Following the military he attended an electronics school in Chicago and then gained him employment with Collins Radio at Cedar Rapids. Seven years later he left Collins for government service as an electronics specialist.

IVAN HUNTER, GOWRIE, IA, was a farm implement mechanic before he entered military service at Ft. Dodge, Iowa, on September 9, 1942.. He received training at Jefferson Barracks, MO; McCarran Field, Las Vegas, NV and McDill Field, Tampa, FL. He was deployed on June 15, 1944, to Thorpe Abbotts, England as a tail gunner assigned to the 418th Squadron of the 100th Bomb Group.

On July 28, 1944, Ivan flew his first mission. His goal of thirty-five missions required for rotation back to the United States was interrupted on November 10,1944, his thirty-third mission, during a raid on a German airfield at Weisbaden, Germany. Flying "tail end Charlie" at 29,000 feet, flak knocked out one engine of his plane and killed his navigator. They struggled to maintain altitude by throwing out everything they could but the crew bailed out of their aircraft after the engine caught fire. Ivan normally kept his shoes near his parachute with the shoelaces tied together. He took his shoes with him as he bailed out and free fell about 10,000 feet before he opened his chute. His greeting party when he hit the ground near Trier, Germany, was the German Army. After being taken to a guardhouse where he was reunited with other crew members, they were trucked to Koblenz where they spent the night. They were then put on a train for a town north of Koblenz for interrogation and placed in solitary confinement. At that point they were issued a suitcase containing a towel, underwear, a sweater and miscellaneous items, before they were put on another train for Stalag Luft 4 near the Baltic Sea.

Chapter Twenty-Two

Ivan was assigned to a POW barracks that had bunks three tiers high. He received one meal a day of a stew and 3-5 brickettes of coal a day for the stove in his room that held 24 men. One-third loaf of bread, described as sawdust, was provided daily per man. Red Cross parcels containing eleven pounds of food were doled out to the prisoners. The contents were not issued all at once to prevent hoarding for possible escape. POWs were allowed to walk around the compound during the day but were "locked down" in their barracks nightly at about 7PM.

In January, 1945, as Allied armies began to close in on the area near the prison camp, the POWs were loaded in boxcars and shipped by train to Nurnberg, an eight day trip. At Nurnberg the barracks were longer, less men to a compartment and only two tiered bunks. Sleep was difficult. Mattress pads filled with paper rested on only three wood slats. The mattresses were infested with sand fleas. Camp life was no different, the same routine, no work details and constant waiting. Food that was provided came mainly from Red Cross parcels. No bread was provided. Rations provided by the Germans was dehydrated greens enriched with the protein of weevils.

In April, 1945, the prisoners were told they were being transferred to Moosburg about 150 kilometers distant, and they would be walking. This required a trip of about two weeks. Their guards appeared to be World War I veterans with little ambition. POWs had to live off the land as they went. That's where Ivan's shoes came in handy to prevent blisters and frostbite. Soap, cigarettes and candy from Red Cross parcels were used to trade with farmers for food. During the trip POWs learned of the death of President Roosevelt.

On April 29, their camp was entered by American troops. Two months later and about 50 pounds lighter, Ivan was home. He received his discharge on October 27, 1945, at San Antonio, TX. Ivan's unit received two Presidential Citations. He was also awarded, among other medals, the Purple Heart, Distinguished Flying Cross and Air Medal. After the war Ivan worked for the Soil Conservation Service and farmed. He has retired from both. Ivan is an active attendee at National and State POW organizations and has served on the Board of Directors of the Iowa Chapter, Eighth Air Force Historical Society.

JACK HURLEY, DES MOINES, IA, was part of a replacement crew sent to Seething near Norwich, England in May, 1944, as part of the 714th Squadron of the 448th Bomb Group. One of their first missions was in support of the D-Day invasion where the crew was able to view the spectacle of Allied forces below them as well as in the skies.

On June 27, 1944, a mission was ordered to bomb the rail yards near Creil, France. After "bombs away", German anti-aircraft batteries made hits on Jack's B-24 in the nose section and between the number one and two engines. Making their turn back toward England it was obvious the aircraft would not be able to continue in the air. The bail out alarm was given and the crew exited the airplane. The tail gunner, the only married man of the crew, had his parachute catch on the airplane when it was opened too soon and he went down with the airplane. The bombardier was shot and killed by German forces as he descended in his parachute. Four crew men were taken prisoner by the Germans and spent the rest of the war as Prisoners of War. Four crew men, including Jack were found by French Underground members and hidden from the Germans for eight weeks until they could make it back to Allied hands.

STAVER HYNDMAN, CHEROKEE, IA, was employed in Cherokee before World War II as a factory worker for a firm that made agricultural products. He entered military service at Camp Dodge at Des Moines in October 1942.

After Basic Training at Jefferson Barracks, MO, Staver was sent to aircraft mechanics school in Kansas City, MO. While there the Army Air Corps sent out a call for volunteers for pilots, navigators and bombardiers. He took a series of tests and soon found himself an aviation cadet headed for flight training. Staver completed Primary Flight Training at Tulare, CA and Basic Flight School at Merced, CA. He graduated from Advanced Flight Training in February 1944 at Douglas, AZ, where he won his wings and was promoted to the rank of Second Lieutenant. At Hobbs, NM he began B-17 pilot training. Staver met his crew at Alexander, LA and began crew training in preparation for overseas deployment.

Staver received a new B-17G at Lincoln, NE. He and his crew flew to Nuts Corner, Ireland by way of Goose Bay, Labrador and Rekyjavik, Iceland. The airplane was left in Ireland and the crew proceeded to England by ship and eventually arrived at Nuthampstead, England, and the 398th Bomb Group.

Staver flew 35 combat missions and was rotated back to the United States. He almost didn't make it. On November 21, 1944, his Group was assigned to bomb the heavily defended synthetic oil refinery at Merseburg, Germany. Anti-aircraft batteries ringed Merseburg and some of the Luftwaffe's best fighter units were nearby. Of the thirteen aircraft in his squadron, only three returned from the mission. Ten aircraft lost during the mission (100 men) were the result of slashing attacks by German Focke-Wulf 190 fighters.

As they approached the target, clouds and contrails became thick which reduced visibility. The plane to the left and slightly behind Staver's took anti-aircraft hits that damaged an engine and shot out their oxygen system. The plane left the formation to try and struggle home.

Weather worsened to the extent airplanes in the formation could not see each other. They were ordered to gain altitude to find "daylight". Other Squadrons became hopelessly lost and abandoned the mission or found targets of opportunity to drop their bombs. Staver's squadron, however, made a run on the target despite no air-to-air radio contact with other aircraft due to electrical problems. On the bomb run the airplanes were within range of over 400 anti-aircraft guns that protected the refinery. Flak exploded in mass profusion. A plane far to Staver's right took a hit in Engine No. 1 and then the Number 2 engine quit. The plane disappeared into the clouds with its bombs stuck in their racks and the fuses "hot". It was later found out that the top turret gunner/engineer pried the bombs out of the bomb bay area. The crew also jettisoned anything they could that was heavy including the ball turret and made a belly landing in a field near Paris.

As they turned toward the target the squadron was faced with an off-course bomber squadron that approached them out of the clouds at the same altitude. Staver's squadron climbed to avoid a collision. A decision was made to abandon the bombing attack and only one of the three squadrons of the 398th actually completed the bomb run on the target.

Staver's squadron could not release their bombs for fear of dropping them on other bombers below and eventually dropped them when away from their scheduled course. Problems continued to plague the airplanes in Staver's squadron. The lead airplane had electrical problems and its bomb bay doors had to be hand-cranked open. Another airplane's bomb bay doors were frozen open and had to be hand-cranked shut. In another aircraft a tail gunner's oxygen system had been shot out. When he didn't respond to a routine oxygen check of crew members, he was found motionless and blue. He was revived by the pilot with a walk-around bottle of oxygen.

At this time two waves of enemy fighters attacked the bombers head-on. The fighters came so close to the bomber formation Staver saw faces of the Luftwaffe pilots. The first wave shot down three bombers. One of them exploded during its spin to earth. The second wave of fighters shot down the B-17 to the right rear of Staver. Of the thirty crewmembers in his squadron that were shot down, only twelve survived and they were taken Prisoner of War.

A cannon shell from a Luftwaffe fighter ripped into Staver's navigator wounding him severely in the groin area. Other cannon hits shot out two engines and did minor damage to a third engine. His plane's entire hydraulic system was shredded and the electrical system damaged. While first aid was rendered the navigator, Staver attempted to fly the stricken aircraft back to England. They realized they were not going to make it. He attempted a wheels-down landing (with no brakes) at a Royal Air Force base in Belgium. As he tried to land on a muddy field, the landing gear folded. Staver was able to spin the airplane around to a stop before he would crash into a construction area at the end of the runway. No one was injured in the landing. The navigator was immediately dispatched to a hospital and fully recovered from his wounds. Despite flak, fighters, weather, radio problems, equipment failures, oxygen problems, and bail outs it was apparent to all those that flew this mission they were lucky any survived.

Staver received the Distinguished Flying Cross for the Merseburg mission. He also was awarded the Air Medal with six clusters, WWII Victory and European Theater of Operation Medals.

After discharge from military service at Sioux City, Iowa, in October, 1945, Staver returned to his pre-war job in Cherokee. Shortly thereafter he began working for the U S Postal Service from which he retired in 1984.

Right - Staver and his crew at 398th BG, Nuthampstead, England. Staver, Pilot, is back row, second from left.

HAROLD JACKSON, WATERLOO, IA, graduated from high school and had been employed with John Deere Tractor Company in Waterloo only a short time when Harold and a friend bought an airplane. He was in Waco, Texas, when he enlisted in the Army Air Corps in January, 1943.

Harold was sent to Sheppard Field, Wichita Falls, Texas, for Basic Training and Meteorology School. He was then sent to Radio Operator School at Scott Field, Illinois, before being

assigned to an aircrew at Salt Lake City, Utah and overseas training at Casper, Wyoming. Harold and his crew picked up a new airplane at Lincoln, Nebraska, and flew the northern route to Scotland via Goose Bay Labrador. In route and still over open sea they became lost. Just before they would run out of fuel, and in dense overcast, the pilot spotted a break in the clouds and dove through it. They had just arrived over land and spotted a landing strip. The landing strip however was filled with railroad rails. The decision was made to set the plane down anyway and they crashed landed. British soldiers appeared from the hills around them and told them they had just flown over Scapa Flow, a British naval base. Naval gunners had almost fired on them to shoot them down. A transport plane was brought in to evacuate Harold and his crew.

Harold took advanced radio school in Ireland and other training before beginning the first of thirty-five combat missions as a Radio Operator with the 44th Bomb Group at Shipdham, England. Most memorable to him were low-level missions to bomb German submarine pens at coastal cities and German troops at St. Lo, France, in support of attacking British forces. It was Harold's responsibility during a bombing mission on Dusseldorf, Germany, to kick out bombs "hung up" in his aircraft's bomb bay area.

As Harold and his crew prepared to takeoff for a mission to Berlin their base was immersed in dense fog. "We were lined up nose-to-tail and took off at thirty second intervals, turned at a prescribed time and climbed in order to form up for the mission. There were a lot of collisions at times because of the weather." Of the twenty-seven aircraft that took off for the mission in dense fog, nine were shot down during the mission.

Harold returned to the United States at the completion of his tour in the Spring of 1945. He was sent to Laredo, Texas, for Gun Camera and Radio Operator School before transferr to Westover Field, Boston, MA in a teaching capacity. Harold was discharged from military service September 20, 1945. He had been awarded the Distinguished Flying Cross, Air Medal with four oak leaf clusters, ETO Ribbon and World War II Victory Medal.

After the war Harold was employed by the Carnation Milk Company. He retired thirty years later from their quality control program.

Right - Harold and enlisted men of his crew at 44th BG, Shipdham, England. Harold, Radio Operator, is front row, left.

JERROLD JACOBSEN, CEDAR FALLS, IA, was in high school when America entered World War II. After graduation he enlisted in the Army Air Corps in June, 1943, and was sent to Shepard Field, Wichita Falls, Texas for Basic Training. Accepted for the Aviation Cadet Program he was sent to Jefferson College, St Louis, Missouri, as part of the College Training Detachment Program to take aviation related classroom courses.

At an Army Air Corps Classification Center at San Antonio, Texas, Jerrold was assigned to attend Bombardier's School at Childress, Texas. He graduated in June, 1944, and was awarded his wings and commission as a Second Lieutenant. He was then assigned to an aircrew and completed overseas training with them at Casper, Wyoming. After training the crew picked up a new aircraft at Topeka, Kansas, and began their flight to the European Theater of Operations. Jerrold, however, was given orders to attend a Radar School at Boca Raton, Florida, and Navigation School at Langley Field, Virginia. His crew departed for overseas without him. He subsequently received word his crew was lost during their flight while near Newfoundland.

Jerrold finished his training and was flown to Scotland and then rode by train to the 467th Bomb Group at Rackheath, England. He would fly four combat missions before V-E Day including an attack on Germany's jet headquarters. Most memorable however, was a bombing mission to Czechoslovakia. At the start of their bomb run, one engine of Jerrold's aircraft malfunctioned and quit running. Another engine was lost when hit by flak. The crew was able to make it to France where they made a forced landing near a town close to the Belgium border that had recently been taken by Allied ground forces.

Following Victory in Europe, Jerrold returned to the United States and after furlough spent thirty days in Santa Ana, California. He was transferred to Boca Raton, Florida, where "we just layed around" with no special duties. He received his discharge from military service November 1, 1945, and had been awarded the European Theater of Operations Medal and World War II Victory Medal.

After the war Jerrold entered Grinnell College. After he earned his Bachelor's Degree he entered the University of Iowa Law School. He graduated, passed the Iowa Bar Examination and then entered his family's law practice at Cedar Falls which he still owns.

Jerrold had the distinction of a father-son combination in military service during World War II. His father, a World War I veteran re-entered military service during World War II. He was with the Thirteenth Armored Division and rose to the rank of Colonel.

ALFRED HENRY JANSS ATLANTIC, IA, graduated from high school in May, 1943, and enlisted in the Army Air Corps a short time later.

While stationed at Santa Ana, California, Alfred was selected for training as a navigator. After intensive training for eighteen weeks at Hondo, Texas, he earned his wings and commission as a second lieutenant. Alfred received further training with his flight crew in the B-24 Liberator at Walla Walla, Washington, before being sent overseas.

Deployed in 1944, Alfred was assigned as a navigator with the 789th Bomb Squadron of the 467th Bomb Group at Rackheath, England. Alfred had completed numerous missions and was nearing the end of his tour of duty when his crew was scheduled for a mission on Sunday, March 18, 1945. The target was a raid on Rheinmetal factories in Berlin which manufactured heavy guns, bombs and torpedoes. This was to be the largest aerial assault on Berlin to date with 1,327 bombers. Although the formation was attacked by a score of the new German jet fighters, the ME-262, Alfred's airplane, B-24 H, serial number 42-52546 was hit by intense anti-aircraft fire in the bomb-bay area of the aircraft. Some crew members were able to bail out of the stricken airplane and taken prisoner of war. One crew member struck an airplane below his when bailing out and was killed. Alfred and two others perished with the aircraft.

Alfred was twenty years old at the time of his death. He was posthumously awarded three Purple Hearts, a Citation of Honor, and the Air Medal for Meritorious Achievement in aerial combat.

BERTRAND, 'BUD' JENSON, CEDAR RAPIDS, IA, worked at Pinicon Ford corn processing plant in Cedar Rapids until he was drafted into the Army Air Corps October 23, 1942. He was sent to Sheppard Field, Wichita Falls, Texas, for Basic Training. He then spent the next twenty-two weeks at Radio Operator School at Chicago, Illinois where he was able to transmit thirty-five words a minute by Morse Code.

Bud was assigned to an aircrew and trained with them at Pyote, Texas and Dyersburg, Tennessee, in preparation for overseas deployment. In October, 1943, Bud and his crew boarded the ocean liner "Queen Elizabeth" with other American troops and sailed to Grennock, Scotland. He was assigned to the 379th BG, Kimbolton, England.

Bud flew twenty-five combat missions as Radio Operator/Aerial Gunner aboard a B-17 bomber named "London Avenger". On a December 20, 1943 mission to bomb a Focke Wolfe aircraft plant at Bremen, Germany, "we were flying tail end Charlie in the formation. "Flak" from an anti-aircraft burst off the nose of our plane killed our bombardier and wounded the navigator. We were still able to stay in formation and make it back to England."

Bud flew two Schweinfurt, ball bearing plant missions, "one was bad and one not so bad". "On a raid to Merseburg we had two engines knocked out from "flak". We kept losing altitude and threw out everything we could to maintain altitude. When we dropped the ball turret out, our plane jumped up from loss of weight. We were trying to call MFDF stations to find out where we were. They would call back our coordinates. We navigated back to England on radio calls and were able to make one last pass at an emergency field before we landed there out of gas."

Bud claimed credit for one ME-109 shot down. "He came at us from the left. I fired at him and he blew up about a hundred yards from our ship."

After Bud completed his required twenty-five missions he volunteered to remain in England and teach at a Battlefield Indoctrination School. Radio operators from all branches of the services were checked for reception qualification, "trying to get everyone up to speed". When he returned to the United States in June, 1945, he had received no furlough since his entry into military service in October, 1942, other than periods of rest and relaxation at King Henry VIII's hunting lodge in England.

Bud received his discharge from military service June 24, 1945, at Jefferson Barracks, St. Louis, Missouri. He had been awarded, among other medals, the Distinguished Flying Cross, Air Medal with three oak leaf clusters, European Theater of Operations Medal with four battle stars and the World War II Victory Medal.

Bud was employed as a bricklayer and millwright helper after the war. He became the first founding Board Chairman of Kirkwood Community College; was Chairman of the college's Board of Directors; and spent fourteen years on the Cedar Rapids Community School Board, four of which were as President.

Iowans of the Mighty Eighth

Right - Bud, Radio Operator at 369th BG, Kimbolton, England, is back row, center.

ELMER C. JOHANSMEIER, BURLINGTON, IA, was a mechanic working for an auto dealer before the outbreak of World War II. The dealer was forced to close due to rationing. Elmer gained employment at the Army Munitions Plant at Middletown, IA.

He was drafted into military service in December, 1942, at Camp Dodge, Iowa, and sent to Miami Beach, Florida, for Basic Training. Elmer completed Driving School at Chanute Field, Illinois, where he became qualified to drive all military vehicles including tanks. He later graduated from a Truck Driver and Dispatcher Course at Kelly Field, Texas. While there, the 2003 Ordnance and Maintenance Company was preparing for deployment overseas and needed a mechanic. Elmer was the best qualified and was re-assigned to them.

Elmer boarded the "Queen Elizabeth" with twenty-three thousand other American troops for Europe. "Bunks were stacked clear to the ceiling. Troops spent twenty-four hours below decks and twenty-four hours on deck." To feed this number of troops required there be a "constant chow line". Elmer was designated a ship's runner requiring he be on duty twenty-four hours a day. He had the benefit of sleeping in the 2003rd's headquarters compartment and have access to the dining room at any time.

Elmer's duties with the 2003rd were in support of the Eighth Air Force. Their headquarters was in a manor house near the town of Risley, England. Enlisted personnel were quartered in quonset huts near the manor house. Elmer traveled all over England where he performed maintenance work on Eighth bases, made deliveries, and serviced vehicles including jeeps, trucks, bulldozers, and cranes. He also served as an armorer, calibrated instruments and assembled bomb truck carriers. Glenn Miller's orchestra performed from the roof of the manor house mess hall to G.I.s sitting on the lawn.

Elmer returned to the United States in the latter part of 1945 aboard the "Queen Mary. He received his discharge from military service in Illinois on Christmas Day, 1945. In the three years Elmer was in service and married, he never received a furlough home.

After the war Elmer worked for twenty-three years as a service technician for John Deere dealers. He then became head of mobile equipment for a fertilizer plant until he retired.

FRANCIS JOHNSON, CEDAR RAPIDS, IA, was employed by Lockheed-Vega in California from 1941-43 where he built aircraft ailerons and elevators. Although continued employment in a vital industry would have allowed him deferment from the Draft, Francis enlisted in the Army Air Corps in January, 1944. After Basic Training at Buckley Field, Colorado, and Aerial Gunnery School at Kingman, Arizona, Francis was assigned to an air crew at Lincoln, NE. The crew trained together at Dyersburg, Tennessee in preparation for deployment overseas.

On January 12, 1945, Francis boarded a ship at Boston, MA and sailed for England and assignment to the 92nd Bomb Group at Podington as a tail gunner. Francis flew sixteen combat missions. On only his second mission flak blew out one engine on his B-17. The propeller began wind milling and the crew was ordered to bail out. Luckily they were over territory occupied by Allied forces and were eventually returned to their base.

On February 3, 1945, as part of a 1,000 plane raid on Berlin, Francis, from his tail gunner position, saw two bombers in his formation disintegrate when they took direct hits in the bomb bay area during their bomb run. On March 12, 1945, in route to bomb submarine pens at Swinemunde, Germany, his aircraft lost one engine from flak. Another engine was not running properly. To avoid a mid-air collision his pilot pulled their aircraft up abruptly causing the six 1,000 pound bombs they were carrying to break loose and fall through the bomb bay doors. Crippled, they fell behind the remaining aircraft in their bomb group and losing altitude were faced with the possibility of having to ditch in the North Sea. They were able to reach Malmo, Sweden, a neutral county and interned for the remainder of the war.

Francis was released on May 28, 1945. He sailed for America on June 15, 1945, aboard the Queen Mary with 18,000 other troops. After a ninety day furlough Francis reported to Ellington Field, Texas and discharged from military service in November of that year. He had been awarded, among other decorations, the Air Medal with two oak leaf clusters and the ETO Medal with two battle stars.

Francis retired after thirty-five years as a mechanical engineer with Rockwell-Collins in Cedar Rapids.

Right - Francis and his crew at 92nd BG, Podington, England. Francis, Ball Turret Gunner, is back row, right.

MAYNARD JOHNSON, SIBLEY, IA, as a young man "rode the rails". He hopped freight trains to see America. He also worked for the Civilian Conservation Corps where he cut stone for outdoor stairs in Dolliver State Park, drove a truck for a construction company, and completed civilian pilot training. In December, 1942, Maynard underwent surgery and had a disk removed from his back. After release from medical care in March 1943, he enlisted in the Army Air Corp.

Maynard completed Basic Training at Augusta, Georgia. He completed other phases of training at Macon, Georgia and Tallahassee, Florida, in preparation for shipment to the Pacific Theater of Operations. This included six weeks of judo and karate training at Keesler Field, Mississippi. Maynard was then shipped back to Macon, placed in a trucking unit and shipped instead, to the European Theater of Operations. "There were nine thousand of us on board the ship "General John Pope". It took us eight days to sail to Scotland in stormy seas without any escort."

Maynard was assigned to the 2465th Trucking Company at the First Strategic Air Depot at Honington, England. He was placed in charge of a fleet of trucks and twenty-five drivers. Bombs were hauled from various railheads to the Depot where they were dispersed to American air bases throughout England. Each truck could carry twenty-five 500 pound bombs and pull a trailer loaded with another five 500 pound bombs. Maynard recalled his fleet had seventeen flat tires in one day from metal objects on runways and grassy areas of the bases.

In December, 1944 during the Battle of the Bulge, Maynard was transferred to Belgium to haul gasoline and supplies to air bases captured by American ground forces. While there he volunteered to rescue a downed American B-17 bomber from a swampy area twelve miles behind German lines. A skirmish was fought with German troops but the aircraft was freed from its mire, re-fueled and flown back to Allied hands.

Maynard remained in Belgium until V-E Day, Victory in Europe, and then returned to England. When it came his turn for rotation back to the United States he was assigned to a cargo ship which took seventeen days to make the voyage.

In February, 1946, Maynard received his discharge from military service. He had been awarded the World War II Victory Medal and the ETO Ribbon with two battle stars. In civilian life Maynard farmed and hauled livestock. At one time he owned a fleet of five corn shelling trucks. He resumed flying lessons and earned a private pilot's license. He owned two Cessna 120 aircraft over the course of twenty-six years and flew with the Civil Air Patrol for ten years.

VICTOR L. JOHNSON, NASHUA, IA, entered on duty with the military service at Charles City, IA in December, 1943. After Basic Training at Amarillo, TX and Aerial Gunner's School at Las Vegas, NV, he was assigned to a B-17 crew and trained with them at Alexandria, LA as a ball turret gunner.

In October, 1944, Victor was sent to Lincoln, NE, and boarded a train for Providence, RI. On December 11, 1944, he boarded a troop ship at Boston, MA for an eleven day trip across the Atlantic to Liverpool, England and eventually arrived at the 92nd Bomb Group, at Podington, England.

Victor flew his first combat mission on January 6, 1945. On February 25, 1945, he flew his fourteenth mission. His aircraft took a flak hit in the number four engine just as they came off the bomb run. Victor grabbed his parachute harness and put it on just as the wing of the aircraft caught fire. At the bail out order "I took a deep breath and jumped. I knew we were supposed to free fall for a while before pulling the rip cord but I pulled it right away. I passed out from lack of oxygen and woke up swinging back and forth as I drifted down. Germans soldiers took me prisoner right away. I was trucked to a jail in a little town and then to another town where the rest of my crew was. They put me on a train to Frankfurt. On the way we were strafed by American planes. At Frankfurt they attempted to interrogate me and placed me in solitary confinement. I got to know every nail in the ceiling of that cell."

Victor was then placed in a railroad boxcar and sent to Stalag 3A at Nuremberg. "We never had any food except a green soup that tasted like grass. Any weevils in the food you just ate. They gave us a dark bread you had to toast in order to eat. There were 50-60 of us in double-bunked barracks with no heat. There was a lot of dysentery."

As Russian and American ground forces began to close in on Germany "they took us out of the prison camp. They took our flight clothes away and gave us an overcoat, blanket, shoes and a Red Cross parcel. We had to march guarded by elderly German guards. During the march three American P-51s came over and one of them strafed us. The pilot must have realized what was going on because he kept the other two planes from attacking. From then on we had a plane over us everyday to keep track of our progress and where we were going."

"Along the march we slept in ditches, woods, and barnyards. They marched us to another camp where we were liberated. General Patton came in a tank and broke the fence down. The Army set up kitchens to feed us. We sat until May 8, 1945, when the war ended. Then C-47 cargo planes flew in and took us to Camp Lucky Strike in France. I left for the United States on June 11, 1945, aboard the "USS Sea Robin"."

Victor was discharged from military service in December, 1945. He had been awarded the Air Medal with two oak leaf clusters, the ETO, World War II Victory and the POW Medal. He returned to his hometown of Charles City and worked at the Oliver Tractor Plant until it closed, then attended barber college. Victor is still in business cutting hair in Nashua.

Right - Victor and his crew at 92nd BG, Podington, England. Victor is back row, fourth from the left.

OLIVER W. "Ollie" JOINER, MONROE, IA. entered military service January 8, 1943, at Fort Crook, Nebraska. After basic training at Miami Beach and radio schools at Chicago and Truax Field, Madison, Wisconsin he attended Control Net System School at Tomah, Wisconsin.

Ollie had short stays at Hammer Field and March Field, before he joined the 383rd Fighter Squadron, 364th Fighter Group at Oxnard, California. He sailed on the "Queen Elizabeth" and arrived Honington, England, February 9, 1944. Ollie served as CNS man that gave homings to pilots. He also directed the base dance orchestra, "The Goldbricks". The band played English clubs for a 10-shilling note and free Scotch or beer. Red Cross dances were played for free. One English club provided them with hard cider. "A young guitar player who did not drink thought it was the best thing he ever tasted without realizing what he was drinking. Needless to say he was very happy as the night wore on."

Although it had nothing to do with fighting the war, Ollie thought playing in the base band helped with morale. The land on which his base was located was owned by the Duke of Grafton. He selected the Goldbricks to play at a ball being held at his estate. The band arrived early and strolled around the ballroom to look at life-size paintings of past Dukes. The orchestra was approached by an elegantly gowned lady who came up to them and said" Would you gentlemen like to know the history of the Duke of Grafton's family?" What else could they say but "yes". She stated "The first Duke of Grafton was the illegitimate son of King Charles the Second by one of his mistresses." During intermissions she would appear in the room where the band had been taken to enjoy food and spent the whole intermission talking to the band, asking about the United States and the band members' families. They all felt they had indeed met a Lady, in every meaning of the word.

Ollie returned to the United States September 20, 1945. After military service he entered college and received his B.A. degree in two and a half years and then went on to earn his Master Degree from Drake University.

Ollie taught music in Nebraska and Iowa schools for six and a half years and was superintendent of schools for twenty-five years. He retired in 1980.

In his retirement Ollie served on the Executive Board of the Iowa High School Music Association. He composed fight songs for two Nebraska colleges and was active on the Board of the 364th Fight Group association and served as its President for one year.

DARWIN JOLIFFE, DAYTON, IA, was working as a riveter building PBY airplanes for Consolidated Aircraft Company in San Diego, California, when he was drafted into the Army Air Corps in October, 1942. After Basic Training at Chanute Field, Illinois he was sent to Keesler Field, Biloxi, Mississippi for Aircraft Mechanics School and Laredo, Texas, for Aerial Gunnery School.

Assigned to an air crew he completed overseas training with the crew at Salina, Kansas, in October, 1943. Assigned to the Pacific Theater of Operations, the crew picked up a new aircraft at Topeka, Kansas and headed West. Over Nebraska they developed problems with a propeller governor on one engine. A supercharger blew on another engine. Fully loaded with gasoline, mail and supplies they could not maintain altitude and were forced to make an emergency landing at McCook Army Air Base, Nebraska. At that time one wheel would not lock into the down position. In an attempt to pull up and gain altitude they did not have sufficient power for their weight, stalled and struck a power line. They crashed landed in a corn field injuring two crew members who were pinned in the wreckage. The two later received medical discharges.

Darwin and his crew were sent back to Topeka to pick up another aircraft and this time assigned to the European Theater of Operations. While flying to the East Coast in winter, their wings "iced up" over Detroit and they were forced to return to Topeka. This time they were routed through Florida, Puerto Rico, South America and Africa to England. When they arrived in South America their pilot was relieved of his duties due to mental stress. They were given another pilot and continued the balance of their flight without incident. Darwin managed to secure a Cocker Spaniel puppy while there and it flew with them to England resting comfortably in a shoebox.

Darwin was assigned to the 446th BG at Bungay, England, and flew thirty-one missions as an aerial gunner. Five missions were described as short. Missions to bomb synthetic oil fields near Leipzig were long missions where they encountered heavy "flak" and were attacked by yellow nosed German fighter planes. Darwin's tail gunner shot down one fighter. "The lead bombardier really hit the target. We didn't want to go back."

On a mission over France "flak" knocked out their radio and oxygen systems causing them to "fly down on the deck" to get back to base. While on a mission over Frankfurt "flak" hit the wing of their aircraft. It also shorted out wiring causing the aircraft to fill with smoke. "We dropped out of formation and most of us went into the bomb bay area with oxygen bottles to get ready to bail out when someone found the problem. "Flak" had cut a wire. It was repaired and we flew back to base."

"My dog, slept on my bed. It would be with the crew chief while I was on a mission and would be at the hard stand waiting for me when I returned from a mission."

Darwin's crew was placed on standby for a February, 1944, mission to Berlin. Each of his crewmembers were used as replacements for any crew needing someone to fill in. ""Flak" was intense. To me it seemed like four bursts around us. One in front and two on the sides. You didn't want to be there when the fourth one exploded." It was on this mission that Darwin's Engineer flying as a replacement in another aircraft, went down with the plane.

Darwin flew two missions on D-Day and two missions to St. Lo, France in support of ground forces after the invasion. "All missions were scary. No one mission stands out from the others. With "flak" bursting outside I don't see how we got through it."

He returned to the United States in September, 1944 and was sent to Pueblo, Colorado, where he was taken off flight status and worked in the base sheet metal shop on B-24 bombers. In May, 1945, the base changed over to B-29 bombers and were preparing to go to Japan. However the war ended and Darwin received his discharge from military service in October, 1945. He had been awarded the Distinguished Flying Cross, Air Medal with three oak leaf clusters, ETO and World War II Victory Medals.

Darwin returned to farming and operated a corn shelling business until he began working for the Farmers Coop Elevator at Bradgate, Iowa. He retired in 1985 and has been active in woodworking and craft projects with his wife for twenty years.

Right - Darwin and his crew at 446th BG, Bungay, England. Darwin, Aerial Gunner, is front row, second from right.

JACK JONES, PANORA, IA, was originally from Des Moines. He graduated from high school in June, 1941 and attended his first semester at Drake University. He enlisted in the Army Air Corps in 1942 under the Aviation Cadet Program and was placed in a "hold" status. He quit school and worked at the Des Moines Ordnance Plant until he was called to active duty later in the year.

After Basic Training at Jefferson Barracks, St. Louis, Missouri, Jack attended the University of Missouri as part of the College Training Detachment Program

where he took courses that included mathematics and physics. While there he and other aviation cadets were billeted in fraternity houses. Also attending the university were one thousand sailors taking engineering courses. Each morning, marching to classes, the campus would be serenaded by the sailors singing "Anchors Aweigh" and the aviation cadets singing the "Air Corps Song".

Jack was then sent to a classification center at San Antonio, Texas, for testing and physical examination. He was classified as "ground duty only" and sent to Shepard Field, Texas for more Basic Training. He was then re-assigned to Radio School at Sioux Falls, South Dakota. At the end of 1943 and near the end of the training program "they took a whole class of us and sent us to Scott Field, Illinois to get us ready for shipment overseas. We were put on a train to Camp Kilmer, New Jersey, where we boarded a ship as part of a convoy bound for England. We landed at Liverpool and unloaded at night in the middle of an air raid."

Jack was assigned to the 453rd Bomb Group at Old Buckenham, England. He took aerial gunnery training over "The Wash" of England and trained to learn how to jam German radar and radar controlled anti-aircraft weapons.

While never officially part of an aircrew, Jack flew thirty-five combat missions. He sat behind the pilot with three transmitters and one receiver. "Every time I would pickup a German radar signal I would jam it and record the time. It worked. We would see flak being shot in perfect patterns but it would explode either way below, behind or above us. There were two of us operators and we would rotate missions."

His missions included participation in low-level supply missions to American ground forces crossing the Rhine. "I don't know why I was on this mission, I turned the radar off. One minute we could see Americans waving at us and the next minute Germans shooting at us."

On a mission to Cologne Jack's aircraft received many flak hits and was forced to make an emergency landing at a matted airstrip in Belgium. "The weight of the airplane tore up the matting and the aircraft pretty bad. We were transported to Brussels where we were flown back to base. During the Battle of the Bulge I could hear aircraft taking off in bad weather. You would occasionally hear the roar of the plane on takeoff, then silence, and then "boom" when it crashed."

The 453rd was removed from operations in early April, 1945 for possible re-deployment to the Pacific Theater, Jack was transferred to the 389th Bomb Group, Headquarters for the Second Air Division at Hethel, England. While there he flew his last four missions. After the war ended in Europe Jack flew back to the United States and was eventually re-assigned to B-29 bombers at Santa Ana, California. While there only two days, he got blood poisoning and remained in the hospital until war's end.

Jack received a medical discharge from military service in October, 1945. He had been awarded the Air Medal, ETO Ribbon and World War II Victory Medal. Although he had been treated for blood poisoning he subsequently learned this was not the cause of his ailment. Whatever the problem, it cleared after he got married. He resumed his education at Drake University under the GI Bill of Rights and eventually earned a Doctorate Degree in Education at the University of Nebraska. His career included teaching school, administrative duties as school principal before he began teaching school administration, and leadership classes at Drake University from which he retired.

VERNE JOSIFEK, CEDAR RAPIDS, IA, was a crew chief with the 361st Fighter Group based at Bottisham and Little Walden,

England. The fighter group flew P-47 Thunderbolts but eventually made the transition to the P-51 Mustang. Verne had had in-line engine schooling while the rest of the mechanics had radial engine training. As a result, Verne was assigned as crew chief on the first P-51 assigned to the Group for training. According to Verne, it was a piece of junk when it arrived. It was his job to take care of the plane, but every pilot in the Group was trying to put hours in on this plane to become proficient. This required many extra hours, often working through the night to keep the plane in flying condition.

When the operational P-51s arrived, there was not room for him to be a crew chief, so an existing crew chief volunteered to give up his Staff Sergeant rank to Verne if he could be assigned to Verne's crew as an assistant crew chief.

Verne received a Bronze Star for keeping a plane in operating condition for 200 hours without any mechanical problems resulting in aborted missions. At one point Verne had gotten somewhere near 900 hours out of an engine without an engine change. "The bigwigs wanted to get to 1000 hours to try and set some type of record but Verne insisted the engine was in need of change and told his pilot not to fly it. An engine change was ordered. When the plane was taxied down to the main hanger for the change no one could believe the engine was still running. It was popping and cracking like no one had heard before.

As the war was winding down and it was obvious the Air Corps would be focusing more on spit and polish, memos were issued to concentrate on having the planes in good shine. The quickest way to do this was spray aviation fuel on the planes despite conservation efforts. Aviation fuel was also used as dry cleaning solution to wash uniforms.

Verne also played in a band formed by members of the 361st. It was not an official base band but they were very successful often playing at jobs three times a week. High ranking officers on the base liked the band and often would send their staff cars to the flight line to pick up Verne and get him to band jobs. The band played at the Stage Door Canteen in the Rainbow Corner Red Cross Club in London on both VE day and on VJ Day.

After the war when it came time for the men to go home, Verne had earned enough points through the Bronze Medal and bronze battle stars he got for servicing the aircraft in particular campaigns that he was due to be rotated. He was single and having too much fun playing with the band and really didn't want to go home early.

Verne recalls one incident when someone sneaked a "party girl" on the base and hid her for several days in an air raid shelter. The shelters were almost never used as they were never attacked while in England. Verne described it as comical to see the foot race from the mess hall after chow. Guys were sneaking food to the girl in hopes of being "rewarded". After a while officers got to wondering why there were so many men around the air raid shelter all the time and they discovered the girl.

Right - Verne receives the Bronze Star from Brig. Gen. Jesse Auton at 361st FG, Little Walden, England.

MAURICE KAHL, LEHIGH, IA, entered the Army Air Corps in 1942. After Basic Training he was sent to Aerial Gunnery School before assignment to an air crew and training with them in preparation for overseas deployment. In late 1943, Maurice and his crew flew the southern route through Puerto Rico, South America and Africa to the 458th Bomb Group based at Horsham St. Faith, England.

Assigned as a B-24 tail gunner Maurice flew several missions before medical reasons prevented him from continuing in a flight status. He remained at Horsham St Faiths working in armaments, primarily patching and repair of damaged aircraft. His original crew continued missions with a replacement gunner until they were all subsequently killed in action.

Maurice returned to the United States aboard the Queen Mary shortly before the war was won in Europe. He was then transferred to Sioux Falls, South Dakota, for B-29 training in preparation for deployment to the Pacific Theater of Operations. Victory over Japan precluded further military service and Maurice was discharged from the Air Corps. He had been awarded the Air Medal, World War II Victory Medal and the ETO Ribbon, among other medals.

Maurice returned to Iowa became a carpenter and worked in construction while farming until his retirement.

FRANCIS KAPLER, WATERLOO, IA, was managing the family café in Hudson, Iowa when the Japanese attacked American bases on the island of Oahu in the Hawaiian Islands on December 7, 1941. Previously he had inherited seventy dollars. "It was more money than I had ever seen. I went to the Waterloo airport and asked how much it would cost to learn how to fly. I was told seventy dollars. So, I plopped down the money and began taking lessons. I soloed twice before December 7 and had my log book signed by Jonathan Livingston. "

Early in 1942 Francis tried to enlist in the Army Air Corps as part of the Aviation Cadet Program. He passed the written examination but failed the physical due to an abnormality in his feet. "It made me so mad I went across the hall and joined the Army." He was sent to El Paso, Texas for Basic Training and spent one year in training for the coast artillery. Francis then boarded a troop train for New Jersey. He noticed ads for volunteers to join the Army Air Corps and become pilots. He re-took the tests while in New Jersey and passed them all including the physical.

Francis completed Pre-flight Training at San Antonio, Texas. Next came Primary Flight at Brady, Texas. Basic Flight and Advanced Flight Training was taken at Waco, Texas where he received his wings and commission as a second lieutenant upon graduation. After two-engine flight training Francis was assigned to nine weeks of B-26 training at Del Rio, Texas. During the nine weeks, nine B-26 Marauders, also known as the "Widow Maker", were lost in training accidents. "The problem was that you couldn't fly slower than 150 miles per hour and it required a six thousand foot runway. I once landed a B-26 at Los Angeles Airport that only had a 4,000-foot runway. I managed to stop in front of a big fence at the end.

Francis was assigned to fly the B-26 and tow targets for B-17 aerial gunners in training at Alamagordo, New Mexico and Rapid City, South Dakota. He received assignment as Co-Pilot to a B-17 crew. In July, 1944, a new plane was picked up by Francis and his crew at Kearney, Nebraska, for their flight to the European Theater of Operations. In route their aircraft was struck by lightning while over New York state. "It appeared as if there was a ball of fire off the nose of the aircraft. We had a wire outside the airplane as an antennae. The wire led to a spool of the wire in the back of the airplane where one of our crew was sleeping with his head resting on the spool. The lightning melted the spool of wire and never hurt our man. Our instruments were going haywire because the lightning melted some of the wiring. We landed at Iceland and spent three days there while the whole airplane was re-wired. We then delivered the aircraft to Valley, Wales and rode by train to the 385th BG at Great Ashfield."

Francis flew twenty-seven combat missions. During a mission on August 27, 1944, weather prevented Francis's bomb group from holding formation after it passed the coast of Europe. During the confusion their aircraft passed over enemy territory at a point they would least want to be, the island of Helgoland. The island, located in the North Sea between Wilhelmshaven, Germany and Denmark, bristled with German anti-aircraft guns. Their aircraft took hits that knocked out number three and four engines, both of which began to windmill. "This caused us to lose additional speed. We had turned back and were over the North Sea. We opened the bomb bay doors and threw out everything we could to lose weight, including our bombs, armor plating, guns, ammunition and even our bombsight. We still couldn't maintain altitude. We were able to fly about an hour toward England but could tell we weren't going to make it. I had to make a dead stick landing in the North Sea that had fifteen-foot swells. We hit the water and went under then came to the surface. We had practiced ditching procedures before so each man knew what he had to do. We had two life rafts inflated and got them out. In the cockpit we went out the windows. We had one life raft that wouldn't inflate."

"We spent four hours in the water in our lifeboats bobbing up and down with the swells. At the bottom of the swell there was a wall of water all around us. We had radioed a "Mayday" signal so everyone knew where we were. We eventually saw a P-38 flying a search pattern so we shot off some flares and he saw us. Later a British boat picked us up."

During his tour of duty Francis spent three weeks in the base hospital which prevented him from finishing the required number of missions with his original crew. He was re-assigned to fly weather reconnaissance in stripped down B-17s with only a five-man crew. "A plane would take off at midnight, another one at two in the morning and another one an hour before a mission was to leave to gain weather data. Although we had limited defense in the air, we were never jumped by German fighters. English weather was terrible to fly in and caused a lot of accidents and mid-air collisions. We would peel off on a landing pattern at ten-second intervals with virtually no visibility many times. One mistake and it was all over."

In May, 1945, Francis boarded the "Ile de France" ocean liner for his return to the United States. He reported to Los Angeles where "we did nothing" until he got orders he could go home and be discharged. He was at home when Japan surrendered to the United States in September, 1945. Francis had been awarded, among other medals, the Air Medal with four oak leaf clusters. ETO Ribbon with battle stars, and the World War II Victory Medal.

After the war he became a flying instructor at Waterloo then spent twenty-eight years in the restaurant business. He retired after fourteen years as a representative with the Iowa Restaurant and Beverage Association.

Right - Francis and crew at 385th BG, Great Ashfield, England. Francis, Pilot, is back row, right

DOUG KEEN, CHEROKEE, IA,

grew up in Libertyville, Illinois. While still a senior in high school he signed up for the Army Air Corps Aviation Cadet Program and successfully passed written and physical examinations for acceptance. After graduation from high school in June, 1943, he was inducted into military service.

Doug attended ground school at the University of Tennessee before completing Pre-flight Training at Maxwell Field, Montgomery, Alabama. While in Primary Flight Training at Bennettsville, South Carolina, all cadets were "washed out" of training because of an existing over-supply of trained pilots. He then completed Aerial Gunnery School at Ft. Myers, Florida, and in December, 1944, was assigned to a B-29 bomber aircrew for training at Pratt, Kansas.

The 20th Air Force located in the captured Marianas Islands of Saipan, Guam and Tinian in the Summer and Fall of 1944, began bombing Japan. A buildup of air forces continued throughout the first half of 1945. It was intended that with the surrender of Germany, the Eighth Air Force would be transferred from Europe to the island of Okinawa once that island was re-captured from the Japanese. The massive bombardment of Japan with the combined forces of the 8th and 20th would to aid American invasion forces if Japan would not sue for peace.

Okinawa was invaded on April 1, 1945, and considered secure for arrival of Eighth Air Force aircraft at the end of June. The war in Europe had ended only a month earlier and build-up of Eighth air forces would be slow. Three air crews of the Eighth that had trained on the B-29 were sent to the Marianas to gain combat experience and brief following Eighth Air Force crews on what to expect once they began to arrive in numbers. Doug and his crew were assigned to the 330th Bomb Group at Guam and arrived on the island in mid-July, 1945. On July 17, he flew his first mission against Japan, as a member of the 346th Bomb Group of the Eighth Air Force attached to the 330th Bomb Group of the 20th Air Force. Doug flew eleven combat missions before the war ended with the dropping of atomic bombs on Hiroshima and Nagasaka, Japan. Japan sued for peace on August 15, 1945, and formally surrendered September 2 of that year.

"We flew both day and night missions during our tour. Each mission was of 12-13 hours duration, all over water. When Iwo Jima was captured by the Marines, B-29 crews were really grateful for this emergency landing field. B-29 crews could land there if they were shot up or running low on fuel. We landed on Iwo Jima twice. Once because an engine had been damaged by anti-aircraft fire over Japan. Another guy and I took off for the site of a recent battle and found a Japanese tank. We climbed on top of the tank, looked in and saw a Japanese combat boot with the foot still left inside. We also climbed to the top of Mount Suribachi, the volcanic landmark made famous after the American flag-raising by six Marines. We looked right down on "Blue Beach", the main invasion beach. The Japanese poured incredibly intense fire down on the Marines from there. Now, just a few weeks after the invasion, the entire beach and landing area was filled with row after row of white crosses. I found the grave of a high school friend and took a photograph to take back to his family."

Doug's last missions flown while attached to the 20th Air Force was on August 30, 1945, when American Prisoners of War were picked up at Osaka, Japan and then on September 2, 1945, when a "Show of Force" flight was made over Tokyo Bay during surrender proceedings aboard the "USS Missouri".

Doug remained on Guam until October, 1945, and then joined his Eighth Air Force unit on Okinawa. His Bomb Group had arrived on the island just as the war was ending and never flew a mission, yet, three combat crews remain the only Eighth Air Force crews to bomb the Empire of Japan. He received his discharge from military service April 14, 1946 at Ft. Sheridan, Illinois, and had been awarded, among others, the Air Medal and Pacific Theater of Operations Medal.

Doug was severely injured in an auto accident shortly after discharge and spent a year recovering in a Veterans hospital. He then attended Lake Forest College for two years before graduating from Northwestern University with a degree in education. He taught school before he returned to college for additional education and counseling credits. Doug worked many years at the Cherokee Mental Health Institute as a counselor before retiring in 1988. He now resides in Arizona.

ROBERT KELLEY, LISBON, IA,

had graduated from high school and was on an athletic scholarship at Millikin College, Decatur, Illinois, when World War II called him to military service. Accepted into the Aviation Cadet Program he took Pre-flight Training at Montgomery, Alabama; Primary Flight Training at Camden, South Carolina; Basic BT 113 at Sumter,

South Carolina and Advanced Training at Shaw Field, Georgia.

After crew assignment and overseas training Robert and his crew left the United States on Easter morning, 1944, and flew via Iceland to Grafton-Underwood, England, home of the 384th Bomb Group. Robert flew formation practice for a few days before he flew the first of his thirty-one missions. It was a bombing raid on Posen, Poland, a trip of 1500 miles. Their Group encountered heavy "flak" when they entered Germany. He saw the B-17 next to him shot down by a German fighter plane. "I could see the German pilot plain as day."

Robert's third and sixth missions were to heavily defended Berlin. In his B-17 named "Hot Rock" other missions were flown to targets at Saarbrucken, Mannheim, and Bremen, Germany; Cherbourgh, Caen, and Normandy, France on D-Day. The last missions on his tour were in the St. Lo, France area in support of the Allied breakout into France.

In June, 1944, Robert was part of an experimental mission that carried 100 pound bombs with "wings" under each wing of his B-17. With other aircraft armed in the same manner, the formation flew into the Ruhr Valley. Within 50-60 miles of the target, the planes were put into a dive reaching 350 miles an hour. The bombs were released to "sail" on to the target. German propaganda claimed churches and hospitals were hit. No damage assessment was made and Robert never talked to anyone else who had participated in this mission to determine its effectiveness.

Robert was discharged from military service in November, 1947. He had been awarded, among other medals, the Distinguished Flying Cross, Air Medal with three oak leaf clusters, ETO and World War II Victory Medals.

He operated a truck body business for thirty years and a black angus farm for twelve years. In fourteen months Robert built his own experimental airplane in the basement of his home. A Glastar, he had it certified and flew it in his retirement, a dream come true.

Right - Robert and his crew at 384th BG, Grafton Underwood, England. Robert, Pilot, is front row, second from left.

EDWARD KELLY, CORYDON, IA, entered the U.S. Army in November, 1942. He was stationed with the 91st Division in Oregon "going nowhere" when he volunteered for the Army Air Corps. Ed was sent to Buckley Field, Colorado, for Armament School and then to Laredo, Texas, for Aerial Gunnery School.

At March Field, California, he was assigned to an air crew and completed phase training for overseas deployment. In November, 1944, he boarded the ocean liner "Ile de France" for "a terrible trip" to Scotland. The seas were rough, stormy and "everyone got sick". After arrival he boarded a train for the 44th Bomb Group at Shipdham, England.

Ed flew twenty-eight missions as an aerial gunner. His first mission followed custom at the 44th. The newest crews flew the oldest planes. "Immediately on takeoff we lost engine number three. In a very short time number four engine went out. We were informed that our field was fogged in and that we would have to proceed to an air base in Scotland." The crew dumped everything they could within the plane to lighten their load. This included their bombs which were jettisoned somewhere over The Wash of England. They made it safely to the base in Scotland. "If it had not been for the skill of the pilot we would not have made it."

Another mission Ed described as the Purple Heart mission was also on one of the base's oldest airplanes. "It was equipped with an Emerson nose turret. Our nose gunner was completely ignorant of all aspects of its operation. As a result the turret swung around and opened a gash over the gunner's eyebrow. Flying a "milk run" mission the pilot was anxious to complete the mission for credit. It was agreed that if they didn't have to abort the mission for any reason he would make sure the gunner got the Purple Heart Medal (for wounds sustained in action with the enemy). After the mission the crew visited the gunner at the base hospital and there on the pillow in all its resplendent glory rested the Purple Heart."

During the Battle of the Bulge Ed flew low-level supply missions in support of ground forces. Armament was stripped from B-24 bombers. Crates of supplies were roped together in the bomb bay area and hooked to the bomb releases. "When alerted the bomb bay was emptied and we in the back of the plane pushed other supplies out. Then all hell broke loose. We could see a German officer firing his pistol at our airplane. A machine gun on the ground managed to shoot off part of the wing on the airplane next to us. The plane went into the ground and hit a tree. We found out later that several of the crew were killed. The radar operator (don't ask me what a radar operator was doing on this mission) survived and was taken prisoner by the Germans. He later returned to our base after escaping."

A crew man on one of the planes in the low-level raid became entangled in the ropes attached to the supplies and was dragged out of his aircraft. "At our mission briefing a Colonel who was not on the mission threatened not to give us credit for a mission because "The Germans got most of the supplies you dropped"".

An unusual experience occurred during one mission when Ed's Group was attacked by ME-109 German fighter planes. "One of the fighters pushed its nose into our formation. I looked over the left waist gunner's shoulder and could see the plane with a pilot that was probably dead at the controls. The waist gunner poured a long burst into the plane causing it to break in two and go into a steep dive."

On another mission to bomb a railyard identified by smoke bombs, the wind changed causing the smoke to blow over a village. The Group bombed the town which had no military targets.

Ed flew back to the United States in June, 1945. When he landed at Bangor, Maine, the aircraft was taken from the crew. Ed boarded a train for Sioux Falls, South Dakota, where he was assigned to the discharge section of the air base. He received his own discharge in October, 1945. He had been awarded, among other medals, the Air Medal, World War II Victory Medal and the ETO Ribbon.

Ed entered Buena Vista College in September, 1946, and earned his Bachelor's Degree. After teaching school for a year he quit to enter farming. Ten years later he returned to teach primarily English and Spanish for twenty-eight years at various schools and earn a Masters Degree in Comparative Literature. He retired from the Corydon school system.

GEORGE KESSELRING, GUTHRIE CENTER, IA, graduated from High School in 1941. He then helped his father raise crops on rented farms. When America entered World War II farming was a vital industry which would give an exemption from the draft and military service. While getting a field ready for planting he heard a loud roar and saw a low flying P-51 fly past.

From that moment on he was hooked on aviation. To enter the Aviation Cadet Program George took night classes in science and math at Perry, IA and was able to successfully pass the entrance examination without benefit of college training. He enlisted in the Army Air Corps in September, 1942 at Des Moines, IA.

George was sent home to wait for an opening in the Program and was subsequently called to active duty on February 2, 1943. He reported to Lackland Army Air Field, San Antonio, Texas. After Basic Training, Primary Flight Training was taken at Corsicana, Texas; Basic Training at Greenville, Texas, and Advanced Training at Frederick, Oklahoma. Upon completion of training he was commissioned a Second Lieutenant.

In April, 1944, George was assigned a crew for overseas training and eventually deployed to England by ship in November and assigned to the 91st Bomb Group at Bassingbourn. On No-

Chapter Twenty-Two

vember 26, 1944, George flew his first combat mission to bomb a railway viaduct at Altenbeken, Germany.

George flew thirty-five combat missions. He described himself as a truck driver, "we picked up a load here and delivered it there. Its just that the people receiving the merchandise really didn't want it, and would do whatever it took to see that it didn't get to its destination."

His third mission was on November 30, 1944, a raid on the synthetic oil plant at Zeitz, Germany. When he was ready to begin the bomb run on the target his number three engine started smoking, could not be "feathered", and caught fire. The engine vibrated, the fire was out of control, and in danger of blowing up. The possibility of bailing out over enemy territory was considered when the vibrating propeller wore itself out and stopped, but the fire blew itself out and they left the formation alone at reduced speed for the return trip to England. After they jettisoned their bombs a flight of American P-51 fighters escorted them back to base.

George's fourth mission was on December 4, 1944, to bomb rail yards at Kassel, Germany. He described it as "a crazy mission, doomed to failure from the start. The lead airplane appeared to fly all over Germany and couldn't seem to find a target. The formation was in the air so long that when we landed back at Bassingbourn we had only twenty minutes of fuel left."

Sunday, December 24 the mission was directed toward airdromes at Frankfort, Germany, in support of the Battle of the Bulge. The battle had reached a desperate stage for Allied ground forces. Weather had prevented air forces from supplying American troops and attack German troops until December 23 when weather cleared. On the 24th weather over England was still not good but the Mighty Eighth made it in the air. Weather over the target had cleared and it was destroyed. Return to England was another problem. Weather at all but three Eighth Air Force bases had them closed down, including Bassingbourn. George and the rest of the 91st landed at Bury St Edmunds, home of the 94th BG. "It was completely loaded with B-17s. Many of us had to sleep in our airplanes. They didn't have enough room or food for all of us."

George's ninth mission was a raid on a rail center in the middle of Kassel, Germany. "One of our planes blew up on takeoff with all killed. Two other planes collided over the English Channel. The Group had to bomb a secondary target but the lead airplane missed finding the target and required a second bomb run. This gave enemy anti-aircraft batteries a second chance." George's plane took five hits which shot our their glycol system. Engine number two couldn't be feathered. A piece of flak just missed their number four gas tank. A three inch hole was made in the ball turret hitting the gunner. A piece of plexiglass was broken from the nose section, and a large piece of flak entered below George's seat and struck the co-pilot.

Very few missions were flown that would be considered "milk runs". Battle damage was sustained on almost all missions that could have resulted in loss of the airplane and serious injuries to the crew. Not to be disregarded was the possibility of accidents, mechanical failure and collisions with so many aircraft involved. On George's thirteenth mission the number two engine on "Sweet 17" caught fire as they were rolling down the runway for takeoff. Going ninety miles per hour at the time, the throttles were cut and they were able to stop before running off the runway. They were able to get another aircraft and continue with the mission.

George's co-pilot was seriously wounded from flak that entered the cockpit on their eighteenth mission. They had dropped their bombs on target and on the return flight to England believed they were over friendly territory. The formation dropped in altitude to get off oxygen. Unfortunately they were still over enemy territory and anti-aircraft fire shot at them was intense and accurate. Low on fuel George was forced to land his aircraft at a captured airfield in France with only eight gallons of fuel remaining. Their plane had 178 holes in it.

Mission thirty-three, to bomb an ordnance depot in Germany saw several of the new German jet fighters, the ME-262, flying through their formation without being fired on by gunners for fear of hitting their own planes.

A mission of April 11, 1945, called for their Group to bomb an open field. Known to mission planners but unknown to flight crews, the open field contained an extensive underground fuel storage tank system. According to George, " the whole field exploded".

George's last mission was a rare "milk run" but it was on Friday the 13th of April, 1945. As it turned out the mission was short in duration instead of the usual twelve to thirteen hours, there was no flak and no enemy fighters. His tour was over.

Although George had completed his thirty-five missions, some of his crew had not. With two missions to go, his ball turret gunner was blown out of his turret from a cannon blast fired by a German fighter plane. The gunner dangled from the ball area for a few seconds but lost his grip and fell to earth without a parachute.

George was at Liverpool, England to board a ship for the return trip to America when news came of the surrender of Germany. George decided to remain in the Air Force and make it a career. He retired August 31, 1963 at the rank of Major and had served in all phases of Personnel. He had been awarded the Air Medal with five oak leaf clusters, European Theater of Operations with three Bronze Service Stars, and World War II Victory Medal, among others. George now resides at Van Buren, Arkansas.

Right - George and his crew at 91st BG, Bassingbourn, England. George is front row, second from left.

Right - B-17 "Sweet 17" flown by George Kesselring, Guthrie Center, 91st BG

DARRELL KIDDIE, DES MOINES, IA, entered on duty with the Army Air Corps at Des Moines, Iowa, in January, 1943. He was assigned to the 303rd Bomb Group at Molesworth, England. Darrell flew the first of twelve combat missions as a bombardier on March 6, 1945, on a bombing raid of Essen, Germany. His other missions included targets on marshalling yards, airfields, oil refineries and strategic bridges to deny German ground forces of strategic materials to continue fighting. One raid included a bombing of German headquarters at Yassen, Germany.

Between missions Darrell participated on his base skeet shooting team which won the European Theater of Operations championship. He was discharged from military service in September, 1945, and had been awarded the Air Medal, ETO Ribbon and WWII Victory Medal.

Darrell retired from H.E. Sorensen Company, a furniture distributor, after thirty-five years with the firm. Before his death he was inducted into the North High School Hall of Fame as an outstanding baseball player.

Right - Darrell and crew at 303rd BG, Molesworth, England. Darrell, Navigator, is back row, second from right.

ROSS KING, SIOUX CITY, IA, graduated from high school in May, 1942 and worked as a bookkeeper until he was drafted into the infantry in March, 1943, at Camp Crook, Omaha, Nebraska.

After he completed basic infantry training Ross volunteered for the Aviation Cadet Program. He passed required testing at San Antonio, Texas in September, 1943, and was sent to

Oklahoma City University under the College Detachment Training Program. Because of a glut of applicants waiting pilot training Ross was sent to Aerial Gunnery School at Harlingen, Texas. Upon completion of training he attended Navigation School at San Marcos, Texas. He graduated in November, 1944, and was awarded his wings and commission as a Second Lieutenant.

Ross was deployed overseas in March, 1945, and was assigned as a Navigator to the 364th Squadron of the 305th Bomb Group at Chelveston, England. He participated in "a few" missions until V-E Day (Victory in Europe). Ross and his Bomb Group were then sent to St. Trond, Belgium, to conduct aerial photography of Europe and North Africa. "During photography we had to fly specific routes and be on course at all times." His squadron also photographed Iceland and the North Pole and in December, 1945, moved to Lechfeld, Germany, near Munich where they continued their aerial photography. "The Russians wouldn't let us fly East beyond a certain point."

In early 1946 Ross returned to the United States and received his discharge from military service in June, 1946. Under the G.I. Bill of Rights he entered the University of Iowa, graduated and passed examinations to become a Certified Public Accountant. He has subsequently retired after a career as a C.P.A. at Sioux City and enjoys playing golf.

CARL KITCHEN, WATERLOO, IA, graduated from Northern Illinois School of Optometry in June, 1940, and set up his practice in Creston, Iowa. After America's entry into World War II he enlisted in the Army Air Corps in October, 1942. He was not called to active duty until February 23, 1943.

Carl was sent to Jefferson Barracks, St Louis, Missouri, and then to Oshkosh, Wisconsin, for College Detachment Training under the Aviation Cadet Program. The next three stages of flight training were taken in California; Pre-flight Training at Santa Ana; Primary Flight Training at Visalia and Basic Flight Training at Bakersfield. Advanced Flight Training was completed at Pecos, Texas in May, 1944 whereupon Carl was awarded his Wings and commission as a Second Lieutenant. He then reported to Kingman, Arizona for Co-Pilot Transition Training on the B-17 bomber.

Carl was assigned to an air crew at Lincoln, Nebraska and trained with them at Ardmore, Oklahoma in preparation for deployment to the European Theater of Operations. In December, 1944, Carl and his crew flew to Gander, Newfoundland, for refueling. The temperature was forty-five degrees below zero. They took off in a blizzard for Iceland, the next stop in their trip where they spent Christmas, 1944. After flying to Prestwick, Scotland, they flew on to Belfast, Ireland where they spent New Years Eve. Their aircraft was taken from them for retrofit and they were put aboard a boat for Wales. It was then a train ride to Eye, England and the 490th Bomb Group.

Carl would fly twenty-seven combat missions beginning January 14, 1945 until April 24, 1945. Most missions were flown as the number three aircraft off of the lead airplane. On the bomb run during a mission to Munich flak from German anti-aircraft guns was intense. "I didn't know if I was gonna get through this. I was lucky compared to a lot of them."

His last mission, to Czechoslovakia was considered his most memorable. It was then their Group was attacked by the new German jet, the ME-262. "Our formation was all spread out due to a navigation error and we were in the middle. In trying to "form up" the jet hit us and shot down two B-17s. Gunners couldn't track the jets and get shots off at them."

After Victory in Europe, Carl flew missions to Belgium and Holland dropping food supplies to those who had lived a starvation existence under Nazi rule. His aircraft named "Moy's Boys" also flew Ninth Air Force WACs on a sightseeing tour of Europe to witness the results of Eighth Air Force bombings.

In July, 1945, Carl flew back to the United States in his combat aircraft. After leaving Wales for Iceland they flew into bad weather and subsequently received a radio message that Iceland was "socked in" and they were to return to Prestwick, Scotland. They did not have sufficient fuel to return and continued on their flight. Carl was able to find a "hole" in the weather and safely land.

Carl was scheduled to take B-29 training in Florida and was home on leave when the war ended. He was separated from military service and returned to Iowa and resumed his optometry business. Carl practiced in Estherville, Iowa, for thirteen years before moving to Cedar Rapids. He continued in the Air Force Reserves for twenty years and retired in 1966.

During his twenty-seven combat missions Carl never lost an engine, never aborted a mission and never lost a crewman. He was awarded the Air Medal with three oak leaf clusters, the ETO Ribbon and World War II Victory Medal.

ROBERT KLOSER, CARROLL, IA, was helping his father in a family farm seed business when he enlisted in the Army Air Corps January 10, 1942. Bob was sent to Sheppard Field, Wichita Falls, Texas for Basic Training. After training he performed orderly room duties for a short time at McClelland Field, California, before being transferred to Second Air Depot Group at Alameda, California. He worked in the orderly room at Alameda before the entire group was shipped by train to the East Coast in May, 1942.

Bob boarded an English ship that was part of a convoy and sailed for Bristol, Wales, a voyage that lasted two weeks. He was initially assigned to the 15th Bomb Squadron at Molesworth, England, a base subsequently occupied by the 303rd Bomb Group. The 15th remained only a few months at Molesworth before it was reassigned to the 12th Air Force in North Africa.

Bob was then transferred back to orderly room duties with the Second Base Air Depot Group at Burtonwood, England.

The Group performed major maintenance and repair of aircraft and served as a "hardware supply and flying equipment store" for other air bases. Bob was successful in switching assignments from the orderly room to mail room duties where he remained until the end of the war. In October, 1945 he boarded the "Queen Mary" for return to the United States. Bob received his discharge from military service within two weeks and had been awarded the ETO Ribbon and World War II Victory medal.

Bob returned to civilian life and re-joined his father in the family seed business until retirement in 1986.

RUSSELL KNIGHT, IOWA CITY, IA, worked for Douglas Aircraft Company until he enlisted in the Army Air Corps in October, 1942. He was sent to Midland, Texas, for Basic Training and applied for the Aviation Cadet Program. Russell was accepted and completed Pre-Flight Training at San Antonio, Texas. He was in Primary Flight Training under civilian instructors at Vernon, Texas, when he was "washed out" of further training due to a personality conflict with one instructor.

Russell was assigned to Aerial Gunnery School at Panama City, Florida where he excelled and was chosen to compete in a gunnery tournament at Las Vegas, Nevada. Upon graduation he was assigned to an aircrew at Salt Lake City, Utah and completed overseas training with the crew at Peterson Field, Colorado Springs, Colorado, in April, 1944. The crew then picked up a new B-24 bomber at Topeka, Kansas, and flew to England through Florida, Puerto Rico, South America and Africa.

Russell was assigned to the 466th Bomb Group at Attlebridge. He flew thirty-one combat missions that included three straight missions in three days to bomb targets at Munich, Germany. "The worst thing about the missions was the "flak". We rarely came back without holes in our plane. We must have gotten a direct hit by a dud anti-aircraft shell. The leading edge of our right wing between the number three and four engines had a groove in it that only could have come from a shell."

On another mission "we were carrying 150 pound cluster bombs. On our way back to England we were near the English Channel when we heard a big noise and saw one of our bomb bay doors fly back past us. One cluster of three bombs hadn't released when we dropped our bombs. Two of the bombs feel free but one bomb was still hung on cables and was swinging under our plane. We couldn't land or would be blown apart. We didn't have any tools to cut the bomb loose. One guy on our crew had a mess kit and a fingernail file. We were told to fly up and down the English Channel and try to free the bomb. If we were going to run out of gas before we could get it free, then we were supposed to bail out and let the plane fall into the Channel." Taking turns the aircrew was successful in filing through three-quarter inch steel cable with the fingernail file and release the bomb into the water. They then flew back to their base.

"The saddest part of our missions was trying to climb in altitude to assembly and formation through fog and overcast. A lot of bases were close to each other and air traffic patterns crossed. A lot of young men lost their lives in mid-air collisions."

"Our co-pilot was at the controls flying in "soupy" weather during one mission when he got vertigo. You don't know whether you are flying upward, downward, or level. The pilot had to take over and remain at the controls for the balance of the flight."

Russell completed his required number of missions in October, 1944, and returned to the United States aboard the ship "New Amsterdam". Aboard ship were about three thousand German prisoners of war. "I had to help guard them. I was down in the lowest level of the ship at the rear. I could hear the ship's propellers from where I was at."

After a short stint at Truax Field, Madison, Wisconsin, Russell was detailed to Idaho where he and others relieved other soldiers fighting forest fires. In October, 1945, he was discharged from military service at Tacoma, Washington. Russell had been awarded the Distinguished Flying Cross, Air Medal with three oak leaf clusters, European Theater of Operations and World War II Victory Medals.

In civilian life, Russell retired from the University of Iowa where he was the Manager of the Physical Power Plant.

Right - Russell's crew at Attlebridge, England, and their B-24 named "Madame Shoo Shoo". Russell, Aerial Gunner, is front row, second from the left.

WILLIAM KNOWLING, IOWA CITY, IA, was working on the family farm and raising turkeys when the Japanese attacked the American naval base at Pearl Harbor, HI. He attended a welding and riveting school and then secured employment with Consolidated Aircraft Company in San Diego, CA. Bill worked there for one year when it was obvious more and more men left employment to enter military service and their positions were filled by women. He wanted to become a pilot but believed he had no chance for entry into the Aviation Cadet Program because it required two years college. A new rule was issued making it possible to pass a general knowledge test and become eligible for flight training.

Determined to be a pilot Bill returned to Iowa in the Fall of 1942, took the test for the Aviation Cadet Program, passed, and was immediately sworn into the Army Air Corps. He completed all stages of flight training in Texas and graduated December 5,

1943, with a commission as a second lieutenant. Bill and several other newly commissioned pilots were without assignments and sent to Salt Lake City, UT, which served as a holding station. He eventually reported to New Orleans, LA for P-47 Thunderbolt training and on graduation was sent to Boston for overseas duty.

In May, 1944, Bill boarded a troop ship, the "Isle of France", which set sail for Scotland in a convoy. Because of the time it took to sail across the Atlantic, he took refresher training in the P-47. It was during this time the Allies invaded Normandy.

Bill was assigned as a replacement pilot with the 353rd Fighter Group which had sustained high losses in dive bombing and strafing enemy targets. This was due mostly to pilots that had failed to provide top cover for themselves. Bill flew his first mission in the middle of June, 1944, in support of D-Day invasion forces. He received some "flak" from German anti- aircraft batteries but none that interfered with operation of his aircraft.

Bill flew between thirty and thirty-five missions in the P-47. Because of its lack of fuel range his Group replaced the Thunderbolt with the P-51 Mustang. Although he had received very little training in the P-51 he made the transition to the new aircraft easily. Bill's Fighter Group began its heaviest flying in the Fall and Winter of 1944. English weather was not cooperative and often required they fly at tree top level to visually find their base near the East coast of England. He named a P-51 assigned to him "Miss Maureen" after his fiance, Maureen Siegel of Andrew, IA, who after the war became his bride.

During Operation Market Garden, the airborne assault on Holland, Bill was patrolling and protecting ground troops. Two squadrons of his Group had turned back to England as their fuel ran low. Bill and his squadron then noticed a box of German fighters heading their way. The Germans went into a circling tactic that made it difficult to attack them without being shot down. Bill's squadron, however, attacked and was successful in downing fifteen enemy fighters. Bill was credited with one.

Most of Bill's missions were flying escort for bomber groups and strafing troop convoys, airfields and railroad traffic. He had high praise for the bombers particularly on the bomb run when they had to fly through heavy flak to release their bombs. His squadron often escorted crippled bombers back to England. "The 3,000 bomber raids were something to see. If the weather was bad we wouldn't have a problem finding our base. We could follow the stream of bombers back to England."

In December, 1944, Bill completed the required 275 hours of combat flying which totaled 69 missions. He had been credited with one aerial victory, one probable and one destroyed on the ground. He remained in England and taught new pilots their Group tactics. On one occasion he wanted to demonstrate how to make a fighter pass at a bomber. He advised a student to follow him and made a pass at an American bomber group. When the bombers believed they were being attacked by Germans they fired at Bill and the student. They quickly flew away without being harmed.

Bill returned to the United States in June, 1945, aboard a troop ship. After a furlough he attended an instructor's school to teach instrument flying until his discharge from military service in September, 1945. Bill was awarded the Distinguished Flying Cross, Air Medal with five oak leaf clusters and the European Theater of Operations Medal with four battle stars.

Right - Pilots at the 353rd Fighter Group. Bill is on the extreme left

Above left - Bill in his P-51 "Miss Maureen" named after his wife Maureen Seigel (*above right*) of Andrew, Iowa.

DUANE KRITCHMAN, DES MOINES, IA, was a first year college student when he entered the Army Air Corps as an eighteen year old on December 5, 1942. He entered the cadet pilot training program but was subsequently rushed into emergency gunnery training to meet overseas demands.

While in cadet training he was placed with athletes "plucked" from their senior year in college and included notable sports personalities. A roommate was Stan Mauldon, who became a pilot and was an All-American tackle from an undefeated University of Texas football team and played professional football after the war. He played softball with Enos Slaughter of the St Louis Cardinal baseball team. He peeled potatoes with the brother of the famed catcher of the New York Yankees, Bill Dickey. The mess sergeant threatened to put them both in the guardhouse. On a humorous note, while he sat in the rear cockpit of an AT-6 trainer, Duane managed to shoot a hole in the wing of his own airplane while flying over the Gulf of Mexico. What impressed Duane the most was that a naïve young man as himself could be flung into a group of well known athletes, many older than him, and be accepted without arrogance or prejudice. He felt it an honor to have known them, some of which never returned from the war.

Duane was deployed to England as a left waist gunner and ball turret gunner with the 327th Squadron of the 92nd Bomb Group at Podington. His first combat mission was as a substitute waist gunner with a crew who had lost their waist gunner on a previous mission. His second mission was with his original crew on a raid on Munich during which they endured a prolonged attack from German fighter planes. Other missions to follow were to Brunswick, Saarbruchen, Leipzig, Merseburg and Berlin. On one mission to Berlin, oxygen to the crew was lost while over the English Channel. They returned to base and faced the fury of a Commanding Officer who felt they should never leave the Group unless all four engines failed. He assigned them an additional combat mission than was required. The C.O. later realized that without oxygen they couldn't fly at the altitudes they were scheduled and rescinded the penalty.

Foggy weather played a part in a disaster witnessed by Duane and his crew as they prepared to take off on a mission to bomb Orly Airfield outside Paris in advance of D-Day. The B-17s were loaded with six, 1000 pound bombs each. One bomber failed to become airborne and ran into the woods beyond their airfield. The next plane was already on its takeoff run and stopped halfway down the runway after hearing a radio command or saw warning flares to stop. The pilot turned the B-17 around and started to taxi back down the runway. The pilots of the next plane either didn't receive a radio command or see the flares and with throttles wide open began its takeoff and collided head on with the taxiing airplane. From the resulting explosion twenty-one lives were lost. The runway was so badly damaged it took three days and nights for it to be repaired. Duane and his crew, as well as others, had abandoned their airplane and ran from the explosions. An ambulance arriving at the scene got there when a delayed explosion occurred.

Within the 92nd it appeared that policy dictated more experienced bomb crews would receive new aircraft that arrived at the base. Newer crews flew the older B-17s. Duane's crew received a new airplane on his seventeenth or eighteenth mission. He gained acceptance from his crew members when he suggested they name their aircraft "Heaven's Above". Duane also flew with other crews made up of wounded fliers returned to duty and remnants of other crews. During this period he and his crew, unable to make it back to Podington, were forced on three occasions, to land badly damaged B-17s at other bases.

Duane echoed the feeling of flight crew members when he stated, "Nothing in flying could have been accomplished without the supreme work effort of the ground crewmen who got little reward. "Nothing can be written without describing the admiration felt for the B-17 and its integrity in accepting immense battle damage. Many of the rewarding inspirational scenes of my experience was seeing a B-17, or riding in one, out of formation, without any reason for still being airborne, struggling to return to England. You carry a debt to that plane for the rest of your life. Almost all missions had unforgettable personal and visual experiences."

"Looking back, the military was not my way-I thought, but the engineer on my crew was employed at Boeing and Douglas Aircraft after the war for the balance of his life. All of the dress clothing purchased by me most of my life was from a friend's store who was a B-26 pilot in the 9th Air Force. My business partner was badly wounded on his nineteenth mission as a B-17 bombardier. My best friend was a gunner on a B-24 in the 15th Air Force. A schoolmate was a radio operator on a B-17 shot down over Germany. One cousin became a B-17 co-pilot and pilot. Another, a B-17 navigator that served in both World War II and Korea, one a B-29 engineer in the Pacific, another a P-38 fighter pilot in the Pacific and yet another failed his pilot test physical and became an Eighth Air Force truck driver. My wife had a cousin who worked for Curtis-Wright and North American and his brother-in-law was an F-101 pilot. Somehow the aura of the air force may never have really let me go at that."

Duane found it difficult to describe many events with detail but remembered many very well. "The pathos, the inequities, the unfairness of war is intolerable without daily grim humor, and forgetfulness". Like so many others the question is always asked to themselves, "Why was I spared when so many were cut down so young?"

Duane ended the war a Staff Sergeant. He returned to the United States aboard the "Queen Mary" for discharge from military service. He was awarded among other medals, the Distinguished Flying Cross and Air Medal with three clusters. Duane has served on the Board of the Eighth Air Force Historical Society and has actively supported the Central Iowa Wing of the Iowa Chapter.

BYRD LANGE, DES MOINES, IA, graduated from high school and worked as a shipping clerk when he enlisted in the Army Air Corps July 15, 1942. He was sent to Sheppard Field, Wichita Falls, Texas, for Basic Training. He was then assigned to Radio School at Scott Field, Illinois where he spent four months learning aircraft radio repair and maintenance.

After completion of training Byrd was sent to Atlantic City, New Jersey where the military occupied hotels along the Boardwalk as an overseas replacement center. From there, "about a hundred of us were sent to Halifax, Canada where we boarded an old French boat used by the British and set sail for Liverpool, England.

The ship was dirty, everyone got seasick, there was vomit all over the deck of the ship. The food was so bad. They fed us sardines for breakfast and there was nearly a revolt by the men over the food. They finally brought out some pork and beans and to this day I can eat them any time, hot or cold. One day out of Liverpool they dragged out hoses and washed down the ship."

After docking at Liverpool that had been repeatedly bombed by the Germans, Byrd was sent by train to Hardwick, England, home of the 93rd Bomb Group. "There were only five planes in the 330th Bomb Squadron when I arrived. At the end of the war in Europe we had twenty-five. We saw some B-24 bombers flying low in formation down the field on many occasions. We didn't know they were practicing to became part of the famous raid on Ploesti oil fields in August, 1943. Two of our men received the Congressional Medal of Honor for their actions during the raid."

Byrd's assignment was aircraft radio maintenance and repair of radios that malfunctioned or received battle damage. "From ten o'clock at night until two o'clock in the morning we would check out all the radios in the aircraft to make sure they were working properly. When the planes returned from a mission we would be waiting to check them out again and make any repairs."

Byrd remained in that assignment until V-E Day (Victory in Europe) and was treated to an aerial sightseeing trip to view the bomb damage inflicted on Nazi-occupied territory by the Eighth Air Force. In the middle of June, 1945, he sailed back to America aboard the "Queen Mary". In September, 1945, he received his discharge from military service at Jefferson Barracks, St Louis, Missouri. He had been awarded the European Theater of Operations Medal with ten battle stars and the World War II Victory Medal, among others.

In civilian life after the war Byrd worked for Northwestern Bell Telephone Company for thirty-one years.

Right - Byrd on his bicycle in front of his living quarters.

Left - Byrd, the middle person in the back row in front of his living quarters with co-workers

Bottom - 26 Lange Comm. Section 05-Communications Section of the 330th Squadron, 93rd Bomb Group, Hardwick, England. Byrd is fourth from right in the front row.

LYLE LATIMER, FARRAGUT, IA, was a public school principal when World War II began. He entered the Army Air Corps June 16, 1942, at Fort Crook, Nebraska.

Lyle was accepted into the Aviation Cadet Program at san Antonio, Texas. He took Primary Flight Training at Stockton, Texas until he was "washed out" of the program. He was assigned to Armorers School at Lowry Field, Colorado and Aerial Gunnery School at Harlingen, Texas.

Iowans of the Mighty Eighth

On April 21, 1944, Lyle was deployed to the European Theater of Operations as a tail gunner with the 44th Bomb Group at Shipdham, England. He flew thirty-one combat missions in  two and one-half months. His most memorable mission was his twenty-seventh, a bomb raid on Hamburg, Germany. Heavy flak was thrown at their formation on the bomb run. Lyle's left waist gunner was wounded in his upper leg. The crew's radioman although drenched by gasoline spray from three crippled engines rendered first aid to the gunner and then took over his gun position. Alone over the North Sea and subject to Luftwaffe fighter attack, an American P-51 Mustang fighter flew alongside their aircraft and escorted them all the way back to their base.

Other missions flown by Lyle included those in support of ground fighting after D-Day and breakthrough of German strongholds. Lyle was awarded the Distinguished Flying Cross, Air Medal with four oak leaf clusters, ETO Ribbon and World War II Victory Medal. He was discharged from the military June 25, 1945, and returned to teaching and school administration.

Right - Lyle receeivess the Distinguished Flying Cross from General Leon Johnson who waas a recipient of the Congressional Medal of Honor.

Right - Lyle and his crew at Topeka, Kansas, enroute to the European Theater of Opeations and the 44th BG, Shipdham, England.

WALTER LIENEMANN, MINBURN, IA, was farming in the DeSoto, Iowa, area when he was drafted into the Army Air Corps on October 12, 1942. He was sent to Jefferson Barracks, St. Louis, Missouri, for Basic Training and then to Aircraft Mechanics School at Kansas City, Missouri. After graduation Walt was transferred to Jacksonville, Florida, where he worked on the air base flight line servicing aircraft before attending Aerial Gunnery School at Panama City in Florida.

After gunnery school Walt was sent to a classification center at Salt Lake City, Utah where he was assigned to an air crew. The crew trained together at Casper, Wyoming in preparation for overseas deployment. They then picked up a new B-24 at Topeka, Kansas, named "Wolf Wagon" and began their flight to the European Theater of Operations. On arrival at Stone, England, their aircraft was taken from them and they proceeded by truck to the 392nd Bomb Group at Wendling.

Walter flew twenty-three missions as tail and waist gunner. On September 11, 1944, during a bombing mission on targets at Munich, Germany, his aircraft took numerous flak hits. His navigator was wounded when a piece of flak struck him in his side. Walt was busy at the time throwing out "chaf" in an attempt to confuse German radar controlled anti-aircraft batteries. He returned to his gun position when a German jet, an ME-262 dove on their formation. "I didn't have my gun charged. The jet attacked and shot down a plane next to us. I grabbed my gun, charged it and got off some bursts. I saw the German pilot when he went through the formation. I was too late to get him. Our radio operator gave the navigator morphine for his wounds and took care of him."

The war ended after Walt had completed twenty-three missions and he flew back to the United States at the end of May, 1945. He received his discharge from military service in September of that year and had been awarded the Air Medal with three oak leaf clusters, ETO Ribbon with three battle stars and the World War II Victory Medal.

Walt returned to farming in the DeSoto area until he bought another farm near Minburn, Iowa, and moved there.

IVAN LINDAMAN, APLINGTON, IA, worked for a construction company and helped on the family farm prior to World War II. He was drafted into the Army on October 15, 1942, at Camp Dodge, Iowa.

Ivan was sent to Camp Roberts, California, for training as a 37mm anti-tank gunner. He transferred to the Army Air Corps and was sent to Santa Ana, California,  for pilot training in September, 1943. Training sites included Lemoore, California; Ft. Sumner and Roswell, New Mexico. He was assigned to an air crew and trained with them at Gulfport, Mississippi, in preparation for deployment to the European Theater of Operations.

Ivan was assigned to the 366th Squadron of the 305th Bomb Group at Chelveston, England. He flew twenty-one combat missions as pilot and served as Operations Officer and Squadron Commander. After the war ended in Europe his Bomb Group was transferred to St. Troud, Belgium where the Group flew flights to photograph all of Europe, Iceland and the North Pole for a project called "Casey Jones". The Group was subsequently moved to Leichfield Air Base near Munich in connection with the Project. The Casey Jones Project expanded to include tours of duty for Ivan at Foggia, Italy; Tunis, Tunisia, and Roberts Field in Liberia.

Ivan was discharged from the Army Air Corps in June, 1946, at Camp McCoy, Wisconsin. He had been awarded, among other medals, the Air Medal with two Oak Leaf Clusters, the Commendation Medal, ETO Theater Medal with two bronze battle stars and the World War II Victory Medal.

Right - Ivan beside B-17 at Chelveston, England, bearing 305th BG motto "Can Do"

Right - Ivan on base at 305th BG

GILBERT LINDBERG, WEST BRANCH, IA, was in the construction business with his father. He enlisted in the Army Air Corps on January 6, 1940, at Chanute Field, IL. Gilbert sensed

Chapter Twenty-Two

America would be going to war and felt that by enlisting beforehand he would have a better chance of going to flight school.

After Basic Training Gilbert was assigned to a unit personnel assignment and rose to the rank of staff sergeant. He applied for flight training and sent to Nashville, TN, for classification. He qualified for pilot training and took Pre-Flight Training at Maxwell Field, AL; Primary at McBride, MO; Basic at Malden, MO; and Twin-Engine Advanced Training at Blythville, AR,  where he received his wings and commission as a Second Lieutenant. Next came B-17 Transition Training at Lockbourne Field, Columbus, OH, followed by crew assignment and training at Drew Field, FL.

Gilbert and his crew picked up a B-17 at Savannah, GA, in June, 1944, and headed for England with a flight plan through Greiner Field, NH; Gander, Newfoundland and Iceland. Near Labrador their compass "wasn't faithful" . Gilbert was watching the negative compass which indicated they were flying in a southerly direction. He called his navigator and asked how they were doing. The navigator replied "We're right on". Gilbert asked him if he had checked other compasses and their position. There was a moment of silence before the navigator answered "Oh My God". They were going the wrong direction.

Assigned to the 384th Bomb Group at Grafton Underwood, Gilbert flew fifteen combat missions. During one mission, a raid on Anklam, Germany, "my bombardier couldn't get rid of his bombs. Everyone else dropped their bombs except us. We had been climbing in altitude until we were supposed to drop our bombs then loose altitude and go like hell to get home." With the bomb load still aboard and the mission requiring eleven hours flight time, they were running low on fuel. The bombardier discovered he had forgotten to turn on the intervolumeter switch. The bombs were dropped in the countryside and they were able to make it back to base on the remaining fuel.

Aircrews in England were becoming over-strength allowing Gilbert to return home before the required thirty-five missions and before the war in Europe had ended. He was sent to Lubbock, TX for instrument training before reporting to Lockbourne AAB, Columbus, OH, to teach other combat returnees advanced four-engine instrument flying. He was released from active duty to the Air Force Reserve before V-J Day having been awarded the Air Medal.

Gilbert worked in Chicago for ten years as a contractor building houses before settling in Iowa to farm near West Branch.

WILMER LINK, DUBUQUE, IA, worked as a sheet metal worker with Lockheed Aircraft Company at the start of World War II. He eventually returned to Dubuque and enlisted in the Army Air Corps at Camp Dodge, Iowa, in September, 1943. He applied for the Aviation Cadet Program. After Basic Training at Shepard Field, Wichita Falls, TX, his entry into the Cadet Program was delayed for six weeks due to a large number of applicants ahead of him. In the meantime  Wilmer was sent to Hobbs, NM, a B-17 pilot training base where he assisted in overhauling engines. The six week delay turned into six months before he reported for Cadet Training.

In April, 1944, all Aviation Cadets were "washed out" at the convenience of the government. The excess of Cadets required personnel for other crew positions. Wilmer then attended Aerial Gunnery School at Yuma, AZ. After graduation he reported to Lincoln, NE, for crew assignment. While there he took a Flight Engineer test, passed, and was sent to Ardmore, OK for Flight Engineer School.

In October, 1944, Wilmer boarded the "Queen Elizabeth" with thirteen thousand other troops for a five day sail across the Atlantic Ocean to England. He was assigned to the 379th Bomb Group at Kimbollton.

Wilmer flew twenty-eight combat missions. His first mission on December 18, 1944, was a bombing raid on Koblenz. He flew seven missions in what remained of December. Eight missions were flown in January mostly in support of American troops during the Battle of the Bulge. In February their crew began flying as lead aircraft.

Wilmer included among his most memorable missions a January 13, 1945, raid on Mannheim,Germany. on January 13, 1945. In route their aircraft flew in "prop wash". "We were bouncing all over the place. On the bomb run we didn't drop our bombs and we had to make a second bomb run." This exposed them to more accurate flak from German anti-aircraft batteries.

On February 16, 1945, during a raid in the Ruhr Valley "we got hit over the target. Flak knocked out rudder control cables preventing the pilot from turning on the bomb run. While the rest of the formation turned toward England, we flew deeper into enemy territory. We had a "green" co-pilot who didn't realize for a long time his controls worked . We hitched onto another bomb Group and flew towards home. Flak had also cut hydraulic lines and we lost the fluid. To prevent landing with no brakes we urinated in the hydraulic tank behind the co-pilot's seat and wrapped the leak in the line with rags. It worked and we didn't lose hydraulic pressure until we landed and stopped."

After the war ended in Europe it was customary to take ground crews on sightseeing flights over Germany and other targeted countries to view the damage their Group had inflicted on the enemy. Instead of going on one flight, Wilmer went to visit a friend. His aircraft was involved in a mid-air collision that killed all aboard.

Wilmer, along with a B-17 bomber, was transferred to the 55th Fighter Group. Selected for duty as part of the occupational air forces at Kaufbeuren, Germany, Wilmer became a crew chief on a C-47 aircraft and transferred to the Ninth Air Force.

He eventually boarded the ship "George Washington" in December, 1945, for return to the United States. While at sea their ship ran into a severe storm. They were hit sideways nearly capsizing. An SOS was sent but ship's personnel finally gained control of the vessel for the balance of the trip.

Wilmer arrived in Chicago, IL, on Christmas Day, 1945, and received his discharge on the 28th at Rockford, IL. He had been awarded the Air Medal with four oak leaf clusters, the European Theater of Operations Medal with one battle star and the World War II Victory Medal.

Wilmer worked for John Deere Company in Dubuque for thirty-seven years before retirement. His duties included travel throughout the United States and the World teaching service schools and trouble-shooting. The latter part of his career was in design and procurement.

Right - Wilmer and crew at 379th BG, Kimbolton, England. Wilmer is front row, left.

HOWARD LINN, HUBBARD, IA, had worked on a farm as a hired hand and with a local Rural Electric Association installing power poles and lines when he was drafted into military service February 11, 1943. Assigned to the Army Air Corps he was shipped to St Petersburg, FL for Basic Training. Three weeks later he reported to Ft Myers, FL for six weeks Aerial Gunnery School.

In May, 1943, Howard attended Aircraft Mechanics School at Sheppard Field, Wichita Falls, TX on two engine bombers, the B-25 and B-26. This required complete knowledge of hydraulic, electrical, control, oxygen, propeller and intercom systems. Upon completion of training Howard was sent to Salt Lake City, UT where he was assigned to an air crew and then shipped to Biggs Field, El Paso, TX where he joined his crew for training prior to deployment overseas. Howard trained as Flight Engineer, upper turret and left waist gunner.

In April, 1944, Howard and his crew picked up a new B-24 Liberator bomber at Herrington, Kansas and flew to Nuts Corner, Ireland, via a southern route. They flew from Florida to Trinidad, British Guinea, Brazil, and Africa, a ten day trip touching four continents. Their final destination was North Pickenham, England, home of the newly organized 492nd Bomb Group.

Howard flew his first mission on May 14, 1944, a raid on Murseburg, Germany. His second mission on May 19 changed his life dramatically. Scheduled to bomb a target at Brunswick, Germany, they were escorted part way to the target by P-51 Mustang fighters. When they reached the limit of their fuel range, the P-51s turned back to England. P-38 fighters scheduled to continue the escort, failed to show and Howard's formation was attacked head on by German fighter aircraft.

The lead bomber in their formation was hit and went down with no parachutes exiting the aircraft. Another head on pass by the Luftwaffe hit Howard's plane causing the number three engine to burst into flames. Smoke began coming out of the leading edge of their left wing. It burst into flames sending smoke and a fiery inferno within the aircraft. Howard snapped on his parachute and bailed out of the B-24 along with three other crew members before the aircraft exploded killing the remaining six crew men. One of those that bailed out with Howard fell 21,000 feet without his parachute opening.

Howard fell until he could see trees rushing towards him then pulled his rip cord. He landed in a forest clearing, unhooked his parachute and ran into the woods. He hid under a brush pile and later heard voices of what he believed to be a search party looking for him. Howard spent the night in the forest unsure of where he was but certain he was in Northern Germany. At that point his escape map was useless until he could determine where he was.

At dawn he started walking west through the forest wearing the inner liner of his flying suit and his flying boots. His shoes, strapped to his parachute, had been forgotten in his haste to escape capture after landing in the forest clearing. Howard came to a village and decided to walk through it. A fifteen-year old boy standing in a doorway spotted Howard and waved down a motorcycle policeman who captured him.

Howard was taken to a building in the village and place in a barbed wire enclosure. Later in the day he was taken by a Luftwaffe officer to a forced labor camp where two other American airmen were being held. They were all transported to an interrogation center at Frankfurt, GE, where attempts to interrogate them resulted in only name, rank and serial number. The interrogators already knew the background of Howard's military training and some personal family data.

With other prisoners of war, Howard was loaded in a railroad car and given only a loaf of heavy, sour, dark bread for his trip to Stalag Luft IV prison camp about a hundred miles Northeast of Berlin. The prison camp was comprised of four compounds. Each compound was surrounded with a barbed wire fence with guard towers every 200 feet. Tower guards were armed with machine guns. Guards also walked between the towers. At night guard dogs were turned loose to roam the prison compound after the prisoners were locked in their barracks.

Each prisoner was issued a mattress and pillow filled with wood shavings infested with fleas. Food was poor and sparse, barely sufficient to keep a person alive. An eleven pound Red Cross parcel containing canned food items was supposed to be given each prisoner every week. Instead a parcel had to be shared with seven other prisoners. When German guards were seen smoking American cigarettes it became obvious where their Red Cross parcels were going. They did receive sports equipment, playing cards and additional blankets from the Red Cross.

With nothing to do all day and locked in their barracks at night, idle time had to be occupied to prevent depression, boredom or going "stir crazy". Howard witnessed two prisoners shot while attempting obvious escapes in the open and in broad daylight, victims of depression.

In July, 1944, the Russian Army began closing in on Germany. Prisoners of War from Stalag VI were taken to Stalag IV. Included in the prisoners was a shirt-tail relative of Howard's whom he spotted walking across his compound.

On Christmas day, 1944, the German Prison Commandant turned on the camp's floodlights and allowed the prisoners out of their barracks until midnight. They were given extra food supplemented by Red Cross parcels. Christmas carols were sung by the men. "It was like lighting a candle in an otherwise dark world."

In February, 1945, the Russian Army was closing in on Stalag IV. The prisoners were told they had to evacuate the camp, would be walking for two or three days and to take with them what they needed and could carry. The POWs gathered the most needed items they had to withstand the winter and were marched for 52 days in snow, ice and cold. They slept on open ground and in barns on straw laid on top of manure. Food was scrounged from the countryside. Dysentery and illness reduced the number of prisoners from two thousand to fifteen hundred. A buddy system for sleeping was developed. Pairs of POWs shared blankets, overcoats and body heat to survive.

The POWs arrived at Hanover, Germany, at the end of March, 1945, and had barely begun to get settled at their new camp when it was decided to move them again. Allied armies were closing the ring around Germany. They were marched another thirty-five days finally stopping in a woods. Their guards suddenly disappeared and on May 2, 1945, four English soldiers in a jeep drove into their encampment. They were free at last! Told to walk toward American lines the POWs reached them the next day. Then came the long awaited showers, delousing, clean clothes, shaves, haircuts and food.

Howard boarded a Liberty ship at Le Havre, France and sailed for the United States. After an extended furlough at home he received his discharge from military service on October 26, 1945.

Howard was able to return to Germany and visit his crash site near Niedernstoecken. He visited Rodewald, Germany, the village where he was captured and met the fifteen year old boy, now seventy, who had turned him in to a policeman on May 19, 1944, after he had parachuted from his flaming aircraft. The fifteen-year old German had also became a prisoner of war – of the Americans.

Highlights of this biography were taken from an account "World War II and my Prisoner of War Experiences" written by Howard 49 years after the war ended.

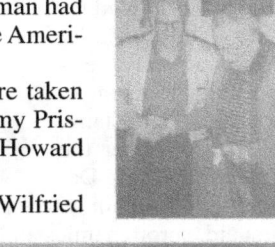

Right - Howard on the left, meets Wilfried Beermann, who as a fifteen year old turned Howard in to German authorities after Howard had been shot down and was trying to evade capture.

Right - Howard and his crew, 492nd BG, North Pickenham, England. Howard is front row, center.

RAYMOND LISCHER, CRESTON, IA, attended Iowa State College from 1939 to 1941. He then worked as a Fireman on the CB&Q Railroad until October l, 1942, when he entered military service. Ray attended Pre-Flight Training at Santa Ana, CA; Primary on the PT-22 at King City, CA; Basic BT-13 at Chico, CA and Cessna AT-6 at Stockton, CA.

On March 6, 1944, Ray left Kearney, NE on a flight to Ireland and then on to Thorpe Abbotts, England, where he was assigned as a pilot with the 100th Bomb Group. Ray flew thirty-five combat missions. Six of those missions were to bomb Berlin, the heart of Nazi Germany. Of his eleven crew members, nine are still alive 55 years after the end of World War II.

Ray received the Distinguished Flying Cross and Air Medal with four oak leaf clusters. He received his discharge from the military on July 25, 1945, at Jefferson Barracks, St Louis, MO.

After the war Ray returned to the CB&Q Railroad as an Engineer and farmed for twenty-five years.

Right - Ray's crew at 100th Bomb Group, Thorpe Abbotts, England. Ray, Pilot, is front row, right

Chapter Twenty-Two

RUSSELL LOGUE, NORWALK, IA, had attended Morningside College at Sioux City and Drake University in Des Moines before he entered the Army Air Corps in 1942. He was accepted into the Aviation Cadet Program and completed Basic Training at Santa Ana, California, before being shipped to Roswell, New Mexico for Bombardier School. On his final test ride Russell was 'washed out' of the program. He found out later he had passed the training but due to an over abundance of bombardiers in training, he and others in alphabetical splits, were arbitrarily eliminated.

Russell was re-assigned to Radio School at Scott Field, Illinois and Aerial Gunnery School at Yuma, Arizona, before assignment to an aircrew at Tonopah, Nevada, for overseas training. Poor aircraft maintenance was believed responsible for an air crash during training missions. Russell's crew refused to fly an aircraft leaking oil from two engines. They were held in a briefing room for five hours until another crew agreed to fly the plane. On takeoff the plane crashed killing all aboard. "This caused a hell of a shake up and maintenance got much better after that."

During overseas training, Russell's ability to site targets was noticed by a Training Officer. He was asked to attend "Mickey School", radar bombing training, which would also earn him a commission as a Second Lieutenant. To do so would cause him to lose a dependent allotment he had deducted from his pay to support his father and dependent siblings at home, so he turned down the promotion opportunity.

Russell was deployed to England in December, 1944, as a radio operator with the 392nd Bomb Group at Wendling. He flew nineteen combat missions. His first mission was flown with a pilot who was making his final mission before rotation back to the United States. They returned to Wendling in a snowstorm with only two working engines. The other two had been shot out by flak during their mission. Unable to see their runway, Russell took a radio direction finding and relayed the information to the pilot. He continued to give the pilot headings so directional corrections could be made. Their first pass "we flew right down the runway but we were too far down it before the pilot saw it, so we flew past and went around again. On our second try we landed on the snow covered runway. Unable to stop because of the snow we slid off the end of the runway and stopped in a ditch. No one was hurt."

"Coming back from our third mission, our base at Wendling was fogged in and we were running low on fuel. I remember our pilot telling us on the intercom that he couldn't find a hole in the fog anywhere. He asked if we should bail out and one of the crew answered "I think we should climb up a little bit first because we just flew under a cow's belly". We climbed to about 5000 feet, leveled out the fuel, put on the auto-pilot and bailed out. Our engineer balked at the door and I pushed him out. As he left the plane his helmet flew off and I thought he had been decapitated. As we floated down our bombardier was singing "There will be a hot time in the town of Berlin". When I landed I broke my back and right foot. We never did find out where our plane crashed but we had it headed back out to the English Channel."

After recuperating from his injuries, Russell returned to combat. During one mission a bomb "hung up" on its shackles in the bomb bay area. Russell, without parachute at 20,000 feet and the bomb bay doors open, walked out on the narrow catwalk to manually release the bomb.

Russell recalled amusing incidents of life on his airbase. A keg of beer covered with a blanket was kept in their barracks. Rations of coke to fuel the only stove in their hut were meager and called for "midnight requisitioning" of the base supply. The coke would be hidden under their bunks. One gunner, an American Indian, loved to drink and spent a lot of time in the "brig" because of his obsession with alcohol. "He would go out and come in loaded and shake the guy in the bunk below him awake. One night the lower bunkmate wasn't asleep when he was roused and shot his .45 pistol right up through the top bunk. This scared the hell out of "Chief", as he was called, and that was the last time he ever shook anyone awake. The MP's came to check out the shooting and smelled everyone's .45 to see who had fired the shot. They never found out because most of us had two pistols, one to use and one to smell.

After his nineteenth mission Russell returned to the United States and received his discharge from military service in October, 1945, at Sioux Falls, South Dakota. He returned to school at Drake University and later spent forty years as a manager for a propane and agribusiness company. Russell and his wife operated a show horse farm for twelve years before retirement. He made a sentimental return to his old base at Wendling and a local pub in the year 2000.

ROGER BRUCE LORD, IOWA FALLS, IA, was twenty-three years old, married, had a son, had graduated from college and taught school for one year when he enlisted into military service. Bruce was not called to active duty until February, 1943. He was promptly sent to the Classification Center at San Antonio and eventually entered the Aviation Cadet Program. After washing out in the Pilot Training portion he chose to become a bombardier and was sent to Albuquerque, NM for training. Gunnery school was also taken at Kingman, AZ.

Crew assignment and training took place at Midland, TX and Avon Park, FL. In January, 1944 he was deployed to the 486th Bomb Group at Sudbury, England. The D-Day invasion of Normandy took place while Bruce was in route through Labrador, Greenland and Iceland.

Bruce flew thirty-six combat missions from June, 1944 to January, 1945. He considered a raid on synthetic oil plants at Mersberg, Germany his most memorable. When he returned to base after the mission, 242 holes were counted in his aircraft. The crew chief had only counted halfway around the airplane. A piece of flak found on the floor of his airplane had a seven-digit serial number on it. The last four numbers matched the last four numbers of Bruce's military service number.

During missions and especially on the bomb run, Bruce saw many B-17s explode when hit by anti-aircraft fire. Sometimes parachutes were seen exiting the stricken aircraft and at other times none were seen to bail out.

While on the bomb run during one mission the number three engine on his airplane was hit. Unable to maintain speed with the formation they dropped out of the attack and headed for home alone. Unprotected from enemy fighter attack they were able to limp back to Sudbury, and made it home one hour before their Group returned.

One of Bruce's pilots flying in another aircraft, was killed on his last mission before rotation back to the United States.

Bruce was discharged from military service in June, 1945. He had been awarded, among other medals, the Air Medal with six oak leaf clusters, ETO Ribbon and World War II Victory Medal. He returned to college, obtained his masters degree and resumed teaching. He entered education administration as a school principal and eventually superintendent of schools until he retired in 1970.

LLOYD LUND, EMMETSBURG, IA, helped on the family farm until he enlisted in the Army Air Corps in November, 1942. He was sent to Jefferson Barracks, St. Louis, Missouri, for Basic Training and while there got double pneumonia. He applied for the Aviation Cadet Program, passed testing, and was sent to college at Eau Claire, Wisconsin under the College Training De-

tachment Program where he completed courses in meteorology, first aid, aerodynamics and mathematics.

Lloyd was sent to Santa Ana, California for Pre-Flight Training; Phoenix, Arizona, for Primary Flight Training and LeMoore, California for Basic Flight Training. He was commissioned a Second Lieutenant and awarded his wings after completing Advanced Flight Training at Ft. Sumner, New Mexico.

B-17 Transition Training was completed at Tampa, Florida before he was assigned an aircrew and completed overseas training with them at Gulfport, Mississippi and Roswell, New Mexico. In November, 1944 Lloyd and his crew were assigned a new B-17 bomber and flew to the European Theater of Operations from Bangor, Maine. "We were the third plane that took off. The fifth plane caught its wing on deep snow lining the runway, crashed and killed all aboard."

After landing in Iceland despite German attempts to jam their radio, Lloyd and his crew flew on to Shannon, Ireland, where their aircraft was taken from them for installation of additional armor and other items to make the aircraft combat ready. Lloyd was sent to the Combat Crew Replacement Center at Stone, England, and assigned to the 305th BG at Chelveston.

Lloyd flew twenty-two combat missions, of which the majority were flown as lead aircraft for the bomb group. During one mission "flak" knocked out one of our engines and it caught fire". "We went into a dive to try and put out the fire. Fire can cause the wings to melt. The fire went out but then we lost a second and then a third engine and we were forced to land at an airstrip near Brussells, Belgium, that had just been taken by Allied ground forces. The Germans had flak guns mounted on railroad flat cars and would go all over the country where ever our formations were flying."

"The first German jet fighter we saw collided with our Deputy lead plane and both planes just disintegrated."

No member of Lloyd's crew was lost to combat. His Flight Engineer was killed when a bomber on takeoff lost control from "prop wash" and crashed into a barracks where the Flight Engineer stayed.

After V-E Day, Lloyd flew missions for the "Casey Jones" project, an operation that photographed Europe from the air. He returned to the United States and was discharged from military service at Santa Ana, California, in the Fall of 1945, just in time to return to Iowa and combine the family soy bean crop. Lloyd was awarded the Distinguished Flying Cross for superior leadership and exceptional flying ability in adverse weather conditions and during enemy fighter attacks. He also received the Air Medal with two oak leaf clusters, ETO and World War II Victory Medals. In civilian life Lloyd farmed in the Cylinder, Iowa, area until retirement.

Right - Lloyd and his crew at 305th BG, Chelveston. England. Lloyd, Pilot, is back row, left.

DONALD J LYNAM, GREENFIELD, IA, was an Iowa State College Engineering student prior to America's entry into World War II. He enlisted into military service September 14, 1942 at San Antonio, Texas. He completed Aircraft Mechanics School at Amarillo, Texas, Aerial Gunnery School at Kingman, Arizona, Gunnery Instruction at Ft. Myers, Florida and Laredo, Texas.

Donald was deployed to Debach, England, November 21, 1944. He was assigned as a gunnery instructor and waist gunner with the 493rd Bomb Group, the last bomb group of the Eighth Air Force to become operational in World War II.

Donald's most memorable mission was participation in food missions to the Netherlands. Still held by the Germans, the Netherlands had been flooded to prevent the Allies from taking the territory. The Dutch people were reduced to near starvation under Nazi rule. Despite war, the Germans allowed American airplanes to drop food to the Dutch with the provision they would not be fired upon if they flew a certain route. "It was heartwarming to see the starving people waving and smiling at the American formations when food was dropped to them."

Donald was discharged from the military on November 19, 1945, at Sioux City, Iowa. His primary occupation in Post-World War II was as a construction engineer.

FRANCIS P. LYNAM, ATLANTIC, IA, was attending Northwest Missouri State College when he was drafted into the US Army the latter part of 1942. He was sent to Jefferson Barracks, St Louis, Missouri for Basic Training and then attended Grinnell College in Iowa under the College Training Detachment Program. Francis was transferred to the Army Air Corps and sent to Lincoln, Nebraska for Air Corps Basic Training before being assigned to Aerial Gunnery School at Las Vegas, Nevada.

Francis reported to Tampa, Florida where he was assigned to an aircrew and completed combat training with them at Tampa for eventual deployment overseas. In July, 1944 he boarded a British ship with eighteen thousand other American troops and sailed to Scotland. From there he rode by train to his assigned base with the 447th Bomb Group at Rattlesden, England. Francis would fly thirty combat missions as ball turret gunner. His first mission, was on August 26, 1944. He completed his required number of missions by November of that year.

At the turn to the bomb run on Berlin, Germany, " enemy fighters flew right over us and attacked the Group behind us. Several bombers were shot down. This Group then came up and flew the bomb run under us."

On his eighth mission Earl's squadron was to dump propaganda leaflets over the city of Mainz, Germany. "We came over the target last and the lowest. We got hit by flak and lost two engines but we made it back to our base. After we landed we counted over two hundred holes in our plane "Little Herbie". No one was wounded or injured in his thirty missions.

Francis returned to the United States aboard the ocean liner "New Amsterdam". He reported to Kingman, Arizona where he participated in dismantling air bases before reporting to Sioux City, Iowa, in November, 1945, for discharge from the military. Francis had been awarded the Air Medal, ETO Ribbon and World War II Victory Medals, among others.

Francis returned to Northwest Missouri State College where he earned his bachelor's degree. After farming for sixteen years he owned a wholesale and retail lumber yard in Atlantic from which he has since retired.

Right - Francis's crew at 447th BG, Rattlesden, England. Francis, Ball Turret Gunner, is front row, right.

RICHARD (DICK) LYNCH, CONRAD, IA, graduated from high school when he was sixteen and farmed with his father until he enlisted in the Army Air Corps. Dick was sent to Biloxi, Mississippi, for Basic Training. He was ready to enter the Aviation Cadet Program when volunteers were needed for aerial gunners. Dick volunteered and was sent to Harlingen, TX, for training.

After gunnery school Dick was assigned to an aircrew. They were sent to Riverside, CA for training to mold themselves into an effective combat team. It was at Riverside Dick and his crew almost became a fatal training statistic. On a training mission during foggy weather they advised the control tower they were desperately low on fuel. Ordered to fly on to Blythe, CA they told the tower they did not have enough fuel to fly there. At that point one engine quit running. A second engine ran out of fuel as they approached the Riverside runway. They cleared a fence at the end of the runway by inches and landed just as the final two engines ran out of fuel. A tow truck had to pull the aircraft off the runway.

Dick and his crew were then sent to Hamilton Field, CA near San Francisco. They were issued winter clothing which indicated they were not headed for the Pacific Theater of Operations. They boarded a troop train for Camp Kilmer, NJ, and then the "Queen Mary" for a seven-day cruise to Scotland. In the lower hold of the ship, bunks were stacked five high, but seasickness did not seem to be a problem with the troops. From Scotland Dick's crew was trucked to their base at Shipdam, home of the 44th Bomb Group.

Dick flew thirty-three combat missions. One of his most memorable was a low-level mission on March 24, 1945, to Wesels re-supplying paratroopers and glider forces. Flying at 300 feet they dropped their supplies. The airplanes flying on both sides of Dick's bomber were hit by ground fire and crashed. "We crossed the dropping zone into the glider area then bullets began flying. A crew on our wing went down and blew sky high, then another, it was terrible. I wasn't scared until after we got back across the Rhine then I really was nervous. We had twenty-two holes in our plane."

May 8, 1945, was V-E Day, Victory in Europe. "No one at our base was excited. Just another day. I wondered how the people at home were taking it"

"May ll, 1945, we flew our ground crew on a tour of Northern Germany towns and Holland."

Dick returned to the United States and was discharged from the military on June l, 1945. He had been awarded the Air Medal with four oak leaf clusters, ETO Medal with a battle star and World War II Victory Medal. He resumed farming in the Conrad area and played semi-pro baseball and AAU basketball. Dick served on the Board of the Farmers Coop for thirteen years, the local school board for twelve years, and board of directors at his bank for nearly thirty years.

In 1996 Dick returned to France on a tour with the 44th Bomb Group. The tour included the dedication of a memorial to the 44th in the center of a French town. A lady on the tour was two years old when her pilot father was killed when shot down near that town. No remains were recovered at the crash site. The aircraft exploded and burned on contact with the ground. After the dedication a man told of a memorial in the woods outside of town where an American plane had crashed during the war. The tour walked a half-mile to the woods and found the crash site. It had been fenced in and a memorial stone erected, dedicated to the crew. A man came forward and presented the lady on the tour with her father's dog tags he had recovered at the crash site fifty-two years earlier.

Right - Dick and his crew at 44th BG, Shipdham, England. Dick is front row, right.

JAMES MAIRS, MARSHALLTOWN, IA, had attended college for one year before America's entry into World War II and was working at Boeing Aircraft, Wichita, KS, when he was drafted into military service. After classification he entered the Cadet Program at San Antonio, TX where he was to become a navigator, pilot or bombardier. He completed aerial gunnery training at Harlingen, TX; Pre-flight, flight and Advanced flight training in Navigation School at Ellington Field, TX.

After being assigned to an aircrew and training together to mold themselves into an effective combat team, they picked up a new B-17 at Lincoln, NE, and proceeded to England. Their route took them across the North Atlantic through Labrador, Greenland, and Iceland to Wales. Their plane was taken from them and they boarded a train for the final leg of their trip to the 398th Bomb Group at Nuthampstead. A new B-17 was assigned to them on arrival that was promptly named "Norma Kay".

Jim flew the first of thirty-five missions in September, 1944. Only four or five missions were completed that his aircraft hadn't sustained major damage. Although he didn't navigate for the entire Wing on missions, he was still required to maintain navigation and logs of their location in case they got hit and had to fall out of formation. Jim would then be able to advise the pilot where they were and how to get back to base. Wind at various altitudes caused problems gauging where they were and what speed to maintain. "Pilots not listening to their navigator also caused problems." Their Group once bombed Pilsen, Czechoslovakia, when they weren't supposed to "because the pilot didn't listen to the lead navigator."

During one mission Jim was bending over his navigational charts spread on his desk behind the bombardier. For some reason he stood up and did something, then turned back to his charts. There was a hole in the charts from a piece of flak where his head would have been had he remained in his seat. "I never worried beforehand about not making it back from a mission. I was too busy. I didn't have much free time. If I wasn't flying missions, I was in the classroom or doing personal things."

Jim finished his tour with all of his crew. "I was lucky I didn't fly in 1942-43 when there was no fighter escort. As it was, if you finished your tour you were lucky." On one mission the engine next to Jim's position in the aircraft was struck by a German .88 shell that didn't detonate. The shell lodged in the engine and caused loss of airspeed. They fell behind the formation and were subject to enemy fighter attack as a straggler. "We turned for home but soon realized we weren't going to make it on the fuel we had." Jim found the nearest Eighth Air Force Base in England and made arrangements for landing there if they could make it. When they landed, and as the plane was rolling down the runway, it ran out of gas.

When flying at high altitudes the temperature inside their aircraft was 35-50 degrees below zero. The thin air required the crew wear oxygen masks anytime above 10,000 feet. An oxygen check with each crewmember every ten minutes was required. Each crewmember was required to respond whether or not they were alright. On one mission the tail gunner did not respond to an oxygen check. A waist gunner took an oxygen bottle and went to check on him. When the waist gunner did not come back or respond to his own oxygen check the other waist gunner went to see what was wrong. He found both men passed out. Condensation had caused the tail gunner's mask to freeze and cut off his oxygen supply. The waist gunner's bottle had run out of oxygen. Both were revived.

Jim's crew flew seven or eight missions to Cologne. After making the bomb run on one of the missions and they turned for "home". Jim's pilot, who had learned the day before his wife had given birth to a baby, did not straighten the plane out but kept making a 360 degree turn over Cologne muttering over the radio "Baby, go see my wife and baby". The Co-Pilot had to shake the pilot off the controls and take command of the aircraft. The crew was given "flak" leave after they returned to base.

Three missions were flown in support of American troops surrounded in the Battle of the Bulge. "These were the only short missions we had" bombing German troops on December 28, 29, and 31 of 1944.

Jim returned to the United States in February, 1945 aboard the "Queen Mary". He was discharged from military service in October of that year at Sheppard Field, Texas, and had been awarded, among other medals, the Air Medal with six oak leaf clusters, ETO Ribbon and World War II Victory Medal.

Jim returned to college, received his Bachelor's degree and began a career teaching and coaching athletics.

Right - Jim and his crew at 398th BG, Nuthampstead, England. Jim, Navigator, is back row, right.

ROBERT MANAHL, EVANSDALE, IA,

worked at Chamberlain Manufacturing, Cedar Rapids, Iowa, where he made wringers for washing machines. After the Japanese attack on Pearl Harbor, Robert was "laid off" from his job in May, 1942, and he enlisted in the Army Air Corps.

Only nine days into Basic Training, there was an urgent need for Aircraft Mechanics. Robert volunteered, was accepted and sent to Chanute Field, Illinois to attend Mechanics School where two shifts a day were taking courses. Following graduation Robert was sent to Eglin Field, Florida, to take part in experimental development of a glide bomb.

To avoid a high rate of aircraft losses a one ton glide bomb was conceived that would be released from an aircraft while still distant from the target. The bomb was encased in a balsa wood frame with sixteen foot wings, a gyro and a twelve volt battery to maintain flight. Testing of the glide bomb took place at Tonapah, Nevada. From there Robert returned to Eglin Field, and was then deployed overseas. On April 6, 1943, Robert left Halifax, Nova Scotia, aboard the ship "Louis Pasteur" with fifteen hundred other Americans and 4,500 Australians and Canadians for a zig-zag voyage to Liverpool, England.

Robert was assigned to the 544th Squadron of the 384th Bomb Group at Grafton Underwood. The glide bomb project was abandoned and Robert worked as an aircraft mechanic until the end of the war in Europe. He was able to make pleasure flights over Germany to view the devastation caused by Eighth Air Force bombing. He was then flown to France to remove guns, armor plating and other equipment from B-17s and install seats. The aircraft were flown to Africa and used to haul troops to the Pacific Theater of Operations.

In September, 1945, Robert boarded the "Queen Elizabeth" at Southampton for return to the United States. He left behind a bicycle he had made from scrapped airplane parts for transportation from his barracks to airplane hard stands.

Robert was discharged at Fort Snelling, Minnesota, on September 28, 1945. He had been awarded the ETO ribbon with one battle star, World War II Victory Medal and a Distinguished Unit Ribbon. Robert retired from the U S Postal Service after twenty-eight years as a letter carrier.

Top Right - Ground crew at 544 Bomb Squadron of 384th Bomb Group, Grafton Underwood, England. Robert, crew chief, is under engine number one next to man on end in dark coveralls.

DONALD MARNER, IOWA CITY, IA,

joined the Army Air Corps in November, 1942 at Camp Dodge, IA. After Basic Training at Lake Charles, LA, he was sent to Victoria, TX; Mobile, AL; and New Orleans before attending Mechanics School at Kelly Field, San Antonio, TX. He applied for Cadet Pilot Training and Aerial Gunnery School but was denied acceptance because of an over-abundance of applicants.

Assigned to an air crew Donald was sent to Salt Lake City, Utah for crew training before deployment overseas aboard the British Ocean Liner "Mauritania". After arrival at Liverpool, England, Donald was sent to Sheffield for further combat training before he boarded a train to London. While in London he saw the effects of German bombing attacks on the city and experienced his first air raid when a V-1 rocket, called a "Doodlebug", exploded nearby showering him with glass, plaster and debris. He was now more than ready to leave London for his base at Lieston with the 357th Fighter Group.

Donald's base was three miles from the North Sea and only sixty miles from Nazi occupied Holland. In July and August, 1944, "V-1 rockets were flying constantly from launching sites in Holland toward London. Anti-aircraft guns were moved to the base in hope of shooting them down before they reached their target. Several of the guns were crewed by ATS women who seemed to have a good eye for shooting them down. One evening I watched them shoot down at least twenty of the thirty-two that came over. Air raid alerts occurred day and night from buzz bombs flying overhead often at tree top level. This continued into late 1944 when vapor trails from the V-2 rocket then began to appear."

Donald's duties included delivery of 108 gallon drop tanks to hard stands on the base and installation on the P-51 Mustang fighter. Ground crews often worked all night to get the Group's aircraft ready for the next day's missions. Early in the morning they "ran up" the engines to ensure there were no coolant, fuel or oil leaks.

From his base Donald witnessed hundreds of bombers flying overhead to their targets in Germany; formations of gliders, fighters and bombers in route to Holland for Operation Market Garden, and on December 24, 1944, a formation of bombers 400 miles long in route to bomb Germany. Meanwhile fighter pilots from his Group continued to tally a high rate of aerial victories. By the end of the war in Europe the 357th had destroyed 609 _ German planes in the air and 106 _ on the ground. They had the fastest rate of aerial victories of any fighter group and the highest rate of victories in a single mission, 59. Kit Carson, also an Iowan in the Group shot down five German planes in a single mission. His individual total was 27 enemy aircraft shot down.

Donald's base was also used as an emergency field for crippled bombers and other aircraft attempting to return to their own base. He participated in rescue efforts to remove wounded from the planes. Several crashes occurred on the base and mid-air collisions overhead. Tragically one of these was a Group fighter pilot returning from his last mission before going home. In buzzing the base he was not able to pull out of a dive in time to avoid hitting a tree. The airplane exploded killing the pilot.

After V-E Day, Donald left England for Cherbourg, France. He traveled to his next duty assignment through Normandy, Paris, and Germany and saw the destruction of war. For the next eight months he was assigned as part of an occupation force at the Neubiberg Air Base which had been a permanent base for the Luftwaffe.

On April 3, 1946, Donald boarded a train for the French coast where he caught a Liberty Ship for New York. He was discharged from military service at Camp McCoy, WI, and had been awarded, among other medals, the European Theater of Operations Medal with five battle stars and Unit Citation with an oak leaf cluster.

RAY MARNER, JR, IOWA CITY, IA, attended the University of Iowa from 1940 through May of 1942. He enlisted in the Army Air Corps in August, 1942, at Camp Dodge, Iowa. Following Basic Training at Sheppard Field, Texas, Ray was sent to an Engineer and Operations School in Denver, CO.

Ray was deployed overseas in February, 1943, as a Personnel and Supply Sergeant assigned to the 506th Squadron of the 44th Bomb Group at Shipdham, England. He boarded the "S.S. Chantilly" in New York Harbor on February 27. An old French ship taken over by the British in 1940, the Chantilly was described as being in bad repair. The crew was composed mainly of Hindu natives from Calcutta, India. "The Chantilly" was the only ship carrying troops in a convoy of seventy-four other ships. It was placed near the rear of the convoy with only three other ships behind them. It took seventeen days to sail to Glasgow, Scotland. "Besides poor sleeping arrangements, seasickness, and the worst food any of us had ever eaten, the first eleven days were uneventful."

The next day "we heard an explosion and the muster bell ring". "We headed up the gangway to the deck in time to see an oil tanker sink and two other ships damaged by torpedoes. The Captain of our ship had seen the first torpedo coming at us and changed course in time for it to miss us. Around midnight we were attacked again. It was too dark to really see how much damage was being done, but we knew it was bad. Around 3A.M. we heard another explosion and either a munitions ship or a tanker with high octane gas was hit. The flames grew larger and larger lighting the entire area. At dawn we found we were alone. The three ships behind us and the three ahead of us were either sunk or changed position. We were sitting ducks. We were the slowest ship on the sea but luckily no more attacks were forthcoming."

"After we arrived at our base I was walking from our living quarters to the flight line when a staff car stopped and offered me a ride. I got in the back seat with then Colonel Leon Johnson who wanted to know all about our trip over the Atlantic and the submarine attack. He was our Group Commanding Officer and won the Congressional Medal of Honor."

In addition to requisitioning and issuing supplies for base personnel, Ray also had the unpleasant task of recovering personal effects from the living quarters of aircrew who were killed or missing in action. "We had an 1800 square foot building that was stacked to the ceiling with barracks bags."

"There were a lot of V-1 and V-2 rockets that went over our base. They seemed to be going over all night. Some were real low. During a pass to London I stayed at a Red Cross Club. The buzz bombs bumped me out of bed a few times."

Ray returned to the United States in June, 1945, and eventually discharged at Jefferson Barracks, St. Louis, MO in September. He was been awarded the World War II Victory Medal, Good Conduct Medal and the European Theater of Operations Medal with nine battle stars. His unit had also received two Presidential Unit Citations for their raids on Kiel, Germany and Ploesti, Romania.

FRED MAROLD, WATERLOO, IA, was an accounting major at the University of Wisconsin with one semester remaining before graduation when he was drafted into the Army Air Corps in June 1942. After Basic Training at Jefferson Barracks, St Louis, Missouri, Fred was assigned to Clerical School at Ft Logan, Colorado, an eight week course. He was then transferred to Pueblo, Colorado; Salt Lake City, Utah; and Wendover, Utah to perform clerical duties for aircrews training at those locations.

At the end of February, 1943, he boarded a troop ship at Camp Kilmer, New Jersey, and sailed for Glasgow, Scotland in a convoy of other ships. The first ten days of the voyage were uneventful. The night of March 10 at 630PM a tanker in the convoy was hit and sunk by torpedoes fired from German submarines. Troops aboard Fred's ship were ordered to stay on deck. Later that night another tanker was torpedoed and sunk. The convoy proceeded to Scotland without further incident.

Fred was assigned to perform clerical duties in the communications section of the 44th Bomb Group at Shipdham, England. During his tour he performed the same functions with the 482nd BG at Alconbury and the 36th Squadron at Watford on the outskirts of London. While on frequent trips to London he met and dated a British girl. It was an hour and a half ride on the British Underground from northwest London to where she lived in the extreme southeast part of the city.

Following the end of the war in Europe Fred returned to the United States on October 16, 1945, aboard the "Queen Mary". Six days later he received his discharge from the military. Although school had started Fred was able to enroll for the Fall Semester at the University of Wisconsin. He graduated in January, 1946, passed his CPA exam and married the British girl he had met in London. Fred became a partner in a CPA firm in Waterloo from which he retired in 1982.

CLEMENT MARSDEN, AMES, IA, graduated from Iowa State Teachers College at Cedar Falls, Iowa, in June of 1941. He taught school and coached athletics at Glidden, Iowa, during the 1941-42 school year. He then enlisted in the Army Air Corps and was sent to Jefferson Barracks, St Louis, Missouri, for Basic Training. Following Basic, Clem was sent to Power Turret School in Texas and applied for the Aviation Cadet Program. In September, 1943, he graduated from Navigation School at Hondo, Texas, and received his wings and commission as a Second Lieutenant.

Following crew assignment at Ephrata, Washington, Clem and his crew trained at Wendover, Utah, in final preparation for overseas deployment. In January, 1944, they left Grand Island, Nebraska, to begin their cross-Atlantic flight to England. Weather forced them to land in Ireland but they eventually reached their final destination of the 457th Bomb Group at Glatton, England.

Clem flew thirty combat missions against Nazi Germany including five missions to Berlin. His first two missions were on March 22, 1944, to Berlin and two days later to Schweinfurt, a rough beginning for any tour of duty. The last nineteen missions Clem served as lead navigator for his squadron. He was wounded in the back from a piece of "flak" and another piece was found imbedded in his parachute. Only one crew member was lost to enemy action. During one mission "flak" tore through their ball turret striking the gunner in the head.

Clem's last mission was flown on September 3, 1944. He returned to the United States shortly thereafter aboard a tanker ship and was re-assigned to Ellington Field, Houston, Texas, as a physical training instructor. Clem received his discharge from military service in September, 1945, having been awarded the Distinguished Flying Cross, Air Medal with five oak leaf clusters, Purple Heart, European Theater of Operations and World War II Victory Medals.

Following the war Clem taught school and coached athletics in Wisconsin and Ogden, Iowa. He re-entered college at Drake University, Des Moines, Iowa and obtained his Masters Degree in Education in 1951. He taught mathematics and coached basketball and track at Harlan, Iowa, where his 1954 track team was state champion. Clem later served as high school principal at Eldora, Iowa, until retirement.

Right - Clem and his crew at 457th BG, Glatton, England. Clem, Navigator, is front row, second from right.

REX MCDOWELL, WATERLOO, IA, helped on the family farm near Grinnell, Iowa, before World War II. He was drafted into military service in October, 1942, and assigned to the Army Air Corps because of high test scores in mechanical ability. After Basic Training at Wichita Falls, Texas, he stayed there to attend an Aircraft Mechanics School. An advanced Mechanics School was attended at Chanute Field, Illinois, before Rex was transferred to Walla Walla, Washington, and Redmond, Oregon, to service aircraft used by crews training for overseas deployment.

Rex then boarded a train at Seattle, Washington, for Camp Kilmer, New Jersey where he sailed on an old luxury liner for Glasgow, Scotland. He was assigned to the 44th Bomb Group at Shipdham, England, as part of a ground crew assigned to a B-24 bomber.

Rex went through several flight crews, all of which were able to finish their required number of missions for rotation back to America. He helped fuel and maintain the engines and systems of his aircraft including replacement of rubber fuel tanks. His last crew nearly didn't complete their missions. The plane landed with over 200 flak holes in it and the Radio Operator and Flight Engineer had been killed in action.

After the war ended in Europe, Rex was taken on sightseeing flights over Europe to see the devastation caused by Eighth Air Force bombing. He was able to fly back to the United States aboard a B-24 from Wales through Iceland and Greenland to Maine. In route the aircraft hit an air pocket and almost went down. The pilot was able to pull the airplane out of a dive with little air space remaining.

After discharge from military service at Sioux Falls, South Dakota in October, 1945, Rex returned to farming from which he retired.

THOMAS MCELHERNE, AMES, IA, graduated from high school in June, 1942, and completed one year at the then Iowa State College when he was drafted into the Army Air Corps in August, 1943.

Tom was sent to Amarillo, Texas, for Basic Training and Aircraft Mechanics School. He then attended Aerial Gunnery School at Las Vegas, Nevada, before crew assignment and overseas training at Sioux City, Iowa.

The crew picked up a new B-17 bomber at Lincoln, Nebraska in January, 1945 and began the long flight to Valley, Wales through Goose Bay, Labrador and Iceland. Tom was assigned to the 388th Bomb Group at Knettishall, England as Flight Engineer and Top Turret Gunner.

On March 23, 1945, on a mission to bomb targets in Dortmund, Germany, their aircraft took anti-aircraft hits in the wing, The bomb bay area was on fire and Tom and his crew bailed out of their aircraft. "I free fell for a long way. We were told that when you could see windows on buildings it was time to pull the rip cord." Tom landed in a wooded area, got out of his parachute harness and started running. Children pointed out to soldiers where Tom came down. He later learned his pilot had been killed by civilians and one of their waist gunners severely beaten. The civilian population was indoctrinated that American flyers were gangsters and should be shot. Tom was captured by a German soldier and taken to a police station. He was interrogated by an S.S. Officer who, in his frustration at not receiving information other than name, rank and serial number, stormed out of the interview telling him "You are a prisoner of war."

Tom was then taken to a roadhouse where other American POWs were being collected. They received medical attention and some bread and sausages. While waiting at a train station to be shipped to Stalag 11B near Fallingbostel, Germany, "a German soldier on furlough who had lost his mother and sister to American bombers wanted to kill us. A German soldier guarding us stood between us and the other German soldier and told him "you'll have to kill one of your own to do that"". The soldier on leave then left.

In route to the prison camp, the train the POWs were on, was strafed by American fighter planes. "We bailed out of the boxcars with the German guards. It was decided we would walk the remaining distance to a train station in Hanover where we were to catch another train for the last leg of the trip to the camp. While there we had to go to a bomb shelter. The station was bombed all night long. There was fifteen of us and about 50-60 guards under a lot of concrete."

At Stalag 11B, Tom was housed in a building with a fence around it. A lot of Russian prisoners were in his building. No one was allowed outside. Bunks were stacked three high with only slats to sleep on. There was one table and a stove. For heat, a tree stump was placed inside the fence with an axe. Prisoners had to chop apart the stump for firewood. Slats from their bunks were also used. Food consisted of a soup in which an unknown vegetable had been cooked and removed. At times they would receive three boiled potatoes and perhaps some bread. Twice during his imprisonment he received Red Cross parcels which had to be shared with three or four other servicemen. There were no toilets, just a hole in the ground.

As Allied forces began to close the ring on Germany, the prison camp was evacuated in groups of several hundred at a time. The POWs were guarded by infirm or elderly German soldiers and required to walk. At night they stayed in any nearby woods or in farm buildings. One morning, near Denmark, the POWs awoke to find the German guards gone. They were soon liberated by English soldiers. American jeeps and trucks pulling howitzers followed. The POWs walked in the direction the jeeps came from until they were told to congregate near a captured airstrip. Transport planes flew the prisoners to France where they were trucked to Camp Lucky Strike. In route they saw soldiers celebrating. Germany had surrendered. After food, rest, showers, delousing and new clothes Tom and his crew were flown back to Knettishall for a victory celebration. Tom could not attend, he had contracted yellow jaundice.

Tom returned to the United States by Victory Ship. He reported to Ft Sheridan near Chicago, Illinois, and received his discharge in November, 1945. Tom had been awarded, among other medals, the Air Medal with two oak leaf clusters, and the ETO and World War II Victory Medals.

Tom returned to college at Ames and subsequently became a Chemical Engineer with the Iowa Department of Transportation from which he retired.

Right - Tom's crew at 388th Bomb Group, Knettishall, England. Tom was Flight Engineer and Top Turret Gunner.

ROBERT W. MCELREE, OELWEIN, IA, was working at a Wilson Meat Company processing plant when the United States entered World War II. He had tried to get into the Navy on three occasions but was turned down. Drafted into the Army in October, 1942, he was sent to St Petersburg, FL for Basic Training and then to Gulfport, MS for Mechanic's School. When it became known volunteers were wanted to become Aerial Gunners, Robert was interested but learned there was a height restriction of six feet. He was six feet two inches. He applied anyway and during the physical slouched down when they measured his height.

The doctor, aware of what Robert was doing and how much he wanted to become a gunner, passed him as being six feet tall.

In March, 1943, Robert attended Aerial Gunner's School at Panama City, FL. At the end of the course, "Man I was proud. I really wanted to be a gunner." He was assigned to an aircrew at Moses Lake, Washington. He completed crew training at Lewiston, Montana. In October, 1943, Robert and his crew left Bangor, ME for Prestwick, Scotland through Labrador and Iceland. They eventually arrived at Polebrook, England and the 351st Bomb Group.

Robert flew twenty-six combat missions as Flight Engineer and Gunner. His first mission was November 26, 1943, a raid on the seaport of Bremen, Germany. One B-24 in their group was hit by flak. "I saw one wing break off of the plane, go up and over the aircraft before it went down. I knew then there was a war on."

On December 31, 1943, Robert flew an eleven hour mission to bomb an aircraft plant at Bordeaux. Because of the distance they had no fighter escort. "The target area was clouded over so we went to another target even further away. There was a lot of flak and fighters. One plane behind us got hit and was all on fire. We lost eight or nine planes that day. No one made it back to base." Aircraft were running out of fuel and the crews bailing out. "We had to land at an English base. The airplane ahead of us ran out of gas when it hit the runway. We were coming in behind it and had to swerve to miss hitting it. We counted over 200 holes in our plane and stopped counting. No one was hurt in our crew."

"We had a lot of close calls. Twice we were at the door ready to bail out but each time the pilot got the plane under control. We just kept going on missions and coming back."

Memories of other missions include that of March 4, 1944 when Robert's crew was leading the Group. "We were flying at 27,000 feet. It was sixty-eight degrees below zero. We had to bomb a secondary target because our main target was clouded over." On March 6, 1944, the first raid on Berlin, "we lost sixty nine heavy bombers. What a mess. I saw pieces of planes flying past us. We went back two days later and had little or no opposition." On another mission when one bomb "hung up" in the bomb bay area, Robert and another gunner, neither of which were wearing parachutes, had to release the armed bomb. Robert held onto the other gunner while he reached out over the open bomb bay to release the bomb.

Even on an overnight pass to London Robert couldn't escape the war. While he stayed in a hotel near Hyde Park a German air raid took place. Nearby anti-aircraft batteries "were really loud because they were so close to us. We could hear flak landing on the roof of the hotel. The next day was alright and we wandered around and saw some sites."

In April, 1944 Robert returned to the United States aboard the "USS George Washington", an eleven day voyage. He had volunteered for a second tour of duty in England and in June, 1944, returned aboard the "Queen Mary".

Robert was attending B-29 Flight Engineer Training School when the war ended. At the time of his discharge he had been awarded the Air Medal with four oak leaf clusters, a Presidential Unit Citation, the ETO Medal with three battle stars and World War II Victory Medal. Robert had shot down three ME-109 German Fighters as aerial gunner.

After the war Robert returned to Wilson Packing Company until it closed in 1959 and then became a driver/salesman for an area beer distributor until he retired.

Chapter Twenty-Two

Right - Roberet and crew at 351st BG, Polebrook. Robert is front row, second from left.

ROBERT MEGCHELSEN, WASHINGTON, IA, graduated from high school in 1941. He helped on the family farm until drafted into military service on January 18, 1943 at Camp Dodge, IA. Assigned to the Army Air Corps John was sent to St. Petersburg, FL where he and other inductees were billeted in a hotel. They drilled on the hotel grounds before being sent to Clearwater, FL for Basic Training.

John attended Armorer School at Lowry and Buckley Fields, CO and Aerial Gunnery School at Kingman, AZ. Following graduation he was sent to Euphrata, WA where he was assigned to an aircrew. The crew trained at Kearney, NE, to prepare themselves for deployment overseas and combat.

Following a furlough John and his crew left Kearney on Thanksgiving Day, 1943, for England. The trip would take them to Syracuse, NY, and Presque Isle, Maine, in route to Newfoundland where they stayed for two weeks because of snow and bad weather. Other aircraft being ferried to England were also forced to land at Newfoundland due to the weather and airplanes began to backup on the base. They finally were able to take off for the final leg of their trip on December 17, 1943, through Nutts Corner, Ireland to Stone, England.

John and his crew were replacements for heavy losses sustained by the Eighth Air Force during October, 1943. There were assigned to the 91st Bomb Group at Bassingbourn.

John flew thirty combat missions as tail gunner. Assigned a B-17 bomber named "Black Magic" the crew changed the name to "Lassie Come Home" depicting a pin up girl rather than the Lassie of filmdom.

On a March 8, 1944, mission to Berlin one engine on his aircraft caught on fire after taking a flak hit from anti-aircraft fire. The pilot put the airplane into a dive and was successful in putting out the fire.

The following day, March 9, it was back to Berlin. Again flak took its toll on John's airplane. The horizontal stabilizers were shot up, one front tire was rendered flat, the tail wheel was shot off and the windshield was cracked. Numerous hits in the wings and fuselage were also taken. When they landed back at Bassingbourn on only one tire, they came to a stop only after they ran off the runway. Fortunately no one was hurt.

Most of John's original crew members had completed their thirty missions when he flew on his final mission required for rotation back to the United States. John was flying as a replacement with a different flight crew. It was on the eve of D-Day when they took off. John's pilot couldn't find their Bomb Group in "forming up" over England. He "hooked onto" another Group and assisted them in bombing their target. On their return to Bassingbourn the pilot dropped down under their bomb group and called John from his tail gunner position to the nose of the aircraft. They buzzed the control tower in John's honor, symbolic of finishing a tour of duty.

Following D-Day John remained at the 91st BG where he assisted ground crews until he was rotated back to America. John was awarded the Distinguished Flying Cross, Air Medal with three oak leaf clusters, European Theater of Operations Medal with two battle stars and Presidential Unit Citation. John was employed as a rural mail carrier in Washington, Iowa, and has since retired.

Right - John and his crew at 91st BG, Bassingbourn, England. John, Tail Gunner, is front row, fourth from left.

Right - John, on right, and another crew member survey damage to aircraft stuck in mud after it landed with no brakes and ran off the runway at 91st BG, Bassingbourn, England.

WILLIAM 'BILL' MEHEGAN, CEDAR RAPIDS, IA, was working for Quaker Oats Company before World War II. He enlisted in the Army Air Corps in June, 1942, at Kelly Field, Texas, and entered the Aviation Cadet Program.

After "washing out" of the Pilot Training portion of the Cadet Program, Bill attended Bombardier's School at Midland, Texas and Aerial Gunnery School at Laredo, Texas.

Assigned to an air crew Bill completed overseas Phase Training at Murdock Lake, California. In April, 1944, Bill and his crew began their cross-Atlantic flight to England from Fresno, CA. Their route took them to Puerto Rico; British Guinea; Brazil; Dakar; Morocco and Valley, Wales. Additional crew training was taken in Ireland prior to combat operations.

Assigned as a replacement crew to the 453rd Bomb Group at Old Buckenham, England, Bill flew fifteen missions as bombardier. The Executive Officer of his Group was film star Jimmy Stewart who held the rank of major at the time and was later promoted to Lieutenant Colonel.

During one mission to bomb a target in Hamburg, Germany, flak knocked out the two port engines of Bill's aircraft. On their return to England they continually lost altitude and distance from the rest of their formation. American P-51 fighters were called and escorted them to their base. The return flight was complicated by the two running engines. They were on the same side of the aircraft and caused difficulty in his ability to maintain control of the aircraft. Unable to join in the landing pattern for fear of stalling, Bill's pilot brought their aircraft in to land on a straight run to the runway.

Bill's fifteenth mission was a raid on an aircraft engine plant at Halle, Germany. Over the target two direct hits were taken in their aircraft. One in the nose and one in the bomb bay area. Bill's navigator and tail gunner were blown out of the airplane without parachutes. Except for Bill and a gunner, the balance of his crew were killed. Bill bailed out, was captured by German farmers and turned over to the military.

After numerous attempts to interrogate him without success, he was transported to Stalag Luft I. Despite a near starvation diet provided by his captors, overcrowding and primitive living conditions, each piece of paper, tin, and cloth was utilized by the inmates to make life more bearable. Necessity is often said to be the mother of invention and the inmates ingenuity in using what they could knew no bounds. To relieve boredom Bill was instrumental in establishing stage plays at the prison camp. Scripts were written from books at the prison library. Guards on leave in Berlin would often bring back props for use on stage.

After Germany surrendered Bill began recuperation at Camp Lucky Strike, a former German fighter base. After de-lousing, shaves, showers, decent food and new clothes Bill was flown out of Germany on a B-17 bomber to England. He boarded a Victory Ship for the voyage back to America. Bill was discharged from military service in January, 1946. He had been awarded the Air Medal with oak leaf clusters, ETO, WWII and POW medals.

Bill entered college under the GI Bill at the University of Iowa but later transferred and graduated from Coe College in Cedar Rapids with a Bachelor and Masters degree. He retired from teaching school in Michigan and New York An actor, Bill estimated he has produced and participated in over 600 stage plays.

LEON MEHRING, CEDAR RAPIDS, IA, enlisted in military service in 1943 while still in high school. After graduation he was called to active duty on November 27, 1943, and was sent to Buckley Field, Colorado, for Basic Training and Dyersburg, Tennessee for B-17 mechanic's training. While there he volunteered for Aerial Gunners School, was accepted, and on May 1,

1944, sent to Las Vegas, Nevada, for training. Upon completion of training Leon was assigned to an aircrew at Tampa, Florida, and trained with the crew at Gulfport, Mississippi, for overseas deployment.

Leon and his crew picked up a new B-17 bomber at Hunter Field, Georgia, and left for Europe on January 7, 1945. They stopped at Bangor, Maine and Goose Bay, Labrador in route. At Goose Bay snow lined both sides of the runway thirty feet high. When they took off in a blinding snowstorm the propeller on number four engine hit a snow bank and the engine started to vibrate. They were denied permission to return to base because the next plane after theirs had crashed on takeoff. Leon and his crew proceeded to Greenland with just three engines. Unable to land at Greenland because of weather, they continued on to Iceland. After a propeller change they flew on to England, and arrived January 17, 1945. They were assigned to the 305th Bomb Group, 364th Squadron, at Chelveston.

Leon flew his first combat mission January 20, 1945. He would fly eleven missions; five as left waist gunner and six as ball turret gunner. On a February 25, 1945, mission to bomb a target at Wurzburg, Germany, Leon was at left waist. It was an early morning wakeup and breakfast. Fog was so bad they couldn't see across the street. Solid clouds ranged up to 12,000 feet. They were told it is a "must" mission and the weatherman predicted the front would lift by the time they got back to England in the afternoon. At takeoff they couldn't see the runway lights on either side. The pilot lined up in what he hoped was the middle of the runway and told the crew to watch for runway lights and let him know what side they were on so he could use the brakes to keep them on the runway.

They made it off the ground but did not break into the clear until they were at 15,000 feet. Three other bomb groups within five miles of each other were also taking off within the solid weather front.

When they arrived over the target it was one of those clear days when they could actually see the target – the one and only mission Leon was able to see the bombs hit and explode. After "bombs away" they returned to England. The weather front had not moved. The base commander decided to let the Group's planes down by circling and descending so many feet per minute, but everyone was on their own. There was bound to be some collisions but Leon's crew was never told of any. Every crew member was at his position in the airplane blinking lamps on and off to warn other planes of their presence. Round and round they went over the English Channel for what seemed an eternity before they broke out in the clear, over water. When they did, another B-17 was flying in formation with them. The two planes never saw each other and were both heading directly at a large ship in front of them. Leon's plane broke left and the other B-17 went right. He wondered later what the sailors were thinking as two B-17s buzzed them.

Pilot to navigator, "Give us a heading for home." Navigator: "I'm lost, I can only point you to the coast line." The ball turret gunner thought everything was alright now and began to listen to music instead of the intercom. The pilot told the crew their fuel was getting very low and unless they sight a landing field soon they would have to make a crash landing. Suddenly the co-pilot saw a long flame off to the right. It was an emergency field on the coast that burned fuel along the runway to lift the fog. The pilot told the crew they were going in for a landing now, there was no time for a go-around because one engine was beginning to sputter from lack of fuel.

The ball turret gunner was still listening to music. Leon banged on the turret, opened the hatch and yelled for him to get out of there. The guns were straight down. The gunner came out. There was no time to stow the turret for landing. The guns hit the runway and became horseshoes, the oxygen tank broke open but did not burst into flames. Before they come to a stop at the end of the runway two more engines had cut out. They taxied only a short way on one engine before it gave out. After refueling they flew back to their base, got something to eat and fell into bed. They would fly another mission tomorrow.

On February 20, 1945, the target was Berlin. They were told there would be a tail wind of over 100 miles per hour all the way to Berlin. Flak was heavy. It was all around them. Understandably, nineteen year old Leon was terrified. After "bombs away" they turned for home straight into a headwind. Fuel consumption was heavy and they seemed to be getting nowhere. The Group Commander ordered the formation to drop to 10,000 feet to see if the wind would be less, but no such luck. At that altitude they were off oxygen, took off their gloves and had more freedom. They were sitting ducks for enemy fighters at their slow ground speed but they were never attacked. Over France, the fuel was getting short and the crew was ordered to throw out everything hey could to make the plane lighter. This included flak helmets, jackets, and ammunition. Leon opened his gun cover and a .50 caliber shell exploded. His hands and eyes were burned from the powder. He was blinded. The engineer poured sulfa powder on

Leon's face and hands. Leon didn't remember anything more until he was put in an ambulance and taken to the base hospital for treatment.

Leon didn't fly again until March 21, 1945, on a mission to Nijmegan with Disney bombs. Meanwhile he went on R&R to a British Legion dance and met the love of his life, Vera Handshaw, whom he would later marry and would have five children.

After the war ended in Europe, the 305th was sent to St. Troud, Belgium, as part of a program to photograph all of Europe from 20,000 feet. In August, 1945, his Squadron was sent to Iceland to photograph the island and the North Pole until October, 1945, when they returned to St. Troud. Leon got a ten day leave, returned to England, married Vera and went to London for their honeymoon.

The Group moved to Leichfield Air Base near Munich in December, 1945. In the move Leon drove a weapons carrier and was able to see the bomb damage done to German cities. "Nothing remained of Cologne except a church."

Leon returned to England in January, 1946, for three days. When it was time to return to Germany, Vera went to the airport to see him leave. Mechanical problems and weather delayed his flight for three more days. With no luggage or papers to prove they were married Leon and Vera were refused a room at a local hotel. The R.A.F. gave them blankets and a mattress and for three nights Leon and Vera slept in a B-17 radio room. Leon later became ill with hepatitis and was hospitalized. After six weeks he was sent back to the United States by ship. Leon was discharged from the military on April 27, 1946. Vera followed in July and the couple made their home in Montana before moving to Iowa.

Right - Leon and his crew at 305th BG, Chelveston, England, in front of "Miss Dee Day". Leon, waist gunner is front row, second from left.

ROBERT MESSERLY, JANESVILLE, IA, worked for Rath Packing Plant in Waterloo, Iowa, when in May, 1942, he enlisted in the Army Air Corps at Des Moines. At the time of his induction Bob weighed 118 pounds. The doctor that conducted his physical told him that "if you weighed a half pound less I wouldn't take you". The doctor passed him to go into the Army as a non-combatant. Bob was sent to Rockford, IL, for Basic Training and then to Euphrata, WA for dental and medical training as a medic.

Bob was then sent to Tucson, Az where the 80th Medical Unit was being formed for deployment overseas. In April, 1943 Bob boarded a ship as part of a convoy that would take fourteen days to cross the Atlantic. They sailed into a storm enroute. When the storm cleared no other ships in the convoy were in sight. Bob recalls a young soldier on board his ship crying "I don't want to die. The Germans are going to get us", meaning torpedoed. Soon the convoy reformed including destroyer escort and they proceeded to England without incident.

Assigned to the 486th Bomb Group at Sudbury, Bob was responsible for meeting inbound aircraft with casualties aboard and other medical duties.

Bob returned to the United States in August, 1945, a four day trip aboard the Queen Elizabeth. He was discharged from the military in October, 1945, at St Louis, MO, having been awarded the World War II Victory, the ETO and Good Conduct Medals.

Bob owned and operated a general store in Finchford, Iowa, for thirty-two years before he retired in 1981.

JOHN E MEYER, WAVERLY, IA, was a senior in college when the Japanese attacked Pearl Harbor. After graduation he enlisted in the Army Air Corps in August of 1942. "My parents objected to me enlisting in the Air Corps. I had graduated from the College of Pharmacy and could easily have gotten into the medical corps. My dad said I could be sitting back of the lines in a hospital where I had a bed every night and good food. He would rather have a live coward than a dead hero. I used to think about that."

Given a choice of military schools to attend, John elected to choose training as a Bombardier. Assigned to a flight crew they went to Colorado Springs, CO, for crew training. They were then dispatched to Topeka, KS, where they picked up a new airplane and headed for England via the southern route through South America and Africa. Assigned to the 466th Bomb Group at Attlebridge, England, John and his crew flew training missions in preparation for D-Day, June 6, 1944. On the eve of D-Day, their base was closed down. No one was allowed to leave and all leaves were cancelled. "We knew then that this was it. We were told to go to bed early. We were awakened at about eleven o'clock that evening, went to the mess hall to eat and then to mission briefing. We were told the weather would be clear, we would have a clear shot at the target and we would be going on the bomb run at a low altitude, making us vulnerable to anti-aircraft fire. We had to be accurate in our bombing because we would be bombing just ahead of our landing forces so we had to be in a precise location at the precise time. Movie Tone News was filming our preparation for the mission. This was one of the greatest time in history and here I was taking part in it."

John's squadron took off, formed up and headed for the English Channel. At the coast they flew into a cloud layer and broke through it above the clouds. To their surprise there was no one else in sight. They were all by themselves above the clouds with an airplane belly full of bombs to help with the invasion. The pilot flew in behind another squadron and John dropped the bombs when the lead aircraft of the Group dropped theirs. They encountered no anti-aircraft fire and saw no enemy fighter planes.

The next day's mission took them across the Channel where John described the sight as standing in the top stands of a football stadium with everything laid out ahead of you out on the floor. "I could see everything, ships going back and forth, the Navy bombarding the shore, planes diving and dropping bombs. It was a sight I'll never forget, a front seat to the biggest adventure of our time. We didn't know how long it would take but we knew we were going to win the war. It was a great time to be alive, it really was."

John was discharged from the Air Corps in December, 1945, as a First Lieutenant. He had been awarded the Distinguished Flying Cross, Air Medal with three oak leaf clusters, European Theater of Operations Medal with three campaign stars, and World War II Victory Medal.

FREDERICK MILLER, DES MOINES, IA, had attended Iowa State College, Ames, Iowa, for one year and was in the Air Force

Reserve Officers Training Corps. He then enlisted in the Army Air Corps in November, 1942 at Camp Dodge, Iowa and was sent to Lowry Field, Colorado where he completed Bombsight and Automatic Pilot Schools.

In the summer of 1943 Fred was sent to the East Coast where he boarded a ship bound for England and the European Theater of Operations. "My hammock was in the bow of the ship. Its not the place down below you would want to be. It's a long way from there to get out of the ship in case you had to."

Fred was assigned to the 390th Bomb Group at Framlingham as a bombsight and auto- pilot mechanic. Repairs were made to those instruments that had suffered battle damage. He also tested the lead bomber's auto-pilot the night before each mission as well as the instruments on other aircraft on a daily basis.

On June 21, 1944, Fred flew on a shuttle flight to Russia. Oil refinery targets at Ruhland, Germany, were bombed. The target was too far away to make a return trip to England. With the cooperation of the Russian Government the bombers flew on to Russia where they were to be refueled, rearmed and another target bombed on the return to England. "Each aircraft on the mission took a ground crew person with a specialty to make needed repairs once we landed in Russia. I also served as waist gunner." That evening German aircraft bombed and strafed the Russian airfield and destroyed the majority of the American bombers. "We were at an airfield near there and believed they would come and bomb us the next night so we took off and flew to a Fifteenth Air Force airfield in Italy."

A target at Drohibycz, Poland, was bombed on June 25th. Fred's formation returned to the airfield in Italy that night and then bombed a target in France July 5 when they returned to England. Fred received the Bronze Star for his role in the Shuttle Mission.

In June, 1945, Fred returned to the United States aboard a war weary B-17 bomber that was to be scrapped for its metal. He was transferred to Sioux Falls, South Dakota, where he and other military personnel helped farmers. He was discharged from military service in September, 1945, and returned to Iowa State College where he earned a B.S. degree in mechanical engineering. Fred then worked for Honeywell Corporation until he became the Chief Engineer for General Growth Development Corporation designing shopping malls.

Right - 568th Bombsight Unit at 390th Bomb Group, Framlingham, England. Fred, Bombsight and Auto Pilot Specialist, is second row, right.

GERALD MILLER, DES MOINES, IA, worked in a grocery store until he was drafted into the Army Air Corps in late 1942. He was sent to Sheppard Field, Wichita Falls, Texas, for Basic Training. Then came Radio School at Scott Field, Illinois and Aerial Gunnery School at Harlingen, Texas. Following completion of training Gerald was assigned to an aircrew at Salt Lake City, Utah, and completed overseas training with his crew at Casper, Wyoming.

The crew then picked up a new B-24 bomber at Wichita, Kansas, and flew to Ireland through Bangor, Maine; Gander, Newfoundland and Iceland. At Ireland their aircraft was taken from them for installation of additional equipment for combat. Gerald sailed across the Irish Sea to Scotland and then was transported to the Eighth Air Force Replacement Center at Stone, England.

Gerald was assigned to the 458th Bomb Group at Horsham St. Faith, England as Radio Operator and Top Turret Gunner. His first missions, two of them, came on D-Day, June 6, 1944. "On the first mission we flew at about two thousand feet. It was a fabulous sight to see the invasion forces. It looked like you could jump from one boat to another all the way across the English Channel. We bombed coastal defenses. On the second mission later that day we flew at about twenty thousand feet and bomber further inland."

Gerald's sixteenth and last mission came on July 12, 1944. While on the bomb run to bomb railroad marshalling yards at Munich, Germany, the number three engine of their airplane was hit by "flak". "We couldn't keep up with our bomb group so we peeled off losing speed and altitude. We got close to Switzerland and the pilot gave us the choice of landing in Switzerland or trying to make it back to England. We elected to try for England. While over Belgium we ran out of gas. The pilot ordered everyone to bail out. I remember our tail gunner wouldn't jump. The pilot told the crew he has to jump cause we were going down and were going to crash. One guy yelled back to the pilot, "he's gone, I pushed him."

"At the time we were only about sixteen miles into Belgium from the German border. Everyone had bailed out but three of us. When the plane went into a dive it took all of us pulling on the controls to level the plane out so we could jump. What an experience. I remembered all the instructions they told us about bailing out. When I went out the bomb bay I tumbled and tumbled in the air. I remember them telling us to spread our legs and arms and it worked. I straightened out. They also said "Pull the D-ring hard". When I did I thought it had broke. The ring was in my hand and I was terrified. But the next thing I knew the parachute inflated. We were over a forest near the town of Givry. There were a lot of people because they saw our plane go down. I tried to steer the parachute clear of the trees but in doing so the parachute started to collapse. So I quit doing that and landed in trees headfirst. I was suspended from the trees upside down and was able to swing myself to a limb, get out of the parachute and get down to the ground. I started running and saw two guys following me. They caught up with me and motioned for me to follow them. They were part of the "Army Blanche", the Belgian resistance to Germany."

"I was taken to an old castle where in the basement there was a Belgian girl who spoke English. I was told to put on some women's clothing in order to get rid of my American flight clothes. When it was dark two guides led me through the forest to a spot where I was to cover myself with leaves and branches and to wait. They returned and took me to a farmhouse where the farm couple fed me wine. I passed out and woke up when it was daylight. I hid in their barn and then for two or three nights traveled at night with the guides and hid in the daytime. On the third night I hid in a potato field while the guides went somewhere. They came back and took me to a big farmhouse where two elderly ladies were hiding five other American flyers. One of them had been at the farmhouse for over a year. The other four were all members of the same aircrew. In hiding the Americans they were making their contribution to the war effort. We were now only one mile from the French border near the town of Blarnegeis. The roads were well patrolled by German forces."

"We spent our days learning to speak French and playing cards. If the house was to be searched there were panels in the walls that could be opened and closed to allow us to hide in the walls. We could climb to the third floor of the house where there was a cupola on top of the roof and we could see the country-side and German troops on the roads near there."

"We ate potatoes and carrots from the fields. The two elderly ladies baked the best bread I have ever eaten in an open-hearth oven. We were wearing civilians clothes provided by the Underground. One morning we woke up and heard shooting. A tank battle was going on near the town. The Germans pulled out of the area and American G.I.s showed up and got out of their tanks. As a group, the six of us walked to them. They pointed their guns at us. We told them we were Americans. They didn't believe us. We showed them our dog tags. They still didn't believe us and started asking us all kinds of questions about America and where we were from. After I said I was from Iowa, I saw a sergeant leave and come back shortly with a Lieutenant Colonel."

The Colonel asked which one of us claimed to be from Iowa. I replied that it was me. He then asked me what town I was from. When I replied, Des Moines, he asked several questions about Des Moines that I answered correctly. I saw a name tag on his uniform and recalled that a person with the same name had been on the Des Moines School Board and after he retired an elementary school in the city had been named after him. When I pointed this out to the Colonel there was no doubt who we were.

The Colonel explained that we had to go with his armored forces as they had no way to send us back behind the lines. I really hated to say goodbye to those two ladies who treated us so nice. For five days we were with the Third Armored Division all the way to the Rhine River. Along the way we picked up about two to three thousand German prisoners and took them with us too."

"The Colonel gave me a set of his uniforms and I was an instant Lieutenant Colonel. I told him I would have to take the officer's insignia off. He said leave it on. I was the luckiest guy in the world to run into a guy from Des Moines and even on the advancement with the Third Armored Division I slept in the General's foxhole. He got word to his wife that I was recovered. She in turn called my wife and over lunch in Younker's Department Store Tea Room, told her I was safe. It was several week's later the government officially notified my wife I was safe.

Red Ball Express supply trucks arrived at the Rhine River to replenish the armored forces. When their trucks were emptied we loaded all the German prisoners of war in them and headed for Paris. The Germans were placed in a prisoner of war camp. From there I was flown back to England and returned to the 458th Bomb Group. I was able to meet a pilot our family had raised as a brother. He had been assigned to the 458th and arrived after I had gotten shot down. What a reunion."

"I was given the option of finishing my missions or going home. Naturally I flew back to the United States almost immediately. It was November, 1944. After furlough I was assigned to the Air Transport Command ferrying B-25 and B-29 bombers from Love Field, Dallas, Texas. I was then told I could have a three day furlough because I was being transferred to India to fly C-46 cargo planes "over the hump" to supply Allied ground forces. For those three days I stayed at the base and reported to sick call each day. The doctor then grounded me permanently so I wouldn't have to go to India. I then taught ground school to pilots who had completed their overseas tours."

Gerald received his discharge from military service in October, 1945. He had received the Purple Heart Medal, Air Medal with two oak leaf clusters, European Theater of Operations and World War II Victory Medals.

In civilian life Gerald and his brother owned and operated Miller's Super Value Grocery Store on Army Post Road in Des Moines for thirty-five years. He owes his life to the Belgian Resistance fighters of the "Army Blanche".

Right - Gerald's aircrew, 458th BG, Horsham St. Faith, England. Gerald, Radio Operator, is third from the left in back row.

Right - Some members of the "Army Blanche", Belgian Resistance. Man on the left is Marcel Guddond, a guide who lead Gerald through the night to safe havens. The woman is Madame Biron, one of two ladies on whose farm Gerald hid from German forces.

Right - Madama Julie Biron on left and Anna Missalin, the two ladies on whose Belgian farm Gerald and five other American flyers hid after being shot down over Germany

Right - Madames Biron and Missalin and the six downed American flyers hid by them from German troops. Gerald is third man from the right. Man on the right hid at the Belgian farm for over a year before all were freed by American ground troops. The other four men were members of the same aircrew shot down. "Flicka" the dog is being held for the picture by Anna on the right.

HARVEY A MILLER, CLARKSVILLE, IA, was drafted into the Army Air Corps on February 15, 1943 and sent to Jefferson Barracks, St. Louis, Missouri, for Basic Training. He then completed Aircraft Mechanics School at Sheppard Field, Wichita Falls, Texas and Aerial Gunnery School at St. Petersburg, Florida.

Harvey was assigned to an aircrew

and completed overseas training at Salt Lake City, Utah in March, 1944. The crew picked up a new B-24 bomber at Harrington, Kansas, and flew to the European Theater of Operations via a southern route. This took them to South America and stops in Africa before they reached Sudbury, England, home of the 486th Bomb Group.

Harvey flew the first of his thirty combat missions as an aerial gunner on May 3, 1944. Attacks on German submarine pens were his most memorable. The area was well protected by fighter aircraft and anti-aircraft batteries. Bombs made no impact on German submarine operations. "The concrete protecting the pens was so thick bombs didn't do any damage."

He finished his thirtieth mission only three and a half months after his arrival in England. "Our airplane never received any serious damage and only our tail gunner was injured when he got hit by flak in the foot. We were just lucky." Harvey returned to the United States aboard the Queen Mary in September, 1944. He became an instructor at Keesler Field, Mississippi until he received his discharge from military service. Harvey had been awarded, among other medals, the Distinguished Flying Cross, Air Medal with three oak leaf clusters, the ETO Ribbon and World War II Victory Medal.

Right - Harvey and his crew at 486th BG, Sudbury, England. Harvey, Aerial Gunner, is front row, second from left.

JACK MODLIN, DAWSON, IA, was farming prior to World War II. He enlisted in the Army Air Corps and called to active duty in January, 1943. After Basic Training at Jefferson Barracks, St. Louis, Missouri, Jack reported to Coe College, Cedar Rapids, Iowa, under the College Training Detachment Program as an Aviation Cadet. The Air Corps subsequently believed they had sufficient personnel in training as Pilots, Co-Pilots, Bombardiers and Navigators and further training was discontinued. Jack was sent to Santa Ana, California for classification and then to Engineer School at Amarillo, Texas. He spent a year in training at Amarillo learning everything he could about the B-17 bomber from nose to tail. He was then sent to Las Vegas, Nevada for Aerial Gunnery School.

Jack was assigned to an air crew at Lincoln, Nebraska and trained with the crew at Alexandria, Louisiana in preparation for overseas deployment. In November, 1944, he and twenty-one thousand other American servicemen boarded the "Queen Elizabeth" ocean liner for Grennock, Scotland. From there he was trained to his new home, Horham, England, and the 95th Bomb Group.

Jack flew thirty-two combat missions as Flight Engineer and gunner. This included two food missions to Holland while the war was still being waged against Germany. A truce between combatants allowed American bombers to fly within a specified corridor to drop food supplies to the starving Dutch who had been under Nazi rule. After the war ended in Europe Jack flew two missions to pick up French prisoners of war suffering from typhus.

On January 5, 1945, during a mission to Frankfurt, Germany, "They threw everything they had at us (flak). We lost three engines and with only one engine, we were losing altitude and running out of gas. We spotted a temporary landing strip made of steel mats in Belgium just behind the front lines. A crashed C-47 sat at the end of the runway. Rudy (Rudy Nelson, Pilot, Marion, Iowa) sat the plane down and was able to stop it in front of the C-47." English troops occupying the runway wanted the bomber out of there in order to receive supplies. Not realizing the aircraft only had one working engine they asked Rudy how much gas he needed to take off and get back to England. Rudy replied "1700 gallons". The ground forces were supplied with only 5- gallon gas cans. Jack and his crew were trucked to Brussells, Belgium where they stayed at the Metropole Hotel for three days. Two to three hundred other airmen were staying in and around Brussell also waiting for flights back to their bases in England. It was a week before they were successful in being flown back to Horham.

Other targets bombed during his missions included oil refineries, marshalling yards and bridges before Jack returned to the United States by air in June, 1945. He was in B-29 training at Sioux Falls, South Dakota, in preparation for deployment to the Pacific Theater of Operations when the war ended. Jack received his discharge from military service October 18, 1945, having been awarded, among other medals, the Air Medal with five oak leaf clusters, ETO Ribbon with three battle stars and the World War II Victory Medal. Jack returned to farming in the Dawson, Iowa, area.

Right - Jack's crew, 95th BG, Horham, England. Jack, Flight Engineer, is back row, left. His pilot, Rudy Nelson from Maraion, Iowa, is front row, left.

LOYD MORSE, FORT DODGE, IA, was born and raised in Emporia, Kansas. He served in the National Guard from 1936-1939. After America's entry into World War II he enlisted in the Army Air Corps and called to active duty February 2, 1942.

After Basic Training at Sheppard Field, Wichita Falls, Texas, Loyd was sent to Tucson, Arizona for re-assignment where

"about a thousand of us were marched into the desert. We set up ten rows of tents, ten to a row, and lived there until reassigned". Loyd applied for the Aviation Cadet Program, was accepted, and sent to Alexandria, Louisiana, for Pre-Flight Training; Primary Flight and Basic Flight Training in Arkansas; and Advanced Flight Training at Superior, Indiana. He graduated July 28, 1943 and received his wings and commission as a Second Lieutenant.

After two weeks of B-24 bomber training at Boise, Idaho, Loyd was assigned an air crew and trained with them at Wendover, Utah, in preparation for overseas deployment. In September, 1943 the Bomb Group was transferred to Sioux City, Iowa, to take sixty new bombers to the European Theater of Operations. Loyd flew the southern route through Puerto Rico; British Guinea; Brazil; Dakar, Africa and Marrakesh to England. Getting to England took longer than expected. While at Puerto Rico, ground crews pre-flighting the engines on Loyd's aircraft accidentally released the brakes. When the aircraft started rolling the brakes were put on with such force the nose wheel collapsed dumping the plane on its nose. It was thirty days before Loyd and his crew continued their trip to the 448th Bomb Group at Seething, England.

Loyd flew eighteen combat missions beginning Christmas Eve, 1943. "At that stage of the war it was estimated only seven out of one hundred bomb crews would survive their required twenty-five missions."

Munich was bombed four straight days by Loyd's bomb group. The fourth day, his eighteenth mission, Loyd's aircraft was hit by "flak" causing them to lose fuel. Unable to make it back to England they landed at an air base in Switzerland, a neutral country in the war. Combatants that landed in Switzerland or forced down by violating a neutral country's airspace were interned for the duration of the war. Officers of Loyd's crew were billeted in a resort hotel while enlisted personnel were housed elsewhere. To escape and be caught meant prison.

With no special duties to perform and nothing to do, boredom became the biggest problem for the internees. Anxious to leave and get back to the war, Loyd and two other officers decided to escape. They climbed aboard a train and hid in automobiles being shipped on railroad cars. The train took them to a city in northwest Switzerland. Loyd had studied the German language spoken in that part of Switzerland and was able to purchase railroad tickets which took them to the city of Geneva. On the train ride, Loyd sat across the aisle from three German officers. At Geneva they were assisted by the French Underground and reached American troops after hiking through mountains for ten days.

After return to England, Loyd was shipped back to the United States on November 3, 1944. If he were to continue to fly missions, be shot down and captured, he would be interrogated and possibly tortured to reveal Underground sources and routes. As a result, escapees were rotated home.

Loyd spent a brief period at Santa Monica, California before being transferred to Panama City, Florida, where he flew missions carrying aerial gunners firing at tow targets. He then spent five months at Victorville, California training in radar navigation before separation from military service June 10, 1945.

He joined the Air National Guard at Fort Dodge in 1950 in time to be recalled to active duty during the Korean War. He became a Radar Officer after attending an Electronics School and then was shipped to Korea. His training allowed B-29 bombers to bomb enemy front lines at night using auto-track radar. He would lock onto planes with the radar, guide them to the target and relay to them when to release the bombs.

Loyd remained with the Air National Guard until he retired September 12, 1978 at the rank of Colonel. He had been awarded the Air Medal with three oak leaf clusters, ETO Ribbon, World War II Victory Medal and those associated with the Korean War. He spent fifty-four years in life insurance of which forty years were spent with one firm.

NORMAN MUTCHLER, WAVERLY, IA, was raised in Michigan and enrolled at Morningside College, Sioux City, IA, in the Fall of 1942. When he turned eighteen he enlisted in the Army Air Corps with hopes of becoming a fighter pilot. After Basic Training at Sheppard Field, Texas, he entered the College Training Detachment Program at Kansas State University. Courses were taken in Math, Science, Physics and how to survive in the Pacific Islands.

Norm was sent to the Classification Center at San Antonio, Texas, and assigned to pilot training. Next came the progression of flight training in single, double and four engine aircraft.

He received his wings at Lackland Field, Waco, TX. Half of the graduating class went to B-46 training while Norm's half of the class attended administrative school at San Antonio. He was then sent to Boca Raton, FL for B-17 Co-Pilot School and Radar Training School for graduate navigators. Norm flew five navigators on night training missions for five hours. Each navigator spent one hour at the Mickey seat.

Norm eventually was sent to Avon Park, FL for crew assignment and training for overseas deployment. In early February, 1945, he boarded the "Queen Mary" and sailed for Glasgow, Scotland. No warship escort was provided since the Queen was faster than enemy submarines.

Norm was assigned to the 486th Bomb Group at Sudbury, England, where he flew three combat missions. One was a 500 foot low-level flight to Linz, Austria where thirty-two French slave laborers were picked up and flown to Paris. He had to be sprayed with delousing powder before and after the mission to avoid being infested. He described the refugees as "poor, starved and looking like animals".

Another mission was a ten hour flight to Engelstadt, Germany, where fragmentation bombs were dropped on a railroad area.

After the war and discharge from military service, Norm returned to Morningside College where he earned his bachelor's degree. Following graduation he taught and coached high school athletics. He later gave up teaching to enter the sporting goods business. Norm continued his love of flying and flew for his own pleasure until 1964. He completed requirements for an instructor's certificate and taught flying for twelve years.

ORVILLE MYERS, PANORA, IA, enlisted in the Army Air Corps in February, 1941, ten months before America was thrust into World War II. Originally from Oregon, Orville was sent to Hamilton Field, California for Basic Training and a Curtis-Wright Technical School on aircraft engines at Glendale, CA.

After schooling he reported to Portland, Oregon Army Air Base where he worked on the flight line maintaining P-47 aircraft for pilots in training. Orville had a Model A Ford car at the time and decided to visit a friend attending college at Corvallis, Oregon. While there he heard the news of the Japanese attack on Pearl Harbor. All military service personnel were ordered to report immediately to their bases and Orville started to return to Portland. In route a front wheel came off the car and he drove into a ditch. He made it back to his base by hitchhiking.

Orville was then sent to Payne Field, Everett, Washington to work on P-38 fighter aircraft. While there he applied for pilot training, was accepted and sent to Hemet, California to begin flight school. He "washed out" then applied for Navigation School. Lack of mathematics in his schooling prevented him from completing the course and Orville was sent to Laredo, Texas for Aerial Gunnery School.

Upon completion of training, Orville was assigned to an air crew at Topeka, Kansas and in August, 1944 flew through New Hampshire, Labrador and Iceland to the 93rd Bomb Group at Hardwick, England.

Orville flew thirty-five combat missions between September 25, 1944 and March 25, 1945. During the Battle of the Bulge Orville flew low-level supply missions to American ground troops. "We had German ground troops shooting at us, even with pistols."

When they returned from one mission "we ran into a snowstorm. You couldn't even see our wingtips. There were a lot of mid-air collisions between our planes, but our pilot got us out of there and we flew on to Scotland."

In his thirty-five missions no crewmember was injured. Long missions required the crew remain on oxygen for up to eight hours was not fondly recalled. "We never got too close to other crews in our quonset hut. It seemed they weren't there that long, being shot down." A close call came on his second mission, a bombing raid on Hamm, Germany, where flak knocked out two of their engines. "The pilot ordered us to throw out everything we could. Constantly losing altitude it was our choice if we wanted to bail out rather than risk crashing or ditching in the water. We decided to stay with the aircraft and we made it back to base."

After he completed his required number of missions, Orville returned to the United States aboard a Victory Ship. He reported to Ft. Lewis, Washington, where, despite plenty of points to qualify, there was a delay in obtaining his discharge. He decided to re-enlist until he learned he would be sent to the Pacific Theater of Operations. He finally got his discharge. Orville had been awarded the Air Medal with five oak leaf clusters, ETO Ribbon with battle stars, and World War II Victory Medal.

Orville resumed his education in civilian life and earned his Bachelor's and Master's Degree. He became a high school teacher and coach, then a Superintendent of Schools before he accepted an Elementary Principal position in Iowa's East Buchanan School System where he remained for twenty-three years until retirement.

Right - Orville's crew at 93rd BG, Hardwick, England. Orville, Top Turret Gunner, is back row, fourth from the left.

Right - Orville at his gun position

ROBERT MYERS, TIFFIN, IA, graduated from high school in 1942. He then attended American Technical School in Des Moines where he was taught aircraft fabrication. In September, 1942, Robert was employed by North American Aviation, Kansas City, MO, where the B-25 bomber was made. He worked on 700 B-25s all of which bore the red star insignia of Russia. The airplanes were flown to Alaska by American pilots and turned over to Russian pilots who would fly them on to Russia.

Robert was drafted into the Army April 15, 1943, and sent to Miami Beach, FL for Basic Training. While in training he had to perform beach patrol against infiltration by enemy saboteurs or spies. From the top of his hotel where he was billeted he could see ships on fire out on the ocean at night exploding from attack by German submarines.

After Basic Training Robert was sent to Chanute Field, Illinois, to attend Sheet Metal School and then Tinker Field, Oklahoma, where the C-47 cargo plane was assembled at a Douglas Aircraft Plant. In October, 1943, he was sent by train to Camp Kilmer, NJ, where he boarded a ship as part of a convoy that sailed for Scotland.

Robert was assigned to Base Air Depot #2 at Wharton, England, where 10,000 personnel were assigned to fulfill engine, structural support functions and modifications for aircraft assigned to a multitude of Eighth Air Force bases. P-51 Mustang fighters that arrived in crates at English ports were transported to the Base Depot for assembly. Engines for both the B-24 and the P-51 were overhauled; armor plating was installed on the outside of the B-24 next to the pilot and co-pilot positions; oxygen bottles and life raft positions in the B-24 were moved from where installed by the factory; gas tanks were installed behind the pilot in the P-51B; radio and instrument modifications were made; and major structural repairs were made to aircraft suffering battle damage. War weary planes had their bomb bay doors riveted shut and were used to drop supplies through escape hatches to the Underground on low-level flights. The necessity of getting aircraft to the war zone depended on getting planes built at the factory transported to the war zone as soon as possible so Base Depots could perform modifications to get them ready for combat.

When the war ended in Europe, Robert and others not seeking discharge from the military at that time, had the opportunity to remain in Europe for up to three, three month periods. Robert agreed to stay for nine months. He was transferred to the Ninth Air Force and assigned to the 86th Fighter Group which had been transferred to Schweinfurt, Germany. To get to Schweinfurt in August, 1945, Robert sailed from England to Cherbourg, France. After arrival, and with no official orders on where to report, Robert and some friends went to Paris and stayed there until military authorities returned them to Cherbourg. Once again, with no official orders and no duty, they went to Paris again and once again were eventually returned to Cherbourg. Robert and his crew did make it to Schweinfurt where Americans forces used a captured air field for their P-47 Thunderbolts. Robert was the Chief of Maintenance until he returned to the United States and was discharged at Camp McCoy, WI, on April 23, 1946.

Robert gained employment with Wilson Packing Company in Cedar Rapids until he entered government service with the Veterans Administration in Iowa City, IA. He has subsequently retired.

Right - Bob and personnel at BAD2, Wharton, England. Bob is standing above and to the right of engine number two with arams folded.

ROBERT G. NELSON, SIOUX CITY, IA, had worked with the U.S. Post Office and U.S. Rubber Company in Detroit prior

Chapter Twenty-Two

to World War II. He entered military service on April 13, 1943, at Fort Custer, Michigan.

He attended Aerial Gunnery School at Lowry Field, Colorado and Kingman, Arizona. After assignment to an aircrew at Salt Lake City, Utah, Robert trained with his crew at Sioux City, Iowa, in preparation for overseas deployment. The crew picked up a new B-17 on April 3, 1944, and flew through Bangor, Maine, and Gandor, Newfoundland to Prestwick, Scotland. At Stone, England, Robert and his crew were assigned to the 94th Bomb Group at Bury St, Edmunds, England.

Robert flew thirty-two combat missions as ball turret gunner. On a mission to bomb submarine pens at Kiel, Germany, "we had to make two passes over the target before we could see what we were supposed to bomb. We had armor piercing bombs that were supposed to penetrate fortifications protecting the German subs. "Flak" was intense especially on the second pass. We got a lot of holes in our plane but no one got hurt except our flight engineer. A piece of "flak" hit him in the chest. He was wearing a flak suit. The shrapnel still penetrated the suit and he received a minor wound for which he was awarded the Purple Heart Medal."

On another mission "it was somewhere in the mountains in Yugoslavia". "We dropped supplies to Marshall Tito's forces. It was a low-level mission, gratifying and different from how we normally flew bombing missions."

After Robert completed his tour of missions he returned to the United States in September, 1944. He rotated between various bases attending Photography School and serving as Duty Sergeant until the end of the war. He was discharged from military service on October 10, 1945, at Lowry Field, Colorado, and had been awarded the Distinguished Flying Cross, Air Medal with three oak leaf clusters, ETO Ribbon and World War II Victory Medal.

Robert is retired from a career as a floor covering business owner.

Right - Robert's crew at 94th BG, Bury St. Edmunds, England. Robert, Ball Turret Gunner, is back row, second from right.

RUDY NELSON, CEDAR RAPIDS, IA, met his flight crew in Alexandria, Louisiana, in September, 1944. By December, 1944, they had been deployed to Horham, England with the 95th Bomb Group and were completing their first mission over Nazi-held territory.

Rudy completed 32 missions in a nine month span. Some of the missions were in 1000 plane raids, and according to Rudy, not many of the missions could be classified as "milk runs". Anti-aircraft fire was faced on every mission as well as the Luftwaffe. Often on their return to England they found holes spattered throughout the fuselage.

His second mission appeared to be his last when their B-17 Flying Fortress was forced down over Belgium, but luckily, they found themselves behind Allied lines. "Can't say we were ever that worried. One crew member was married at the time, so he

was a bit more nervous about getting back."

Upon completion of their 32 missions Rudy returned to the United States on June 18, 1945. His crew had the distinction of having had no casualties. The only wound suffered was a scratch on the bombardier's finger. In 1959 Rudy and his crew held their first reunion since the war ended. Meeting in Chicago they were missing one crew member who had died the year before. They have continued their reunions every five years thereafter.

After the war and with a degree in Electrical Engineering, Rudy embarked on a career at Collins Radio Group of Rockwell International, in Cedar Rapids, Iowa, as a Reliability Engineer and has since retired. Rudy has served the Iowa Chapter of the Eighth Air Force Historical Society as its President and on the Board of Directors for many years. After Rudy's tenure as President of the Historical Society ended in 1996, two of his crew members made a surprise visit to the Chapter's annual reunion wearing "Rudy's Crew" ball hats, quite a tribute to the man who had brought them home from 32 missions with only a scratch.

Right - Rudy's crewe, 95th BG, Horham, England. Rudy, Pilot, is front row, left. Jack Modlin of Dawson, Iowa, Flight Engineer, is back row, left.

ARLON NESSA, HUBBARD, IA, worked in a combination hardware, general store and post office at Garden City, Iowa, prior to World War II. He enlisted in the Army Air Corps in March, 1942, and was sent to Jefferson Barracks, MO, for Basic Training. Arlon was then sent to McDill Field, Florida where the 91st Bomb Group was being formed and learned aircraft mechanics through "on the job training".

In September, 1942, Arlon and 18,000 other American troops boarded the "Queen Mary" for Scotland. They stayed in port five days before sailing in order to outfit the "Queen" with machine guns on deck. On arrival in Scotland he boarded a train for his new home, Bassingbourn, England, a former Royal Air Force base.

Arlon was a crew chief and had three other mechanics assigned to him, responsible for maintenance of one B-17 bomber. While armorers, radio specialists and sheet metal workers performed specific functions on aircraft, Arlon and his crew were responsible for the mechanical operation of their aircraft. They changed engines, tires, and wings, installed fuel tanks and performed pre-flight checks before the aircraft took off for missions. Ground crews worked tirelessly, often through the night, to get their aircraft ready for missions. If and when their aircraft returned from a mission they began their maintenance routine all over again at the end of a long day to get it ready for the next day.

Iowans of the Mighty Eighth

Air crews on D-Day flew three missions in support of Allied ground forces. To ground crews it was also their "Longest Day". Aircraft assigned to him until they were either lost in combat or salvaged, included "Queenie", "Wee Willie" and "Ack Ack Annie".

Initially ground crews were billeted with aircrew enlisted men in former RAF barracks on the base. When air crew losses mounted it was found to have a direct effect on morale of the ground crew and they were assigned separate facilities.

In June, 1945, after nearly three years in England, Arlon flew back to the United States via Iceland and Greenland. After thirty days furlough he began training on the B-29 Super Fortress in Florida. When the Atomic Bomb was dropped on Hiroshima and Nagasaki, Japan, further military service was precluded and Arlon received his discharge September 19, 1945. He had been awarded the European Theater of Operations Medal with six battle stars for the American Air Offensive, Normandy, Northern France, the Rhineland, Ardennes and Central European Campaigns as well as the Distinguished Unit Citation.

KERMIT NEUBAUER, IOWA FALLS, IA, completed high school in the Spring of 1940 when he was only sixteen years old. He then attended a nine month training course at a trade school in Omaha, NE, in aircraft-drafting and blueprinting. This allowed him to secure employment with Curtis-Wright Aircraft Corporation in Buffalo, New York through December,
1942. He then returned to Iowa Falls to attend Ellsworth College and help on the family farm.

In July, 1943, Kermit enlisted in the Army Air Corps and was promptly sent to Sheppard Field, Texas, for basic training as an aviation cadet. Much to his dislike superior officers on the Cadet Board changed his training status to that of aerial gunnery and he was sent to Las Vegas, Nevada for training. Training consisted of flying in a B-17 firing the .50 caliber machine gun at targets towed by another aircraft and trap and skeet shooting on the ground. He graduated from aerial gunnery school in 1943 and met the balance of his ten- man crew at Salt Lake City, Utah. The crew was sent to Ardmore, Oklahoma, for seven weeks of overseas training. Kermit trained as a tail gunner which required he crawl on his hands and knees through a little door leading to the tail section of the aircraft. He had to sit on a bicycle styled seat with his knees and feet bent behind him for nearly the entire mission.

Kermit was assigned to the 94th Bomb Group and deployed to Rougham, England, near Bury St. Edmunds. He was assigned to a barracks that housed 32 airmen and got a sobering welcome when he went to his assigned bed the first day. Another airman asked him what position he flew. Kermit replied "tail". The airman said the last guy that occupied that bed was also a tail gunner and they washed him out of the airplane's tail with a hose after his last mission.

It was the crew's responsibility to check each night with the Operations Office to see if they were scheduled for a mission the next day. On three occasions to start his tour of duty he was awakened in the wee small hours of the morning and told he was flying although he hadn't been scheduled. He saw his first action as a replacement gunner.

On Kermit's fifth mission, a raid on Bremen, Germany, his airplane received a direct hit from enemy flak. One engine and the aircraft's oxygen system were knocked out. The pilot feathered (shut off) the engine and dropped in altitude below ten thousand feet so they could breath without oxygen support. At a lower altitude and reduced speed they were at the mercy of additional flak bursts and enemy fighters. While they limped home to England an American P-47 Thunderbolt fighter flew alongside and escorted them back to the English Channel.

On two successive missions the tail section of Kermit's plane was so heavily damaged ground crews had to replace the elevator and rudder. Amazingly he was not hurt. After another mission over 140 holes were counted in Kermit's aircraft. No one was wounded, yet a close friend of his was killed in another airplane which had only one hole in it.

Kermit's twenty-eighth mission was a raid on Mersberg, Germany synthetic fuel facilities. After "bombs away" and heading home they were suddenly attacked by German fighter planes which "annihilated our high squadron and then came after my squadron which was flying the lead squadron". "Our navigator was wounded, our oxygen system was destroyed, our hydraulics ruined, number four engine was shot out and there was a large hole in the right wing. With no oxygen system and poor condition of the airplane we were forced to drop in altitude. We lost our way and found out we were over Guernsey Island in the English Channel, which was held by the Germans." They received small arms fire from German troops stationed there. An American P-51 fighter arrived to guide them back to England. On arrival over their base with no hydraulics, the landing gear on "You Is My Ideal", the name of their B-17, had to be hand-cranked down. Since they still didn't have any brakes it was decided that as the airplane touched down on the runway the crew would let out a parachute at each waist gunner's position to inflate and slow the airplane. One parachute opened ahead of the other and caused the plane to "ground loop". They came to an abrupt stop and no one was seriously injured.

Kermit flew thirty-two missions as tail gunner, two more than was required. On November 1, 1944, he boarded the "Queen Mary" for a seven day voyage back to the United States. On board were 2,500 wounded GIs and 3,000 other military personnel heading home. Kermit volunteered to help take care of the wounded during the night. He was so happy to see the Statute of Liberty, Kermit tossed his helmet overboard at the Statute's feet. After a furlough he finished his military service as a gunnery instructor.

Kermit was awarded, among other medals, the Distinguished Flying Cross, Air Medal with three oak leaf clusters, Unit Presidential Citation with a cluster, European Theater of Operations Medal with four battle stars, and World War II Victory Medal.

KENNETH NEWSOM, DES MOINES, IA, was in high school when America entered World War II. Following graduation he learned Consolidated Aircraft in San Diego was hiring plant workers. He traveled to San Diego only to be told no help was needed at the time. To enhance his chances for employment he began attending a sheet metal workers school and worked nights in a
drug store earning eighteen dollars a week. He secured employment with Consolidated constructing wing spar sections on B-24

bombers. He changed employment to Aurora Aircraft in engine assembly until he got his Draft notice for induction in early 1943. He was selected for the Army Air Corps.

Kenneth was sent to Basic Training at Fresno, California; Aircraft Mechanics School at Biloxi, Mississippi and Aerial Gunnery School at Harlingen, Texas. Following graduation he was assigned as a replacement with the 486th Bomb Group being formed at Tucson, Arizona.

In March, 1944, Kenneth boarded a ship at Camp Kilmer, New Jersey, along with eighteen thousand other soldiers and sailed to the Firth of Clyde. The voyage took thirteen days. The troops were fed two meals a day.

The 486th Bomb Group was based at Sudbury, England. Kenneth flew twenty-five combat missions as tail gunner. Midway through Kenneth's missions the Group changed from flying the B-24 Liberator bomber to the Boeing B-17 bomber.

Kenneth flew a few missions as ball turret gunner. Once such mission was to Bremen when he was called to fly as a replacement. During the bomb run "I heard a big thump. A German .88 shell came up right through the plane's radio compartment and exploded above us. No one was injured. It must have been set to detonate at a specific altitude and we were just lucky. During missions when anti-aircraft shells are being shot at us and the "flak" starts flying you crunch up like trying to squeeze into the shell of a turtle."

"In route to a mission to Berlin we were supposed to fly routes that were absent of flak. Evidently we flew too close to the German island of Helgoland. Flak knocked out one third of our oxygen supply and we had to abort the mission and return back to England alone at low altitude."

"Most of our missions we took off at night. They used to get us up at eleven o'clock or midnight. We would go eat and then attend the general briefing. When they pulled the cover off the flag and you saw the red yard from our base to the target, you could hear a pin drop. About one-third of the time when we would get up that early and go through all the routine they would cancel the mission.

In November, 1944, Kenneth returned to the United States and reported to Santa Ana, California. After R&R at Spokane he finished the war in B-24 line maintenance and was discharged in October, 1945. He had been awarded the Air Medal with three oak leaf clusters, ETO Ribbon with four battle stars and the World War II Victory Medal.

In civilian life Kenneth worked in the building profession his entire career.

ALBERT NICHOLS, DES MOINES, IA, had attended college for one year, worked for Boyt Leather Company and built mobile home trailers for defense plant workers before he entered military service. He had joined the National Guard when he was sixteen and subsequently passed examinations for the Army Air Corps pilot training program. Albert was called to active duty in November, 1942, under a delayed entry program until he reached the age of eighteen.

Albert completed Pre-Flight Training at Santa Ana, California; Primary Flight at Glendale, Arizona; and Basic Flight at Pecos, Texas. After Advanced Flight Training at Marfa, Texas, Albert received his wings and commission as a second lieutenant. He then completed B-17 Transition Training at Roswell, New Mexico, before he reported to Salt Lake City, Utah, where an air crew was assigned to him. He trained with his crew at Tampa, Florida, in preparation for overseas deployment. After six additional weeks at Langley Field, Virginia, in radar crew training, Albert and his crew picked up a new B-17 and flew to Valley, Wales, through Bangor, Maine, and Gander, Newfoundland. He was assigned to the 452nd Bomb Group at Deopham Green, England.

Albert flew thirty combat missions of which twenty missions were flown as lead or deputy lead pilot. His first mission was on August 7, 1944, to a target in France. His most memorable mission was on August 25, 1944, to bomb Politz, Germany. During the bomb run two engines were lost to German "flak". As they lost speed and altitude they were forced to leave their formation and try to make it back to England alone. A P-51 Mustang, an American fighter plane, flew escort with them while over Germany. From 26,000 feet it was questionable whether or not they would be able to make it back to England. A decision had to be made whether to fly to Sweden where they would be interned for the duration of the war or try to make it across 600 miles of the North Sea to England on only two engines. To crash land in the North Sea could mean certain death from exposure to the icy waters. The crew chose to try and make it to England. They were able to make it to their base through gradual descent. They ran out of fuel as they landed. For his actions Albert was awarded the Distinguished Flying Cross.

Albert participated in the second shuttle mission to Russia in September, 1944. A target was bombed at Chemnitz, Germany. Instead of returning to England the bombers flew on the Poltava, Russia. They were refueled, re-armed and two days later bombed a target at Diosgyor, Yugoslavia, on the return to England. While in Russia, Albert had his first taste of vodka and was not impressed with its taste.

On December 31, 1944, Albert flew his last mission, a raid on Hamburg, Germany, submarine pens. "We got hit by both fighters and German flak. When we turned on the I.P. to make a run for the target the headwind was so strong it took us twenty-five minutes to fly fifteen miles. We were like sitting ducks. We lost seven planes from our Group. When we landed at our base I landed long on the runway and had to stop fast. Our tires were fifteen ply. I stopped so fast I ground them down and one wheel went flat."

Albert returned to the United States aboard a Liberty ship that took seventeen days to sail to America. His quarters were in the bow of the ship and the seas were "heavy". The boat pitched up and down constantly. He visited the enlisted men's quarters in the hold of the ship. "Their bunks were stacked clear to the ceiling. It was hot down there and putrid with all the guys seasick and throwing up."

After furlough Albert was sent to Tucson, Arizona, where he trained with a crew in the B-29 bomber for possible deployment to the Pacific Theater of Operations. While on a train to Topeka, Kansas, to pick up a new aircraft, he learned the Atomic bomb had been dropped on Japan. This precluded further training and he received his discharge from military service in October, 1945 at Sioux City, Iowa. He had been awarded two Distinguished Flying Crosses, the Air Medal with four oak leaf clusters, European Theater of Operations and World War II Victory Medals.

After the war Albert built houses and apartments and in 1979 began building and renting storage units in the Des Moines area.

Iowans of the Mighty Eighth

FLOYD NIELSEN, POCAHONTAS, IA, had received two, six month deferments from military service because of farming and then enlisted in the Army Air Corps in September, 1943. He was sent to Keesler Field, Biloxi, Mississippi for Basic Training before attending Aerial Gunnery School at Panama City, Florida.

He was assigned to an air crew and completed overseas flight training at Charleston, South Carolina before Floyd and his crew flew a new B-24 bomber to Prestwick, Scotland and then to Valley, Wales. Additional flight training was taken in Ireland before Floyd was assigned to the 25th BG(Reconnaissance) at Watton, England. His unit, the 652nd, was a Heavy Weather Squadron.

Floyd worked on the flight line at Watton for two to three months as an aircraft mechanic when the unit changed from flying the B-24 to the Boeing B-17 bomber. His squadron was responsible for weather flights over the Atlantic Ocean to take air pressure and wind direction readings for meteorologists. A meteorologist was included in each crew. Floyd served as an aerial gunner.

"At Lands End, England, we would fly toward Iceland. Every one hundred miles we would go down to twenty-five feet above the ocean to take a pressure reading. We would also drop a smoke bomb onto the water, take a sighting, then fly at a ninety degree angle to take another reading. From those readings they could predict wind speed and direction. We would then climb back to altitude for another one hundred miles and drop down and do the same thing. When we got near Iceland we would be at thirty thousand feet and fly a fifty-mile box to determine what is now known as the jet stream. Our flights would be ten to twelve hours long. When you were down to twenty-five feet above the ocean it was like being in a bowl with water above you on all sides."

Flights were also made to the Azores for weather purposes. "These were day and night straight flights taking readings down and back.

Once at his base at Watton a German JU-88 "strafed our base. We saw it coming and ran for the slit trenches. He made one pass through our base and flew off. It must have been no more than a nuisance attack because no one was hit and no damage was sustained to any aircraft or facility."

On V-E Day, May 8, 1945. "I celebrated by getting on top of our barracks roof, which was a flat roof, and shooting off a whole case of different colored flares with a Very pistol. We kept flying weather missions until August, 1945." Floyd had flown thirty-three missions and was slated to go to Paris for a month to assist in aerial photography of Europe. Instead he flew back to the United States on September 23, 1945. After furlough he received his discharge from military service at Santa Ana, California. He had been awarded the Air Medal, European Theater of Operations and World War II Victory Medal.

After the war Floyd returned to farming and still operates the family farm in semi-retirement.

MILO NOBLE, CHEROKEE, IA, was farming at the outbreak of World War II. He has the distinction of serving in two branches of the military. He enlisted in the Naval Reserve in November, 1942, but was discharged a year later because of a surplus of personnel. He then enlisted in the Army Air Corps at Ft McArthur, CA, and was sent to Buckley Field, CO for basic training.

After Basic, Milo attended radio school at Scott Field, IL and aerial gunnery school at Harlingen, TX. He was assigned to a combat crew and trained with them at Tucson, AZ prior to being shipped overseas.

In February, 1945, Milo and his crew picked up a new B-24 bomber at Lincoln, Nebraska and flew to Valley, Wales by way of Goose Bay, Labrador. They rode by train to their new home, with the 785th Squadron of the 466th Bomb Group at Attlebridge, England. Prior to Milo's arrival his squadron had flown fifty-five consecutive missions without a loss.

During the summer of 1944 the 466th Bomb Group in addition to flying bombing missions, also flew fuel supplies in support of ground forces in France after D-Day. Over two million gallons of fuel in 5 gallon cans, aircraft drop tanks and in bomb bay containers were delivered to Allied ground and air forces.

Milo flew fifteen missions as nose gunner and toggleir. A toggleir released bombs from his aircraft when he saw bombs being released from the lead aircraft in the formation. A mission to Berlin to bomb the German capitol was on a Sunday. Raised in a very devout family that didn't work on Sundays and Grace was said at all three daily meals, Milo was now on his way to Berlin to drop bombs and possibly kill people on the Sabbath. Suddenly his electrically heated flying suit shorted out and lost temperature. At their altitude in a non-pressurized airplane temperature within the aircraft was below zero. Milo had to continually bang his hands against the side of the nose turret to maintain circulation in his fingers and be able to release his bombs on cue. He was successful, target strikes were good and Milo knew he had done his part.

During another mission flown in his bomber named "Lady Jake", they suffered an anti-aircraft hit in the right wing. The 88 mm shell pierced the underside of the wing and exploded above the wing. Luck was with them that day and they made it back to base. Examination of the wing after the mission disclosed the shell had grazed the side of the fuel tank and the main wing spar. The main wire cable controlling the function of the aileron on that wing was frayed and only three tiny strands of wire were all that kept the pilot in control of the aircraft.

After the war ended in Europe Milo was sent to St. Petersburg, FL as a medical supply sergeant, an assignment he described as being "a round peg in a square hole". The assignment required a Staff Sergeant and Milo had been chosen. This assignment lasted four months until December, 1945 when he was sent to Greensboro, NC for discharge from military service. He carried with him all the shipping orders for the group of personnel going with him for discharge. Milo put the orders in his B-4 bag and on arrival, stowed it under his bunk. The soldiers sat for three days with no action toward their discharge. The men began complaining about the delay. One night it dawned on Milo the delay was because the orders everyone was waiting for was in his bag. He slipped out of the barracks early the next morning and turned the orders over to the proper personnel saying absolutely nothing to the men about his error. He thought the risk associated with that mistake was comparable to a combat mission if the soldiers had found out that he was the cause for the delay.

Milo was awarded, among other medals, the Air Medal with one oak leaf cluster, ETO Ribbon with two bronze battle stars and World War II Victory Medal. He worked as a carpenter and cabinet-maker in Portland, OR, after the war then returned to Iowa in 1951 to farm.

Right - Milo and his crew of "Lady Jake", 466th BG, Attlebridge, England. Milo is front row, extreme right.

VERNON NYHUS, MASON CITY, IA, had taken a truck sheet metal course and gained employment with Lockheed Aircraft Company at Burbank, California, before World War II He was drafted in the Army Air Corps during February, 1943 and sent to Sheppard Field, Wichita Falls, Texas, for Basic Training.

Vern completed Radio School at Scott Field, Illinois and Aerial Gunnery School at Kingman, Arizona before assignment to an aircrew. The crew trained at Tampa, Florida in preparation for overseas deployment.

In March, 1944 Vern and his crew picked up a new B-17 bomber and flew through Labrador and Iceland to Nutts Corner, Ireland. They were assigned to the 390th Bomb Group at Framlingham, England. "For six weeks we didn't have anything to do." It wasn't until September 21, 1944, that Vern flew the first of his thirty-five combat missions at Radio Operator/Gunner.

"Flak on our missions was always accurate and we would come back to base with a lot of holes in our plane. Went the anti-aircraft shells would explode it would throw the airplane upward. You could hear the shrapnel hitting the plane. We never had anyone hurt but a piece of flak flew past my head and hit a cross-member of our plane behind me. Flak also knocked out an engine on one mission. The whole plane shook and vibrated when the engine's propeller wind-milled out of control. We made it back to base and when we landed the wind-milling prop broke loose and flew away from the plane."

Vern participated in a mission that dropped supplies to Jews fighting the Germans in the city of Warsaw during what was known as the Warsaw Ghetto Uprising. They flew on to Poltava, Russia, after dropping the supplies since it was too far on limited fuel to return to their base in England. At Poltava, they were refueled and re-armed and bombed a rail center in Hungary on their return to England.

Vern returned to the United States during November, 1944 and remained stationed at Ft. Worth, Texas, until his discharge from military service September 10, 1945. Vern had been awarded the Distinguished Flying Cross, Air Medal with five oak leaf clusters and the ETO Ribbon with battle stars. Vern worked in construction as a heavy equipment operator until retirement. He sang as a member of the River City Barbershop Quartet for thirty years.

Right - Vern's crew at 390th BG, Framlingham, England. Vern, Radio Operator/Gunner, is back row, second from left.

REV. JAMES E. O'CONNOR, PEOSTA, IA, was a college student prior to World War II. He entered military service December 1, 1942. After Basic Training he was accepted into the Aviation Cadet Program and earned his wings and commission as a Second Lieutenant at Freeman Field, Indiana. In February, 1944, he as sent to a Distribution Center at Salt Lake City, UT.

Day and night from training fields all over the United States, pilots, bombardiers, navigators, engineers, radio operators and gunners were pouring into the Center. Rosters were being tabulated, airmen assigned to particular aircrews, destinations plotted for additional training and troop trains dispatched.

Father O'Connor was sent to Ardmore, OK, where he met his crew. They trained together until the middle of May, 1944, then were shipped to Kearney, NE, where they were assigned a new B-17 bomber. Father Jim and his crew flew through New Hampshire and Newfoundland in route to Nutts Corner, Ireland. On arrival their aircraft was taken from them and they were flown to Stone, England, another distribution center. Sent on to Bovingdon, near London, they attended pre-combat courses in Luftwaffe tactics, ditching and escape procedures as well as gunnery instruction. While there they were awakened by the roar of hundreds of aircraft flying overhead. It was the beginning of D-Day, June 6, 1944. Four days later they arrived at their new home, the 388th Bomb Group at Knettishall. They occupied bunks in a barracks that had belonged to a crew shot down a couple days before.

Father O'Connor flew thirty-five combat missions as co-pilot. The majority of missions were on a B-17 named "Skipper and the Kids". His first mission, July 4, 1944, was to the southeast of Paris to bomb a railroad bridge in order to cut off supplies and

reinforcements of German troops. His thirty-fifth mission was to the heavily defended oil refinery complex at Merseburg, Germany. Intervening missions were targeted toward marshalling yards, war production centers, fuel and oil refineries and in support of Allied ground troops.

During his seventh mission, a raid on the ball bearing plants at Schweinfurt, Germany, Father James flew "tail end Charlie". "The sky was black with flak, the worst I had ever seen. Flak was exploding all around our aircraft, tossing us around and shredding our plane with shrapnel." Flak had taken out the rudder and trim cables and at the moment of landing back at their base, they suddenly realized flak had also punctured one of their wheels. "We had no way of knowing before landing that a tire was punctured by flak. To be surprised by a blowout while landing at about 65 m.p.h. was a roller coaster experience. This happened to us when we returned from two other missions. Each time we managed to pull off the runway into the infield in order to clear the landing strip for other incoming ships. Some had wounded aboard, were damaged or dangerously low on fuel."

A chemical plant at Ludwigshaven, Germany was the target of an August 14, 1944 mission flown by Father James. "Flak was intense and accurate. A large piece came through the right side of the ship, passed over my knees and smashed into the instrument panel, sending up a shower of glass splinters from the gauges. The noise was deafening, and the pilot and I looked at one another wide-eyed expecting to see one or the other decapitated."

Two days later during a raid on oil refineries at Magdeburg, Germany, "a plane flying off our right wing was involved in a mid-air collision. The ship above it dropped down and sheared off the tail of the plane below it with its props. I still have a picture in my mind of the tail gunner's face as he looked up into the propellers just above his head. The ship went down out of control with all crewmembers killed. Our ship lost the No. 2 engine from a flak hit and we were unable to feather the prop. The propeller windmilled, so we had to evacuate the bombardier and navigator from the nose due to the probability of the prop breaking off from the shaft and flying through the side of the aircraft." They were forced to drop out of formation deep in the heart of Germany and try to make it back to their base alone. Another engine had evidently taken a flak hit and began to lose oil and pressure. Losing altitude their chances of survival against enemy fighters were slim. Fortunately American P-51s and P-47s flew alongside and escorted them to the English Channel. "We finally crossed the Channel at about 1,000 feet. We were down to our last few hundred feet as we arrived at our base."

On his twenty-eighth mission, September 28, 1944, the target was again the oil refineries at Merseburg. Their aircraft took up to one hundred flak hits, one of which wounded their tail gunner. Their number two engine was shot out and another engine lost half power. "Upon landing we discovered our hydraulic system had been shot out and we had no brakes. We simply coasted to a stop off the end of the runway. Our airplane's ground crew in assessing our damage couldn't understand why the No. 2 engine didn't fall right off the wing and the whole ship collapse."

After his final mission Father O'Connor returned to the United States and was assigned to the Air Transport Command at Bradley Field, CN. He began ferrying bombers and fighters returned from England to Oklahoma and Texas until his discharge from military service April 1, 1945. He had been awarded the Distinguished Flying Cross, Air Medal with four oak leaf clusters and the European Theater of Operations Ribbon with three battle stars.

Father O'Connor entered Notre Dame University then transferred to DePaul University in Chicago where he received his Bachelor's Degree. In 1949 he joined the Trappists, a contemplative order within the Catholic Church and entered New Melleray Abbey near Peosta in Dubuque County. He was ordained as a priest in the Order of Cistercians of Strict Observance in 1954.

Fifty years after World War II, Father O'Connor was contacted by his former pilot for a reunion with his former B-17 crew members. Unable to leave the monastery his pilot, flight engineer and three aerial gunners came to the Abbey with their wives to meet with him. Four of the five surviving crew members returned again four years later, in 1999.

Father O'Connor recorded his World War II experiences in a booklet titled "The Year I Can't Forget" (A Combat Crew Diary) from which excerpts were taken for this biographical account.

RUSSELL ORWIG, BETTENDORF, IA, was helping on the family farm when the Japanese attacked Pearl Harbor on December 7, 1941. With consent of his parents he enlisted in the Army Air Corps on December 11, 1941 and was sent to Jefferson Barracks, St Louis, MO for testing and evaluation. Further training involved Armaments School at Lowry Field, CO and Bendix Turret School at South Bend, IN.

From June to August, 1942 Russell flew coastal patrol at Tyndall Field, FL. He was then assigned to a B-26 crew at McDill Field, Tampa, FL and trained with them at Lake Charles LA from February through May, 1943 until deployment overseas.

Russell boarded the "Queen Elizabeth" for a five day sail across the Atlantic to Scotland. Near the end of the voyage the ship turned 180 degrees and sailed for half a day before turning back on course for its destination. This action was taken to avoid a German U-Boat "Wolf Pack" converging on the "QE's" original course.

Beginning in July, 1943, Russell flew his first thirteen missions with the 386th Bomb Group as an aerial gunner out of Boxted, England. With a 500 mile range limit the B-26 squadrons attacked German targets in France, Belgium and Holland. A raid on the Luftwaffe Schipol Air Base near Amsterdam, Holland, required they begin their bomb run at 12,000 feet. Over 160 German anti-aircraft guns protected the area. Russell and his crew returned from the mission with over one hundred-sixty flak holes in their plane but no injuries were sustained by the crew or damage to vital aircraft equipment.

A fatal mishap nearly occurred during takeoff on another mission. A 4,000 pound bomb load had been loaded in their B-26, "Miss Muriel", named after the Pilot's girlfriend. While rolling down the runway to takeoff the Co-Pilot in reaching to adjust flaps accidentally retracted their landing gear causing them to belly-land on the runway. When they came to a stop Russell was successful in scrambling out an escape hatch in the side of the fuselage under the tail.

In October, 1943, B-26 Squadrons of the 386th Bomb Group were transferred out of the Eighth Air Force to become the Ninth Air Force at Great Dunmow, England.

Russell went on to fly seventy-six missions. The last few missions were in support of Allied D-Day ground forces. In July, 1944, he was sent back to the United States on furlough. Russell returned to the United Kingdom in September, 1944, to continue flying more missions. After flying only one more mission he was sent back to America to become an aerial gunner instructor at Laredo, TX, until his discharge from military service. Russell had been awarded the Distinguished Flying Cross, Air Medal with thirteen oak leaf clusters and the European Theater of Operations Medal with four battle stars.

Following military service Russell entered college under the GI Bill. He secured employment in the Purchasing Department of John Deere Company. He retired in the 1980's.

Right - Russell and his crewe at 386th BG(M), in front of their B-26 "Miss Muriel". Russell is on the extreme right.

KENNETH C. OSETH, CEDAR RAPIDS, IA, was employed in construction when America was thrust into World War II with the Japanese sneak attack on military bases on the island of Oahu, Hawaiian Islands, December 7, 1941.

Kenneth was inducted into the Army Air Corps August 25, 1942. After Basic Training additional training was taken at Gulfport, Mississippi; Nashville, Tennessee, and Fort Myers, Florida. On November 19, 1943 he was deployed to Bury St. Edmunds, England, as a waist gunner with the 94th Bomb Group.

Kenneth flew 25 combat missions, the most memorable of which, was a January 11, 1944, mission to bomb Messerschmitt aircraft factories at Brunswick, Germany. When his formation of   bombers approached the point where they were to begin their bomb run, the mission was cancelled and all aircraft ordered to return to England. Twenty aircraft flying in the lead formation including that of Ken's didn't receive the order to abort the mission. On the bomb run clouds obscured the target. The lead pilot ordered what was left of the bombers to make a wide circle and another bomb run on the target. German fighter planes were waiting for them and pressed their attack. Ten of the twenty bombers were shot down.

The tail gunner's machine guns on Ken's aircraft froze from too much oil on them. He kept his calm and was able to radio the pilot when and where to move their aircraft to avoid being hit by fire from the enemy fighters. This was accomplished by watching the path of tracers shot with regular ammunition. Once over the target on the second run bombs that were released hit their target. Ken was credited with shooting down one enemy fighter.

Ken was discharged from the Army Air Corps on September 25, 1945 at Amarillo, Texas. He had been awarded the Distinguished Flying Cross, Air Medal with three oak leaf clusters, ETO ribbon and World War II Victory Medal. He returned to factory work in Cedar Rapids and has since retired.

Right - Ken's crew at 94th BG, Bury St. Edmunds, England. Ken, Waist Gunner, is back row, left.

MARVIN OTTO, ALTA, IA, was working as a farm hand when he enlisted in the Army Air Corps in March, 1942. After Basic Training at Jefferson Barracks, St. Louis, Missouri, Marvin was sent to Tallahassee, Florida, Waycross and Augusta, Georgia before he boarded the ocean liner "Aquatania" at New York in May, 1943, and sailed to England. "There were   twenty-two thousand American troops on board the ship. We took one day longer to get to England because German submarines were spotted ahead of us and we detoured around them."

Marvin was assigned to the 100th Service Group. "In England our unit was split in half. My half went to set up three air fields being built. We put up Nissen huts, mechanic facilities and bomb and ammo storage dumps." His last field was Rattlesden, England where he was permanently assigned as support.

Marvin's duties included supervision of bomb and ammunition delivery to the base and maintenance of a perpetual inventory of their supply. Ammunition delivered loose in ammo boxes were loaded into ammunition belt links.

He was involved in the recovery of sixteen bombs buried in the ground at Rattlesden from a bomber that dropped them when it exploded in the air. Some of the bombs contained delayed action fuses. Each bomb when located was disarmed.

A B-17 that returned from a mission to Berlin had a large "flak" hole in the left side of the fuselage. The radio operator's compartment had been totally destroyed and the radio operator blown out of the aircraft. One bomb bay door had been blown away. The aircraft landed with one flat tire and the ball turret guns pointing downward dragging on the runway. One bomb had not released over the target and was jammed in the wreckage  of the bomb bay area. While fuel leaked from the aircraft and sparks emitted from the electrical system, Marvin disarmed the bomb and removed it from the aircraft. For his actions he was awarded the Soldier's Medal.

In November, 1944, Marvin returned to the United States for re-assignment to the Pacific Theater of Operations. At Santa Ana, California, he was transferred to Carlsbad, New Mexico Army Air Base, a bombardier's training station. Marvin remained at Carlsbad providing practice bomb support until he received his discharge from military service in October, 1945.

Marvin returned to Iowa and farmed for ten years. He was then employed by DeKalb Seed Corn Company where he remained until retirement.

THOMAS PAGE, OSCEOLA, IA, graduated from high school in 1942 and enlisted in the Aviation Cadet Program. A pneumonia scar was detected during his physical examination and his entry into military service was delayed for six months on two occasions to allow the scar to heal or disappear. He volunteered for the Draft in June, 1943, and was sent to Buckley Field, Colo-   rado, for Basic Training. After Aerial Gunnery School at Kingman, Arizona, he was assigned to an air crew at Salt Lake City, Utah, and sent to Dyersburg, Tennessee, for overseas training.

Tom and his crew picked up a new B-17 bomber at Kearney, Nebraska, for their flight through Gander, Newfoundland to Nutts Corner, Ireland. On arrival their aircraft was taken from them and they proceeded to Stone, England, for assignment. Tom was assigned to the 94th Bomb Group at Bury St Edmunds, England as a tail gunner. Beginning July 8, 1944, he flew twenty-eight missions in two and a half months.

During these missions he witnessed two mid-air collisions in his Bomb Group while they flew in formation. On one occasion he noticed debris flying past his tail gunner windows. A lower flying aircraft bounced upwards in turbulence. Its propellers severed another B-17 in half causing it to immediately go nose down to earth. The other plane managed to climb and circle with its nose broken off and flight deck crushed. He saw the bombardier fall out of the aircraft with no parachute. No parachutes were seen escaping from the two aircraft. After another collision between two B-17s, seven parachutes were counted escaping the stricken airplanes.

On a mission to bomb railroad marshalling yards near Paris visibility was obscured over the target and Tom's Group prepared to circle and make a second bomb run. One of his aircraft's engines was not running to full capacity. An anti-aircraft shell pierced one of their wings and created a big hole. The self-sealing tanks in the wing worked, for about ten minutes, then began leaking fuel. They "feathered" that engine. The engine quit and then began to windmill. With only two engines and losing altitude rapidly they dropped out of formation and turned back toward England. They jettisoned their bombs near a farm and were able to land at an RAF Spitfire base. A car came out to meet them driven by a Scottish officer wearing a kilt, Tam, and carrying a swagger stick. He greeted them and said he had always wanted to view the inside of a B-17. Meanwhile Fuel continued to leak from the wing tanks and oxygen supply lines hissed from the stricken aircraft. The Scottish officer decided now was not the right time.

Another damaged B-17 landed at the same RAF base. The Co-Pilot had been killed by a large piece of "flak", and the Pilot hit in the Achilles Tendon of one foot. The Flight Engineer had landed the aircraft.

After he completed his tour of duty, Tom returned to the United States aboard the "HMS Samara". He was utilized as a submarine lookout and gunner aboard ship. After he reported to Santa Ana, California, for re-assignment he was sent to Truax Field, Madison, Wisconsin. No special duties were required of him and he actually worked part time at Ray O Vac battery company while still in the military.

Tom was re-assigned to Boca Raton, Florida, where he worked in the base personnel office. He then volunteered for B-29 training but World War II ended and precluded that assignment. After transferring to Buckley Field, Colorado, and working in the base Headquarters Office, he was re-assigned to Lowery Field, Colorado, where in the Fall of 1945 he was discharged from military service. Tom had been awarded the Air Medal with oak leaf clusters, World War II Victory and ETO medals. Tom is a retired rural carrier from the U.S. Postal Service.

Right - Tom and his crew at 94th BG, Bury St. Edmunds, England. Tom, Tail Gunner, is back row, second from left.

BERNARD PALMQUIST, RED OAK, IA, was with the 100th Bomb Group, Thorpe Abbotts, England.

For seventeen missions Bernie and his crew had all flown together. When the crew returned from a pass they learned they were scheduled for a mission the next day, May 7. Their regular airplane was still in repair from an April 28th mission so they would fly in a replacement B-17. Bernie was in the hospital some distance from Thorpe Abbotts and for the first time would not fly with the crew on a mission.

"While forming up after take-off, the top turret gunner was firing flares from a Very pistol when a live flare flew back into the nearly full box of flares, starting a very quick and smokey fire. The pilot called for "ready to bail out" and the men in the rear grabbed for their parachutes. The plane went into a tight spin and everyone was pinned back to the fuselage. As the airplane flattened somewhat, but still in steep descent, they tried to open the main hatch just in front of the tail. The door was made to open with a latch for entering the aircraft, but had an emergency handle that pulled the hinge pins and the door out when exiting the airplane for escape."

"As they pulled the handle, the top pin pulled out. The cable broke leaving the bottom pin stuck tight. The top of the door gapped open enough to start through, but a body with a chute and harness was too bulky to get through. The first man got stuck. The next man kicked him on through and got stuck himself. The next man then pushed him out, etc. The fifth man out was the spare ball gunner taking my place. He was a big boy and got stuck tight. While the last man was pushing him he accidentally pulled his rip cord. His chest pack was outside. It opened pulling him outside and back striking the tail and breaking his back."

"The last man was Madsen. He was big, got stuck and had nobody left to help him. He got his chute outside and pulled the rip cord. Out he went clearing the tail okay. The chute gave him a hard jerk and the next second he hit the ground. Three or four hundred yards away, the plane went into the ground. It had a full bomb and gas load. The gas went off first, then the bombs, creating a large crater in the ground. The four officers in front were still aboard. Why the bombardier and navigator didn't get out no one knows. They should have had plenty of time and had an escape hatch in the nose section."

The crash was near a church at the edge of a small English village. The English Earl who lived nearby wrote the pilot's wife about how proud she should be of the young man that stayed at the controls of his aircraft in order to miss the town and avoid much more loss of life.

The control tower at Thorpe Abbotts is now a museum cared for by a local group known as "Friends of the Eighth". Bernie would like to return to the base someday, maybe share a pint of mild and bitters at the Fox and Hounds pub just outside the main gate of his base at a crossroads known as Brock-Dish. He'd visit the crash site and see the grave in the little church yard with a marker put up by the local people giving the names of four good boys sleeping far from home.

STANLEY PATTERSON, MASON CITY, IA, graduated from Hamilton Business College in 1941 and was employed as an accountant when he was drafted into the Army Air Corps on November 7, 1941, one month before the Japanese attack on Pearl Harbor.

He was sent for Basic Training and Medical Administrative School at Camp Grant, Illinois.

Upon completion of training Stan was sent to Salt Lake City, Utah where the 305th Bomb Group was being formed and he met the flight surgeon doctor for whom he would work. The Group trained at Muroc Lake, California during June, July, and August, of 1942, where Stan worked in the dispensary. At the conclusion of training the Group began overseas deployment. Stan went by train to Fort Dix, New Jersey where he boarded the "Queen Mary" for Greenock, Scotland. The Group was initially assigned to

Grafton Underwood, England but transferred to Chelveston in December, 1942.

Stan operated the base dispensary, completed medical reports and dealt with "sick call". He was a member of the emergency crew that waited by the runway and removed casualties from aircraft that returned from missions or were in nearby crashes. Two B-17s collided over Chelveston. Stan was part of the team that recovered twenty bodies from the wreckage.

When the 305th moved to Belgium after V-E Day, Stan operated the base dispensary until September, 1945, when he returned to the United States aboard the "Queen Mary". in September, 1945. He received his discharge in October of that year and had been awarded, among other medals, the World War II Victory Medal and the ETO Ribbon with two battle stars.

Stan worked for ten years with the Iowa Employment Security Commission based in Mason City as a Veteran's Placement Specialist until he transferred within the agency to become an Unemployment Insurance Tax Auditor. He retired in 1985.

LESLIE PEDERSEN, WEST BRANCH, IA, was farming at the outbreak of World War II. He enlisted in the military April, 1942, at Fort Des Moines, IA. After Basic Training, Leslie attended Delgado Aircraft Engineer School, New Orleans, LA and Engine Specialists Course at Indiana Central College, Indianapolis, IN.

Leslie was deployed to Wattisham Air Base, England in May,1944, as a mechanic with the 479th Fighter Group. The Group had formerly flown the P-38 Lockheed Lightning but had converted to the North American P-51 Mustang when Leslie arrived. He was a crew chief responsible for maintenance and repair of fighter aircraft assigned to him as well as work performed on the aircraft by armorers, radiomen, and other specialists. He also had to install fuel drop tanks for long-range missions, do pre-flight checks on the aircraft and have it warmed up, ready for take-off when the pilot arrived. Often the pilot would have to fly three missions a day. It was not unusual for Leslie to be on the flight line from 3:00 A.M. until Midnight.

Although the pilot only saw his crew chief a few minutes before and after a mission, their living quarters were far apart and they had a different social life, a strong bond existed between the two. The most important person, the one who held the pilot's life in his hands, was his crew chief who had the final say on whether the high powered fighter was ready and fit to fly. If the crew chief made a mistake his pilot might not come back from a mission. Leslie's pilot, a Lt. Edward Sims, flew until the war ended without a "hitch" from engine, oxygen equipment, guns or other features of his airplane. Leslie received the Bronze Star Medal for having the first fighter plane in the Eighth Air Force to fly over 400 hours without a mechanical failure or return.

His long hours on the flight line was not without hazard and the nuisance of buzz bombs launched from Germany. Located in what was termed "doodle-bug alley" buzz bombs "came over all the time especially at night". "Some came tree top high. Once, thirty-seven landed within a one- mile radius of our base during a twenty-four hour period.

"I would occasionally fly in a P-51 that had a jump seat behind the Pilot. Once Lt. Sims and I flew over the White Cliffs of Dover and London. Flying over London was strictly forbidden. We risked being shot down by anti-aircraft fire mistaken as Germans. Sims later admitted "We shouldn't have done that", but no one turned us in, no one found out and we were young and having fun."

Leslie received his discharge from military service in November, 1945, at Camp McCoy, WI. He returned to government service as a Federal Protection Officer for twenty years. Leslie and his pilot, Edward Sims exchanged Christmas cards after the war and in 1990 were reunited in Florida for the first time in forty-five years.

Right - Leslie, on left, on wing of P-51 he maintaianed at 479th Fighter Group, Wattisham, England.

RALPH PENDER, CEDAR FALLS, IA, was working as a machinist for Douglas Aircraft Company in Santa Monica, California at the time of America's entry into World War II. He enlisted in the Army Air Corps in 1942 and was sent to Douglas, Arizona for what was supposed to be Basic Training. Instead "I was assigned a tool box, put on the air base flight line and told to go to work", as an aircraft mechanic without formal training.

Ralph was subsequently sent to Kingman, Arizona for Aerial Gunnery School. Upon completion of training he was assigned to an aircrew and sent to Drew Field, Tampa, Florida for training prior to overseas deployment. "We lived in locker room facilities under the grandstand of a baseball diamond."

In January, 1944, Ralph and his crew picked up a new B-17 bomber at Savannah, Georgia and began their cross-Atlantic flight to Scotland via Bangor, Maine and Gander, Newfoundland. On arrival their aircraft was taken from them for installation of additional armament and the crew was trucked to Knettishall, England, home of the 388th Bomb Group.

Ralph flew twenty-five missions as Engineer. "My job was to know just about everything about the aircraft and be able to not only monitor smooth running of the engines but make repairs to operating cables and some parts while in flight."

His first mission, in March, 1944, was to Ludwigshaven, Germany. "I was scared to death. We didn't see any German fighters but there was a lot of flak." His most memorable mission was a raid on the Rumanian oil fields at Ploesti. In contrast to previous attacks on the oil fields which were carried out at low-level, Ralph's bomb group flew at 32,000 feet. "The German flak still reached us. It would explode below us, then above us and then right on us. They zeroed in on us."

During one mission Ralph's aircraft took flak hits in the wing that punctured the fuel tanks. Luckily the aircraft didn't explode but the holes in the wing were too large for the self-sealing tanks to prevent leakage of all their gasoline. "We were able to make it back to France and land at an airstrip American ground forces had captured the previous day. We spent three days there repairing the aircraft and getting fuel to fly back to England. German fighters strafed us but we were in bunkers and no one got hurt."

When we got back to our base our footlockers in our barracks had been looted. No one expected us to return from the mission after they saw us go down."

Ralph flew two missions to Holland to drop food to starving Dutch citizens who had lived under Nazi rule. "They outlined a large circle we were to drop the supplies in. The food was in "gunny sacks" loaded in the bomb bay area of our plane. Some sacks got "hung up" and I had to go down in the bomb bay and kick them free. We had to make three passes over the drop zone to empty the plane."

Ralph also flew missions to Germany after V-E Day to pick up American prisoners of war and return them to England. He returned to the United States on June 30, 1945, and reported to Jefferson Barracks at St. Louis, Missouri. He was then re-assigned to Rapid City, South Dakota for B-29 bomber training. When atomic bombs were dropped on two Japanese cities and the war ended, further training was cancelled. Ralph was sent to Deming, New Mexico, where "we just laid around until they transferred me to Sioux City, Iowa, for discharge in November, 1945." Ralph had been awarded, among other medals, the Air Medal with three oak leaf clusters, ETO Ribbon and World War II Victory Medal.

Ralph drove an ice cream truck route serving grocery stores and restaurants until retirement.

Right - Ralph and his crew at 388th BG, Knettishall, England. Ralph, Flight Engineer is back row, right.

JACK PERRIN, CHEROKEE, IA, was in college at Iowa State Teacher's College (now the University of Northern Iowa) at Cedar Falls when Japan attacked American bases in the Hawaiian Islands on December 7, 1941. He immediately entered military service at Omaha, NE.

Jack was sent to Santa Ana, CA for Basic Training. After Basic, he was transferred to Marfa Field,

TX where he was assigned to the headquarters squadron of a twin-engine flying school. He worked for a short time in the printing pressroom and then was shifted to Central files where he worked for almost two years as a file clerk. By the Spring of 1944, the Army Air Corps needed replacement aerial gunners. Jack took a series of tests, passed, and during the summer of 1944 attended Aerial Gunnery School at Las Vegas, NV. He was assigned to an air crew at Lincoln, NE. After crew training at Ardmore, OK he was deployed to England in January, 1945, aboard the "Ile de France", France's largest ocean liner. He was assigned to the 568th Squadron of the 390th Bomb Group at Framlingham, England, as a tail gunner.

Jack flew twenty-two combat missions. His first was on February 6, 1945, a mission to bomb railroad marshalling yards at Chemnitz, Germany. Russian forces were approaching Chemnitz from the east and the destruction of the rail ways in the city would greatly hinder German reinforcements to the front. On approach to the target, his B-17 bomber took a "flak" hit to the right wing. An engine was damaged and caused them to lose their place in the formation, fall behind and lose altitude. Another engine began to have trouble and quit running which made them extremely vulnerable to enemy fighter attack. Luckily no fighter resistance appeared. Alone over Germany the crew was left with two options, try to make England and risk ditching in the English Channel or North Sea or head for Allied lines and try to land at a base in Belgium. They were able to find a P-38 reconnaissance airfield in Belgium that had a runway of pierced steel planking. The planking could not hold the weight of a heavy bomber and was damaged, but they were safe. Three days later they were back at their home base in Framlingham.

In March, 1945 Jack witnessed an attack by Germany's new jet fighter, the Messerschmitt ME 262, on a formation of B-17 bombers. Jack called out the fighter's approach and saw him blast the right wing and fuel tank of a B-17 on his right. The bomber went down but the crew was able to parachute out of the airplane. Jack continued to call out the ME 262's position, but couldn't talk fast enough because the jet's speed was too fast. He knew there was no way a hand-held .50 caliber machine gun nor any of the power-operated gun turrets could track the jet to get shots at it.

Flew flew missions at the end of the war to drop food and medical supplies to starving Dutch civilians. Portions of The Netherlands had been flooded by the Germans and many areas could not be reached over land. On one mission, a large "X" had been drawn on a soccer field as a target for American bombardiers. The canned goods and other supplies missed, crashing through the roof of a nearby barn, smashing out the side walls allowing livestock in the barn to escape.

Jack's most memorable experience came as part of a flight crew to return American prisoners of war from Linz, Austria. A constant companion of Jack's growing up in Cherokee was a Jim Thomas. After the Japanese attack on Pearl Harbor Jim was too young to enlist in the military with Jack. Instead Jim went to Canada and enlisted in the Royal Air Force. He became part of a Lancaster bomber crew that "got shot up pretty bad and Jim was wounded. After he got out of the hospital he was put on another flight crew and got shot down again. This time he was captured and spent two years in a POW camp. I found out he was missing and later that he was a POW. When we flew into Linz they tried to get POWs sorted by Bomb Groups so that a plane from that bomb group would take them back to England. After we returned to our base, we lined up along the sidewalk to the mess hall to let the POWs eat first. This guy walked past me and I couldn't tell but I thought it was Jim. The guy had lost so much weight. When I saw the back of his head I knew it was Jim and yelled out his name. What a reunion. We spent seven days in London partying and I almost missed my plane to fly back home."

Jack completed twenty-two missions and held the rank of staff sergeant. He had been awarded the Air Medal with three oak leaf clusters and ETO Ribbon with three Battle Stars. One battle star was for the first napalm mission flown by an aircrew of the United States.

Jack was discharged from the military in September, 1945, at Sioux Falls, SD. He started a mink ranch that raised the animals for the luxury fur market. His ranch eventually became one of the largest mink ranches in the United States. Jack retired in 1985.

Right - Jack's crew at 390th Bomb Group, Framlingham, England. Jack, Aerial Gunner, is back row, left.

EUGENE PERSON, MANSON, IA, enlisted in the Army Air Corps October 28, 1943, as an Aviation Cadet. On December 1, 1943, he reported to Camp Dodge, Iowa and was sent to Amarillo, Texas for Basic Training. He then volunteered for Engineering School at Keesler Field, Biloxi, Mississippi, followed by Aerial Gunnery School at Tyndall Air Base near Panama City, Florida.

Gene was assigned to an aircrew and completed Transitional Training with them at Charleston, South Carolina. Additional training was taken at Westover Air Base in Massachusetts before they reported to Mitchell Field, New York in March, 1945, to fly a new B-24 bomber to Valley, Wales. Their route took them through Presque Isle, Maine; Goose Bay, Labrador and Meeks Field, Iceland. At Valley, Wales, their aircraft was left to be fitted with guns, bomb racks and additional armor and they proceed to the 466th Bomb Group at Attlebridge, England.

Gene flew the first of twelve combat missions on March 29, 1945, a bombing raid on Wilhelmshaven, Germany. On his second mission, to Brunswick, Germany, the target was covered by clouds and all aircraft were recalled from the mission. Gene went into the bomb bay and replaced safety pins in their bombs to render them safe before they landed back at their base. On his third mission flak knocked out his aircraft's number two and four engines. They managed to make it back across the English Channel by throwing out everything in the aircraft to lighten their load. The pilot was able to locate a fighter base to make an emergency landing. The runway however, was too short. On landing their aircraft ran off the end of the runway and crashed through a stone fence. The right landing gear folded. The pilot shut off the master switch on the magnetos to avoid the risk of fire from gasoline leaks.

On his fourth mission their bomb group saw Germany's jet fighter, the ME-262. A cannon shell fired at Gene's plane missed him in the turret but dug into the half deck behind the pilot and failed to explode. On his sixth mission Gene was credited with shooting down one and a half enemy fighters.

On May 6, 1945, with the end of the war in sight Gene's ground crew was taken on an aerial tour of Germany at tree top level to see bomb damage that had been inflicted by the Eighth Air Force. Gene left England for the United States by airplane. His route took him through Iceland and Labrador. The plane landed at Labrador with only fifteen minutes fuel remaining.

After discharge from military service Gene worked for AT&T for awhile before spending thirty-one years at Hormel Packing. He is active with the Eighth Air Force Historical Society and was an original founder of the Iowa Chapter. He is the Wing Commander of the Northwest portion of the state and organizes quarterly meetings for membership in that area.

Right - Gene's crew and their B-24 named "Earthquake McGoon" at 466th BG, Attlebridge, England. Gene, Flight Engineer/Gunner, is front row, left.

ARTHUR PETERSEN, MASON CITY, IA, worked at Montgomery Wards and attended college when he joined the army in February, 1942. He was sent to Aberdeen Proving Grounds for Basic Training and an Armaments School to learn ammunition, bombs, fuses, gases and weapons.

Art was assigned to the 305th Bomb Group which had been activated at Salt Lake City, Utah. He issued ammunition required for crews training at Spokane and Muroc Lake, California. He later attended a Bomb Reconnaissance School to study German bombs.

On September 5, 1942 Art boarded the ocean liner "Queen Mary" bound for England, and reported to the 305th at Grafton-Underwood. The Group was moved to Chelveston, England in December, 1942.

Part of Art's duties was loading loose ammunition in belt links including armor-piercing, tracers and incendiary .50 caliber ammunition shells. "The aircraft held ten or twelve 500-pound bombs in the bomb bays. We also loaded incendiary bombs to start fires and fragmentary bombs that would be dropped on enemy ground troops." Art maintained custody of bomb fuses until the bombs were assembled and loaded in aircraft bomb bay racks.

After the war ended in Europe Art was sent to St. Trond, Belgium with the 305th as part of American occupation forces. He returned to the United States in September, 1945 aboard the ship "Maraposa". Art received his discharge from military service October 4, 1945. He had been awarded, among other medals, the ETO Ribbon with six battle stars, two Distinguished Unit Citations, and World War II Victory Medal.

Art was in military service for thirty-seven months during which time he never received a furlough home. His parents never saw him as a soldier except while in uniform after he received his discharge.

LAVERN PETERS, BEDFORD, IA, was a dairy plant worker prior to World War II. After entry into the Army Air Corps he attended Waldorf College, Spartanburg, SC; Aerial Gunnery school at Tyndall Field, FL, and armor/gunnery school at Buckley Field, CO.

He was deployed to Hethel air Base near Norwich, England during December, 1944 as a waist gunner with the 389th Bomb Group. On arrival at Hethel and barracks assignment he learned eighteen previous occupants of the barracks were having their belongings removed. They were members of three aircrews lost on a prior mission.

Lavern flew twenty-four combat missions. A mission on April 7, 1945, was the first time his bomb group led an Eighth Air Force mission over Europe. This was also the day Hermann Goering, Germany's Luftwaffe commander instituted "ramstaffel", suicide missions against American bombers. Goering had recruited 300 pilots to ram 300 American bombers. The trade-off was supposed to be the loss of 300 pilots against 3000 American air crewmen and have a demoralizing effect on American policy of daylight strategic bombing. The pilots were instructed to begin firing at a bomber from long range and continue all the way to the point of ramming the aircraft. The pilot was supposed to bail out at the last moment, if possible. Several instances of ramming did occur, one of which killed Lavern's commanding officer. A German ME-109 pilot with a severely damaged plane crashed across the cockpit area of the lead bomber cutting off the nose of the aircraft causing it to crash into the wing of another bomber. Both bombers went down.

On March 24, 1945, Lavern's crew was one of approximately 350 crews assigned to a special mission in which ammunition, waist guns and oxygen were removed from bombers assigned to the mission. The bottoms of fuselages were lined with flak vests for protection against small arms fire. Instead of carrying bombs, the bomb bay area was filled with parachute packs to which were attached ammunition, medical supplies and weapons. Instead of the usual mission at 20,000 feet, the planes flew to their target at an altitude of 400 feet. They dropped supplies to airborne troops who had parachuted into the Rhine River area near the small town of Wesel and were preparing to cross the Rhine into Germany.

In route to the target Lavern recalled seeing C-47 cargo planes returning to England with cables attached. They had just released gliders containing the troops. He saw many of the gliders wrecked on the ground as a result of landing or enemy fire. Paratroopers were seen hanging in trees, shot before they could get free of their parachutes. On the run to the drop area it was discovered one parachute in their plane was on fire, hit by ground fire incendiary shells. Lavern and the other waist gunner entered the bomb bay area on the catwalk and were able to throw it from the aircraft. The low-level flight of the planes made them easy prey from German small arms and cannon fire. Fourteen B-24s were lost and 104 aircraft returned to base damaged. Two squadrons of planes had to make a second run through the gauntlet of enemy fire to make sure their cargo was dropped in the right area for the ground troops.

Memories from other missions include a variety of experiences Allied bomber crews encountered during their tour of duty in England during World War II. Lavern witnessed one of his closest friends get shot down on his fourth mission. He had his barracks strafed by an enemy fighter plane; listened to the sputter of a German buzz-bomb just before it exploded near his barracks and watched enormous V-2 rockets that had been launched from the Baltic Sea area against England. Flying through heavy barrages of anti-aircraft flak bursts was the most terrifying of his experiences. He also encountered some of the first German jets, watched German ships disperse prior to American bombing raids on submarine pens, and was attacked by German fighter aircraft while their bomb group was trying to land at their base.

Lavern received his discharge from military service on October 27, 1945. He had been awarded, among other medals, the Air Medal with three oak leaf clusters, ETO Ribbon with battle stars, World War II Victory Medal and Presidential Unit Citation. Lavern retired in 1998 after serving as a Postmaster for twenty-nine years.

ROBERT W. PETERS, GRINNELL, IA, was married just six weeks before Pearl Harbor. He was employed as a cost accountant, but enlisted in the Army Air Corps at Des Moines, Iowa, on September 4, 1942, and called to active duty in March, 1943.

Bob's training was spent entirely in Texas, taking Aviation Cadet training at San Antonio, Pre-flight at Ellington Field, Gunnery School at Harlingen and Navigation School at Hondo.

After assignment to an aircrew and completion of overseas training, Bob and his crew picked up a new B-24 bomber at Topeka, Kansas, in April, 1944, for deployment to England. Bob had been assigned as a navigator with the 445th Bomb Group at Tibenham. They named their aircraft "Heavenly Body". After arrival the airplane was taken from them and they were eventually assigned another airplane.

Bob flew thirty-five combat missions. His first mission, was a bomb raid on marshalling yards at St Lo, France, in support of the D-Day invasion. It was on this mission that ground winds shifted smoke marking the target and caused some bombs from most of the Bomb Groups to fall on friendly troops. He recalled that on D-Day, it was unbelievable, even at 20,000 feet, to see the English Channel filled with ships and boats from the invasion and support forces. The sky with filled with airplanes going to and from France on bombing and strafing missions. During the three months following the Normandy invasion, the 445th had the highest bombing accuracy rate in the Eighth Air Force.

A close call came on return from one mission. One engine had been damaged and was not working. Their left landing gear had been destroyed by flak. Only the right landing gear worked. The pilot attempted a one-legged landing with no brakes. It was decided the crew would open parachutes out the waist gunner's windows in a braking attempt. According to Bob, "The pilot brought the plane down beautifully on the right wheel holding it there. When the parachutes were opened the one on the left side inflated prematurely and caused us to make an immediate left turn off the runway. But we stopped and everyone was safe with no injuries."

Bob went on R&R to London with the Co-Pilot of his plane. As they exited a railroad station, a German buzz bomb exploded about three blocks from them. The Co-Pilot turned around, got back on a train and returned to their base never to go to London again.

In October, 1944, Bob returned to the United States aboard the *Queen Mary*.

With so many G.I.s aboard sleeping quarters were doubled. In space for two there were four. In cabin space for ten, twenty were assigned. He recalls singer/actor/dancer Fred Astaire was also aboard and spent almost every waking moment entertaining the troops on the way home.

Bob went on to make the Air Force a career. He flew 33 combat mission in the Korean War aboard a B-29 based at Okinawa of the 307th A-Bomb Unit. On a night mission over the Yalu River they were attacked by MIG jets. The MIGs flew so fast and at night they could not be seen or tracked by B-29 gunners. When he landed back at Seoul his B-29 had been shot up so badly it was deemed not repairable and was scrapped.

On October 23, 1951, twenty-three B-29s were lost on a mission over North Korea when MIGs, waiting above the clouds, pounced on the formation. Allegedly the American Press had published advance information of the raid and it was leaked to the North Koreans. Bob's crew, had been scheduled for the mission but was grounded in Japan when fuel tanks were discovered leaking and could not be immediately repaired.

Bob retired from the military in 1967. He had been awarded two Distinguished Flying Crosses and six Air Medals. He and his wife Mim had two sons and adopted two daughters. Mim discovered she was pregnant with their first son when Bob entered World War II. She thought she was pregnant again just before the Korean War. When Bob came home and told her he was going to Korea, she knew then another child had to be on the way.

JOSEPH R. PFIFFNER, WATERLOO, IA, was farming when he enlisted in the Army Air Corps in November, 1943. He was sent to Jefferson Barracks, St. Louis, Missouri for Basic Training and then Laredo, Texas for Aerial Gunnery School. Joe was then assigned to an air crew and trained with them at McGowan Field, Boise, Idaho in preparation for overseas deployment.

At the end of August, 1944, Joe boarded a ship at Massachusetts which became part of a convoy bound for Ireland. He eventually reached the 458th Bomb Group, Horsham St. Faiths, England. While there two A-26 light attack bombers buzzed his airbase after completing their required number of missions for rotation back to the United States. The planes hit a high wire and crashed killing all aboard.

Joe flew twenty-eight missions as an Aerial Gunner. He began his tour hauling gasoline in wing tanks to forward bases in support of General Patton's tank forces. The mission required only one waist gunner. Joe and the other gunner drew cards with the high man going on the mission. Joe drew an eight and the other gunner drew a king. The aircraft they were to fly in crashed on takeoff killing the entire crew.

Joe's first mission was on October 26, 1944, a bombing raid on a target at Perleburg, Germany. Due to weather conditions their Group flew to Belgium before "forming up". A weather front had moved in and they were required to fly in fog. The wings on Joe's aircraft "iced up" and the airplane went into a dive. The pilot ordered the crew to bail out. Joe bailed out but hadn't tightened the harness around himself. When the chute opened he learned his mistake as it "nearly tore me apart". Floating toward earth he notice a big town below. He attempted to drift away from the town but his parachute canopy nearly collapsed. He landed in a pasture with other crewmembers and saw civilians rushing toward them with pitchforks. Fortunately American GIs arrived to prevent any mistaken identity that they were Germans. Joe and his crew were flown back to their base in England.

Joe's missions included those to Berlin with its heavy concentration of anti-aircraft batteries. He and his crew were never seriously hit by flak or enemy fighters. He did see, however many American planes fall. "Their flak guns followed every plane, like they were shooting at the plane's contrails", knowing the next formation would have to fly right into it.

Following the end of the war in Europe Joe and his crew ferried an airplane back to the United States. He volunteered to be a B-29 gunnery instructor and was transferred to Santa Ana, California. This required further training on his part at Laredo, Texas. The Japanese surrender precluded further service and Joe was discharged from the military in October, 1945. He had been awarded, among other medals, the Air Medal with oak leaf clusters, ETO Ribbon and the World War II Victory Medal.

Joe returned to Iowa and worked in construction building cement mixers until he started his own electrical business which he operated for thirty-five years until retirement. In his spare time he built his own airplane which he flew for twenty years.

Bottom Left - Joe at his waist gunner position

Right - Joe and his crew at 458th BG, Horsham St Faith, England. Joe, Aerial Gunner, is front row, center.

ROY PICHT, AMES, IA, had civilian employment as a PX helper and deliveryman at Fitzsimmons Military Hospital in Denver, CO; attended a Government School on Aircraft Engine Maintenance and was a hydraulic mechanic at Lowry Field, CO.

Roy entered military service on June 16, 1943, at Denver. He served at bases in Utah, Idaho and Nevada before he was deployed overseas on New Year's Day, 1944. Roy was based at Horsham St. Faith, England, with the 458th Bomb Group as an assistant crew chief and was later promoted to crew chief.

Roy and his crew were responsible for ensuring aircraft assigned to them were in perfect mechanical condition and ready for missions. This often required changing engines overnight and scavenging parts from irreparable aircraft to meet mission demands., One particular memory was witnessing a B-24 with all four engines out make a successful "dead stick" landing from six thousand feet, a spectacular feat in view of the weight of the aircraft.

Roy was awarded six bronze campaign stars to his European Theater of Operations Medal. After he returned to the United States, he served at Sioux Falls, South Dakota, Randolph Field, San Antonio, Texas, and at Carlsbad, New Mexico.

Roy was discharged from the military at San Antonio on October 19, 1945.

JAMES PIERCE, GRINNELL, IA, was employed at Maytag Company, Newton, Iowa, when he enlisted in military service August 24, 1943 at Camp Dodge, Iowa.

James was sent to Aerial Gunnery School at Las Vegas, Nevada; Aerial Gunnery School, Ardmore, Oklahoma, and Airplane and Engine Mechanic School at Amarillo, Texas.

While at Ardmore he was scheduled to practice parachuting from an airplane. Another student quipped "why practice, its got to be right the first time".

James was assigned to an aircrew as a ball turret gunner with the 303rd Bomb Group. He and his crew flew to their base at Molesworth, England May 27, 1944. He flew eleven combat missions. When he returned from his first mission seventy-two holes were found in his airplane named "Paper Doll". No one in the crew suffered any wounds or injuries. His eleventh mission was a bomb raid on Leipzig, Germany. Their airplane unknowingly to them, had been shorted 500 gallons of fuel in preparation for the mission. Over the English Channel the pilot realized they were not going to make it back to their base but managed to bring the aircraft over land as fuel ran out. He gave the order for the crew to bail out. James was the third crewmember out the escape hatch. At that time the airplane was down to about 3,000 feet. He remembered thinking of everything in his lifetime on the way down until he landed in a wheat field. Other were not so fortunate. One crewmember opened his parachute too soon. It caught on the airplane and he was dragged down with it. The pilot stayed too long with the airplane, failed to jump, and died in the crash. He was deemed a hero in guiding his plane back over land for the crew to bail out rather than over water.

After eleven missions the war was over and James was fortunate to be sent home on a military airplane with eight other crewmen and a cargo of mail. Among other medals, James was awarded the Air Medal, European Theater of Operations and World War II Victory Medal. He was discharged from the military March 14, 1946, at Ft Leavenworth, Kansas. His primary occupation after the war was as a meat cutter and store meat department manager.

GEORGE POPELKA, CEDAR RAPIDS, IA, had attended Iowa State College, was married and had worked in a plant making machine gun mounts before he enlisted in the Army Air Corps in 1943. He was sent to Jefferson Barracks, St. Louis, Missouri, for Basic Training. He enrolled in the Aviation Cadet Program and attended Iowa Wesleyan College at Mt. Pleasant, Iowa, as

part of the College Detachment Training Program before further flight training. He elected to become a bombardier and was sent to Deming, New Mexico, for navigation/bombardier training and Aerial Gunnery School at Kingman, Arizona.

George was assigned to an air crew and trained with them at Pyote, Texas before they picked up a new B-17 bomber at Kearney, Nebraska, and headed overseas. They flew through Gander, Newfoundland, to Prestwick, Scotland, then boarded a train for the last leg of their trip to the 390th Bomb Group at Framlingham, England.

George flew the first of his thirty-five combat missions June 29, 1944. Most memorable of his missions included a shuttle to Poltava, Russia. They were scheduled to bomb a target in Poland then fly on to Poltava where they would be refueled and re-armed. They would return to England the next day and bomb another target in route. Their aircraft was hit by flak over Poland which disabled their aircraft to the extent they couldn't maintain speed and altitude with the rest of their Group. Unable to make it to Poltava they landed at the nearest Russian airfield. Their aircraft was deemed not repairable and they were flown by the Russians to Egypt. After stops in Libya and Casablanca, Americans flew them back to England.

During a mission to Aachan, Germany, flak knocked out two engines of George's aircraft. Unable to maintain altitude the crew bailed out over American held territory except for the Pilot and Co-pilot who went down with the airplane and were killed. One other crewmember, too frozen with fear to pull the rip cord, fell to earth without opening his parachute.

A mission on July 14, 1944, was a low-level flight to drop supplies, weapons and ammunition to the French Underground. George recalled they flew so low they were skimming tree tops. In his crew was another Iowan, Ray Carter, of Hedrick, Iowa.

George flew his thirty-fifth mission on October 30, 1944. He returned to the United States aboard a troop ship and became an instructor at a bombardier school at Carlsbad, New Mexico, testing Chinese aviators.

After war's end George remained in the Air Force Reserve in Cedar Rapids, until he retired with twenty-two years service. He had been awarded the Distinguished Flying Cross, Air Medal with six oak leaf clusters and the ETO Medal with battle stars. George retired as an industrial engineer with Collins Radio and other Cedar Rapids firms.

Right - George and his crew at 490th BG, Framlingham, England. George, Bombardier, is front row, right. Fellow Iowan Aerial Gunner Ray Carter, Hedrick, is back row, left.

LES PORTWOOD, BOONE, IA, graduated from high school in May, 1942. He was drafted into the Army Air Corps in March, 1943 and sent to Provo, Utah for Basic Training. He then attended Medics School at Springfield, Missouri; Flight Surgeons School at Louisville, Kentucky and additional training in those specialties at Fort Wayne, Indiana.

After completion

of training Les was sent to the East Coast where he boarded the "Anthon Castle" ocean liner as part of a 454 ship convoy bound for Glasgow, Scotland. In route a soldier on his ship opened a port hole at night esposing light from the interior of the ship. Les recalled the soldier was court-martialed and the ship was pulled from the convoy to make it to Scotland on its own.

Les was assigned to the 21st Air Depot Group at the Fourth Strategic Air Depot near a small village twelve miles from Ipswich, England. The Depot served several American air bases for engine overhaul, major structural repairs, parts, and new engines. The base also served as an emergency landing strip for Allied aircraft returning to England in event of bad weather or too crippled to make it to their own base.

Les worked in the dental clinic of the base hospital and responded to all emergencies in and around the base with other medical personnel. This included the recovery of bodies from crash sites and wounded aboard returning aircraft. Emergency first aid was provided for wounded before they could be transported to a major medical facility.

After Victory in Europe Les returned to the United States in August, 1945 aboard a Victory ship. The day his ship docked in New York harbor the war with Japan ended. A band playing "Sentimental Journey" was on hand to greet them.

Les reported to temporary duty assignments at Macon, Georgia and Jacksonville, Florida before returning to Rantoul, Illinois for discharge from military service. He attended a business college in Minnesota under the GI Bill of Rights and eventually became Investment Manager and Assistant Treasurer at Iowa State University.

STANLEY POTTER, MARION, IA, had graduated from high school and worked for his father in a small business before World War II. In February, 1943, he enlisted in the Army Air Corps and was sent to Jefferson Barracks, St. Louis, Missouri for Basic Training.

Stanley was accepted in the Aviation Cadet Program and sent to college at Hastings, Nebraska to take courses as part of the College Training Detachment Program. He took a series of tests at Santa Ana, California to determine his best qualifications. Although he wanted to become a fighter pilot a good friend talked him into becoming a bombardier. He was accepted and attended Bombardier's School at Deming, New Mexico, followed by Aerial Gunnery School at Kingman, Arizona.

Assigned to an air crew at Rattlesnake Air Base, Pyote, Texas, Stan and his crew trained together prior to overseas deployment. In early 1944 they flew a northern route from Bangor, Maine to Ireland. Their aircraft was loaded with candy, cigarettes and nylon stockings in the bomb bay area. On arrival in Ireland the Commanding Officer of the base ordered them to unload and leave their "extra cargo".

Stan was assigned to the 385th Bomb Group at Great Ashfield, England, and flew thirty-five combat missions as bombardier. It took three missions to realize he was really in a war. When his aircraft was jumped by German fighters he realized the enemy also had guns. "I grew up in a hurry." Stan received credit for one enemy fighter shot down. "It was a common trick for German fighters to hit a switch discharging oil over a hot pan causing smoke to make it appear they were on fire and going down."

Stan's Group bombed German ground forces at St. Lo, France, after D-Day. Smoke marking their target was shifted by winds. This caused some bombs to drop on Allied forces. The next day Stan's crew and five other crews volunteered for a low-level mission to bomb an important bridge in a valley to prevent German reinforcements from reaching the front. As they approached the target area they popped over a large hill into the valley. The bridge came upon them too quickly to release their bombs. They saw German armor and troops massed near the bridge. Too tempting a target to pass up the six planes made a twenty mile turn to try and deceive the enemy into thinking they were leaving. A second bomb run was made with their gunners strafing the ground. The bombs were released on target in the middle of the German armor. "We could see the Germans firing at us with 88s, rifles, machine guns and pistols. We bombed the living hell out of them, did a helluva job. I've never seen such explosions and destruction. Tanks were flying through the air." A photo recon mission to photograph the destruction confirmed what Stan and the other crews saw. In leading the flight of bombers back to destroy the tanks Stan was awarded the Distinguished Flying Cross.

His most scariest moments were before and after a mission. "If you weren't scared, something is wrong with you, but there is always some character to keep things lightened up – we were just like brothers".

While on a mission to Brux, Czechoslovakia, to bomb an experimental testing station site, Stan's formation was joined by a B-17 bomber not of his Group. The crew aboard the bomber attempted to convince the formation to change their direction heading. Suspicions were aroused about the identity of the bomber and it was shot down. It was a bomber captured by the Germans to infiltrate American bomber formations, create havoc and even shoot down other American planes. "The pilot spoke perfect English."

Stan flew in a B-17 named "Perry's Pirates' for most of his missions. During a mission on November ll, 1944, shrapnel from a flak burst came up his pant leg and hit him in the groin. Stan pulled out the jagged piece of metal himself, got temporary medical attention and was able to finish the mission.

Stan completed his required thirty-five missions and was home by Christmas, 1944. After recuperating from his wounds at Ft General Wright near Spokane he was assigned to Pilot Training in Texas. While there World War II ended with Japan's surrender. Stan was discharged from military service at Jefferson Barracks on September 29, 1945. He had received the Purple Heart, Distinguished Flying Cross, Air Medal with six oak leaf clusters, ETO ribbon, World War II Victory Medal and a Distinguished Unit Citation.

After the war Stan helped start West Side Transport and subsequently retired from the company while its General Manager.

Right - Stan and his crew at 385th BG, Great Ashfield, England. Stan, Bombardier, is back row, right.

ROBERT PREIS, WEST BURLINGTON, IA, enlisted in the Army Air Corps in December, 1942. After Basic Training at Jefferson Barracks, St. Louis, Missouri, he attended College Training Detachment at Michigan State University. He then entered the Aviation Cadet Program at San Antonio, Texas. Robert received his wings and commission as a second lieutenant at Frederick, Texas.

After being assigned an air crew, overseas training was taken at Walla Walla, Washington, in preparation for deployment to the European Theater of Operations. After training the crew was sent to the East Coast where they boarded the "Aquatania" for a voyage of five days to England. Robert was assigned to the 493rd Bomb Group at Debach, the last operational Group formed in the Eighth Air Force. The Group had recently switched from the B-24 bomber to the B-17. Trained in the B-24 Robert had to take an additional eight hours transition training in the B-17.

His first combat mission was on December 14, 1944, a raid on Hanover, Germany. On his seventh mission, January 14, 1945, flying a B-17 named "Pair of Dice Kids", their target was Derben, just outside Berlin. "On the way to the mission we had a run away prop and had to feather it so that caused us to drop out of formation and be susceptible to the fighters in the area. We dropped our bombs and tried to get back to Debach, That was impossible because of the loss of power and the lack of gas that was lost. We decided to head for Finland. As we were heading North we were hit by flak from anti-aircraft batteries over Rostov, Germany, and lost another engine. They shot the hell out of us. We wound up over Sweden. A Swedish fighter plane flew alongside and motioned us to follow him. We were to land at an airstrip at Malmo at the southern tip of Sweden. We had one shot to land as we lost another engine on the final approach and couldn't go around and try to land again. We landed without incident on a grass field. We had 168 flak holes in our aircraft. We were later told that if you fly across any part of Sweden you must land or be shot down."

"A Major in the Swedish Army entered the plane and recited the Rules of the Geneva Convention on Neutral Countries and told us we would be interned. We had to hand over our handguns ending our participation in the war. They billeted us in a retirement home." They were not confined as prisoners but were free to do most anything. That included skiing, going to dances, swimming at the beach, but not escape. To do so and be re-captured meant internment in a prison.

When the war ended in Europe Robert assisted in repair of aircraft interned in Sweden and flying them back to England. He made eight trips.

Robert returned to the United States in a Liberty Ship that took fourteen days to sail across the Atlantic. Once stateside he volunteered to join an A-26 Group but the war ended precluding further military service at that time. Robert returned to Iowa and attended the University of Iowa. Following graduation he entered the insurance business. Robert stayed in the Air Force Reserves until retirement on September 25, 1983.

Right - Robert and his crew of 493rd BG, Debach, England, while interned in Sweden for duration of war after crash landing in the neutral country. Robert is front row, third from left.

FRANCIS PRENDERGAST, CALLENDAR, IA, was farming prior to America's entry into World War II. After the Japanese attacked Pearl Harbor on December 7, 1941, he wanted to enlist in the Army Air Corps. In order to qualify for pilot training he took night classes in trigonometry and physics in Ft. Dodge, Iowa, before enlisting in June, 1942.

Accepted for the Aviation Cadet Program at San Antonio, Texas, Francis began Primary pilot training at Fort Stockton, Texas, and then opted for Navigation School at San Marcus, Texas. Upon graduation in December, 1943, Francis received his wings and commission as a Second Lieutenant. He was assigned to a B-17 air crew at Kearney, Nebraska, and began training for overseas deployment.

In March, 1944, Francis and his crew arrived in England and were assigned to the 447th Bomb Group at Rattlesden. His first of thirty-four missions came on May 13, 1944, when his Group was assigned to bomb aircraft repair facilities north of Berlin, Germany. "Flak" from German anti-aircraft batteries was intense. In addition, German fighter aircraft attacked the bombing formation and Francis was able to shoot down a Focke-Wulf 190. "He dove close to our plane, within 150 feet. I pulled the trigger on my machine gun and hit him across the fuselage. I could see the pilot and saw him flinch like he got hit. He went down and I didn't see him parachute out."

Francis flew two missions on D-Day, June 6, 1944, in support of the Allied invasion. It was a memorable day not only from the invasion standpoint, but returning from the second mission of the day his aircraft ran off the end of the runway at their base and struck another bomber fully loaded with gasoline and bombs. They didn't explode.

His missions also included four raids on Berlin and a mission when two engines of his aircraft was destroyed by flak. One of the engines was ripped from the airplane. Despite the damage they were able to return to their base in England safely.

Francis completed his last mission in September, 1944, and was sent back to the United States where he attended a flight instructors school at Selma Air Base in Louisiana. He was then assigned to San Marcus, Texas, as a navigation instructor until the end of World War II. He was then transferred to the Air Transport Command in Bermuda as a navigator on a C-54 and also on B-17s equipped for air-sea rescue. In October, 1948, Francis was placed on inactive reserve and separated from military service. He returned to Iowa and attended Iowa State University under the GI Bill of Rights and resumed farming. He subsequently joined the Iowa Air National Guard until retirement in June, 1964, at the rank of Lieutenant Colonel. During his military service he had been awarded, among other medals, the Distinguished Flying Cross and three Air Medals.

Francis established and currently operates a farm service and realty company in Ft. Dodge in addition to farming almost three thousand acres.

RAYMOND PRITCHARD, DES MOINES, IA, worked for Standard Oil Company in Des Moines when he was drafted into the Army Air Corps in October, 1941. He completed Basic Training at Sheppard Field, Texas, before he was assigned to Aircraft Mechanics School with Boeing Aircraft Company in Seattle Washington.

After schooling Ray performed line maintenance duty for aircrews in training at Tampa, Florida and Walla Walla, Washington. He volunteered for flight service and was sent to Wendover, Utah for Aerial Gunnery School. Ray was assigned to an aircrew and completed phases of overseas training at Blythe, California; Pyote, Texas and Dyersburg, Tennessee. He and his crew then picked up a new aircraft at Savannah, Georgia and flew to Valley, Wales through Goose Bay, Labrador and Iceland. Ray was assigned to the 384th Bomb Group at Grafton Underwood, England.

Ray flew nine combat missions. The most memorable of which was his last mission, on April 25, 1945, a bombing raid on the Skoda Armament Works at Pilsen, Czechoslovakia. "We had to make three bomb runs on the target before it could be seen visually. The flak was murderous. When we got back our tail gunner had a large hole in the tail section right behind his position. We found him lying on his back laughing and looking up where the flak had come through the plane and missed him."

After V-E Day (Victory in Europe) Ray was sent to Istres, France, where his Bomb Group began moving American troops to staging areas for return to the United States. Ray left France in early December, 1945 and returned to England where he boarded the German ocean liner "Europa" to sail back to America

Ray received his discharge from militaray service on December 24, 1945 at Camp Grant, Illinois. He had been awarded the Air Medal, European Theater of Operations and World War II Victory Medals.

Ray retired from the U. S. Postal Service in 1974.

Chapter Twenty-Two

ELMER PRUSHA, TAMA, IA, went to Des Moines, Iowa to enlist in the Marines in 1942. He was told enlistments were closed and other services were also full at the time except for one opening in the Army Air Corps. He believed the Air Corps required either some college credits or at least two years of study before a person would be accepted for pilot training. The recruiter told him that requirement had been waived and he could enlist but wouldn't be called to active duty right away.

Elmer entered military service in 1942 and was sent to College Detachment Training at Kearney State College, Kearney, Nebraska. He then attended Bombardier, Navigation, Geography, and Gunnery schools. He always finished first or near the top in each class.

After assignment to an aircrew and completion of overseas training Elmer was deployed to England through Goose Bay, Labrador to Nutts Corner, Ireland. He eventually reached his assigned base at Molesworth, England, with the 303rd Bomb Group. Elmer flew thirty-two combat missions, the last sixteen as Lead Bombardier for the entire bomb group. "I would take 90-100 planes to the target. The other planes would drop their bombs when mine were released. If I missed the target, so did they."

On August 5, 1944 during a mission to Liege, Belgium, cloud cover prevented release of their bombs on target. The entire formation circled to make a second bomb run. On the second run another formation also closing on the target "screwed up" calibrations on Elmer's bomb sight and required the formation to circle again and make a third run on the target. This time through a break in the clouds and at the right moment Elmer was able to sight the target and release his bombs. The objective was destroyed. Elmer received the Distinguished Flying Cross for his actions on this mission.

He recalled that he was never afraid before any mission until his twenty-fifth. "I just figured I'd never make it. When I had twenty-five missions in I thought I made it this far, maybe I'm going to make it after all. I liked all the missions I flew-when you're young and not afraid you give everything up."

During a sightseeing pass to London with a crewmate, Elmer stood at his hotel window watching a buzz bomb fall on the city. His friend dove underneath a bed and yelled at Elmer to get away from the window in case the explosion burst the glass. Elmer calmly replied "I can't see it if I'm not at the window". According to Elmer, once the buzz bomb ran out of fuel, it was about four seconds until it hit the ground and exploded. While in London, Elmer was also approached by a Piccadilly Commando (lady of the evening). His reply "We came over here to save your ass, not buy your ass" to which she said "S.O.B. Yanks".

Elmer ended his military career with the Distinguished Flying Cross and Air Medal with four clusters. After the war he assisted his father in a newly established garage for vehicle sales and auto repairs.

KENNETH RANSON, CEDAR RAPIDS, IA, worked on the assembly line at Lockheed Aircraft building belly tanks when he learned of the Japanese sneak attack on American bases in the Hawaiian Islands on December 7, 1941. Ken enlisted into military service on that date and was sent to a crew chief technical school at Wichita Falls, Texas. At that time he admits "I didn't know the tail of an airplane from an engine." After a year at the school he was reassigned to attend a technical school back at Lockheed After graduation Ken was sent to Hamilton Field, CA.

From there he boarded a train headed for Payne Field at Everett, Washington, with orders that would send him to the Aleutian Islands. In route the train was stopped and Ken was ordered to return to California on another train. This train was also stopped, this time near a San Francisco air base where he and others reported to the base flight line to pre-flight a squadron of P-38s ordered to fly a practice alert and search for submarines in the San Francisco area.

Ken was eventually sent to New York by train where he boarded the "Queen Elizabeth" for Glasgow, Scotland. The ship sailed south for six hundred miles "to get rid of a sub" before it continued on its voyage.

Ken was assigned as a crew chief with the 20th Fighter Group at Kings Cliffe, England. Initially a P-38 Group, the Group switched to the P-51 Mustang in 1944. During his tour of duty Ken was assigned to the aircraft of four different pilots. All finished their tour of duty without casualty. His last pilot received half credit for an enemy fighter shot down flying "Ran's and Reich's Wreck", named after Ken and the pilot.

Without prior experience or weapon knowledge Ken flew three missions as a B-17 tail gunner with a bomb group located near his base. During one mission he saw the P-51 he maintained flying as escort with the bombers.

As a crew chief Ken's usual day started at 4:00 A.M. with a pre-flight of his assigned aircraft. Maintenance included monitor of oil and hydraulic fluid levels, spark plugs, tires, brakes, and check of struts and ailerons. During the last year of the war Ken and another mechanic lived in a tent near their aircraft. Sabotage had become a problem in the hard stand area. It diminished after Ken fired shots at shadows lurking near an airplane.

After the war ended in Europe Ken was sent to a Paris air base where he assisted in staging loaded bombers destined for Berlin, Germany, during initial stages of the Berlin airlift.

On September 19, 1945, Ken boarded the "Queen Elizabeth" for America and discharge from military service. When he returned to civilian life Ken worked for several firms before permanent employment with FMC-Link Belt from which he retired.

JEAN RAY, COLFAX, IA, was drafted into military service August 25, 1942, and sent to Fort Leavenworth, Kansas. While at Leavenworth "we were given IQ tests to determine what branch of the Army we were best fitted. As it turned out I passed high enough to go into the Army Air Force however when asked by a sergeant in charge which branch I would like, I stated that I would like to get into an armored outfit. Good, he says, we'll put you in the air force. So there I was."

"After receiving my uniform, which fit like a potato sack I was transferred with many other recruits to Sheppard Field, Texas, to receive my basic training." Jean would later attend Radio School at Sioux Falls, South Dakota, be assigned to an aircrew and deployed to the 100th Bomb Group at Thorpe Abbotts, England.

While on a mission over Germany in September, 1943, another B-17 bomber in his formation struck the tail section of Jean's aircraft. Jean parachuted from his stricken aircraft. On landing behind enemy lines he was taken prisoner of war and interned at Stalag Luft XVIIB, at Krems, Austria.

On April 8, 1944, after nineteen months captivity the German military evacuated the prisoner of war camp to flee the advance of the Russian Army. Carrying their meager possessions and with little or no food the POWs were forced to walk West toward American lines. On April 26 the column of prisoners, after living off the land, bartering with Austrian civilians for food and sleeping in whatever shelter could be found or made, they arrived at a forest. Weak from years of living on a starvation diet and little or no exercise, the forest was to be the final destination for the exhausted POWs. Shelters were made of logs and pine boughs to protect them from constant rain and occasional snow. On May 2, American soldiers arrived at their camp and disarmed the POW's German guards.

A diary maintained by Jean during the forced march describing conditions under which the POWs existed has been transcribed and included in the "Forced Marches" portion of the POW chapter.

Right - Jean's crew, 100th Bomb Group, Thorpe Abbotts, England, Jean, Radio Operator, is back row, second from left.

AL RAZOR, COLLINS, IA, lived in Des Moines prior to America's entry into World War II. Along with his father and brothers, Al helped in the construction of a dam and bridge at Blackstone, Virginia, an Army base at Terre Haute, Indiana, and a naval base at Ogden, Utah. When he returned to Des Moines he was drafted into the Army in February, 1943.

After Basic Training at Miami Beach, Florida, Al was assigned to the 2457th Quartermaster Truck Company that began overseas deployment on July 25, 1943. Al and 22,000 other United States troops boarded the "Queen Mary" and left New York for Scotland. Al was assigned to a ship's cabin with eighteen other men. There were three sets of bunks stacked three high. Each night nine men would sleep in the cabin and nine would sleep on the deck of the ship. Their roles were reversed the next night.

Al's Company was attached to the Eighth Air Force and based at Wattisham, England. The base was formerly home to the 68th Observation Group and then the 479th Fighter Group. The base was utilized as a supply distribution point and Al, as a truck driver, delivered bombs and other supplies to 8th Air Force bases all over East Anglia.

On one occasion Al's truck was loaded with P-47 drop tanks. His orders only read "To Whom it may Concern". At that stage of the war in Europe drop tanks had not been used and Al felt no one knew what the drop tanks were. He spent three days and nights on the road trying to deliver the tanks to bases before it was determined where they were supposed to be delivered. By that time he had driven all the way to Wales.

On October 1, 1944, Al and several others from his Company were transferred to a new Quartermaster Truck Company being formed in Western England. They traveled by Army truck to their new base and decided to make a rest stop at a small English village. Al and a friend thought this was a good opportunity to get a haircut. While they were gone, the truck and rest of the transferred personnel drove on to their destination without realizing Al and his friend were missing. Al and his friend found separate lodging for the night with plans to meet the next morning at a specified place and time when they would try and find transportation to their new base. When Al's friend didn't show the next day Al boarded a train for his new base. He reported in to his new Company Commander who made no mention of Al being late. Al's friend, subsequently reported in to the Company Commander while in a highly intoxicated condition. It just so happened the Base Commander was in the office at the same time. Al's friend naturally wound up in the stockade for a week.

Al's Company was transferred to France and assigned to the Ninth Air Force. When the German ground offensive broke out in December, 1944, in what would become the Battle of the Bulge, Al was transferred to the Infantry. He was sent to England for weapons refresher training. "Eisenhower had signed an order that any soldier thirty-one years or older would be exempt from transfer to the infantry. When I had originally applied to become a pilot I was told I was too old. When I wanted to be an aerial gunner I was told I was too old. When they transferred me to the infantry I was three days over thirty-one, too old, so I went back to France and the truck company."

Al returned to the United States aboard a Liberty Ship and received his discharge from military service March 18, 1946. He is retired from a career of contract construction.

DARRELL REED, CHEROKEE, IA, worked part-time at a local movie theater while in high school. After graduation in 1943 he was drafted into the Army Air Corps and reported to Camp Dodge near Des Moines, IA, for induction.

Darrell was sent to Buckley Field, Denver, CO for Basic Training and then attended the University of Denver for a short time under the College Detachment Program for pilots, co-pilots and navigators. In December, 1943, he attended Radio Operator's School at Sioux Falls, South Dakota, and then Aerial Gunnery School at Yuma Army Air Base, Arizona. Darrell was assigned to an aircrew and completed combat crew training at Boise, Idaho and Topeka, Kansas. Darrell and his crew then reported to Camp Miles Standish, Massachusetts, where, on December 9, 1944, they boarded the "USS Mt Vernon" for England. He arrived at the 445th Bomb Group at Tibenham, England, where they would fly the B-24 into combat on December 20, Darrell's first wedding anniversary.

He arrived at Tibenham at a time when German fighter activity against bomber formations was dwindling however German defenses still fired devastating flak barrages. Just three months prior, on September 27, the 445th had lost 30 B-24s on a single mission (300 men). Darrell flew twenty-two missions as a radio operator/gunner on two different B-24s named "Olde King Cole" and "Q Queeny". The Group claimed the highest above average bombing accuracy of any group in the Second Bombardment Division in the last six months of the war.

Chapter Twenty-Two

Darrell's sixteenth mission, on March 24, 1945, was to Wessel, Germany in support of an Allied crossing of the Rhine River. All other missions had been flown at altitudes in excess of 20,000 however this mission was to be totally different. At briefing on March 23, aircrews were told they would be flying a low-level supply mission in support of U.S. troops as they crossed the last natural defensive barrier for Germany in the west-the Rhine River. The balance of the day was spent at his aircraft, which was stripped of all its extra weight and loaded with supplies that had been stacked next to the airplane. This included ammo, mortars, food, medical supplies, gasoline, telephone wire and countless other items. Large bags were hung on the shackles in the bomb bar area. The ball turret was removed and netting stretched across the opening as well as across the rear escape hatch. Smaller supplies were set directly on these nets. The pilot told his crew Command had said "We're asking for volunteers for an extremely dangerous mission. Heavy casualties are expected. It is absolutely vital that this mission be successful."

As he waited to take-off the next morning Darrell noticed the sky full of C-47 transport airplanes loaded with paratroopers. Others were pulling gliders. After take-off Darrell's aircraft reached its prescribed altitude over the White Cliffs of Dover and began a slow descent. By the time they neared the target area they had descended to 150 feet. Darrell could clearly see the destruction of war, dead animals and men, towns on fire, and burned fields.

A pontoon bridge had been built across the Rhine over which men and equipment crossed. As Darrell's aircraft came to a clearing where they were supposed to drop their supplies, the pilot slowed the plane to almost a stall. At the sound of an alarm bell, the crews cut the nets over the ball turret opening and escape hatch and the supplies dropped from the plane. Darrell's position was between the rear bomb bay and the ball turret opening. As the cords were cut, he lost his balance and plunged toward the ball turret opening. An Associated Press reporter flying in the plane that day quickly lunged forward, grabbed Darrell';s parachute harness and pulled him to safety saving his life. An air crewman from another B-24 was seen falling out of his airplane. Darrell stated the body almost bounced up to their altitude.

After the drop Darrell's pilot dropped down to an altitude of fifty feet to avoid ground fire. German soldiers shot at their airplane from rooftops, sometimes shooting down at them. A B-24 on their right was hit and crashed. Darrell's airplane was so low the pilot couldn't bank for fear of catching a wing. The deputy group commanding officer was flying ahead of Darrell's airplane. It either caught a wing on something or was hit by ground fire but smashed into the ground and erupted into a huge ball of fire. Wreckage was strewn for a half mile. There were no survivors. The Commanding Officer had finished his tour of duty and had been scheduled to leave for the United States. He purposely stayed behind to fly this mission.

After the supply drop Darrell's pilot scrambled for altitude. Before getting there he dodged church steeples, factory smokestacks, and tall trees. On the way home and out of harms way, Darrell was able to breathe a sign of relief, his sixteenth mission was almost his last.

Darrell received his military discharge at Sioux City, Iowa, in November, 1945. He had been awarded, among other medals, the Air Medal with three clusters, WWII Victory Medal and ETO Medal among others.

After the war Darrell was employed for many years at the Cherokee Creamery and worked part-time as projectionist at the local movie theater. He also worked part-time at the Cherokee Community Center.

Right - Darrell and crew at Boise, Idaho, training for overseas deployment. Darrell is front row, second from left.

ROBERT C. REEVES, WATERLOO, IA, was born and raised in Des Moines, IA. He graduated from East High School in June, 1941 and then attended Iowa State College, Ames, IA, as a student in Mechanical Engineering. Bob was inducted into military service September 13, 1943. He was assigned to barrack number 13, bed number 13, served 13 days on K.P. (kitchen police), and was discharged from service on March 13, 1946. He considers himself extremely lucky and is not at all superstitious about the number 13.

After flight and gunnery training Bob was assigned to crew number 9077 and shipped overseas to Bassingbourn, England home of the 322nd Bomb Squadron, 91st Bomb Group.

Bob recalls returning from one mission with 158 flak holes in his airplane. A mission on March 8, 1945, was to bomb the synthetic rubber factory at Halle, Germany. On the bomb run the bomb racks malfunctioned and the plane load of Composition B bombs were brought back to their base. After they had been armed, the bombs would detonate after a free fall of only four feet. "We hoped we wouldn't hit an air pocket. We were unsuccessful in dropping our bombs over the target, and therefore could not keep up with the rest of our formation on the way back. We fell back, but were lucky to have fighter escort back to the coast. We tried again to drop our bombs over the English Channel but couldn't."

"We landed at Bassingbourn with the full load of bombs and "greased it on", but as we turned off the runway one of our main tires blew out. We thought the bombs would blow next. You should have seen us get out of that plane and run for our lives." After another mission 158 flak holes were counted in their aircraft.

Bob and his wife Lorraine were married April 1, 1951 in Fargo, ND. They have a daughter Hallie, a son Lincoln, and two grand-daughters.

Bob and Lorraine both received their bachelor degrees in music from Sherwood Music School, Chicago, IL. Bob received his Master of Music degree from the University of Northern Iowa in 1963. Both are now retired after teaching music for 35 years. They own and operate four Cessna airplanes. Bob is a commercial pilot, checked out in 14 different airplanes and has over 2,000 hours of "pilot in command" time. He flies his personal airplane once a week all year round as he has done for the past twenty-five years. Their son is an ATP pilot with U.S. Airways, flying the F-1- out of Charlotte, NC. Both of Bob and Lorraine's children have degrees in music. Hallie is a performing violinist and teacher in Houston, TX.

Bob has served the Iowa Chapter of the 8th AFHS as Northwest Iowa Wing Commander for several years.

Iowans of the Mighty Eighth

Right - Bob and his crew, 91st BG, Bassingbourn, England. Bob, tail gunner, is back row, right

HERBERT REIS, EARLY, IA, worked as a farm hand until he had saved enough money to attend an Engine Mechanics course at the National School of Aeronautics in Kansas City, Missouri.

After completing the four-month course he gained employment with Continental Motors in Detroit, Michigan, testing aircraft engines. While in Detroit the Japanese attacked American military bases in the Hawaiian Islands on December 7, 1941, thrusting the United States into World War II.

Herb enlisted in the Army Air Corps in October, 1942 and was sent to Miami Beach, Florida for Basic Training. He then attended Xavier University at Cincinnati, Ohio, until sent to Nashville, Tennessee, a classification center. Herb was assigned to Navigation School at Monroe, Louisiana and Aerial Gunnery School at Ft. Myers, Florida. He returned to Monroe for Advanced Navigation School and on graduation in May, 1944 was awarded his wings and commission as a Second Lieutenant.'

After assignment to an aircrew at Lincoln, Nebraska, Herb trained with the crew at Boise, Idaho, in preparation for combat. In July, 1944, he boarded a ship at Camp Kilmer, New Jersey, bound for the European Theater of Operations. After a months additional training at Cookstown, Ireland, Herb flew the first of thirty combat missions with the 453rd Bomb Group at Old Buckenham, England.

After Herb's seventh mission his crew was made Lead crew which reduced the number of missions required for rotation back to the United States from thirty-five to thirty. On a mission to bomb targets near Kassel, Germany, "we got hit hard by flak. We never lost an engine but we had one hundred forty-two holes in our plane." Two crewmembers received only scratches from flak that pierced the aircraft. Herb's pilot received one of those scratches, across his forehead. Had the pilot been leaning forward only slightly he would have been killed.

On another mission "our bombardier passed out while on the bomb run. He had lost his oxygen. While he was being tended to I operated the toggle switch to drop our bombs when the lead plane dropped theirs".

Herb completed his missions in April, 1945 and was on a boat at Southampton, England, ready to sail to the United States when the war ended in Europe. He received his separation from military service in October, 1945 but remained in the Air Force Reserve where he attained the rank of Major. Placed on an inactive status in 1970, Herb received his official discharge in 1980.

After return to civilian life, Herb owned and operated a service station and towing service in Early for over thirty years before retiring and turning the business over to his sons.

HARLEY RIESGAARD, EXIRA, IA, was working on the family farm when he enlisted in the Army Air Corps in February, 1944. After Basic Training at Biloxi, Mississippi, he completed Aerial Gunnery School at Las Vegas, Nevada.

Harley was then sent to Savannah, Georgia, where he was assigned to an aircrew and trained with them at Savannah in preparation for deployment to the European Theater of Operations.

In the Fall of 1944, Harley and his crew flew to Valley, Wales where their aircraft was taken from them for installation of additional armament and other retro-fitting. The crew proceeded to Stone, England where they received assignment to the 452nd Bomb Group at Deopham Green.

Harley flew thirty-four combat missions as a B-17 bomber waist gunner. His most memorable mission was a raid on targets at Frankfurt, Germany. "Flak" from German anti-aircraft guns was extremely heavy over the target area. Flak knocked out one engine of his aircraft and shortly thereafter, two other engines were lost. Unable to maintain altitude, everything available in the aircraft such as guns and ammunition were thrown out of the aircraft to reduce their weight, including the ball turret. The pilot was able to fly the aircraft until they were behind Allied lines to avoid capture by the Germans should they have to bail out. Unable to continue flying further, the pilot belly-landed their airplane named "3 Deuces" in a wheat field in France. "We sat in the radio room in crash position. We had been trained on what to do. It wasn't too bad, the pilot did a great job. We got out of the airplane real fast as soon as we stopped and ran in case it would blow up. American soldiers showed up right away. They took us to an airstrip where there was another B-17 that had been forced to land and was repaired, so we flew it back to our base."

Harley returned to the United States on a French ship in May, 1945. He reported to Santa Ana, California for re-classification and was sent to Mission, Texas, until his discharge in September, 1945. Harley had been awarded, among other medals, the Air Medal with four oak leaf clusters, ETO Ribbon with three battle stars and the World War II Victory Medal.

Harley returned to Iowa and resumed farming

Right - Harley's crew at 452nd BG, Deopham Green, England. Harley, Waist Gunner, is back row, right.

WILLIAM C. RICH, CLEAR LAKE, IA, was a student at Iowa State College, Ames, Iowa. He entered the military in February, 1943, at Jefferson Barracks, Missouri. He criss-crossed the United States to take pilot training. Training was taken at Oshkosh, Wisconsin; Santa Ana, Oxnard, Chico and Stockton, California; Roswell, New Mexico and Tampa, Florida.

Bill was deployed to England in February, 1945, as a pilot with the 487th Bomb Group at Lavenham, England. He flew thirteen missions before the war ended. A mercy mission to Austria in June, 1945, was the most memorable of his experiences. Boxed food was delivered to an airport near Lenz for starving civilians.

French prisoners of war, men, women and children were taken aboard his plane and flown to a steel mat landing strip near Paris. The POWs were off-loaded and his plane and crew returned to England. To feed starving people, attend to their needs and return them to their homeland was extremely heart warming.

Bill was awarded the Air Medal with oak leaf clusters, European Theater of Operations and World War II Victory Medals. He was discharged in October, 1945, at Santa Ana, CA.

Right - Bill and his crew at 487th BG, Lavenham, England. Bill, Pilot, is front row, second from the left.

DONALD RICHARDS, WATERLOO, IA, attended high school in Burlington, Iowa, and took a machine shop course. He secured employment after school hours as an assistant to the Engineer of Burlington Instrument Company which held government contracts in war projects. After graduation John continued employment on a full time basis. He tried to enter the Coast Guard and the Navy but failed the physical because of eyesight. He was able to enlist in the Army on July 7, 1942, as a non-combatant and declined a deferment because of wartime employment with the instrument company.

After Basic Training at Cheyenne, Wyoming, Donald attended a machine shop course at an Ordnance School; an Automotive Specialist Course at San Antonio, Texas and a drafting course at Jackson, Mississippi. Donald was assigned to the 2006th Ordnance Company at Langley, Virginia, attached to the Eighth Air Force.

On July 8, 1943, the Ordnance Company was deployed to England aboard the ocean liner "Aquatania". One night the ship "ran into a German sub and outran it". A wolf pack was waiting for the liner. "The ship's Captain turned everything off on the ship, drifted out of the ring of submarines and then headed for its destination, the Firth of Clyde."

On arrival at its base near the small English village of Melchbourne, the Company was split in half with half the personnel being assigned to a motor pool and the other half to machine shop work. Donald's duties included making metal parts and tools from metal casings, operating engine lathes, milling machines, drill presses and power hack saws. They constructed Nissen huts, tools and parts for all branches of military service including the British, and bomb rack hooks. A cardboard bomb containing propaganda leaflets was developed that would detonate and free the leaflets at a designated altitude. Donald was the one person available that was able to mill and repair the warped head on a General's twelve- cylinder vehicle.

Donald returned to the United States aboard the "U S S Wasp" on January 5, 1946. One day out of England, instead of returning to port to avoid a storm, the ship's Captain sailed South running directly into the storm. An SOS was sent after part of the deck was torn from the ship and hangar decks as well as lower decks were awash from sea water. The ship was able to continue and make it to America. All personnel were without food for three days during the trip until repairs could be made.

After discharge from military service Donald returned to Burlington Instrument Company and attended Burlington Junior College and Iowa State Teachers College at Cedar Falls, Iowa. He graduated in 1950 and began a teaching career, the last thirty years of which were in the Waterloo school system as an Industrial Arts instructor. Donald retired in 1984

DARRAH L. ROBERTS, IOWA FALLS, IA, was farming in the Iowa Falls area prior to World War II. He entered the military July 1, 1942 at Des Moines, Iowa, and underwent pilot training at various airfields in Texas.

Deployed to Ramsburg, England, May 16, 1944, Darrah was later transferred to Norwich with the 368th Fighter Squadron, 359th Fighter Group. Darrah flew twenty-two combat missions as a C-47 pilot with the 9th Air Force after serving briefly with the Mighty Eighth. He also flew as a pilot on General Eisenhower's staff.

Darrah was awarded the Air Medal with two oak leaf clusters and the European Theater of Operations ribbon with eight battle stars. His Group received a Presidential Unit Citation

Darrah was discharged from the military on January 3, 1947, at Randolph Field, Texas. He resumed farming in the Iowa Falls area until he was recalled for the Korean War in 1950 and served as a senior pilot in Japan.

Darrah is the author of a book on his World War II experiences entitled "The Flashing Green Light – A Pilots View of WWII".

GLENN ROBINSON, DES MOINES, IA, was born and raised in the Iowa Falls, Iowa, area. He graduated from Ellsworth Junior College at Iowa Falls and in 1941 flew forty hours instruction in the Civilian Pilot Training Program (CPT). He completed aerobatics in 1942, cross-country in 1943 and went to Kansas City to obtain his commercial pilot's license and instrument rating with Trans-World Airlines.

He was informed the Air Corps had a glut on pilots in training and all members of the Civilian Pilot Training Program who had received a deferment from the Selective Service System until their training was completed, would be referred back to their draft boards. Glenn had enlisted in the Air Force Reserve in order to fly in the CPT. He was called to active duty from the Reserves in September, 1943 and sent to Sheppard Field, Wichita Falls, Texas, for Basic Training.

The Air Corps then called for volunteers to become bombardiers or navigators. Glenn was selected and sent to Butler University as part of the College Training Detachment Program to take college courses before Air Corps training. "We lived in the college field house in the balcony. Our bunks were stair-stepped" In the winter of 1944 the Air Corps terminated the need for bombardiers or navigators and Glenn was sent to Laredo, Texas, for Aerial Gunnery School.

After gunnery training Glenn was assigned to an aircrew and trained with them at Charleston, South Carolina. He was then sent to New York City where he boarded the "Queen Mary" for Scotland.

Glenn was assigned to the 491st Bomb Group at North Pickenham, England. He flew twenty-eight missions as an aerial gunner. After one mission "we counted over 500 hits on our aircraft including five 20 millimeter hits in our tail. No one was hurt and we made it home alright." His most memorable mission was a low-level flight dropping supplies to the British Army. "Me and the tail gunner were kicking out supplies through the bomb bay. We also went on a mission to bomb the bridge across the Rhine at Remagen. We missed it." He also served as a toggelier, in place of a bombardier. The toggelier released bombs from his aircraft when the lead bombers in the formation released theirs. This eliminated the need for additional Norden bombsights and training of bombardiers.

Glenn returned to the United States aboard the ocean liner "Isle de France". He reported to Wisconsin for re-assignment and was sent to the State of Washington to fire forest fires that were plaguing the West Coast. He remained there until October, 1945, when he received his discharge from military service. He had been awarded the Air Medal with three oak leaf clusters, European Theater of Operations and World War II Victory Medals, among others.

In civilian life Glenn farmed in the Iowa Falls area until he returned to schooling at the American Institute of Business in Des Moines. He then gained employment with the Sate of Iowa in the Collections Section of the Iowa Department of Revenue. Glenn retired in 1983.

PAUL DALE ROBINSON, ALBIA, IA, was in high school when America officially entered World War II. He enlisted in the Army Air Corps in February 1943 and was sent to St. Petersburg, Florida, for Basic Training.

After Basic, Dale was assigned to Radio School at Scott Field, Illinois. He then returned to Florida for Aerial Gunnery School at Ft. Myers

and crew assignment and overseas training back at St Petersburg.

In the Summer of 1944 Dale and his crew were assigned a new radar equipped B-17 at Langley Field, Virginia, and flew to England. Initially assigned to the 100th Bomb Group, Dale and his crew were transferred to the 401st Bomb Group at Nuthampstead. Additional training took place in formation flying before Dale flew his first combat mission. His commanding officer constantly stressed that all aircraft in the squadron were to fly in tight formation for self-protection and better bombing accuracy. Dale believed this was extremely beneficial as his squadron, in thirty-two combat missions, were not attacked by enemy fighter aircraft.

Losses however, came heavily from "flak". During a mission to bomb a ball bearing plant near Munich his bomb group lost twenty-three of the thirty-six aircraft sent. Most of the losses came during the bomb run when they had to fly straight and level at a prescribed altitude. Dale flew with his original crew for seven missions. He and his pilot flew their remaining missions with other crews in the lead position for their Group.

In January, 1945, Dale and ten other air men took a train to Scotland to catch a plane back to the United States. In their revelry and excitement of going home it took them two weeks to reach Scotland. When they arrived at the designated air base their plane had already left. They returned to America aboard a Liberty ship with 500 other servicemen and 500 German prisoners of war. The POWs were put in the hold of the ship and guarded on work details by Dale and other GIs.

After arrival home and furlough, Dale reported to Waco, Texas, where he worked in the air base control tower for a short time. He was then transferred to Independence, Kansas where he assisted in stripping and storing machine guns from bombers. He received his discharge from military service in the Spring of 1945. Dale had been awarded, among other decorations, the Air Medal with five oak leaf clusters, ETO ribbon and the World War II Victory Medal.

Dale worked for a few years with John Deere Company in Ottumwa, Iowa, as a tool and die maker. He then worked for thirty-five years as a dispatcher for Burlington Northern Railroad which allowed him to farm at the same time for forty years until his retirement

Right - Dale and his crew at 401st BG, Deenethorpe, England. Dale, Radio Operator, is front row, second from right.

ROGER H. ROBINSON, DAVENPORT, IA, was a machinist apprentice at John Deere Company and took courses at Augustana College prior to World War II. He was inducted into the Army Air Corps in November, 1941, and sent to Sheppard Field, Wichita Falls, Texas, for Basic Training. He then graduated from Armaments School at Lowry Field near Denver, Colorado in

April, 1942 and was assigned as an armorer, to the 31st Fighter Group at New Orleans, Louisiana. The 31st was equipped with the P-39, Bell "Airacobra" fighter plane and was in the process of intensive training for deployment overeseas.

Roger boarded the "Queen Elizabeth" at Ft. Dix, New Jersey, on June 4, 1942, for Greenock, Scotland. In route he was assigned to man a gun on the poop deck of the ship and therefore had the privilege to eat meals at any time and "buck" chow lines.

The 31st Fighter Group was the first American fighter group to arrive in England and based at Atcham until August, 1942. Weather on the Atlantic prevented the P-39 from being flown across the "pond" and the 31st was initially equipped with the Spitfire Mark V fighter. The three squadrons of the Group were stationed at different bases and made fighter sweeps across the English Channel to strafe Nazi targets and provide fighter escort for medium bombers. They became the first American fighter group to engage in combat in the European Theater of Operations when they assisted the British in a raid on Dieppe, France, on August 19, 1942, and also scored the first aerial combat victory.

Under a cloud of secrecy the 31st was ordered, in October, 1942, to pack up and board a train which took them back to Greenock, Scotland. They boarded an English transport ship and sailed south, then through the Strait of Gibraltar. On November 8, 1942, D Day of Operation Torch, the Allied invasion of North Africa, they landed at Oran, Algeria. The 31st had been officially transferred from the 8th to the 12th Air Force. They were transported by truck to Tafaraoui Airdrome twenty-five miles inland as ground was taken from German forces, to provide air cover for further action from the invasion.

Roger made many moves during his stay in North Africa depending on the fortunes of war. This included a move to Casablanca during the summit conference of Roosevelt, Churchill and Stalin, and to Tunisia where he saw the destruction of tanks and other military equipment at Kasserine Pass. As armorer, weapons were cleaned and repaired. Sightings down gun barrels of fighter aircraft were taken to determine bullet point of convergence. Blowing sand in Africa required weapons be covered at all times to ensure proper operation. While the Group flew the Spitfire, British personnel were assigned to help them learn mechanics of the aircraft.

Roger and the 31st moved to Sicily after the island was invaded. He then went in with British troops during the invasion of Salerno on September 8, 1943. His Group was made part of the 15th Air Force based at Foggia, Italy, equipped with the American P-51 fighter.

Roger returned to the United States aboard the "USS America" from Naples, Italy, to New York. During furlough he was married before he reported for further duty at Miami Beach, FL. He received his discharge from military service in May, 1945. Until his retirement Roger was employed by Red Jacket Pump Company for thirty-two years as a draftsman, purchasing agent and project engineer.

GEORGE ROEPKE, TRAER, IA, formerly of Oelwein, worked in a grocery store prior to World War II. He enlisted in the Army Air Corps at Ft. Des Moines on May 11, 1942, and was sent to Jefferson Barracks, MO, for Basic Training.

George was chosen to attend the Casey Jones School of Aeronautics, a Mechanics School in New Jersey and the Bell Aircraft School at Niagara Falls, NY. Additional training was taken at Fresno, CA, before assignment to the 357th Fighter Group at Hamilton Field, CA. After bombing and gunnery training near Tonapah, NV, the fighter group began their overseas movement on a troop train to the East Coast.

On November, 23, 1943, George boarded the "Queen Elizabeth" for a six day zig-zag sail to England. Eventually arriving at Leiston, England, George became a crew chief responsible for the maintenance and repair of one P-51 Mustang fighter aircraft. While other ground personnel maintained the propeller, oxygen equipment, instruments and machine guns George was responsible for the mechanical operation of the engine. His sterling record of no engine malfunctions and ability to keep his aircraft airborne earned him the Bronze Star.

During his tour with the 357th until war's end, George went through two P-51s and three pilots. One P-51 was shot down and the pilot believed killed in action. At a Group reunion after the war he was surprised to see the pilot, Charles Goss, in attendance. He had bailed out and was taken prisoner of war. Two other pilots flying George's P-51 went on to score six aerial victories, one probably destroyed and many others damaged in aerial combat and ground strafing attacks.

Immediately after Victory in Europe George was sent to Neubiberg, Germany, near Munich as part of occupational forces. At Dachau Concentration Camp he witnessed the deplorable state of prisoners held there. George paid a return visit to the site fifty years later under much different conditions.

In late September, 1945, George was placed high on the list of persons eligible for return to the United States. He had lost two brothers in ground fighting in Europe. One in the Italian Campaign and one during the D-Day invasion. He sailed for America on the "Aquatainia" and discharge from military service October 12, 1945, at Jefferson Barracks, MO.

George was employed by the United States Postal Service in Traer, Iowa, until his retirement in 1983. He remains active in the 357th Fighter Group Association attending their reunions and maintaining contact with friends he made during this period of American history.

VIRGIL ROETHLER, ALGONA, IA, was farming in Kossuth County until he was inducted into the Army Air Corps in January, 1943 at Camp Dodge, Iowa. He was sent to Amarillo, Texas, for Basic Training where he tested for the Aviation Cadet Program, passed and was accepted for pilot training.

Virgil was sent to Missoula, Montana, for Pilot Training but after only two weeks the Cadet Program was cancelled for "the convenience of the government" and he was sent back to Amarillo. Virgil was then sent to Biloxi, Mississippi, for Flight Engineer Training and Panama City, Florida, for Aerial Gunnery School.

After completion of training Virgil was assigned to an aircrew at Springfield, Massachusetts, and trained with the crew at Charleston, South Carolina and Havanna, Cuba, in preparation for overseas deployment.

Virgil and his crew flew to Stone, England, through Hempstead, New York; Bangor, Maine; Goose Bay, Labrador; Keflivik, Iceland and Prestwick, Scotland. He was assigned to the 445th Bomb Group at Tibenham, England, as Flight Engineer.

Virgil flew sixteen combat missions, twelve supply missions and three missions over Rouen, Germany, which were not counted as missions because they encountered no enemy fire.

On one mission, an overload of bombs aboard their aircraft and a strong headwind caused them to crash on takeoff. No one was hurt but as the sliding plane stopped, Virgil yelled, "Lets get the hell out of here". He pulled open an escape hatch but was the last person out of the aircraft because everyone else climbed over the top of him to get out.

Virgil's most memorable missions were those to Peenemunde, Germany, site of German rocket testing and launches toward England. He learned years later through an article in "Readers Digest", the site was where Germany was working with heavy water for development of a nuclear bomb.

His longest mission was to Ludwigshafen, Germany, where aircraft facilities that produced the ME-109 fighter were produced. His aircraft carried only enough fuel to make a safe return to England if they encountered no difficulty.

A mission to Kassel, Germany, will never be forgotten. A maximum effort, meaning all available aircraft, was dispatched to the target. On the way to the target the main bomber stream made a left turn toward Kassel but Virgil's squadron, for some unexplained reason, didn't turn. They went straight ahead and were left isolated. Nine ME-109s German fighters escorting some of their own aircraft saw the squadron all alone and attacked. There were twenty-five to twenty-eight planes in Virgil's squadron. The l09's "shot the bloody hell out of them". Virgil's crew was the only plane to make it back to their home base. A couple others made it back to England and made emergency landings at other bases, but the rest of his squadron was lost. ("They never found out who made the SNAFU but it must have been someone high up or else someone would have gotten court-martialed over the screw-up.")

After return to the United States, Virgil was scheduled to begin training on the B-29 Super Fortress in preparation for deployment to the Pacific Theater of Operations. Meanwhile the atomic bomb was dropped on Japan precluding his training and he was sent to Sioux Falls, South Dakota, until further notice.

Since this was fairly close to Spirit Lake, Iowa, site of a popular amusement park, Virgil and friends took off for there for fun and games. When they returned to Sioux Falls Virgil discovered his unit was gone. They had shipped out. Virgil was given a train ticket to Harlingen, Texas, where he was given the choice of becoming a cook or an MP (Military Police). He chose to become an MP.

"His first assignment was to go to the bank and pick up the payroll. He was not told which bank or how to go about it. So he commandeered several jeeps from the motor pool, took a bunch of armed MPs and found out which bank held the payroll. They pulled up in front of the bank. Some of the MPs got out with their guns and guarded the jeep while Virgil and several others went into the bank and got the money. Back at the base Virgil piled the $350,000 in cash on the floor of the Day Room. The Officer of the Day didn't show up to relieve him of the money, so Virgil sat in the dark all night with a gun guarding the payroll."

The base at Harlingen was closed and Virgil was sent to San Antonio, Texas, for a criminal investigation assignment until he received his discharge from military service at Ft. Leonard Wood, Missouri, on May 5, 1946.

Virgil returned to the Algona, Iowa, area and farmed until retirement in 1981.

Right - Virgil at 445th Bomb Group

Right - Virgil and his crew at 445th Bomb Group, Tibenham, England.

OLAF ROGNESS, CEDAR RAPIDS, IA, operated a service station in Minnesota prior to World War II. He enlisted in the Army Air Corps March 7, 1942 and was sent to Jefferson Barracks, St. Louis, Missouri, for Basic Training. Olaf was then assigned to Provo, Utah where he worked in the air base post office.

In the Fall of 1943, Olaf reported to Camp Kilmer, New Jersey, where he boarded the ocean liner "Brittania" with other troops bound for England. Although the voyage across the Atlantic was made in only a few days, stormy seas were encountered most of the way. Many of the troops became seasick. Despite only two meals served on board the ship each day, Olaf recalled the dining room was never full.

Olaf was initially assigned to a bomb group that sustained a series of losses in combat. He was subsequently transferred to the 466th Bomb Group at Attlebridge where he served in the base post office until the end of the war in Europe. In the Fall of 1945 he sailed home aboard the "Queen Mary" and after reporting to Sioux Falls, South Dakota, received his military discharge.

After the war Olaf was employed in sales with Conoco Oil Company in Milwaukee, Wisconsin. He later joined Pure Oil Company from which he retired.

BLAIR ROSSOW, PANORA, IA, grew up in the Lohrville, Iowa, area. He was employed by Martin Aircraft in Baltimore, Maryland when he enlisted in the Army Air Corps September 29, 1942. He was transferred to six different locations before he was able to complete Basic Training.

Initially sent to Camp Lee, Virginia he and others were put aboard one railroad car attached to a passenger train and shipped to Sacramento, California. The train took ten days to cross the United States via a zig-zag route, many delays with no heat and very little food provided. Blair caught pneumonia in route and was hospitalized. He was then sent to Stockton, California and eventually across San Francisco Bay to San Bruno. At San Bruno "it rained constantly. They had a Japanese internment camp set up on a race track where the Japanese were housed in shanties and lived in deplorable conditions. They moved them out and moved us in. We ate "slop" cooked in big iron kettles. The ground became so soaked they kept moving us to higher ground and finally I got shipped to Miami Beach, Florida to finish Basic."

"I was put in an MP unit and when I complained I wanted out of that they made me a drill instructor. I told them I wanted to fly. That's why I joined the Air Corps." In October, 1943, Blair was re-assigned to Aircraft Mechanics School at Sheppard Field, Wichita Falls, Texas, a five month course. Then came Aerial Gunnery School at Tyndall Field, Florida.

After the completion of training Blair was assigned to an air crew at Salt Lake City, Utah. He came down with pneumonia again, complicated by scarlet fever while in route to crew training in Arizona. Following release from the hospital he completed crew training with another crew, and was sent to Topeka, Kansas to pick up a new B-24 bomber to take to the European Theater of Operations. The landed at Valley, Wales in May, 1944, where their aircraft was taken from them for installation of additional armament. Blair and his crew continued to the 34th Bomb Group at Mendelsham, England.

Additional gunnery and practice formation flying took place before Blair would fly the first of thirty-two combat missions with the 34th as nose gunner, ball or top turret gunner. His early missions were to targets in France in support of the D-Day invasion. His later missions included two missions to heavily defended Merseburg, Munster and Berlin. His last mission was to Cologne, Germany where virtually all that remained standing in the city was a cathedral.

"We rarely came back to base with all four engines intact. Most of the time we were limping home on only two engines due to "flak"". Weather was an obstacle as much as flak and German fighters. On one mission fog caused our aircraft to "ice up". We couldn't climb. There were a lot of mid-air collisions. We couldn't bomb the target so dropped our bombs on a target of opportunity. On the trip back to our base in the fog we came in on a radar beam. We were looking out for church steeples and landed at a base that wasn't our own." After another mission, in clear weather, "our pilot over-compensated on the landing and we lit on the grass infield. It was a bumpy ride but everyone was O.K."

Blair's aircraft was hit hard by flak on another mission. Fog had settled in around Mendelsham and the runway lights were turned on to aid pilots. "While landing there were two explosions. Two bombers had collided in mid-air. Some crewmembers were able to parachute to safety but base anti-aircraft guns opened up on the guys thinking it was a German airborne invasion. A German fighter had also stalked the 34th on its return to England and shot down two planes while they were very vulnerable – landing."

Blair and his crew normally flew in a B-24 named "Queenie". On one mission, "Queenie" was grounded for repair. They were assigned to another aircraft named "Bambi". Blair made a pre-flight check of the aircraft and found oil pressure beyond limitations on two engines and other borderline problems. He reported these finding to his pilot who recommended the aircraft be grounded. Blair's crew was ordered to take the aircraft on the mission. After takeoff, they lost one engine due to failure but were denied permission to abort the mission. They continued on the mission unable to maintain speed and altitude with their Group. Over the target the 34th was hit hard by flak and lost several aircraft. Blair's aircraft flying well below them and an easy target was hardly fired upon. As they returned to base over the North Sea and constantly lost altitude, an unidentified aircraft flew with them trying to guide them to a landing strip. Two patrol boats appeared and with one boat on each side of the aircraft directed them to an emergency landing field.

Blair returned to the United States by ship on December 11, 1944. He received his discharge from military service in September, 1945 having been awarded, among other medals, the Distinguished Flying Cross, Air Medal with three oak leaf clusters, the ETO Ribbon with five battle stars and World War II Victory Medal.

Blair retired in 1977 after thirty-one years as a lineman with Iowa Public Service Company.

Right - Blair in flight gear

Right - Blair and his crew at 34th BG, Mendelsham, England. Blair, Aerial Gunner, is front row, left.

LOWELL ROTHBART, DEWITT, IA, was farming when he entered military service on September 5, 1941, at Ft. Des Moines, Iowa, two months before Pearl Harbor was attacked. He was sent to Jefferson Barracks near St. Louis, Missouri for Basic Training. From there he attended Airplane Mechanics School at Chanute Field, Illinois and Bell Aircraft Maintenance, Niagara Falls, New York.

Upon graduation in April, 1942, Lowell reported to the 20th Fighter Group at Myrtle Beach, South Carolina. In the next nine months the 20th moved to Charlotte, North Carolina; Spartansburg, South Carolina; Drew Field, Sarasota, Florida; Paine Field, Everett, Washington; Pendleton Army Air Base, Oregon; and Tumwater Air Base, Olympia, Washington. Lowell performed aircraft maintenance at these locations for pilots in training.

The Fighter Group then moved to March Field, Riverside, California. Lowell was assigned to attend Lockheed Aircraft Maintenance School at Burbank, California.

On August 11, 1943, the Fighter Group left California in three trains for the East Coast. Nine days later they boarded the luxury liner "Queen Elizabeth" with 19,600 other soldiers for Grenock, Scotland. To accommodate that many men, officers were billeted 20-30 men in a stateroom that normally held 2-3 persons. Enlisted men were housed below deck for a 24-hour shift followed by 24 hours on deck. "That way it doubled the troops using the quarters. On arrival in the Firth of Clyde the ship dropped anchor five miles at sea because no dock space was available that could handle a ship the size of the "QE". They rode to shore in small boats. It took five days to unload the ship. From there the 20th rode by train to their new base at Kings Cliff, England.

"Kings Cliff was one of the poorest airfields in England. The buildings were old and inadequate. Facilities were practically non-existent and mud was plentiful." Lowell was an assistant engineering chief that serviced planes that were in need of more than routine service. "I had a crew of 20 men and we worked most of the time in the evenings." Lowell was promoted to Crew Chief assigned to one P-38 flown by fellow Iowan, Lt. Richard (Steamboat) Garrett of Ferguson, Iowa. "He named his plane "Shorty" and flew 25 missions claiming one German aircraft shot down, several "probables" and several train engines destroyed on strafing missions."

Lowell attended a Merlin Rolls Royce Engine Maintenance School at Derby, England, in connection with the fighter group's conversion from the P-38 to the P-51 Mustang. He was promoted to Flight Chief and was in charge of thirteen men to perform maintenance and repair of fighters in "B" Flight.

"During D-Day we were really kept busy. The planes were flying 24 hours a day. We broke up our men on the flight line so they would not have to be on duty more than eight hours a day. Flight Chiefs worked 12-hour days, two on a shift to take care of all the aircraft and men 24 hours a day. This lasted about 15 days, long enough for the ground troops to have a good hold in France. The sky was a constant blur with bombers and fighter planes all day long."

"On July 4, 1944, I witnessed the death of one of our sergeants. He was killed while riding his bicycle on the perimeter track. A P-38 ran into him from the back and cut him up. His body was sent back to the U.S. for burial."

The 20th Fighter Group flew 321 missions after its arrival in England and had the best P-51 maintenance record in the Eighth

Air Force in the latter months of the war. Their last mission was flown on April 25, 1945.

On September 14, 1945, four months after Victory in Europe, Lowell sailed for the United States on a Kaiser Liberty ship "SS Robert E. Burnside". The sail home took seventeen days. The ship had boiler trouble necessitating a stop at Newfoundland for repair. While there it snowed three feet in a three-hour period. When they arrived at New York, the ship was quarantined because two men had died in route and were kept in the ship's cooler. One had died from an unknown cause and the other from drinking two-fifths of Cognac.

Lowell was discharged at Ft. Sheridan, Illinois, on October 9, 1945. He had been awarded the European Theater of Operations Medal with six battle stars, World War II Victory and American Defense Medals.

After the war Lowell worked as a tool setter with Caterpillar Company until his retirement in November, 1982.

Right - Lowell and other aircraft mechanics at 20th Fighter Group, Kings Cliffe, England.

Right - Lowell in front of P-38 he maintained, flown by Richard (Steamboat) Garrett, 20th FG.

JOHN RUPPERT, IOWA CITY, IA, graduated from high school in June, 1943, and entered the Army Air Corps in July. Sent for Basic Training at Miami Beach, FL he then entered the Aviation Cadet Program at Huntington, West Virginia and San Antonio, TX.

Due to a surplus of pilot applicants, cadets were encouraged to volunteer for other training. John was sent to Radio School at Sioux Falls, SD, but elected to become an aerial gunner and was transferred to Las Vegas, NV, for training.

After crew assignment and combat training at Gulfport, MS, John and his crew picked up a new B-17 bomber at Savannah, GA, and headed for England via the northern route through Labrador, Greenland and Iceland. John flew thirteen combat missions as tail gunner with the 447th Bomb Group, Rattlesden, England.

On his thirteenth mission one engine of their aircraft was lost due to mechanical problems or anti-aircraft fire. Realizing they would not make it back to their base, John's pilot gave his crew the chance to bail out of their stricken aircraft over territory recently taken from the Nazis. The pilot indicated he was going to try and land at a former Luftwaffe air base in France. The crew decided to stay with the airplane. Despite the poor condition of the bombed out runway they landed safely. A French farmer brought them food in exchange for a few gallons of fuel from their airplane. The Norden bombsight was removed for savekeeping. John and his crew were sent to Paris where they were granted a pass until they could be returned to England. John recalled being constantly confronted by Military Police because they were dressed only in their flight clothing and had no other clothes. Their passes indicated they were "missing in action personnel".

John returned to the United States by Victory Ship and was discharged from military service September 6, 1945, having been awarded among other medals, the Air Medal with an oak lead cluster, European Theater of Operations and World War II Victory Medals.

Right - John and his crew at 447th BG, Rattlesden, England. John, Aerial Gunner, is back row, center.

BRUCE RUST, SHEFFIELD, IA, was a welder at Cedar Rapids, Iowa, when he enlisted in the Army on January 5, 1942. He spent thirteen months in the infantry before he transferred to the Army Air Corps in response to a need for "Flying Sergeants".

After Basic Training at Santa Ana, California, he began Primary Flight Training but was washed out due to color blindness in one eye. Bruce was sent to Los Angeles, California to attend Motor Mechanics School and then served for one year as a night foreman at Kingman, Arizona Air Base. When he learned Aerial Gunners were needed he volunteered and remained at Kingman for that training. Assigned to an aircrew he trained with them at Ardmore, Oklahoma, before they picked up a new B-17 and headed for the European Theater of Operations. After landing at Valley, Wales, in February, 1944, their aircraft was taken from them for installation of additional armament and they proceeded to the 94th Bomb Group at Bury St. Edmunds, England.

Bruce flew fifteen combat missions as tail gunner beginning the day after D-Day, June 6, 1944. On one mission to Regensburg, Germany, their bomb group encountered heavy flak tearing forty holes in Bruce's aircraft. One engine was lost. The navigator's life was saved when struck by a piece of flak because he was wearing his flak suit. He only suffered two broken ribs.

On a mission to Berlin, the lead aircraft for the raid used a togglier to signal when the group was to drop their bombs. Forty miles from the target, while leaning forward, the bill of the togglier's cap hit the bomb switch and released his bombs. All other aircraft then dropped their bombs. The formation had to abort the mission before they could reach the target area.

After the war was over in Europe, Bruce was sent to Germany as part of the occupational force. In addition to his normal duties he worked nights as a bouncer in a nightclub frequented by American troops. He returned to the United States aboard the ocean liner "Queen Mary" in November, 1945 and received his discharge from military service the beginning of December. He had been awarded, among other medals, the Air Medal with oak leaf cluster, ETO Ribbon and World War II Victory Medal.

Bruce returned to the Sheffield area where he worked as a carpenter and bricklayer in construction and at one time owned a local Ford Motor dealership.

Right - Bruce's crew at 94th BG, Bury St Edmunds, England. Bruce, Aerial Gunner, is front row, center.

WARREN RYAN, GRINNELL, IA, graduated from high school in 1938 and was helping on the family farm when the war in Europe was spreading and the Battle of Britain began. Warren's main source of world news came from newsreels at the local theater. Before America's entry into World War II, Americans had come to the aid of Britain and flew in the Royal Air Force, Eagle Squadron. Warren had taken private flying lessons, was interested in aviation and wanted to help. He attempted to enlist in the Royal Canadian Air Force but was told two years college was required so he returned home.

After the attack by the Japanese on Pearl Harbor catapulted America into World War II, Warren attempted enlistment in the Army and Navy believing the U.S. Army Air Corps also required two years college training. When he learned the Air Corps had waived the college requirement, Warren enlisted in the Summer of 1942. A backlog of enlistees in training prevented him from being called to active duty until January, 1943. He was placed in the Aviation Cadet Program for training to be either a Pilot, Navigator or Bombardier. He attended Pre-Flight and Primary Flight Training but was cut from the program. Warren was re-assigned to Radio School at Scott Field, Illinois and then Aerial Gunnery School.

Morse Code was a major part of the radio school. To pass, Warren had to be able to send 23 unrelated letter groups a minute. Airplane radios didn't have voice radio that would reach all the way back to their base. Warren flew thirty-five missions as radioman. During missions he had to stay tuned to the home base to let them know by Morse Code when bombs were "away" toward the target and results. He also served as an alternate waist gunner while under attack from enemy fighters.

Warren was married after he completed gunnery school and spent his honeymoon on furlough before being sent overseas to join the 96th Bomb Group at Snetterton Heath, England. A new airplane was picked up at Lincoln, Nebraska, and he and his crew flew to New Hampshire; Goose Bay, Labrador; Iceland and then to Wales where they found public transportation to their base.

Warren kept a diary of his activities which indicated that between combat missions his time was occupied by continual training in radio, practice missions, target identification and evasion tactics. Many missions were "scrubbed" because of the English weather.

Warren flew his first combat mission on October 22, 1944. During the thirty-five missions flown hardly a mission was completed without damage to his airplane from flak (anti-aircraft guns). The Germans became experts in firing intense and accurate barrages at the American formations. During his fifth mission, a raid on Merseburg, Warren saw two airplanes explode in the air and another plane abandoned after it was hit by flak. Sixteen planes became stragglers on the return trip home to England due to battle damage and were susceptible to fighter attack. Five of the planes had casualties aboard.

Warren's thirteenth and seventeenth missions were raids on Hamburg to bomb submarine pens. Hitler's submarine force was highly protected by intense concentrations of anti-aircraft batteries and Luftwaffe fighters. On the two missions Warren saw ten bombers go down. His eighteenth mission, to Hohenbudburg, Warren's plane took several flak hits that cut hydraulic lines. With no brakes the Pilot, on reaching Snetterton Heath, landed the airplane at the beginning of the runway. According to Warren, "we rolled and rolled and were finally stopped by a parked truck." No injuries occurred.

His thirty-fourth mission was described as the toughest. Germans threw up heavy flak and his Bomb Group lost six planes including the two lead planes. Along with them went fifty-four crewmen. His final and thirty-fifth mission was on March 21, 1945, again to Hamburg enduring intense flak and enemy fighters.

While overseas Warren learned that his wife Clara was pregnant. At the completion of his tour he sailed for America in what turned out to be a two week trip. On arrival at New York he attended a steak fry for those aboard ship and immediately afterward boarded a train for home. The train arrived in St Louis, Missouri, on May 8, 1945 where he learned the war in Europe was over. Warren made it home in time to be at Clara's side when the baby was born on May 10.

Warren was discharged from military service June 18, 1945. He had been awarded the Air Medal with four Oak Leaf Clusters, European Theater of Operations and World War II Victory Medal. He resumed farming in the Grinnell area and has since retired.

Right - Warren, second from left in back row, and crew at 96th BG, Snetterton Heath, England.,

EVERETT SANDERSFELD, SOUTH AMANA, IA, was farming and newly married before America's entry into World War II. Inducted into military service March 12, 1942, at Ft. Des Moines, IA, his father and brother would operate Everett's farm during his absence.

He was sent to Jefferson Barracks near St. Louis, Missouri, for Basic Training where he found himself marching, doing KP (kitchen police),

learning his General Orders, military courtesy, and answering questionnaires which would determine his future role in the military. From there he was sent to Tallahassee, FL and Augusta, GA, and eventually left New York for England aboard the ocean liner "Aquitania". The liner was the sister ship of the "Lusitania" torpedoed by a German submarine without warning in World War I.

It took eleven days and nights on a zig-zag route to arrive at Scotland. Rough seas were encountered and tossed the ship around "like a cork". Water swept over the deck and ran under the soldier's bunks. Oatmeal served on board was thick with little white worms so Everett subsisted on candy bars for most of the trip.

Assigned to the 385th Bomb Group at Knettishall as a mechanic, Everett had received no training other than two weeks of classroom study. Responsible for maintenance, repair and inspection of aircraft engines, accessories, instruments and air frames he credits his hangar crew chief with providing most of his training.

As a member of the ground crew he watched in amazement B-17 bombers lined up for takeoff, getting into formation once airborne and heading for their target. On hand when the bombers returned he saw many land on one front wheel or forced to belly land with no front wheels. In the first mission flown by the Group on his arrival, twenty of twenty-one aircraft dispatched, were lost. Also at that stage of the war it was not uncommon for the Luftwaffe to follow British bombers back to their bases after night bombings and attack American bombers taking off in the early morning hours for their missions.

Buzz bombs sent by the Germans flew over Knettishall. One bomb exploded nearby and the crater left by the explosion was described as "big enough to set a house in". On a visit to London to attend church a buzz bomb struck nearby and caused flying glass that cut people on the street.

Everett described base food as good except for the powdered eggs. Coca Cola he felt, didn't taste like that purchased in America. British tea wagons visited the base daily to serve tea and provide snacks.

Everett recalled one instance of a B-17 returning from a mission in extreme fog and overcast with its instruments shot out. A P-51 fighter was flying alongside communicating with the B-17 pilot assisting him in finding and landing at their base.

In another instance one B-17 failed to make sufficient manifold pressure to get completely airborne on its takeoff and came down in a field. The crew was unharmed and were loaded in another airplane and sent on the mission.

A base party was held when the Group completed its 200th mission. On hand was General Doolittle the Eighth Air Force Commander. In addition to plenty of food, the day off was celebrated with softball games, tug of war between crews and chasing greased pigs. Glenn Miller's orchestra played at the evening base dance. The next day the plane carrying Miller to Paris in advance of his band was lost without a trace.

After V-E Day (Victory in Europe), Everett returned to the United States aboard a merchant marine ship. Unlike the miserable trip he experienced going to England, he ate excellent food and fruit on the return trip. He was sent to Sioux Falls, South Dakota, to train on the B-29 Superfortress in preparation for deployment to the Pacific Theater of Operations however, the war ended with the dropping of Atomic bombs on Hiroshima and Nagasaki.

Everett was discharged from the military at Sioux Falls on October 22, 1945, and returned to farming at South Amana.

CARL SCHARF, FORT DODGE, IA, enlisted in the Army Air Corps in May, 1942. He completed pilot training in the Aviation Cadet Program in November, 1943, earning his wings and commission as a Second Lieutenant. B-24 Transition training was completed at Liberal, Kansas before he was assigned an air crew and trained them at Casper, Wyoming, and McCook, Nebraska, in preparation for deployment to the European Theater of Operations.

A new aircraft was picked up at Topeka, Kansas, for their overseas flight to Nutts Corner, Ireland. On arrival their bomber was taken from them and they were assigned to the 392nd Bomb Group, 576th Bomb Squadron at Wendling, England.

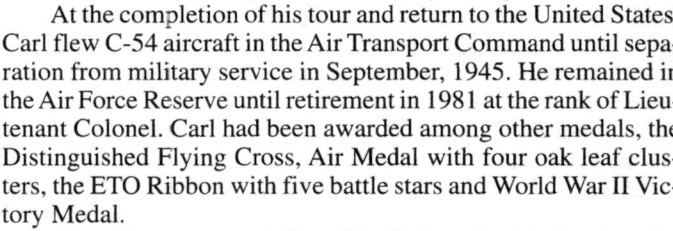

Carl flew thirty-three combat missions, fifteen of which were flown as either Squadron or Deputy Group lead aircraft.

At the completion of his tour and return to the United States, Carl flew C-54 aircraft in the Air Transport Command until separation from military service in September, 1945. He remained in the Air Force Reserve until retirement in 1981 at the rank of Lieutenant Colonel. Carl had been awarded among other medals, the Distinguished Flying Cross, Air Medal with four oak leaf clusters, the ETO Ribbon with five battle stars and World War II Victory Medal.

After his return to civilian life Carl worked in farm equipment manufacturing and was a vocational –technical instructor at Iowa Central Community College at Fort Dodge until retirement.

PAUL SCHERB, WAVERLY, IA, enlisted in the Army Air Corps, August 7, 1942. He filled out a form asking his preference in what he would like to do in the service. As all service men know this usually doesn't mean anything particularly in wartime. Meteorology was his first choice and he got it.

As an enlisted man, he was first trained as an observer, a two and half month course. If qualified, additional training in forecasting was available taking another five to six months. Officer's meteorology training was more in-depth concerning weather phenomenon and forecasting techniques. Training took place at Wendover, UT; San Bernadino, Palmdale and Victorville, CA. Deployed to England he was assigned to the 18th and 21st Weather Squadrons at Hethel and Bungay, England.

Forecasters performed their work in base control towers. Although essentially non-hazardous when compared to flight crews their work was none the less important. In order for aircrews to fly and be able to complete their missions they had to know what the weather conditions were to and from the target as well as over the target areas. Some weather they could fly in and some they couldn't. It was the meteorologists responsibility to accumulate weather data, plot it on charts and make forecasts. Forecasts were made not only for the base they were at but other bases scheduled for missions. Four officers, two forecasters and eight observers worked in shifts twenty-four hours a day.

Paul was discharged from military service December 27, 1945.

LOREN SCHIPULL, EAGLE GROVE, IA, was attending college at Ames, Iowa when he enlisted in the Army Air Corps in October, 1942. He was not called to active duty until February, 1943, and sent to Jefferson Barracks, St Louis, Missouri, for Basic Training. Accepted into the Aviation Cadet Program, Loren attended Milwaukee State Teachers College where he took courses in math and physics under the College Detachment Training Program.

Following completion of schooling Loren reported to Santa Ana, California for classification and Pre-flight Training. Primary Flight Training was taken at Blythe and Basic Flight Training at Taft, California, before Advanced Flight Training at Marfa, Texas, where he received his wings and commission as a Second Lieutenant.

Loren flew B-17s towing targets for aerial gunners in training at Kingman, Arizona before he reported to Lincoln, Nebraska for crew assignment and training with the crew at Alexandria, Louisiana.

In August, 1944, Loren flew to the European Theater of Operations assigned to the 398th Bomb Group at Nuthampstead, England. He flew half of his thirty-five combat missions as Co-pilot before taking over as First Pilot.

Loren's third mission, a raid on Brux, Czechoslovakia, was his most memorable. "Turning on the bomb run and seeing the flak ahead of us, I never thought we would make it through it." He was hit in the hand by a piece of flak but was not seriously wounded. He never received serious damage to his aircraft and never lost a crew member to wounds. His last mission was flown on February 3, 1945. He had completed more missions than the rest of his crew and remained at Nuthampstead ferrying downed and repaired aircraft until his crew finished their tour of duty.

Loren was in Prescott, Scotland waiting for a boat back to the United States when the war ended in Europe. He received his separation from military service in June, 1945, having been awarded the Air Medal with five oak leaf clusters, ETO Ribbon and World War II Victory Medal, among others. He returned to Iowa where he farmed until retirement.

RAYMOND C. SCHLEIHS, JOHNSTON, IA, attended Iowa State College and was employed by General Motors Diesel Plant and Rock Island Railroad before he enlisted in the Army Air Corps at Fort Des Moines, Iowa, on March 12, 1942.

Ray completed Mechanic and Propeller Specialist schools at Chanute Field, Illinois and then graduated from Pilot School at Stockton, California. He was assigned to an air crew and trained with them in preparation for overseas deployment. They flew a new B-17 to Ireland and later were assigned to the 390th Bomb Group at Framlingham, England. Ray flew thirty-five combat missions including a shuttle mission to Russia. With the cooperation of the Russian Government, targets out of B-17 range to make a return flight to England, would be bombed. They would fly on to Russia where they would be refueled and re-armed to bomb a target on their return to England. On this particular mission a German fighter plane shadowed the bomber formation to Russia to find out their destination. That night, while the B-17s were parked on the airfield, German bombers attacked and destroyed sixty American bombers.

After he returned to the United States Ray began flying B-29s at Alexandria, Louisiana, until separated from military service on September 13, 1945, at Jefferson Barracks, St. Louis, Missouri. Ray had been awarded the Distinguished Flying Cross, Air Medal with four oak leaf clusters, European Theater of Operations and World War II Victory Medals.

Ray began a career as Sales and Service Engineer for an Iron Foundry whose products were used by American Railroads. He is active in the Johnston Lions Club and has given talks to middle school students on World War II.

ROBERT J SCHREINER, WATERLOO, IA, attended Iowa State Teachers College at Cedar Falls, Iowa, (Now University of Northern Iowa) and worked nights at John Deere Company as a machinist He entered military service at Camp Dodge, Iowa, on December 12, 1942.

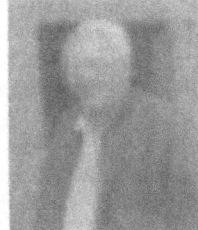

Robert was sent to Jefferson Barracks, Missouri, for Basic Training. He then began a series of cross-country trips to attend training that included: Fort Belvoir, Virginia, for Map Reproduction School; Greensboro, North Carolina, for Aviation Cadets; Presbyterian College, Clinton, South Carolina, for College Training Detachment; Nashville, Tennessee, for Classification; Maxwell Field, Montgomery, Alabama, for Pre-flight; and Emery Riddle Flying School, Arcadia, Florida, for Primary Flight Training. The Air Corps needed aerial gunners more than pilots and Robert was re-assigned to Buckley Field, Colorado, for Armaments School; Harlingen, Texas, for Aerial Gunnery School; and Walla Walla, Washington, for Crew Formation and Training. He sailed on the "Aquitania" and arrived at Glasgow, Scotland, November 23, 1944. Robert was assigned to the 863rd Bomb Squadron of the 493rd Bomb Group, Debach, England.

A crew that shared the Nissen hut with Robert was shot down while flying off his left wing. Six were killed and three taken prisoner of war. Robert's plane was required to make a forced landing in France from left wing damage and subsequent loss of fuel that prevented them from making it back to base. He also participated in two food missions to Holland. The Germans agreed to a truce period to allow food be dropped to starving Dutch. "It was very heart warming to be greeted with the people on rooftops, spelling out "Thanks, Yanks" in tulips and waving in appreciation."

Robert returned to the United States, June 12, 1945, after flying thirty combat missions. For the next four months until discharge on October 6, 1945, he served at Ft. Sheridan, Illinois; Santa Ana, California, and finished at Victoria, Texas, as a physical education instructor.

After military service Robert returned to school and graduated from the University of Iowa Law School in June of 1951. He entered the banking profession and retired in 1986.

Right - Bob, Waist Gunner, beside his B-17 at 493rd BG, Debach, England

CLARENCE SCHUCHMANN, HAWKEYE, IA, received his wings in May, 1943, at La Junta, Colorado. He then completed transition courses on the B-25 and B-17 before he was transferred to Euphrata, WA, where he became part of the 457th Bomb Group in training. Additional training was taken at Wendover, UT and Grand Island, NE. While at Grand Island one engine of his plane was taking on excessive amounts of oil and had to be changed. Clarence called his girl friend in Iowa. She came to see him and they were married. Three days later he took off for Glatton, England. Clark Gable, stationed at Polebrook was a good friend of his commanding officer and came to Clarence's base occasionally.

On his first combat mission Clarence's radio operator was killed when hit by a piece of flak in the forehead. The next day their flak helmets were issued.

His fourth mission was on February 25, 1944, a 750 bomber attack on three Messerschmitt production centers and a ball bearing plant at Stuttgart, Germany. Three of his aircraft's four engines were shot out north of Paris on the way home and three crew members were wounded. The bombardier had glass in his eyes and they were bleeding. The engineer had glass in his neck and the tail gunner was wounded. They had to get the ball turret gunner out of his turret as it was smeared with oil. They fell back from the formation lucky they could fly at all. They made it back to England which was overcast from low lying clouds. When they got through the clouds they were at about one thousand feet over a B-17 base (Deenethorpe). When they tried to land, their remaining engine did not respond to the throttle. The flight engineer shot off a red flare to indicate they had wounded aboard and landed down wind just ahead of the base's returning Group. "I was afraid of the gas blowing up so I shut off the switches. His engineer advised that if Clarence wanted brakes he would have to turn on the switches. The plane did stop and didn't blow. Clarence received a commendation for his down-wind, dead stick landing without injury to his plane or crew. Twenty-three of the twenty-four planes that completed the mission suffered battle damage. One was destroyed on landing and two were lost to enemy action.

March 20, 1944, was a scheduled mission to Frankfurt, Germany, to bomb the Alfred Treves plant, manufacturer of 50% of Germany's aircraft and submarine piston rings and 75% of their hydraulic brakes. The mission was aborted when only about 80 miles from Frankfurt due to bad weather and lack of visibility. In leading the top squadron, Clarence rolled out of a left turn. The right wing man did not and came directly at them for what was about to be a mid-air collision. Clarence's co-pilot pulled the stick back in his lap. Clarence opened the throttle wide open and they went over on their back going into a spin. They recovered after a 10,000 foot fall. Out of formation in bad weather they were on their own. They broke into the clear at one point to discover three ME-109 German fighters beneath them. The enemy did not attempt to engage them and Clarence headed for the nearest cloud bank for cover. They were lucky they made it back to their base. Everyone in their bomb group saw them go down in a spin and took it for granted they crashed. No one knew a B-17 could recover from a tail spin with a full bomb load.

Schweinfurt was the objective on March 24, 1944. When the bombardier went to salvo the bombs they wouldn't release. With the bomb bay doors open and still loaded they could not maintain sufficient speed to stay with the formation. Three crew members went into the bomb bay and released the bombs individually. The bomb shackles holding the bombs were put in backwards making them inoperative. At this time an Me-109 hit them with a .20 millimeter shell in the vertical stabilizer ahead of the rudder. With the rudder peddles jumping around they were still able to fly. They stayed on the side of their group away from where fighters were attacking. When they made it back to their base they tried a stall before they landed and the plane seemed to handle better so the decision was made to land tail up. It worked.

During his tour, Clarence's gunners were credited with thirteen German planes shot down. Other planes were shot down but couldn't be authenticated for credit.

Clarence was awarded the Distinguished Flying Cross with one cluster, Air Medal with five clusters, European Theater of Operations and World War II Victory Medals.

Right - Clarence and crew after a mission. Clarence, Pilot, is back row, second from right.

VICTOR SCHWEER, WEST LIBERTY, IA, was working for a canning factory prior to World War II. Although drafted into military service in 1942, Victor was not called to active duty until after the farm harvest season had ended. After Basic Training at Amarillo, TX, he entered the Cadet Detachment Training at Norfolk, NE, to take courses in mathematics and meteorology.

The Air Corps needed aerial gunners. For the good of the service Aviation Cadets were "washed out" and Victor was sent to Las Vegas, NV for Aerial Gunnery School.

Following completion of gunnery training Victor met his crew at Tampa, FL. They trained together as a combat team at Gulfport, MS. They picked up a new airplane at Savannah, GA to begin their cross-Atlantic flight to Valley, Wales.

Assigned to the 100th Bomb Group at Thorpe Abbots, England, Victor flew twenty-nine combat missions as a B-17 tail gunner. Six missions were flown to Holland after V-E Day to drop food supplies to the Dutch who were near starvation after years of Nazi rule. In appreciation, red tulips were planted spelling "Thank you" over which the American bombers flew.

Victor was credited with downing one German ME-262 jet fighter. As the jet began to close in on his aircraft to shoot it down, Victor started firing while the jet was out of range and continued firing until it flew into his stream of bullets. The jet started smoking and headed for the ground. Victor saw the pilot bail out and open his parachute.

On another mission flak from German anti-aircraft guns blew out the entire tail gunner's dome and a large part of the aircraft's tail. Victor said he felt "a hell of a jolt, a tremendous gust of air, and our plane started vibrating". The pilot was able to trim the aircraft to avoid the vibration. Victor's guns had jammed and he had just crawled out of the tail gunner's position when the flak hit his position.

On a mission to bomb Heidelberg, Germany, "we were taking flak below us. Their guns couldn't quite reach us. Flak was denting the underside of our aircraft. That which pierced the plane just dropped on the floor. We had 108 holes in our plane when we got back to base".

One of the new German jets was a small airplane called a Komet. It had no wheels and only about twenty minutes of flying time. It would fly into American bomber formations to gauge speed, altitude and direction which would be radioed ahead for

Luftwaffe fighters and flak batteries. In his tail position Victor was suddenly surprise to see a Komet flying right along his airplane. "The pilot stared me in the eye then suddenly flew away. It scared the hell out of me."

On a pass to London, Victor and some friends were seeing the sights. They stayed at a Red Cross Club in Piccadilly Square where servicemen could stay overnight. "We stayed in a room where bunks were three high. I was in the top bunk. Air raid sirens went off, a V-2 rocket was headed for London. We ignored the sirens. It landed close enough to us, I was knocked out of the top bunk onto the floor and covered with plaster. All the windows were blown out of our room. We never ignored any sirens after that."

Victor received his discharge at Patterson Field, OH. He was employed in marketing at Rath Packing Company in Waterloo, IA, for twenty-one years, and the Louis Rich Turkey Processing Plant in West Liberty. Victor and his wife bought a local jewelry store which they operated for twenty-five years. Although retired, Victor still works occasionally at the jewelry store lending his expertise to new owners.

CLAYTON SCOTT, OSCEOLA, IA, was working on the family farm prior to World War II. He had spent one year as an aircraft fabricator manufacturing the Curtis P-40 at Buffalo, New York.

Clayton entered the military on March 29, 1942 at Buffalo, New York. After Basic Training he was received Bombardier Training at Ellington Field and Big Springs,

Texas; Aerial Gunnery School at Las Vegas, Nevada; Rated Aircraft Observer(Bombardier) and Radar Bombardier Training at Boca Raton, Florida.

He was deployed to England in July, 1944, with the 381st Bomb Group at Ridgewell, England, a B-17 group. He received further Radar Bombardier Training at Alconbury and transferred to the 492nd Bomb Group in B-24s at Harrington, England.

Clayton flew thirty combat missions as Radar Bombardier. His nineteenth mission was a bombing raid on a railroad yard at Wilhelmshaven, Germany, an 885 mile mission. He recalled that it was more dangerous on the ground before taking off for the mission. An RAF Spitfire taking off from their base attempted a barrel-roll just off the end of the runway. He was turning back to land in the opposite direction but didn't make it. His engine "konked out". Clayton and a friend were walking from the briefing room for their mission and saw the RAF fighter coming right at them. They dove into a roadside ditch full of mud and water. The Spitfire hit the tops of trees then knocked over a large tree directly across the road from them. The airplane skidded through the rear of the base Finance Office coming to rest near their briefing room. The wings and engine were torn off and the pilot's body thrown out. The wheels, guns and ammunition were scattered between them and where the fuselage came to rest. Clayton arrived at his aircraft on the flight line covered with mud. His pilot asked if he still felt like flying the mission. He did.

Clayton retired from the Air Force on May 1, 1954 as a Lieutenant Colonel having been awarded, among other medals, the Distinguished Flying Cross, Air Medal with three oak leaf clusters, Air Force Commendation Medal with one oak leaf cluster and the ETO Ribbon with three battle stars. Since retirement Clayton was Executive Secretary of Clark County Development.

LAVERNE M. SEDORE, FAIRFIELD, IA, was born in Southeast Iowa and graduated from Agency High School in the Spring of 1940. He worked at Morrell's Packing Plant in Ottumwa, Iowa until enlistment in the Army Air Corps, October 12, 1942, at Des Moines, Iowa. After Basic Training at Jefferson Barracks, St.

Louis, Missouri, and College Training Detachment schooling at Creighton University, Omaha, Nebraska, Laverne was sent to classification at Santa Ana, Californian.

He entered nine weeks of Pilot Ground School, nine weeks of Primary Flight Training near Visalia, California, nine weeks of Basic Flight Training at Chico, California, nine weeks of Advanced Flight Training and a month of Co-Pilot Training at Las Vegas, Nevada. Laverne was then sent to McDill Field, Tampa, Florida, for staging and crew assignment.

Laverne was deployed to Debach, England in January, 1945, with the 493rd Bomb Group. His first of twenty-five missions was on January 7, 1945. His most memorable mission was flying food to starving people in the Netherlands. "Our bombers were loaded with food. We flew across the Channel at low altitude and dropped the food on a racetrack on the outskirts of Amsterdam. These people knew we were coming. They were there by the thousands. We came over so low, we could see their mouths were open and they were waving like crazy. We did that for two consecutive days. It was a real upper."

After Germany's surrender, Laverne returned to the United States for B-29 training and deployment to the Pacific Theater of Operations. In the meantime, Japan surrendered. Laverne was discharged from military service on October 15, 1945, and returned to Iowa to join his father in farming. He quit farming in 1984 to drive a contract mail route. He retired eight years later and continues to provide community service by driving for Meals on Wheels.

Right - Laverne and his crew at 493rd BG, Debach, England. C0-Pilot Laverne is back row, second from right.

WENDELL C. 'CHUCK' SESSIONS, CEDAR RAPIDS, IA, worked for General Electric Company as a Laboratory Technician before World War II. He entered military service October 27, 1942, at Springfield, Massachusetts.

Chuck attended B-17 Engine School at Amarillo, Texas. He was accepted into the Aviation Cadet Program and sent to Iowa Wesleyan College,

Mt. Pleasant, Iowa, for schooling as part of the College Training Detachment Program. Pre-Flight Training was taken at Santa Ana,

California; Primary Training at Hemet, California; Basic Flight Training at Taft, California; Advanced Flight Training at Pecos, Texas; and B-17 Transition Training, Roswell, New Mexico. After assignment with an aircrew, overseas training was taken with the crew at Gulfport, Mississippi.

Chuck was deployed overseas January 6. 1945, as First Pilot and assigned to the 490th Bomb Group at Eye, England. He flew thirty-three combat missions, the most memorable of which, was his second mission. Heavy enemy flak taken by their plane caused engine failure and made it impossible to return to their base. They were forced to make a landing at Eindhoven, Holland, behind Allied lines. They were picked up by British forces and returned to England.

Chuck was discharged from military service, September 6, 1946, at Drew Field, Florida. He had been awarded the Air Medal with oak leaf clusters, ETO Ribbon with battle stars, and World War II Victory Medal. His unit received a Presidential Unit Citation and was a unit that suffered the lowest missing in action losses of an Eighth Air Force unit in combat for extended periods of time.

Since the war he served as Vice President of Operations for Vigortone Agriculture Products, a Division of Beatrice Foods.

Right - Chuck and his crew at 490th BG, Eye, England. Chuck, Pilot, is back row, left.

A. DONALD SEXTON, NEWTON, IA, had nearly completed his first year of engineering at the University of Iowa when he entered military service on February 21, 1943. As part of the College Detachment Training Program he attended Milwaukee State Teachers College until June, 1943, when he was sent to Santa Ana, CA, for Classification. This included ten hours flying time in a Piper Cub to determine if he was suited for flying. He passed this successfully and moved to Pre-Flight Training also at Santa Ana and then Primary Flight Training at Scottsdale, AZ. Donald then took Basic Flight Training at Lemore, CA, Advanced Flight Training at Pecos, TX and four engine training in New Mexico.

On his twenty-first birthday Donald was assigned to a flight crew at Lincoln, Nebraska. He trained with his crew at Dyersburg, Tennessee. They returned to Lincoln in January, 1945, and boarded a train for New York. Donald's crew sailed on the "Queen Elizabeth" to England following a zig-zag route to prevent submarine attack. They eventually reached Stone, England where they received assignment to Polebrook as a replacement crew with the 351st Bomb Group. Polebrook was a former RAF base with tarpaper shacks for housing. The weather was always cold. Flying at high altitudes meant the inside of a B-17 could reach between 30 to 60 degrees below zero during missions. The only way to get warm after a mission and de-briefing was to go to bed.

Between January and the end of the war Donald flew twenty-eight combat missions. Although the appearance of Luftwaffe fighters had been greatly reduced, flak bursts from German anti-aircraft batteries was a constant threat that could destroy or cause serious damage to bomber formations let alone death or injury to aircrews. Routes were flown to targets to minimize the risk of flak. Chaf (aluminum strips) were dumped from aircraft to confuse German radar operators directing barrages against them particularly when overcast skies prevented visual observation of American bombers. Donald did witness a plane in formation ahead of him explode from a direct hit. He found out later a friend from Dubuque he had met in training perished in that plane.

Donald flew back to the United States after V-E Day and received his discharge from military service in June, 1945, at Jefferson Barracks, St. Louis, Missouri. He had been awarded the Air Medal with three oak leaf clusters, ETO Ribbon and World War II Victory Medal.

He returned to the College of Engineering at the University of Iowa where he received his Bachelors and Master of Science in Engineering Degrees. Donald was employed by Maytag in Newton until his retirement in 1984. He stayed in the Air Force Reserve until October, 1983.

Right - Donald and his crew at 351st BG, Polebrook, England. Donald, Pilot, is front row, left. Fellow Iowan Lee Gingery, Shenandoah, is back row, fourth from left.

DICK SHEPARD, JANESVILLE, IA, entered the Army Air Corps in March, 1943. He flew eight missions as a tail gunner for the Eighth Air Force with the 855th Bomb Squadron of the 491st Bomb Group. These included missions that dropped food to the Dutch and supplies to ground forces in support of D-Day.

Dick was then transferred to the Fifteen Air Force in Italy where twenty-five missions were flown in the B-24. On his twenty-fifth mission, a raid on the marshalling yards in Berlin, Dick's airplane took a direct hit in a gas tank just before it turned on the bomb run. Fortunately the airplane didn't explode. They rapidly lost fuel and jettisoned their bomb load and all equipment they could to lighten the aircraft and headed for Russia. Near Lodz, Poland, they circled an airfield and were initially shot at by Russian fighter planes. Dick's pilot lowered their planes wheels and opened the bomb bay doors as a sign of surrender. Down to one thousand feet with two engines out and a third engine on fire they landed without the fighters resuming their attack and successfully put out the engine fire.

Dick and his crew were guarded by Russian soldiers at first and then were housed at a hotel in Lodz once their identity was established. "After five or six days we were sent to Odessa where a DC-3 flown by a Russian pilot with an American Co-Pilot arrived to pick us up. We were flown to Persia, issued new clothing, and then flown to Palestine where we refueled for a flight to Cairo, Egypt. The Air Transport Command came to take us back to our base in Italy."

"While in Poland, an American P-51 with engine trouble landed where we were. He was only there a short time. I gave the pilot a letter to mail to my mother telling her I was alright. She received the note two days before getting a telegram that I was Missing in Action.

Dick was discharged from military service in September, 1945. He had been awarded the Air Medal with five oak leaf clusters, European Theater of Operations Medal with eleven battle stars, and World War II Victory Medal. Dick worked for a company making concrete mixers until retirement.

ELLSWORTH SHIELDS, WAVERLY, IA, attended the University of Wisconsin in the Fall of 1942. He was drafted into the Army Air Corps April 23, 1943. He completed training as a Radio Operator/Aerial Gunner and assigned to a B-24 Liberator bomber crew with the 752nd Squadron, 458th Bomb Group stationed at Horsham St. Faith, England.

Ellsworth flew 35 combat missions and nine gasoline supply missions in support of General Patton's advance through France in September, 1944, and Belgium during the Battle of the Bulge. Before leaving on any mission Ellsworth always took the opportunity to go to the base chapel and pray. "Most of the time it was about coming home safely from the mission. When we were waiting to start up our engines I would say my prayers too."

"The first several missions bothered me because I knew our bombs didn't always hit the military target and they had to hit some homes. When there was cloud cover over the target and we couldn't drop our bombs we always had an alternate target to fly to. If that was covered we would try to drop our bombs on railroad yards or factories that made war armaments. On the bomb run when the pilot had to fly steady and straight to drop our bombs on target is when I got to know the Lord very well. I didn't want to die. I wanted to live and recited the 23rd Psalm. Flak on the bomb run was intense. The Germans were good at tracking us and getting their shells right up where we were. It either damaged a plane, damaged it to the extent it wasn't flyable, or it exploded killing or wounding crewmembers. Once a bomber started to go down it was very hard to bail out. Centrifugal force pinned a person inside the aircraft."

"We were all young men but we had courage, courage to do the job we were trained for. We were frightened but it was important we do our job as a team. Because of our training, friendship and teamwork we worked together and developed a comradeship. We were of different faiths so we did our own thing in going to the chapel or praying in the bomber when being hit hard by flak or German aircraft."

On January 26, 1945, Ellsworth's plane was hit severely with flak and started going down. "We had three men on board wounded. It looked like we were going to crash and I was sure I was going to die. I thought of my parents and my sisters. I would be gone. I felt sorry for them. But then I had a wonderful feeling that I would be going home to the Lord. The pilot managed to land the plane behind Allied lines northeast of Paris in a snowy cornfield with only two main wheels. The front wheel had been shot off by flak over the target."

The nine gasoline supply flights were flown with only five crew members instead of the usual ten. "The gas fumes in the bombers were very heavy because we had these five gallon gas tanks in the bomb bay. All that was needed was a spark and you would blow up. Our flight engineer used to say "I'm going to keep the bomb bay doors partially open to let in fresh air come in all the time", which was good. Later they did that on other missions because it made sense."

"Once, in heavy fog we almost crashed into another B-24. Can you imagine a big B-24 right below you in heavy fog and you are trying to find your base. You see these big props right below you not fifty feet. If it moved a little higher, twenty of us would have been gone and two bombers. Another time we landed and a big tire blew as we were taxiing. If it would have blown as we touched in landing we would have cart wheeled off the runway."

Ellsworth completed his 35 missions required for rotation back to the United States by the age of twenty. He was discharged October 7, 1945, having been awarded, among others, the Air Medal with four oak leaf clusters, European Theater of Operations Medal, and the World War II Victory Medal.

Ellsworth returned to college and graduated from the University of Wisconsin, Milwaukee, in 1948. He chose life insurance as a career and worked for one company for over forty-one years working in all positions from sales to Vice-President of Field

Right - Ellsworth and his crew at 458th BG, Horsham St Faith, England. Ellsworth, Radio Operator/Aerial Gunner, is back row, second from right.

KEITH SHIRK, DES MOINES, IA, was taking Civilian Flight Training while a student at Iowa State College in Ames prior to the start of World War II. He enlisted in the Army Air Corps in May, 1942, but was not called to active duty until February, 1943. He was sent to Jefferson Barracks, St. Louis, Missouri, for Basic Training.

Keith entered the Aviation Cadet Pro-

gram and took Pre-Flight Training at Creighton University, Omaha, Nebraska, in March, 1943. Additional flight training included Pre-flight School at San Antonio, Texas; Primary Flight Training at Corsicana, Texas and Basic Flight Training at Greenville, Texas. In November, 1943, he attended Twin Engine Advanced Training at Frederick, Oklahoma. He graduated in January, 1944, and was commissioned a Second Lieutenant. Keith reported to Liberal, Kansas, in January, 1944, for Transition Training in preparation for overseas deployment. A massive snow storm hit Liberal. "The snow banks were so high only the tops of the airplane's rudders were visible." With training slowed because of the snow, it was not until June, 1944, that Keith went to Tonopah, Nevada for Crew Training and eventually to Camp Kilmer, Jew Jersey, where in September, 1944, he and his crew were shipped to England with the 389th Bomb Group.

Keith's first mission was as an observer on a bomb raid to Hamburg, Germany. The next day, October 7, 1944, he flew his first mission with his own crew. The target was Kassel, Germany, where they experienced heavy flak over the target area. "After dropping bombs and turning off target, Navigator Dunn was looking out the right blister window when bombardier White called his attention to something on the left side of the plane. Dunn pulled his head out of the window just as a piece of flak hit the window and passed through the plane and exited by my left foot. If Dunn hadn't withdrawn his head just then he would have been killed. I was flying and we were gaining on the formation so I made a couple of power reductions on the supercharger control. We were still gaining so I reached up and pulled the throttles back and noticed that the manifold pressure was dropping. I switched to the spare inverter that supplies A C power to the supercharger, but it did no good. The supercharger control did not work. The engineer tried to find the trouble but couldn't. By this time we could not maintain speed and could not keep up with the rest of the formation. We could not maintain enough manifold pressure so we descended to an altitude of 12,000 feet where we could fly without the supercharger and made it back to base alone. After we got home we found all the gaskets in the manifold system were blown out. Two wires leading to the supercharger control had been cut by the piece of flak. With power cut, the engine's waste gates went to the fully closed position and pressure built up quickly. When the throttles were opened, the system would not hold enough pressure to fly at higher altitude."

Fog required an instrument takeoff on December 19, 1944, for a mission behind German lines during the Battle of the Bulge. "We could only see two runway lights ahead of the plane so I asked the Co-pilot to watch the lights on the right side and the engineer to watch the lights on the left and to let me know if we were getting close to them. At 90 m.p.h. the engineer shouted "look out we are running off the runway, we're going to hit the lights"". I called full flaps-emergency power and hauled back on the yoke and we jumped into the air. I kicked the right rudder. As the flaps came down the nose wanted to come up so I had to hold a lot of pressure on the yoke to keep the plane level. We didn't have enough speed to fly so we had to get back down to the runway. It seemed to take a long time to hold the plane down and get back to the runway. We finally bounced at about 110 m.p.h. I felt we could hold it so called 'gear up'. As the speed continued to increase we started to climb. We raised the flaps slowly. By the time we got the flaps up we were at 700 feet and broke out into the clear. We set the controls to normal power and continued on with the mission."

Several missions found them returning to base on only three engines. On one of these landings using a short runway Keith had to 'ground loop' the plane to stop before running off the end of the runway. This caused a tire to blow but all hands were safe.

Keith's last mission was on March 9, 1945, on a raid to Munster, Germany. He returned home to Grundy Center on May 8, V-E Day.

Keith married Ann Hellmich on May 19 and headed for California. After three weeks he was sent to Jefferson Barracks, Missouri, where he received his discharge from military service on July 19, 19455. Keith received, among other decorations, the Distinguished Flying Cross, Air Medal with four oak leaf clusters, ETO Ribbon and World War II Victory Medal. He and his bride were in Ames, Iowa o n VJ Day where they made arrangements to return to Iowa State in the Fall Quarter. After graduation Keith was a structural engineer.

ROBERT G. SHULER, DES MOINES, IA, was in school and worked for a short time with Caterpillar to get funds for college when he enlisted in the Army Air Corps, June 3, 1942, at Pekin, Illinois. He was sent to the Nebraska School of Engineering at Lincoln, Nebraska, and Lockheed Air Terminal at Ontario, California.

On October 20, 1943, he was deployed with the 79th Squadron, 20th Fighter Group, Kingscliffe, England, as a draftsman for squadron intelligence. His job was to make maps and charts for pilots. He was also responsible for painting names or slogans and pictures on planes that fighter pilots wanted on their assigned aircraft.

He was discharged from military service, September 29,1 945, at Ft Sheridan, Illinois. Robert had been awarded the ETO Ribbon with two battle stars, and the World War II Victory Medal.

Robert resumed his education after the war and became a university instructor, business owner and artist.

W. A. SINGER, AMES, IA, graduated from the University of Iowa in June, 1942. A member of the Army Air Corps Reserve he was called to active duty in October of that year and sent to San Antonio, Texas, for classification under the Aviation Cadet Program. He was assigned to Saxton, Missouri, for Primary Flight Training but "washed out" because of shin splints. He was

re-assigned to Aerial Gunnery School at Hondo, Texas. Upon completion of training he returned to San Antonio where he learned of an opening in Navigator's School at Ellington Field, Houston. Bill volunteered and was accepted. Upon graduation he was assigned to an air crew at Tampa, Florida, where they trained in preparation for overseas deployment. In addition to flying practice missions they practiced procedures in case of fire aboard their aircraft, ditching in water and bailing out of the airplane.

In May, 1944, Bill and his crew were assigned a new bomber at Savannah, Georgia, to fly, with others, to Europe. The day they were to leave Savannah the first two planes ahead of them burst into flames on takeoff killing all crew members. Further takeoffs were cancelled. An inspection of aircraft disclosed an oxygen design problem had caused an instantaneous fire and the aircraft to explode. Changes to the aircraft were made before Bill and his crew finally left, flying across the North Atlantic toward Belfast, Ireland. On takeoff their own aircraft blew an engine manifold. Nearing Belfast cloud cover over the land and ocean prevented celestial and dead reckoning sightings. A radio heading given by the Belfast airport was their only navigational tool. They landed at the busy airport with only one-quarter inch of fuel remaining in their tanks.

Before flying combat missions Bill took additional instruction at Stone, England, in the "G-Box", radar equipment installed in the ball turret area of aircraft. Assigned to the 384th Bomb Group at Grafton Underwood Bill and his crew were hungry for information. Old timers, those with a few missions under their belts grudgingly gave information on what to expect. They didn't want to make friends for fear their new found friends would be lost on a mission. He did meet fellow Iowans Bill Green, a University of Iowa football player and Duane Bennett from Newton.

Bill's first mission was to bomb submarine pens at Brest, France. "I was a nervous wreck, no enemy fighters attacked us nor was there any "flak" . He would fly his first three missions with his original crew. Thereafter he was made lead Navigator for his squadron or deputy lead for his bomb group.

On his seventeenth mission, October 11, 1944, "we turned on the I.P. and became level. Right after we dropped our bombs we got hit. Two engines were shot out and a third engine was running at half power. We tried to get across the Ruhr and got hit by "flak" again. A German fighter made a pass at us and blew a big hole in the fuselage but didn't press any further attacks. Our pilot was unconscious and we spun down about three or four thousand feet before the Co-Pilot could get control of the aircraft. We pulled the Pilot out of his seat and wrapped his wounds. I was wounded in the left leg but helped the Co-Pilot by operating the rudder with my right foot. We belly landed in a potato field near a dense forest. When we came to a stop we thought the plane would explode. We got everyone out and away from the airplane. I realized I left a .45 caliber pistol in the plane. I ran back to the plane and shot out the G-Box equipment and instruments."

"Civilians came after us with pitchforks, but a German army patrol came and backed the civilians down. One German guard even gave us apples to eat. I tore off a piece of cardboard, wrote down my mothers name and address and gave it to the guard. The guard would later become a Prisoner of War and wrote my mother. I still have his letter."

Bill received medical treatment for his wounds at Traben Trabach, Germany, where one of the nurses brought cognac from the village, sneaked it into the hospital and gave it to patients.

After interrogation at Frankfurt, Germany, Bill was shipped to Wetzler, Germany, for clean uniforms, showers and decent food before being transported to Stalag Luft III located near Zagan, Poland, 110 kilometers southeast of Berlin. Bill was hospitalized most of his internment. His wounds took a long time to heal and he had an allergic reaction to sulpha drugs administered to him. His head was put in a plaster cast. Following release from the prison hospital he was put in the South Compound of Stalag Luft III with about 200 other Americans. The prison had three escape tunnels being dug named "Tom, Dick and Harry". The entrance to "Tom" was through a covert hole in the shower room. To prevent detection by German guards a prisoner would pretend to take a shower during guard inspections.

During his internment the prisoners never got their full allotment of Red Cross parcels. What parcels they did receive had to be shared with other POWs. Occasionally trucks carrying the parcels would be strafed and destroyed.

As the Russian Army began to close in on Germany, the POWs were moved. They were required to march further away from the front lines, without food, transport or sleeping facilities. They were initially herded into 40X8 railroad cars (designed to haul 40 men or eight horses). It was impossible to lay down and Bill, as well as other POWs, got sick with diarrhea. There were no sanitary facilities in the boxcars. Their train took them to Nurnberg. From there they were to march toward Berchtesgaden in Bavaria. Other than what could be scavenged from the land, they had no food except for remnants from Red Cross parcels, They had to sleep in open fields or in whatever shelter could be found. One night Bill and two other POWs decided to escape across a plowed field into some woods. They wound up walking in circles for hours. The only food they had was a jar of jam and a jar of margarine and one of the POWs got sick. They spent the night in a rabbit hutch in the woods while a tank battle took place near them. With their condition deteriorating the trio decided to get re-captured. They approached a house in a nearby village and were met by a Hungarian SS Officer who promptly took them to a jail.

They were treated well and given food. After 4-5 days American Airborne soldiers arrived and freed them. They had to stay with the airborne unit which required they march 10-12 miles a day and sleep wherever a comfortable place could be found in an open field or barn. They arrived at a small town in Bavaria which had a hospital for Jewish prisoners. The Germans had fled in advance of the Americans leaving the tortured, starving prisoners and skeletal remains of others.

The next morning American tanks arrived in the town and Bill was officially liberated, May 2, 1945. He and other POWs were trucked to Moosburg, Germany, a large POW center where C-47 cargo planes arrived to fly out 40-45 thousand Allied POWs.

Taken to LeHavre, France, site of Camp Lucky Strike, Bill received a haircut, shave and shower, new uniform and food. During his processing period, rest and relaxation included a trip to Paris. Because of the large number of POWs to receive partial back pay, finance officers were located at several locations within the camp to handle the volume. It didn't take long for some to realize that if you went from one finance location to another, they couldn't keep track of what was being paid out to who and a GI could double or triple his pay. Bill went to Paris well-healed for a good time.

Bill boarded a Liberty Ship at LeHavre for Newport News, Virginia. After he arrived home he got married and then reported to Miami Beach, Florida, for more R&R and a promotion. He was declared surplus because of Japan's surrender in the Pacific and discharged from military service in November, 1945.

Meanwhile Bill entered University of Iowa Law School in September, 1945. He graduated in February, 1947, and practiced law until his retirement at age 79. Bill stayed in the Air Force Reserves. He was recalled to active duty during the Korean War and became Adjutant of the Troop Carrier Squadron out of Des Moines. He also served as Assistant Staff Judge Advocate at SAC Headquarters and received two promotions within a twenty-one year span. Bill retired from the Reserves after twenty-six years with the rank of full Colonel.

Right - Bill and his crew at Grafton Underwood following successful raid on German rocket site at Peenemunde. Bill is back row, third from right.

WILLARD SPANGLER, EVERLY, IA, was manager of the United Farmers Telephone Company in Everly prior to entering the Army Air Corps on February 25, 1943. He was sent to Jefferson Barracks, St. Louis, Missouri, for Basic Training. Additional training took place in the Southeastern United States. Pilot Training was taken at Maxwell Field, Alabama, and he attended other schools in Nashville, Tennessee; Albany and Macon, Georgia.

Willard was deployed to Knettishall, England, in April, 1944, as a Co-pilot with the 388th Bomb Group. On his thirteenth mission, August 2, 1944, his plane took three direct hits from German anti-aircraft fire while over France. One of the hits was at his aircraft's number three engine next to his co-pilot position. He was wounded with severe neck, shoulder and back injuries which rendered him unconscious. Upon wakening, he discovered the nose of the airplane had been blown off, the airplane was on fire, and none of the other crew members were aboard, having bailed out, except for the bombardier who was trapped in the wreckage. Willard stayed with the plane and was able to make a forced landing but was taken prisoner of war by the Germans.

Willard was sent to Stalag Luft III, Prisoner of War Camp, which consisted of American, Canadian and British POWs. During his internment the food he received was a leafy soup. He got little if any meat or bread and no medical attention. Red Cross parcels destined for the prisoners were not distributed but were kept stored in a nearby church. When Willard was liberated by the Allies in April, 1945, he weighed only 96 pounds as a result of malnutrition at the hands of his German captors.

He was discharged from military service in 1945 at San Antonio, Texas, and had been awarded, among other medals, the Distinguished Flying Cross, Air Medal with oak leaf cluster, ETO Ribbon and World War II Victory Medal. Since the war Willard served as Postmaster at Everly for thirty years until retirement.

ROBERT W. STAFFORD, AMES, IA, was a freshman student at Iowa State College. After the first quarter of school he enlisted into the Army Air Corps on the first anniversary of the Japanese attack on Pearl Harbor, December 7, 1942. He was not called to active duty until March, 1943 and sent to Jefferson Barracks, St. Louis, Missouri, for Basic Training.

Bob applied for and was accepted into the Aviation Cadet Program. After Basic Training he was sent to Monmouth College under the College Detachment Training Program to take courses in Mathematics, Physics, and other courses related to aviation. He then reported to Santa Ana, California, for Pre-Flight Training and Scottsdale, Arizona, for Primary Flight Training. After completion of Basic Flight Training at Pecos, Texas, Bob was assigned to an aircrew as Co-Pilot and completed B-17 Transition Training with the crew in preparation for overseas deployment. He was awarded his wings and commissioned as a Second Lieutenant in March, 1944.

In June, 1944, Bob sailed from Camp Kilmer, New Jersey to England and assignment with the 94th Bomb Group at Bury St. Edmunds, England. Additional training in formation flying, communications and aerial gunnery was required of all replacement crews before they flew their first mission. Bob flew the first of thirty combat missions on August 1, 1944, to bomb targets in Mannheim, Germany, in a B-17 nicknamed "Gremlin's Hotel". He would eventually fly four missions to Mainz, Germany, site of tank manufacturing and flying rocket assembly plants. Two missions were flown to heavily defended Merseburg, Germany to bomb synthetic oil refineries.

After eight missions Bob's crew was designated as a "lead crew" which meant their aircraft would be the lead plane in a squadron or group formation, depending on assignment at the time. It also meant they would be required to fly only thirty missions instead of thirty-five before rotation back to the United States. As Co-Pilot of a lead aircraft Robert had to give up his seat to a Command Officer flying on the mission. Bob was relegated to flying the mission in the tail gunner's position and act as formation control officer. He reported to the pilot and command officer on aircraft that were not maintaining formation, where enemy fighters were attacking, flak was being concentrated and damaged bombers from fighter and anti-aircraft fire.

In Bob's thirty missions no member of his crew was seriously injured. They were plagued with consistent bad weather flying in England and the North Sea from snow, fog, heavy overcast and icing problems that could have caused their aircraft to crash or be involved in a mid-air collision. A mission on November 29, 1944, required they take off from their base, with a full bomb and fuel load, in heavy snow. They managed to lift off just before they run out of runway but struck a fence. They managed to remain aloft, but another bomber following behind them struck the same fence and crashed killing all aboard.

On February 6, 1945, weather conditions and strong head winds during a mission to Valenciennes, France, exhausted the fuel supply of Bob's aircraft. Unable to make the return flight to England they were forced to land at a recently captured German airfield in France. After obtaining additional fuel they flew back to their base where it was disclosed, after examination of their aircraft, the plane was not air-worthy and shouldn't have been flown.

Bob's last mission was flown on March 24, 1945, a mission to Varrelbusch, Germany.

After return to the United States and discharge he entered Northwestern University. While in school he joined the Air Force Reserve. After graduation he secured employment with an insurance company in Des Moines and joined the Iowa Air National Guard. He was recalled to active duty as a Finance Officer during the Korean War. After his tour of duty Bob returned to Ames, Iowa, where he gained employment in a local bank and subsequently retired from the bank as its President.

Bob remained in the Air National Guard until 1966 when he retired at the rank of Colonel. During his military career Bob received the Distinguished Flying Cross, Air Medal with four oak leaf Clusters, European Theater of Operations and World War II Victory Medals. His Bomb Group was cited by the President for the historic bombing of the Muhlembau aircraft assembly plants at Brunswick, Germany. His Air Division also received a Presidential Citation for a shuttle run to Africa after bombing Messerschmitt aircraft assembly plants at Regensburg, Germany in August, 1943.

Right - Bob at the 94th Bomb Group, Bury St Edmunds, England

ERVIN STAMP, HOLSTEIN, IA, was farming at the outbreak of America's entry into World War II. He enlisted in the Army Air Corps at Camp Dodge near Des Moines in 1942 and was sent to Bakersfield, California for Basic Training. From there he was assigned to Marana Army Air Field near Tucson, Arizona where he performed pre-flight duties on aircraft. He was then transferred to the fueling section "gassing planes."

After two years in Arizona Ervin was sent to Salt Lake City,

Utah, in May, 1944, where he was in charge of a group of non-commissioned officers assigned to build a dry firing range. He was then sent by troop train to Boston, Massachusetts where he boarded the ocean liner "Mauritania" for a zig-zag voyage to Liverpool, England and eventual assignment with the 20th Fighter Group at Kings Cliffe, England. Ervin's specialty was as a heavy equipment driver. He was also a member of a recovery crew at crash sites. He recalled a P-38 fighter took off from the base and failed to gain altitude. "The pilot dropped the wing tanks and crashed right side up. The plane caught on fire and shells were going off all over the place. The pilot got out and was in the chow line with us the next morning."

Ervin also served in the re-fueling section of the 306th Bomb Group. After V-E Day he was sent to the French Morocco in North Africa for a short tour of duty before transferring back to England as a heavy equipment driver. He drove a semi-truck and trailer hauling supplies. He recalled one trip hauling empty fighter aircraft wing tanks. When he stopped at a small English village the townspeople thought he was hauling bombs and were filled with terror until he banged on the sides of the tanks with his hand and explained he was not carrying bombs. Erwin also was sent to Germany as part of the occupation forces until March 31, 1946, when he boarded a boat for return to the United States. In route the ship encountered two storms which virtually lifted the ship out of the water and causing widespread seasickness.

Erwin received his discharge from military service in 1946 at Camp McCoy, Wisconsin. He had been awarded the European Theater of Operations Medal and World War II Victory Medal.

Erwin retired from the U.S. Postal Service as a rural mail carrier.

Right - Erwin, on the right, as a heavy equipment driver at 20th Fighter Group, Kings Cliffe, England.

RICHARD STEELMAN, FORT DODGE, IA, was attending Hamilton Business College in Mason City, Iowa, when the United States entered World War II. He hitch-hiked to Seattle, Washington, with some friends and worked in a shipyard until he enlisted in the Army Air Corps July 18, 1942. He was not called to active duty until February 2, 1943, during which time he helped operate a skating rink owned by his family.

Dick was accepted into the Aviation Cadet Program and sent to a classification center at San Antonio, Texas, where he also took Pre-Flight Training. Primary Flight Training was taken at Pine Bluff, Arkansas; Basic Flight at Coffeyville, Kansas, and Advanced Flight Training at Altus, Oklahoma. He graduated December 5, 1943 and was awarded his wings and commission as a Second Lieutenant. Transitional flight training on the B-24 bomber was taken at Liberal, Kansas, before being assigned a flight crew and training with them for overseas deployment at Tonapah, Nevada.

Assigned to the European Theater of Operations as a replacement crew, Dick and his crew rode a train to Camp Kilmer, New Jersey, where they boarded the ocean liner "Ile de France" in September, 1944. With thirteen thousand other American troops they sailed to Scotland, a voyage that took them six days to complete. The ship maintained a zig-zag route to avoid detection by German submarines.

After classification at Stone, England, and ten days orientation in Ireland, Dick was assigned to the 93rd Bomb Group at Hardwick. He flew thirty-five combat missions from October 2, 1944 to April, 1945. On his fourth mission he took off in heavy overcast to "form up" with his squadron and Group. Breaking into clear weather his Group could not be found and he was forced to fly an oval pattern to try and find them meanwhile using precious fuel. Unsuccessful in finding them he continued the mission with another bomb group. On the homeward trip he realized there was not sufficient fuel to make it back to base. "May Day" calls went unanswered. He was able to land at a base about twenty miles from Dunkirk, France. After receiving fuel they returned to England. Two RAF Spitfire fighters flew alongside and checked them out to make sure there were American crews aboard. Germans sometimes used captured American fighters and bombers to infiltrate bomb groups to shoot down aircraft.

In his thirty-five missions, Dick was sent to Magdeburg, Germany, three times, to Hamburg, Germany, four times to bomb submarine pens and to Berlin twice, all heavily defended targets.

His next to last mission was to Hamminkeln, Germany, a low-level mission to drop supplies to American paratroops and ground forces crossing the Rhine River. The aircraft flew at an altitude of 250-400 feet. "I was so low at times I had to raise the aircraft up over haystacks and chimneys." In the drop zone both American and German troops could be seen including dead American paratroopers hanging in trees where they were killed.

Dick's last mission was to Wilhelmshaven, Germany on March 30, 1945. In his thirty-five missions no crewmember was injured and no serious hits by flak were sustained by his aircraft.

He returned to the United States on July 3, 1945 aboard the "SS Brazil". After reporting to Santa Ana, California, he was transferred to Phoenix, Arizona, where he flew B-24s carrying radar operators on training missions. Dick was separated from military service in September, 1945, having been awarded the Air Medal with oak leaf clusters, ETO Ribbon with battle stars and the World War II Victory Medal.

Until his retirement Dick owned and operated a roller skating rink in Fort Dodge for twenty-five years.

MORRIS STEFFEN, CUMBERLAND, IA, was helping on the family farm when he was drafted into the Army Air Corps in September, 1942. After processing at Ft. Leavenworth, Kansas, he was sent to Charlotte, North Carolina, for Basic Training.

Assigned to the 1735th Ordnance Company, Morris completed training at Waycross and Atlanta, Georgia before being shipped to New York.

He and his unit boarded the ocean liner "Aquatania" for Scotland. The unit was than sent to England by train and the unit was split. Morris was assigned to the 385th Bomb Group at Great Ashfield.

Morris was responsible for storage and issue of ammunition, bombs and bomb fuses. He handled bomb hoists and carts to lift and transport ordnance to places of storage and had to know safety regulations in handling the bombs, their fuses and ammunition. This included hand loading machine gun bullets into their links for use aboard bomber aircraft. When bombs were transported from English ports to his base by truck, Morris was responsible for their safe unloading.

After Victory in Europe, V-E Day, Morris was included in aerial sightseeing tours of Germany, Holland and France flown by bomber crews at his base. He returned to the United States by ship and eventually received his discharge from military service at Sioux Falls, South Dakota on October 27, 1945.

Morris returned to Iowa and resumed farming from which he has subsequently retired.

WAYNE STELLISH, AURELIA, IA, was helping his father farm before he entered military service at Camp Dodge, Des Moines, IA, in August 1942. He was sent to Morris Field, Charlotte, SC for training as a medic. More personnel were needed for the Eighth Air Force buildup in England and Wayne soon found himself assigned to the Signal Corps attached to the 4th Station Complement Squadron.

Wayne boarded the "Queen Mary" in June, 1943, along with 25,000 other soldiers and sailed for Grenock, Scotland. He recalled that after having been at sea for several days, all the Americans were glad to see a friendly shoreline. The soldiers headed for the starboard side of the ship as she nestled into port. "We actually made the ship list to the starboard side. Finally MPs got us somewhat evenly separated and the ship leveled out." Wayne remembers some Scottish fanfare that took place while the GIs were debarking from the ship. "The Scots had bagpipers on shore as we left the ship. They played those pipes and marched up and down the dockside as we set foot on Scotland. Those pipers played constantly until the ship had completely unloaded its cargo. They were so glad to see us."

Shortly after his arrival, Wayne was sent to a Royal Air Force Airfield Control School at Swindon, England. "We went into the school as corporals, but were told that upon completion we'd graduate as second lieutenants. The commanding officer didn't care for our unit as a whole, so we completed the course as corporals, graduated as corporals, and remained corporals. This was my first exposure as to how the Army could operate at times."

Wayne was assigned to the 368 Bombardment Squadron, 306th Bomb Group at Thurleigh, England, where he would remain until the end of the war and then become part of the Army of Occupation at Giebelstadt, Germany.

The 306th Bomb Group was assigned to the Eighth Air Force in September, 1942 at Thurleigh. They had the distinction of being the oldest operational bomb group in the Mighty Eighth and having been stationed at one base in England longer than any other group. Their combat operations began on October 9, 1942 with raids to the industrial area of Lille, France and the German airfields at Courtrai. The final mission for the 306th was April 19, 1945, against marshalling yard targets at Elsterwerda and Falkenberg, Germany. The 306th was awarded two Distinguished Unit Citations. One for a January 11, 1944 raid on the Halberstadt and Oschersleben aircraft industries and the second on February 22, 1944 for their strike against Luftwaffe fighter production plants at Bernberg, Germany.

As the B-17s of the 306th took off from and returned to Thurleigh, they flew over a small, checkered caravan trailer at the end of the main runway. This was Wayne's haunt for almost three years. "The main purpose of the caravan was to maintain visual contact with the airplanes taking off and landing. We were there to help the planes when it was foggy, help aircraft line up with the landing runway using flares or radio, and giving Aldis lamp signals to planes without radios in operating condition." Mounted on the roof of the caravan was the plexiglass nose of a B-17 which allowed the controller to have visual sightings of a formation as it approached the air base. In one incident, a B-17 missed the runway and flew so low over the caravan its ball turret scraped the top of the caravan damaging both the trailer and the airplane. Wayne was not in the trailer at the time.

In another incident, "It was a really foggy day, and there were planes in the air ready to land. Suddenly here comes a B-17 roaring out of the fog, right past me in the caravan. But his gear's still up and he wants to land this thing. I screamed into the radio that his gear was still up. The pilot gunned the ship and the Fortress slowly struggled back to a safer altitude, dropped its gear, and made a good landing later." Wayne's actions undoubtedly saved the lives of the aircrew.

Foggy English weather created immense problems in landings and takeoffs. A mission flown on October 22, 1944 was marked by two mid-air collisions involving the 306th. The first came while the group was climbing from Cromer to the Dutch coast enroute to Munster, Germany. Two planes in the formation collided. One exploded and virtually disappeared. The other fell to earth in a spin. One man was the sole survivor of the two crews.

Later that same day, fog was responsible for the second disaster. The 306th was due back at Thurleigh from their raid. Ground crews started to gather to watch the planes come home. Clouds were down to 800 feet and Wayne was in his caravan. One squadron was approaching the base from the east when another squadron broke out of the fog from the south. Both squadron leaders saw each other and were in radio contact. They agreed the squadron from the east would climb and the squadron from the south would descend. All was going well until the last B-17 from the south pulled up instead of down and crashed into the tail end Fortress of the other squadron. A tremendous explosion occurred directly over Wayne's caravan. All nineteen crew members were killed. Bodies were scattered over the airbase and falling debris caused several fires. "It was a terrible collision, just terrible" Wayne recalled. "And it happened right over my position in the caravan. Falling debris fell all around me."

Wayne was one of the last members of the 306th to leave Thurleigh long after the war was over. There was one B-17 left and ten servicemen remaining at the base. Before we took off to go to Gielbestadt, Germany, I walked through the previously busy headquarters building. "Nothing much was there anymore. The cold wind was banging the window shutters against the side of the building. The once active base was basically like a ghost town now", Wayne remembered.

Wayne received his discharge from the Army Air Corps in March, 1946 at Camp McCoy, WI. He had been awarded The World War II Victory Medal, Good Conduct Medal, Distinguished Unit Badge and the European Service Medal. While overseas, Wayne met and courted a special Irish lady, Ann, who became his bride. The Stellishes farmed for many years in the Aurelia area until retirement.

Right - Control tower personnel at 306th BG, Thurleigh, England. Wayne is front row, second from the right.

GEORGE STERLER, SHELDON, IA, was helping on the family farm when he enlisted in the Army Air Corps during April, 1942. Accepted into the Aviation Cadet Program at San Antonio, Texas, George completed all stages of flight training within the state. He graduated from Advanced Flight Training at Waco in April, 1943, which earned him his wings and commission as a Second Lieutenant.

George completed B-17 training at Pyote, Texas as Co-Pilot. He was assigned to an aircrew and trained with the crew at Dyersburg, Tennessee, in preparation for overseas deployment. He was sent back to Pyote where he was assigned to another air crew as Pilot. Overseas training was then re-taken with the new crew at Delhart, Texas. Following completion of training the Air Transport Command split George's crew in half, putting five men in each of two new aircraft to fly to the European Theater of Operations.

George flew twenty-eight combat missions beginning January 24, 1944 and ending on May 7, 1944 with a bombing raid on Berlin, Germany. The next day, May 8, George began his twenty-ninth mission, a return to the Berlin area to bomb a target at Brunswick, Germany.

He was leading a low squadron and preparing to turn on the bomb run when they were attacked head-on by a group of thirty to forty ME-109 German fighter planes. Enemy shells ripped into George's aircraft and tore off the right wing between engines number 3 and 4 causing it to go into a diving spin. George gave the order for his crew to bail out but their plane exploded in mid-air. George was blown out of the aircraft and pulled the rip cord on his parachute before he lost consciousness. He woke in time to see the ground coming up at him. When he landed he broke his leg. He saw civilians coming after him with pitchforks. Luckily two German soldiers arrived before the civilians and protected George from being attacked by them. George later learned that only one other crew member, his tail gunner, had survived the explosion aboard his aircraft.

George eventually was shipped to Frankfurt, Germany for interrogation and placed in solitary confinement. He was later placed in a German hospital to receive treatment for his broken leg. He was released from the hospital on D-Day, June 6, 1944, and with other POWs, placed in a railroad boxcar and shipped to Stalag Luft III prison camp at Sagan, Poland.

As the Russian Army advanced on Germany, the prisoners of Stalag Luft III were ordered out of their barracks in sub-zero weather on January 28, 1945 and marched to Spremberg, Germany. The winter of '44 was one of Europe's worst winters. They were locked in railroad boxcars without food or water, unable to sit or lay down and shipped to Nurnberg, Germany. Two months later as Allied armies advanced farther into Germany, the prisoners were marched again, this time from Nurnberg to Moosburg, another German POW camp, ninety miles away.

On April 29, 1945, General George Patton's Third Army liberated the POWs at Moosburg. They were eventually flown to Camp Lucky Strike at Le Havre, France where they received food, clothes, de-lousing, shaves, showers and medical treatment before they were shipped back to the United States.

George returned to the United States and was separated from military service in December, 1945. He remained in the Air Force Reserves for five years before obtaining his official discharge. He had been awarded the Distinguished Flying Cross, Air Medal with four oak leaf clusters, ETO Ribbon with battle stars and the Purple Heart for wounds received in battle.

George was a rural carrier with the U.S. Postal Service until retirement.

Right - George's crew at 96th Bomb Group, Snetterton Heath, England. George, Pilot, is front row, left.

ELMER STEVEN, SPENCER, IA, was a farmer, carpenter and implement mechanic before World War II. After entering the Army Air Corps in 1943 he was sent to Teletype Maintenance School at Chanute Field, Illinois.

Elmer was deployed to the European Theater of Operations April 4, 1943, and was assigned as a teletype maintenance mechanic at the 339th Fighter Group, Fowlmere, England. He remained in that position until the end of the war in Europe. Elmer returned to the United States in October, 1945, and received his discharge from military service at the end of that month.

He was awarded the World War II Victory Medal, and ETO Ribbon with one battle star.

Elmer returned to civilian life at Spencer and was an auto mechanic until his retirement.

EUGENE STIENTJES, PELLA, IA, took flying lessons while in high school under the Civilian Pilot Training program and earned his private pilot's license. After two years at Central College in Pella he enrolled for the Fall semester of 1942 at the University of Iowa. Early in 1943 he enlisted in the Army Air Corps Aviation Cadet Program and was sent to San Antonio, Texas.

After Pre-Flight and Primary Flight Training at Stamford, Texas; and Basic Flight at Garden City, Kansas, Eugene returned to Texas for Advanced Flight Training. He received his wings and commission as a Second Lieutenant at Ellington Field, Houston, Texas in December, 1943. In order graduate a pilot had to earn his "green card". With an instructor flying in the back seat of an AT-10 Trainer, Eugene sat in the front seat with a shroud over his head so he could not see. The instructor flew the aircraft for twenty minutes then told Eugene to take over the controls and "take us home". Not knowing where they were and using only the aircraft's instruments he was required to successfully land the aircraft back at their base, which he did.

Although Eugene graduated in twin engine aircraft he was sent to Boise, Idaho, a B-24 Training base, as a Co-Pilot and assigned to an aircrew. It was while training together for overseas deployment that he learned to fly the B-24. On May 1, 1944, Eugene and his crew flew to Florida to begin a single aircraft flight to Ireland. They had no radio or radar to guide them and inflatable gas tanks in the bomb bay area for extra fuel. Their route took them through Trinidad; Brazil; across the equator where they encountered severe thunderstorms to Dakar, Africa and Morocco. After two weeks ground school in Ireland Eugene and his crew were assigned to the 93rd Bomb Group near Hardwick, England.

Beginning May 30, 1944, Eugene flew thirty-four combat missions in seventy days.

His first mission began at 4:30 A.M. with wakeup, breakfast, briefing on weather, route to fly, and where they were expected to encounter enemy flak and fighters. German anti-aircraft guns were 88mm or 150mm. When 88mm shells were fired, the explosion in the air was black and sent shrapnel in all directions. When 150mm shells were fired a red flash would be seen and then black smoke. No enemy fighters attacked their Group on their first mission but anti-aircraft fire was heavy.

Eugene flew thirty-two of his missions with his original crew and no crew member was lost. On one mission flak busted their windshield and Eugene was knocked unconscious. Their aircraft fell from twenty-one thousand to ten thousand feet before the pilot could regain control of the aircraft.

On a mission to bomb synthetic oil refineries at Politz, Germany, their engines' superchargers were lost and caused them to lose altitude and return to their base at a very vulnerable 8,000 feet. Two engines were lost on a mission to Holland. Unable to hold altitude they attempted to return to England. To lighten their load they threw everything they could out of the aircraft. Meanwhile weather had closed in over England and visibility was down to 700 feet. An American P-47 Thunderbolt fighter flew as escort and signaled them where their airfield was. "Our wheels reached the fully down position just as we hit the runway."

Eugene returned to the United States in September, 1944, and was re-assigned to Victorville, California, to attend a Radar Navigation School. He became a B-24 First Pilot and flew for one year at Victorville before he received his discharge in September, 1945. Eugene had received the Distinguished Flying Cross, Air Medal with three oak leaf clusters, ETO ribbon with battle stars and the World War II Victory Medal.

He returned to Pella and bought into his father's Gambles department store. After twenty-seven years he became Purchasing Manager of Pella's Rolscreen Corporation from which he retired in 1986.

Right - Eugene and his crew, 93rd BG, Hardwick, England. Eugene, Co-Pilot, is back row, left.

NORMAN STROM, DES MOINES, IA, was a carpenter and sheet metal worker prior to World War II. He enlisted in the Army Air Corps in August, 1942, but was not called to active duty until November of that year. Norm was accepted into the Aviation Cadet Program and completed Pre-Flight Training at Santa Ana, Primary Flight Training at King City and Basic Flight at Lancaster, California. Advanced Flight training was completed at Douglas, Arizona, where he received his wings and commission as a Second Lieutenant. B-17 Transition Training was completed at Hobbs, New Mexico.

Norman was deployed to the 92nd Bomb Group at Podington, England in August, 1944, as a Pilot. He flew thirty-five combat missions. During a mission in November, 1944, the number two and three engines of his bomber were lost as they neared the Initial Point. The engines had to be feathered and his bomber began to lose altitude at a rate of 500 feet per minute. Norm ordered all possible equipment jettisoned and warned the Radio Operator to stand by to transmit emergency signals. Norm was able to fly the aircraft to reach the English Channel where they jettisoned their bomb load. The aircraft continued to lose altitude. He was informed the ball turret could not be jettisoned whereupon Norm went to the rear of the aircraft and was able to release the turret into the English Channel. As they neared the English coast the number four engine became inoperative. Heavy overcast over England prevented visual flight. As he let the aircraft down through the overcast they finally broke into the clear at only three hundred feet and were able to land at an emergency airfield.

During a mission to bomb fuel plants at Merseberg, Germany, "planes were falling all around us. The "flak" was so thick you couldn't see anything but "flak". We lost eight of the twelve planes in our squadron."

"We had fighter cover all the way to the target on missions to the center of Germany. If the target was covered by clouds we hit another target. Once "bombs away" was called out we wanted to get the hell out of there cause fighters would attack us once we got out of the "flak"."

"On one mission we took a direct hit from "flak" in the bomb bay area when the doors were open but we were able to fly home with a huge hole in the side of the plane. "

Norm returned to the United States in January, 1945 ands was assigned to the Air Transport Command flying all types of war-weary aircraft to airplane graveyards in the Southwest United States. He was in Great Falls, Montana, when he learned that President Roosevelt had died.

Norm was discharged from military service at Scott Field, Illinois, in January, 1946. He had been awarded the Distinguished Flying Cross, Air Medal with oak leaf clusters, the ETO Ribbon with battle stars and the World War II Victory medal.

Right - Battle damage to "The Gay Divorcee", Norm's B-17

Chapter Twenty-Two

Right - Norm "behind the wheel" of his B-17 at Podington, England.

Right - Sporting a new moustache

GEORGE STURTZ, BOONE, IA, was employed as an aircraft sheet metal worker before World War II. He enlisted in the Army Air Corps October 24, 1942, at Ft Crook, Nebraska, and was sent to Buckley Field, Colorado, for Armament School and Ft Myers, Florida, for Aerial Gunnery School.

On November 30, 1944, George was deployed to the 91st Bomb Group at Bassingbourn, England, as a tail gunner and airplane armorer. He flew thirty-four combat missions, the first of which was a bomb raid in the heart of Germany - Berlin, a tough way to start.

George was discharged from military service, September 15, 1945, at Jefferson Barracks, Missouri. He had been awarded the Air Medal with four oak leaf clusters, the European Theater of Operations Ribbon with three battle stars and the World War II Victory Medal.

ROBERT SUCKOW, NEWTON, IA, was a college student and shoe store manager before World War II. He enlisted in the Army Air Corps at Chanute Field, IL, in April, 1941, eight months before America's entry into World War II.

After attending administrative clerical school at Lowry Field, CO, Bob spent nine months in adminsitrative duties as an enlisted man. He was accepted to attend Officer's Candidate School (OCS) at Miami Beach, FL, and subsequently served as an Administrative and Personnel Officer at Scott Field, Belleville, IL.

Bob later applied and was accepted for pilot training at Cimaron Field, KS and Altus Air Corps Base, OK. Following four engine training on the B-24 at Ft. Worth, TX and Combat Staging Training at Mountain Home Air Base, ID, Bob and his crew were deployed to England on November 1, 1944.

Assigned to the 445th Bomb Group at Tibenham, Bob served as Pilot, Command Pilot, and Squadron Operations Officer and Personnel Officer. Seven combat missions were flown as Command Pilot responsible for getting several squadrons assembled after take-off, flight to the target, the bomb run, and return flight to base. Squadron Operations Officer duties included aircraft scheduling for missions and continuous training of aircrews.

Bob's most memorable mission came on February 2, 1945, a low level mission to Halberstadt, Germany, to attack rolling stock supplying Hitler's war machine during the Battle of the Bulge. Fluent in German, Bob was utilized by the British Broadcasting Company in London to beam propaganda over Germany to advise them it was not our intent to kill or injure civilians in the bombing raids but to end the war as soon as possible.

Bob was awarded the Air Medal with oak leaf cluster in addition to campaign medals. After the war he was employed as a manager in the Controller General's Office and as an independent management consultant. He remained active in the Air Force Reserve and retired at the rank of Lieutenant Colonel.

JOHN Q. SWIFT, MANCHESTER, IA, was attending college when the United States entered World War II. He finished the school year and enlisted in the Army Air Corps in the Fall of 1942 after being turned down for naval aviation because he was too heavy. He wasn't called to active duty until January, 1943.

After basic training at Jefferson Barracks, St. Louis, John was sent to Iowa Wesleyan College, Mt Pleasant, under the College Training Detachment Program. From there he entered the Aviation Cadet Program at Santa Ana, CA where he began his flight training.

John received his wings at Douglas, AZ, took Co-Pilot training at Las Vegas and after being assigned a crew trained with them at Alexandria, LA.

In August, 1944, he picked up a new B-17 at Kearney, NE and flew the northern route through New Hampshire, Labrador, Iceland and Wales to England. Assigned to the 94th Bomb Group at Bury St. Edmunds, John flew thirty-five combat missions. On October 7, 1944, the twelve aircraft in his 331st Squadron were attacked by enemy fighters just before they began their bomb run to their target. American fighter escorts had been lured away from the bomber formation on what turned out to be Luftwaffe decoys. "Forty to fifty German fighters came in from our tail in three or four waves stacked in stair step formation." Of the twelve bombers in the 331st Squadron nine were shot down and one crashed landed in Belgium. John's airplane was one of the two that made it back to base. "It made a believer out of me."

John flew home in April, 1945 after completing his required number of mission. He then attended Fighter Pilot School at Greenwood, Mississippi. After training he was assigned to the Fighter Ferry Command flying P-51 Mustangs and P-47 Thunderbolts throughout the United States as needed.

John was separated from military service in October, 1945, to return to the Air Force Reserve. He received his official discharge in 1955 having been awarded the Air Medal with six oak leaf clusters.

Following the war John returned to school. He received his law degree from Creighton University in Omaha in 1949 and entered the family law practice in Manchester. John and his wife had seven sons and three daughters. He remains semi-active in the family law firm now operated by a son.

Right - John and his crew at 94th BG, Bury St. Edmunds, England. John is front row, second from left.

W. L. SYPAL, DES MOINES, IA, entered on duty with the Army Air Corps at Fort Crook, Nebraska, and was sent to Fort Lauderdale, Florida, for Basic Training. He then completed Advanced Radio School at Truax Field, Madison and Tomah, Wisconsin before duty assignments at Miami, Florida; Baton Rouge,

Louisiana; Dehlhart, Texas; Bruning, Nebraska, and in Washington State.

W.L. left Ft. Lewis, Washington, aboard a merchant ship for what would become a thirty day voyage to his next duty assignment, Ie Shima, a small island off the coast of Okinawa. "On the island was an area known as "Chocolate Hill" filled with Japanese in caves. The Navy and Air Corps leveled it."

W.L. was assigned to the 465th Squadron of the 507th Fighter Group, a P-47 unit of the 301st Wing, of the Twentieth Air Force as a communications specialist. His duties included operation and maintenance of a control net system providing bearings to bring pilots back to base. He also maintained and repaired other radio equipment as needed.

"When Doolittle showed up to command Eighth Air Force units sent to the Pacific Theater of Operations, he told us you are now in the 8th, change those patches" (Air Force insignia on uniforms).

At war's end W.L. sailed home in seven days aboard the "USS Sea Bass" and received his military discharge on December 24, 1945. He had been awarded the Pacific Theater of Operations and World War II Victory Medals.

In civilian life W.L. was a general insurance agent with his own firm. In addition to metal and woodworking hobbies, he played in community bands and at one time formed his own band. He continues to shoot rifles, shotguns and handguns competitively.

CHESTER TAYLOR, SPENCER, IA, was originally from Springfield, Missouri, and a brakeman on the Frisco Railroad when America entered World War II. He was drafted into the Army in August 1943. While at Ft. Leonard Wood, Missouri, he was transferred to the Army Air Corps after scoring high on a series of hearing tests.

After Air Corps Basic Training at Amarillo, Texas, he was sent to Radio school at Sioux Falls, South Dakota. The course lasted nearly five months and required he became proficient in use of the Morse Code. He was then sent to Aerial Gunnery School at Yuma, Arizona. Following completion of training he was retained at Yuma until the end of World War II where he served as an instructor in radio and aerial gunnery.

In late 1945 Chester helped close down the Yuma Air Base and was then transferred to Randolph Field, Texas, and Tyler, Texas until discharge from military service in March, 1946.

After he returned to civilian life Chester was an auto mechanic and Conoco service station owner before he worked twenty years with Arnold Motor Supply from where he retired.

RICHARD C. TAYLOR, CEDAR RAPIDS, IA, graduated from high school at Lehigh, Iowa, when he was seventeen and secured employment with Link-Belt Ordnance in Chicago as a machinist until he was old enough to enlist in the Army Air Corps. Although he passed tests for pilot training he was sent to Virginia to become part of a coast artillery unit. The error in assignment was corrected and he was sent to Presbyterian University, Clinton, South Carolina, under the College Training Detachment Program before beginning pilot training at Union City, Tennessee.

He received his wings and commission as a Second Lieutenant in August, 1943. After B-17 Transition Training at Sebring, Florida, a new B-17 bomber was assigned to him. He and his crew then began their overseas flight to the European Theater of Operations. They landed at Prestwick, Scotland, and then rode by train to the 388th Bomb Group at Knettishall, England.

Richard flew six combat missions. While only nineteen years old, he was made lead pilot. Lead pilot required that he fly every other mission for his Group. Off days were spent in London at debriefings from his prior mission. While at one meeting he attended a dance where he met and danced with Winston Churchill's daughter Sarah.

Richard would fly over twenty more missions that included shuttle missions to Russia. Targets south of Berlin that were too far for a round-trip back to England were bombed and the aircraft flown to a base at Poltava, Russia. There they were re-fueled and re-armed for another mission on their return to England. Unknown to the bomber crews a German fighter trailed them to their destination. That night German bombers bombed the aircraft sitting on the ground. Forty-four bombers were destroyed and twenty-six damaged.

As the war closed in on the Germans, Richard's aircraft, in addition to bombs, also dropped propaganda leaflets announcing "Sie Kommen"" (We're Coming). Numerous leaflet drops were made over Germany to convince enemy troops to surrender with promises of humane treatment and food.

Following V-E Day Richard and his crew flew back to the United States. They were assigned to Sioux Falls, South Dakota for B-29 training and continued service in the Pacific Theater against Japan. Before training could commence the war ended. He received his discharge from military service and had been awarded among other medals the Air Medal with oak leaf clusters, ETO Ribbon and World War II Victory Medal.

Richard resumed his education at the University of Iowa, graduating in 1949. He began a career from which he retired fifty years later as a self-employed sales representative for manufacturers of electronic products.

Right - Richard and his crew, 388th Bomb Group, Knettishall, England. Richard, Pilot, is back row, second from right.

SYDNEY THOMAS, WATERLOO, IA, was inducted into military service at Camp Dodge, Iowa, on February 9, 1943. After Basic Training he attended Pre-Meteorology School at the University of Wisconsin. On graduation from the school in September, 1943, he attended an additional meteorology school at the University of Chicago. Syd graduated in June, 1944, and received a direct commission as a Second Lieuten-

Chapter Twenty-Two

ant.

Syd was assigned to a base weather station at Mabry Field, Tennessee. He then trained in aerial weather reconnaissance at Will Rogers Field, Oklahoma City,
Oklahoma, to determine weather over intended targets, weather to and from the target as well as weather that could be expected over Eighth Air Force bases. He was then deployed to the European Theater of Operations in March, 1945. and assigned to the 652nd Squadron of the 25th Bomb Group at Watton and then Alconbury, England. Two other squadrons of the Group also performed reconnaissance functions. One squadron flew weather missions over the European continent while the other squadron was involved in photo reconnaissance.

Sydney served as Weather Officer. He was on a B-17 aircrew that flew weather missions over the Atlantic Ocean. His duties included accurate accumulation of weather data to the east of Britain. Weather from the Atlantic reached the United Kingdom first and it allowed them to track weather fronts. B-17 bombers were modified to carry weather instruments for observance of pressure, temperature and humidity. Fuel tanks installed in the bomb bay area carried additional fuel for a maximum flying time of 20-22 hours. Missions lasted an average of almost fourteen hours.

"Ten routes were flown from England. Our unit flew two of the routes. The Royal Air Force flew the others. From our base we would fly a mission code named "Sharon". This took us over Lands End, England, to the Atlantic Ocean and on to the Azores. After resting for 24 hours we flew the same pattern back to England. Weather observations and various readings were taken every fifty miles to include visibility, precipitation, turbulence, airframe icing, cloud types and tenths of sky covered by each layer, dry and wet bulb temperatures, and barometer readings. Every one hundred miles wind speed and direction was determined using drift meters and smoke bombs at fifty to one hundred foot levels. Every 500 miles readings were taken at every one thousand foot levels up to 25-30, 000 feet. At the end of each leg of a mission, weather data was put into a five digit international weather system , then encoded into a secret cipher and transmitted back to England.

"The other mission flown by our squadron was code named "Allah" and was flown due west of England for about 700 miles, turned south for about 700 miles and then back to England."

In addition to weather flights and data accumulated by Royal Air Force and other United States units, forecasters were aided by the capture of a German "Enigma" machine. The machine was used to produce coded messages of military plans and operations including weather data. The German code that had previously been unbreakable by Allied cryptographers was solved. Weather reports transmitted from German submarines, other ships and weather stations were decoded and provided weather conditions over most of Europe. "Weather forecasting played a great role in the outcome of World War II. We were able to capture weather information all over Europe and track frontal passes. Accurate weather forecasting over Allied bases and targets and the European continent was needed for bombing operations to be successful. It also allowed forecasters to predict a "window of opportunity", a break in the weather, for the Allied landing in Normandy on D-Day, June 6, 1944."

Because fog was such a problem the British developed a system called "Fido" late in the war. Emergency landing strips built near the English Channel were re-designed to be exceedingly long and wide. Petrol would be burned around the runways to burn away fog." This aided bombers and fighters returning from missions to not only find an emergency landing strip when their own base was "socked in" but those aircraft low on fuel or suffering from battle damage and in dire need of landing.

It was generally conceded that Allied forces in Europe had two enemies- the Germans and the weather. The weather changed rapidly. Aircrews often had to takeoff in low overcast and fly through clouds to assemble before starting for the target. Mid-air collisions resulted causing many loss of life.

After Victory in Europe, Syd continued to fly weather missions until September, 1945, to aid aircraft returning to the United States and other non-combat related missions over Europe. He was based as part of American occupation forces at Bad Kissengen, Germany, as a weather officer.

Syd returned to the United States in June, 1946, and received his separation from military service at Camp McCoy, Wisconsin, August 17, 1946. He had been awarded, among other medals, the Air Medal with one oak leaf cluster, Army of Occupation, World War II Victory, and ETO Medals.

In civilian life Syd returned to college and earned a law degree from the University of Michigan. He was a partner in a law firm in Waterloo area until retirement.

Right - Syd's crew at Alconbury, England. Syd, Weather Officer, is on the right.

DONALD E. THOMPSON, MARION, IA, was called to active duty in February, 1943, from the Air Force Enlisted Reserve Corps. He attended Classification and Pre-flight Training at Santa Ana, California, before he completed additional stages of flight training, all in California. Primary Flight Training was taken at Visalia, Basic Flight Training at Minter Field, and Ad-
vanced Flight Training at Mather Field. Transition to the B-17 was held at Hobbs, New Mexico. With his newly assigned aircrew, overseas training was taken at Dyersburg, Tennessee before deployment to Grafton Underwood, England with the 384th Bomb Group.

Donald received his pilot's wings two months before his twentieth birthday. With it came the responsibility of molding himself and his crew into an effective combat crew. It was a memorable day for him when he and his crew walked out on the flight line at Hunter Field, Savannah, Georgia, to the B-17 that would take them to England and combat.

Included in Donald's missions was one on April 25, 1945, a raid on the Skoda Plant at Pilsen, Czechoslovakia. What they didn't know at the time was this raid was to be the last bombing mission flown over Europe on a German target. The end of what had become the greatest aerial strike force the world had ever known. Flak was expected to be heavy over the target area and their plane received several minor hits. They saw two planes from their Group hit by flak and go down. Fortunately the planes were controllable and a landing in Allied territory was made.

The last bombs were dropped at 11:16 A.M. by a bomb group from Grafton Underwood. Ironically the first bombs dropped by the Eighth Air Force in Europe were also by a bomb group at Grafton, the 97th BG, which had been stationed there but subsequently reassigned to North Africa.

Most important there would be no mission for tomorrow.

Donald retired as a Lieutenant Colonel in the Air Force Reserve after thirty years service. He farmed near Central City, Iowa, and was active in the Cedar Rapids Senior Squadron and Iowa Wing of the Civil Air Patrol. Retired, Donald retired to Marion, Iowa.

GERALD THOMPSON, DES MOINES, IA, was formerly from Leland, Iowa. In 1942 while attending Waldorf College at Forest City, Iowa, he enlisted in the Army Air Corps Aviation Cadet Program.

He was sent, under the College Training Detachment Program, to Michigan State University for Pre-Flight Training and where courses in physics and mathematics were also taken. Gerald then completed Primary Flight Training at Thunderbird Field near Phoenix, Arizona; Basic Flight Training at Polaris Flight Academy, Lancaster,  California, and Advanced Flight Training at Marfa Air Base. Upon graduation he received his wings and commission as a Second Lieutenant.

Transition Flight Training to the B-17 four engine bomber was completed at Hobbs, New Mexico before Gerald was assigned an aircrew. The crew trained for overseas deployment at Alexandria, Louisiana.

In December, 1944, Gerald was deployed to the 91st Bomb Group at Bassingbourn, England. He was in the same squadron and had the same crew chief that had maintained the "Memphis Belle" B-17, the first aircrew to complete their tour of duty with the Eighth Air Force.

His commanding officer met independently with each replacement crew as they were assigned to the 324th Bomb Squadron. Most sobering was his statement "you are not expected to complete your tour of duty". With these words as a reminder, Gerald and his crew were able to complete twenty-five missions before war's end.

"On the evening before a mission there was a posting of the crews that were to participate the following day. We got up at three or four in the morning for preparation and briefing. When we returned from a mission it was sometimes as late as eight in the evening. We were de-briefed on events of the mission and information we had on enemy opposition.

Our crew flew missions on three successive days before we got a day off. During the Battle of the Bulge we flew nine missions in ten days. In order to succeed on a mission one had to free one's mind for the task by accepting the idea that you would not live through it."

Gerald flew six missions to Berlin where they had to endure concentrated German anti-aircraft fire and enemy fighters defending the city. Five missions were flown to industrial areas in the Ruhr Valley that included Essen, Dortmund and Gelsenkirken.

Near the end of the war in Europe Gerald's last mission was flown to bomb Dresden, Germany. The advance of Russian ground forces into Germany caused fleeing civilians to flood into population centers. Many were killed when Dresden was bombed.

When discharged from military service, Gerald had received the Air Medal with three oak leaf clusters, European Theater of Operations and World War II Victory Medals, among others.

After the war Gerald earned his Bachelors, Masters and PHD degrees from the University of Iowa. For four years he served as an assistant professor of economics at the University of Toledo, Ohio, before becoming a professor of economics at the University of Nebraska, in 1954. He served on the faculty at Harvard under the Ford Foundation Fellowship, was a visiting professor of statistics at the University of Michigan and has authored numerous publications in economics and statistics.

WILLIAM TOMASEK, WAUCOMA, IA, entered military service September 23, 1942. After basic training and gunnery school he was assigned to the 388th Bomb Group based at Knettishall, England.

Bill flew twenty-five combat missions between November 26, 1943, and March 2, 1944. On December 5, 1943, his third combat mission was a bomb raid on targets at Bordeaux, France. His plane was hit by flak that knocked out two engines. His pilot attempted to land on the Jersey Islands, British islands in the English Channel then held by the Germans. They signaled they were surrendering and wanted to land but were not allowed to do so.

According to Bill, "we were only fifty feet off the ground. It was so foggy the German fighters couldn't see us, so we kept on by shifting gasoline from one engine to another and eventually got up to 2,500 feet. The navigator didn't know where we were at. We had to bail out when fuel was running out. Some bailed out over land, the rest into the Channel."

"I landed on what you might call a lilac bush. I was lucky. I lost my flying shoes and cap, but had another pair of shoes with me." About 150 feet away was a farmhouse. With his firearm ready he knocked on the door. Hearing the people talk in English he then knew he was in England. Within fifteen minutes after bailing out he was in an English home having tea and tarts. All crewmembers that bailed out including those that went into the water were safe.

Bill arrived back in the United States after he completed his required missions on April 7, 1944. Among his decorations is the Distinguished Flying Cross, Air Medal with oak leaf clusters, ETO Ribbon and World War II Victory Medal.

VERNON TORRESON, WALLINGFORD, IA, was working on a farm at the outbreak of World War II. He enlisted in the Army Air Corps at Camp Dodge, Iowa, on December 18, 1942. Vernon was sent to St Petersburg, Florida, for Basic Training before he attended Radio School at the Stevens Hotel, Chicago, Illinois.

Deployed to the European Theater of Operations in February, 1944, he was assigned as a radio operator/aerial gunner with the 452nd Bomb Group at Deopham Green, England. Vernon flew thirty-one combat missions. During one mission, a raid on oil plants at Brux, Czechoslavokia, the bomber formation was attacked by German ME-410 Zestorers while in route back to England. Eleven of fourteen bombers in Vernon's squadron were shot down.

He also participated in a shuttle mission to Russia. Long-range German targets were bombed by American aircraft from England. Unable to return to their base because of the distance involved, the aircraft flew on to Russian bases where they were re-fueled and re-armed and targets again bombed on their return to England. On this particular mission a German high altitude airplane shadowed the bomber formation to their destination. That night the Luftwaffe attacked the Russian base where they were staying. The Russians had virtually no or ineffective anti-aircraft guns to defend themselves and many American bombers were destroyed on the ground. It took three weeks for Vernon to make it back to his base in England.

Vernon finished his tour of duty and returned to the United States in August, 1944. He received his discharge from military service on October 15, 1945, at Sioux City, Iowa. He had been awarded, among other medals, the Distinguished Flying Cross, Air Medal with three oak leaf clusters, ETO Ribbon with two battle stars and the World War II Victory Medal.

Right - Vern's enlisted men's crew, 452nd Bomb Group, Deopham Green, England. Vern, Aerial Gunner, is standing on the right.

RALPH D. TROUT, LOGAN, IA, was a substitute letter carrier with the Post Office at Logan, Iowa, prior to World War II. He entered military service July 9, 1942, at Camp Robinson, Little Rock, Arkansas. He transferred to the Army Air Corps April 2, 1943, and attended Armament School at Lowry Field, Colorado, Aerial Gunnery School at Tyndall Field, Florida. Overseas training was completed at Sioux City, Iowa, with his newly assigned crew.

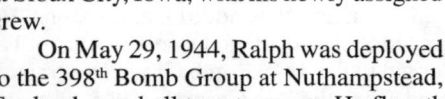

On May 29, 1944, Ralph was deployed to the 398th Bomb Group at Nuthampstead, England, as a ball turret gunner. He flew thirty combat missions in the tight confines of the ball turret. This included three straight missions to Munich, Germany in July, 1944, and two long distance missions to Brux, Czechoslavokia, to bomb synthetic oil plants. On the second mission to Brux, weather obscured the target area and also a secondary target. A target of opportunity was chosen and the bombs dropped. They had survived intense flak over three targets in one day.

Prior to one mission and after a pre-flight check of the turret to make sure it was working properly, Ralph put on his heated flight suit. After takeoff and assembly he entered the ball turret, plugged in his intercom and heated suit extension cord onto his suit. After donning his oxygen mask he had to keep watch for enemy fighters. Suddenly it felt cold. He checked all the connection from his clothing and everything seemed all right. He had one last place to check, the heated suit extension cord in the outlet under the seat. Literally standing on his head to reach the plug in the small turret, he managed with considerable difficulty to lock the plug in the outlet. Warmth began to come into his suit. Had he not been able to do so he would have frozen to death.

Ralph's last mission was to Zeitz, Germany. His regular pilot had completed his required missions. The balance of the crew had to fly with other crews to complete their tour. Ralph went as ball turret to one crew. His tail gunner, Felix Byrne went with another crew. Somewhere over Germany word came through the intercom that the plane on their left side was going down after being hit by flak. In it was his friend Felix. Ralph watched as the plane fell all the way to earth. No parachutes were seen to exit the aircraft.

Ralph was discharged from military service August 20, 1945, at Jefferson Barracks, Missouri. He had received the Distinguished Flying Cross, Air Medal with three oak leaf clusters, ETO Ribbon and World War II Victory Medal. He returned to his job with the Post Office in Logan but was recalled to active duty as a Second Lieutenant during the Korean War and served from October 8, 1950 to March 7, 1952 as Base Postal Officer at Scott Air Force Base, Illinois.

HARLYN TURNER, DUBUQUE, IA, worked for a sash and door company in Dubuque prior to World War II. He enlisted in military service when he was seventeen years old but was not called to active duty until November, 1942, after he had turned eighteen.

Harlyn took Basic Training at St. Petersburg, Florida, where inductees were billeted in a hotel. Next came Aerial Gunnery School at Wendover, Utah, before being assigned to an aircrew. He competed three phases of training in preparation for deployment overseas at Clovis, North Dakota; Blythe, California and Langley, Virginia.

In February, 1944 Harlyn boarded the "Queen Mary" for England. After arrival his crew took further training in Ireland and then reported to Stone, England for assignment as a replacement crew. Harlyn was assigned to the 446th Bomb Group at Bungay. As he settled in at his living quarters in a quonset hut, Harlyn and his crew learned they were assigned bunks that had just been used by a crew shot down the previous day.

Harlyn flew thirty combat missions as a ball turret gunner. Although missions to Brunswick, Germany, were considered the roughest due to enemy flak and continued fighter attacks by the Luftwaffe, he remembered his thirtieth mission as the most memorable. It was a raid on targets at Munich, Germany. While on the bomb run his aircraft was hit by flak. One engine was shot out which reduced their speed and they were unable to keep up with the rest of their formation. Harlyn and his crew in their B-24 named "Little Rollo" became stragglers. The Luftwaffe attacked to finish them off but American P-51 Mustangs and P-38 Lightning fighters suddenly roared by their aircraft, drove off the German fighters and then escorted them safely back to their base.

During an attack on V-1 and V-2 rocket launch sites their B-24 took an anti-aircraft shell through the right wing which also pierced the fuel tank. Fortunately the fuel did not explode, they had completed their bomb run and were not far from the English coast. They dropped out of formation to prevent fuel from leaking on other aircraft and were able to make it back to their base.

After he completed his required number of missions, Harlyn returned to the United Stated aboard a Navy ship in November,

Iowans of the Mighty Eighth

1944. He became a gunnery instructor at Kingman, Arizona, and was then transferred to Laredo, TX, in the same capacity until he received his discharge from military service in September, 1945.

Harlyn re-entered military service in June, 1947 as a B-29 waist gunner. He retired from the Air Force in October, 1970 as a Chief Master Sergeant. He served at posts throughout the world in the Training Command as a technical instructor and Aeronomics Chief. He had been awarded among other medals the Distinguished Flying Cross, Air Medal, European Theater of Operations and World War II Victory Medals.

During the early part of his Air Force career after World War II, Harlyn was stationed at Okinawa. A typhoon was headed for the island. This required all aircraft be dispersed to other bases in the Pacific. Harlyn and his crew flew a plane to Guam. Another B-29 was reported missing and a search organized to locate it. Harlyn and his crew took off to assist in the search. They later developed electrical problems aboard their aircraft, got lost and were running out of fuel when a small island was spotted. The island, named Faia, was formerly held by the Japanese during World War II. American forces had overrun the island and then abandoned it. The island had no airstrip. Harlyn's crew ditched their aircraft in shallow water off the coast of the island and radioed their location for help. Unsure of what to expect in meeting the local natives, they found them to be friendly and helpful. Harlyn and his crew were rescued three days later.

In March, 2002, Harlyn and his grandson were special guests of the King of Faia who held a celebration to promote the island. Faia now has an airstrip precluding the island be supplied strictly by boat and also provides a means to export salt and fruit from the island. It was Harlyn's hope on his visit, to recover pieces of his former aircraft and the radio he used to call for help which had been left behind.

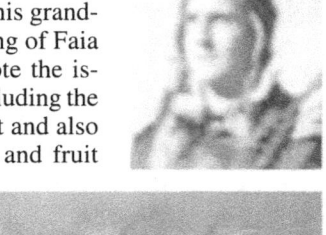

Right - Harlyn as gunnery instructor with the 466th BG, after completing 31 missions.

Right - Harlyn and .50 caliber machine gun

Right - Harlyn and crew at 446th BG, Bungay, England. Harlyn, Aerial Gunner, is back row, second from the right.

GLENN UNDERWOOD, SHENANDOAH, IA, was an automotive parts manager prior to World War II. Eleven months after the Japanese sneak attack on American military bases in the Hawaiian Islands he entered military service at Ft. Crook, near Omaha, Nebraska.

Glenn was assigned to Aerial Gun-

nery School at Pyote, Texas. After completion of training and assignment to an aircrew he was deployed to the European Theater of Operations as a tail gunner with the 447th Bomb Group at Rattlesden, England.

On March 27, 1944, over Merignac, France, enemy fighters attacked aircraft of the 447th and shot out two engines on Glenn's B-17. Unable to fly back to England, Glenn's pilot made a forced landing behind German lines and the crew was taken Prisoner of War. After Victory in Europe, Glenn was liberated and returned to the United States.

On November 3, 1945, Glenn received his discharge from military service at Santa Ana, California. He had been awarded the Purple Heart for wounds received in action, the Bronze Star, Air Medal, ETO Ribbon and World War II Victory Medal.

Glenn gave up civilian life to return to military service during the Korean War. After the end of hostilities he resumed his pre-war occupation as an automotive parts manager.

WILLIAM (BILL) VANCE, DES MOINES, IA, was employed by a dental supply company prior to World War II. After the Japanese attack on Pearl Harbor he entered the Army Air Corps at Ft. Des Moines, Iowa, on January 14, 1942.

Bill attended Armaments School at Lowry Field, Colorado, and was then transferred to a P-38 fighter squadron at San Diego, California.

From there he was sent to Aerial Gunnery School at Las Vegas, Nevada. Bill was then assigned to the 534th Squadron of the 381st Bomb Group as a ball turret gunner and deployed to Ridgewell, England, in May, 1943.

Bill completed his required twenty-five missions by November, 1943. His most memorable mission was to Schweinfurt, Germany on August 17, 1943, when his Wing endured heavy flak and enemy fighters. His Group lost eleven aircraft and the 91st and 351st Bomb Group lost ten aircraft each.

Bill received a direct commission as a Second Lieutenant in January, 1944. He was transferred to the 384th Bomb Group at Grafton Underwood, England, and flew additional missions. He was sent back to the United States to attend Observer's School at Laredo, Texas and returned to the 384th Bomb Group as a trainer.

Bill was discharged from the Air Corps in 1945 with the rank of Captain. He had been awarded the Distinguished Flying Cross, Air Medal with three oak leaf clusters, Distinguished Unit Citation, Certificate of Valor, ETO Ribbon and World War II Victory Medal.

Right - Bill after receiving direct commission as a Second Lieutenant, with trainees at 384th BG, Grafton Underwood, England. Bill is on the left in the back row.

DICK VANDUYN, IOWA CITY, IA, was originally from Waterloo, IA, and worked on a line crew for American Telegraph and Telephone out of Chicago covering the whole Upper Midwest prior to World War II. He entered military service in August, 1942, at Waterloo and was sent to Basic Training at Miami Beach, Florida. From there he attended Signal School at Fort

Monmouth, New Jersey, and had short assignments at Tampa and Bradenton, Florida, before winding up with the 36th Flight Group at Detroit, Michigan.

In July, 1943, Dick boarded a ship on the East Coast manned by British Merchant Marine and sailed for England. He had to sleep on the deck of the ship in quarters made of plywood with bunks fashioned from 2X4 boards. After arrival at Liverpool the ship was unloaded in record time. Evidently the Germans had bombed the harbor at Liverpool the night before and had miscalculated the arrival of his ship filled with American troops. Dick was then trucked to his new base, BAD 2 (Base Air Depot) at Wharton.

BAD2 was a new base with a complement of ten thousand soldiers. Telephones had to be installed and lines strung all over the base including hangars. The telephone switchboard was operated by eighteen American soldiers at night and British girls during the day. Dick's free time was spent visiting various sights around England including the resort city of Blackpool. While visiting the promenade area along the beach Dick met the love of his life, Joyce Evans of Wolverhampton, who he married after the war ended in Europe.

Dick returned to the United States in February, 1946, aboard a Liberty ship in rough seas and storms. The ship's captain had to sail south through the Azores to get into calmer waters. After return to civilian life, Dick returned to AT&T in Chicago as a lineman but subsequently entered management and among his assignments operated their office at Ewart, Iowa, before retiring.

Right - Dick and his telephone crewe at BAD2, Wharton, England. Dick is on the far left.

JAMES VAN GINKEL, ATLANTIC, IA, enlisted in the Army Air Corps in August, 1942. He was not called to active duty until January, 1943. Chosen for the Aviation Cadet Program he completed all his flight training in Texas. He graduated from Advanced Flight Training at Lubbock in 1944, and received his wings and commission as a Second Lieutenant.

James then attended Transition School for B-24 pilots at Liberal, Kansas. Because of a backlog of pilots waiting to attend the school he was sent to various bases for two months as an instructor. After graduation from transition school James was assigned to an air crew at Lincoln, Nebraska, and trained with the crew at Mountain Home, Idaho, before picking up a new B-24 bomber in July, 1944, and flying to Valley, Wales. After a week's orientation in Ireland, James reported to the 466th Bomb Group at Attlebridge, England. He arrived just after the Bomb Group had completed its one-hundredth mission and celebrated with a party. A banner that announced the accomplishment of the Group was still displayed on the front of one of the base hangars when he arrived.

Attlebridge was described as a pub and a church at a stop on the British railroad. The base was located about twenty miles Northeast of the city of Norwich, England.

James flew thirty-five combat missions as Co-Pilot and Pilot. Initially assigned as a Co-Pilot, James's pilot was killed during an early mission when, flying as an observer on a mission, another plane in their Group came down on top of his aircraft and cut off its tail. James then became First Pilot after a replacement pilot had completed his tour of duty.

Although German "flak" was encountered on every mission, James recalled Dresden as the most intense. It was a grueling eight hour flight to and from the target. His crew suffered no injuries nor did his aircraft receive any substantial damage during his remaining missions. He credits the P-51 Mustang and its ability to escort bombers all the way to and from targets as saving his life during his missions. James completed his tour in March, 1945, and returned to the United States. He was assigned to the 6th Ferry Group at Long Beach, California until his discharge in December, 1945. James had been awarded, among other medals, the Air Medal with oak leaf clusters, ETO Ribbon with battle stars and World War II Victory Medal.

After return to civilian life he enrolled at the University of Iowa and earned his Bachelor's Degree in Business Administration. James worked for Rath Packing Company in Waterloo for two years and saved his money to enter Drake Law School. In June, 1953, he graduated from Law School, got married and gained employment as a Special Agent with the FBI, all in the same month. In November, 1956, James established a law practice in Atlantic which he still operates with his son.

Right - James' crew at 466th BG, Attlebridge, England. James, Pilot, is back row, third from the left.

LAVERNE VARENHORST, STORM LAKE, IA, graduated from high school in June, 1941. He was drafted into the U.S. Army in December, 1942 with the Fourteenth Armored Division at Ft. Smith, Arkansas. In response to a need for pilots, Verne successfully passed examinations qualifying him for pilot training and transfer to the Army Air Corps.

Verne completed all stages of pilot training in Texas. Pre-Flight was taken at San Antonio; Primary at Bonham; Basic Flight Training at Paris, and Advanced Flight Training at Lubbock. He earned his wings and commission as a Second Lieutenant in March, 1944.

After assignment to an air crew, combat training in preparation for overseas deployment was taken at Drew Field, Florida.

Verne flew twenty-five combat missions without serious damage to his aircraft or injury to any of his aircrew. He returned to the United States in June, 1945 aboard the Victory Ship "La Grande Victory". The return voyage was not as happy as planned as most all the troops aboard ship suffered continual bouts of seasickness.

Iowans of the Mighty Eighth

After re-assignment to Santa Ana, California, Verne received his discharge from military service in late 1945. He had been awarded, among other medals, the Air Medal, European Theater of Operations and World War II Victory Medals. After return to civilian life Verne was self-employed in retail business and currently owns and operates a fabric shop in Storm Lake.

WILLIAM VINT, BEAMAN, IA, had completed one year of study at Iowa State College. In 1943 he enlisted in the Army Air Corps and was sent to Jefferson Barracks, St. Louis, Missouri, for Basic Training. He was then sent to Butler University as part of the College Training Detachment Program where he took science courses. While at a Classification Center at San Antonio, Texas, he learned volunteers were needed for aerial gunners. Bill volunteered, was accepted, and was sent to Lowry Field, Denver, Colorado, for Armorer/Gunner School. More gunnery schooling was taken at Kingman, Arizona, before being sent to Drew Field, Tampa, Florida, for crew assignment and training as a Togglier.

A togglier sits in the bombardier's position in the nose of the aircraft but without a bombsight. The Norden bombsight was carried in only about six of the thirty-six airplanes in a Bomb Group. When bombs were dropped by the bombardier in the lead aircraft, the togglier in following aircraft released their bombs.

Deployed to England in November, 1944, Bill was assigned to the 96th Bomb Group at Snetterton Heath. He flew twenty-seven combat mission aboard "Pilgrim's Progress" the name of his plane. His crew was eventually made lead aircraft and required a qualified bombardier. Bill had to return to his position as waist gunner. In all his missions only his tail gunner was wounded, and that was by flak.

Bill flew missions in support of the Battle of the Bulge and twice flew missions to Berlin. One mission to Berlin, on February 3, 1945, had over 1000 bombers participating in the raid. After their bomb run and turn for home the aircraft's radio was tuned to the British Broadcasting Company (BBC) so their crew could listen to an account of their raid. The bombing was so intense that while returning to Snetterton Heath Bill saw bombers coming and going to and from the target "as far as the eye could see". The Luftwaffe put up its maximum effort in fighter defense but Bill did not recall seeing any attack their formation.

During his stay at Snetterton Heath Bill experienced only one attack on his base. An enemy fighter came in at night and strafed the base once before flying away. No major damage occurred.

During another mission he saw the lead aircraft in his Group get hit by flak. "The plane seemed to go up and then dove straight down. "

Bill was discharged from military service in October, 1945, at Santa Cruz, Californai. He had been awarded, among other medals, the Air Medal with three oak leaf clusters, ETO Ribbon and World War II Victory Medal. Bill returned to Iowa and resumed farming.

There were five boys in Bill's high school graduating class. Three of them were in the Eighth Air Force. They were based near each other and occasionally got together.

Right - Darwin in front of his B-17 "Pilgrim's Progress"
Right - Darwin and his crew at 96th BG, Snetterton Heath, England. Darwin is back row, left.

ROBERT W. WARD was a pilot in the 361st Fighter Group. He initially enlisted in the Marines at San Diego, CA, but as he put it, "got kicked out of the Marines" because his teeth were not good enough. He spent six weeks waiting for the paperwork to be processed and utilized this time to become quite proficient as a gambler. He was later described as the best gambler in the 361st. Everyone from the squadron commander on down owed him money.

Before each mission Bob's crew chief would give him a lucky silver dollar. In return Bob would give the crew chief his little black book listing everyone who owed him money. Then Bob would ceremoniously relieve himself on his plane's tail wheel and go on the mission. On return, the lucky silver dollar and black book would change hands.

After the Marines passed on Bob he enlisted in the Army and was sent to Jefferson Barracks, Missouri, for Basic Training. During processing he was asked if he had been in the military before and he told them he was in the Marines for six weeks. This exempted him from basic training and he was assigned to a barrage balloon unit in Michigan with the rank of Corporal.

Bob applied and was accepted into the Aviation Cadet Program. He flew primary trainers and worked his way up to flying the P-40 for most of his fighter training. Before being assigned to the 361st he was given a manual on the P-51 and asked to read it. He was then asked if he could fly it. After he was shown how to start the plane he strapped himself in and took off.

Bob was deployed to England by ship and arrived on D-Day. The ship was moved north and hid along the coast until after D-Day, because of a suspected attack from German fighters. He was added to the roster of the 361st as a First Lieutenant on July 1, 1944. He completed his tour with the 361st while they were in Belgium in March of 1945 and had been promoted to Captain. He was credited with destroying two enemy aircraft in the air.

Bob's first P-51 was a B model named "Ginya" after his wife Virginia. Another of his planes was a D Model named "Little Larry" after his son who had just been born. Bob finished the war with two confirmed aerial victories and one damaged. He had strafed many ground targets.

An unusual part of his role with the 361st was to have his plane specially fitted with a camera in the bottom of the tail mounted at a 15 degree angle. After the rest of the planes in his Group had strafed or bombed a target he flew through the target area to record what damage had been inflicted. By this time the target's defenses were well alerted. Bob could only hope that by streaking past at 520 miles per hour they would be shooting where he had been.

Bob's last mission was strafing German trucks which were close to some trees. As he concentrated on hitting his target, he realized at the last second that he was too low. He hauled back on the stick and just barely made it. After that his plane began to act up. The crew chief found that struts installed at the aircraft factory had been removed or modified to fit the camera. Another pilot flew Bob's plane to see if he could figure out the problem. When the plane was not back when expected and it started to get dark, Bob got worried. No one would tell him anything. It was not until the pilot finally showed up that Bob learned the plane's wings had fallen off at the gun ports when doing some turns and maneuvers. The plane went into a tumble in the air and the pilot tried to get out. He forgot to unbuckle his seat belt before he pulled the canopy release. When the canopy let loose the force of the plane's gyrations ripped him out of the airplane with the seat still strapped to his butt. Free falling through space with a P-51 seat strapped to his behind, he was finally able to get the seat belt unbuckled, being careful not to unbuckle the parachute straps as well. The seat tumbled through the air and narrowly missed falling on a farmer. The pilot was not seriously injured.

On another mission Bob began a strafing run on a train. He saw a farmer with a horse and cart who Bob knew not to fire at, but the farmer panicked and tried to run and apparently ran into the train. The cart and horse tumbled into a ditch.

Bob had a brother who was fighting with ground forces near the front lines. When Bob was due for some time off he and a couple friends drove to the front areas for a visit. They took advantage of a curfew imposed on German civilians who had to stay inside their homes after 8:30 at night. They "liberated" two German motorcycles from outside a house and took them back to their base for available transportation. The motorcycles had been left behind by the retreating German Army.

Bob's funniest recollection of a mission was one day when he escorted bombers. He had to use the relief tube, which was a simple device resembling a funnel with a line going to the outside of the aircraft for automatic disposal of urine. Missions were often six, eight or more hours long. Using the tube was a challenge at the altitude they were flying, it was very cold and there were several layers of clothing to contend with. Bob had one hand free to fly with and with the other he used the tube. He noticed it was not draining properly. Usually the pressure of the air streaming past the airplane made the tube empty immediately, so something was wrong. At this point Bob was holding the full funnel end up to try to get it to drain so he could go some more, and of course he was still flying with the one free hand. By this time they were over enemy territory where it was standard procedure to arm the aircraft's guns so that by using the trigger button he could fire the six 50 caliber guns in the wings. He had armed the guns and was still contending with an almost full funnel when he accidentally hit his own gun button. The sound of his own guns going off was very similar to the sound of 30mm fire from German aircraft when they were firing at you. He immediately took evasive action wondering where the guy on his tail had come from. He realized quickly what had happened. Other pilots in his Group called on the radio to ask what had happened.

He told them he was OK, but inside the cockpit, what had previously been sitting in the funnel was now everywhere. The unwanted liquid had instantly frozen to the inside of the canopy and the faces of his instruments. He had to scrape off the frozen substance to see the instruments and for visibility out of the canopy.

It was standard procedure to let down rather quickly from altitude, shoot past the field and get in line to land. He parked his plane just as the frozen material thawed and the crew chief jumped up on the wing. When the ground crew cleaned up the cockpit they found the relief tube had been twisted somewhere before it exited the aircraft.

Robert W Ward was originally from Toledo, Iowa but later moved to Marshalltown. He passed away in October of 1995.

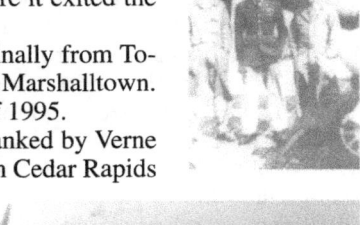

Right - Bob, in center, flanked by Verne Josifek, Bob's crew chief from Cedar Rapids on his left. Man on Bob's right is Verne's assistant, Harry Hiney.

Right - Bob in front of his P-51 at the 361st Fighter Group.

JACK WEAVER, ESTHERVILLE, IA, entered the Army Air Corps on October 9, 1942. He was a radio operator and aerial gunner with the 384th Bomb Group based at Grafton Underwood, England. Jack's duties aboard the aircraft consisted of operating airborne transmitting and receiving equipment and making necessary flight maintenance on the radio equipment.

Jack flew thirty combat missions beginning December 31, 1943 on a bombing mission to Orsona, France and ending August 25, 1944 with a raid on Anklam, Germany. During his second mission a crew member fell out of the aircraft's bomb bay area without a parachute. His ninth mission, a bombing raid on Oberpfoffenhofen, Germany, was considered the worst. "Fighters came through the formation head on. We lost two engines and had one engine on fire, so we had to leave the formation and limp back to England. I only wore my flak suit on three missions. On this mission flak came through the aircraft and hit my chest protector and cut the cord to my microphone. The flak suit saved my life."

Jack received his discharge from military service on October 3, 1945 at Sioux City, Iowa, having been awarded, among other medals, the Distinguished Flying Cross, Air Medal with oak leaf clusters, the ETO Ribbon with battle stars and World War II Victory Medal.

Jack worked for thirty nine years at Morrell Packing Plant in Estherville. Since retirement he has been an active volunteer at the local hospital and with other organizations in the community.

LOREN WEAVERLING, MASON CITY, IA, attended Radar School at Boca Raton, Florida. Upon completion of training he was assigned to the 487th Fighter Squadron of the 352nd Fighter Group at Bodney, England, as a Radar and Radio Mechanic.

Loren was assigned at one time or another to four different P-51 Mustang fighter aircraft. It was his responsibility to maintain the electronics on these aircraft. One of the fighters was flown by George Preddy who had twenty-seven and a half aerial victories in the European Theater. Another pilot in his fighter group was severely reprimanded when he flew a P-47 Thuderbolt upside down under the George Washington Bridge. His pilot, Robert Berkshire, was shot down on a mission over Europe but managed to escape German troops and make his way back to Bodney.

After the invasion of Europe and as territory was taken from the Germans, new bases in Europe were established. Loren crossed the English Channel by boat to a new base in France. His ship was accidentally rammed by a French frigate and started to take on water. It had to be towed. The towline was cut twice when it was feared the ship would sink. On arrival at Le Havre, France, the ship did sink.

Loren and other ground personnel were trucked to a small village near Brussels, Belgium where they lived in tents with wood stoves. Sparks from the fire in the stoves burned holes in their tents. While there an air battle took place above their new encampment. The 487th Squadron shot down twenty-three German planes in one day and received a Distinguished Unit Citation for its actions. One German fighter, a FW-190, was shot down by an American fighter that was taking off down its runway.

Loren regularly sent home the "Stars and Stripes" to his wife. The May 8, 1945, issue with the headlines "Germany Quits" is a prized issue.

NEIL WEBSTER, GUTTENBERG, IA, in 1939 was working as a technician at a small radio station in Greenwood, Mississippi, earning ten dollars a week. In November of that year he enlisted in the Army Air Corps for a two year hitch in Hawaii. He was sent to Ft. McLellan, Alabama, where he received his medical shots and initial allotment of military clothing. He then   boarded the "USS Hunter Ligget" at an East Coast port to sail through the Panama Canal to San Francisco where they would then leave for Hawaii.

After leaving San Francisco "we ran into some bad weather and many of the men were very sick. At chow time many of the men would pick up their metal planes full of food, take one look at it and then throw up. The head was also full of guys heaving while on the stools. When we got to Honolulu one of the sergeants asked me where I had hidden out as they had been looking for me for three days for k.p.(kitchen police). I wasn't hiding and didn't hear my name being called for the detail."

The Air Corps men that arrived in Hawaii took courses in military history and courtesy and were then assigned to various jobs. "I was fortunate to be chosen as a control tower operator. In addition to air traffic control we also had to play Retreat each day at 5:00 PM over a public address system. One of the pranks we would pull was to wait until someone was in the middle of the parade ground and then we would play Retreat. The G.I. would have to stop, come to attention and salute the Flag. Water sprinklers on the parade ground would come on and drench the poor guy."

"When some guy would come back to the barracks late, drunk and crawl into bed, we would lift his bunk up without waking him and place it on footlockers so that when he got up in the morning he would step out not taking into account how high we was and hit the floor. We would also put electric shaver hair in his sheets or short sheet him."

"As control tower operators our job was to see that the airplanes had a clear space to take off and land in the proper order. We gave wind speed and direction, saw that all aircraft radio transmitters checked in and were on the proper frequency. Written records had to be of all landings and take offs and any other information that might be useful."

In November, 1941 Neil and another G.I. were boxing with no gloves on and he broke a bone in his hand. He had to go to Tripler General Hospital to have his hand bandaged and put in a plaster cast. He was required to stay in the hospital and remained there until 7:55 A.M., December 7, 1941, when the Japanese attacked Pearl Harbor and airfields on Oahu. "We were hustled out of the hospital to make room for battle casualties and sent to a nearby school taken over by the military for patients. I stayed there overnight but next day got a ride back to Hickam Field. No one turned me loose or took off my cast. I took the cast off myself when I got back to the field. I took over my regular shift of duties and was issued a .45 caliber pistol. Our barracks suffered bomb damage so I was slept in our transmitter building.

Neil was then sent to Christmas Island two thousand miles south of Hawaii where he was placed in charge of control tower operations. "Our equipment consisted of a very old transmitter and receiver. Power was supplied by a two cylinder motor generator which was inadequate and we later received power from the airfield diesel generators." The island was a landing point for planes going from Hawaii to Australia. "We had very little refrigeration and drank warm cokes and ate mostly canned food. Water contained twice as much iodine as required and was almost impossible to drink."

After seven months on the island, Neil applied for Signal Corps Officer Training School. He passed the required exams, was accepted for training, and was sent back to Oahu to catch a ship for the United States. He attended Officer's Candidate School at Ft. Monmouth, New Jersey, and on December 31, 1942 was commissioned a Second Lieutenant. He was assigned to the 29th Signal Company at Tobyhanna, Pennsylvania, and deployed to Blackpool, England aboard a ship.

Neil was assigned to the 55th Fighter Group at Nuthampsted, England, which flew the Lockheed P-38 Lightning. After a short time the Group was transferred to Colchester, England, and eventually changed to the P-51 Mustang fighter. "Our Signal Company was responsible for supplying tubes and radios to the Fighter Group. We could get complete transmitters but had a difficult time getting tubes. We also supplied batteries, flashlites and other signal items to telephone operators, telephone linemen, crypto analysis, Signal Headquarters and motor pool.

Toward the end of the war Neil was assigned to an advance party to go to Kaufburen, Germany, a flight training station for German Luftwaffe pilots. The advance party was to prepare the field for transfer of the Group to the European mainland. "All underground telephone circuits had been cut and we had no circuit diagrams to use for repair. He stayed there for only three weeks before he returned to England to be sent back to the United States aboard the "Queen Mary."

After separation from military service Neil remained in the Air Force Reserves until official discharge in 1980. He is retired from a career in an electronics business.

DENNIS WEIDEMAN, FORT DODGE, IA, was a Co-Pilot and First Pilot with the 384th Bomb Group based at Grafton Underwood, England. He flew thirty-five combat missions and was awarded, among other medals, the Distinguished Flying Cross, Air Medal with oak leaf clusters, ETO Ribbon and World War II Victory Medal. Following World War II, Dennis was founder and partner in Specialty Machine and Manufacturing Company in Fort Dodge until illness forced his retirement.

Right - Dennis and his crew. Dennis is second from the left in the back row.

RICHARD WERNER, VAN HORNE, IA, was farming prior to World War II. On December 16,1943, he was drafted into the Army Air Corps. He was called to active duty January 6, 1944, and sent to Amarillo, Texas, for Basic Training. He was then scheduled to begin pilot training but his class was "washed out" because of a glut in pilots in training and Richard was sent to Kingman, Arizona, for Aerial Gunnery School.

Richard was then assigned to an aircrew and trained with them at Tampa, Florida, in preparation for overseas deployment. The crew then picked up a new B-17 bomber at Savannah, Georgia, to begin their flight to the European Theater of Operations. Their trip was delayed when his bombardier was taken off the crew to become an instructor and they had to wait until a replacement was assigned. On November 26, 1944, Thanksgiving Day, they were able to start their flight to Valley, Wales, through Bangor, Maine and Goose Bay, Labrador. On arrival their aircraft was taken from them for installation of additional equipment and armament. They were assigned to the 384th Bomb Group at Grafton Underwood, England.

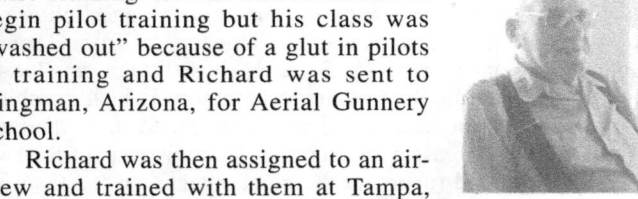

Richard flew thirty-five combat missions as tail gunner beginning December 18, 1944. After five days off he flew twelve missions in sixteen days. This included missions flown five days in a row mostly toward targets in support of the Battle of the Bulge.

His most memorable mission was on February 26, 1945, to Berlin. "The Brits bombed Germany at night and we bombed them during the day. It was like a big belt with the British returning home when we were going to Germany. A big "flak" burst hit below our plane. It was like a big puff ball. From where I was in the tail of the plane I could really feel the concussion. It lifted me off the floor of the plane. We just wanted to finish our missions and get out of the war." Richard flew his last mission on March 18, 1945, also to Berlin.

Richard returned to the United States April 25, 1945. He was scheduled to attend a B-29 bomber power school but instead attended a forest fire school in the state of Washington. He helped fight fires burning in Idaho forests until reassignment to San Diego, California, where he received his discharge from military service on October 9, 1945. Richard had been awarded the Air Medal with five oak leaf clusters, European Theater of Operations medal with three battle stars and World War II Victory Medal. He returned to Iowa and resumed farming.

WILFRED 'BILL' WERNER, MUSCATINE, IA, entered the Reserve Corps in 1942 and spent eight months at a Radio Mechanics School at Des Moines, Iowa. "Although I was in a Signal Corps unit throughout the war, the eight months I spent at Des Moines was the last time I would see the inside of a radio." He was called to active duty in April, 1943, and sent to Camp Kohler, at Sacramento, California.

He was then sent to Fresno, California, "where all Signal Corps personnel were being formed into military companies.

Bill then went by military troop train for Camp Kilmer, New Jersey, where he boarded the ocean liner "Queen Mary" for Scotland. "There was from fifteen to sixteen thousand G.I.s on board. When we got to Scotland me and a Second Lieutenant were ordered to take a train to London. The Lieutenant had control of our files and he told me he would meet me when we got there. When we got off the train we were divided by unit designation. I never saw the Lieutenant again and he had our files. I was told to join up with one of the bomb groups that was on the train and I went with them to some airbase, but it was full.. Then I was sent to another airbase and it was full. I wound up at Honington, England, and placed in the 6th Mobile Reclamation and Repair Group. We would go to crash sites and salvage what we could from wrecks or repair aircraft so they could be flown out from where they were."

Bill was then sent to the 896th Signal Company at Honington as a motor messenger. Everyday he had to deliver "Secret" dispatches and messages to various Eighth Air Force bases in the Third Air Division. He was then assigned to the base message center where he received and sent all messages for the base.

Honington was the location of the First Strategic Air Depot reponsible for major repair, supply and service to fourteen bomb groups. "Honington was a former Royal Air Force base with three story concrete barracks with steam heat. The 364th Fighter Group then arrived at Honington and took over our quarters. We had to move to plywood barracks, that weren't insulated and heated only by a pot-bellied stove that burned coke."

Bill was transferred to Alconbury, England, with the 3011th Signal Company as the message center chief before he moved to the mainland of Europe as part of occupation forces at Erlangen, Germany, site of a German truck repair facility.

In February, 1946, Bill boarded the ship "Le Jeune", a captured German ship for the voyage home to America. He received his discharge from military service at Camp McCoy, Wisconsin in March, 1946, and had been awarded the European Theater of Operations and World War II Victory Medals, among others.

In civilian life, Bill retired from a career in the lumber business.

Iowans of the Mighty Eighth

Right - Bill and his jeep with 896th Signal Company, Honington, England

LEWIS WEST, DES MOINES, IA, worked at the Army Ordnance Plant in Ankeny, Iowa, before America's entry into World War II. He was drafted into the Army Air Corps February 1, 1943 at Camp Dodge, Iowa, and sent to St. Petersburg, Florida, for Basic Training. He attended Communications School at Scott Field, Illinois and Radio Mechanics School at Truax Field, Madison, Wisconsin before assignment to Advanced Combined Net System School.

Lewis reported to the 479th Fighter Group at Glendale, California, where the Group was being formed. The Group was then sent to Camp Kilmer, New Jersey, where Lewis boarded the ocean liner "Aquatania" for the United Kingdom. The 479th was stationed at Wattisham, England, a former Royal Air Force base. As a communications specialist Lewis' duties included maintenance of control tower radio equipment and base transmitters and receivers situated about a mile from the base as well as a homing station equipped with a radio direction finder. The sites were manned twenty-four hours a day with two men on location at each site.

In advance of D-Day, June 6, 1944, Lewis was sent to a radio station near the White Cliffs of Dover that was used for back-up communication in case of attack on his base and destruction of its equipment.

Lewis remained in England after V-E Day and was not sent back to the United States until Thanksgiving Day, 1945. He returned aboard the aircraft carrier "USS Enterprise". His unit was then split-up and Lewis received his discharge from military service on December 6, 1945, at Rockford, Illinois. He had been awarded the ETO Ribbon and World War II Victory Medal.

Lewis retired from the U S Postal Service as an Area Maintenance Technician. He remains active with the 479th Fighter Group as its newsletter editor.

HARTLEY "HAP" WESTBROOK, AMES, IA, was originally from Letts, IA. He was in the first quarter of his junior year at the then Iowa State Teachers College at Cedar Falls when the Japanese attacked Pearl Harbor and other American military installations on Oahu in the Hawaiian Islands on December 7, 1941. Hap had earned his pilot's license through the Citizen's Pilot Training program while in college. His instructor was Jon Livingston who in turn had his official pilot's license signed by Orville Wright.

Hap enlisted in the Air Army Corps in January, 1942. He reported to King City, CA for primary training and graduated from the training with film star Jimmy Stewart. He then reported to Moffit Field near San Jose, CA for advanced training. Moffit Field was originally under Naval authority and in the early stages of American military aviation housed dirigibles in huge domed hangars. Doors at each end of the hangar reached from the ground to the top of the hangar. While in training and surprisingly without being identified, Hap was able to prove a BT-13 single engine trainer could be flown through the hangar. To have been caught would have meant a court-martial and dismissal from the training program.

Additional advanced training taken at Chico, California, included cross-country and formation flying. He was involved in another incident. Hap flew his aircraft under the Golden Gate Bridge also without being identified. In wartime and in training this was also another court martial and dismissal offense. Hap received his pilot's wings and commission as a Second Lieutenant on July 27, 1942. After a furlough and getting married, Hap reported to Wiley Post Airfield near Oklahoma City, OK, for B-24 flight training. While there he accepted temporary duty in Louisiana flying submarine patrol over the Gulf of Mexico.

In August, 1942, Hap boarded the "Queen Mary" with maintenance crews and set sail to Glasgow, Scotland. After arrival he boarded a train for Shipdham, England, and assignment with the 44th Bomb Group.

Nineteen forty-two was the infant stage of the air war on Germany which was to last three years. Long range fighter escort was to come later in the war. Until then losses from German fighter attacks and anti-aircraft batteries caused staggering losses during American daylight strategic bombing. British bombing missions were at night to avoid losses but failed to be directed toward military targets with accuracy. The missions of the two air forces provided for round-the-clock attacks on the German industrial and military machine.

The first mission of the 44th BG was on November 7, 1942, a diversionary flight to draw German fighters away from the bomb groups proceeding to a target. Hap's first mission came on December 6, 1942, one day short of a year after Pearl Harbor. He flew another twelve missions predominately in B-24s named "Suzy Q" and "Miss Dianne". May 14, 1942, changed his life forever.

On May 14 the 44th Bomb Group was to bomb the Krupp Submarine Works at Kiel, Germany. Seaports and submarine pens and facilities were bombed to keep the "life line" of supplies open from America to England. Flying "tail end Charlie", the least desired spot in the formation, Hap and the balance of the 44th had to fly behind slower B-17 bombers assigned to the raid. This required not only that they fly at a reduced speed but at a lower altitude making them extremely vulnerable to anti-aircraft fire and fighter attack.

Before they began their bomb run, Hap's formation was attacked by German Focke-Wulf 190 fighters that sent five bombers to earth. A fighter attacked the rear of Hap's B-24. The rear hatch gunner, tail gunner and waist gunner were killed. Two engines of his aircraft were knocked out and a third engine was on fire. Hap was shot in the shoulder and shrapnel had hit him in the leg but he still managed to jettison their bomb load.

The crew had to bail out of their stricken aircraft. Hap had to push one of his crewmen out the escape hatch after he froze, terror stricken and was unable to jump. Hap later learned the man survived the war as a POW.

Chapter Twenty-Two

Hap tried to control the aircraft but it began a circular descent that carried him out to sea. He bailed out and landed in the icy North Sea that crested seven-foot waves. Hap was able to free himself from his parachute and flying boots and inflate one half of his Mae West life vest. The other half had been punctured by a bullet hole.

It was estimated a human could only survive fifteen or twenty minutes in the cold water of the North Sea. Hap bobbed in the water until he lost consciousness. Later that day a Swedish fishing boat pulled him out of the water believing him dead. They felt a pulse coming from Hap and took him to the boat's hot engine room and stripped him of his clothes to "thaw out". After he regained consciousness Hap was fed hot soup, given medial attention to his wounds and turned over to German authorities.

Hap was taken to a German interrogation center near Berlin for questioning. Interrogators knew in advance that he had attended Iowa Teachers College, was married, knew his wife's first name, and that he had been deployed to England aboard the "Queen Mary". He gave the Germans only name, rank and serial number. Hap was transported to Stalag Luft III, a prison camp that contained a compound of American air force officers. Other compounds in the camp contained Russian and Polish laborers, and British and Canadian airmen.

Two twelve foot high barbed wire fences with barbed wire entanglements between the fences surrounded the camp. The inner wire was charged with high voltage electricity. Another single wire fence twelve feet inside the other fences was a designated no-trespass area. To cross the no-trespass fence could result in being shot by guards. The POWs were locked at night in their barracks built off the ground. Guard dogs were released in the prison compounds at night to prevent escapes. Guards armed with machine guns were in towers every 150 feet while other guards patrolled the ground outside of the compounds.

Barracks were pre-fabricated buildings of plywood construction divided into rooms for eight persons, later to be increased in number as the war progressed. The latrine (toilet) was at the far end of a barracks consisting of a concrete tank with holes cut into it. The lavatory was a concrete trough with faucets. No shower facilities existed in Hap's barracks until the prisoners were able to improvise one. Mattresses and pillows were filled with straw. Each prisoner received one brick of coal per week for heating his barracks in a single stove. Food was watery soup often containing unidentified objects that were alive and dark bread that tasted of sawdust. Red Cross parcels containing food items and cigarettes designed to supplement their meager diet was delivered to each prisoner, one parcel per week. They were often slow in coming.

As confinement lingered so did boredom. Clothes and shoes began to wear out, but American ingenuity is best when tested. At Hap's suggestion tools were made from metal scraps and a shoe repair facility, barbershop and theater for plays established. The YMCA provided sports equipment and musical instruments. Playing cards were made from cardboard. Soup can labels were boiled down to make paint and brushes were fashioned from human hair.

Escape was foremost in each prisoner's mind. At Stalag III it became a game to try and escape. One escapee's fate is unknown. He hid in a pile of human excrement piled on a cart after a Polish laborer had cleaned the concrete latrines. The cart was then pulled out of prison for disposal. Several unsuccessful attempts were made to "hoodwink" German guards. To get caught meant solitary confinement. Constant pleadings from the prison commandant were made to the prison population to not try and escape. The commandant's own fate as an officer depended on prisoner compliance. All that changed with The Great Escape. Utilizing the talents of the diverse population of the prison compound and maintaining secrecy, tunnels were dug, German uniforms made, and documents forged.

Late one night seventy-six British and Canadian airmen escaped their compound through a tunnel. More were supposed to escape, but the tunnel opening outside the compound was discovered by a German guard before any others could exit. The plot had taken months to prepare, get rid of dirt from the tunnel excavation and maintain security. The Germans were known to place English speaking officers in prison compounds disguised as Allied airmen to ferret out escape plans and intelligence information.

All but three of the seventy-six escapees were caught. After re-capture, fifty of them were lined up outside the prison compound and shot by German guards. The prison commandant was relieved of his duties.

In January, 1945, as the Russian Army advanced toward their prison camp, the POWs were notified the camp would be evacuated. The night of January 27, 1945, in fifteen degree temperature, icy winds and snow a foot deep on the ground the POWs were marched for six days covering sixty miles. Hap developed frostbite in his right foot and was barely able to walk. To stop meant being shot by guards. At a rest stop he fashioned a sled for his foot to relieve pressure on it and with an arm around a friend supporting him, he was able to continue the march. At another rest stop, in a vacant pottery factory, he was able to discharge fluid that had swollen his feet and lance the sores. The prisoners were marched to Spremberg, Germany, where they were loaded in railroad cars and shipped 200 miles to Nurnberg, Germany. They were then marched another eighty miles to Moosburg, Germany, site of Stalag VII. "The camp was best described as a vermin-ridden hellhole."

Although escape would have been easy because of their superiority of numbers, the POWs knew Allied forces were near. On April 28, 1945, an American tank crashed through the front gate of the prison compound. General George Patton exited the tank. He ordered the prisoners to remain at the camp until transportation could be arranged. Meanwhile food and medical supplies were delivered to the POWs.

Hap weighed 165 pounds when he entered military service. When he was released from the prison camp he was down to 118 pounds. Hap was flown to a processing camp in Belgium for hot showers, delousing, shaves, haircuts, new clothes, hot food and clean beds. In May, 1945, he boarded a Liberty ship for America and a reunion with his bride and family.

Hap remained in military service until 1947 when he received his discharge. He remained active in the Air Force Reserve while he managed the municipal airport at Guthrie Center, Iowa, and marketed Cessna aircraft. As he prepared to take over management of the municipal airport at Atlantic, Iowa, Hap was called to active duty during the Korean War. After he received his discharge from the military, Hap resumed operation of the Atlantic airport, a job he held for 24 years. After leaving the Air Force, the Governor of Iowa contacted Hap to organize the Iowa National Guard and become its first and Chief Pilot. He accepted and spent years promoting the Air Guard and teaching recruits to fly before he retired as a Lieutenant Colonel.

Hap moved his flying service to the Ames, Iowa, Municipal Airport. He eventually owned twenty-two airplanes, was named Airport Operator of the Year by the Flying Farmers Association, and continued to sell Cessna and other aircraft for over fifty years.

Iowans of the Mighty Eighth

On June 24, 2000, Hap was inducted into the Iowa Aviation Hall of Fame at ceremonies held at the Antique Aircraft Preservation Museum at Greenfield, IA.

After twenty-three years of military service Hap had been awarded, among other decorations, the Purple Heart, Air Medal with two oak leaf clusters and the Prisoner of War Medal. During his aviation career he logged over 30,000 hours in flight.

The 44th Bomb Group operated from England longer, claimed more enemy fighters, and sustained the highest missing in action losses of any other B-24 Group. Hap's favorite quote is "Our bombers were escorted from our base in England to the English coast by Spitfires, and we were escorted to the target and back by Messerschmitts."

Portions of some war-time experiences were taken from the book "An Iowa Pilot Named Hap", by Norman Rudi, McMillen Publishing Company, Ames, Ia., Library of Congress Control Number 2001092394, ISBN Number 1-888223-25-1

ORVILLE WHITCANACK, CANTRIL, IA, had farmed and worked in an aircraft plant in Burbank, CA when America entered World War II. Recently married, his wife Mary moved to her parent's home when Orville was drafted into the Army Air Corps on December 13, 1942, at Camp Dodge, IA.

After basic training Orville attended Airplane Mechanics School at Sheppard Field, Texas and Willow Run, Michigan; Gunnery School at Laredo, Texas; and Airplane Instrument Mechanics School at Chanute Field, Illinois. After assignment to a flight crew at Salt Lake City, Utah, Orville trained with them at Blythe, California, in preparation for overseas deployment. On May 6, 1944, Orville and his crew flew to England through Labrador, Ireland and Wales.

Orville flew thirty-two combat missions as Flight Engineer with the 493rd Bomb Group stationed at Debach, England. He was responsible for engine operatiion, fuel consumption and operation of all equipment aboard his aircraft. Prior to one mission Orville discovered something with his plane he considered to be unsafe and refused to take it on a mission. A superior officer stated there was nothing seriously wrong with the airplane and ordered Orville's crew to fly it on the mission. Orville still refused. They were eventually assigned another aircraft and flew the mission. Their original airplane was also refused by another crew's flight engineer for the same reason detected by Orville. A third crew took the airplane, crashed, and all on board were killed.

As they returned from one mission their Group was flying along the Rhine River in Germany. Suddenly a plane next to Orville's took a direct hit from flak, burst into flames, broke up and went down. "I was looking at the plane. It was so close I could see one guy's face and his eyes. He was there one minute and the next was gone. It gives you a weird feeling to see your buddies go that way." The Germans had anti-aircraft guns mounted on barges floating up and down the Rhine River.

On September 3, 1945, Orville was discharged from military service at Jefferson Barracks, Missouri. He had been awarded the Bronze Star, Air Medal with four oak leaf clusters, ETO Ribbon with four battle stars, and World War II Victory Medal.

After the war he was a service station partner, farmed and eventually went into securities and investment sales. Orville died October 18, 1984. He wife Mary maintains membership in the Eighth Air Force Historical Society, frequent contact with remaining crew members and their spouses and has compiled a book on the history of Orville's crew.

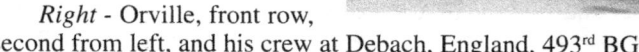

Right - Orville, front row, second from left, and his crew at Debach, England, 493rd BG

ROBERT WHITE, BURLINGTON, IA, attended Texas A&M University until he enlisted into military service March 5, 1941, at Houston, Texas. Following Basic Training at Randolph Field, Texas, Robert was sent to Chanute Field, Illinois, for Mechanics School on December 7, 1941, Pearl Harbor Day. Upon graduation and after furlough, Robert was sent to Coffeyville, KS, where he became a supply sergeant.

Robert was deployed to England in August, 1943, assigned to the 99th Station Complement at Bury St Edmunds with the 94th BG. He was subsequently re-assigned to the 420th Sub Depot at Debach, England, with the 493rd BG.

Robert recalled three incidents that stand out in his memory of base life in England. One of the top gamblers on the base at Debach returned to his barracks by taxi late one night. When the taxi door was opened the interior lights went on inside the vehicle. A German fighter in the area then swooped down and strafed the base. Fortunately no one was hurt. Buzz bombs were a constant threat, "coming over all the time between 5-11 P.M. They were solid coming over. British artillery was good at blowing them up." One evening he went to a "gin mill" at Yarmouth, a port city. The bars closed at 10 P.M. When he exited the bar with many sailors, the Shore Patrol and Military Police were waiting. The drunken sailors went after the military policemen and a large brawl took place. Robert made a hasty exit.

Robert returned to the United States in August, 1945 aboard the Liberty Boat "Athlon Castle" along with ten thousand other troops. During the voyage they learned the Atomic Bomb had been dropped on Hiroshima, Japan.

Following the war Robert returned to college at the University of Texas. After graduation he served as Deputy City Assessor in Texas for nineteen years and thirteen years as a combined city and county assessor.

MELVIN WILE, POMEROY, IA, entered the U.S. Army Air Corps at Des Moines, Iowa, on April 7, 1942. After Basic Training he completed Aircraft Mechanics School at Sheppard Field, Texas and Aerial Gunnery School at San Diego, California. Melvin was then assigned to an aircrew at Salt Lake City, Utah, and completed overseas training with his crew at Clovis and Alamagordo, New Mexico.

On June 12, 1943, Melvin and his crew picked up a new B-24 Liberator bomber and flew to England via Maine, Labrador and Scotland. They were assigned to the 389th Bomb Group at Hethel, England.

Chapter Twenty-Two

Melvin flew his first combat mission in July, 1943, a bombing raid on German submarine facilities at LeHavre, France. During the mission they lost hydraulics to their aircraft causing them to have no brakes. The pilot ordered his entire crew to the tail of the aircraft on landing to weigh it down and cause it to drag on the runway in order to stop.

Melvin's bomb group was ordered to North Africa, along with two other bomb groups of the Eighth Air Force, to take part in the first bombing raid on oil fields at Ploesti, Romania. Mechanical trouble in route caused Melvin and his crew to land at Gibraltor. They had to return to England to pick up another aircraft. Once they arrived in North Africa they were designated an extra crew and placed on stand-by for the raid in case another aircrew was forced out of the mission. "What planes returned from the mission either had no fuel in their tanks when they landed or no oil in the engines."

Melvin's tenth mission was on December 22, 1943, a bombing raid on ammunition dumps and railroad marshalling yards near Osnabruck, Germany. "Right after our fighter escort left us, German fighters attacked. All four of our engines were knocked out. Machine gun bullets from the German fighers came up through the floor of our aircraft. The bullets ran up the side of my leg shredding my flight suit. One bullet struck me in the arm. I was also wounded by flak in the leg. The B-24 doesn't glide very well without power and we went down. When we crashed landed me and our tail gunner were thrown from the airplane. I was knocked unconscious. When I woke up I was surrounded by German soldiers. My tail gunner and I were taken to a Doctor's office for medical treatment. That night we were handcuffed to a double bunk bed. I slept on the top bunk. The tail gunner was in such pain he kept waking me up all night before he died."

Melvin received medical treatment at three different German hospitals. When he was carried on a stretcher by German guards from one hospital, irate German citizens surrounded Melvin and the guards with the intent to lynch him. A woman began beating Melvin with a parasol but he was protected by the guards who took him to a railroad station and then sneaked him out a rear door to a rail car.

Melvin was assigned to Stalag Luft VI at Heydekrug, East Prussia. Later, when the Russian Army began to advance toward the camp, the Prisoners of War were evacuated to prevent their liberation. They were placed in the hold of barges that sailed to Poland. "There were so many of us in the hold of the ship you couldn't move. There was a single light bulb. They must have hauled grain in the barges at one time or another. Rats came out of hiding and began running all over the place. All we could do was swat them away. When we got out of the barges they forced us to run four miles to our new prison camp, Stalag 4 (Gross Tychow, Pomerania). As we ran the guards poked at us with bayonets on the end of their rifles."

In February, 1945, as the Russian Army again began to close in on the prison camp, the Prisoners of War were evacuated. "They forced us to march for eighty-three days covering over six hundred miles. We had to live off the land. When we would come near Allied armies again they would march us in a different direction. I swear we crossed the same bridge three times in those eighty-three days. We were all full of lice."

"In April, 1945, we were herded into an opera house at Betterfeldt, Germany. An American plane flew over and dropped leaflets telling us the American Army was coming." On April 26 near Halle, Germany, Melvin was liberated. He was sent to Camp Lucky Strike near LeHavre, France where he received medical treatment, clothing, de-lousing, food, pay and processing. He subsequently boarded a ship for a twelve day voyage across the Atlantic to America. After furlough he received his discharge from military service on September 7, 1945. Melvin had been awarded the Purple Heart, Air Medal, and European Theater of Operations Medal. He received his Prisoner of War Medal nearly thirty years later.

Melvin returned to Iowa and farmed until retirement in 1981.

GALEN WILEY, BOONE, IA, was working as a clerk in a J.C. Penney store when he was inducted into the Army Air Corps in June, 1942. After Basic Training he attended Aircraft Mechanics School at Lincoln, Nebraska. He then applied and was accepted for pilot training in the Aviation Cadet Program.

Galen completed Pre-Flight Training at Santa Ana, California; Primary and Basic Flight Training at Ontario, California, before Advanced Flight and B-17 training at Ft Sumner and Roswell, New Mexico.

Galen was assigned an aircrew and trained with them at Dyersburg, Tennessee, for overseas deployment. In June, 1944, Galen and his crew flew to the European Theater of Operations through Gander, Newfoundland to Valley, Wales.

Galen was assigned to the 305th Bomb Group at Chelveston, England. He flew 36 missions in four months primarily in a B-17 named "Lucky Lady". This was one mission more than what was required for rotation back to the United States.

First mission jitters for the crew came on June 18, 1944, when, in the crew's belief, they were to bomb Hamburg, Germany. "I don't think I was scared, but I wondered a lot about that first mission. What was it going to be like? We didn't see any enemy fighters, but there was a lot of flak." "When we got back, we had a de-briefing, and the officer asked our navigator "what time was the paper away?" "What paper?" It turned out we had dropped propaganda leaflets over the target instead of regular bombs."

Galen flew five missions to Munich, four of them in a row. Other targets included heavily defended Berlin, Bremen, and Pennemunde, site of Germany's rocket bases, as well as missions to destroy artificial petroleum and ball bearing plants. During one mission the Group's Commanding Officer (C.O.) was the lead plane. Galen's aircraft was following the C.O.'s aircraft and saw it take a direct hit from flak that sheared off the tail and sent it straight down to earth. Only one crewman survived. He was able to exit the aircraft and open his parachute.

In September, 1944, three missions were flown in support of "Operation Market Garden" the airborne invasion at Arnhem, Holland, to secure bridges in conjunction with a breakout of ground forces from Belgium.

During another mission Galen's aircraft took heavy flak during their bomb run. His navigator noticed a two-foot hole in the right wing. Upon return to base and further examination of the damage they were able to see the fuel tank on the edge of the hole. "Lucky Lady" had lived up to her name.

After the occupation of France, Galen was assigned to fly war correspondents to Paris including well-known Life Magazine cameraman Frank Capra. Galen's navigator had stocked their aircraft with cigarettes and stockings for the ladies of Paris in anticipation of having a good time during their short stay. On

Iowans of the Mighty Eighth

approach to Le Borget Airport the left landing gear would not lock in place. All possible efforts failed to secure the landing gear. Rather than attempt a one wheeled landing, crash and close the runway to the airport needed for troop supply, Galen was ordered to return to England.

On approach to his base, Galen was told to attempt a one wheel landing on the grass next to the runway "because they thought the soft ground would be better". He had to hold the left wing up using the controls as long as possible. With all passengers in crash position Galen was able to keep the left wing horizontal until reduced speed lowered it gently to the ground. No one was seriously injured. Said Galen's navigator "Galen did a masterful job. What a great pilot!"

Galen received his discharge from military service in June, 1945. He had been awarded the Distinguished Flying Cross, Air Medal with three oak leaf clusters, ETO Ribbon and World War II Victory Medal. Galen returned to Boone where he flew with the Air National Guard for thirty years, and served as Boone City Clerk until retirement in 1982. He was also part of the planning group for a new Boone Municipal Airport and after retirement was appointed to the Airport Commission as its' Secretary.

Right - Galen and his crew after one-wheeled landing. Galen, Pilot, is third from the right.

DONALD WILSON, ELDORA, IA, had completed his freshman year at the University of Iowa when he entered active duty with the Army Air Corps on August 18, 1943 at Camp Dodge, Iowa.

After Basic Training Donald attended Texas Tech University for Pre-Flight Training as part of the Aviation Cadet Program. He volunteered to become an Aerial Gunner and was sent to Kingman, Arizona, for training.

After assignment to an aircrew and overseas training Donald was deployed to Bassingbourn, England, on October 23, 1944, as a ball turret gunner with the 91st Bomb Group. Donald flew thirty-five combat missions including Christmas Eve, 1944, when 2,034 heavy bombers and 936 fighters attacked various targets in Germany, the greatest single force of airplanes ever dispatched in history. On that mission Donald's aircraft was hit by "flak" that knocked out three of the four engines on his aircraft and caused them to make a forced landing in Belgium. Fortunately they landed behind Allied lines and were returned to England. Four days later Donald and his crew were in the air on a mission to Remagen, Germany.

Donald's last mission was on March 17, 1945. He returned to the United States in April and was re-assigned to Aerial Gunnery Instructor's School at Laredo, Texas. He then served as a gunnery instructor on the B-29 Super Fortress at Pueblo, Colorado, until he received his military discharge October 27, 1945, at Sioux City, Iowa. Donald had been awarded, among other medals, the Air Medal with five oak leaf clusters, ETO Medal with three bronze stars and the World War II Victory Medal.

Donald returned to the University of Iowa where he earned his Bachelors Degree in Political Science. He entered Law School, earned his Law Degree and practiced law for over fifty years until retirement.

Right - Don and his crew at 91st BG, Bassingbourn, England. Don, Ball Turret Gunner, is back row, second from left.

JAMES WILSON, WATERLOO, IA, was stationed with the 379th Bomb Group at Kimbolton, England, as a flight engineer and top turret gunner. On May 7, 1944, while flying his fourteenth mission over Berlin, enemy fighters and anti-aircraft guns caused one engine of his B-17 bomber to leak oil. Soon two engines were knocked out and one of them was on fire. The pilot

gave the crew two choices. They could bail out over what was German-occupied Holland or ride the plane down and crash land. Jim and three other crewmembers bailed out. The plane had continually lost altitude on its return flight. Jim bailed out while at only 1500 feet and landed on the ground very hard. German soldiers nearby saw them bail out and came looking for them hollering "Komrad, Komrad"

Uncertain whether to surrender and spent the rest of the war in a prison camp or try to evade capture and possibly be shot as a spy, Jim and his three crew members decided they would try to contact the Dutch Underground and make it back to England. As the German soldiers came after them, a sixteen year old Dutch boy appeared and said in broken English, "Come, we will fly you to England." They followed the boy to a farmhouse where they were given civilian clothing and taken to a hole in the ground, a small cave, where they hid for three nights. They were given milk, black bread and cheese.

The fourth night the farm family came for them. They were picked up in a small car driven by a local policeman who took them to a church surrounded by a hedge in the town of Heerveen. The airmen got behind the hedge and crawled to a house near the church. Inside was a Jewish doctor, a tall man and his wife. Jim and his crewmen stayed at the house for the rest of May and all of June and July, 1944.

To stay in one place was very risky, especially for those hiding the Americans. Not long before they arrived at Heerveen someone in the Dutch Underground had killed a Nazi sympathizer. The Nazis were anxious to find the killer and from time to time they would take a prominent person hostage in hopes of forcing the identity of the killer. The tall man at their house was a local railroad company controller and it was feared he would be singled out as a hostage and Jim and his fellow evaders, captured. The Germans also came for their victims after curfew. Each night Jim and his crew sneaked into the nearby church and slept in a little space in back of the organ. In the morning they would return to the house.

The Dutch people were starved by the Nazis and food was in short supply. It was while hiding at Heerveen that Jim had his twentieth birthday as well as the Dutch woman hiding them. To Jim's surprise he was treated with roast beef and fresh strawberries.

The Underground wanted to move the downed airmen to South Holland that required a train ride to their next hiding place. Jim was given the identity of a dead man fourteen years older than Jim but with his own picture on the identification. Jim's tail gunner was supposed to be a deaf mute. Jim had learned to speak Dutch and felt he could handle himself in most situations. They were supposed to sit together but somehow got separated and had to sit apart. Jim had always worn his West High School class ring with the insignia turned under to show only the gold band on the top of his hand. On this occasion he had forgotten to turn the ring under. He realized his mistake when a man on the train sitting across from him kept staring at the ring. Fortunately the man did not say anything and at the first opportunity Jim turned the ring upside down.

After switching trains, riding with and seeing German soldiers everywhere, Jim and his tail gunner got off the train when they saw their contact, the Underground leader, exit the train. They were taken to a camp hidden deep in a forest. There were 90 people in the camp living in cabins about a mile apart from each other. It was in a restricted area, set aside by the Germans for anti-aircraft gunnery practice. Food was scare and limited to one meal a day, mostly potatoes. Beds were wooden bunks with straw mattresses. There were no showers and the campers went days without bathing. Jim became a good friend with a nine-year old Jewish boy that he talked with and gave him food. The nine-year old never forgot Jim and in 1960 sent him a poem of their friendship.

After six weeks in the camp Jim was sent to a farmhouse near the town of Epe. The farmers wanted to help the two American flyers. Earlier in the war she witnessed two American servicemen shot down. They parachuted into some trees near her house and were gunned down by German soldiers who left them hanging in the trees. While there Jim and his tail gunner lived in a barn behind the house and helped with the farm work.

One night they left the farm in a truck to cross the Rhine River under cover of darkness. There were two groups, about twenty to a truck. "One group went on ahead and I came in the second truck. We had papers that stated we were conscripted workers being given a weekend of recreation in the City. I was sitting at the very back of the truck. That delay saved our lives. When we got near the place where we were to cross the river, the other group ahead of us had been discovered. We could hear shooting and screaming, and then all was quiet. We got out of there and hid by the road and spent the night in the woods. We stayed there until one afternoon I decided to go get help. I walked down the road until I met a farmer. I told him our plight and he said he couldn't do anything but to stay right there. About an hour later two girls carrying wine and potatoes showed up. We were given bicycles and rode to the town of Barneveldt where we spent the winter in a barn."

In March, 1945, Jim and his tail gunner were able to cross the Rhine River in a small boat. The Germans were patrolling the area and they were fortunate not to get caught. They were then taken to the town of Sliedricht where Canadian ground forces had arrived. Jim was able to get a ride for himself and his tail gunner to the Canadian headquarters. He went into the Canadian mess hall to eat, but found he was only able to eat a small piece of meat and a forkful of potatoes. It was not until months later that Jim was capable of eating a regular meal, having suffered from malnutrition during his ordeal.

Jim was turned over to the American Army and sent to Camp Lucky Strike near Le Havre, France for repatriation. While there he learned his pilot and the rest of his crew that stayed aboard their flaming aircraft, had made a successful crash landing on two engines and were taken prisoner of war. The crew looked healthy while Jim had lost one eye due to malnutrition and pain in the eye was terrible. After a medical stay at Rouen, France, until June 20, 1945, he boarded the ship "George Washington" for New York City.

"When we arrived in New York harbor I saw a sight I shall never forget: the Statue of Liberty. What a thrill! I shall never forget that moment. When I saw her I said a little prayer. I thanked God for being with me, for bringing me home safe, and I vowed that when I got back home and if I got married and had a home of my own I would fly the Stars and Stripes out in front of my house every single day of my life. And I have kept that promise."

After stays in O'Halloran Hospital, New York City and O'Riley General Hospital, Springfield, Missouri, Jim received his discharge from military service on May 7, 1946.

He had been shot down on May 7, 1944; liberated on May 7, 1945; and discharged on May 7, 1946.

Jim's parents received a telegram from the War Department informing them that he was missing in action over Germany on May 7, 1944. They had not known anything more for over a year and everyone but his mother believed that he was dead. While Jim was at Camp Lucky Strike, Herb Plambeck, a broadcaster for radio station WHO, Des Moines visited field hospitals and camps to interview servicemen from Iowa. Jim was interviewed by Plambeck, The taped interview was broadcast later back in Iowa and heard by H.R. Gross, a friend of the Wilson family. He called the Wilson's to announce that "Jim is Alive!!"

After the war Jim worked for John Deere, New York Life, Black Hawk County, the City of Waterloo and as Field Representative for a U.S. Senator. His involvement in civic organizations was extensive: Waterloo Auxiliary Police, American Legion, Optimists, Kiwanis, Masons and Boy Scouts. He received numerous awards and honors in each organization. He has traveled to the Netherlands for reunions of escapees and those who helped them. He also met working on a dairy farm in Idaho, the sixteen year boy who helped him escape capture when he parachuted from his aircraft and German soldiers were coming after him.

The contents of this biography are excerpts taken from an un-copyrighted booklet published by the Grout Museum, Waterloo, Iowa, and the University of Northern Iowa, entitled "The Jim Wilson Story". Written by George F. Day as told by James Reece Wilson.

Right - Jim and his crewe at 379th BG, Kimbolton, England. Jim is back row, left.

CLEON WOOD, CEDAR FALLS, IA, was employed as a pump assembler and tester prior to World War II. He entered the Army Air Corps on September 18, 1942, at Camp Dodge, Iowa. Cleon attended four military schools in four states beginning with Base A&E School at Amarillo, Texas; Lockheed Factory School, Burbank, California; Aerial

Gunnery at Kingman, Arizona and Engineering Specialties School at Chanute Field, Illinois.

Cleon was deployed to Deopham Green, England, with the 452nd Bomb Group as a top turret gunner and flight engineer. He flew thirty-one combat missions. His first mission was on April 9, 1944, a bomb raid on a Focke-Wolfe component parts factory at Poznan, Poland, a rough initiation to combat. On the return flight to England, their formation came under heavy fighter attack by German FW-190 fighters. The fighters attacked from the rear of the formation. The plane next to Cleon had its tail broken off and then exploded. His own plane's horizontal stabilizer was hit by 20 mm cannon fire and flew apart. It didn't affect the ability of the plane to fly and they returned to base safely.

On D-Day, June 6, 1944, Cleon flew missions to attack enemy positions in front of Allied invasion forces. He will never forget the sight of the vast armada of ships and landing craft heading for the Normandy beaches.

Cleon was awarded the Distinguished Flying Cross, Air Medal with three oak leaf clusters and two battle stars on his European Theater of Operations Medal. He was discharged from military service October 22, 1945, at Savannah, Georgia. Cleon was a draftsman-designer after the war until retirement.

JOHN WOOLWAY, DES MOINES, IA, graduated from high school in 1943. He was drafted into the Army Air Corps and sent to Amarillo, Texas, for Basic Training. He then completed Armaments School at Lowry Field, Colorado and Aerial Gunnery School at Laredo, Texas.

John was assigned to an aircrew and completed overseas training with the them at Briggs Field, El Paso, Texas. In August, 1944, the crew picked up a new B-24 bomber at Wichita, Kansas and flew to Bangor, Maine where fuel tank problems had to be repaired. From there they flew to Valley, Wales by way of Goose Bay, Labrador and Iceland.

After additional aerial gunnery training in Northern Ireland John was assigned as a waist gunner to the 453rd Bomb Group at Old Buckenham, England. He flew twenty-eight combat missions before the war ended in Europe. His most memorable mission was his second, on October 12, 1944. While on the bomb run flying straight and level, a flight of B-17 bombers passed through their formation. "It was like everyone for themselves". One B-17 clipped the left wing of John's aircraft and tore off 3 and one half feet of the wing. "The collision knocked me to the floor of the aircraft. When I stood up I had my parachute on. I don't know how or remember putting it on. The pilot never lost control of the plane and we made it back to England and landed at an air field at Mansten.

John's last mission was to bomb a German airfield at Leipzig, Germany. "I remember it was visual bombing and our bombardier run our bombs right up the runway. A German plane at the end of the runway never made it off the ground."

John was in Norwich, England on V-E Day. "They had a parade. A company of British soldiers wore hob-nailed boots. What a sound they made with the metal on the soles of the boots hitting the pavement. A company of WACs also marched in the parade and I remember some British women yelling "look at all those nylons." The WACs were wearing nylon stockings, an item in very short supply due to the needs of war.

John flew back to the United States and was discharged from military service in July, 1945, at Sioux City, Iowa. He had been awarded, among other medals, the Air Medal with four oak leaf clusters, ETO Ribbon with three battle stars and World War II Victory medal.

In civilian life John retired from Northwestern Bell Telephone Company in 1986 where he had been a data tester.

Right - John's crew at 453rd BG, Old Buckenham, England. John, Aerial Gunner, is front row, left.

THOMAS WRIGHT, DES MOINES, IA, graduated from Dowling High School in Des Moines in 1941 and attended Dowling College for one year. He then worked for Boyt Leather where he made pack saddles for mules until he enlisted in the Army Air Corps on December 9, 1942.

At that time he had to have three letters of recommendation and had to have

his teeth fixed before he would be accepted for military service. He was accepted and sent to Jefferson Barracks, St. Louis, Missouri, for Basic Training. Five months were then spent at Michigan State University under the College Training Detachment Program taking courses in physics, meteorology, history and photography. The training program "was run just like West Point, discipline, marching, exercise and classes."

Thomas was then sent to the San Antonio, Texas Classification Center where, on the basis of test scores, Thomas was assigned to attended Navigator School at San Marcos, Texas. Upon graduation he received his wings and commission as a Second Lieutenant. Thomas was assigned to an aircrew and trained with them in Idaho in preparation for overseas deployment. Thomas and his crew then reported to Camp Kilmer, New Jersey, where he boarded the "SS Brazil" bound for Liverpool, England. The voyage took ten days. Nine men were billeted in a stateroom designed to accommodate two persons. After arrival additional training was completed in Ireland before Thomas was assigned as a Navigator with the 453rd Bomb Group at Old Buckenham, England. In his unit were actors Jimmy Stewart and Walter Mathau.

On September 26, 1944, Thomas flew the first of his thirty-five combat missions to bomb railroad marshalling yards at Hamm, Germany. Included in his missions were five flown to bomb oil targets at Magdeberg, Germany.

During a mission to Mainz, Germany, "the German gunners were on target. To comprehend the awesome sounds, visualize hundreds of rocks continually striking both sides of your automobile out of a clear blue sky. The shrapnel from the "flak" would go right through the airplane. The very core of the airplane's structure began to shudder and the engines were sputtering. The intense roaring of these sounds when combed with the shouting on the intercom made all of us feel that "this is it'. My drift meter was struck and shattered to pieces. Better it than me since I was right in the path.

Thomas completed his required missions on March 3, 1945, and returned to the United States aboard the Liberty ship "SS

Willy Weigle", a hospital ship full of wounded. "Halfway across the Atlantic we learned that President Roosevelt had died."

After furlough Thomas reported to Santa Ana, California, where he received his separation from military service in June, 1945. He had been awarded among other medals, the Air Medal with five oak leaf clusters, ETO Ribbon with three battle stars and the World War II Victory Medal.

Thomas attended Drake University where he earned his law degree and then worked as an attorney for Employers Mutual Insurance Company in Des Moines for over forty years.

Right - Tom and his crew at 453rd BG, Old Buckenham, England. Tom, Navigator, is front row, second from left.

MARVIN WUNSCHEL, IDA GROVE, IA, entered military service at Camp Dodge, Iowa, on January 25, 1973. He was sent to St. Petersburg, Florida, for Basic Training and then to Buckley Field, Colorado. In July, 1943, he attended Armaments School at Lowry Field, Colorado and then completed Aerial Gunnery School at Tyndall Field, Florida.

Marvin was sent to Salt Lake City, Utah; Tucson, Arizona, and Biggs Field, Texas before crew assignment and training for overseas deployment at McCook, Nebraska. In April, 1944 Marvin and his crew picked up a new airplane at Lincoln, Nebraska and flew to England through Bangor, Maine and Greenland.

Marvin was assigned to the 493rd Bomb Group at Debach, England, as a Top Turret Gunner. He flew thirty-one combat missions. Three missions were flown to bomb heavily defended chemical works at Ludwigshaven. He flew missions against synthetic fuel facilties at Merseberg and two missions to oil refineries and railroad marshalling yards at Bremen. Railroad marshalling yards at Cologne were bombed by Marvin's crew on two occasions. Aircraft factories at Kassel and robot plane parts at Russelsheim were also attacked. Missions were also flown in support of Allied ground forces. "Flak" installations outside of Rotterdam, Holland, and transportation facilities to deny the enemy supplies for its troops were bombed around Cologne.

Marvin completed his tour of missions and returned to the United States on November 26, 1944, aboard a ship that took thirteen days to cross the Atlantic Ocean. After furlough he was assigned to short duty assignments at Santa Ana, California and Laredo, Texas. In April, 1945 he reported to Las Vegas, Nevada where he received his discharge from military service on October 19, 1945. Marvin had been awarded the Air Medal with four oak leaf clusters, European Theater of Operations Medal with four battle stars and the World War II Victory Medal.

Following military service Marvin returned to farming from which he has retired.

Chapter Twenty-Two

Right - Marvin's crew at the 493rd BG, Debach, England. Marvin, Top Turret Gunner is second from the right in the front row.

ALLEN YASHACK, DIAGONAL, IA, was working on a survey crew when he enlisted in the Army Air Corps Reserve in September, 1942. He was called to active duty in March, 1943 and sent to Santa Ana, California, for Basic Training. He was chosen for Bombardier's School at Roswell, New Mexico, but was "washed out" when it was determined the Air Corps had too many bombardiers in training and re-assigned him to Aerial Gunnery School at Laredo, Texas. After completion of training Allen was sent to Sioux City, Iowa, Army Air Base where he was assigned to an air crew and trained with them at Sioux City for overseas combat training.

In March, 1944, Allen and his crew flew to Thurleigh, England, home of the 306th Bomb Group. He flew twelve combat missions. On his scheduled seventh mission he was grounded because of ear problems. "I thought my ears would explode". A replacement gunner was assigned to Allen's position and the aircraft crashed on takeoff killing all aboard except the tail gunner.

Allen was placed in an anti-aircraft assignment "mainly shooting at buzz bombs that were launched against England and flew over our base." After he recovered from his medical problems he was assigned to another aircrew and flew five more missions. When his new crew finished their required twenty-five missions in October, 1944, Allen was sent back to the United States with them. He spent a year at Lowry Field, Colorado, before he received his discharge from military service in November, 1945. He had been awarded the Air Medal with one oak leaf cluster, ETO Ribbon with battle stars, and the World War II Victory Medal.

In 1980 Allen retired after twenty-sevens years as the Diagonal Postmaster.

JEROME YEAROUS, CEDAR FALLS, IA, helped on the family farm near Fayette, Iowa, until he enlisted in the Army Air Corps September 26, 1942. After Basic Training he was sent to Luke Field, Arizona for Engine School and remained there until the Spring of 1943. He passed examinations for Pilot Training and attended Superior State Teachers College in Wisconsin

under the College Training Detachment Program until he could begin Pre-Flight Training at Santa Ana, California. Doctors detected Jerome had previously suffered a broken leg and "washed" him out of flight training.

He was then sent to Chanute Field, Illinois, to attend Mechanics School. Additional training was taken at Kearns, Utah, where conditions were described by some as "the Germans had concentration camps. The Americans had Kearns, Utah."

Jerome was assigned to Sioux City, Iowa Air Base where he performed maintenance of aircraft on the flight line for aircrews in training. "Some of the pilots had never flown multi-engine aircraft and we basically had to train them to fly the B-17. The flight engineers they brought in for the aircrews had all been exposed to the mumps. Overnight me and several other mechanics were made instant flight engineers and assigned to an aircrew. We picked up a new plane at Grand Island, Nebraska and flew to Valley, Wales. We were the first plane to take-off and had it loaded with mail. I didn't like the way the plane was loaded, its center of gravity, and got the mail moved around to balance the plane. We stopped at Gander, Newfoundland, and then flew to Wales. We were the only plane that made it, the others had to take another route and refuel."

Assigned to the 306th Bomb Group at Thurleigh, England, Jerome flew twenty-eight combat missions. His first mission was on June 15, 1944. Eleven missions were flown as lead aircraft.

On August 6, 1944, their target was an airfield at Brandenburg, Germany. "We got hit by about thirty-five German fighters. Eight American P-51 fighters plowed right into them. I saw five enemy fighters go down. I think one P-51 got three of them. We were hit by "flak" that cut wires in the wiring harness. It caused a short in the landing gear and flaps that caused the wheels to go down and lock and "full flaps". We had to run at full power to stay aloft and made no forward progress. It didn't do any good to crank the wheels up because they would go down again. We were six to eight hundred miles from England and an "easy mark" for both "flak" and German fighters. I went into the bomb bay with a portable oxygen tank, peeled off wrapping and found the wires. I knew where the short was. I cut the wires, opened the bomb bay doors and cranked up the wheels. We made it to England where we cranked the wheels back down to land."

On his ninth mission, July 20, 1944, "we encountered the worst "flak" I had ever seen and our waist gunner got hit, but survived." "It was after a raid on an ordnance plant, a Tiger Tank factory at Kassel, Germany, that Commanding General Doolilttle raised the number of missions required for rotation back to the United States. We only had to fly twenty-eight.

"I can say that General Patton bought me a drink. We were in a hotel bar at Bedford, England, when General Patton came in the door, looked around, and stated "buy these fly boys a drink and put it on my tab." "Once, while on furlough to London we went to Picadilly Circus. One guy in our crew was from Kansas. He saw the statue of Lord Nelson on a horse and being a little tipsy decided he was going to climb on the statue and sit on the horse too. Military Police got him off and we convinced them not to take him to jail, we would take care of him. We went to a Red Cross Club for coffee and doughnuts to sober him up. He was leaning back in a chair and tipped over. He said he had to go to the bathroom so we let him go alone. When he came back he was carrying a mop and bucket. He was going to wash down the horse Lord Nelson sat on because of pigeon droppings. He said "these British don't take care of their horses."

Jerome's last mission was flown on his birthday, November 16, 1944. He returned to the United States and was assigned to Muroc Field, California where he supervised maintenance on the B-29 bomber. He received his discharge from military service September 28, 1945, and had been awarded the Distinguished Flying Cross, Air Medal with five oak leaf clusters, ETO Ribbon with six battle stars and the World War II Victory Medal.

Jerome is retired from a career as a real estate broker.

Right - Jerome's crew, 306th Bomb Group, Thurleigh, England. Jerome, Flight Engineer, is back row, third from left.

WILLIAM 'BILL' ZACHAR, DAVENPORT, IA, was originally from Philadelphia, PA. Just out of high school and working at various jobs he enlisted in the Army Air Corps on September 21, 1941, to pick his branch of military service. After Basic Training at Fort Meade, Maryland, he attended Aircraft Mechanics School at Wichita Falls, Texas. While there the Japanese attacked American bases on the Hawaiian Island of Oahu officially marking America's entry into World War II.

Beginning in February, 1942, Bill trained in several phases of mechanics at Boise, Idaho; Alamagordo, New Mexico and Biggs Field, El Paso, Texas, covering all aspect of an aircraft. On September 5, 1942, at Jersey City, New Jersey, he boarded the "Queen Mary" along with 14,000 other American troops for a five day voyage to Greenock, Scotland. From there he took a train to the 303rd Bomb Group at Molesworth, England.

Bill was assigned to a crew chief as part of a four-man crew maintaining and servicing a B-17 bomber. "We were green, pioneers, we didn't know what we were doing." Bill credits his crew chief with expert supervision and training in turning his crew into "seasoned veterans". The 303rd didn't receive aircraft until October of 1942. "We got six B-17s at first and these were lost in combat right away."

Bill eventually was promoted to Crew Chief and to Master Sergeant. On his crew each mechanic was assigned to one engine of the aircraft for which he was responsible.

After early wakeup and breakfast on mission day, Bill performed pre-flight on his assigned bomber by starting the engines and checking their operation. Bombs were often loaded the night before the mission and fuel tanks topped off. The aircrew gave Bill their wallets and some personal effects to hold if and when they returned from the mission. When a flare was shot for aircrews to start engines, Bill guided his aircraft to the taxiway. After aircrews were gone ground crews often returned to their barracks for sleep until the estimated time of arrival of their aircraft back at the base to "sweat out" who would or wouldn't return from the mission. Bill set up a tent near the hard stand of his aircraft to be close at hand when his aircraft returned.

If an aircraft was lost on the mission the ground crew was assigned another bomber on the base or assigned to assist other crews. On return the cowling of each engine was removed and a post-flight inspection conducted including oil consumption. It was his responsibility to get the aircraft ready for the next mission. That included cleaning the interior of the plane.

Aircraft engines were re-built at a factory in Birmingham, England. Oil consumption rates were constantly monitored to foretell when to change engines on an aircraft. When bits of metal were found in the oil, engines were changed. Aircraft engines rebuilt at a factory reduced the amount of time and work spent in overhauling engines at Sub-Depots. "We installed the new engines ourselves."

During his term of service at Molesworth, Bill went through seven aircraft either lost in combat or retired as battle-weary. Several aircraft at the 303rd flew over one hundred missions including one credited with 135 missions. One of Bill's airplanes, the "Bonnie B" flew ninety-three missions with only seven aborts.

On Memorial Day of 1945, Bill and other ground crews were flown to Casablanca as part of the "Green Project", to service transport planes that would ferry troops to the Far East in preparation for the invasion of Japan. While in a chow line getting ready to eat a meal word came that the Atomic Bomb had been dropped on Japan.

Bill flew back to the United States and was discharged from military service at Ft. Dix, New Jersey on September 14, 1945. He had received the World War II victory medal and the ETO ribbon with six battle stars.

Bill entered Drexel University at Philadelphia under the GI Bill. He graduated with a Bachelor's Degree in Industrial Engineering in June, 1952, and subsequently earned a Masters Degree in Professional Management. After employment with a firm in Philadelphia for twelve years Bill joined the space program with General Electric at Daytona, Florida. A Reliability Engineer for six years, he was involved in America's first space flights. After America put a man on the moon many engineers were "reduced in force" from the space program. Bill gained employment at Rock Island Arsenal to teach in the Systems Engineering Department. He retired in 1986.

WAYNE ZEIGLER, IOWA FALLS, IA, was working on the family farm when America entered WWII. He entered military service October 26, 1942, at Camp Dodge, Des Moines, Iowa. Wayne was sent to Basic Training at Jefferson Barracks, St Louis, Missouri. He was accepted into the Aviation Cadet Program and attended College Detachment Training   at Creighton University, Omaha Nebraska, before the four stages of flight training were taken, all in California. Pre-Flight Training was at Santa Ana; Primary Flight Training at Visalia; Basic Flight Training, at Chico and Victorville; and Advanced Flight Training at Stockton. Wayne completed Co-pilot Flight Training at Indian Springs, Nevada, before assignment to an aircrew and training with them at Alexandria, Louisiana, in preparation for overseas assignment.

Wayne was deployed to England, October 7, 1944, as a Co-Pilot assigned to the 548th Squadron, 385th Bomb Group, Great Ashfield, Suffolk, England. He later became First Pilot. He flew 28 combat missions, three food missions to Holland to drop supplies to Dutch civilians starved under Nazi rule, and one mission to Linz, Austria, to fly 30 French Prisoners of War back to Paris.

Wayne's most memorable mission was on January 2, 1945, to destroy German Tiger tanks behind front lines during the Battle of the Bulge. They were to bomb at 24,000 ft. While at 22,000 feet and nearly to the target, they lost their two engines on the right wing. The formation continued to the target. Wayne's aircraft was left behind as they began to lose altitude. "We turned back hoping to reach Allied territory. The tops of the clouds were at about 10,000 feet. By the time we got down to 12,000 feet, the number 3 engine was out of oil and coming apart causing severe vibration and shaking the B-17 to the point that we were unable to control it. We decided we should bail out before we got in the clouds. We put the B-17 on autopilot and left the plane." Wayne left the plane through the escape hatch just behind the #2 propeller. " I saw the tail of the plane flash by as I tumbled and saw the ground coming up through a break in the clouds. It was then I pulled the ripcord. I was falling head first. Suddenly the main chute opened. It jerked me draining the blood from my head and I blacked out."

"When I came to, the canopy was bobbing over my head. Everything was quiet and peaceful. I heard an airplane engine diving and getting louder. My first thought was that a German fighter had spotted me. I looked around frantically but couldn't see anything. The sound faded away and right away started to come back. I thought he's coming back to finish me off and I expected machine gun bullets to come through from somewhere but the roar faded away again. Right away it started getting real loud. My B-17 had broken away from the autopilot and came diving out of the clouds turning right into me. I thought it was going to snag my chute, but about 100 yards out, the B-17 flopped over on its right wing and dove into the ground under me. It blew up in a ball of fire and completely disappeared. All that was left was a small black column of smoke. The concussion and sound of the explosion hit me in 2 or 3 seconds. I couldn't take my eyes off the spot praying all the crew got out. All of a sudden I realized I wasn't looking down at it but out in front of me and the horizon was high. I was drifting backwards. I looked down and a fence went under my feet about 15 ft below. I started to look over my left shoulder to see where I was going to land. I came down on my left hip. It was like an explosion in my head when it snapped down on my chest and I bit through my tongue."

"When I came to I was laying face down spitting some blood in a patch of snow. I felt my left hip and leg hurting and rolled on my right side. I looked up at two men- one holding a pitch fork right over my head. I didn't move and neither did he. I had some amnesia and couldn't figure out why I was in such a strange place. I looked down the hill and there were 12 to 15 men, women and children running toward me. Soon everyone was around me talking something I couldn't understand. When I started to pull in the shroud lines to unhook the parachute, they realized I was not armed and the crowd gathered up my chute and two men hoisted me on my right leg. I caught sight of the back column of smoke beyond a grove of trees and then I remembered what happended and thought they were Germans."

"A black car with a white star on the side drove up on a dirt road at the bottom of the hill. They motioned they wanted to carry me down there. I refused, so two men got on each side of me and I hobbled down the hill. The two men in the car turned out to be French military police and they spoke English. They asked me who I was and what happended. After I told them, they told the crowd and they became joyous and offered me a big glass of the strongest liquor that I ever tasted, which turned out to be 100 proof home brew. The French soldiers told me the Germans had just retreated and I came down just twenty miles on the Allied side of the front line of the Battle of the Bulge. (Three years ago when I went back to St. Quentin, I met Maurice, the 12 year old boy who stood by his father holding the pitchfork over me. I only found out in June, 1999, when Maurice Brasset came to Iowa Falls to visit me, that the crowd around me thought I was a German. Maurice's father told them not to shoot me as he thought I might be an American)."

"The two military police took me to a school in St. Quentin, which was converted to a military hospital. They x-rayed me and found I had no broken bones. I was in the hospital for about two and a half weeks until I could walk. They put me on orders to find my own way back to England. They took me to an infantry replacement depot. That didn't appeal to me. I asked the Commanding Officer to take me to the nearest fighter base. The Commanding Officer at the fighter base radioed an air base in Brussells and they sent a jeep and driver down for me. I caught a ride on an English transport plane back to England. I walked back into my squadron on January 28th, nearly a month after I bailed out. On February 3, I was on my next mission, to Berlin."

Wayne was awarded the Air Medal with four oak leaf clusters, ETO Ribbon and World War II Victory Medal. He received his discharge from military service on October 23, 1945, at Jefferson Barracks, St Louis, Missouri. His post war occupation consisted of being a farm training instructor for veterans, an agriculture loan officer and real estate salesman. Wayne is active in the Eighth Air Force Historical Society, Iowa Chapter, where he has served as Vice-President.

Right - Wayne and his crew, 385th BG, Great Ashfield, England. Wayne, Pilot, is front row, right.

PICTURE CREDITS

All photographs of individuals were provided by the individual themselves or in the case of deceased, by the next of kin, except as noted in the narrative. Credit for all other photographs are as follows:

Purpose-cartoon, 8th AF News, Feb 1995

Call to Arms-2WASPS, Ia Historical Society

Home Front-Armband, author; Ration Stamps and Bond Books, author; cartoon, "Yank", 12/22/44; B-24 Production and Willow Run, 8th AF News Feb, 1996;

Training-3 training classes, Steve Elliott; 3 training photos Randolph Field, Kay Cunningham;Sheppard Field, Lowell Blizzard; loading ammo, bombardier, Kay Cunningham; ball turret, 8th AF News May 1995; Turret instruction, Roberly Howe; 3 aerial photos, Kay Cunningham; crew positions, B-17 manual;

Deployment-fantail of ship, Lowell Blizzard

British Home Front-bombing of London, 8th AF News March 2000; Bus and V-1 Rocket diving, 8th AF News March 2000; V-1 Rocket flying, Steve Elliott;

American and German Bombers and Fighters, Charles R Taylor, art prints

Base Locations-High Wycombe, James Hoy;

Bases- 96th BG Control Tower, William Vint

17s at Bassingbourn, Robert Megchelsen

392nd Control Tower, Joseph Barnes

390th Control Tower, Frederick Miller

379th Air Base, 379th Newsletter, 4/95

Base Life-Bomb Storage, Frederick Miller

Cartoon, "Yank" 11/2/45;

2 SAD repair shops, Bill Clark; trucks at Storage Depot, 8th AF News February, 1994

Clubmobile, Nancy Foster

Lady Moe, Lowell Blizzard;

Blue Lion Pub, Howard Linn

Flying Fortress Pub, Frances Kapler

Red Cross Light and Theater Guide, author

Bob Hope and Frances Langford-Wayne Stellish

Manor House, Elmer Johansmeier

Christmas Party Scenes(2), 8th AF News

Christmas Party, 305th, 8th AF News, 10/91

November 1993; Christmas Party at SAD3, William Clark;

Special Units- Propagand Leaflets, author;

Spitfire artprint, Charles R Taylor; Omaha Beach defenses, Kay Cunningham; 3 weather flight routes, Sydney Thomas;

Targets- 15 aerial photos, Kay Cunningham

Mission Preparation- B-17 in snow, Mrs Cynde Clingan; 466th Control Tower, Gene Person

Takeoff and Assembly-17s of 305BG,Leon Mehring;

Fighter Escort and OperationsP51s(3), Kay Cunningham;

Ground Crew 356th, Duff Coleman;

Iowans of the Mighty Eighth

Flight to Target- flak guns(2), 8th AF News, 6/99 and Kay Cunningham; 17s in formation, Arlon Nessa; 17s contrails, Leroy Edwards
17s in formation, Darrell Kiddie
bomber formation
ME410, Everett Sandersfeld; downed B17, Lowell Blizzard
Bomb Run-Flak (1)-Orville Myers (2)Howard Breson;Bombs Away 379BG, Howard Breson;
Bombs Away 305, Leon Mehring
B24 dropping napalm, Joseph Barnes
B24 in trouble, Lyle Latimer
Bomb Salvo, Joseph Barnes
B17 going straight down, Darrell Kiddie
B17 stabilizer gone, Kay Cunningham
Home at Last-B-24 landing, Gene Person
Battle damage wing, George Armington
Battle damage ball turret, Robert Megchelsen
Battle damage
B17 on fire and broke apart, Robert Houser
Ambulances at 305BG, Donald Richards
Silhouette, Kay Cunningham.
Special Missions- aerial photo, Kay Cunningham
Damaged aircraft at Poltava-Frederick Miller
Victory-Food drops to Dutch (4) John Fernhout
Liverpool Harbor, Clarence Henderson
POWs- capture photos(4), 8th AF News, 12/98, 8/98,11/96,12/2001; aerial photo, Stalag Luft I, Kay Cunningham; prison compound and barracks drawing, Stalag Luft III, by Bob Neary, Copyright 1946;
Forced Marches (2) Jim Brown; Liberation, 8th AF News
Remembrance-Memorial Stones, 92nd Robert Dougherty; 385th Wayne Zeigler; 445th Morris Brandenburger;American Air Museum, 8th AF News, 5/97; Memorial Windows, 355th, 8th AF News 8/94; 385th Wayne Zeigler;386th BG, 8th AF News 2/92
Cemetery, Madingley(3), Joan Allen;
Control Tower(2), Framlingham,Framlingham Times Newsletter, 9/01

BIBLIOGRAPHY

The Mighty Eighth, Roger A. Freeman, A History of the Units, Men and Machines of the U.S. Eighth Air Force, Orion Books, New York, Copyright 1970
The Mighty Eighth War Manual, Roger A Freeman, Cassell & Co., London, England. Copyright, 1984, 2001
Time/Life, The Air War in Europe, Time Incorporated, 1979
Time/Life, Prelude to War, Time Incorporated, 1976
Time/Life, Liberation, Time Incorporated, 1978
Time/Life, Victory in Europe, Time Incorporated, 1982
Time/Life, The Aftermath, Europe, Time Incorporated, 1982
Round the Clock, Philip Kaplan, Random House, 1993
Little Friends, Philip Kaplan, Random House, 1991
Impact, Volume 5, The Air Force Historical Foundation, Historical Times, Inc. 1982
Impact, Volume 6, The Air Force Historical Foundation, Historical Times, Inc. 1982

Publications by Iowans

A Neighborhood of Eagles, Norman Rudi, McMillen Publishing, Ames, Iowa, 2003, ISBN 1-888223-41-3
An Iowa Pilot Named Hap, Norman Rudi, McMillen Publishing, Ames, Iowa, 2001, ISBN 1-888223-25-1
A Wing and a Prayer, Harry H. Crosby, Robson Books, London, England, 1993
Flying High in Iowa, Howard W Greiner, Indian Hills Publishing, Albia, Iowa, 1999
Nicknames, Wars and Corporate Games, Lee Emerson Gingery, Park Publishing, 1991
On the Edge of Survival, Frederick Clark, GSI Publishers, Howey-in-the-Hills, Florida, ISBN 0-9715162-0-0
Waverly's Heroes, Sara Busch, G&R Publishing, Waverly, Iowa, 2000
Yanks Over Europe, American Flyers in World War II, Jerome Klinkowitz, University Press of Kentucky, Lexington, Kentucky, 1996

NON-COPYRIGHTED, INFORMAL PUBLICATIONS BY IOWANS

B-24 H Crew, Mission History, Ray Carlson, Navigator
Clarence, 546th Sqdn, 384 Bomb Group, Clarence Hightshoe
Drop Tanks, The Wartime Experience of Donald W Marner, 1942-46
Reflections, Howard Hobbs
The Jim Wilson Story, George F Day
The Year I Can't Forget, A Combat Crew Diary, Jim O'Connor
World War II and My Prisoner of War Experiences, Howard Linn
Wiley's Crew #3481, Navigator's Narrative, Harry Kues

Suggested Readings on

EIGHTH AIR FORCE WORLD WAR II

So many books and accounts have been written on the Eighth Air Force in World War II by individuals on their experiences or on operations of the Mighty Eighth as a military unit, it would be impossible to list all the publications. I can only suggest those publications within my library I consider most interesting to the casual reader or military and aviation enthusiast.

A Dying Breed, Neal B Dillon, Hellgate Press, 2000
A Mighty Fortress, Charles Alling, Casemate Publishing, 2002
A Neighborhood of Eagles, Norman Rudi, McMillen Publishing, 2003
A Pilot Named Hap, Norman Rudi, McMillen Publishing, 2001
A Wing and A Prayer, Harry Crosby, Robson Books, 1993
Bomber, Famous Bomber Missions of WWII, Robert Jackson, St Martins Press, 1980
Bomber Pilot, A Memoir of World War II, Philip Ardery, The University Press of Kentucky, 1978
Bombers, The Aircrew Experience, Philip Kaplan, Barnes & Noble, 2000
Combat, He Wrote, Charles Hudson, Airborne Publishing, 1994
Eighth Air Force Bomber Stories, J H Hayes Publishing, London, 1991
First Over Germany, Russell A Strong, Hunter Printing, 1990
Gabby, Francis Gabreski, Orion Books, 1991
Half a Wing, Three Engines and a Prayer, Brian D. O'Neill, McGraw/Hill, 1999
History of the 487th Bomb Group, DeJong, Turner Publishing, Paducah, KY, 2004
Hunters in the Sky, James R Whelan, Regnery Gateway, 1991
Little Friends, Philip Kaplan, Random House, 1991
Log of the Liberators, Steve Birdsall, Doubleday, 1973
Ninety-Second Bomb Group, Turner Publishing, Paducah, KY, 1996
One Day Into Twenty Three, E T Moriarty, 1987
One Last Look, Philip Kaplan, Abbeville Press, 1983
On the Edge of Survival, Frederick W Clark, GSI Publishers
Round the Clock, Philip Kaplan, Random House, 1993
Second Air Division, Turner Publishing, Paducah, KY, 1994
Serenade to the Big Bird, Bert Stiles, Schiffer Military History, 2001
Silent Heroes, Sherri Greene Ottis, University Press of Kentucky, 2001
Spitfires, Thunderbolts, and Warm Beer, Philip D Caine, Brassey's, 1995
Stalag Luft III, Arthur Durand, Louisiana State University Press, 1988
The American Airman in Europe, Roger Freeman, Motorbooks International, 1991
The Lucky Bastard Club, Eugene Fletcher, University of Washington Press, 1992
The Mighty Eighth, Roger A Freeman, Orion Books, 1970
The Mighty Eighth in Color, Roger A Freeman, Specialty Press, 1992
The Wrong Stuff, Truman Smith, Southern Heritage Press, 1996
Those Who Fall, John Muirhead, Random House, 1986
Three Sixty-Fourth Fighter Group, Walsworth Publishing, 1991
Time Out for War, Ed Cury, Rainbow Books, 1988
Tomlin's Crew, A Bombardier's Story, J W Smallwood, Sunflower University Press, 1992
Winged Victory, Geoffrey Perret, Random House, 1993
Wings of Morning, Thomas Childers, Addison-Wesley Publishing, 1995
Yanks Over Europe, Jerome Klinkowitz, University Press of Kentucky, 1996
Zemke's Wolfpack, William N Hess, Motorbooks International, 1992

INDEX

Roster not included in index.

-A-
Abernathy - 86, 306
Abigt - 137, 150, 158, 306
Abraham - 194, 249
Adam - 194
Adams - 158, 166, 194, 249
Adkins - 252
Ahlwardt - 194, 246, 247
Albert - 81, 122, 130, 307
Alfrey - 96, 308
Allen - 34, 37, 61, 194, 246, 472
AllenPanora - 252
Alling - 474
Alvestad - 194, 248
Anderegg - 247
Anderson - 158, 194, 195, 246, 249
Andrews - 166
Ardery - 474
Arihood - 195, 246
Arlenger - 152
Armington - 118, 253, 472
Arn - 252
Arnold - 158
Astaire - 130
Aucker - 195, 249
Ausborn - 308
Autenreith - 130, 195, 249
Autry - 14
Avery - 4
Avit - 252

-B-
Baas - 195, 247
Bachman - 195, 247
Bagley - 158, 195, 248
Bailey - 246
Baker - 61, 158, 195, 246, 249, 309
Ball - 196, 247
Balmer - 152
Baltisberger - 309
Baltisburger - 78, 79, 81, 93, 162, 163
Bamburg - 196, 249
Barnes - 75, 93, 310, 471, 472
Barnett - 196, 245, 247, 249
Barron - 196, 246
Barton - 196, 248
Basbcock - 158
Bavender - 254
Baxter - 196, 247
Beam - 76, 119, 311
Beaman - 254
Beaslely - 162
Beasley - 158
Beaumonte - 155, 156
Becker - 196, 248
Beckman - 29, 128, 196, 247, 311
Beedle - 196, 247
Beigel - 158
Beilstein - 158, 162
Bembenek - 158
Benedict - 197, 249
Bengford - 197, 248
Bennett - 197, 247
Benson - 249
Benton - 197, 247
Benz - 197, 248
Bereskin - 158
Bergquist - 158
Bernstein - 197, 247, 249
Berry - 31, 103, 110, 131, 312
Berve - 158
Betten - 59, 312
Bettis - 245, 246, 248
Betzel - 158
Birdsall - 474
Bishop - 158, 197, 249
Black - 198, 248
Blackbum - 166
Blaylock - 198, 247
Blizzard - 125, 127, 312, 471, 472
Blue - 198, 248
Boat - 158
Boatright - 158
Bobcat - 162
Bockeloo - 198, 249
Bogard - 137, 143, 144, 151, 313
Boice - 77, 104, 132, 314
Boone - 198, 248
Bottenfield - 126, 314
Bottorff - 198, 246
Bowman - 162
Boyd - 198, 248
Boyer - 96, 315
Bradley - 198, 248
Braland - 36, 37
Branch - 106, 162, 316
Brandenburg - 198, 199, 249
Brandenburger - 62, 316, 472
Braun - 125
Brecht - 199, 249
Bredensteiner - 254
Breson - 120, 317, 472
Bricker - 199, 247
Brim - 199, 247
Brindley - 115, 126, 317
Brinkman - 199, 247
Britson - 31, 98, 130, 318
Broadbent - 110, 318
Brody - 199, 249
Brookhiser - 110, 319
Brooks - 158, 199, 248
Brostrom - 199, 246
Brown - 71, 79, 84, 136, 142, 149, 150, 158, 199, 200, 246, 247, 248, 249, 319, 320, 472
Bruning - 114, 167, 245, 249, 321
Brunner - 254
Buchanan - 200, 249
Buchmiller - 200, 246
Buckley - 114, 115, 167, 200, 249, 322
Budde - 158
Budrevich - 200
Buker - 245, 249
Burke - 200, 245, 248, 249
Burkett - 200, 247
Burks - 249
Burlingham - 158
Burmeister - 255
Burns - 255
Burris - 255, 256
Busch - 473
Busesman - 256
Bush - 14, 200, 248
Bussey - 201, 247
Butler - 136, 140, 158, 322
Byam - 258

-C-
Cadwallader - 36, 37
Caldwell - 245, 249
Callaway - 245, 249
Caine - 474
Campbell - 201, 247, 248, 249, 259
Campney - 137, 144, 151, 158, 323
Caplan - 246
Cardamon - 259
Carder - 158, 258
Carlson - 75, 96, 115, 122, 158, 259, 324, 473
Carmen - 249
Carpenter - 110, 158
Carris - 201, 249
Carson - 50, 158, 201, 247, 257
Carter - 109, 261, 325
Cassaday - 201, 246
Cebuhar - 158
Cecil - 122, 325
Chamberlain - 33
Chambers - 166
Chickering - 245, 249
Childers - 474
Childs - 162
Chipman - 59, 325
Chrisjohn - 84, 167, 326
Chrissinger - 201, 246
Christensen - 158, 201, 246
Christman - 158
Churchill - 80, 155, 170

Iowans of the Mighty Eighth

Clark - 30, 61, 79, 158, 162, 163, 202, 248, 262, 326, 327, 328, 471, 473, 474
Claude - 101, 114, 329
Clausen - 158
Claussen - 158
Clemons - 202, 247
Cline - 202, 247
Clingan - 128, 330, 471
Clyman - 158
Cochran - 202, 249
Cohen - 202, 249
Coleman - 4, 330, 472
Collins - 5
Colt - 158
Combs - 158
Comeggs - 248
Comegys - 202
Conklin - 66, 68, 110, 167, 330
Conley - 202, 247
Connell - 117, 331
Connelly - 202, 247
Connolly - 202, 247
Conrad - 263
Conrow - 158
Conway - 158
Cook - 158, 203, 246
Cooke - 203, 248
Cooper - 28, 203, 247, 331
Copley - 162
Corbin - 203, 246
Corderman - 331
Core - 203, 248
Cornelius - 158
Cornick - 203, 247
Cotton - 158
Couchman - 203, 249
Cowley - 203, 247
Cox - 63, 158, 332
Coy - 203, 248
Crawford - 333
Cregar - 262
Croft - 204, 247, 248
Croker - 263
Croner - 79, 123, 333
Cropp - 96, 126, 333
Crosby - 473, 474
Cruse - 204, 247
Cunningham - 4, 18, 72, 73, 263, 471, 472
Cury - 474
Cutting - 204, 248

-D-

Dahlen - 204, 246
Dahlgran - 334
Dailey - 204, 246
Daily - 204, 248
Darling - 81, 98, 111, 334
Daskam - 204, 249
Daudel - 263
Davidson - 84, 136, 140, 158, 335
Davis - 158, 245, 249
Dawson - 158
Day - 473
Decker - 158
Dedrickson - 122, 336
Deetlefon - 245
Degan - 105, 336
Della Betta - 204, 249
DeLorbe - 114, 129, 337
Demery - 205, 248
Dengle - 158
Dennis - 17
Dennison - 205, 247
Denny - 205, 248
Detillion - 159
Detlefon - 249
Devaney - 205, 247
Dewey - 205, 248
Dewild - 159
Dexter - 71, 130, 337
Diaz - 205, 248
Dickenson - 249
Dickerson - 205
Dideriksen - 205, 246
Differding - 205, 248
Dille - 206, 249
Dillon - 474
Dimaggio - 14
Dimig - 159
Dinkel - 159
Dinker - 246
Dirks - 108, 338
Dittmer - 206, 249
Doenitz - 125
Dombrowski - 263
Doolittle - 133, 141
Doorley - 206, 249
Dougherty - 68, 69, 101, 338, 472
Douglas - 65, 245, 249
Douglass - 339
Douroumes - 206, 249
Doyle - 159
Drahos - 166
Duff - 264
Duffy - 159, 206, 247
Dulin - 206, 247
Dulter - 247
Dumont - 159
Dunker - 206
Durand - 143, 474
Durrett - 206, 246
Dutler - 206
Dvorak - 17
Dyvig - 137, 143, 151, 157, 339

-E-

Earnest - 265
Eastwood - 64, 340
Eberle - 35, 37
Ecknosh - 249
Eckrosh - 207
Edder - 152, 156
Edel - 207, 249
Edens - 265
Edgeton - 265
Edgington - 207, 248
Edmondson - 207, 247
Edward - 67
Edwards - 116, 341, 472
Egenes - 207, 249
Egge - 207, 247
Elliott - 4, 49, 63, 65, 66, 341, 471
Emerson - 207, 247, 249
En-lai - 11
Engeman - 208, 248
Epplen - 247
Eppler - 208
Erbe - 265
Erbes - 266
Erdman - 208, 249
Estes - 78, 113, 342
Estle - 208, 249
Evans - 37
Evers - 208, 249
Every - 159

-F-

Fagen - 117, 343
Farmer - 109, 344
Farnham - 266
Feese - 208, 248
Fennell - 119, 344
Ferguson - 123, 344
Fernhout - 127, 345, 472
Ferrel - 61, 345
Feyerabend - 166
Field - 471
Fillman - 159
Finkle - 266
Fischer - 110, 159, 346
Fisher - 208, 246
Fitch - 208, 247, 248
Fitzgerald - 113, 346
Fix - 58, 167, 347
Flaherty - 159
Flaugh - 209, 246
Fleege - 209, 248
Fletcher - 474
Floden - 267
Florine - 268
Fluegel - 209, 247
Focht - 209, 249
Ford - 14, 31, 64, 104, 168, 209, 247, 347
Forte - 209, 248
Foster - 66, 159, 268, 348, 471
Found - 209, 249
Fouts - 115, 348
Fox - 57, 349
Frampton - 77, 107, 130, 349
Franco - 11, 12
Frank - 65, 350
Franklin - 64, 169, 350
Frederick - 249
Freeman - 473, 474
Friedmann - 209, 247
Friend - 209, 248
Fritz - 159
Froah - 350
Frost - 131, 351
Fullerton - 159

-G-

Gable - 14
Gabreski - 474
Gage - 351
Galbraith - 245, 246
Gale - 269
Gallager - 159
Gallagher - 114, 159, 162, 352
Gallup - 210, 248
Gamble - 210, 249
Gammela - 249
Gangstad - 210, 248
Gant - 210, 249
Gard - 159
Garrett - 49
Gartman - 76, 119, 352
Gaskel - 159
Gast - 159
Gee - 210, 246
Geitz - 353
Gerbers - 159
Gibson - 159
Gidel - 51, 353
Gilleon - 159
Gillespie - 107, 354
Gilligan - 210, 249
Gillmeier - 210, 248
Gilroy - 159

Index

Ginder - 210, 246
Gingery - 115, 126, 355, 473
Gjerde - 210
Gjerke - 249
Gladfelder - 159
Glasscock - 211, 246
Glaza - 72, 73, 162, 269
Glover - 79, 162, 163, 355
Goebbels - 125
Goering - 33
Goff - 81, 105, 112, 356
Golbski - 211, 249
Gommela - 211
Goring - 13
Gorman - 211, 248
Gracik - 162
Grady - 211, 249
Graham - 174
Granzow - 270
Graper - 211, 248
Gray - 270
Green - 211, 247
Greiner - 138, 159, 357, 473
Grigg - 211
Grimes - 245, 246
Grow - 212, 247
Grubb - 37, 269, 358
Grundon - 358
Gudgel - 159
Gunnar - 159
Gunsolley - 212, 249
Gustafson - 138, 159, 358

-H-

Haas - 83, 103, 114, 115, 129, 359
Hagedorn - 270
Haight - 162
Haines - 159
Hall - 212, 249
Hally - 212, 247
Halverson - 99, 360
Hamann - 159
Hames - 159
Hamilton - 74, 93, 118, 361
Hammond - 212, 247
Hancock - 57, 271
Handley - 212, 248
Handshaw - 37
Hanna - 167, 271
Hannaman - 159
Hansen - 115, 272, 361
Harder - 162
Hare - 159
Harken - 114, 122, 362
Harker - 159

Harl - 212, 249
Harms - 159
Harrenstein - 212, 248
Harrer - 159
Hartkoph - 212, 249
Hartz - 362
Haugen - 159
Hayes - 159, 213, 246
Hebbeln - 272
Hegg - 213, 247
Heitland - 62, 363
Heline - 213, 249
Hellberg - 31, 85, 169, 363
Hemenway - 159
Henderson - 110, 364, 472
Henrickson - 17
Henryson - 63, 120, 364
Herman - 166, 213, 249
Hess - 213, 248, 474
Higdon - 32, 112, 365
Highsmith - 166
Hightshoe - 112, 162, 163, 365, 473
Hill - 76, 110, 123, 130, 170, 272, 367
Hilton - 213, 249
Hindenburg - 11
Hinds - 81, 93, 368
Histed - 213, 248
Hitler - 10, 11, 12, 13, 33, 80, 82, 89, 125, 127, 132, 149, 152
Hobbs - 31, 138, 139, 147, 152, 159, 368, 473
Hodson - 213
Hoegh - 28, 59, 370
Hoff - 159, 273
Hoffman - 100, 105, 126, 370
Hohl - 82, 85, 371
Holiday - 213, 249
Hollis - 214, 249
Holscher - 273
Hoover - 159
Hope - 69, 471
Hopp - 159
Hotle - 166
Houser - 64, 125, 371, 472
Hovden - 214, 247
Hovey - 214, 246
Hovson - 247
Howard - 159, 214, 246
Howe - 60, 273, 274, 471
Hoy - 73, 126, 372, 471
Hruska - 62, 373
Hubbard - 245, 246, 373
Huddle - 159

Hudson - 159, 474
Huebner - 214, 247, 248
Huff - 159
Huggard - 93, 374
Huggins - 33, 68
Hughes - 214, 248
Humke - 214, 249
Humphrey - 159, 214, 247
Hunter - 137, 143, 151, 159, 215, 248, 374
Hurley - 162, 164, 274, 375
Huston - 215, 246
Hutchcroft - 275
Hutton - 215, 248
Hyndman - 84, 117, 375

-I-

Ibeling - 276
Ingvolstad - 276
Inman - 215, 247
Iverson - 159

-J-

Jackson - 75, 159, 376, 474
Jacobs - 215, 246
Jacobsen - 113, 376
Jacobson - 215, 246
Janish - 159
Janss - 215, 249, 276, 377
Jaquis - 166
Jaspers - 166
Jeane - 159
Jeffrey - 215, 248
Jenson - 119, 131, 377
Johansmeier - 29, 61, 378, 471
Johnson - 14, 61, 130, 138, 146, 150, 152, 159, 166, 215, 216, 246, 248, 378, 379
Joiner - 68, 379
Joliffe - 32, 110, 380
Jones - 77, 159, 380
Jordan - 159
Jorgensen - 216, 247
Josifek - 63, 64, 68, 381
Joslin - 159
Joyce - 216
Joycer - 247

-K-

Kahl - 382
Kai-shek - 11
Kajewski - 276
Kallen - 14
Kaplan - 174, 473, 474
Kapler - 31, 78, 382, 471
Kassa - 159

Kearney - 159
Keefe - 216, 247
Keen - 131, 383
Kehm - 159
Kelley - 162, 167, 216, 247, 249, 384
Kelly - 29, 88, 95, 122, 159, 384
Kemmann - 217
Kempker - 217, 248
Kennedy - 217, 246
Kesselring - 167, 384
Kiddie - 385, 472
Kilbourn - 277
Kilgore - 159
Kill - 246
Killian - 162
Killion - 217, 247
Kincart - 159
King - 130, 159, 386
Kinyon - 277
Kipka - 159
Kirkpatrick - 217, 246
Kitchen - 31, 106, 386
Kitzman - 159
Klinkowitz - 473, 474
Kloser - 60, 61, 386
Klosterman - 277
Knap - 159
Knight - 116, 159, 387
Knoll - 217, 249
Knowling - 85, 99, 387
Knutson - 217, 248
Koehler - 277
Koenig - 159
Kohlhaas - 217, 248
Koll - 217
Kolmerer - 218, 248
Konrad - 277
Kooima - 218, 247
Kopf - 218, 248
Kozik - 159
Kraft - 218, 250
Krapf - 248
Krejci - 159
Kritchman - 75, 388
Krogh - 218, 248
Kropf - 218
Krumm - 166
Kruse - 159
Krutosku - 159
Kudej - 218, 246
Kudij - 248
Kues - 473
Kuhlmeier - 218, 249
Kussman - 219, 248, 249

-L-

Ladd - 14
Lamansky - 219, 248
Lampe - 159
Landen - 219
Lane - 159
Lange - 389
Langford - 69, 471
Larrew - 162
Larsen - 219, 249, 278
Larson - 219, 246, 247
Latimer - 102, 109, 389, 472
Laucamp - 219, 246
Lauger - 159
Lawr - 219, 250
Leaf - 219, 246
LeClere - 159, 278
Leeds - 220, 247
LeMay - 111
Lenin - 12
Leon - 31
Lerow - 159
Lesher - 220, 248
Lewis - 14, 162, 220, 246, 247, 248
Lichter - 279
Lichty - 220, 247
Liddick - 159
Lienemann - 106, 390
Lindaman - 96, 130, 390
Lindberg - 31, 114, 390
Lindbloom - 220, 247
Lindquist - 220, 249
Lines - 159
Link - 109, 129, 391
Linn - 32, 137, 143, 144, 151, 159, 173, 392, 471, 473
Lischer - 393
Livingston - 159
Lock - 34, 37
Loesser - 14
Logue - 76, 118, 173, 393
Long - 159
Longman - 159
Lord - 394
Lough - 159
Loughry - 279
Lowe - 159
Lowman - 220, 249
Lowry - 160, 221, 247
Lund - 221, 250, 394
Lundquist - 221, 247
Lynam - 128, 395
Lynch - 57, 88, 123, 126, 173, 395
Lyons - 279

-M-

Mace - 222
Machen - 222
Macher - 249
MacKenzie - 222, 247
Macklin - 160
Macksey - 160
Macloud - 160
Madland - 160
Maew - 248
Magin - 222
Maillard - 222, 246
Mairs - 17, 98, 396
Mallory - 249
Malloy - 222
Manahl - 62, 66, 397
Mandelbaum - 222, 248
Manderscheid - 280
MaoTse-tung - 11
Maring - 222, 248
Marks - 222, 247
Marner - 29, 63, 130, 397, 398, 473
Marold - 29, 61, 398
Marsden - 110, 398
Matz - 223, 247
Maule - 280
Maxon - 160
McBride - 160
McCabe - 162
McCalley - 113, 280, 281
McCarthy - 70, 221, 250
McCartie - 246
McCarty - 160
McCord - 221, 249
McCowen - 162
McCreevy - 281
McCune - 221, 248
McDowell - 64, 399
McElherne - 126, 138, 145, 151, 160, 399
McElree - 83, 105, 400
McGee - 160, 281
McGinnis - 221, 247
McGreevy - 160, 282
McKern - 221, 249
McMullin - 160
McMurray - 160
McWilliam - 249
McWilliams - 221
Means - 223, 247
Megchelsen - 31, 117, 168, 401, 471, 472
Mehegan - 136, 140, 160, 401
Mehring - 31, 36, 37, 92, 118, 130, 402, 471, 472
Meline - 223, 246
Melton - 223, 248
Menefee - 223, 247
Mercer - 223, 250
Merfeld - 223, 250
Messeri - 160
Messerly - 29, 60, 223, 249, 403
Messmer - 223, 247
Meston - 160
Mettler - 160
Metz - 160
Meyer - 87, 121, 160, 224, 247, 283, 403
Michaelsen - 224
Michaelson - 248
Mileham - 283
Miller - 14, 68, 69, 79, 81, 123, 124, 160, 162, 164, 169, 403, 404, 405, 471, 472
Milliken - 166
Mincks - 224, 248
Mitchell - 224, 247, 249
Modlin - 113, 406
Moeller - 224, 250
Mohr - 162, 224, 246
Moline - 224, 247
Monroe - 224, 249
Monson - 160
Montag - 225, 250
Moore - 7, 283
Moorhead - 160
Morgart - 225, 249
Moriarty - 474
Morman - 225
Mormon - 248
Morris - 225, 249, 250
Morrison - 160
Morrow - 160
Morse - 32, 79, 160, 166, 406
Morton - 225, 247
Mose - 246
Moses - 15, 225, 249
Mowry - 160
Moy - 284
Muirhead - 474
Mulder - 160
Murillo - 225, 249
Murphy - 162, 225, 245, 247
Murray - 226, 247
Mussolini - 11
Mutchler - 127, 407
Myers - 65, 77, 131, 226, 246, 407, 408, 472

-N-

Nacos - 160
Naden - 226, 250
Nagle - 166, 226, 248
Nappier - 226, 246
Narvis - 245, 247
Nasos - 162
Neary - 145, 157, 472
Nelson - 82, 113, 162, 226, 248, 250, 408, 409
Nessa - 63, 131, 409, 472
Neubauer - 93, 102, 112, 130, 410
Neuhauser - 160
Newbrough - 285
Newell - 160
Newsom - 94, 108, 410
Newson - 168
Nichols - 102, 160, 226, 250, 411
Nicklas - 160
Nielsen - 74, 125, 226, 412
Nielson - 250
Nixon - 14
Noble - 98, 111, 412
Nodstrom - 160
Nonneman - 160
Nord - 227, 249
Nordman - 162
Norgaard - 160
Norquist - 227, 247
Norvet - 160
Nowels - 227, 247
Nyhus - 117, 413

-O-

O'Brien - 246
O'Connell - 227, 246
O'Connor - 102, 117, 169, 227, 247, 250, 413, 473
Oge - 162
Olson - 160, 227, 247
Omer - 248
O'Neill - 474
Ong - 160
Orr - 227, 249
Orwig - 29, 52, 95, 414
Oseth - 81, 168, 414
Ottis - 474
Otto - 29, 57, 59, 415
Ove - 285
Owens - 227, 247

-P-

Padget - 228, 247
Page - 94, 95, 415
Palmquist - 96, 416
Parizek - 228, 247

Index

Parkhill - 160
Passica - 160
Patel - 4
Patterson - 60, 160, 228, 250, 416
Patton - 87, 122, 150, 151, 152, 155, 156
Paup - 228, 248
Peabody - 174
Peacock - 228, 249
Pease - 228, 248
Peck - 228, 246
Pedersen - 63, 417
Pender - 113, 126, 128, 417
Peppmeir - 160
Perret - 474
Perrin - 106, 127, 128, 418
Perry - 160
Person - 130, 419, 471, 472
Pessica - 228, 250
Peters - 19, 87, 88, 105, 117, 121, 122, 130, 169, 229, 250, 286, 419, 420
Petersen - 59, 130, 131, 419
Petrus - 228, 248
Pfiffner - 76, 87, 97, 122, 421
Phillips - 156, 229, 247
Piatt - 229, 249
Picht - 62, 421
Pierce - 93, 160, 421
Pike - 160
Pilcher - 160
Pitsenbarger - 249
Pitsenburger - 229
Pogge - 229, 250
Pollard - 160
Polly - 160
Popelka - 4, 103, 123, 124, 261, 422
Portwood - 30, 60, 130, 422
Potter - 122, 423
Powell - 229, 246
Powers - 160
Pratt - 229, 247, 286
Preis - 166, 423
Prendergast - 105, 424
Price - 229, 247
Prior - 229, 249
Pritchard - 108, 424
Prudhon - 230, 250
Prusha - 92, 425
Puls - 286, 287
Pusateri - 29, 287

-R-
Rabenold - 160
Raecker - 288
Raim - 160
Ralston - 160, 230, 250
Ranson - 63, 64, 131, 425
Rapps - 230, 248
Rasko - 160
Rasmussen - 160
Raspotnik - 230, 250
Rathbun - 160
Ray - 139, 147, 148, 152, 157, 160, 425
Raynie - 230, 248
Razor - 48, 61, 426
Reed - 88, 123, 162, 426
Reeve - 230, 247
Reeves - 116, 167, 427
Reinartson - 230, 248
Reis - 107, 428
Reisgaard - 113
Renolds - 160
Reynolds - 230, 248
Rice - 230, 249
Rich - 127, 428
Richards - 30, 57, 129, 429, 472
Richardson - 160
Rickerl - 247
Rickert - 231, 249
Riekegl - 231
Riesgaard - 428
Rinisland - 231, 248
Ritchey - 231, 248
Roberts - 15, 161, 231, 246, 429
Robinson - 59, 429, 430
Roepke - 63, 131, 431
Roethler - 431
Rogers - 231, 249
Rogness - 17, 432
Rohde - 231, 247
Rohloff - 231, 248
Roland - 231
Rolfe - 160
Rolland - 250
Roosevelt - 80
Rossow - 77, 168, 432
Rothbart - 28, 49, 64, 130, 433
Rowlison - 232, 247
Rudi - 473, 474
Ruggles - 160
Ruppert - 113, 434
Rush - 232, 247, 248
Russell - 260
Rust - 107, 131, 160, 434
Rutt - 232, 247
Ryan - 117, 126, 435
Rydberg - 232, 247

-S-
Sackett - 232, 249
Saffell - 160
Sage - 160
Sandersfeld - 30, 62, 68, 70, 435, 472
Sanderson - 232, 250
Sanneman - 232, 246
Santillan - 232, 247
Saunders - 160
Schaen - 233, 248
Scharf - 436
Scharff - 233, 248
Schaupp - 233, 248
Scherb - 74, 436
Scherranan - 248
Scherrman - 233
Scherz - 233, 250
Schinker - 160
Schipull - 109, 436
Schleihs - 123, 437
Schmelzer - 63, 289
Schmidt - 160
Schneider - 233, 248
Schobert - 288
Schoder - 53
Schoedlerman - 248
Schoelerman - 233
Schoer - 233, 246
Schreiner - 128, 437
Schuchman - 96
Schuchmann - 437
Schulte - 288
Schultz - 160, 289
Schwartz - 14
Schweer - 110, 438
Scott - 95, 160, 167, 439
Seaquist - 233, 248
Sedore - 128, 439
Seeger - 234, 250
Seerley - 234
Seiberling - 160
Selk - 234
Sessions - 108, 113, 439
Sexton - 440
Seyfer - 173, 290
Shaeffer - 234, 246
Shannon - 234, 246
Sharp - 234, 250
Shaw - 234, 247
Shepard - 440
Sheppard - 234, 247
Sherrets - 160
Shields - 77, 122, 441
Shirk - 92, 126, 441
Shuler - 100, 442
Sickels - 290, 291
Siebels - 290
Sil - 234
Sill - 246
Simmons - 160, 235, 248
Simpson - 235, 246
Singer - 136, 142, 149, 150, 160, 167, 442
Skubal - 235, 247
Slager - 235, 248
Smalley - 235, 248
Smallwood - 474
Smeltzer - 235, 248
Smith - 160, 235, 236, 246, 247, 248, 249, 250, 474
Snodgrass - 236, 246
Soesbe - 236, 249
Sondag - 236, 246
Sonneborn - 245
Sorden - 160, 291
Soseman - 160
Sowles - 236, 249
Spanger - 150
Spangler - 137, 142, 143, 160, 443
Speer - 82
Spencer - 160
Spicer - 236, 248
Sporrey - 237, 248
Springer - 237, 248
Sprout - 237, 246
Srout - 237, 250
Stafford - 444
Stainbrook - 250
Stalin - 12, 155
Stamp - 129, 444
Staton - 160
Steelman - 76, 97, 445
Steen - 237, 248
Steffen - 59, 445
Stelle - 237, 250
Stellish - 75, 131, 446, 471
Stenseth - 291
Stepanek - 245
Stephens - 160
Sterler - 136, 142, 149, 160, 447
Sterling - 237, 247
Steussy - 160
Steven - 37, 61, 447
Stevens - 237, 250
Stevenson - 160
Stewart - 14, 160
Stientjes - 101, 119, 447
Stiles - 474
Stine - 291
Stockman - 237, 247

Iowans of the Mighty Eighth

Stoll - 238, 250
Stone - 238, 248
Stookesberry - 238, 247
Storm - 245
Straub - 238, 250
Stricker - 245
Strom - 110, 448
Strong - 474
Struble - 238
Struchen - 292
Stuble - 246
Stuckey - 160
Stump - 238, 249
Sturtz - 449
Suckow - 71, 449
Sullivan - 238, 250
Sumpter - 238, 246
Sunberg - 238, 249
Swan - 239, 249
Swanger - 160
Swartzendruber - 239, 248
Sweeny - 245
Swift - 83, 449
Sypal - 132, 449

-T-
Taylor - 4, 16, 71, 72, 123, 239, 246, 248, 450, 471
Terrell - 245
Teter - 239, 247
Thieman - 161
Thomas - 74, 130, 161, 239, 248, 249, 450, 471
Thompson - 25, 93, 161, 239, 248, 249, 293, 451, 452
Thulin - 240, 247
Tibbets - 6
Tiegland - 161
Tillotson - 240, 248
Tilton - 293
Timmins - 161

Toerber - 245
Tomasek - 78, 452
Tomke - 161
Tomlin - 240, 247
Tomlinson - 240, 246
Torreson - 123, 452
Trettin - 240, 249
Trout - 98, 453
Truman - 155
Turner - 101, 161, 167, 168, 240, 246, 453
Turnquist - 240, 249
Tuttle - 240, 248

-U-
Ulstad - 293
Underwood - 138, 161, 167, 454

-V-
Vaderweid - 166
Van Alstine - 240, 248
Van Ausdall - 241, 246
Van De Voorde - 241, 248
Van Duyn - 37, 65, 129, 454
Van Dyke - 293
Van Ginkel - 101, 455
Vance - 81, 245, 454
Vander Schaaf - 241, 249
Vaneschen - 161
Varenhorst - 37, 455
Varland - 17
Vavra - 241, 248
Vejda - 162
Velve - 248
Vermeer - 241, 247, 248
Versteegh - 245
Vevle - 241, 248
Vint - 85, 107, 456, 471
Vogel - 161
Volz - 162
Vrathny - 293

Vratny - 161

-W-
Waggoner - 241, 249
Wagner - 242, 248
Wagoner - 242, 248
Walker - 161, 242, 249
Walton - 161
Ward - 63, 86, 100, 161, 242, 246, 247, 456
Warren - 242, 248
Wassom - 141
Waters - 161
Watson - 161
Watt - 242, 249
Watterson - 242, 247
Watts - 161
Weander - 242, 246
Weaver - 105, 457
Weaverling - 457
Webster - 458
Weck - 243, 249
Weede - 243, 247
Weiby - 243, 246
Weideman - 459
Weiss - 243, 248
Wells - 161, 243, 246
Weltz - 243, 250
Wenstrand - 245
Wente - 243, 247, 249
Wentz - 243
Werner - 57, 109, 459
West - 460
Westbrook - 137, 142, 143, 149, 161, 167, 460
Westell - 161
Whalen - 243, 249
Wharton - 294
Wheeler - 244, 247
Whelan - 474
Whitacre - 161

Whitcanack - 58, 112, 462
White - 37, 61, 246, 462
Whitehand - 244, 250
Whitehead - 161
Whitney - 163
Whiton-Perry - 295
Whittington - 161
Wilcox - 244, 247, 248
Wile - 137, 139, 144, 151, 161, 462
Wiley - 116, 167, 463
Williams - 245, 246
Willson - 244, 247
Wilson - 10, 12, 79, 130, 162, 164, 244, 246, 248, 464, 473
Winter - 244, 246
Wirtz - 296
Wolfe - 161, 245, 247, 249
Wombacher - 295, 296
Wood - 112, 465
Woolums - 296
Woolway - 108, 466
Wright - 108, 466
Wulfekuhle - 245, 247
Wunschel - 467
Wurtz - 161

-Y-
Yashack - 467
Yearous - 101, 467
Yoder - 245, 249
Young - 245, 248

-Z-
Zachar - 62, 131, 468
Zeigler - 103, 122, 173, 469, 472
Zimmer - 245, 246